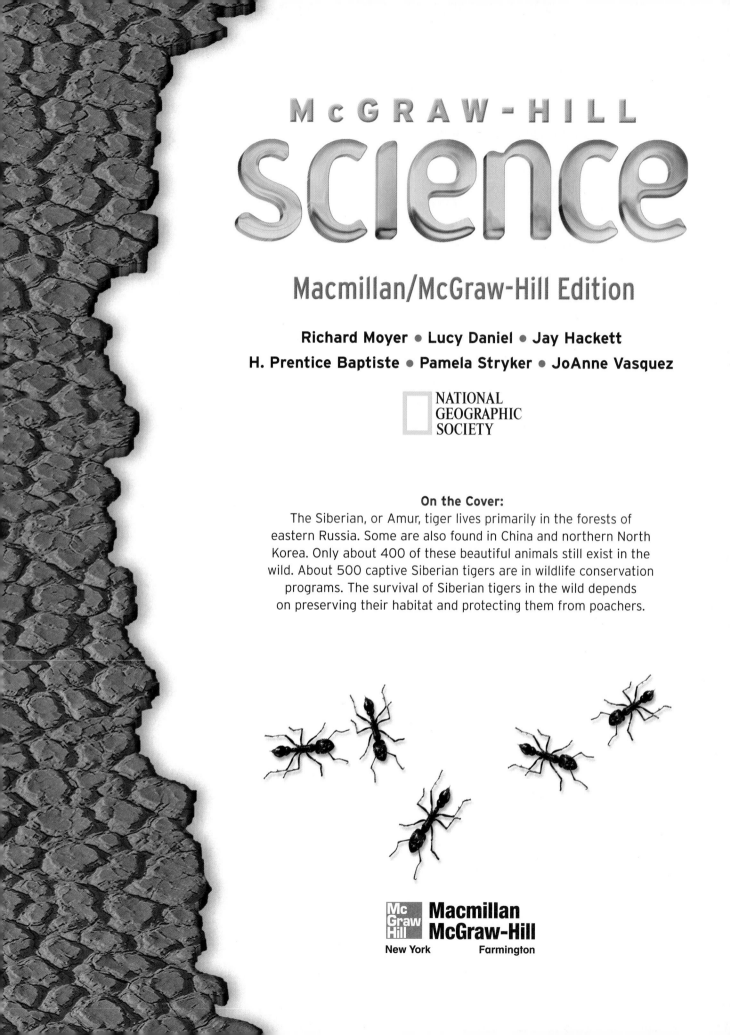

McGRAW-HILL
SCIENCE

Macmillan/McGraw-Hill Edition

Richard Moyer • Lucy Daniel • Jay Hackett
H. Prentice Baptiste • Pamela Stryker • JoAnne Vasquez

NATIONAL
GEOGRAPHIC
SOCIETY

On the Cover:
The Siberian, or Amur, tiger lives primarily in the forests of
eastern Russia. Some are also found in China and northern North
Korea. Only about 400 of these beautiful animals still exist in the
wild. About 500 captive Siberian tigers are in wildlife conservation
programs. The survival of Siberian tigers in the wild depends
on preserving their habitat and protecting them from poachers.

Mc
Graw
Hill
**Macmillan
McGraw-Hill**
New York   **Farmington**

Program Authors

Dr. Lucy H. Daniel
Teacher, Consultant
Rutherford County Schools, North Carolina

Dr. Jay Hackett
Professor Emeritus of Earth Sciences
University of Northern Colorado

Dr. Richard H. Moyer
Professor of Science Education
University of Michigan-Dearborn

Dr. H. Prentice Baptiste
Professor of Science and Multicultural Education
New Mexico State University
Las Cruces, New Mexico

Pamela Stryker, M.Ed.
Elementary Educator and Science Consultant
Eanes Independent School District
Austin, Texas

Dr. JoAnne Vasquez
Elementary Science Education Consultant
Mesa Public Schools, Arizona
NSTA Past President

NATIONAL
GEOGRAPHIC
SOCIETY

Washington, D.C.

The features in this textbook entitled "Invitation to Science," "Amazing Stories," and "People in Science," as well as the unit openers, were developed in collaboration with the National Geographic Society's School Publishing Division.

RFB&D
learning through listening

Students with print disabilities may be eligible to obtain an accessible, audio version of the pupil edition of this textbook. Please call Recording for the Blind & Dyslexic at 1-800-221-4792 for complete information.

Macmillan/McGraw-Hill

A Division of The McGraw·Hill Companies

Published by Macmillan/McGraw-Hill, of McGraw-Hill Education, a division of The McGraw-Hill Companies, Inc., Two Penn Plaza, New York, New York 10121.

Printed in the United States of America

ISBN 0-02-280038-7 / 5

11 12 13 071 07 06 05 04

Teacher Reviewers

Peoria, IL
Rolling Acres Middle School
Gail Truho

Rockford, IL
Rockford Public Schools
Dr. Sharon Wynstra
Science Coordinator

Newark, NJ
Alexander Street School
Cheryl Simeonidis

Albuquerque, NM
Jackie Costales
Science Coordinator, Montgomery Complex

Poughkeepsie, NY
St. Peter's School
Monica Crolius

Columbus, OH
St. Mary's School
Linda Cotter
Joby Easley

Keizer, OR
Cummings Elementary
Deanna Havel

McMinnville, OR
McMinnville School District
Kristin Ward

Salem, OR
Fruitland Elementary
  Mike Knudson

Four Corners Elementary
  Bethany Ayers
  Sivhong Hanson
  Cheryl Kirkelie
  Julie Wells

Salem-Keizer Public Schools
  Rachael Harms
  Sue Smith,
  Science Specialist

Yoshikai Elementary
  Joyce Davenport

Norristown, PA
St. Teresa of Avila
Fran Fiordimondo

Pittsburgh, PA
Chartiers Valley Intermediate School
Rosemary Hutter

Memphis, TN
Memphis City Schools
Quincy Hathorn
District Science Facilitator

Life Science

Consultants

Dr. Carol Baskin
University of Kentucky
Lexington, KY

Dr. Joe W. Crim
University of Georgia
Athens, GA

Dr. Marie DiBerardino
Allegheny University of
Health Sciences
Philadelphia, PA

Dr. R. E. Duhrkopf
Baylor University
Waco, TX

Dr. Dennis L. Nelson
Montana State University
Bozeman, MT

Dr. Fred Sack
Ohio State University
Columbus, OH

Dr. Martin VanDyke
Denver, CO

Dr. E. Peter Volpe
Mercer University
Macon, GA

Earth Science

Consultants

Dr. Clarke Alexander
Skidaway Institute of
Oceanography
Savannah, GA

Dr. Suellen Cabe
Pembroke State University
Pembroke, NC

Dr. Thomas A. Davies
Texas A & M University
College Station, TX

Dr. Ed Geary
Geological Society of America
Boulder, CO

Dr. David C. Kopaska-Merkel
Geological Survey of Alabama
Tuscaloosa, AL

Physical Science

Consultants

Dr. Bonnie Buratti
Jet Propulsion Lab
Pasadena, CA

Dr. Shawn Carlson
Society of Amateur Scientists
San Diego, CA

Dr. Karen Kwitter
Williams College
Williamstown, MA

Dr. Steven Souza
Williamstown, MA

Dr. Joseph P. Straley
University of Kentucky
Lexington, KY

Dr. Thomas Troland
University of Kentucky
Lexington, KY

Dr. Josephine Davis Wallace
University of North Carolina
Charlotte, NC

Consultant for Primary Grades

Donna Harrell Lubcker
East Texas Baptist University
Marshall, TX

Teacher Panelists

Newark, NJ
First Avenue School
Jorge Alameda
Concetta Cioci
Neva Galasso
Bernadette Kazanjian-reviewer
Toby Marks
Janet Mayer-reviewer
Maria Tutela

Brooklyn, NY
P.S. 31
 Janet Mantel
 Paige McGlone
 Madeline Pappas
 Maria Puma-reviewer
P.S. 217
 Rosemary Ahern
 Charles Brown
 Claudia Deeb-reviewer
 Wendy Lerner
P.S. 225
 Christine Calafiore
 Annette Fisher-reviewer

P.S. 250
 Melissa Kane
P.S. 277
 Erica Cohen
 Helena Conti
 Anne Marie Corrado
 Deborah Scott-DiClemente
 Jeanne Fish
 Diane Fromhartz
 Tricia Hinz
 Lisa Iside
 Susan Malament
 Joyce Menkes-reviewer
 Elaine Noto
 Jean Pennacchio
Jeffrey Hampton
Mwaka Yavana

Elmont, NY
Covert Avenue School
Arlene Connelly

Mt. Vernon, NY
Holmes School
Jennifer Cavallaro
Lou Ciofi
George DiFiore
Brenda Durante
Jennifer Hawkins-reviewer
Michelle Mazzotta
Catherine Moringiello
Mary Jane Oria-reviewer
Lucille Pierotti
Pia Vicario-reviewer

Ozone Park, NY
St. Elizabeth School
Joanne Cocchiola-reviewer
Helen DiPietra-reviewer
Barbara Kingston
Madeline Visco

St. Albans, NY
Orvia Williams

Structures of Plants and Animals PAGE A1

Invitation to Science page S1

UNIT B

Life Science

Interactions of Living Things PAGE B1

Earth and Its Resources PAGE C1

Weather and Climate PAGE D1

UNIT E

Physical Science

Properties of Matter and Energy PAGE E1

UNIT F

Physical Science

Motion and Energy PAGE F1

Activities

UNIT D

UNIT E

UNIT F

As you study science, you will learn many new words. You will read about many new ideas. Read these pages. They will help you understand this book.

1. The **Vocabulary** list has all the new words you will learn in the lesson. The page numbers tell you where the words are taught.

2. The name tells you what the lesson is about.

3. **Get Ready** uses the picture on the page to help you start thinking about the lesson.

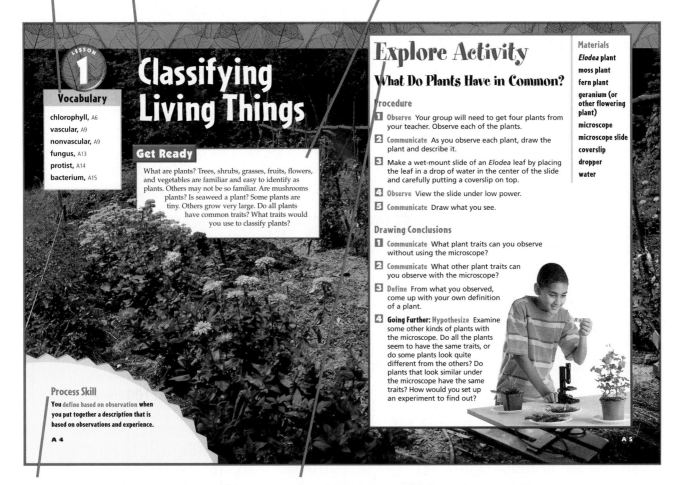

LESSON 1

Classifying Living Things

Vocabulary

chlorophyll, A6
vascular, A9
nonvascular, A9
fungus, A13
protist, A14
bacterium, A15

Get Ready

What are plants? Trees, shrubs, grasses, fruits, flowers, and vegetables are familiar and easy to identify as plants. Others may not be so familiar. Are mushrooms plants? Is seaweed a plant? Some plants are tiny. Others grow very large. Do all plants have common traits? What traits would you use to classify plants?

Process Skill

You **define based on observation when** you put together a description that is based on observations and experience.

A 4

Explore Activity

What Do Plants Have in Common?

Procedure

1. **Observe** Your group will need to get four plants from your teacher. Observe each of the plants.

2. **Communicate** As you observe each plant, draw the plant and describe it.

3. Make a wet-mount slide of an *Elodea* leaf by placing the leaf in a drop of water in the center of the slide and carefully putting a coverslip on top.

4. **Observe** View the slide under low power.

5. **Communicate** Draw what you see.

Drawing Conclusions

1. **Communicate** What plant traits can you observe without using the microscope?

2. **Communicate** What other plant traits can you observe with the microscope?

3. **Define** From what you observed, come up with your own definition of a plant.

4. **Going Further:** **Hypothesize** Examine some other kinds of plants with the microscope. Do all the plants seem to have the same traits, or do some plants look quite different from the others? Do plants that look similar under the microscope have the same traits? How would you set up an experiment to find out?

Materials

Elodea plant
moss plant
fern plant
geranium (or other flowering plant)
microscope
microscope slide
coverslip
dropper
water

A 5

4. This **Process Skill** is used in the Explore Activity.

5. The **Explore Activity** is a hands-on way to learn about the lesson .

As you read a lesson, follow these three steps. They will help you to understand what you are reading.

1. This box contains the **Main Idea** of the lesson. Keep the main idea of the lesson in mind as you read.

2. **Before Reading** Read the large red question before you read the page. Try to answer this question from what you already know.

3. **During Reading** Look for new **Vocabulary** words in yellow. Look at the pictures. They will help you understand what you are reading.

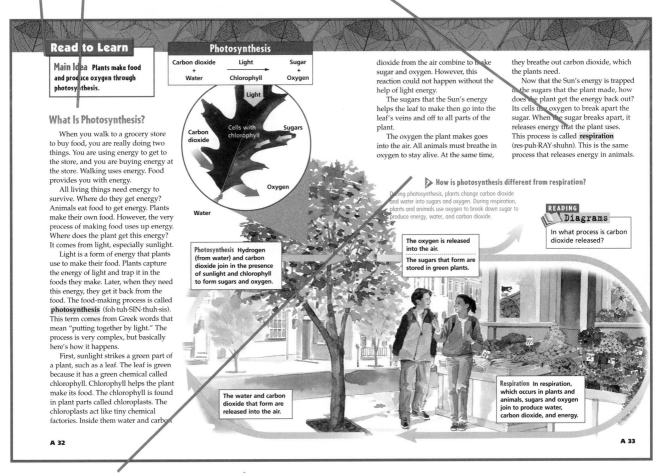

Read to Learn

Main Idea Plants make food and produce oxygen through photosynthesis.

Photosynthesis

| Carbon dioxide + Water | Light → Chlorophyll | Sugar + Oxygen |

Light

Cells with chlorophyll

Carbon dioxide

Sugars

Oxygen

Water

What Is Photosynthesis?

When you walk to a grocery store to buy food, you are really doing two things. You are using energy to get to the store, and you are buying energy at the store. Walking uses energy. Food provides you with energy.

All living things need energy to survive. Where do they get energy? Animals eat food to get energy. Plants make their own food. However, the very process of making food uses up energy. Where does the plant get this energy? It comes from light, especially sunlight.

Light is a form of energy that plants use to make their food. Plants capture the energy of light and trap it in the foods they make. Later, when they need this energy, they get it back from the food. The food-making process is called **photosynthesis** (foh·tuh·SIN·thuh·sis). This term comes from Greek words that mean "putting together by light." The process is very complex, but basically here's how it happens.

First, sunlight strikes a green part of a plant, such as a leaf. The leaf is green because it has a green chemical called chlorophyll. Chlorophyll helps the plant make its food. The chlorophyll is found in plant parts called chloroplasts. The chloroplasts act like tiny chemical factories. Inside them water and carbon

dioxide from the air combine to make sugar and oxygen. However, this reaction could not happen without the help of light energy.

The sugars that the Sun's energy helps the leaf to make then go into the leaf's veins and off to all parts of the plant.

The oxygen the plant makes goes into the air. All animals must breathe in oxygen to stay alive. At the same time,

they breathe out carbon dioxide, which the plants need.

Now that the Sun's energy is trapped in the sugars that the plant made, how does the plant get the energy back out? Its cells use oxygen to break apart the sugar. When the sugar breaks apart, it releases energy that the plant uses. This process is called **respiration** (res·puh·RAY·shuhn). This is the same process that releases energy in animals.

▷ **How is photosynthesis different from respiration?**

During photosynthesis, plants change carbon dioxide and water into sugars and oxygen. During respiration, plants and animals use oxygen to break down sugar to produce energy, water, and carbon dioxide.

Photosynthesis Hydrogen (from water) and carbon dioxide join in the presence of sunlight and chlorophyll to form sugars and oxygen.

The oxygen is released into the air.

The sugars that form are stored in green plants.

The water and carbon dioxide that form are released into the air.

Respiration In respiration, which occurs in plants and animals, sugars and oxygen join to produce water, carbon dioxide, and energy.

READING Diagrams

In what process is carbon dioxide released?

A 32

A 33

4. **After Reading** ▷ This arrow points to a question. It will help you check that you understand what you have read. Try to answer the question before you go to the next large red question.

On one page in each lesson, you will find a question that practices the Chapter Reading Skill. In any chapter you will find one of these skills:

Main idea and supporting details

The *main idea* is what the reading is about. To find the main idea:

- Answer the red question on a page.
- Look for facts that tell more about the main idea. Pictures on the page can add supporting details.

tree must be made of rigid building blocks—rigid cells that support it.

Under the microscope, *Elodea* cells look like boxes. What is one characteristic of boxes? They have walls, which keep them from collapsing into a heap. All plant cells have walls. That's why an oak tree can stand tall and strong.

The cells of all plants work together to keep the plants alive. Different kinds of cells do different kinds of jobs. Each job contributes to the health and survival of the plant. For example, in a tree, cells in leaves make the plant's food. Cells in stems, branches, roots, and the trunk form tubes through

which the food or water is moved, or *transported* (trans·PAWRT·uhd). Other cells may form flowers, fruits, and seeds that allow the tree to reproduce.

Cells are organized into *tissues* (TISH·ewz). The "strings" in celery stalks and the flesh of fruits are examples of plant tissues. Some tissues carry water and minerals to various parts of the plant. Some tissues support the plant.

READING Draw Conclusions
What is one of the things plants have in common that helps an oak tree stand tall and strong?

Cell membrane (holds the cell together)

Nucleus (cell control center)

Mitochondrion (cell energy processor)

Animal Cell
Animal cells do not have a cell wall or chlorophyll.

Vacuole (storage space)

A 7

Draw conclusions

A *conclusion* is a statement of what you learned by putting the facts together. To draw a conclusion:

- Make a list of the facts you read on a page.
- Write your conclusion.

Compare and contrast *Compare* means "to tell how things are alike." *Contrast* means "to tell how things are different."

Sequence of events The *sequence* is the order in which things happen. To find the sequence:
- Ask yourself: "What happened first?" Write it down.
- Then make a list of each thing that happened after that – in order.

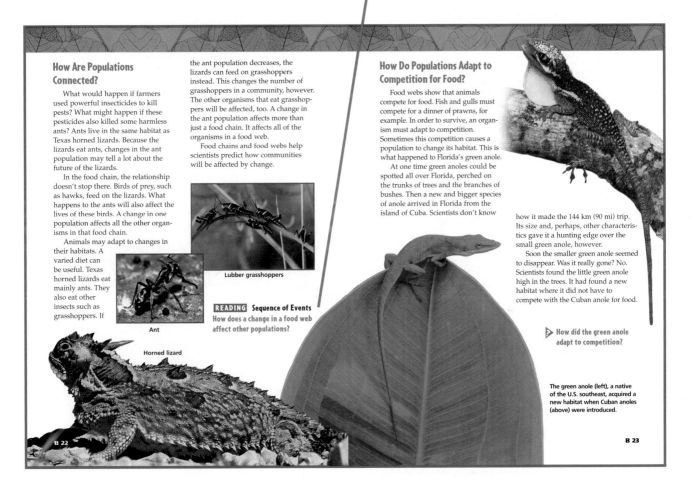

How Are Populations Connected?

What would happen if farmers used powerful insecticides to kill pests? What might happen if these pesticides also killed some harmless ants? Ants live in the same habitat as Texas horned lizards. Because the lizards eat ants, changes in the ant population may tell a lot about the future of the lizards.

In the food chain, the relationship doesn't stop there. Birds of prey, such as hawks, feed on the lizards. What happens to the ants will also affect the lives of these birds. A change in one population affects all the other organisms in that food chain.

Animals may adapt to changes in their habitats. A varied diet can be useful. Texas horned lizards eat mainly ants. They also eat other insects such as grasshoppers. If the ant population decreases, the lizards can feed on grasshoppers instead. This changes the number of grasshoppers in a community, however. The other organisms that eat grasshoppers will be affected, too. A change in the ant population affects more than just a food chain. It affects all of the organisms in a food web.

Food chains and food webs help scientists predict how communities will be affected by change.

Lubber grasshoppers

Ant

Horned lizard

READING Sequence of Events
How does a change in a food web affect other populations?

How Do Populations Adapt to Competition for Food?

Food webs show that animals compete for food. Fish and gulls must compete for a dinner of prawns, for example. In order to survive, an organism must adapt to competition. Sometimes this competition causes a population to change its habitat. This is what happened to Florida's green anole.

At one time green anoles could be spotted all over Florida, perched on the trunks of trees and the branches of bushes. Then a new and bigger species of anole arrived in Florida from the island of Cuba. Scientists don't know how it made the 144 km (90 mi) trip. Its size and, perhaps, other characteristics gave it a hunting edge over the small green anole, however.

Soon the smaller green anole seemed to disappear. Was it really gone? No. Scientists found the little green anole high in the trees. It had found a new habitat where it did not have to compete with the Cuban anole for food.

▷ How did the green anole adapt to competition?

The green anole (left), a native of the U.S. southeast, acquired a new habitat when Cuban anoles (above) were introduced.

B 22

B 23

Cause and effect When you read about something that happened, ask yourself: "What made it happen?"
- A *cause* makes something happen. Beating a drum is a cause.
- The thing that happens is the *effect*. The effect is the sound.

Summarize To summarize:
- Ask yourself what the page you read is about.
- State it in your own words in a sentence or two.

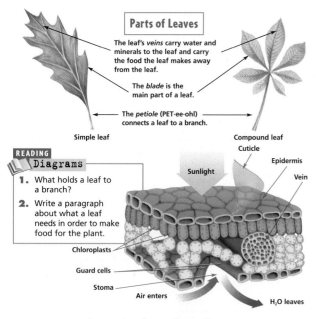

Reading In SCIENCE GRAPHICS

Throughout all chapters of this book, you will get information by reading graphics. Graphics are pictures that are drawn to show information.

Parts of Leaves

The leaf's *veins* carry water and minerals to the leaf and carry the food the leaf makes away from the leaf.

The *blade* is the main part of a leaf.

The *petiole* (PET-ee-ohl) connects a leaf to a branch.

Simple leaf

Compound leaf

Cuticle
Sunlight
Epidermis
Vein
Chloroplasts
Guard cells
Stoma
Air enters
H_2O leaves

READING Diagrams

1. What holds a leaf to a branch?

2. Write a paragraph about what a leaf needs in order to make food for the plant.

diagrams: pictures that show how something works or is put together

maps: drawings that show features of places on Earth's surface. Some maps are drawn to show the weather.

READING Maps

1. Where do you see low pressure systems in the satellite picture? What do the clouds appear to be doing?

2. What kind of weather is happening in different parts of the country in each map? Explain.

Front Symbols
Warm front
Cold front
Occluded front
Stationary front

Energy Pyramid: Land Food Chain

READING Charts

1. What happens to the number of organisms at each level of the pyramid starting from the base?

2. How much more energy from the Sun was available to the grass than to the bluebirds?

charts: lists of information in tables with pictures

Solid
Liquid
PDCB
Liquid
Melting
Mothballs (PDCB)
Solid
Liquid
Water
Melting
Solid
Water
Ice
Time

Temperature (°C)
60
50
40
30
20
10
0
−10
−20
−30

Melting of PDCB and water

READING Graphs

1. What is the melting temperature for water? For PDCB?

2. Does ice or PDCB take longer to melt? Explain how you got your answer.

graphs: lines, bars, or symbols drawn to help you compare amounts

NATIONAL GEOGRAPHIC

Invitation to Science

Some were bigger than a school bus. Some were fierce hunters, armed with giant hooked claws and teeth as long as dinner knives. Some defended themselves with spiked tails. No human ever saw them alive, but their bones are scattered over Earth. What were these creatures? They were dinosaurs, of course. They lived for millions of years. Today they are all gone. Why did the dinosaurs disappear?

Read about a scientist who may have found the answer. As you read, you'll learn about the **Methods of Science**—steps scientists follow to solve problems. Also watch for important science skills shown in **red**.

Dr. Walter Alvarez studies rock layers for clues to the disappearance of the dinosaurs.

Question

One day in the 1970s, Walter Alvarez was digging in a rocky hillside in Italy. Alvarez was **observing** rocks because he is a geologist. A geologist is a scientist who studies Earth's crust. That day Dr. Alvarez found something surprising. He found a layer of ancient rock full of fossils. Above this layer, he found a layer of rock with no fossils in it. Between those two layers, there was a thin, red layer.

Dr. Alvarez knew that the rock layer with the fossils was formed millions of years ago when dinosaurs roamed Earth. The rock layer without fossils formed after the dinosaurs died. What about the red rock layer? As Dr. Alvarez held some of the red rock, many questions came to his mind. Was it deposited on Earth's crust just as the dinosaurs were dying? Could it provide clues about what killed them? Such questions are important. Scientific discovery always starts with good questions about how things work.

The impact of a huge meteorite created Meteor Crater in Arizona.

Hypothesis

Dr. Alvarez **communicated** with other scientists. Scientists communicate to share ideas and to work together. The others helped Dr. Alvarez **measure** the red rock's age. They found that the rock layer was 65 million years old. That means it formed just about the time the dinosaurs became extinct. The scientific team tested the red rock layer further. They discovered that it contained a lot of iridium. Iridium is a metal that is rare on Earth. However, iridium is found in large amounts on meteorites. Meteorites are rocky chunks of matter that travel through space and reach the surface of Earth.

Dr. Alvarez formed an idea based on facts and observations. He **inferred** that the iridium-rich rock came from a meteorite that smashed into Earth about the time the dinosaurs died. When you infer, you reason from evidence. Next Dr. Alvarez formed an important **hypothesis**. He stated that the meteorite was so big that it caused a huge explosion when it struck Earth. The explosion—and all its effects—killed the dinosaurs.

What is a hypothesis? A hypothesis is a possible answer to a question or puzzle. A good hypothesis must do three things.

- It must explain observations.
- It must be testable.
- It must predict new findings.

A **prediction** states possible results of an event or experiment. Dr. Alvarez's hypothesis did predict new findings. You might think of a hypothesis as an "If … then …" statement. For example, if a meteorite killed the dinosaurs, then there should be evidence of its impact somewhere on Earth. Dr. Alvarez's hypothesis also explained observations—such as the reason for the mysterious layer of red rock. Now, could Dr. Alvarez's hypothesis be tested?

This meteorite is on display at the Rose Center for Earth and Space in New York City.

Experiment

A scientific test of a hypothesis is called an experiment. Scientists use variables in their experiments. A variable is one of the things in an experiment that can be changed or controlled.

A good experiment must follow certain rules.

- It must be repeatable.
- It must test only one variable at a time.

This scientist is working with a computer model to study tsunamis, or tidal waves.

Dr. Alvarez and others did many experiments to test his hypothesis. They calculated that the meteorite would need to be about ten kilometers (six miles) wide to leave so much iridium on Earth. Could a meteorite that size cause enough damage to destroy the dinosaurs? To find out, the scientists used computer models. Models represent real objects. Models can show how real objects react to changes in their environment.

The computer models provided the answer. The models showed it would have been possible for a large meteorite to kill the dinosaurs. How? There would have been severe earthquakes around the world. Huge tidal waves—walls of water over 1.6 kilometers (1 mile) high—would have crashed along the coasts. Shock waves would have brought hurricane-like gusts of wind. Wildfires, ignited by the meteorite's debris, would have swept across the globe. The friction between the air and the rocky fragments would have made the air as hot as a furnace. Toxic gases could have formed. After the fires, tidal waves, and earthquakes stopped, temperatures would have dropped far below freezing as dust from the explosion blocked the Sun.

Observation

Scientists around the world began making careful **observations** to look for clues to support Dr. Alvarez's hypothesis. A meteorite big enough to kill the dinosaurs would have left a huge crater when it struck Earth. That impact crater would have been hundreds of kilometers wide. Some traces would still exist. The scientists knew there were some huge craters on Earth. However, none they knew of were the right size and age to have been formed by Dr. Alvarez's meteorite.

Finally, in the 1980s, a huge crater about 200 kilometers (124 miles) wide was identified as an impact crater. Materials in the crater were later found to match those in the layer that Dr. Alvarez had found. The impact crater is off the tip of Mexico's Yucatan Peninsula. Scientists collected and interpreted data about the crater. When scientists **interpret data**, they analyze information that has been gathered. The nature of the crater, its age, and location fit Dr. Alvarez's theory perfectly. Most scientists now believe that the meteorite that made the giant crater also killed the dinosaurs.

This computer image shows the crater scientists believe was created by the meteorite that killed the dinosaurs.

Conclusion

The results of a good experiment should either clearly support or not support the hypothesis. If the results support the hypothesis, then it is possible to state a conclusion, or general rule. If results do not support the hypothesis, then a scientist needs to change the hypothesis or form a new one. New experiments must be done to test the new hypothesis. Through repeated testing, a hypothesis can be improved and refined. Even if the original hypothesis was flawed, it might eventually lead to one that is correct.

Dr. Alvarez used computer models to test his hypothesis. However, his theory was not widely accepted until there was clear evidence from the real world that his theory could be true. Today computer modeling is often used. Still, there is no substitute for solid evidence and experimentation in the real world.

The scientific method is used in simple experiments. It is also used in complex scientific studies that last a long time. Scientists around the world worked for more than 20 years to investigate Walter Alvarez's hypothesis. They made many predictions, measurements, and observations. Today scientists generally agree. A giant, burning meteorite, hurtling to Earth at a terrific speed, is what doomed the dinosaurs 65 million years ago.

Methods of Science

Here is a chart that shows the steps scientists such as Dr. Walter Alvarez follow when solving a problem in science. Scientists don't always follow the steps in the order shown.

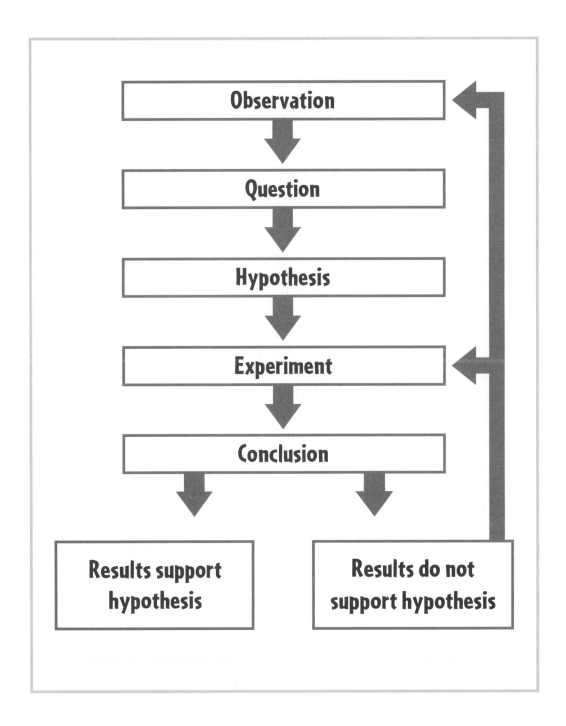

Science Process Skills

Observe to use one or more of the senses to identify or learn about an object or event

Infer to form an idea from facts or observations

Classify to place things that share properties together in groups

Measure to find the size, distance, time, volume, area, mass, weight, or temperature of an object or event

Use numbers to order, count, add, subtract, multiply, and divide to explain data

Communicate to share information

Predict to state possible results of an event or experiment

Interpret data to use the information that has been gathered to answer questions or solve a problem

Form a hypothesis to make a statement that can be tested to answer a question

Use variables to identify things in an experiment that can be changed or controlled

Experiment to perform a test to support or disprove a hypothesis

Make a model to make something to represent an object or event

Define based on observations to put together a description that is based on observations and experience

Science Safety Tips

In the Classroom

- Read all directions. Make sure you understand them. When you see BE CAREFUL!, be sure to follow the safety rule.
- Listen to your teacher for special safety directions. If you don't understand something, ask for help.
- Wash your hands with soap and water before an activity.
- Wear safety goggles when your teacher tells you to wear them. Wear them when working with anything that can fly into your eyes or when working with liquids.
- Wear a safety apron if you work with anything messy or anything that might spill.
- Wipe up a spill right away or ask your teacher for help.
- Tell your teacher if something breaks. If glass breaks, do not clean it up yourself.
- Keep your hair and clothes away from open flames. Tie back long hair, and roll up long sleeves.
- Be careful around a hot plate. Know when it is on and when it is off. Remember that the plate stays hot for a few minutes after it's turned off.

- Keep your hands dry around electrical equipment.
- Don't eat or drink anything during an experiment.
- Put equipment back the way your teacher tells you.
- Dispose of things the way your teacher tells you.
- Clean up your work area after an activity and wash your hands with soap and water.

In the Field

- Go with a trusted adult—such as your teacher or a parent or guardian.
- Do not touch animals or plants without an adult's approval. The animal might bite. The plant might be poison ivy or another dangerous plant.

Responsibility

- Treat living things, the environment, and one another with respect.

Life Science

UNIT A

Structures of Plants and Animals

LOOK!

Is it a plant? Is it an animal?
The leafy sea dragon is
 actually a fish that looks like
seaweed! How do you think
this helps it to survive?

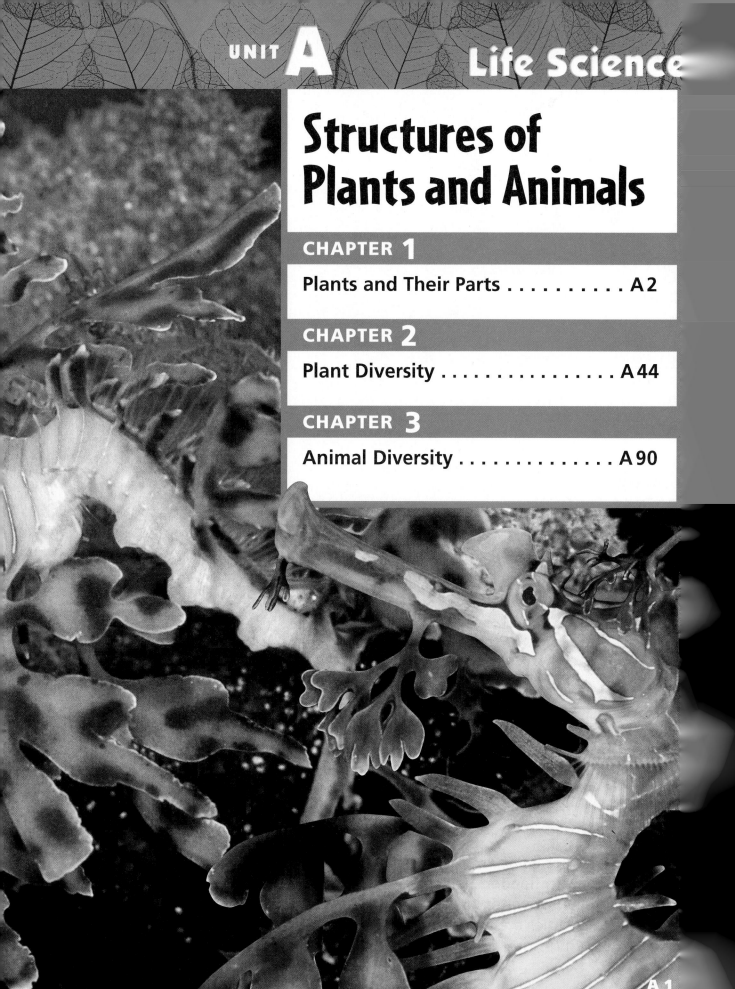

Structures of Plants and Animals

Plants
and Their Parts

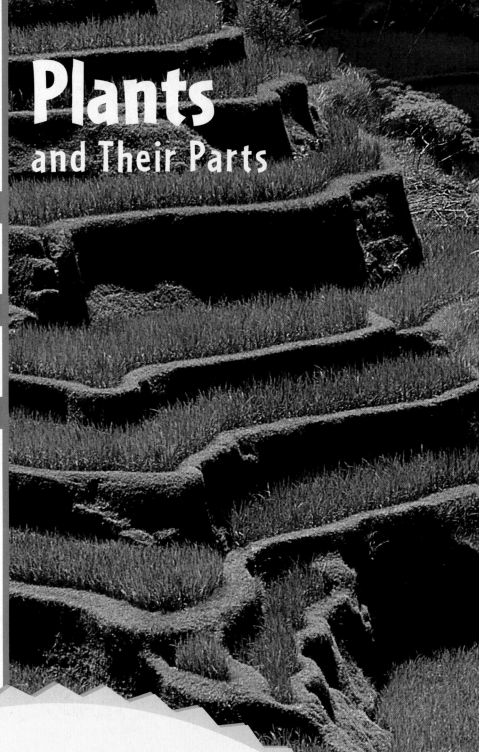

Did You Ever Wonder?

Where does rice come from? Most of the world's rice is grown in Asia, often in flooded fields called paddies. It takes 5,000 liters (1,320 gallons) of water to grow 1 kilogram (2.2 pounds) of rice. These rice paddies are growing on terraces—step-like fields cut into a hillside. Why is rice an important food crop?

A 3

Classifying Living Things

Vocabulary

chlorophyll, A6

vascular, A9

nonvascular, A9

fungus, A13

protist, A14

bacterium, A15

Get Ready

What are plants? Trees, shrubs, grasses, fruits, flowers, and vegetables are familiar and easy to identify as plants. Others may not be so familiar. Are mushrooms plants? Is seaweed a plant? Some plants are tiny. Others grow very large. Do all plants have common traits? What traits would you use to classify plants?

Process Skill

You define based on observation when you put together a description that is based on observations and experience.

Explore Activity

What Do Plants Have in Common?

Materials

Elodea plant

moss plant

fern plant

geranium (or other flowering plant)

microscope

microscope slide

coverslip

dropper

water

Procedure

1. **Observe** Your group will need to get four plants from your teacher. Observe each of the plants.

2. **Communicate** As you observe each plant, draw the plant and describe it.

3. Make a wet-mount slide of an *Elodea* leaf by placing the leaf in a drop of water in the center of the slide and carefully putting a coverslip on top.

4. **Observe** View the slide under low power.

5. **Communicate** Draw what you see.

Drawing Conclusions

1. **Communicate** What plant traits can you observe without using the microscope?

2. **Communicate** What other plant traits can you observe with the microscope?

3. **Define** From what you observed, come up with your own definition of a plant.

4. **Going Further: Hypothesize** Examine some other kinds of plants with the microscope. Do all the plants seem to have the same traits, or do some plants look quite different from the others? Do plants that look similar under the microscope have the same traits? How would you set up an experiment to find out?

Main Idea All plants have common characteristics, such as the same parts and the ability to make food.

What Do Plants Have in Common?

You don't need a microscope to discover that plants are green. That's because their cells contain a green chemical called **chlorophyll** (KLAWR·uh·fil). It allows plants to use the Sun's energy to make their own food. The other things plants need to make food are water and minerals from the soil and carbon dioxide from the air.

If you look at an *Elodea* leaf under a microscope, you will see what looks like little boxes. These are the cells, or basic building blocks, of the *Elodea*. All living things are made up of cells. Plants are made up of many different kinds of cells. All plant cells have certain things in common that help plants live and grow.

Let's look at a tree to find out how its cells help it survive. A tree rises up from the ground. Its rigid trunk supports all its weight. Its roots anchor it into the soil. It doesn't walk, run, or swim. In order to live and grow, the

Plant Cell

Plant cells have rigid walls and contain chlorophyll.

Mitochondrion (cell energy processor—helps supply energy for the cell)

Vacuole (storage space—stores food, water, and wastes)

Chloroplast (contains chlorophyll)

Nucleus (cell control center—directs everything the cell does)

Cell wall (rigid structure surrounding the plant cell)

Cell membrane (holds the cell together)

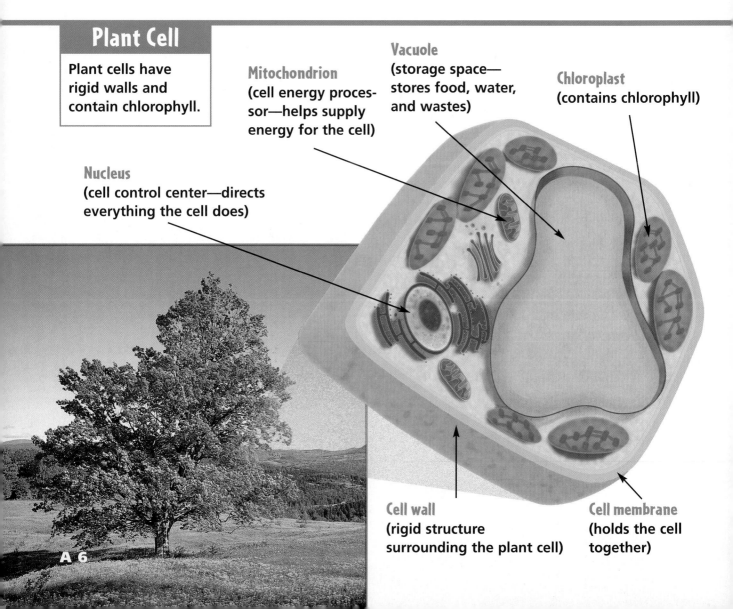

tree must be made of rigid building blocks—rigid cells that support it.

Under the microscope, *Elodea* cells look like boxes. What is one characteristic of boxes? They have walls, which keep them from collapsing into a heap. All plant cells have walls. That's why an oak tree can stand tall and strong.

The cells of all plants work together to keep the plants alive. Different kinds of cells do different kinds of jobs. Each job contributes to the health and survival of the plant. For example, in a tree, cells in leaves make the plant's food. Cells in stems, branches, roots, and the trunk form tubes through which the food or water is moved, or *transported* (trans·PAWRT·uhd). Other cells may form flowers, fruits, and seeds that allow the tree to reproduce.

Cells are organized into *tissues* (TISH·ewz). The "strings" in celery stalks and the flesh of fruits are examples of plant tissues. The tissues that carry water and minerals support the plant.

READING **Draw Conclusions**
What is one of the things plants have in common that helps an oak tree stand tall and strong?

Cell membrane (holds the cell together)

Nucleus (cell control center)

Mitochondrion (cell energy processor)

Vacuole (storage space)

Animal Cell

Animal cells do not have a cell wall or chlorophyll.

What Are the Major Plant Groups?

People have always tried to make sense of their surroundings. One way to do this is to look for patterns. Finding such patterns among plants can help answer very important questions, such as: What plants are good to eat? What plants are poisonous? What plants contain valuable medicines? What plants produce wood that is strong and hard?

The science of finding patterns among living things is called *classification* (klas·uh·fi·KAY·shuhn). Ancient scientists came up with very simple classification systems for plants. These were based on characteristics that anyone could see. Remember, there were no microscopes or other complex instruments in those days. In 350 B.C. the Greek scientist Aristotle classified plants into three large groups—herbs (little plants), shrubs (bigger plants), and trees (the biggest plants). Aristotle's classification system was based on size.

This made sense at the time. However, as scientists learned more about plants, they realized that size was not a sensible way to classify them.

For example, today we know that a tiny blade of grass is more like a bamboo that is as tall as a ten-story building than it is like a moss that grows close to the ground.

Vascular and Nonvascular Plants

By getting a look at what goes on inside plants—not what they look like on the outside—scientists have been able to divide them into two large groups. Let's take a close look inside plants to see what scientists found; something that separates one large group from the other.

READING Charts

Write a paragraph describing the differences between vascular and nonvascular plants. Give two examples of each.

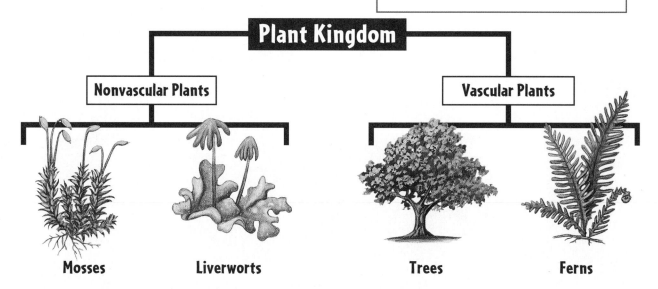

Plant Kingdom

Nonvascular Plants

Mosses   Liverworts

Vascular Plants

Trees   Ferns

First, look inside the stem of a moss. What do you see? You see lots of cells packed together like pieces in a jigsaw puzzle. The cells look very much like one another. Water from outside is passing directly into the cells.

Now, do the same thing with the stem of a corn plant. You see something very different here. Lengths of tubelike cells tunnel up and down the stem. Water taken in by the plant's roots is moving up one set of tubes toward the plant's leaves, flowers, and other parts. At the same time, foods made in the leaves are moving down the other set of tubes, which lead to all of the plant's parts. These tubes are called *vascular tissue.*

Scientists call plants that have this kind of tissue—such as trees and flowering plants—**vascular** (VAS·kyuh·luhr) plants. *Vascular* means "composed of or containing vessels," like the veins and arteries in your body. Scientists call plants that don't have this kind of tissue—such as mosses and other simple plants—**nonvascular** plants. All plants fall into one of these two groups.

▷ **What is the difference between vascular and nonvascular plants?**

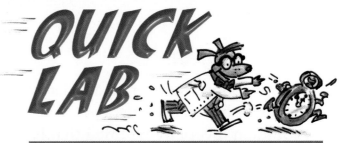

QUICK LAB

FOR SCHOOL OR HOME

Tubelike Plant Parts

1. Observe Use a hand lens to examine the parts of a celery stalk, piece of moss, or leaf. Draw what you see.

2. Hypothesize Make a guess about the function of each structure.

3. Add water to a bottle so the water is about an inch deep. Add a few drops of food coloring to the water.

4. Try putting different plant pieces in the colored water. Observe them after a few minutes. Record what you see.

5. Interpret Data Write an explanation for what you see. Explain why your observations support or don't support your guess.

What Are the Divisions of the Plant Kingdom?

As you've discovered, all plants have certain characteristics in common. Every living thing that has these characteristics belongs to the plant kingdom. A kingdom is the largest subdivision of living things.

While all plants have certain characteristics in common, they have their differences, too. As you have seen, plants may be vascular or non-vascular. However, the plants within each of these two groups are far from identical. This observation prompted scientists to divide nonvascular plants into smaller and smaller

Plant Kingdom

Division: Nonvascular Plants

Vascular Seedless Plants

Hornworts   Mosses   Liverworts   Horsetails

READING
Charts

1. Name two plants you are familiar with and the division you think each belongs to.

2. Pick two plant divisions from the chart. List two ways they are alike. List two ways they are different.

groups. The scientists did the same for vascular plants. They divided vascular plants into seedless plants and plants with seeds. Then they divided seed plants into flowering and nonflowering plants.

The smallest groups would have plants most like one another. The larger groups would have plants least like one another. This meant that the smaller the group, the more closely related were its members.

The chart on these two pages shows the plants divided into groups called *divisions*. These divisions make up the plant kingdom. You will discover the other kingdoms of living things on the following four pages.

▷ **What are some examples of plants belonging to each division of the plant kingdom?**

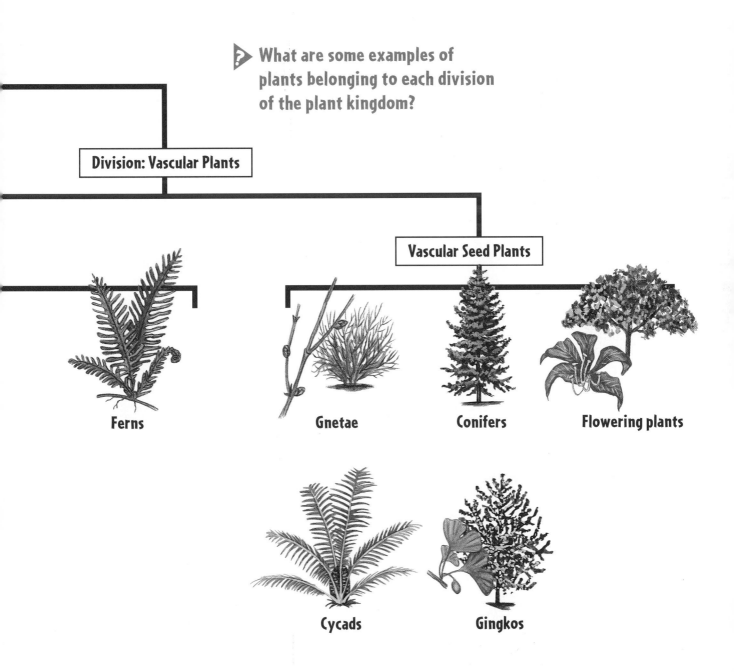

Division: Vascular Plants

Vascular Seed Plants

Ferns   Gnetae   Conifers   Flowering plants

Cycads   Gingkos

What Makes Animals Different from Plants?

Unlike plants, animals cannot make their own food. Animals also differ from plants because animals can move from one place to another during some parts of their lives.

All animals are grouped into one kingdom, known as the animal kingdom. The animal kingdom is divided into smaller and smaller groups. The chart on this page shows two of these groups. The first level contains groups called *phyla* (FIGH·luh) (singular, *phylum*). Some are shown on the left. The next level contains groups called *classes*. Some examples of animals in these groups are shown on the right.

▷ **How are animals different from plants?**

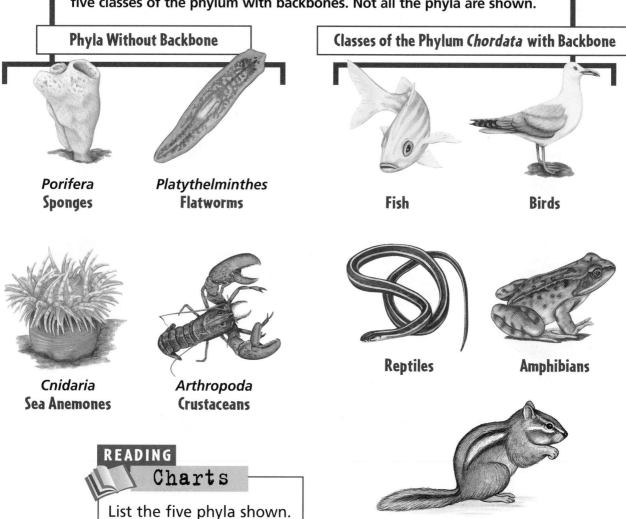

Animal Kingdom

Phyla in the animal kingdom are like divisions in the plant kingdom. On the left are members of four phyla without backbones. On the right are five classes of the phylum with backbones. Not all the phyla are shown.

Phyla Without Backbone

Porifera
Sponges

Platythelminthes
Flatworms

Cnidaria
Sea Anemones

Arthropoda
Crustaceans

Classes of the Phylum *Chordata* with Backbone

Fish

Birds

Reptiles

Amphibians

Mammals

READING
Charts

List the five phyla shown.

What Is a Fungus?

It may be one celled or many celled. It doesn't make its own food as plants do or eat food as animals do. Instead it simply absorbs (takes in) food from decaying dead organisms and wastes in its environment. What is it? It's a **fungus** (FUNG·guhs).

Fungi (FUN·jigh)—the plural of *fungus*—can be very useful living things. Some of them have great flavors. Others contain chemicals that fight diseases. Still others help your bread to rise or turn cheeses sharp and tangy. Fungi in soil break down decaying plants and animals so that their chemicals can be used by living things. You might say that such fungi clean up our environment.

Unfortunately, the fungus kingdom also contains organisms that cause problems for people. Some fungi are poisonous. Some fungi give people itchy diseases, like athlete's foot. Some fungi can spoil food and make you sick. Some fungi coat bathroom tiles and basement walls with smelly black or white fuzz. In the autumn of 1997, one kind of fungus was even responsible for the closing of a library in Staten Island, a part of New York City. The fungus, which grows in damp places like the library's basement, caused people to cough and sneeze as if they had the flu.

The chart on this page shows the groups of the fungus kingdom.

▷ **How are members of the fungus kingdom different from plants?**

Fungus Kingdom

Yeasts, morels, mildews

Molds

Mushrooms, smuts, rusts

READING
Diagrams

1. What are the three main groups of fungi?
2. Make a chart listing things useful fungi can do.

What Is a Protist?

What do you see when you look into a lake, pond, river, or ocean? Sometimes it looks like clear water. However, that "clear" water is home to millions of microscopic living things that belong to the **protist** (PROH·tist) kingdom. This kingdom isn't made up of just microscopic living things. It also includes living things you can see without a microscope, such as seaweed and green pond scum. Although most protists live in water, some inhabit the land.

Some protists are single cells that swim in the water in search of smaller living things to eat. Others, like seaweeds, are made up of groups of the same cells that are linked together. Called algae, these protists don't have to hunt for food. They contain chlorophyll. All they have to do is float on water in the sunlight, soak up the Sun's rays, and make their own food. Still other kinds of protists are one celled, swim around, and contain chlorophyll.

Members of the protist kingdom certainly seem very different. However, if scientists put them in the same kingdom, they must have something in common. You would discover that "something" if you peered at the cells of protists under a microscope. You'd notice a dense, dark structure, called a *nucleus* (NEW·klee·uhs) inside each cell. If you looked very carefully, you'd see that the nucleus was surrounded by a thin envelope. Scientists call this envelope a *membrane* (MEM·brayn). The chart shows some of the groups of the protist kingdom.

▷ **How are some protists like plants?**

Protist Kingdom

Slime molds

Diatoms

Dinoflagellates

Green algae

Euglenas

What Are Bacteria?

Bacteria (bak·TEER·ee·uh) are the tiniest living things. They are also very simple. Some can cause a great deal of trouble, like infections. Others are necessary for animals and plants to survive.

Some kinds of bacteria group together in clusters or chains. Other kinds don't. You can only see bacteria under a microscope. Each *bacterium* (bak·TEER·ee·uhm) is a single cell without a nucleus.

The "ancient" bacteria kingdom includes some fascinating organisms. One type lives in the digestive system of cows. It helps the cow by digesting cellulose, the main substance in grass, which the cow eats but can't digest. Still another kind of "ancient" bacterium lives deep in the ocean, where lava seeps through cracks in the ocean floor. The red-hot lava heats the water up to 105°C. That's hotter than the temperature of boiling water!

The true bacteria kingdom also contains some unusual members. Have you ever seen a blue-green spot in a polar bear's white fur? If so, you detected *cyanobacteria* (sigh·uh·noh·bak·TEER·ee·uh). The prefix *cyano-* means "blue."

Some true bacteria cause diseases in plants and animals. A "strep" throat is caused by a true bacterium. If your stomach aches after eating spoiled food, the culprit is likely to be another true bacterium. More serious diseases like tuberculosis and certain kinds of pneumonia are also caused by true bacteria.

▷ **How are bacteria different from plants and other organisms?**

Bacteria Kingdoms

"Ancient" Bacteria

These bacteria are methanogens. They use carbon dioxide and produce methane (natural gas).

True Bacteria

These bacteria are streptococci—the ones that can give you a strep throat.

What Was "The Vine That Ate the South"?

The Philadelphia Centennial Exposition in 1876 was part of the United States' 100th birthday celebration. Many countries had exhibits. The Japanese, known for their fine gardens, exhibited many unusual plants.

One of those plants was a woody vine. It had hairy green leaves and tiny purple flowers that hung in long clusters. It was called "kudzu" (KOOD·zew).

Today people in America's southern states call it other things: "Mile-a-Minute Vine," "Foot-a-Night Vine," and, more frighteningly, "The Vine That Ate the South."

"The Vine That Ate the South," and "Mile-a-Minute Vine" are exaggerations, but "Foot-a-Night Vine" is not. The plant can grow that much each day. It can spread out over 18 meters (60 feet) in a single summer and choke the life out of other, weaker plants. Fortunately, it dies back in the winter.

How did kudzu escape from Philadelphia? Why does it now cover seven million acres of America's southland? It was pretty. In the late 1800s, homeowners used it to decorate gardens and homes. It was tasty to animals. In the 1920s farmers grew it to feed cows, sheep, and other farm animals. Its huge 2-meter-long (6-foot-long) roots grew to be 18 centimeters (7 inches) in diameter and weighed up to 182 kilograms (400 pounds). Those roots hung on to soil in a tight grip. In the 1940s conservation workers planted it all over the South to keep soil from being washed away by heavy rains.

What nobody counted on was the hardiness of the plant. It grew best in hot, rainy areas. It found an ideal home in the South. There was something else that promoted its rapid growth— its lack of natural enemies. They kept it in check in Japan but not in America. These were insect pests that lived in Japan but not in the American South.

Today kudzu is labeled a weed by the United States Department of Agriculture. Kudzu can be controlled with weed killers.

> **Why did kudzu become such a problem in the South?**

The purple flowers of the kudzu are very beautiful. They smell good, too. Lots of people bought the plants to decorate their properties.

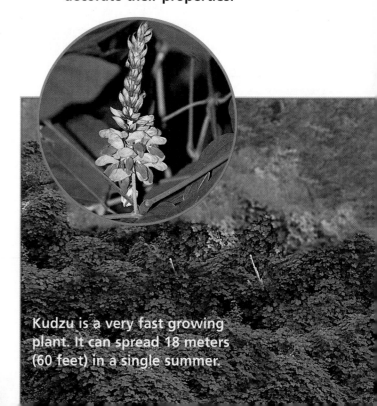

Kudzu is a very fast growing plant. It can spread 18 meters (60 feet) in a single summer.

Why It Matters

There are many different kinds of plants, but they are all very important. Without plants, life would be impossible on Earth. Almost everything you eat comes from plants, or from animals that eat plants.

Think and Write

1. What do plants have in common?

2. How are plants similar to animals, protists, fungi, and bacteria? How are plants different?

3. How are vascular plants different from nonvascular plants?

4. Describe three characteristics of plants.

5. **Critical Thinking** How can plants that are imported from other parts of the world become pests here?

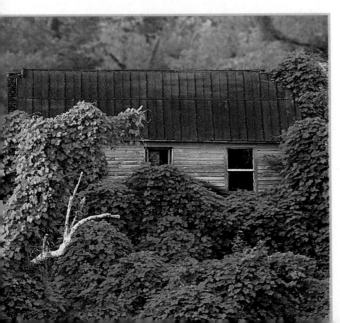

L·I·N·K·S

WRITING LINK

Write a paragraph. Tell what plants are important in your life, and explain why.

MATH LINK

Solve this problem. Under ideal conditions a bacterium can divide into two bacteria every 20 minutes. Then each of those bacteria can divide into two new ones after another 20 minutes. If you start with one bacterium, how many will you have after one hour? After two hours? After three hours? Five hours? Eight hours?

ART LINK

Make a poster. Design a poster using spore prints. Take a ripe mushroom, and remove the stalk. Examine the mushroom cap with a hand lens. Then put the cap, with the underside facing down, on a piece of poster paper. Cover it with a bowl. After three hours, remove the bowl. Experiment with making various designs.

TECHNOLOGY LINK

At the Computer Visit www.mhscience02.com for more links.

Roots, Stems, and Leaves

Vocabulary

xylem, A20

cortex, A20

epidermis, A20

root cap, A20

root hairs, A20

phloem, A21

cambium, A21

chloroplast, A24

transpiration, A25

Get Ready

What do you have in common with a plant? Would you believe that you and a plant have similar needs? Still, there is a big difference. You can move around to get things. You can change things around you—like your room temperature. Plants stay in one place, yet different kinds of plants can survive in very different places. How? What helps plants survive in their surroundings?

Process Skill

You predict when you state possible results of an event or experiment.

Explore Activity

How Do a Plant's Parts Help It Survive?

Materials

cactus

water plant, such as an *Elodea* or a duckweed

flowering plant, such as a geranium

Procedure

1 **Observe** Look at the physical properties of the leaves of each plant. Note the color, size, and shape of the leaves.

2 **Communicate** List any other plant parts that you see.

3 **Communicate** Observe the physical properties of these parts. Record your observations.

Drawing Conclusions

1 **Interpret Data** How do the parts of a cactus help it survive in a hot, dry desert?

2 **Infer** Would the geranium be able to survive in the desert? Why or why not?

3 **Infer** Could the water plant survive out of water? Why or why not?

4 **Going Further: Predict** Could these plants survive outside where you live? Why or why not? For each plant, what conditions would you have to change so that the plant could survive outside where you live?

> **Main Idea** All plants have certain parts with the same functions.

How Do a Plant's Parts Help It Survive?

Some plant roots help you survive. That's because they are foods. Beets, carrots, sweet potatoes, radishes, and turnips are the roots of different plants. How do roots help a plant survive?

Most plants have roots that hold them in the ground. Some plants, like mosses, don't have true roots. Still, mosses have rootlike structures that anchor them. Roots help keep plants from getting swept away by wind and running water. Roots draw up water and minerals from the soil. Plants must have water and minerals to make their own food. Roots also store food for the plant. That's especially true of sweet potato, sugar beet, and carrot plants.

A root gets its start early in the life of a plant. If you were to look at a lima bean as it sprouted, you would see a tiny piece of the young plant growing straight downward. This is the plant's first root.

This root bores deeper and deeper into the soil. Why don't the rough particles of soil rub away and harm the young root? The tip of the root is protected by a layer of tough cells called the root cap.

Parts of a Root

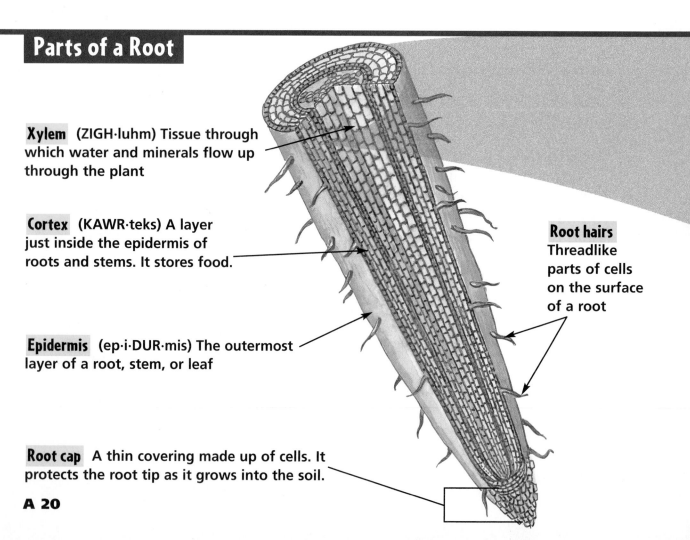

Xylem (ZIGH·luhm) Tissue through which water and minerals flow up through the plant

Cortex (KAWR·teks) A layer just inside the epidermis of roots and stems. It stores food.

Epidermis (ep·i·DUR·mis) The outermost layer of a root, stem, or leaf

Root hairs Threadlike parts of cells on the surface of a root

Root cap A thin covering made up of cells. It protects the root tip as it grows into the soil.

Soon more roots branch out from the sides of the original root. *Taproots* have one large root with a few hairy branching roots. They look like a carrot or a beet. Other roots, like those of grass or rye plants, are made up of only thin hairy branching roots called *fibrous roots*.

Taproots tend to grow deep into the ground and reach water deep down. Fibrous roots spread out near the soil's surface. They collect water where there is little rain that only soaks into the very top layer of soil.

Fibrous roots can make huge networks. The total surface area of the root system of a single rye plant was 639 square meters (6,879 square feet)!

Some plants like orchids, that grow high in the branches of rain forest trees, have *aerial roots*. These roots never touch the ground. They take in moisture from the air. *Prop roots*, like those of a corn plant, grow like fingers out of the bottom of the stem. These roots help prop up the plant.

The structure of a root helps it absorb water and minerals and send them to other parts of the plant. The diagram shows how this happens.

Water and minerals enter the root hairs. They pass through the root's cortex to the xylem. They then move up the xylem, into the plant's stem, and to all parts of the plant.

Phloem (FLOH·em) Tissue through which food from the leaves moves down through a plant

Cambium (KAM·bee·uhm) A layer that separates the xylem from the phloem. The cambium is where new xylem and phloem grow.

READING Draw Conclusions
How do you think fibrous roots would help a plant grow in a dry or desert area?

A 21

How Are Stems Similar?

Some stems are soft and delicate, like those of a young corn plant. Others are hard and tough, like those of a giant redwood tree. No matter what they look like, all stems have certain things in common.

All stems support leaves. Some also support flowers. Stems help leaves reach open places, where the leaves can be bathed in sunlight.

Stems also hold the transportation system for plants. This system lets water and minerals move from the roots to all parts of the plant, especially its leaves. It moves foods made in leaves to all other parts of the plant.

The *xylem* makes up the part of the transportation system that moves water and minerals up from the roots. The *phloem* moves food from the plant's leaves to its other parts. Many stems also have a *cambium*—a layer of cells—that separates the two. In addition, woody stems are protected by a tough outer layer of tissue, called bark.

Soft and woody stems have the same basic parts for transporting water, minerals, and food to all parts of a plant.

Woody stem

Phloem

Cambium

Xylem

Soft stem

READING
Diagrams

How are the xylem, phloem, and cambium arranged differently in a woody stem and in a soft stem?

Strawberry stems, called runners, grow along the ground.

A potato is an underground stem.

Some stems do more than support a plant and give it a transportation system. For example, the stems of plants like potatoes and sugarcane store food for the plants to use later. The potatoes and sugarcane you eat actually are stems. The stems of cactus plants store water, which the plants use during long dry periods in the desert. Still other stems, like those of asparagus, help make the plant's food.

Not all stems grow up into the air. Those of strawberries grow along the ground. That's how a strawberry patch spreads and grows.

The stem of the cactus stores water.

▶ **What are two ways in which all stems are similar?**

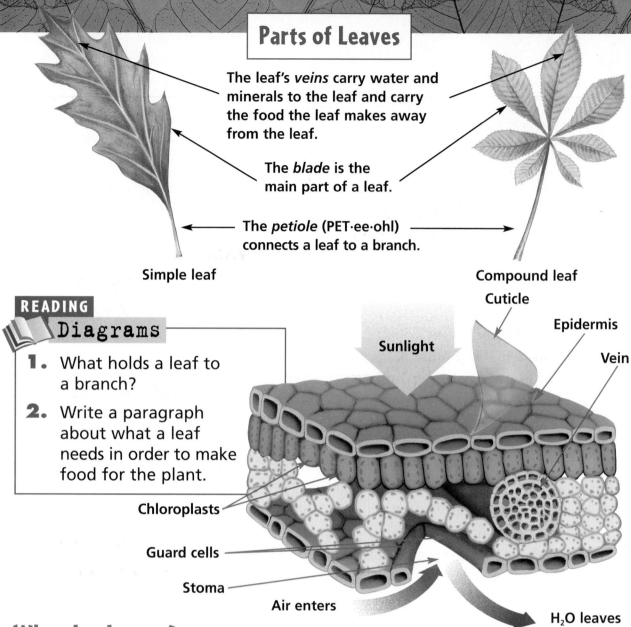

Parts of Leaves

The leaf's *veins* carry water and minerals to the leaf and carry the food the leaf makes away from the leaf.

The *blade* is the main part of a leaf.

The *petiole* (PET·ee·ohl) connects a leaf to a branch.

Simple leaf

Compound leaf

Cuticle

Epidermis

Vein

Sunlight

Chloroplasts

Guard cells

Stoma

Air enters

H₂O leaves

READING

Diagrams

1. What holds a leaf to a branch?

2. Write a paragraph about what a leaf needs in order to make food for the plant.

What Are Leaves?

Leaves come in all shapes and sizes. Most of the leaves you see hang from their plants as single leaves or in groups. Maple and oak trees have single leaves. They're called *simple* leaves.

Horse chestnut and locust leaves come in clusters. These are called *compound* leaves.

The parts of a leaf work together to help keep the plant alive.

The outermost layer of a leaf is its *epidermis*. Cells of the epidermis secrete a waxy coating, called a *cuticle*

(KYEW·ti·kuhl). The cuticle helps keep water from leaving the leaf.

The leaf makes food in cells between the layers of the epidermis. These cells contain **chloroplasts** (KLAWR·uh·plasts), the green food factories of plants. In addition to sunlight, these factories need water, minerals, and the carbon dioxide in air to make food.

The air comes through tiny pores in the bottom of the leaves called *stomata* (STOH·muh·tuh) (singular, *stoma*).

When the stomata are open to let in air, water can also evaporate from the leaf. The job of opening and closing each stoma is performed by two *guard cells* that surround it.

When the plant has plenty of water, the guard cells swell and pull open the stoma. When the plant has too little water, the guard cells shrink and close the stoma.

Importance of Leaves

Many leaves have green, broad, flat surfaces that help "capture" the sunlight the plant needs to make its food. Other leaves have different shapes for different purposes. The spines on a cactus protect the plant. The needles of a pine tree are covered with a wax that keeps the tree from losing too much water. The crunchy layers of an onion store food. The leaves of the garden pea plant wind around objects to give the plant added support.

The leaves of the Venus's-flytrap are colorful insect traps. They snap shut when an insect flies inside.

Leaves are often far from roots, yet they help roots take in water from soil. When water evaporates from the leaves, more water moves up through the plant to replace the lost water. This process is called **transpiration** (tran·spuh·RAY·shuhn).

People eat all parts of plants, including leaves such as lettuce, cabbage, parsley, and spinach. Why are leaves important to you?

▷ **What do leaves do for a plant?**

QUICK LAB

FOR SCHOOL OR HOME

Leaves

1. Collect a variety of different leaves that you eat as food.

2. **Observe** Examine them with a hand lens. Draw what you see.

3. In what ways are the leaves you observed alike? In what ways are they different?

4. Compare the leaves you examined with the leaves your classmates looked at. In what ways are your leaves similar to theirs? In what ways are they different? Record your observations.

How Do Orchids Grow?

Many kinds of orchids are rooted in the ground. However, in tropical rain forests, certain orchids grow high up in the trees, dangling their roots in the air. The orchids' colors "paint" the trees with flashes of red, purple, pink, and orange.

One kind of orchid looks and smells a lot like a certain kind of female bee. The orchid attracts male bees. As the bees go from flower to flower, they help the orchids reproduce.

A sudden shower drenches the tree where the orchid lives. Tiny streams of water trickle down the tree's bark. The orchid's exposed roots soak up some of the water that washes off the tree trunk and branches above. Along with the water come minerals the orchid needs.

The roots of a nearby orchid are very strange. They are flat, as long as you are tall, and wrapped around the branches of a tree like a huge flat worm. In fact, the scientific name of the orchid means "tapeworm leaf."

You might think that this is a strange name for a root. However, in a way, it makes sense. The roots of this plant are green, like leaves! Scientists have discovered that these roots do two jobs for the orchid. They absorb

Dangling their roots in the air, these orchids cling to trees high in the canopy of a tropical rain forest. Their aerial roots soak up water that trickles along tree trunks and branches.

water and minerals that pass by, and like leaves, they make food for the orchid. This orchid needs no leaves, although it has some very little ones covering its stem.

▷ **What makes the roots of some tropical rain forest orchids unusual?**

Why It Matters

We depend on plants for many things. Among them are food, clothing, and shelter. Since plants are needed by all living things, it is important to know how they survive. Part of a plant's ability to survive depends on how well its parts work together to move water and minerals in one direction and food in the other direction. The parts that do this are roots, stems, and leaves.

Think and Write

1. List three things plants need in order to live and grow.

2. Compare and contrast two or more different kinds of roots. Do the same for stems and leaves.

3. How do roots, stems, and leaves help a plant survive?

4. How can rain forest orchids live high up in the trees?

5. **Critical Thinking** How does having flowers that look like bees help a plant survive?

ART LINK

Make a poster. Find out the names of different orchids and where they come from. Make a poster using photographs or drawings of at least two orchids. Under each illustration, write what you know about the orchid.

WRITING LINK

Write an essay. The giant leaves of the royal lily pad are strong enough to hold up the weight of a small child. Research this Amazon plant, and write an essay about it.

MATH LINK

Solve this problem. Find the total surface area of the leaves of a single tree. Use graph paper to estimate the surface area of a single leaf. Then estimate the number of leaves on a single branch. (Find the average of several branches.) Estimate the number of branches on the tree. Find the total number of leaves, then find their total surface area.

TECHNOLOGY LINK

At the Computer Visit www.mhscience02.com for more links.

Plant Power:
M E D I C I N E S

What good are plant parts? Bitter or poisonous chemicals in some plant parts protect them from predators. The chemicals have powerful effects on animals that eat them. They might also be useful in medicines for humans!

Fever Powder of Peru

Missionaries to Peru in the 1600s found natives making a bitter powder. It was ground-up bark from the cinchona, a rare jungle tree. The powder cured the fever of malaria!

Suddenly there was a demand for cinchona bark, and the quinine in it.

Doctors now use artificial quinine and other drugs to treat malaria. However, the parasite that causes malaria is becoming resistant to the drugs. Cinchona bark still works when modern medicine fails!

Poison to Kill Cancer?

Humans have used yews for thousands of years. Spears and bows were made from the wood. The bark yielded a poison.

In the 1960s the National Cancer Institute began looking for plant chemicals that might kill cancer cells.

Pacific yews weren't valued for their wood, so many were cut down and thrown away!

Cinchona

Quinine is a bitter chemical found in the bark of the cinchona tree.

In 1963 they found such a chemical, taxol, in the bark of the Pacific yew.

By the time cancer scientists proved that taxol works against cancer, the Pacific yew was thought to be rapidly disappearing. It was even protected by the federal government for a while. Today scientists make taxol from needles and twigs of all kinds of yews, not just the bark of the Pacific yew.

Many plants may be in danger of extinction. People are destroying Earth's rain forests. If plants die off before they're found, we'll never know if their chemicals could have cured diseases.

MEDICINES FROM PLANTS			
Here are a few medicines made from plant parts.			
PLANT	**PARTS**	**MEDICINE**	**USED FOR**
Belladonna	leaves/roots	atropine	eye disorders
Foxglove	leaves	digitalis	heart problems
Periwinkle	leaves	vinblastine	leukemia
Rauwolfia	roots	reserpine	high blood pressure
Willow	bark	aspirin	reducing pain and fever
Wild Mexican yam	tuberous roots	cortisone	curbing inflammation

What Did I Learn?

1. Cinchona bark is used to
   A protect Pacific yew trees
   B treat malaria
   C make belladonna
   D make aspirin

2. Taxol comes from
   F the bark of Pacific yew trees
   G the bark of cinchona trees
   H periwinkles
   J willow bark

AT THE COMPUTER

Visit www.mhscience02.com to learn more about medicine.

Vocabulary

photosynthesis, A32

respiration, A33

The Importance of Plants

Get Ready

Why are plants important? Plants give us food. They also give us oxygen we need to breathe. What do plants need in order to do this? Did you ever wonder why crops are planted in open fields, not in the shade? What happens to plants that are kept in a dark corner of the room? Do they do as well as plants that get more light? How will a plant change if it does not get sunlight for several days?

Process Skill

You use variables when you identify and separate things in an experiment that can be changed or controlled.

Explore Activity

What Does Light Do for a Plant?

Materials

growing plant (window plants from home or plants from an aquarium)

opaque paper or aluminum foil

Procedure

1 Cover part of a leaf of a growing plant. Be sure to wash your hands after handling plants.

2 **Use Variables** Cover at least four different leaves of the plant in the same way.

3 Place the whole plant in a window that gets lots of light.

4 **Experiment** Remove the foil from one leaf after one class period. How is that leaf different from the uncovered leaves? Record your observations. Then cover the leaf again.

5 **Experiment** Continue your observations. Remove the foil from another leaf after one day, another after two days, and another after a week. Record your observations. Replace the foil each time.

Drawing Conclusions

1 **Observe** After one class period, how was the leaf you had just uncovered different from the uncovered leaves?

2 **Interpret Data** How did the difference you noticed change after a day, two days, and a week?

3 **Infer** How do light and darkness affect the growth of leaves?

4 **Going Further: Use Variables** Remove the coverings from the four leaves, and observe them for another week. How do these leaves respond to being uncovered?

Main Idea Plants make food and produce oxygen through photosynthesis.

What Is Photosynthesis?

When you walk to a grocery store to buy food, you are really doing two things. You are using energy to get to the store, and you are buying energy at the store. Walking uses energy. Food provides you with energy.

All living things need energy to survive. Where do they get energy? Animals eat food to get energy. Plants make their own food. However, the very process of making food uses up energy. Where does the plant get this energy? It comes from light, especially sunlight.

Light is a form of energy that plants use to make their food. Plants capture the energy of light and trap it in the foods they make. Later, when they need this energy, they get it back from the food. The food-making process is called **photosynthesis** (foh·tuh·SIN·thuh·sis). This term comes from Greek words that mean "putting together by light." The process is very complex, but basically here's how it happens.

First, sunlight strikes a green part of a plant, such as a leaf. The leaf is green because it has a green chemical called chlorophyll. Chlorophyll helps the plant make its food. The chlorophyll is found in plant parts called chloroplasts. The chloroplasts act like tiny chemical factories. Inside them water and carbon

Photosynthesis

Carbon dioxide	Light	Sugar
+	→→→	+
Water	Chlorophyll	Oxygen

Light

Cells with chlorophyll

Carbon dioxide

Sugars

Oxygen

Water

Photosynthesis Hydrogen (from water) and carbon dioxide join in the presence of sunlight and chlorophyll to form sugars and oxygen.

The water and carbon dioxide that form are released into the air.

dioxide from the air combine to make sugar and oxygen. However, this reaction could not happen without the help of light energy.

The sugars that the Sun's energy helps the leaf to make then go into the leaf's veins and off to all parts of the plant.

The oxygen the plant makes goes into the air. All animals must breathe in oxygen to stay alive. At the same time, they breathe out carbon dioxide, which the plants need.

Now that the Sun's energy is trapped in the sugars that the plant made, how does the plant get the energy back out? Its cells use oxygen to break apart the sugar. When the sugar breaks apart, it releases energy that the plant uses. This process is called **respiration** (res·puh·RAY·shuhn). This is the same process that releases energy in animals.

> ▶ **How is photosynthesis different from respiration?**

READING
Diagrams

In what process is carbon dioxide released?

The oxygen is released into the air.

The sugars that form are stored in green plants.

Respiration In respiration, which occurs in plants and animals, sugars and oxygen join to produce water, carbon dioxide, and energy.

99¢   29¢ $3.09 $5.00

A 33

In autumn cooling temperatures signal trees to stop making green chlorophyll. The chlorophyll disappears, uncovering other colors.

How Do Leaves Change Color?

Do you live in an area where the leaves change color in the autumn? If so, you may have noticed that the leaves of all plants, except evergreens, change color in the fall. You wake up one morning in September or October, and the trees near where you live are speckled with flashes of yellow, orange, and maybe red.

All the yellows and oranges were inside the leaves ever since summer. However, you couldn't see them because there was too much green chlorophyll there.

It's as if you put some yellow and orange objects in the bottom of a bucket of green paint. The yellow and orange objects would be in there, yet all you would see is green.

However, if you could take out all the green paint, what would you see? The answer is what you see in the fall.

How is the greenness taken out of leaves in the fall?

As temperatures begin to drop, the leaves of trees other than evergreens stop making chlorophyll. Slowly the chlorophyll that remains begins to break down and vanishes. Now you can see the yellow and orange colors. If the weather is especially cool and the sky is clear most of the time, you may see another color—red. This color wasn't in the leaves to begin with. It's made by them in places where the fall climate is cool and clear. Where the climate is warmer and the sky is cloudy a lot of the time, the colors will be mostly yellows and oranges.

READING Draw Conclusions
Where would you expect to see a greater variety of autumn colors—in Vermont or South Carolina?

Process Skill
B U I L D E R

SKILL Experiment

Why Leaves Change Color

To find out why leaves change color in autumn, the first thing you might do is figure out what changes occur in the fall that might cause leaves to change color. Scientists call such changes *variables*. You might identify two of these variables as the amount of daylight and the temperature, both of which go down in the fall.

Next you would make a guess that seems to make sense about which variable causes leaves to change color. This guess is called a *hypothesis*. It is often made in the form of an "*if . . . then . . .*" statement. For example, "*If* the plant doesn't get water, *then* it won't grow." To see if your hypothesis is a good idea, you would perform an experiment. That experiment has to be set up so that it gives a clear answer.

Procedure

1 Look at the drawings. They show three experiments—A, B, C. Study the setups.

2 **Observe** What variable or variables are being tested in the first experiment? Record your answer. What variable or variables are being tested in the other two experiments?

Drawing Conclusions

1 **Infer** Which experiment is testing to see whether light causes leaves to change color? Explain.

2 **Infer** Which experiment is testing to see whether temperature causes leaves to change color? Explain why.

3 **Infer** Which experiment will not give a clear answer? Explain why not.

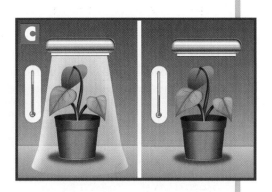

A 35

How Does Water Get from Roots to Leaves?

If you were to dry 1,000 g (2.2 lb) of leaves, you would end up with between 50 and 300 g (1.8–11 oz) of crumbly matter. That's because plants are made up of 70–95 percent water.

Cells in all parts of a plant need water to live and grow. They need water to carry out many vital chemical reactions, including photosynthesis. They also need water to stay firm and not wilt.

Plants constantly lose water through *transpiration*. Over its lifetime an average plant in a mild climate area will lose more than 100 times its weight in water!

It is very important for a plant to efficiently move water from its roots to all its other parts. The diagram on page A37 shows how this is done.

Tropical rain forests pump great amounts of water into the air.

▷ **Why is it important to move water from a plant's roots?**

If a normal plant (left) gets too little water, it will lose firmness and wilt (right).

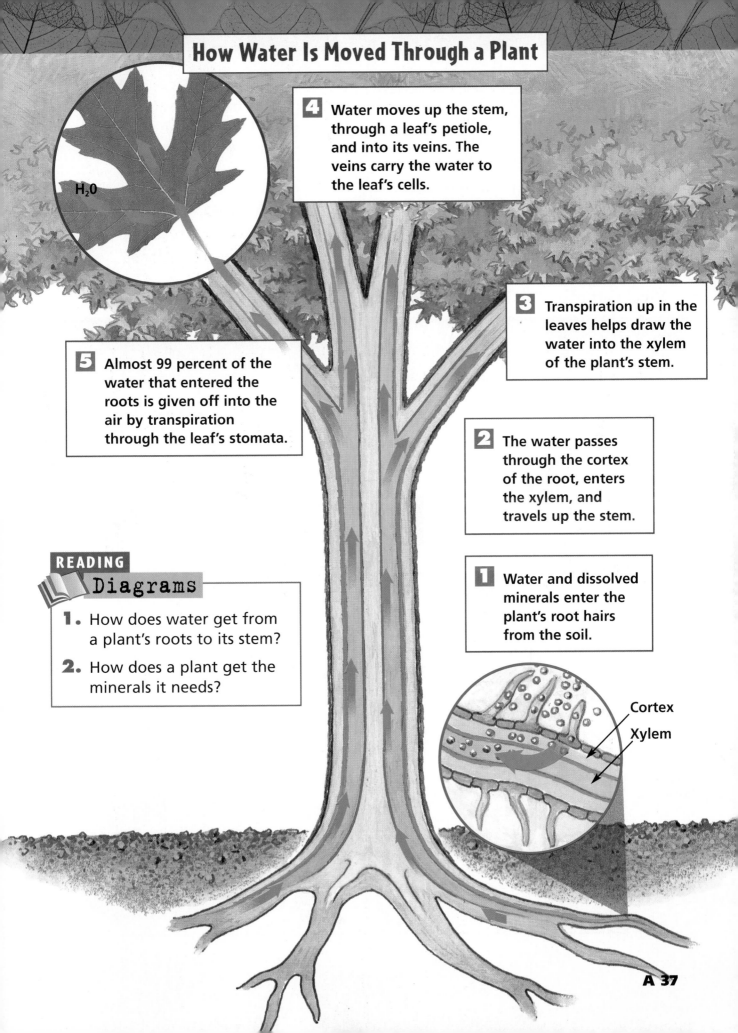

How Water Is Moved Through a Plant

H₂0

4 Water moves up the stem, through a leaf's petiole, and into its veins. The veins carry the water to the leaf's cells.

3 Transpiration up in the leaves helps draw the water into the xylem of the plant's stem.

5 Almost 99 percent of the water that entered the roots is given off into the air by transpiration through the leaf's stomata.

2 The water passes through the cortex of the root, enters the xylem, and travels up the stem.

1 Water and dissolved minerals enter the plant's root hairs from the soil.

READING
Diagrams

1. How does water get from a plant's roots to its stem?

2. How does a plant get the minerals it needs?

Cortex

Xylem

What Parts of Plants Do You Eat?

There probably isn't a part of a plant that you haven't eaten at one time or another. Whether you know it or not, you've eaten roots, stems, leaves, seeds, fruits, flowers, and even the bark and sap of plants. If you don't believe this is true, look at the chart on this page. Which of these plant parts have you eaten?

▷ **What are five examples of plant parts that people use for food?**

READING
Diagrams

What part of a plant is a tomato? A peanut?

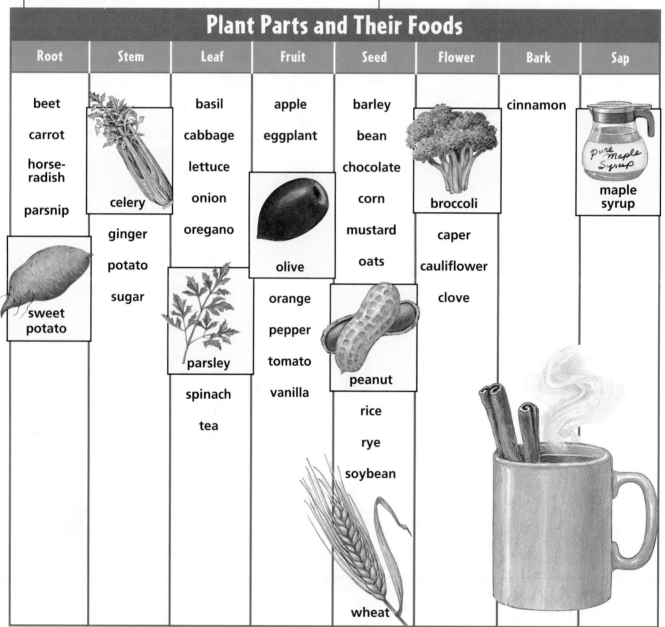

Plant Parts and Their Foods

Root	Stem	Leaf	Fruit	Seed	Flower	Bark	Sap
beet		basil	apple	barley		cinnamon	
carrot		cabbage	eggplant	bean			
horse-radish		lettuce		chocolate			maple syrup
parsnip	celery	onion		corn	broccoli		
	ginger	oregano		mustard	caper		
	potato		olive	oats	cauliflower		
	sugar		orange		clove		
sweet potato		parsley	pepper	peanut			
		spinach	tomato	rice			
		tea	vanilla	rye			
				soybean			
				wheat			

Why It Matters

About 21 percent of the air you breathe is oxygen. You use this oxygen to release energy from the foods you eat.

Most of the oxygen in air comes from plants and other green living things, like algae, that carry on photosynthesis.

Plants and animals need each other in order to survive. Animals need the food and oxygen plants make during photosynthesis. Plants need the carbon dioxide animals give off when they breathe out. Visit www.mhscience02.com to do a research project on photosynthesis.

Think and Write

1. Describe photosynthesis.

2. Describe the process of respiration in plants.

3. Trace the path of water from the soil, through a plant, and into the air.

4. **Experiment** How would you design an experiment to see if the changing temperature or the changing amount of daylight plays a bigger part in why leaves change color in autumn?

5. **Critical Thinking** If there were no plants, would animals be able to survive? Explain.

L·I·N·K·S

LITERATURE LINK

Read *The Power of Green*, the story of some of the plants and protists that live in different areas of the world. When you finish reading, think about the plants and protists that live in your area. Try the activities at the end of the book.

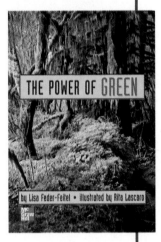

THE POWER OF GREEN

by Lisa Feder-Feitel • Illustrated by Rita Lascaro

ART LINK

Draw an experimental setup. Let's say you thought the amount of rainfall was the reason leaves changed color. Make a set of drawings showing an experiment that would test this hypothesis.

TECHNOLOGY LINK

Science Newsroom CD-ROM Choose *Color My World* to learn more about how leaves change color.

At the Computer Visit www.mhscience02.com for more links.

Cleaning Pollution with Plants

Plants help us in many different ways. They produce oxygen for us to breathe. They provide food for us to eat. We build homes with wood from trees. Lifesaving medicines are made from some plants. Now research shows plants have another amazing use—they help us clean up pollution!

Every year millions of gallons of oil leak into the soil from pipelines, storage tanks, and industrial sites. The usual method of cleanup is to dig up the polluted soil and dispose of it elsewhere. This method is very expensive and disturbs the soil structure.

Researchers Katherine Banks and Paul Schwab have discovered that certain plants—along with tiny soil microbes—will clean up the soil pollutants. The microbes in the soil break down the oil and use it for food. The plants speed up the microbes' activity by getting more oxygen into the soil.

Banks and Schwab have found that certain grasses clean pollution well.

Clover and alfalfa plants also are effective because they increase microbe growth. Finding the right plant, however, can be tricky. Since oil spills occur in different parts of the world, scientists need to use plants that will survive in different climates.

Plants can be used to clean up other kinds of soil pollution, too. Some plants can absorb heavy metals and radioactive material from soil. The plants store the substances in their tissues. Then the plants become toxic and must be destroyed. Mustard plants, for example, can soak up metals, such as lead. In Ukraine, mustard plants were used to remove radiation pollution from the soil around a nuclear plant that exploded.

There are many reasons why using plants may one day be the best way to clean up soil pollution. The method is cheaper, prettier, and powered by an unlimited source of energy—the Sun!

Mustard plants can soak up heavy metals, such as lead. The plants are then burned or dried to recycle the metals.

Researchers Katherine Banks and Paul Schwab of Purdue University discovered that grasses with large root surfaces work well at cleaning up polluted soil.

What Did I Learn?

1. In Ukraine, mustard plants were used to

   A remove pesticides from the soil
   B clean up oil spills in lakes
   C remove radiation pollution from soil
   D clean up oil in parking lots

2. Plants help clean up oil spills by

   F speeding up the "oil-eating" microbes' activity
   G using the oil as plant food
   H absorbing the oil like a paper towel
   J getting more carbon dioxide into the soil

Sunflowers can be used to clean up radioactive wastes from water.

AT THE COMPUTER Visit www.mhscience02.com for more amazing stories and facts about plants.

Chapter 1 Review

Vocabulary

Fill each blank with the best word or words from the list.

cambium, A21
chlorophyll, A6
cortex, A20
epidermis, A20
fungus, A13
phloem, A21
photosynthesis, A32
root cap, A20
transpiration, A25
xylem, A20

1. The outer layer of a root is the _____.

2. Water and minerals flow up through the _____.

3. Foods flow down from the leaves through the _____.

4. Water and minerals then pass through the root's _____ to the xylem.

5. A green chemical called _____ allows plants to use the Sun's energy to make their own foods.

6. A mushroom is a _____.

7. The process by which plants make their own food is called _____.

8. The layer of tough cells that protects the root is called the _____.

9. The process by which water goes out of leaves is known as _____.

10. The _____ separates xylem from phloem.

Test Prep

11. Which of the following is a fungus?

A mold

B moss

C fern

D conifer

12. In the process of making food, plants give off _____.

F sugar

G carbon dioxide

H oxygen

J chloroplasts

13. The green "food factories" of plants are _____.

A chloroplasts

B phloem

C stoma

D epidermis

14. Leaves help roots take in water from soil through the process called _____.

F photosynthesis

G transpiration

H respiration

J perspiration

15. When plants use stored sugar for energy, they go through a process called _____.

  A photosynthesis

  B transpiration

  C respiration

  D perspiration

Concepts and Skills

16. Reading in Science Write a paragraph explaining why ferns can grow taller than mosses.

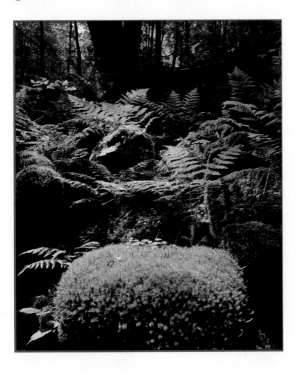

17. Scientific Methods How would you determine how much light a geranium plant needs in order to survive? Write up a design for an experiment that would test this.

18. Decision Making Is there a single correct way to classify an organism? Write a paragraph explaining your answer.

19. Process Skills: Experiment Design an experiment to determine how much mosses, ferns, and grasses depend on water for survival. Write how you would set up the experiment. Write down your hypothesis. Tell what variables you would test.

20. Critical Thinking You dig in the ground and find a fossil of a fern. You then dig deeper and find a fossil of a club moss. What reasoning might let you conclude that club mosses evolved earlier than ferns? Write a paragraph explaining your reasoning.

Boost your test scores!

Be Smart!

Visit www.mhscience02.com

CHAPTER

2

Plant Diversity

Did You Ever Wonder?

Where do orchids grow? Of the thousands of different kinds of orchids, many grow in tropical rain forests. However, about 100 kinds of orchids grow in Europe, Asia, and North America. What do orchids have in common with other flowering plants?

Plants Without Seeds

Vocabulary

rhizoid, A48

spore, A48

frond, A51

rhizome, A51

asexual reproduction, A52

fertilization, A52

sexual reproduction, A52

Get Ready

Have you ever seen plants like these? If so, there were probably none as tall as these. You are looking at ferns in Costa Rica's Monteverde rain forest, one of Earth's dampest places. These ferns grow taller than a six-story building. Their leaves are more than three times longer than you are tall.

Ferns do best in warm, wet places. So do mosses, but mosses grow low to the ground. Why do ferns grow tall while mosses don't? How do the parts of mosses help them live where they do?

Process Skill

You predict when you state possible results of an event or experiment.

Explore Activity

How Do Mosses Get Water?

Materials

hand lens

forceps

dropper

3 microscope slides

coverslip

microscope

moss plant

Procedure

1 **Observe** Place a moss on a paper towel. Use a hand lens to find its rootlike, stemlike, and leaflike parts. Record your observations.

2 **Measure** Use the forceps to remove a leaflike part. Make a wet-mount slide of the part. Observe its cells using the microscope on low power. Determine how thick the leaflike part is by moving the focus up and down.

3 **Observe** Find a capsule-shaped object at the end of the brownish stalk. Observe it with the hand lens. Place the capsule on a slide. Add a drop of water. Place a second slide on top of the capsule. Press down on the top slide with your thumb, and crush the capsule. Carefully remove the top slide and place a coverslip over the crushed capsule. Examine the released structures under low power. Draw what you see.

Drawing Conclusions

1 **Observe** Which parts of the moss are green? Explain why they are green.

2 **Observe** How many cell layers make up the leaflike structure?

3 **Interpret Data** What structures anchor the moss plant? What was the capsule?

4 **Going Further: Predict** What do you think the objects inside the capsule do? How would you test your prediction?

Main Idea Seedless nonvascular plants and seedless vascular plants have different structures but similar life cycles.

How Do Mosses Get Water?

Mosses and their close relatives the liverworts are nonvascular plants. They don't have the long tubelike structures vascular plants have. They cling to damp soil, sheltered rocks, and the shady side of trees. Mosses and liverworts are tiny plants, only 2 to 5 centimeters (about 1 to 2 inches) tall. Mosses' leaves are only one or two cells thick.

Mosses and liverworts don't have roots. However, they stay anchored in one place. That's because they have hairlike fibers that do a job much like roots. The fibers are called **rhizoids** (RIGH·zoydz). Rhizoids, like other parts of mosses and liverworts, can take in water from their surroundings. The water then travels directly from one cell to the next.

Most of the plants you see every day grow from seeds. However, mosses and liverworts are seedless plants. They grow from **spores** . Spores are cells that can develop into new organisms.

Nonvascular

Mosses

Liverworts

Mosses and liverworts grow in damp places. Most are tiny plants, growing only 2 to 5 centimeters (about 1 to 2 inches) tall.

Club mosses

Club mosses produce spores at the ends of stems in structures that look like tiny pine cones.

Spores are tiny structures found inside a capsule called a *spore capsule*.

Many mosses look like green, fuzzy pillows. Many liverworts look more like flat leaves. Ancient people thought that the shape of these plants resembled a liver. That's how they got their name.

Seedless Vascular Plants

True mosses and liverworts are seedless plants. So are their more distant relatives club mosses, spike mosses, horsetails, and ferns. All of them use spores to reproduce. However, mosses and liverworts are different from the other four in a very important way.

Mosses and liverworts don't have a vascular system. Club mosses, spike mosses, horsetails, and ferns do.

The vascular tissue in these plants is made up of long tubelike cells. These cells let water and food move easily over long distances. That is why vascular plants can grow very tall and thick. That is also why nonvascular plants like true mosses and liverworts are so short and delicate. The trunks of the largest ferns can be as thick as your body.

READING **Compare and Contrast**
How do mosses and ferns get water?

Vascular

Horsetails

The stems of horsetails are hollow, have a ring of vascular tissue and joints, and contain a gritty, sandy substance called silica.

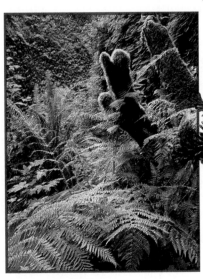

Ferns

Ferns come in all sizes and shapes and live in different kinds of climates.

Spike mosses

Spike mosses, such as this "resurrection plant," live in the desert. Resurrection plants can dry out when there is no rain, but they do not die. They revive when water becomes available again.

QUICK LAB

FOR SCHOOL OR HOME

Ferns

1. **Observe** Carefully examine a fern plant. Look at the stem. Observe how the leaves grow from the stem. Find the veins in the leaves. Draw what you see.

2. **Observe** Find a leaf whose bottom is covered with brownish spots. These are spore cases.

3. **Experiment** Place a drop of water on a clean slide. Use a toothpick to scrape one of the spore cases into the drop of water.

4. **Observe** Examine the spore case under the low power of a microscope. What does the spore case contain?

5. **Infer** What do ferns and mosses have in common?

What Are Ferns?

Ferns once formed huge forests on Earth. You can still find them today in many wooded areas. Many people also grow ferns at home. What are ferns like?

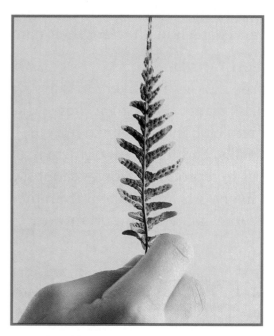

Finding spore cases on the bottom of a fern leaf

Preparing a slide for viewing one spore case

Ferns have leaves that are called **fronds** (FRAHNDZ). They grow above the ground from an underground stem called a **rhizome** (RIGH·zohm). Roots, which anchor the plant to the soil or to a tree, branch out from the rhizome.

The bottom sides of some fronds are covered with rows of brownish or rust-colored spore cases that contain spores. Under the right conditions, the spore cases pop open and spray spores as far away as a few meters. If the spores land in a place where conditions are right for fern growth, the spores will develop into the first stage in a new fern's life cycle.

Spore cases arranged on the bottom of a fern frond will pop open, spraying spores all around. If conditions are right where the spores fall, the spores will produce new fern plants.

> **What are ferns like?**

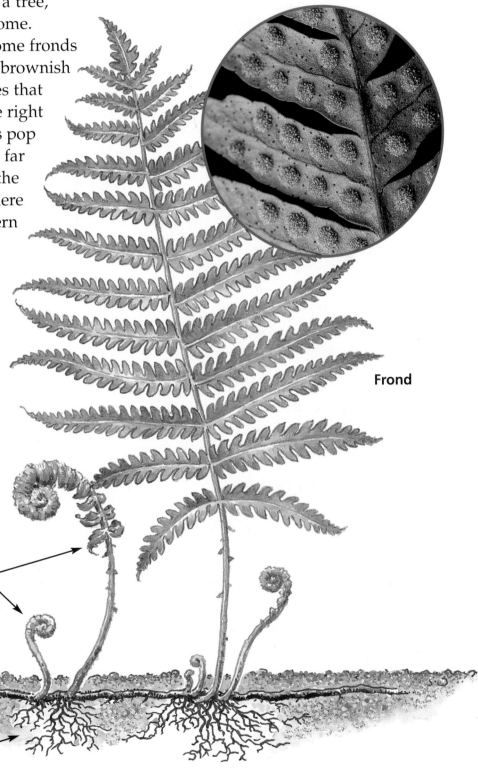

Frond

Young ferns (fiddleheads)

Rhizome

Roots

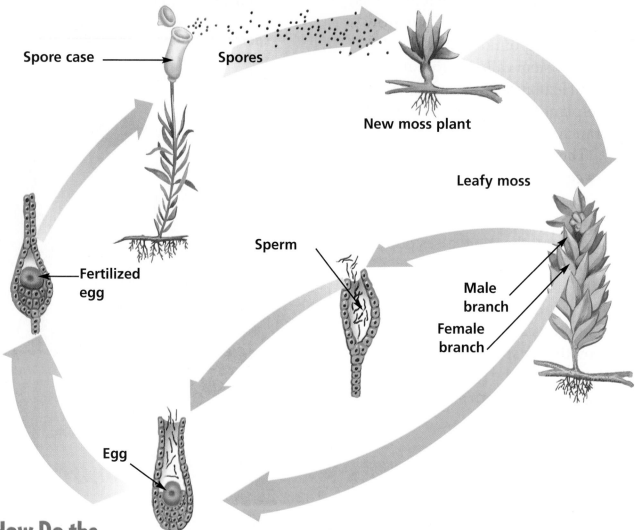

Spore case — Spores

New moss plant

Leafy moss

Sperm

Fertilized egg

Male branch

Female branch

Egg

How Do the Life Cycles of Mosses and Ferns Differ?

Since mosses and ferns use spores to *reproduce* (ree·pruh·DEWS)—make new plants—you might guess that their life cycles are similar. That guess would be correct, but there are differences, too.

The diagrams on these two pages will help you compare and contrast the life cycles of mosses and ferns.

Both mosses and ferns have two separate stages to their life cycles. One stage is when they produce spores.

This stage in the life cycle is called

asexual reproduction (ay·SEK·shew·uhl ree·pruh·DUK·shuhn). That's because the plant needs only one type of cell—the spore—in order to reproduce.

Moss spores grow into leafy moss plants that have male branches and female branches. The male branches produce *sperm*—male sex cells. The female branches produce eggs—female sex cells. When a male sex cell meets a female sex cell, the two may join together. This is called **fertilization** (fur·tuh·luh·ZAY·shuhn).

This stage in the cycle is called **sexual reproduction** (SEK·shew·uhl ree·pruh·DUK·shuhn). That's because

Life Cycle of a Fern

READING
Diagrams

Where are a fern's spores produced?

Spore case

Fern leaf (frond)

Spores

Male branch

Sperm

New fern plant

Female branch

Fertilized egg

Egg

the plant needs both male sex cells and female sex cells in order to reproduce.

The fertilized egg eventually becomes a thin stalk with a spore case on top. When the spore case opens, the spores are released. Spores that land on damp ground may grow into new moss plants, and the cycle begins again.

This process of going from sexual reproduction to asexual reproduction to sexual reproduction again is called *alternation of generations.*

Ferns also reproduce by alternation of generations. Leafy fern plants produce spores on the undersides of their fronds.

Spores landing in shady, moist soil are most likely to grow. The spores grow into small, heart-shaped plants. These plants produce male and female sex cells.

If a male sex cell fertilizes a female sex cell, the fertilized egg starts to form a new plant. The new plant develops into a leafy fern plant. Spore cases on the fern's fronds produce spores, and the cycle begins again.

▷ **In what ways are the life cycles of mosses and ferns alike?**

Mosses

Ferns

Gymnosperms

Angiosperms

420 million years ago

310 million years ago

275 million years ago

130 million years ago

Green algae

What Were the Ancestors of Plants?

The first land plants developed from living things that lived in the water. Which living things were the ancestors of land plants?

Scientists searched for clues linking organisms that lived in water to those that first grew on land. A good place to start was with photosynthetic organisms. These were living things that made their own food.

To narrow the search, the scientific detectives compared the chlorophyll of various simple organisms living today with that of plants. They found the closest match was with green algae.

Scientists found other clues. The cell walls of both green algae and plants contain cellulose. Cellulose can help plants survive on land, since a strong cell wall helps plants stay upright.

There was another clue. Both green algae and plants store food as starch.

Next, scientists hunted for fossils—the preserved remains of living things.

This fernlike plant was found in rock that is over 340 million years old.

Fossils are found mostly in rocks. Scientists have ways of finding out how old different rocks are. If you know the age of a rock, you also know the age of the fossil in it.

Putting all the pieces of this puzzle together, scientists concluded that the first land plants to evolve, or develop, from algae were probably nonvascular plants similar to mosses. These early land plants first appeared about 420 million years ago. Vascular plants appeared more recently. The earliest vascular plants, the ferns, were seedless. The first plants with seeds were gymnosperms, followed by angiosperms, or flowering plants.

▶ **How did scientists find the ancestors of plants?**

Why It Matters

Mosses and ferns were among the first plants to live on land. Today mosses are often the first plants to return to an area where plant life has been destroyed. Mosses help break down rocks into soil. Mosses also help hold on to the soil, making it easier for other plants to survive in the area. Without mosses, perhaps your favorite plants would never have had a chance to grow where they do.

Visit **www.mhscience02.com** to do a research project on seedless plants.

Think and Write

1. Why do mosses grow close to the ground?

2. Why do people sometimes add moss to a garden?

3. How do mosses change rocky areas so other plants can grow?

4. List two differences between mosses and ferns.

5. **Critical Thinking** How do cell walls help plants survive on land?

ART LINK

Make a poster. Find pictures of different kinds of ferns, and make a chart. Label each fern, and write a brief description of where each one can be found. Try to include at least one of the following: interrupted fern, leather fern, strap fern, vine fern, shoestring fern, ostrich fern. How do you think these ferns got their names?

WRITING LINK

Write a guidebook. Put together a guidebook of the kinds of ferns found in your area. Each page should have a photo or drawing of one of the ferns. Include a description of the fern and information on where it can be found in your area.

MATH LINK

Solve this problem. Study the time line on page A54. About how long after early land plants first appeared did gymnosperms appear? About how long after gymnosperms did angiosperms appear?

TECHNOLOGY LINK

 At the Computer Visit **www.mhscience02.com** for more links.

Plants with Seeds

Get Ready

What do flowering plants and evergreens have in common? One way they are alike is they produce seeds. They are seed plants.

How are these plants different? One way they are different is that they have different kinds of leaves. How do these differences help the plants survive?

Process Skill

You **experiment** when you perform a test to support or disprove a hypothesis.

Explore Activity

How Do Seed Plants Differ?

Materials

small pine seedling or other conifer

grass plant

garden plant or houseplant, such as a geranium

hand lens

microscope slide

coverslip

microscope

Procedure

1 **Observe** Examine each plant. Use the hand lens to examine a leaf from each one. Draw each leaf, and label it with the name of the plant it came from.

2 **Observe** Remove a part of the lower epidermis from the grass leaf. Make a wet-mount slide. Examine the slide under low power.

3 **Communicate** Draw what you observe.

4 **Observe** Repeat step 2 with a pine needle and a houseplant leaf (such as a geranium). Draw what you observe.

Drawing Conclusions

1 **Interpret Data** How are the leaves of the three plants alike? How are the leaves of the three plants different from one another?

2 **Infer** Which one of the plants do you think is least like the other two? Explain your reasoning.

3 **Going Further: Experiment** Predict which of the plants you examined could survive best in a dry environment. How do you think the plant's leaves would help it do this? Design an experiment that would test your prediction.

Main Idea One group of seed plants produces seeds on cones, the other group produces seeds inside fruits.

How Do Seed Plants Differ?

How are the leaves of a grass plant, a pine tree, and a geranium different? Two of these plants come from one major group of seed plants, while the other comes from a different group.

Both groups are vascular plants. Both groups reproduce from **seeds**. A seed contains an undeveloped plant and stored food for the young plant.

Most of the plants that you see every day are seed plants. They include grasses, trees, shrubs, and bushes. They all have roots, stems, and leaves. Some, called **angiosperms** (AN·jee·uh·spurmz), produce flowers. The others, called **gymnosperms** (JIM·nuh·spurmz), do not produce flowers. These are the two major groups of seed plants.

The gymnosperms are the oldest seed plants. They include such evergreen trees as pine, fir, cedar, juniper, yew, larch, and spruce.

Gymnosperms first appeared on Earth about 250 million years ago. One hundred million years would pass before the first angiosperms appeared.

The fruits, vegetables, grains, and almost all of the nuts you eat are produced by angiosperms. However, one tasty nut—the pine nut, or pignoli—is a gymnosperm seed. It is the seed of certain pine trees.

Gymnosperms

Gymnosperms include some of the largest and oldest living things.

The seed for this bristlecone pine sprouted about 5,000 years ago.

The giant redwood (left) can grow as tall as a 30-story building.

Conifers are found mostly in the northern parts of the world.

The gymnosperms are divided into four divisions. They are the **conifers** (KAHN·uh·furz), *cycads* (SIGH·kadz), *ginkgoes* (GING·kohz), and *gnetophytes* (NE·toh·fights). Look at the photographs on these pages. You'll notice that these plants look different. However, they all have certain things in common.

Their seeds are produced on the scales of female cones. The seeds are not surrounded by a fruit. The leaves of most gymnosperms look like needles or scales. Most gymnosperms are *evergreens*. Evergreens lose only a few leaves at a time and constantly replace the leaves they have lost.

Some conifers, such as the larch, dawn redwood, and bald cypress, lose their leaves each fall. Plants that do this are called *deciduous* (di·SIJ·ew·uhs).

When gymnosperms evolved, most of Earth was cold and dry. These plants are well adapted to cold, dry climates. For example, the needles of conifers have a very small surface area and are covered with a thick cuticle. They lose less water than the wider leaves of flowering plants.

READING **Compare and Contrast**
How are angiosperms and gymnosperms different?

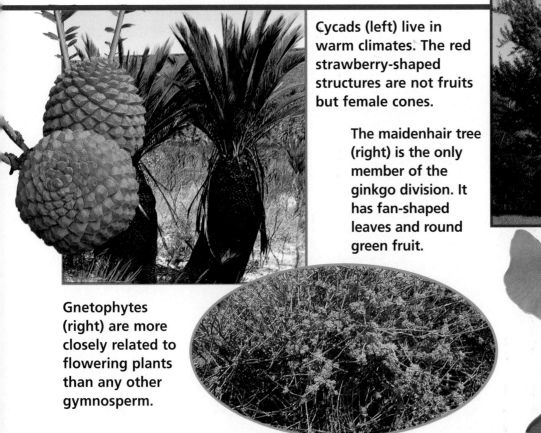

Cycads (left) live in warm climates. The red strawberry-shaped structures are not fruits but female cones.

The maidenhair tree (right) is the only member of the ginkgo division. It has fan-shaped leaves and round green fruit.

Gnetophytes (right) are more closely related to flowering plants than any other gymnosperm.

A 59

What Are Angiosperms?

Angiosperms are the most recently evolved and best-adapted division of seed plants. There are about 235,000 different kinds of angiosperms, which makes them the largest division in the plant kingdom.

Some, like duckweed, float on water and are about the size of a large bee's eye. Duckweed is the smallest flowering plant. The largest flowering plant is the giant eucalyptus tree, which can be 100 m (330 ft) tall and 20 m (66 ft) in circumference.

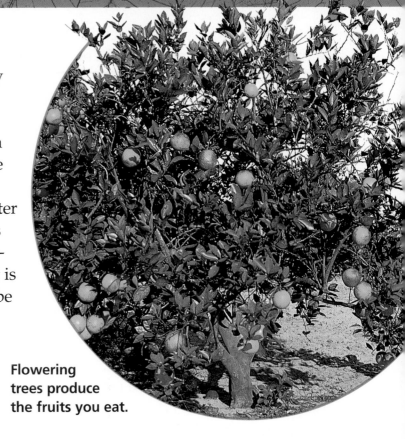

Flowering trees produce the fruits you eat.

Wheat seed

Wheat, an angiosperm, is a grass that produces one of the world's most important food crops.

The world's largest flower belongs to this parasitic plant, "the stinking corpse lily," which lives in Southeast Asia.

Angiosperms live in all climates and in all parts of the world. The saguaro cactus lives in the hot, dry desert. Duckweed and water lilies grow only in the water. Some orchids live high in the air attached to trees in hot, damp rain forests. Other angiosperms flower near the Arctic Circle. Still others grow on the sides of tall mountains. Oddly, a few angiosperms cannot live on their own. They have little or no chlorophyll and are *parasites*. That is, they live off other plants. The plant with the largest flower is this kind of parasitic angiosperm. The flower can be a meter across, as thick as your thumb, and weigh as much as a small dog.

This saguaro cactus lives in the desert of the southwest United States.

How can you tell an angiosperm from a gymnosperm? Angiosperms produce flowers; gymnosperms do not. The seeds of angiosperms are inside a fruit. Gymnosperms do not produce fruits.

▷ **What are two locations where angiosperms live?**

What Are Cotyledons?

Scientists divide the angiosperms into two classes. As you might guess, scientists are able to do this because of some particular characteristic that sets the two classes apart. That characteristic turns out to be the number of an angiosperm's **cotyledons** (kaht·uh·LEE·duhnz). A cotyledon, also called a seed leaf, is a tiny leaflike structure inside a seed.

Some angiosperm seeds contain only one cotyledon. Plants whose seeds contain only one cotyledon are called *monocotyledons*, or **monocots**

(MAHN·uh·kahts) for short. (The prefix *mono-* comes from a Greek word meaning "one.") There are over 60,000 different kinds of monocots. Corn, rice, wheat, grasses, orchids, and coconut palms are examples of monocots.

Angiosperms whose seeds contain two cotyledons are called *dicotyledons*, or **dicots** (DIGH·kahts) for short. (The prefix *di-* comes from a Greek word meaning "two.") There are over 170,000 kinds of dicots. Bean plants, maple trees, rose plants, and cactuses are some of the dicots.

▷ **What are three differences between monocots and dicots?**

Characteristics of Monocots and Dicots

Characteristics	Monocots	Dicots
Cotyledons	One	Two
Leaf veins	Parallel	Branched
Flower parts	Multiples of three	Multiples of four or five
Vascular system	Scattered in bundles	In rings

Process Skill BUILDER

Flowering Plants

In this activity you will observe flowering plants in order to try to classify them. That is, you will examine several plants and try to determine whether each is a monocot or a dicot. As you examine each plant sample, refer to the chart on page A62 to help you classify the sample.

Materials
sample leaves and flowers from various angiosperms

Procedure

1 **Observe** Get together with a few of your classmates and go on a leaf- and flower-collecting field trip. (Make sure to avoid poison ivy, poison oak, and poison sumac leaves. Your teacher can tell you how to spot them.)

2 **Observe** Find a number of different angiosperms. Try to get a sample of a leaf and flower from each plant. If you can't get a flower, a leaf will do.

3 **Interpret Data** Look at the chart of Characteristics of Monocots and Dicots. It will give you clues on how to tell if the sample leaves and flowers you chose are monocots or dicots.

Drawing Conclusions

1 **Observe** Examine the plant parts you have chosen. For each sample leaf, describe how the leaf veins look. For each sample flower, tell how many parts the flower has. Record your answers.

2 **Classify** Mount the leaves and flowers on a heavy sheet of cardboard, and indicate whether each came from a monocot or a dicot.

The awful-smelling jack-in-the-pulpit flower attracts insects that help the plant reproduce.

Why Do Flowers Have Aromas?

The characteristics of living things help them survive in their environment. It would make sense to expect that the aromas of flowers do the same for their plants.

To your nose, some of these aromas are very pleasing. That's why flowers such as roses and jasmines are used in perfumes. However, some flowers, like those of the jack-in-the-pulpit plant, smell awful. Surprisingly, both beautiful and awful aromas attract insects! What is the advantage of this?

When an insect enters the flower, it brushes against a part of the flower that holds tiny grains of dust, called *pollen*. These grains contain the plant's male sex cells.

The pollen sticks to the insect. As the insect moves around the flower—

or moves to another flower on the plant—some of the pollen rubs off on parts of the flower that hold female sex cells. The two sex cells join, and the reproduction of a new plant begins.

Many plants attract one particular kind of insect. The jack-in-the-pulpit attracts dung beetles and flies. These insects generally feed on dead or decaying animals or animal wastes, which smell awful. The insects mistake the aroma of the plant for that of a good meal.

Once inside the flower, the insects discover that its sides are so smooth, they can't climb out. As they rush around inside the flower, they keep transferring pollen to the part of the flower that holds female sex cells.

After about 24 hours, something strange happens. The inside of the flower changes from smooth to wrinkled. Their job done, the insects can now get a foothold, escape, and move on to another flower.

▷ **How does a flower's aroma help it survive?**

L·I·N·K·S

Why It Matters

Almost all of the food you eat that comes from plants is produced by flowering plants. Flowering plants also decorate the landscape and homes with beautiful colors. Some produce chemicals that are used in perfumes and other cosmetics. Others, such as plants used as spices, flavor the foods you eat. Like all plants, flowering plants help keep the balance of gases in the air by using up carbon dioxide and producing oxygen.

Think and Write

1. How are gymnosperms and angiosperms alike? How are they different?

2. How are flowers important to a plant?

3. What are the differences between monocots and dicots?

4. **Observe** List five plants that are angiosperms and five plants that are gymnosperms. Explain what characteristics helped you determine which was which.

5. **Critical Thinking** How have seed plants become adapted to the environment?

WRITING LINK

Write an essay. Write about a day in your life and all the plants that are important to you. Classify the plants as angiosperms or gymnosperms and as monocots or dicots.

ART LINK

Make your own flip books. Illustrate a "year in the life of an angiosperm" by making a flip book. Do the same for a gymnosperm.

SOCIAL STUDIES LINK

Make a crop map. Look at the table showing food crops that come from monocots and dicots. Research where in the world these crops are grown. Then, using a different color for each crop, make a map showing where each of the crops is produced.

Monocots	Dicots
Corn	Apples
Onions	Beans
Rice	Cabbage
Wheat	Tomatoes

TECHNOLOGY LINK

At the Computer Visit www.mhscience02.com for more links.

BANKING ON SEEDS

Where do farmers get the corn seeds they plant each year? Before farmers knew about plant heredity, they just planted leftover seeds from the last year's crop. There were thousands of varieties of corn. Then farmers learned about hybrids.

Ears of corn from a hybrid all become ripe at the same time. They're the same size, so harvesting is easier.

Farmers can breed corn that thrives despite chemical pesticides and fertilizers. Many crops grow faster, produce more food, and store better.

That's the good news about farming. There's bad news, too. If farmers grow just one kind of plant, a disease or pest invasion can wipe out a whole crop.

In 1970, for example, the corn grown in the United States was too similar. Much of it caught the same disease at the same time. Fifteen percent of that year's corn crop was lost. The situation was even worse in Ireland in the 1840s. Almost every Irish farmer grew the same kind of potato. When a potato disease hit, it killed almost the entire Irish potato crop. There was a serious shortage of food, and many Irish people moved to the U.S.

If farmers grow only a few kinds of plants, other plants become extinct. Then animals that depend on a specific kind of plant die out as well.

As hybrids became more common, people became alarmed by the number of plant types dying out. Consequently seeds were collected from existing plants and placed in seed banks. The banks preserve the seeds from plants that otherwise might become extinct. Farmers have also been encouraged to grow more varied crops.

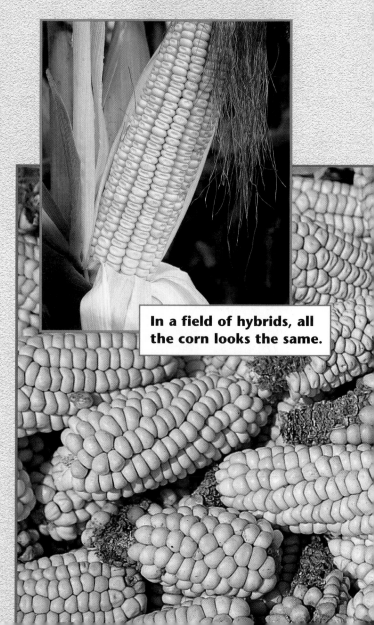

In a field of hybrids, all the corn looks the same.

What Did I Learn?

1. What can growing hybrid corn do?

 A It can make harvesting easier.
 B It can produce plants that are more pest-resistant.
 C both A and B
 D neither A nor B

2. Seed banks were started

 F as a place farmers could buy seeds to feed animals
 G to preserve seeds from plants that might otherwise become extinct
 H to protect seeds from fertilizers
 J to let farmers save seeds for the following year

AT THE COMPUTER

Visit www.mhscience02.com
to learn more about seed banks.

Flowers and Seeds

Get Ready

Have you ever seen bees buzzing around flowers? Don't disturb them. From a distance you might watch as a bee goes from flower to flower. What do you think it is doing? Not just bees, but other insects, such as butterflies, and other animals, such as hummingbirds, hover around flowers as well. What do you think they do for the plants? What do plants use their flowers for?

Process Skill

You **infer** when you form an idea from facts or observations.

Explore Activity

How Do Flowers Differ?

Materials

several large flowers from different plants

hand lens

forceps

dropper

toothpick

Procedure: Design Your Own

1 Decide how you will compare the flowers you look at. You may choose to look for parts that they seem to have in common. Describe what the parts are and how they differ from plant to plant.

2 Begin by removing the outer leaflike parts. Examine them. Draw what they look like.

3 Remove the petals. Examine them. Draw what they look like.

4 **Observe** Examine the rest of the flower as you decide.

5 **Communicate** Draw the parts you examined.

Drawing Conclusions

1 **Communicate** What color is each flower? What do you think the job of the petals is? How would you design an experiment to find out?

2 **Infer** What do you think the various parts of each flower are for? Do you think the same parts of different flowers do the same kinds of jobs for their plants?

3 **Going Further: Infer** Why do you think a plant has flowers? Make a hypothesis. Design an experiment to test your ideas.

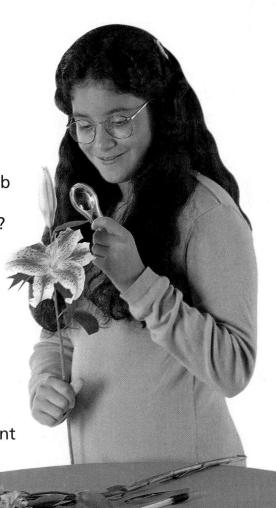

Main Idea Fertilized flowers produce seeds that become new plants.

How Do Flowers Differ?

Not all flowers are alike. Some flowers are *complete flowers*. Complete flowers have sepals, petals, stamens, and pistils. *Incomplete flowers* are missing one of these parts. Some flowers are called perfect. *Perfect flowers* have both female and male parts, that is, both pistils (female parts) and stamens (male parts).

Imperfect flowers have either pistils or stamens, but not both. You might think of these flowers as "female" or "male." Some plants, like corn and oak trees, have separate male and female flowers on the same plant. Other plants,

Parts of a Flower

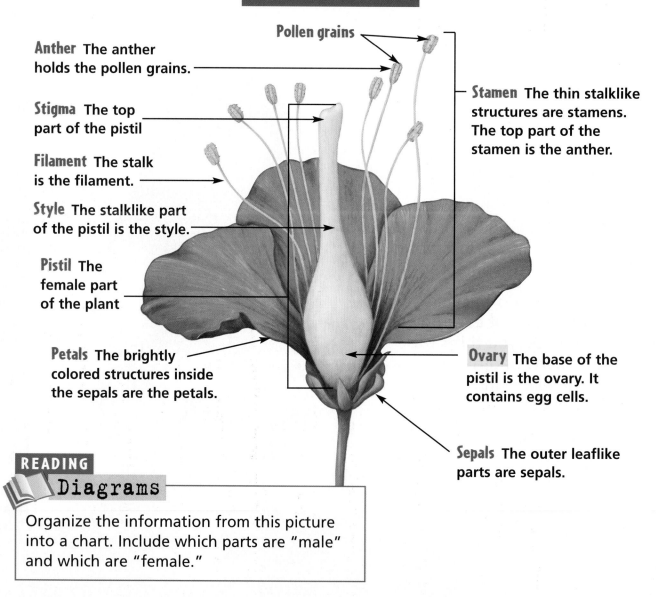

Anther The anther holds the pollen grains.

Stigma The top part of the pistil

Filament The stalk is the filament.

Style The stalklike part of the pistil is the style.

Pistil The female part of the plant

Petals The brightly colored structures inside the sepals are the petals.

Pollen grains

Stamen The thin stalklike structures are stamens. The top part of the stamen is the anther.

Ovary The base of the pistil is the ovary. It contains egg cells.

Sepals The outer leaflike parts are sepals.

READING
Diagrams

Organize the information from this picture into a chart. Include which parts are "male" and which are "female."

flower of another plant, the process is called *cross-pollination*.

On the stigma a tube forms from the pollen grain. The tube grows down the style and into the flower's ovary. Sperm travel down the tube, through the style, and into the ovary. There a sperm cell combines with, or fertilizes, an egg cell. This combining is called *fertilization* (fur·tuh·luh·ZAY·shuhn).

A seed develops from a fertilized egg cell. Under the right conditions, a new plant will develop from the seed. The process of making a new plant from the joining of a sperm and an egg cell is called *sexual reproduction*.

▷ **What are the steps involved in cross-pollination and fertilization?**

Fertilization

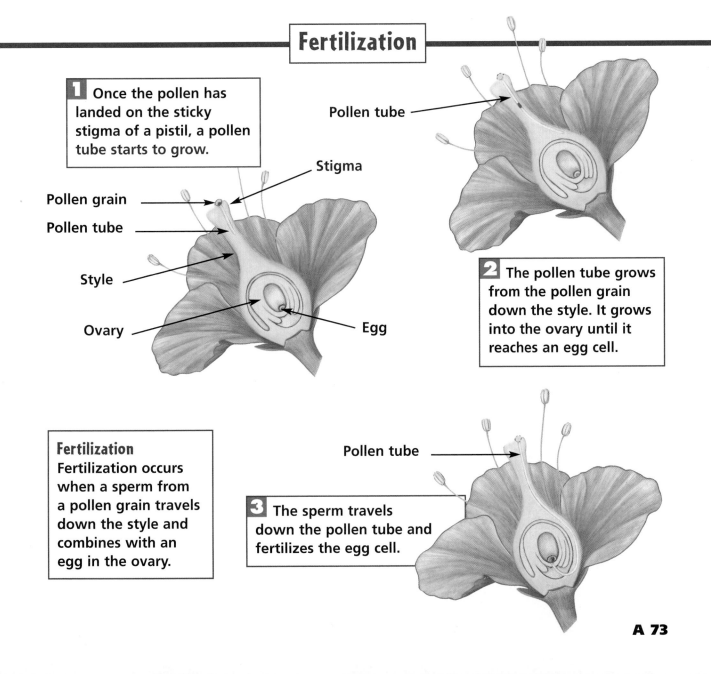

1 Once the pollen has landed on the sticky stigma of a pistil, a pollen tube starts to grow.

Pollen tube

Pollen grain

Pollen tube

Stigma

Style

Ovary

Egg

2 The pollen tube grows from the pollen grain down the style. It grows into the ovary until it reaches an egg cell.

Fertilization
Fertilization occurs when a sperm from a pollen grain travels down the style and combines with an egg in the ovary.

Pollen tube

3 The sperm travels down the pollen tube and fertilizes the egg cell.

Inside a Seed

1. Soak a lima bean in water overnight.

2. Observe Carefully pull apart the two halves of the lima bean. Examine the halves with a hand lens. Draw what you see.

3. Infer Which part is the embryo?

4. On your drawing label the seed coat and the cotyledon where food is stored.

5. Communicate Compare a corn kernel with a lima bean. Describe how its parts are similar to or different from the lima bean.

6. Classify Which seed is a dicot? Which is a monocot? Explain how you know which is which.

What Is in a Seed?

A seed is made up of three main parts. One part is an **embryo** (EM·bree·oh). An embryo is an immature plant. Another part is the cotyledon where food is stored in the form of starch. The third part is the **seed coat**. The seed coat encases the whole seed in a tough, protective covering.

Parts of a Seed

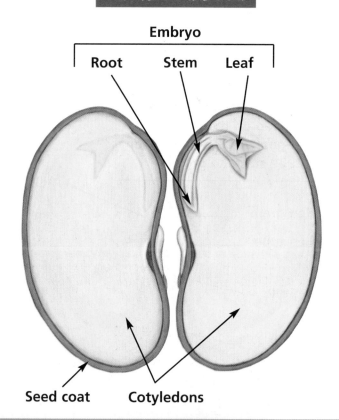

Embryo

Root   Stem   Leaf

Seed coat   Cotyledons

From Seed to Plant

Two things must happen for a seed to produce a new plant. First, the seed must move from the flower to a place where it can sprout. This is called *seed dispersal* (SEED di·SPUR·suhl). Second, the place must provide everything that is needed for sprouting, which is called *germination* (jur·muh·NAY·shuhn). A warm temperature and water are the two most important needs for germination. Food is not needed because the seed has its own supply of stored food.

Usually the seed must move a relatively long distance from its parent plant. Why? Competition from its parent, and plants like it, may make the development of a new plant difficult. For example, nearby plants may block sunlight from reaching the young plant. They may soak up the water or minerals from the soil that the new plant needs.

Seeds have evolved all sorts of adaptations for dispersal. For example, dandelion fruits and cottonwood seeds have feathery "parachutes." These parachutes can be blown great distances by the wind. Animals also help move plant seeds.

Animals eat **fruits**. A fruit is a mature ripened ovary of a plant. The animals digest the soft parts of the fruits but not the hard seeds inside. As the animals move from place to place, they deposit the seeds in their wastes.

Coconut seeds rely on ocean currents and sea breezes to move them.

The seeds of a cocklebur have tiny hooks that cling to the fur of animals or the clothing of people.

Animals eat fruits and the seeds inside.

How Gymnosperms Spread Seeds

Gymnosperms don't produce fruits. They disperse their seeds in other ways. For example, the cones of the balsam fir tree shatter. When they do this, they release winglike seeds that ride on the wind. Animals move cones from place to place. Heavy rains, floods, and streams can disperse them also.

▷ **What do the three main parts of a seed do?**

Male cones

Pollen

Female cones

Ovules

Pine seeds

Seedling

What Is the Life Cycle of a Conifer?

Since gymnosperms don't produce flowers or fruits, their life cycle is not the same as angiosperms. However, there are similarities. As you read on and look at the diagram on this page, make a list of the similarities and differences.

Let's examine the life cycle of a pine tree. A pine tree belongs to a group of gymnosperms called conifers. Pines produce male and female cones on a mature tree. The scales that form the cones carry spore cases that produce the plant's sperm and egg cells. Male cones produce pollen grains, which contain sperm cells.

When pollen grains fall away from a male cone, the wind carries them through the air. If a pollen grain

READING
Diagrams

What are the steps in the life cycle of a conifer?

happens to land on a female cone, a sperm cell from the pollen may fertilize an egg cell in the female cone.

The fertilized cell eventually becomes a seed. As autumn and winter come, the female pine cones fall from the trees. Their seeds scatter on the ground. Sometimes wind or water will carry the seeds far from the tree. If they end up in a place where conditions are right for germination, the seeds will sprout, and a new pine tree will start growing.

 Where are conifer seeds found?

L·I·N·K·S

Why It Matters

Some plants can be grown from pieces of the plant—such as stems, leaves, and roots—rather than from seeds. This is called *vegetative propagation*. It is also called *asexual reproduction* because it happens without sperm and egg cells joining. For example, strawberry plants send shoots into the soil from stems that grow along the ground. Each shoot will make a new strawberry plant.

Flowering plants produce almost all of the plants you eat. People eat flowers, fruits, seeds, leaves, stems, and roots. Flowering plants are also eaten by animals that we eat.

Think and Write

1. Identify the different parts of a flower, and tell what each part does.

2. Explain how seeds are produced.

3. Give at least three examples of how seeds are dispersed.

4. Describe the difference between fertilization and germination.

5. **Critical Thinking** How do you think trees that produce seedless oranges are grown? Write down your prediction. Then do library research to see if your prediction was correct.

WRITING LINK

Write an essay. Research at least two plants—besides strawberries—that can be grown by vegetative propagation. Write an essay discussing what the benefits are of growing plants in this manner.

MATH LINK

Solve this problem. The countries of the world produce about 1.8 billion metric tons of rice, wheat, and corn. A metric ton equals 1,000 kilograms, or 2,205 pounds. How many kilograms of these grains are produced? How many pounds?

TECHNOLOGY LINK

At the Computer Visit **www.mhscience02.com** for more links.

Plant Responses and Adaptations

Get Ready

What happens when you jump up? Why don't you just fly up and away from Earth's surface?

There is a pull between Earth and everything on it. This pull is called gravity.

Does gravity affect how a plant grows? Do a plant's roots, stems, and leaves grow downward? What is happening to this tree as it grows on the side of the hill? Do roots always grow "down" no matter how you plant a seed?

Process Skill

You predict when you state possible results of an event or experiment.

Explore Activity

How Do Roots Grow?

Materials

petri dish (plastic)

2 paper towels

marking pen

tape

4 bean seeds that have been soaked in water overnight

Procedure

1 Soak two paper towels. Wrinkle the paper towels, and place them in the bottom half of the petri dish.

2 Place the four seeds on top of the wet paper towels as shown in diagram 1. Place the seeds so that the curved part is turned toward the center of the dish.

3 Place the top on the petri dish. The top will hold the seeds in the wet paper towels. Seal the top with transparent tape. Draw an arrow on the petri dish with the marking pen as shown in diagram 2. This will show which direction is down. Write the number or name of your group on the petri dish.

4 In a place your teacher provides, stand the petri dish on its edge so the arrow is pointing downward. Tape the petri dish so that it will remain standing. Do not lay the dish down flat.

5 **Predict** Make and record a prediction about the direction you think the roots will grow.

6 **Communicate** Examine the seeds for the next four days. Record the direction of root growth.

Drawing Conclusions

1 **Observe** In what direction were the roots growing on day 1? On day 4?

2 **Interpret Data** Is your prediction supported by your data?

3 **Going Further: Predict** What would happen if a seedling were not able to grow its roots down into the soil? Design an experiment to test your prediction.

Main Idea Plants have certain behaviors and adaptations that help them survive.

What Are Tropisms?

If the flash of a camera goes off near your eyes, you are likely to respond to the bright light by blinking. The flash of light stimulated your blinking. Anything in the environment—light, heat, gravity, and more—that produces such a **response** is called a **stimulus** (STIM·yuh·luhs).

Plants also respond to a stimulus, but they tend to respond more slowly than animals do. Plants slowly bend or curve toward or away from a stimulus. Scientists call this kind of response a **tropism** (TROH·piz·uhm). Tropisms help a plant survive in its environment. For example, as seeds sprout, their roots grow downward. Why do you think the seeds' roots grow downward?

There are several major kinds of tropisms. One of these is *gravitropism*. A plant's roots respond to the stimulus of gravity and grow downward.

The roots of a plant show positive gravitropism. No matter how the plant is tilted, its roots will always grow downward into the soil. The roots grow in the direction Earth's gravity is pulling them. Stems show negative gravitropism. They grow away from the force of gravity. They grow into the air, where their leaves can get the most sunlight.

Light, of course, is very important to plants' survival. Plants respond to changes in light. These responses are called *phototropisms*. (*Photo* comes from a Greek word meaning "light.") If a plant is exposed to light coming from only one direction, its stem will bend in that direction. That is positive phototropism.

If a plant bends toward a stimulus, its change is called a positive tropism. If it bends away, the change is called a negative tropism.

If you examine the roots of a willow tree growing near a stream, you will discover *hydrotropism*. *Hydro* means "water." The willow's roots show positive hydrotropism. They grow toward a source of water.

Some plants, like squash and grape plants, show a response to touch. Grape vines grow around posts farmers stick in the ground. The vines send out threadlike tendrils that coil toward whatever they touch.

People long knew about plant tropisms. However, they didn't always know the process inside a plant that made a plant's parts move. The first clue was discovered by Charles Darwin and his son Francis in the 1870s. Charles Darwin cut off the tips of some very young plant shoots. He left other plants alone. The plants with tips bent toward light. The plants without tips did not. Darwin

The tendrils of this plant respond to touch as they coil around other objects.

concluded that something in the tips was causing the bending, but what?

The second clue was found in the 1920s by Dutch scientist Frits Went. Went guessed that a chemical made only in the shoot's tip was responsible for the bending. He separated many chemicals from shoot tips. One by one he placed them on the cutoff tops of plant shoots. Finally, he found the chemical that let the cut shoots bend toward light.

The chemical is called an *auxin*. Auxins are chemicals that stimulate plant growth. Auxins work on all parts of the plant and cause tropisms of all kinds. How do auxins cause plant parts to bend? When one side of a stem is exposed to light, for example, auxins move to the other side and down. Auxins cause more cells to grow—and some to grow more in length—on the dark side, but not on the side facing the light. This unequal growth causes the stem to bend toward the light.

Charles Darwin showed that when the tip of a plant shoot is cut off, the plant will not bend toward light.

▷ **What are examples of a positive tropism and a negative tropism?**

How Do Plants Survive?

Plants survive in deserts, rain forests, and the Arctic. They survive in all these places because they have adapted to their environment. An **adaptation** (ad·uhp·TAY·shuhn) helps an organism survive in its environment.

Desert plants have adaptations for collecting, storing, and saving water. Cactus plants have roots that absorb water very quickly. The water is stored in the center of the plant. A thick, waterproof, waxy coating helps stop water loss. Finally, the plant's stomata only open at night, when temperatures are cooler. Less water is lost through transpiration.

Carnivorous (meat-eating) plants can't get enough nutrients from the soil. These plants trap and digest insects to get some of the nutrients they need.

Plants like spinach, lettuce, and wheat bloom in late spring and early summer. They are called *long-day* plants. That's because when they bloom, there is much more daylight than darkness. By contrast, *short-day* plants, like strawberries, soybeans, and ragweed, bloom in early spring or in the fall. Short-day plants bloom when there is more darkness and less daylight. This flowering response is called *photoperiodism*.

▶ **What adaptations help plants survive water shortages?**

Short-Day, Long-Day Plants

Plant A
Leaves, no flowers

Leaves and flowers

Plant B
Leaves and flowers

Leaves, no flowers

Light

Light

READING Diagrams

1. Which plant is a long-day plant? Which is a short-day plant?
2. In what season would plant A bloom?

Why Do Plants Compete?

Like all organisms, plants compete with one another for what they need to survive and grow—sunlight, water, and nutrients.

Each plant has its own strategy for winning its battle with other plants. Vines, like ivy and honeysuckle, climb the trunks of trees to get a greater share of sunlight. The trees themselves rise to great heights. They spread their branches to form leafy canopies above the forest. That's why in a forest, trees like oaks and maples have more leaves at their tops.

Have you ever been in a forest full of giant redwoods or other conifers? If so, you probably felt as if you were in a huge building filled with soaring columns. Only when you look high up do you see branches covered with green needles. Trees like these also preserve the nutrients and water in the soil for themselves. They do this by blocking sunlight from reaching the ground. Without sunlight few plants can grow in the soil and soak up nutrients and water near great trees.

▶ **How do plants compete with each other?**

QUICK LAB

FOR SCHOOL OR HOME

Plants Compete for Light

1. Collect samples of various houseplants that grow to different widths and heights.

2. Plant them, with some grass seed, in soil in a paper cup. Record the types of plants you used.

3. **Observe** Examine your plants over the next few days. Draw or photograph their progress.

4. **Observe** Which plants are being shaded by others? Are the plants in the shade doing as well as the plants that are getting more light?

5. **Hypothesize** Design an experiment to test which plants need more light to grow. How could you determine if these plants have anything else in common?

How Do Plants Use Chemicals to Survive?

Some plants use another strategy for keeping other plants at a distance. They produce chemicals that are poisons to other plants. Creosote bushes, which live in dry areas, release such a poison from their roots. The poison keeps the seeds of other plants from germinating. It may even kill other plants that are already growing.

Plants also make chemicals that discourage insects and animals from feeding on or infecting them. The most powerful insect-fighting plant chemical is made by the neem tree of Africa and Asia. This chemical is so strong that if you dissolved a teaspoon of it in a medium-sized swimming pool and sprayed the water on a plant, insects would not feed on it. Some plants, like the hemlock, even make poisons that can kill a person.

Unlike the plant below, which is being eaten by an insect, other plants such as the poison ivy above, produce chemicals that keep insects away or make them sick.

READING **Compare and Contrast**
What are two ways that plants use chemicals to survive?

Why It Matters

How can you tell a tree's age? You can do it by counting its rings. A tree forms a layer of wood each year. This process continues for as long as the tree lives. The size of a tree ring, however, can change depending on whether the weather has been warm and rainy or cold and dry.

Plants respond to changes in their environment. They have to be able to adapt to changes in light, water, and temperature. They need these adaptations in order to survive. Other equally important adaptations help plants reproduce successfully and fight off enemies such as insect pests.

Think and Write

1. What are tropisms? Give an example of one.

2. Where does a cactus store water?

3. How do auxins help plants grow toward the light?

4. Compare the way vines and trees compete for sunlight.

5. **Critical Thinking** What do you think might happen if all plants bloomed at the same time?

L·I·N·K·S

MATH LINK

Solve this problem. How big does a giant *sequoia* (si·KWOY·uh) grow? Research giant sequoias to find how tall they grow, how big around they get, and how much they weigh. Which weighs more—a giant sequoia or a blue whale?

WRITING LINK

Write an essay. Research how a tree's rings can tell scientists about weather conditions in an area, and write an essay on your findings. What can studying a tree's rings tell about how the tree adapted to its environment?

ART LINK

Make a poster. Find pictures illustrating several plant tropisms, and use them to help you design a poster. Include a description of each tropism you illustrate.

TECHNOLOGY LINK

Science Newsroom CD-ROM Choose *Flower Power* to learn more about how flowers attract pollinators.

At the Computer Visit www.mhscience02.com for more links.

How Can Cutting Trees Save Forests?

In Ancient Greece people told of an earlier "Golden Age" when the hills were covered with trees. Their forests were gone by then, and the Greeks discovered that when trees go, soil washes away. Greece has never recovered from the loss of its trees.

About a thousand years later, rich landowners in England saved some forests for hunting and fishing. Some villages had forests that they cut partway down. Trees were cut about 6 feet from the ground every few years. The tall stumps grew new shoots, which could be used for firewood.

Today some of the greatest forests left are in the western part of North America. Lots of rainfall west of the Rocky Mountains helps trees grow larger there than most places in the world. These are the giant redwoods and sequoia trees. Some of these giant trees are more than 2,000 years old!

In the 1850s it took four men 22 days to chop down one of these sequoia trees with hand axes. The trunk was 10 meters (33 feet) across!

Lumber companies eventually built roads into the forests. They hauled in power-driven saws and giant cranes. Whole sections of the forest were cut down at once. That's called clear-cutting. It leaves large bare patches. Forest animals lose their homes. Soil washes into streams, and the fish's environment is changed!

Today there are other ways to use modern tools to cut trees but save the forests. Helicopters can fly in workers and tools. A tree can be cut and lifted away. The other trees, the animals, and the soil all remain in the forest.

What Did I Learn?

1. The giant trees found in the western part of North America are the

    A red oaks and red maples
    B red maples and sequoias
    C redwoods and red maples
    D redwoods and sequoias

2. Clear-cutting

    F leaves large bare patches in the forest
    G prevents soil from being washed away
    H means cutting down only a few trees at a time
    J is done by helicopter

AT THE COMPUTER

Visit www.mhschool.com to learn more about forests.

Chapter 2 Review

Vocabulary

Fill each blank with the best word from the list.

adaptation, A82
angiosperm, A58
cotyledon, A62
frond, A51
fruit, A75
gymnosperm, A58
pollination, A72
spore, A48
stimulus, A80
tropism, A80

1. A plant that has flowers is called a(n) _____.

2. A characteristic that helps an organism survive in its environment is a(n) _____.

3. Transferring a pollen grain from an anther to a stigma is known as _____.

4. Bending toward or away from a stimulus is a(n) _____.

5. A mature ripened ovary is called a(n) _____.

6. A seed plant that does not produce fruits is a(n) _____.

7. A new moss plant is produced by a(n) _____.

8. The leaflike structure of a fern is a(n) _____.

9. A tiny leaflike structure inside a seed is a(n) _____.

10. Something in the environment that produces a response in an organism is a(n) _____.

Test Prep

11. What kinds of plants do very well in hot, damp climates?

    A   apple trees

    B   ferns

    C   fir trees

    D   grains

12. Which of the following are gymnosperms?

    F   apple trees

    G   ferns

    H   fir trees

    J   grains

13. Bees help flowers reproduce through a process called _____.

    A   fertilization

    B   phototropism

    C   transpiration

    D   pollination

14. Tropism is the process of _____.

    F   movement of a plant toward or away from a stimulus

    G   making sugar from sunlight

    H   transporting water along a stem

    J   adaptation to a hot climate

15. What causes sunflowers to bend toward the sunlight?

    A pollination

    B transpiration

    C positive phototropism

    D negative phototropism

Concepts and Skills

16. Reading in Science Write a paragraph explaining the difference between a monocot and a dicot.

Rose

Lily

17. Product Ads Look at the ingredients listed on boxes of breakfast foods. What kinds of plants are most commonly used to make breakfast foods? Write a paragraph explaining why.

18. Scientific Methods Describe two ways that adaptations can help plants survive. Write up a design for an experiment that would test this.

19. Process Skills: Observe Tell which of these plants are angiosperms and which are gymnosperms—bristlecone pine, rose, wheat, oat, fir, cedar, lily, juniper, yew, larch, violet, tomato, spruce, giant redwood tree. Write a paragraph explaining your answer.

20. Critical Thinking If you were lost in the woods in the United States, had no compass, and could not see the sky, how might plants help you infer direction? Write a paragraph explaining your answer.

Boost *your test scores!*

Be Smart!

Visit www.mhscience02.com

Animal Diversity

Did You Ever Wonder?

Where do starfish live? Although starfish live in every ocean on Earth, there are more kinds of starfish in the northern Pacific than anywhere else. Are starfish really fish? What other kinds of animals can you see in this photo?

Animal Structure and Function

Vocabulary

tissue, A94

organ, A94

system, A94

vertebrate, A95

invertebrate, A95

Get Ready

Animals have different traits. These traits include shape, size, body parts, and color. Scientists use such traits to put similar animals into groups. This is not always as easy as it seems. What traits would you use to group animals? Many different kinds of animals visit a watering hole in Africa. How might these animals be grouped?

Process Skill

You **classify** when you place things that share properties together in groups.

Explore Activity

How Are Animals Classified?

Materials

25 pictures of animals

5 sheets of paper

tape

scissors

Procedure

BE CAREFUL! Be careful using scissors.

1 Cut out 25 animal pictures from old magazines.

2 **Classify** Decide on a trait for grouping the pictures. You may group the pictures into three or more groups.

3 **Communicate** Write your reason for placing the pictures in each group.

4 **Infer** Have your classmates determine the basis you used to group the pictures.

Drawing Conclusions

1 Which trait was used most often for grouping the pictures?

2 **Infer** What is the best method for grouping the animals?

3 **Going Further: Infer** Why do you think scientists all over the world use a single system for grouping organisms?

What Traits Are Used to Classify Animals?

The building blocks of living things are cells. Whether an animal grows hair or feathers depends on the kinds of cells it has. Scientists often study the cells of animals in order to best group or classify them.

Similar cells that have the same job or function come together to make a **tissue** . Tissues of different kinds come together to make an **organ** , like a heart or brain.

Finally, a group of organs that work together to do a certain job makes up an organ **system** . For example, a bat's digestive system includes its mouth, stomach, and intestines. Birds have similar organs, but those of bats and cats are more like each other than like those of eagles.

Cells, tissues, organs, and systems—compare them carefully. By doing so, you can make groups that contain animals that are really closely related. They may be closely related even though at first glance they may look very different.

If you were to take a really close look, you would find that the wing of a bat is built more like the front leg of a cat than like the wing of an eagle. Bats have five sets of finger bones inside each wing. Eagles have a single fused finger bone inside each wing.

Eagle

Bat

Cat

The bones in the diagram above have been color-coded to show similar bones in each animal.

Vertebrates and Invertebrates

Scientists could use one similar trait to make a grouping. However, such groups might not make scientific sense. Why not? For example, this might lead to putting birds and bats in the same group because they both have wings and fly. However, these animals are very different.
A bat is more like a cat than an eagle. That is, bats and cats have more similar characteristics than bats and birds do. Why?

For one thing, bats and cats have hair. For another thing, bats and cats feed their young milk. Eagles, like all birds, have feathers, not hair, and they don't feed their young milk. Then how do scientists put animals into different groups?

First, animals are divided into two large groups. One group is made up of animals that have backbones. The members of this group are called **vertebrates**. The members of the other group do not have backbones. They are called **invertebrates**.

As you might expect, vertebrates and invertebrates can be divided into smaller groups. What animals go into which group? Animals with similar traits go into the same groups. On the following pages are some of the groups of invertebrates and vertebrates. They are listed from the simplest to the most complex.

READING Summarize
What trait do scientists use to divide all animals into two main groups?

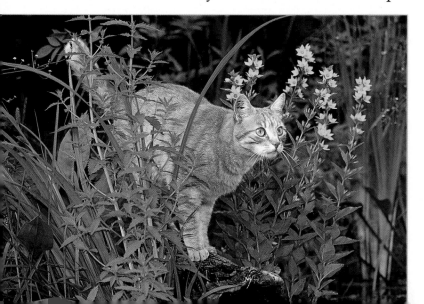

Even though bats and eagles have wings and fly, bats go in the same animal group as cats. Why is this true?

Invertebrates

Sponge

One of the simplest kinds of animals is a sponge. Sponges belong to a group called *Porifera* (pawr·IF·er·ah). A sponge's body is like a hollow tube with lots of holes in it, called pores. Sponges have different kinds of cells that do different jobs. They have some tissues but no organs. Sponges live in water.

Sea anemone

Hydra

Hydras, sea anemones, and jellyfish are the *Cnidaria* (nigh·DAYR·ee·uh). They do not have heads or tails. They live in water. They have soft bodies and tentacles—long threadlike structures. At the end of each tentacle, they have cells that make poisons. They inject the poisons into small animals they kill to eat.

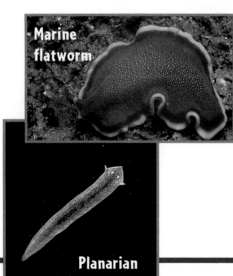

Marine flatworm

Planarian

Flatworms are *Platyhelminthes* (pla·tee·hel·MIN·theez). Their bodies are flat. They have heads and tails. They also have organs cnidarians do not have. Most flatworms do not have true organ systems. Some flatworms live in water. Some live inside other animals.

Roundworms, or *Nematoda* (nee·mah·TOHD·ah), have round bodies, a digestive system, and a simple nervous system. Roundworms live all over Earth, including inside plants and animals.

Hookworm

Earthworms belong to a group called segmented worms, or *Annelida* (AN·el·id·ah). Many segmented worms have eyes and other specialized organs, such as jaws or gills. Each of these animals also has a circulatory, digestive, and nervous system.

Earthworm

Snails, clams, and octopuses belong to the *Mollusca* (MAHL·us·kah), the mollusks. Almost all mollusks have a shell. The shell may be either inside or outside the mollusk's body. Mollusks have three main body parts, a kind of foot, a tissue covering called a mantle, and a compartment holding internal organs. They have gills for breathing. They have jaws or other organs for capturing food. They each have a circulatory system for moving blood. More complex mollusks, like octopuses, have a well-developed brain.

Octopus

Tree snail

Grasshopper

What has a tough outer skeleton, jointed legs, and a body made up of two, three, or more sections? It is an arthropod—a member of the group *Arthropoda* (AHR·thruh·pohd·ah). There are more arthropods on Earth than any other kind of animal. They include insects, spiders, centipedes, millipedes, lobsters, and crabs.

Spider

Lobster

Unlike arthropods, the *Echinodermata* (i·KIGH·noh·durm·ah·tah), or echinoderms, have a skeleton inside their bodies. Most also have a spiny skin and tubelike feet with suction cups.

Starfish

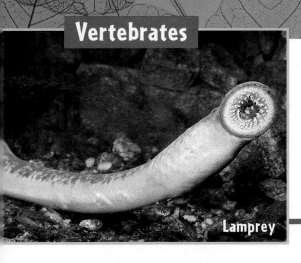

Lamprey

The simplest fish, the *Agnatha* (AG·nah·thuh), do not have jaws or bones. Their skeletons are made of tissue called cartilage. These fish do not have backbones, but each does have a tough nerve cord that runs down its back. They look more like big worms than like fish.

Like those of lampreys and hagfish, the skeletons of sharks and rays are made of cartilage, not bone. However, the cartilage running down their backs is made of a chain of smaller parts called vertebrae. Unlike lampreys and hagfish, sharks and rays have jaws. They also have paired fins. These fish are *Chondrichthyes* (kahn·DRIK·theez).

Shark

Reef sting ray

Tropical fish

Bony fish, or *Osteichthys* (AHS·tee·ik·theez), have bones instead of cartilage. Many have fins that look like fans with spokes in them. These fish have a movable flap over their gills. The movement of this flap lets bony fish breathe while staying still. Unlike sharks, most bony fish have an organ called a swim bladder, or air sac, that allows them to hover at any depth.

Frog

Salamander

Frogs, toads, and salamanders are *Amphibia* (am·FIB·ee·uh), the amphibians. Most adult amphibians have four legs and skin that is not covered with scales. Adult amphibians breathe with lungs instead of gills. In their early stages of life, amphibians live in water. As adults, most live on land.

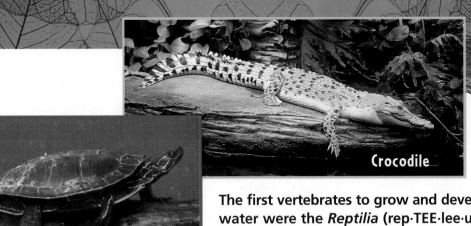

Crocodile

Snake

Turtle

The first vertebrates to grow and develop out of water were the *Reptilia* (rep·TEE·lee·uh), the reptiles. Reptiles breathe through lungs. Most have waterproof scales on their skin that keep them from drying out on land. Their eggs have a leathery or hard covering that protects the eggs from drying out.

Frigate bird

Ostrich

Not all birds can fly, but all birds belong to the group *Aves* (AY·veez). Birds have feathers, walk on two hind limbs, and have front limbs that are wings. Their bones are strong but very lightweight.

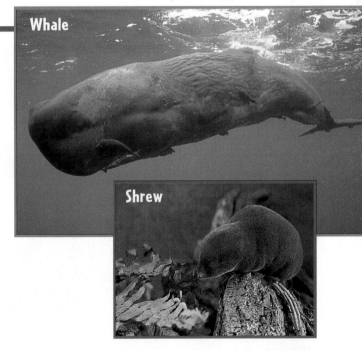

Whale

Shrew

You belong to the group called *Mammalia* (mam·AYL·ee·uh), the mammals. All mammals feed their young milk. At one time or another, all mammals have at least some hair or fur. No other animals have these traits. For their size, most mammals have larger brains than other vertebrates.

Using a Key

How should an animal be classified? Into what group of animals should it be placed?

One way to classify organisms is by using a *classification key*. A classification key lists choices describing characteristics of organisms. It is a series of pairs of statements with directions to follow. These directions will eventually lead you to the identity of the organism you have chosen.

Key to Birds

1. Webbed feet........Go to 3.
    No webbed feet...Go to 2.

2. Hooked bill......Red-tailed hawk
    No hooked bill...Cardinal

3. Flat bill.....Mallard duck
    No flat bill....Go to 4.

4. Pouch...
    Brown pelican
    No pouch...
    Red-faced cormorant

Procedure

1 **Observe** Use the classification key, above right, to identify the birds shown. Starting with the first pair of statements, choose the one that applies to the bird you picked.

2 **Interpret Data** Follow the statement's directions. It will lead you to another pair of statements.

3 Keep following the directions until you come to the identity of the bird you chose.

Drawing Conclusions

Do you think this key would be helpful in identifying birds in your neighborhood? Explain.

Why It Matters

Nature holds many secrets and presents many mysteries. It is the job of scientists to discover the secrets and solve the mysteries. Classifying animals helps do this. Among other things, it shows which animals are most closely related to one another. It also can show the order in which they appeared on Earth. Classification can be thought of as a kind of calendar of life on Earth.

Think and Write

1. Name three traits you might use to classify an animal.
2. What are the building blocks of living things?
3. What is the main difference between an invertebrate and a vertebrate?
4. **Classify** Name a trait you would use to classify a fish as belonging to either the lamprey and hagfish group or the shark and ray group.
5. **Critical Thinking** Which do you think are more closely related—whales and goldfish or whales and mice? Explain.

LITERATURE LINK

Read *Dino Flight*, the story of the discovery of the ancestors of birds. When you finish reading, think about how fossils can give clues to the past. Try the activities at the end of the book.

WRITING LINK

Write an essay. Look at the picture of the animal shown here. It swims underwater. It has a ducklike bill and webbed feet. It lays eggs like a bird, yet its eggshells are like those of a reptile. It is a *platypus*. Write an essay on how you would classify this animal.

MATH LINK

Solve this problem. The smallest bat is 4 centimeters long. The blue whale is 3,300 centimeters long. How much longer is the blue whale than the smallest bat?

TECHNOLOGY LINK

At the Computer Visit www.mhscience02.com for more links.

ANIMAL LIFE CYCLES

What if you saw a tadpole but had never seen a frog? Would people have a hard time convincing you a frog was a grown-up tadpole?

When you see seedlings, you can predict that the fully grown plants will be on stems and have leaves. However, some baby animals look nothing like the adults. They change shape by going through metamorphosis.

Frogs lay eggs in ponds and lakes. The eggs hatch into tadpoles. They must live in water because they have gills, like fish, not lungs.

The tadpoles begin to change. They grow legs. Their tails disappear. They develop lungs and lose their gills. Now they can live on land and in the water!

Insects have two kinds of metamorphosis—complete and incomplete. During complete metamorphosis an egg hatches into a wormlike larva. It eats a lot and grows to become a pupa. This is a resting phase. Many body changes take place. Some larvae spin protective cocoons. Finally, the adult winged insect emerges.

During incomplete metamorphosis the insect changes shape gradually. An egg hatches into a nymph that looks like a small adult without wings. The nymph grows and slowly changes. Finally, it grows wings and becomes an adult.

Eggs

Tadpole with gills

Tadpole with limbs

Young frog

Egg   Larva   Pupa   Adult
                                          Butterfly

What Did I Learn?

1. To go from egg to adult, a frog goes through a process called

A childhood
B adolescence
C the pupa stage
D metamorphosis

2. The stages of complete metamorphosis are

F egg larva pupa adult
G egg larva nymph pupa adult
H egg nymph pupa adult
J egg nymph adult

Egg   Nymph   Adult
                                                Grasshopper

AT THE COMPUTER Visit www.mhscience02.com to learn more about metamorphosis.

Animal Adaptations

Get Ready

Alaska is home to many animals, including the snowshoe hare. You might think this hare is a little strange. Its fur changes color from white in the winter to brown in the summer. How does this help the snowshoe hare survive in its environment?

Process Skill

You experiment when you perform a test to support or disprove a hypothesis.

Explore Activity

How Do Sow Bugs Adapt to Their Environment?

Materials

10 sow bugs

tray

paper towels

water

Procedure

BE CAREFUL! Handle live animals with care. Wash your hands well when you finish this activity.

1 **Observe** Place a sow bug in the center of the tray, and observe it. What traits does it have that enable it to live in the soil and under decaying wood or leaves? Record your observations.

2 **Observe** Touch the sow bug. How does it react?

3 **Experiment** Place all the sow bugs in the center of the tray. Do the animals tend to stay together?

4 **Experiment** Move the sow bugs to one end of the tray. Dampen three or four paper towels, and place them in the opposite end of the tray. Observe for several minutes. Record your observations. When the animals move, do they tend to move faster in the dry section or wet section of the box?

Drawing Conclusions

1 **Infer** How do sow bugs protect themselves?

2 **Infer** Can the behavior of sow bugs when exposed to moisture be related to their survival? If so, how?

3 **Going Further: Experiment** Design an experiment to test the reactions of sow bugs to light. Record your results.

Main Idea Animals have certain characteristics, behaviors, and adaptations that help them survive.

How Do Animals Adapt?

Certain traits animals have help them to survive in their environment. Such traits are called adaptations.

An animal has many adaptations. One important group of adaptations helps the animal keep from getting eaten by a *predator* (an animal that might eat it). How can an animal avoid being eaten?

Through experience, you have learned to avoid certain things. For example, if you see a buzzing black-and-yellow striped insect, you are not likely to try to touch it. Why? You have learned that insects that look like this can give you a painful sting. They are called yellow jackets. Animals that feed on insects have also learned to avoid yellow jackets.

They also avoid a harmless insect called a syrphid (SUHR·fuhd) fly. Why? It looks very much like a yellow jacket. In nature, looking like something else—especially something unpleasant—is called **mimicry**.

Mimicry

One of these insects stings. One does not. To be safe, insect-eating animals avoid both. This helps both the wasp (left) and the harmless syrphid fly (right) to survive. Animals avoid the harmless fly because it mimics a stinging wasp.

When food spoils, it tastes bad. If you don't want to get sick, you quickly dispose of spoiled food. Some birds might like to make a meal out of the good-tasting viceroy butterfly. However, birds often avoid gulping down a viceroy. Why? The viceroy looks like a monarch butterfly, which, birds have learned, tastes awful.

You are probably very careful when you meet a cat you don't know. You have learned that its sharp claws can give you a nasty scratch. Certain predators have learned the same thing about thorny plants. The predators stay away from such plants.

This gives thornbugs protection from being eaten. That's because thornbugs look like thorns. When the bugs cluster on the stem of a plant, a predator mistakes them for the thorns on a plant. The predator stays away, and the thornbugs live to see another day.

Viceroy

Monarch

> **Why is mimicry a good adaptation for an animal to have?**

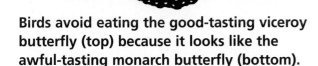

Birds avoid eating the good-tasting viceroy butterfly (top) because it looks like the awful-tasting monarch butterfly (bottom).

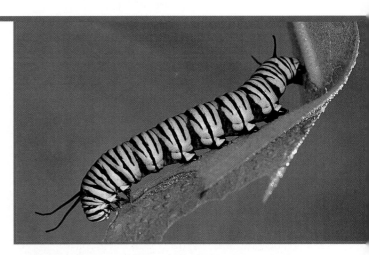

Monarch larvae (caterpillars) feed on milkweed. Milkweed contains a substance that can make animals ill. Birds that have eaten one monarch butterfly learn to avoid eating both monarchs and look-alike viceroys.

The dark "thorn" on the branch is a thornbug. Because thornbugs look like thorns that can scratch, predators stay away.

What Is Camouflage?

At one time or another, most people have dreamed about being invisible. For one thing, if people can't see you, they can't hurt you. You can't make yourself invisible. Neither can animals. Even so, you can make yourself look so much like your surroundings that you are almost invisible.

An animal that does not move, or moves very, very slowly, and looks like its surroundings is camouflaged. **Camouflage** is another important adaptation that helps animals avoid their predators.

There are two basic kinds of camouflage, or blending in with the environment. One has to do with an animal's shape. The other has to do with its color. Let's start off by exploring how shape can camouflage an animal.

What if you were a bird hunting for a butterfly? You would not be tempted to eat a leaf. That is what protects the leaf butterfly from being eaten. The wings of the leaf butterfly are shaped like the leaves of a plant. When this butterfly is perched on the stem of a plant, or resting on a forest floor littered with leaves, it is very hard to see. A bird passes it by as if it were not there.

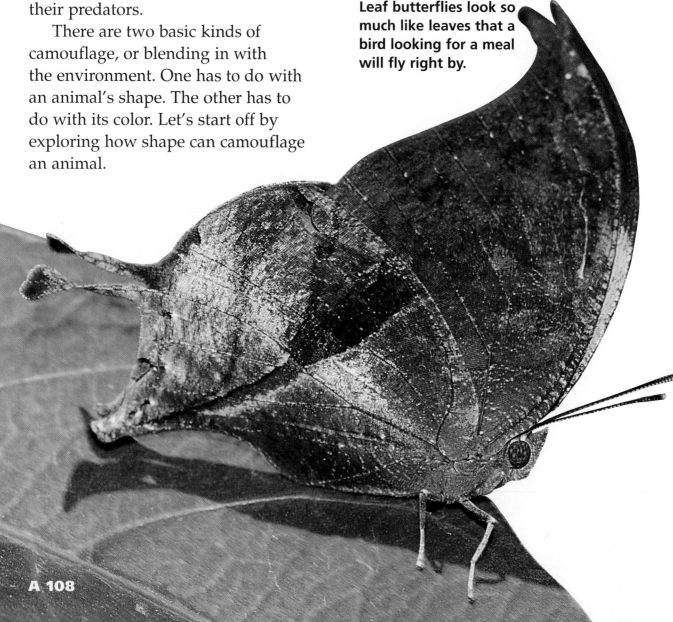

Leaf butterflies look so much like leaves that a bird looking for a meal will fly right by.

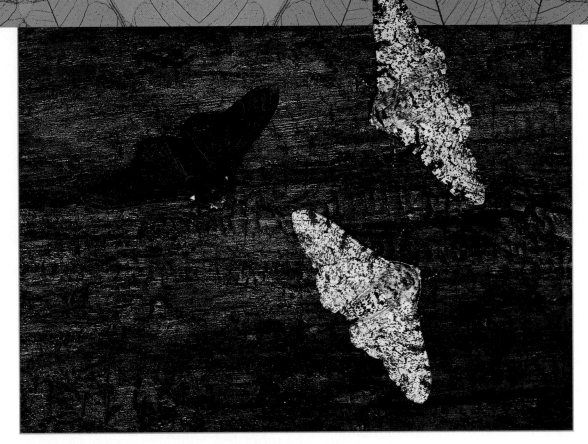

Birds can more easily spot a light-colored peppered moth (right) against a dark background than a dark-colored peppered moth (left) against a dark background.

About 150 years ago, England was home to two kinds of peppered moths. One kind was light colored. The other kind was dark colored. Birds fed on both kinds of moths, many of which clung to the trunks of trees.

However, gradually the light-colored moths seemed to be disappearing. The birds were eating more of these moths than the dark-colored ones. What was causing this?

Nearby factories were pouring dark, sticky smoke into the air. The smoke stuck to the trunks of trees. The light-colored moths stood out against this background. The dark-colored moths blended in with the background.

Since the birds could more easily see the light-colored moths, the birds were eating more light-colored moths than dark-colored moths. This is an example of a kind of camouflage called **protective coloration** . The color of the dark peppered moths protected them from predators.

 How does camouflage help an animal survive?

Nest building is an inherited trait. Robins (left) build their nests of twigs. Penguins (above) build their nests of pebbles.

What Is Inherited?

Animals behave in many different ways. They learn some kinds of behavior, like avoiding bad-tasting insects. You may have noticed learned behaviors in your pet. For example, if your cat cries for food every time it hears the electric can opener, your cat has learned that the sound of the can opener can mean mealtime. No wonder your cat acts disappointed when the canned food turns out to be something it doesn't like. However, not all behaviors are learned. Certain other kinds of behavior seem to be automatic.

Young birds will build the same kinds of nests their parents build. They do this even if the young birds have never seen their parents build a nest. In other words, birds do not learn how to build nests. They do it automatically.

Scientists would say that nest building is *inherited*, or passed down from one generation to the next. An inherited behavior is one that is not learned. It is done automatically. This inherited behavior is called *instinct*. The passing of inherited traits from parents to offspring is called **heredity**.

Many physical traits of an animal are also inherited. For example, the shape of a bird's feet and beak is inherited. The color of its feathers is inherited, too. This is easy to see, since young birds have the same-shaped feet and beaks as their parents.

Hawk

Duck

Woodpecker

The feet and beaks of birds are inherited physical traits. All woodpeckers have feet adapted for grasping the sides of tree trunks. All hawks have feet armed with claws adapted for grabbing smaller animals. All ducks have webbed feet adapted for swimming.

What physical traits are not inherited? Those that the environment can change. If there is not much food around, an animal's weight and size may be smaller than normal. Weight and size are physical traits, but they may not be inherited. Of course, certain animals—such as elephants—tend to be bigger and heavier than others—such as mice. Such tendencies are inherited.

The average weight and size of an elephant is greater than the average weight and size of a mouse. Even so, some elephants will be larger and heavier than others. Some mice will be larger and heavier than other mice. In other words, some traits are affected by both heredity and the environment.

▷ How are animal behaviors that are inherited different from those that are learned?

Although gerbils are smaller than elephants, the environment can make some gerbils bigger than other gerbils and some elephants bigger than other elephants.

Donkey

Horse

Mule

A mule is the hybrid offspring of the mating of a female horse and a male donkey. Many hybrids are sterile and cannot produce offspring of their own. This is true of mules.

What Is a Hybrid?

What looks a little like a horse and a little like a donkey, but isn't either? The answer to this riddle is . . . a mule! It looks the way it does because its male parent was a donkey and its female parent was a horse.

Living things that have parents that are quite different from each other, such as donkeys and horses, are called **hybrids**. People sometimes breed hybrids on purpose, since a hybrid may have more desirable traits than either of its parents.

A mule can do work that neither a donkey nor a horse can do. Mules are often used to carry heavy loads through rugged country. That's because mules do not slip as easily as horses. Mules also have more

endurance than donkeys. Horses and donkeys do not normally mate. Even so, for thousands of years people have been breeding mules.

Crossbreeds

People often mate closely related living things on purpose. They may mate certain crop plants, flowers, dogs, or cats. They do this to produce hearty crops or plants and animals with desirable traits. This process is sometimes called **crossbreeding**. A crossbreed is a product of the mating of individuals from two distinct breeds or varieties of the same *species* (kind of organism). Crossbreeding has produced new breeds of dogs and cats. Cross-breeding has also given us new kinds of corn that resist disease, produce more food on the same area of land, and are more nutritious.

Crossbreeds also occur naturally. If you have found a shady spot under the branches of a London plane tree, you have run across a hybrid. About 2,000 years ago, the oriental plane tree grew in the southern parts of Europe. It was so pretty that people living in northern Europe wanted to grow it there. Unfortunately, the oriental plane tree could not survive the cold northern winters. Then in about 1670, the oriental plane tree crossbred naturally with another kind of plane tree. The offspring, which came to be called the London plane tree, was a new kind of plant that could survive cold winters. Today these lovely trees are found on many streets in northern Europe and in the northern United States.

Cat Breeds

Cat breeds can be divided into two major groups—cats with short hair and cats with long hair. Different breeds of cats also vary in color, in length and texture of hair, and in temperament. Some are quiet and affectionate. Others tend to be vocal and demanding.

QUICK LAB

FOR SCHOOL OR HOME

Find the Hybrid Cat

1. Observe Look at the picture of the Siamese cat. What traits do you think it has been bred for?

2. Observe Look at the picture of the Persian cat. What traits do you think it has been bred for?

3. Observe Look at the picture of the Himalayan cat. What traits do you think it has been bred for?

4. Infer Which cat do you think is the hybrid? Explain your answer.

▷ How is a mule an example of a hybrid?

Persian cat

Siamese cat

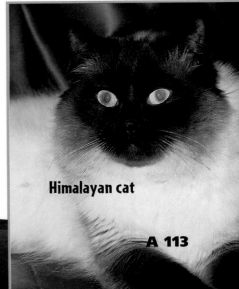

Himalayan cat

Why Is Diversity Important?

Would you rather have a mutt or a purebred dog? Purebred dogs—or other animals—look very much like their parents. They are bred to have certain traits. Mutts, on the other hand, may not look much like either parent. However, they do have a great mix of traits.

A group of dogs made up of mutts is a good example of animal **diversity**. *Diversity* means "different." Animal diversity refers to a group of the same kind of animal—like dogs—in which there are lots of animals with different traits. A group of mutts is made up of individual dogs with very different traits. Is there an advantage to being a mutt? The answer can be yes! Mutts may be healthier than certain purebred dogs. Some purebred dogs are known to have breathing problems. Some have hip problems. However, other purebred dogs come from very healthy breeds.

Threatened Cheetahs

Animal diversity is important. When an environment changes, only those animals that can adapt to the change will survive. If the population is made up of animals with the same traits—and those traits do not help the animals survive in a changing environment—the whole population may die out. This fate threatens the cheetahs of Africa. However, if the population holds animals with different traits, it is more likely that some will survive to keep the population going.

Africa's cheetahs are in trouble. The traits of all cheetahs are so much alike, they have little diversity. This could threaten their survival against a new disease or other changes in their environment.

READING Summarize

Why is diversity important in an animal population?

Why It Matters

Nature favors animal diversity. Hybridization, whether natural or artificial, produces animal diversity. Humans are no exception to this rule. Sometimes people carry traits that could be unhealthy for their children. Diversity among humans reduces the chances of inheriting such traits.

Visit **www.mhscience02.com** to do a research project on animal diversity.

Think and Write

1. What is one adaptation that helps an animal escape a predator?

2. What is an example of an inherited behavior?

3. What is an example of an inherited physical trait?

4. If two different kinds of animals mate and produce offspring, what might you infer about the traits of the offspring?

5. **Critical Thinking** Dark peppered moths cling to trees covered by black soot from factories. If the factories were not allowed to produce sooty smoke, what might happen to the dark peppered moths? Explain.

L·I·N·K·S

ART LINK

Make a display. Research two or three hybrid animals other than the ones discussed in this lesson. Find or make illustrations or models of the hybrid animals as well as their parents. Write descriptions of the hybrids, and add them to your display.

Tiglon

WRITING LINK

Write an essay. Write a paragraph about some of your favorite animal's behaviors. Which of its behaviors are automatic? Which of its behaviors are learned? Write another paragraph about some of your automatic responses. Compare them with some of the things you have learned to do.

TECHNOLOGY LINK

At the Computer Visit **www.mhscience02.com** for more links.

Chapter 3 Review

Vocabulary

Fill each blank with the best word or words from the list.

camouflage, A108
crossbreeding, A113
heredity, A110
hybrid, A112
invertebrate, A96
mimicry, A106
organ, A95
protective coloration, A109
system, A95
vertebrate, A96

1. A(n) _____ is an animal that has a backbone.

2. An animal uses _____ to blend in with the background.

3. Looking like something a predator would not like to eat is an example of _____.

4. The changing color of an arctic hare's coat is an example of _____.

5. A mule is a(n) _____.

6. Tissues come together to form a(n) _____.

7. Organs come together to form a(n) _____.

8. Scientists use _____ to produce heartier crops.

9. The passing down of inherited traits is called _____.

10. A(n) _____ is an animal that does not have a backbone.

Test Prep

11. Insects, spiders, lobsters, and crabs are all _____.
    A mammals
    B amphibians
    C arthropods
    D syrphids

12. The skeletons of sharks are made of _____.
    F scales
    G bones
    H fins
    J cartilage

13. A bird's bones _____.
    A are made of cartilage
    B weigh very little for their size
    C weigh a lot for their size
    D are surprisingly thick

14. Animals with fur are _____.
    F amphibians
    G syrphids
    H either arthropods or mollusks
    J mammals

15. As adults, frogs breathe with _____.
    A gills
    B lungs
    C cartilage
    D mollusks

Concepts and Skills

16. Reading in Science Write a paragraph explaining why a predator might avoid eating a syrphid fly.

17. Scientific Methods The two graphs below show changes in population size between a certain predator and its prey (the animals it eats). Identify which animal is the predator and which is the prey. Write a paragraph giving the reasons for your answer.

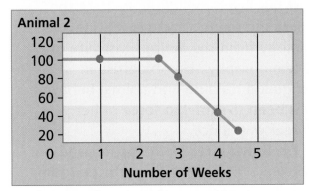

18. Decision Making A company is planning to build a factory near a river that is home to many different kinds of fish. The only thing the company is planning to dump in the river is clean water. However, the temperature of the water they are dumping is 18°C warmer than the warmest temperature the river usually reaches. You are on the planning committee that will decide whether or not to allow the factory to be built there. What factors do you need to consider when making your decision? Write a paragraph discussing these factors and explaining what your decision would be.

19. Process Skills: Classify Many members of different animal groups are found in water. Create a classification key to identify a whale among a hagfish, a shark, and a sea turtle. Write a paragraph explaining how your key works.

20. Critical Thinking You are a marine biologist, a scientist who studies living things in the ocean. You are exploring under the water and come upon a strange fish. You catch it in a net and take it back to your laboratory. What must you find out about the fish in order to classify it? Write your ideas.

Boost *your test scores!*

Be Smart!
Visit www.mhscience02.com

Bioacoustician
Dr. Ann Bowles
Hubbs-Sea World Research Institute

Dr. Doolittle talked with the animals. While his conversations were make-believe, there are scientists called bioacousticians who study how animals communicate, too. The only difference is they focus on understanding the animal instead of the other way around. They also study what animals can hear and the effects of human-made sounds.

Dr. Ann Bowles is a bioacoustician at Hubbs-Sea World Research Institute. She grew up in Peru where her father was helping to build a radio telescope in the desert outside Lima. Her love for animals started when she saw amazing animals like morpho butterflies, llama, and gigantic tadpoles during her family's travels throughout South America.

In college, Dr. Bowles earned a degree in linguistics—the study of human languages. However, she never lost her love of wildlife. In 1994 she completed a doctorate in marine biology from the Scripps Institute of Oceanography. Her expertise in language training and animal behavior has been the driving force of her career ever since.

Dr. Bowles' research has focused on the ways that adult emperor penguins recognize each other by voice. She is now trying to understand how killer whales develop their word-like calls. Information like this may help humans understand how their own language evolved.

Dr. Bowles has also studied the effect of human-made sounds on other animals. Marine animals make life-and-death decisions based on what they hear. Unfortunately, human-made sounds can have a bad effect on marine animals. For example, noise made by shipping traffic can mask communications between whales and blasting can deafen them.

Sometimes, human-made sounds can be beneficial. For example, fishermen's nets now carry pingers, little devices that produce a peeping noise. Many marine mammals find the sound annoying, which keeps them out of nets and traps. Dr. Bowles is trying to understand why these tiny sounds are effective in a noisy ocean. With this information, better pingers can be designed. It's her way of respecting the needs of our animal neighbors.

AT THE COMPUTER

Visit **www.mhscience02.com** to learn more about careers.

Write
ABOUT IT

1. How do adult emperor penguins communicate?

2. Why is it important to study the effect human sounds have on marine animals?

Careers IN SCIENCE

Career Track

Here are some different types of careers related to the study of bioacoustics. You can use the Internet or library resources to find out more about these careers.

- linguist
- naturalist
- marine biologist
- ecologist
- zoologist

Plant Parts Do Their Part

Your goal is to identify plant parts and diagram water movement in a plant.

What to Do

1. Using a hand lens, identify veins and petioles in a leaf; root hairs, cortex, and xylem in a root; and xylem and phloem in a stem. Draw and label diagrams of each part.

2. Draw and label a tree. Show water movement from soil to leaf.

Analyze **Your Results**

Using the words *light*, *chlorophyll*, and *energy* describe how leaf cells use water.

Flowers for Lunch

Your goal is to identify common foods from plant parts.

What to Do

Examine each of several foods. What plant part is it? Create a table using the words below.

Root	Stem	Leaf	Fruit
Seed	Flower	Bark	Sap

Analyze **Your Results**

1. Fill in the table by classifying each of the foods you examined.

2. Make a menu with at least five foods made from plants and identify the source.

Cactus Creature

Your goal is to make a model animal adapted to life in the desert.

What to Do

BE CAREFUL! Handle sharp objects carefully! Examine a cactus with a hand lens. Think of how an animal that lives among cactus would look. Make a model of it.

Analyze **Your Results**

Describe the adaptations you gave your model animal. How would each of these adaptations help the animal survive in the desert? Compare it to a cactus.

Life Science

UNIT B
Interactions of Living Things

NATIONAL GEOGRAPHIC

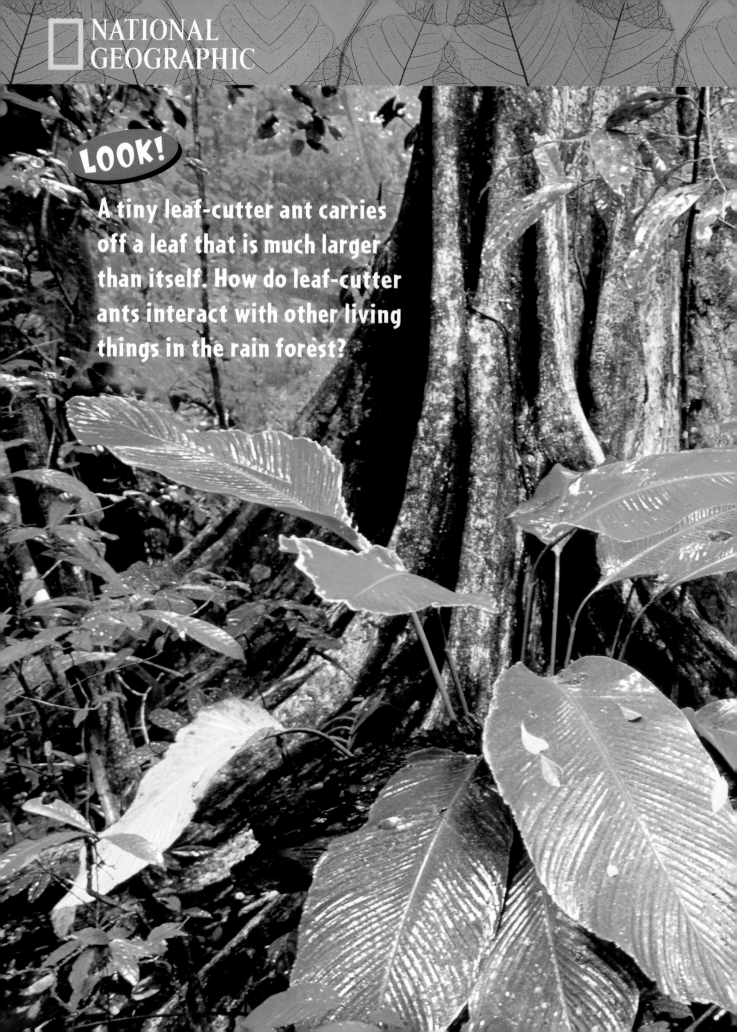

NATIONAL GEOGRAPHIC

LOOK!

A tiny leaf-cutter ant carries off a leaf that is much larger than itself. How do leaf-cutter ants interact with other living things in the rain forest?

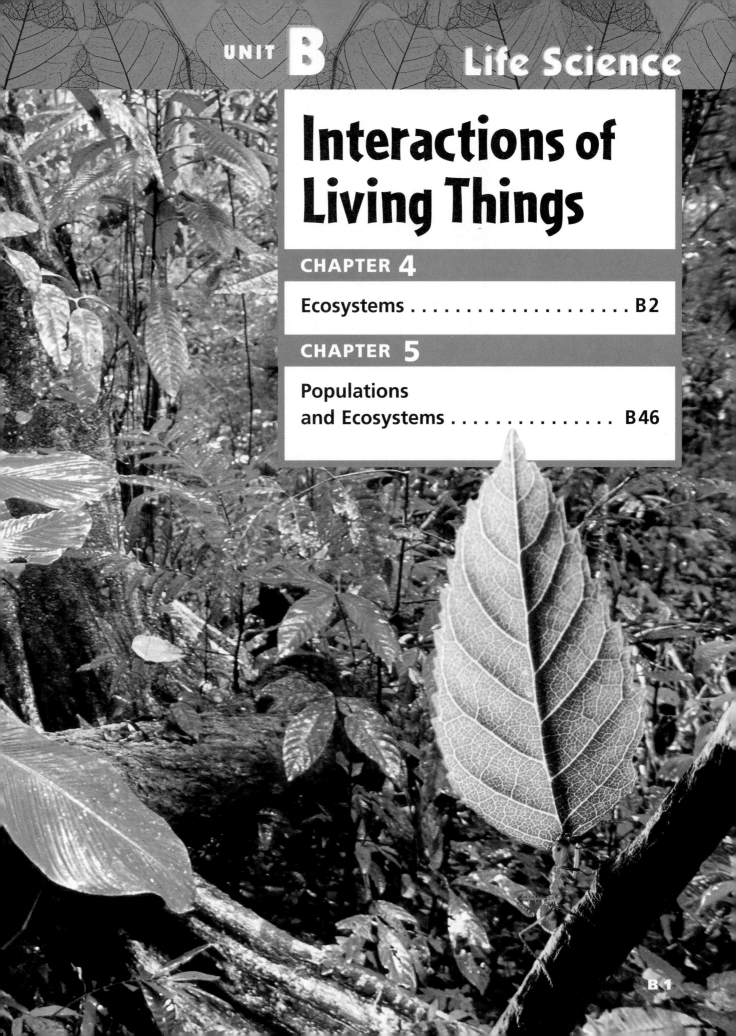

Interactions of Living Things

CHAPTER 4

Ecosystems

Did You Ever Wonder?

What happened to the buffalo? The huge herds of buffalo
that once roamed the grasslands of the United States were
hunted almost to extinction. Today, however, buffalo can once
again be seen in places like Yellowstone National Park. What other
kinds of animals live in the grasslands?

Living Things and Their Environment

Vocabulary

ecosystem, B6

ecology, B6

abiotic factor, B6

biotic factor, B7

population, B10

community, B10

habitat, B11

niche, B11

Get Ready

What do you need in order to survive? Food? Water? Comfortable temperatures? Shelter?

What kinds of things does the animal shown here need to survive? What kinds of things do the plants need? Where do you think they get these things?

Process Skill

You experiment when you perform a test to support or disprove a hypothesis.

Explore Activity

What Do Living Things Need to Survive?

Procedure: Design Your Own

BE CAREFUL! Handle animals and plants gently.

1 For a water environment, add thoroughly washed sand or gravel to the jar. Fill the jar with water. Add a few floating plants, rooted plants with floating leaves, and submerged plants. Add water snails.

2 For a land environment, place a layer of gravel on the bottom of the jar. Cover the gravel layer with a layer of moistened soil. Add plants, and plant grass seeds. Add earthworms, sow bugs, and snails.

3 Place each jar in a lighted area but not in direct sunlight.

4 Cover each jar with its own lid or with a piece of plastic wrap. Record the number and types of living things you used.

5 **Observe** Examine your jars every other day, and record your observations.

Drawing Conclusions

1 **Infer** What are the nonliving parts of your system? What are the living parts of your system?

2 **Infer** What do the living things need to survive? How do you know?

3 **Going Further: Experiment** How could you design an environment that contains both land and water areas?

Materials

wide-mouthed, clear container with lid

washed gravel

pond water or aged tap water

water plants

water snails

soil

small rocks

grass seed and small plants

earthworms, land snails, sow bugs, or other small land animals that eat plants

What Is an Ecosystem?

What or whom do you interact with every day? Living things and nonliving things interact in an **ecosystem**. An ecosystem is all the living and nonliving things in an area. **Ecology** is the study of how all these things interact in order to survive.

An ecosystem may be very small, such as a backyard or pond. Some ecosystems, like the prairie ecosystem of North America, the deserts of Africa, and the rain forests of Brazil, cover large areas of a country or continent. Freshwater ecosystems cover less space than saltwater ecosystems. Saltwater ecosystems can cover entire oceans. It doesn't matter where they are or what they look like, all ecosystems have the same parts.

Abiotic Factors

The nonliving parts of an ecosystem are the **abiotic** (ay·bigh·AHT·ik) **factors**. All living things need certain nonliving things in order to survive. Abiotic factors include water, minerals, sunlight, air, climate, and soil.

All *organisms*, or living things, need water. Their bodies are 50 to 95 percent water. The processes that keep living things alive—like photosynthesis and respiration—can only take place in the presence of water. Living things also need minerals, such as calcium, iron, phosphorus, and nitrogen. Some living things, like plants and algae, need

sunlight to make food. Animals need oxygen to produce energy for their bodies. Plants and algae need carbon dioxide. The environment must also have the right temperature for organisms to survive.

Abiotic Factors

Abiotic factors in an ecosystem include light, water, soil, temperature, air, and minerals.

Biotic Factors

Biotic factors in an ecosystem include plants, animals, fungi, protists, and bacteria.

READING
Diagrams

1. How do these two diagrams differ? What does each diagram show?

2. Which of these two diagrams best shows the abiotic factors in the ecosystem? Explain your answer.

Biotic Factors

The right abiotic factors help make it possible for organisms in an ecosystem to survive. The living parts are animals, plants, fungi, protists, and bacteria. Mushrooms and molds are examples of fungi. Protists include one-celled organisms.

These organisms—animals, plants, fungi, protists, and bacteria—make up the **biotic** (bigh·AHT·ik) **factors**, or living parts, of an ecosystem.

Plants and algae are called *producers*. They produce oxygen and food that animals need. Animals are *consumers*. Animals consume, or eat, plants or animals. Animals also give off carbon dioxide that plants need to make food.

What do the fungi and bacteria contribute? They are a very important part of any ecosystem. Fungi and bacteria are *decomposers*. They *decompose*, or break down, dead plants and animals into useful things like minerals that enrich soil. Plants need these in order to grow.

Each of these kinds of organisms helps the others survive.

▷ **What are five abiotic and five biotic factors in an ecosystem?**

What Is a Prairie Ecosystem Like?

Long ago a "sea of wild grasses" covered North America from central Texas in the south to North Dakota in the north. These were America's prairie lands, the range of the famous song "Home on the Range."

The Blackland Prairie is the largest remaining prairie in America. It stretches 483 km (300 mi) across Texas, from Austin to Clarksville. The Blacklands got their name from the rich black soil the early settlers found there. The settlers found that the summers were hot and long, and that there was enough rain to grow profitable crops, like cotton.

Before the land became farms and ranches, huge herds of buffalo grazed on the prairie grasses. Native Americans once hunted the buffalo on this land for food and clothing as a means of survival.

Buffalo were not the prairie's only inhabitants. Plants and animals of all kinds lived there. At least 50 different kinds of tall and short grasses provided food for plant-eating animals. Many kinds of wildflowers painted the landscape with beautiful colors. These flowers included purple coneflowers, bluebells, yellow sunflowers, and golden daleas. Travelers might have come across oak, hickory, elm, or cedar trees along nearby streams.

The cattle and crops that provide much of our food live on the prairie today. Ranchers and farmers now graze cattle and plant crops such as corn and wheat on the Blacklands.

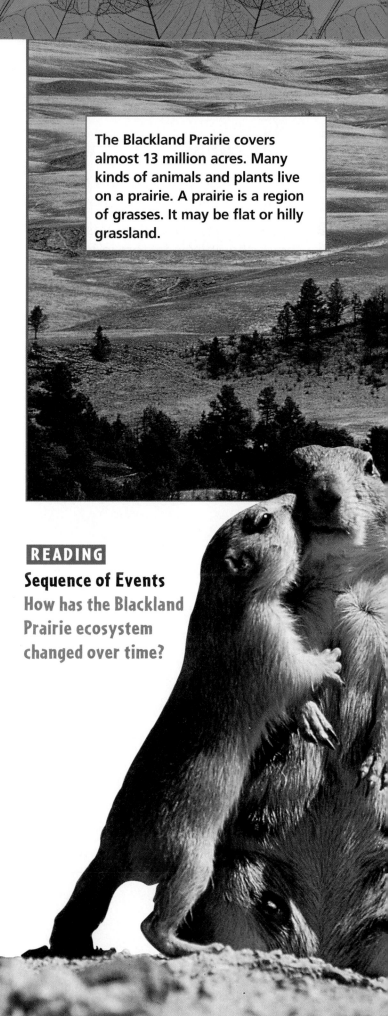

The Blackland Prairie covers almost 13 million acres. Many kinds of animals and plants live on a prairie. A prairie is a region of grasses. It may be flat or hilly grassland.

READING

Sequence of Events
How has the Blackland Prairie ecosystem changed over time?

Armadillo

Clarksville

T E X A S

Dallas

Bobcat

Waco

Cottontail rabbit

Austin

READING

Maps

1. What large cities are on the Blackland Prairie?

2. Why do you think those cities are located where they are?

What Animals Live on the Blackland Prairie?

About 500 species, or different kinds, of animals still live on this prairie. The spotted chorus frog sings in the night near the streams and rivers. Rattlesnakes and lizards seek shelter under rocks.

Birds like pipits, longspurs, and horned larks, as well as 300 other kinds of birds, still live on the Blackland Prairie.

Raccoons, opossums, coyotes, white-tailed deer, and striped skunks live on the Blacklands. Cotton rats, white-footed mice, eastern cottontails, red bats, and bobcats live there, too.

Mountain lions, gray wolves, black bears, and jaguars used to come in search of prey. When people came and built towns, cities, and farms, the buffalo left. The animals that fed on the buffalo left, too. Some animals, however, came to the Blacklands from other places, and stayed. Armadillos arrived from Mexico as the Blacklands' climate warmed up over the past 150 years. Badgers invaded from north-western Texas when their natural homes were cleared for development.

▷ **What are five animals that live on the prairie?**

Prairie dogs

How Are Living Things Organized?

The Blackland Prairie, like all ecosystems, is home to many different organisms. Each kind of organism, whether an animal, plant, fungus, protist, or bacterium, is a member of a different species. All the organisms of a species living in the same area make up a **population**.

The Blackland Prairie has populations of armadillos and badgers. It has little bluestem grass and Indian grass. It has elm trees. It also has pond algae and soil bacteria.

Most people are satisfied with just identifying the populations around them. Scientists, however, want to know how populations interact. Scientists investigate the activities of animals, plants, fungi, protists, and bacteria in the ecosystem. They want to know which animals prey on others. Which animals eat plants? Which insects eat crops? They are interested in how bacteria and fungi make the soil fertile. All these questions need to be answered to understand how an ecosystem stays healthy.

Scientists have to do more than study individual organisms or even individual populations in the ecosystem. They have to study the interactions of all the populations in an area. All the populations living in an area make up a **community**.

 What are populations and communities?

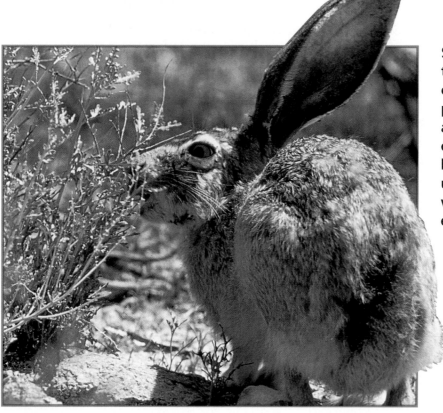

Scientists study the interactions of different populations in an ecosystem's community. This helps them to understand what makes an ecosystem grow.

What Are Niches and Habitats?

The place where an organism lives is called its **habitat**. The chorus frog's habitat is in the scattered ponds of the Blacklands.

Each species in an ecosystem also has a role or place in the activities of its community. The role of an organism in the community is its **niche**.

A species' niche includes many factors. It includes what a species eats and what eats that species. It includes the kind of environment the species needs to live in. It even includes whether the species is active by day or night.

No two populations can have the same niche. Why is this true? To have the same niche, two populations would have to eat the same foods and be eaten by the same predators. They would have to live in the same space and reproduce in the same ways. They would have to grow under the same temperature, moisture, and light conditions, get the same diseases, and look and behave exactly alike. They would have to be identical! No two populations are identical though, so no two populations have the same niche.

Scientists study the habitats and niches of organisms in a community. They do this to see if the community is healthy or in trouble.

The red bat's habitat is above the ground. During the day it hangs from tree branches like a red leaf. At night it streaks through the air looking for food.

▷ **What is the difference between a niche and a habitat?**

The horned lark has its niche on the prairie.

What Happens When Habitats Change?

The world is a place of changes. One day the weather may be dry and cold. The next day it may be wet and warm. Heavy rains may drench the land one spring and summer. The next year's spring and summer may have cloudless skies day after day. This makes habitats change. A good habitat for a certain organism at one time may be a threatening one at another time. How do populations survive difficult times?

The Eastern Spadefoot Toad

The eastern spadefoot toad lives on the Blackland Prairie. This animal reproduces in water and needs water for its daily life. What happens if a drought strikes the Blacklands?

A close look at the toad's hind feet provided scientists with a clue to the answer. Its hind feet are shaped like little spades. They are adapted for digging. That's just what the spadefoot toad does when water is scarce. It digs into the ground and covers itself with soil. This toad can absorb water through its skin. There's a lot of clay in Blacklands soil, and clay holds water well. Usually there is some water in the soil, even though there may not be any water above it. The toad may be able to survive in the soil even during a drought.

Bald eagles were once common on the Blackland Prairie.

American Bald Eagles

Many years ago there were bald eagles on the Blackland Prairie of Texas. Then they disappeared. A few have returned recently, especially around the lakes created by damming rivers. Why did the eagles disappear for a while?

Scientists carefully analyzed data to discover one reason why bald eagles may have vanished from the skies above the Blackland Prairie.

▷ **What happens to animals when habitats change?**

The eastern spadefoot toad can survive in a dry, hot habitat by burrowing into the soil and absorbing water through its skin.

Process Skill BUILDER

Vanishing Bald Eagles

The table below shows the average number of bald eagle eggs that hatched in the wild during a 16-year period. It also shows the level of an insecticide in bald eagle eggs during the same period. What is the relationship between these two variables?

Variables are things that can change. In order to determine what caused the results of an experiment, you need to change one variable at a time. The variable that is changed is called the *independent variable*. A *dependent variable* is one that changes because of the independent variable.

Materials

ruler

Bald Eagle Egg-Hatching Data																
Year	1966	1967	1968	1969	1970	1971	1972*	1973	1974	1975	1976	1977	1978	1979	1980	1981
Average number of young hatched (per nest)	1.28	0.75	0.87	0.82	0.50	0.55	0.60	0.70	0.60	0.81	0.90	0.93	0.91	0.98	1.02	1.27
Insecticide in eggs (parts per million)	42	68	125	119	122	108	82	74	68	59	32	12	13	14	13	13

*pesticide banned

Procedure

1. **Infer** What is the independent variable in the study? What is the dependent variable in the study?

2. **Communicate** Make a line graph showing the average number of young that hatched. Make another line graph showing the amount of insecticide in eggs.

Drawing Conclusions

1. **Use Variables** Based on the graphs, what appears to be the relationship between the amount of insecticide in eggs and the number of young hatched?

2. **Hypothesize** Suggest a reason for the relationship.

What Is the Treasure of the Blackland Prairie?

Have you ever read about a buried treasure? Unlike those stories, the treasure of the Blackland Prairie is not buried underground. The treasure of the Blackland Prairie is the ground.

Prairie soils can often be identified by their dark brown to black *topsoil*. Topsoil is the top layer of soil. The dark color shows the presence of *humus*. Humus is partly decayed plant matter. The decay is produced by the bacteria and fungi.

The rich topsoil is full of minerals that prairie grasses and crops need. Two of the most important minerals are magnesium and calcium. Plants need magnesium in order to make chlorophyll. Calcium is an important element of cell walls in plants.

Today most of the natural grasses that used to sway in the wind like ocean waves are gone from the Blackland Prairie. They have been replaced by "seas" of cultivated grasses. Is this a good thing?

The nutrients in certain prairie soils tend to stay near the surface. That's true because of the low yearly rainfall on prairies. There isn't enough water to carry the nutrients deep into the ground. Farmers take advantage of this by growing crops that have shallow roots, such as corn, wheat, cotton, and sorghum. Sorghum is a grain that is used to feed livestock. What do these crops have in common with the plants that grow naturally on the prairie? They are all classified as grasses.

▷ **How can you describe the soil of the Blackland Prairie?**

Why It Matters

In nature ecosystems tend to stay in balance. One population controls the number in another population. Communities help preserve and enrich the soil. Some organisms contribute to the health and well-being of others. This balance, however, can be upset by the actions of people. Cities are built on the land. Crops are cultivated. The land changes. Its natural inhabitants disappear. People gain certain things but lose others. It is important to make wise decisions when you think of changing an ecosystem. Otherwise you may lose more than you gain.

Think and Write

1. Describe the structure of an ecosystem.
2. What is the difference between a population and a community?
3. How does an animal's habitat relate to its niche?
4. **Use Variables** Give examples of how biotic and abiotic factors interact in an ecosystem.
5. **Critical Thinking** Identify changes caused by human activity in your ecosystem. Explain what was lost and what was gained. Evaluate the results.

L·I·N·K·S

ART LINK

Make a poster. Visit a local ecosystem like a park, pond, or even your backyard. Draw all the living and nonliving things you see. Label the biotic and the abiotic factors you included in your picture.

LITERATURE LINK

Read *The Eagles Are Back!* to learn about two eaglets named Ross and Betsey who were raised in a safe environment and then were returned to the wild. Try the activities at the end of the book.

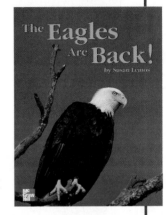

The Eagles Are Back! by Susan Lemos

MATH LINK

Find the range. Using the data on page B13, determine the range of young hatched and the range of insecticide in eggs from 1966 to 1981. Remember, the range is the difference between the largest number and the smallest number in a set of data.

TECHNOLOGY LINK

At the Computer Visit www.mhscience02.com for more links.

Food Chains and Food Webs

Vocabulary

food chain, B18

food web, B20

herbivore, B20

carnivore, B20

predator, B21

prey, B21

scavenger, B21

omnivore, B21

Get Ready

Populations provide energy-rich food for one another. Grasses and other green plants provide food for gazelles. Lions feed on gazelles. What do you think might happen if a drought reduced the number of grasses? How can changes in a population lead to changes in the ecosystem where it lives?

Process Skill

You predict when you state possible results of an event or experiment.

Explore Activity

How Do Populations Interact?

Materials

tape

string

population cards

Procedure

1 Cut out the cards representing the plants and animals in the ecosystem.

2 Label the top of your paper *Sunlight*.

3 Place the plant cards on the paper, and link each to the sunlight with tape and string.

4 Link each plant-eating animal to a plant card. Link each meat-eating animal to its food source. Only two animals can be attached to a food source. Record the links you have made.

5 Fire destroys half the plants. Remove four plant cards. Rearrange the animal cards. Remove animal cards if more than two animals link to any one food source. Record the changes you have made.

Drawing Conclusions

1 **Observe** What has happened to the plant eaters as a result of the fire? To the animal eaters?

2 **Infer** Half of the plants that were lost in the fire grow back again. What happens to the animal populations?

3 **Experiment** Try adding or removing plant or animal cards. What happens to the rest of the populations?

4 **Going Further: Predict** If plants or prey become scarce, their predators may move to a new area. What will happen to the ecosystem the predators move into?

Grasshopper
Food: prairie plants

Meadowlark
Food: crickets, grasshoppers

Ground Squirrel
Food: prairie plants

Bullsnake
Food: mice, rabbits, ground squirrels, birds and eggs.

Red-Tailed Hawk
Food: ground squirrels, mice, rabbits, snakes, lizards, small birds

Prairie Plants
Food: made from water, carbon dioxide, and sunlight

Coyote
Food: rabbits, ground squirrels, meadow mice, other rodents

Main Idea Food chains and food webs describe the feeding relationship in an ecosystem.

What Is a Food Chain?

How important is a small change in a population? Changes in one population can affect several other populations in the same ecosystem. Every population needs energy in order to survive. Where does that energy come from? The energy in an ecosystem comes from the Sun.

You can feel the Sun's energy as it warms your skin. A meadow mouse scurrying through a Blacklands cornfield and a red-tailed hawk diving to snare the mouse can feel it, too. Neither of these animals can directly use the Sun's energy. However, they must have it to move, to breathe, to keep their hearts beating, and to stay alive.

The energy of the Sun is stored in food. The energy in food is passed from one organism to another in a **food chain**. A food chain is the path energy takes from producers to consumers to decomposers.

On the prairie the first organisms in a food chain are plants. Plants capture the Sun's energy during photosynthesis. This energy is stored in foods, or sugars, the plant makes for itself.

What happens when a plant eater such as a grasshopper eats the plant? It takes in the energy-rich sugars. Some of the energy is released for the grasshopper to use. Some of the energy is also stored in its tissues. Some is lost as heat. A Texas horned lizard may snap up the grasshopper, and a red-tailed hawk may eat the lizard. In the prairie community, the hawk is one of the organisms at the top of the food

A Food Chain

A food chain moves the Sun's energy through a community from producers to consumers.

Energy

Grass (producer)

Grasshopper (consumer)

Horned lizard (consumer)

chain. It eats snakes, mice, lizards, rabbits, and other birds.

The red-tailed hawk doesn't eat plants. However, because of the food chain, it gets some of the Sun's energy that was originally stored in plants.

What happens when plants and animals die? They become food for small organisms like crickets, worms, and ants. They are also a food source for microscopic organisms like bacteria.

? What does a food chain show?

READING
Diagrams

1. What are the members of this food chain?

2. Where does the food chain begin? End?

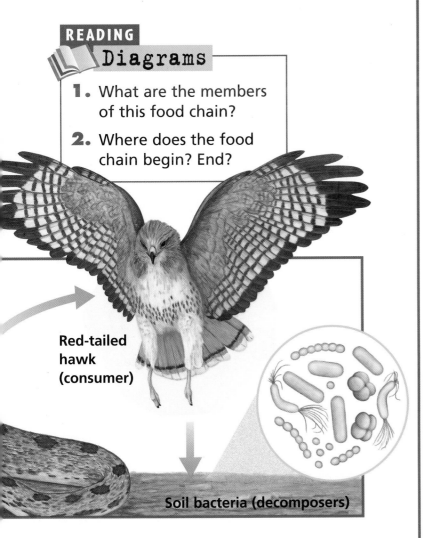

Red-tailed hawk (consumer)

Soil bacteria (decomposers)

QUICK LAB

FOR SCHOOL OR HOME

Getting Food

1. Take a walk outdoors around your home or school. Choose a community to study. Make a list of the living things you see. Don't include people or domestic animals like dogs, cats, and farm animals. You may want to take photos to complete your observations. Use illustrations to complete step 2.

2. **Classify** Organize the organisms into two groups—those that can make their own food (producers) and those that cannot (consumers).

3. **Classify** Which organisms did you list as producers?

4. **Classify** Which organisms did you list as consumers?

5. **Communicate** Draw two or more food chains to show how energy moves through this community.

What Is a Food Web?

Do all organisms eat only one food? Are all organisms eaten by only one type of animal? No. Animals often eat or are eaten by many different things. How can we study all of the things that an animal eats or is eaten by? A food chain only shows the path of energy as it moves from one organism to another. A **food web** shows the relationship between all of the species in a community. It shows how populations must compete for food. A food web is a map of overlapping food chains.

Producers

All food webs begin with *producers*. The producers on land include grasses, trees, and all other organisms that use the Sun's energy to make their own food. In oceans the main producers are algae.

Plant Eaters

Organisms that cannot make their own food are *consumers*. Consumers get energy from the food made by other organisms. Consumers can be grouped according to the type of food they eat. **Herbivores**

(HUR·buh·vawrz) eat producers. Both Earth's land and waters are filled with herbivores—animals that eat plants, algae, and other producers.

Meat Eaters

Herbivores, in turn, are eaten by **carnivores** (KAHR·nuh·vawrz)—animals that eat other animals. All cats, big and small, are carnivores. So are dogs, wolves, foxes, coyotes, and other sharp-toothed animals. The sea also has carnivores. The most frightening of these is the great white shark.

Land Food Web

Snakes • Hawks • Mountain lions • Insect-eating birds • Seed-eating birds • Deer • Rabbits • Mice • Bark beetles • Grass • Grasshoppers • Seeds • Trees • Fungi • Earthworms

READING Diagrams

Which of these animals are predators? Which of these animals are prey?

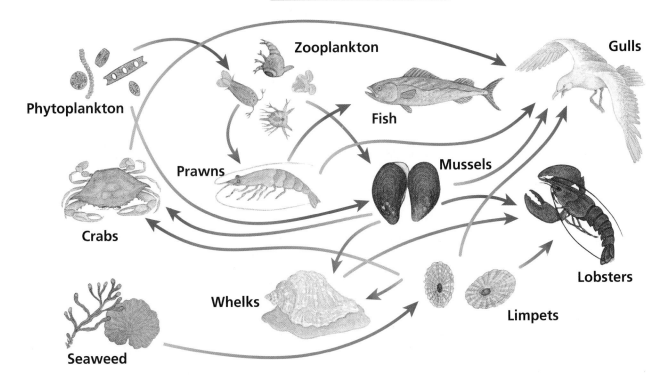

Phytoplankton

Zooplankton

Gulls

Fish

Prawns

Mussels

Crabs

Lobsters

Whelks

Limpets

Seaweed

Other sea dwellers also eat meat. Frolicking seals, playful dolphins, and gentle whales dine on fish, squid, and even penguins.

Living things that hunt other living things for food are **predators**. The hunted are called **prey**. The relationships between predators and prey are a key part of both food chains and food webs.

However, not all meat eaters are predators. Some animals eat meat but don't hunt it. Such meat eaters are called **scavengers**. They feed on the remains of dead animals. Have you ever seen vultures circling a spot of land? Then you have seen scavengers. Crows are also scavengers. You might see them on a road, pecking at the body of an animal.

The sea is home to many scavengers. One of these is the hagfish. It wanders the ocean floor in search of dead or dying fish. Some tiny sea creatures also feed on the remains of dead sea animals.

When an animal eats both animals and plants, it is an **omnivore**. You are an omnivore. Bears are omnivores, too, eating things from berries to salmon.

Decomposers

Every food chain and food web ends with *decomposers* such as worms, insects, bacteria, and fungi. These organisms break down dead matter into substances that can be used by producers. Decomposers break down dead organisms and wastes into simpler substances. Some of these substances are absorbed by the decomposers. Some are returned to the soil.

▷ **What are the parts of a food web?**

How Are Populations Connected?

What would happen if farmers used powerful insecticides to kill pests? What might happen if these pesticides also killed some harmless ants? Ants live in the same habitat as Texas horned lizards. Because the lizards eat ants, changes in the ant population may tell a lot about the future of the lizards.

In the food chain, the relationship doesn't stop there. Birds of prey, such as hawks, feed on the lizards. What happens to the ants will also affect the lives of these birds. A change in one population affects all the other organisms in that food chain.

Animals may adapt to changes in their habitats. A varied diet can be useful. Texas horned lizards eat mainly ants. They also eat other insects such as grasshoppers. If

the ant population decreases, the lizards can feed on grasshoppers instead. This changes the number of grasshoppers in a community, however. The other organisms that eat grasshoppers will be affected, too. A change in the ant population affects more than just a food chain. It affects all of the organisms in a food web.

Food chains and food webs help scientists predict how communities will be affected by change.

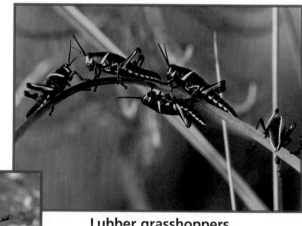

Lubber grasshoppers

Ant

READING **Sequence of Events**
How does a change in a food web affect other populations?

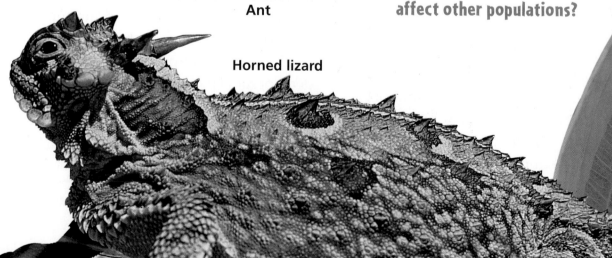

Horned lizard

How Do Populations Adapt to Competition for Food?

Food webs show that animals compete for food. Fish and gulls must compete for a dinner of prawns, for example. In order to survive, an organism must adapt to competition. Sometimes this competition causes a population to change its habitat. This is what happened to Florida's green anole.

At one time green anoles could be spotted all over Florida, perched on the trunks of trees and the branches of bushes. Then a new and bigger species of anole arrived in Florida from the island of Cuba. Scientists don't know how it made the 144 km (90 mi) trip. Its size and, perhaps, other characteristics gave it a hunting edge over the small green anole, however.

Soon the smaller green anole seemed to disappear. Was it really gone? No. Scientists found the little green anole high in the trees. It had found a new habitat where it did not have to compete with the Cuban anole for food.

▷ How did the green anole adapt to competition?

The green anole (left), a native of the U.S. southeast, acquired a new habitat when Cuban anoles (above) were introduced.

Energy Pyramid: Land Food Chain

An energy pyramid shows that less and less food and energy is available as you go from the base to the top of the pyramid.

READING Charts

1. What happens to the number of organisms at each level of the pyramid starting from the base?

2. How much more energy from the Sun was available to the grass than to the bluebirds?

How Does Energy Move in a Community?

Plants capture energy from sunlight. When you eat a plant, how much of that energy do you get? All organisms need energy to live. Producers get energy from the Sun. Consumers get it from the foods they eat. However, energy is lost as it passes from one organism to another in a food chain.

You can see the effect of this in the drawing of the energy pyramid on this page. An energy pyramid shows a number of things. It shows that there is less food at the top of the pyramid than at the base. It also shows that there are fewer organisms as you move from bottom to top.

Consumers get their energy from food. The less food there is, the less energy is available. Energy decreases from the base to the top of the pyramid.

In an ocean community in the Antarctic, algae form the base. Algae are producers that store energy from the Sun. Small fish that live in the icy waters eat some of these algae. The algae that are not eaten are lost to the community. Their energy is not passed up to the next level of the pyramid. Only some of the energy the fish get is passed up to the next level. The fish use some of the energy in swimming and other activities.

Energy Pyramid: Ocean Food Chain

The penguins dive for the small fish and eat as many as they can catch. Many fish get away. Nevertheless, the penguins have snared some energy-rich fish as food. Some of the energy from the fish is stored in the penguins' tissues. Some of the energy is used to heat their bodies. A dip in the frigid water removes some of this heat from the penguins' bodies. Now they have less energy than they took in from the fish.

Rising from below, a leopard seal clamps its sharp teeth around a helpless penguin and eats it. Does this predator get all the energy that was originally in the algae the fish ate? No. Energy has been lost at each level in the pyramid.

Kilogram for kilogram there are fewer fish than algae. There are fewer penguins than fish. There are fewer leopard seals than penguins. That's because there is less food and energy available at each higher level in the energy pyramid. The less food and energy there are, the fewer living things that can be supported.

How much energy is lost from one level of an energy pyramid to the next? Scientists have actually measured it. The startling figure is 90 percent! Of all the Sun's energy captured by the algae, the leopard seal gets only one-tenth of one percent.

▷ **What does an energy pyramid show?**

How Do Food Webs Affect You?

"Red Tide Observed Off the Coast of Maine" might not seem like a scary headline. You might even ignore this important warning. However, it could mean trouble for the average person.

On page B24 you learned that single-celled organisms called algae are at the base of the marine food web. When the algae population increases very rapidly, or blooms, it can turn hundreds of square miles of ocean red. Scientists call this a red tide. Most red tides are not harmful. However, some algae produce poisons. Fire algae are an example. A bloom of these algae is very dangerous to all the species in a food web.

Small fish and mussels feed on the algae. The algae's poison may kill or infect the fish. The decline in the fish population reduces the energy available to the consumers that feed on fish.

How does this affect you? People who eat contaminated fish may become very sick. You are part of a food web, too. Humans are at the top of most food webs. Changes in any population may also affect you.

Deadly red tides, like this one, occur when the population of fire algae greatly increases.

▶ How can changes in a food web affect you?

Why It Matters

If a food chain, food web, or energy pyramid changes, the result might affect humans. On farms a decrease in predators like insect-eating birds might lead to a population explosion of insects. If the insects are plant pests, crops may suffer and food may become scarce. Humans may influence such changes. It is important to monitor how human actions affect the populations of an ecosystem.

Think and Write

1. What is the original source of energy in an ecosystem?

2. Is it possible to have a food chain that has only a producer and a decomposer?

3. What is the relationship between a food chain and a food web?

4. Choose a meat product you eat, and construct a food chain that includes yourself as the final consumer.

5. **Critical Thinking** Explain why there are fewer coyotes than mice in a prairie ecosystem.

L·I·N·K·S

MATH LINK

Use percents. An energy pyramid shows that 90 percent of the energy is lost from one level to the next. If you start with 100,000 units of energy, how much energy does the next level get? The fourth level?

100,000 x 0.10 = ?

100,000 units of energy

WRITING LINK

Write a story. The theme of your story is a changing ecosystem. Make sure the events in your story involve the lives or activities of people.

SOCIAL STUDIES LINK

Conduct research. Investigate what causes red tides. Where and when have they occurred? What can be done to stop them from occurring? Use the Internet or library resources for your research. Write a report to tell what you have learned.

TECHNOLOGY LINK

At the Computer Visit **www.mhscience02.com** for more links.

What Affects Your Food Choices?

Hmmm, a shopper thinks. *Should I buy the oat or the wheat cereal?* In the next aisle, the shopper may decide between whole milk and skim milk, or between peaches and plums.

The shopper is part of a food web, and so are you. However, unless your family grows or hunts its own food, your food choices aren't limited by the food you can grow or catch. Your food choices are based on what's found in the supermarket. How do people decide what foods to buy?

First, we choose foods that look, taste, and smell good to us. However, many of our food choices are affected by advertising. Food advertising encourages people to choose one product over another. A shopper may pick the wheat cereal because of the colorful box. He may buy a certain brand of canned fruit because he has a coupon.

The food industry spends about $10 billion a year on advertising through television, magazines, and newspapers. It spends another $20 billion on coupons, games, and other gimmicks. In one recent year, a candy manufacturer spent $67 million to advertise just one type of candy!

All this advertising encourages people to eat more. It also causes them to choose less healthful foods, like candy and chips, over more healthful foods, such as fruits and vegetables.

The advertising appears to be working. Americans today eat more food per person than they did 20 years ago. More people are overweight than ever before. More people have diseases related to being overweight, such as heart disease, diabetes, and certain cancers.

If you don't base your food choices on advertising, what can you use? Try using the U.S. Department of

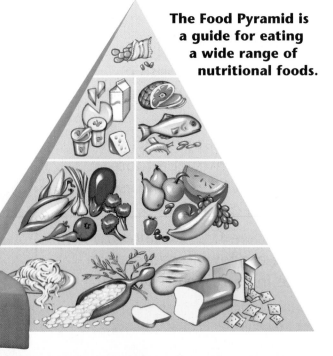

The Food Pyramid is a guide for eating a wide range of nutritional foods.

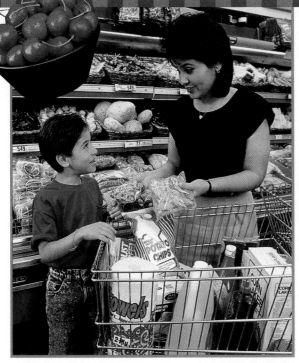

Agriculture's Food Guide Pyramid. It shows the amounts of food you should eat from each group. It's simple to use—just choose more foods from the bottom of the pyramid than from the top.

You should also eat a variety of foods from each food group. For example, look at the Vegetable Group. To eat three servings of vegetables, you might have a large salad at lunch (2 servings), and carrots at dinner (1 serving).

This doesn't mean you can never eat candy, chips, or other "favorite" foods. It just means that foods with fats, oils, and a lot of sugar should be used sparingly.

What Did I Learn?

1. Which of the following is NOT a result of food advertisements?

A People buy more food.
B People eat more food.
C People grow their own vegetables.
D People choose one brand of food over another.

2. According to the Food Guide Pyramid, from which food group should you eat the most servings per day?

F Bread, Cereal, Rice, and Pasta Group
G Vegetable Group
H Fruit Group
J Fats, Oils, and Sweets

AT THE COMPUTER

Visit www.mhscience02.com
to learn more about food choices.

Cycles of Life

Vocabulary

evaporation, B32
condensation, B32
precipitation, B33
water cycle, B33
carbon cycle, B37
nitrogen cycle, B38

Get Ready

Have you ever walked in a grassy field early in the morning after a clear night? What did you observe about the grass? It was probably wet with dew. Where did all this water come from? It hadn't rained in the night. Dew comes from water in the air. How is water stored in the air? How does it change to dew?

Process Skill

You **infer** when you form an idea from facts or observations.

Explore Activity

What Happens to Water?

Materials

plastic food container with clear cover

small bowl or cup filled with water

small tray filled with dry soil

paper towel

100-W lamp (if available)

Procedure

1 Place the dry paper towel, the dry soil, and the bowl of water in the plastic container. Close the container with the lid.

2 **Observe** Place the container under a lamp or in direct sunlight. Observe every ten minutes for a class period. Record your observations.

3 Observe the container on the second day. Record your observations.

Drawing Conclusions

1 What did you observe the first day? What did you observe the second day?

2 **Infer** What was the source of the water? What was the source of the energy that caused changes in the container?

3 What happened to the water?

4 **Going Further: Infer** How did the water move?

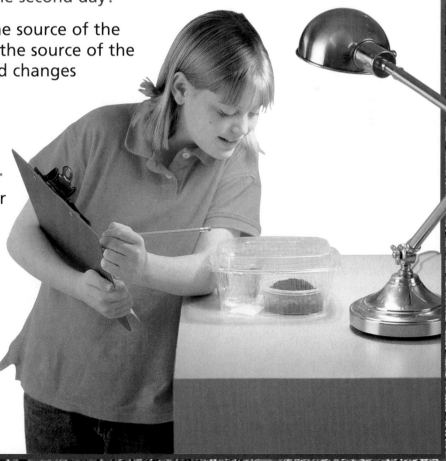

Main Idea Earth's systems recycle materials such as water, carbon, and nitrogen.

What Is the Water Cycle?

What happens to rainwater after it falls? Does it simply vanish? Water moves from one part of the environment to another. It is not lost from an environment. In other words, water is recycled. How is this possible?

Here's how it happens. Heat from the Sun is absorbed by oceans, seas, lakes, streams, ponds, and even puddles. This heat makes the water evaporate and go into the air. **Evaporation** is the process in which a liquid changes into a gas.

As the *water vapor*, or water in its gas state, rises higher and higher into the atmosphere, it cools. When cooled enough, water vapor condenses into tiny water droplets. **Condensation** is

The Water Cycle

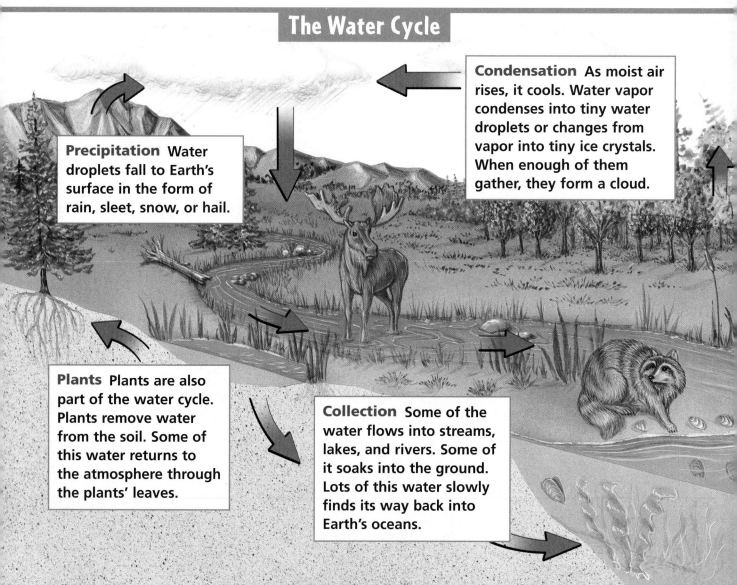

Condensation As moist air rises, it cools. Water vapor condenses into tiny water droplets or changes from vapor into tiny ice crystals. When enough of them gather, they form a cloud.

Precipitation Water droplets fall to Earth's surface in the form of rain, sleet, snow, or hail.

Plants Plants are also part of the water cycle. Plants remove water from the soil. Some of this water returns to the atmosphere through the plants' leaves.

Collection Some of the water flows into streams, lakes, and rivers. Some of it soaks into the ground. Lots of this water slowly finds its way back into Earth's oceans.

the process in which a gas changes into a liquid.

When enough water droplets gather, a cloud is formed. As more and more droplets gather, they become too heavy to stay in the air. They fall to Earth's surface as **precipitation**. Precipitation is any form of water particles—rain, sleet, snow, or hail—that falls to Earth.

On land some of the precipitation seeps into the ground and is stored as *groundwater*. Some of the water, however, flows downhill across the surface. This water becomes *runoff*. It is collected in streams, lakes, or rivers. It slowly finds its way back to the ocean. Here it absorbs heat and evaporates into the atmosphere again. The **water cycle** is the continuous movement of water between Earth's surface and the air, changing from liquid to gas to liquid.

READING Sequence of Events
What are the stages of the water cycle?

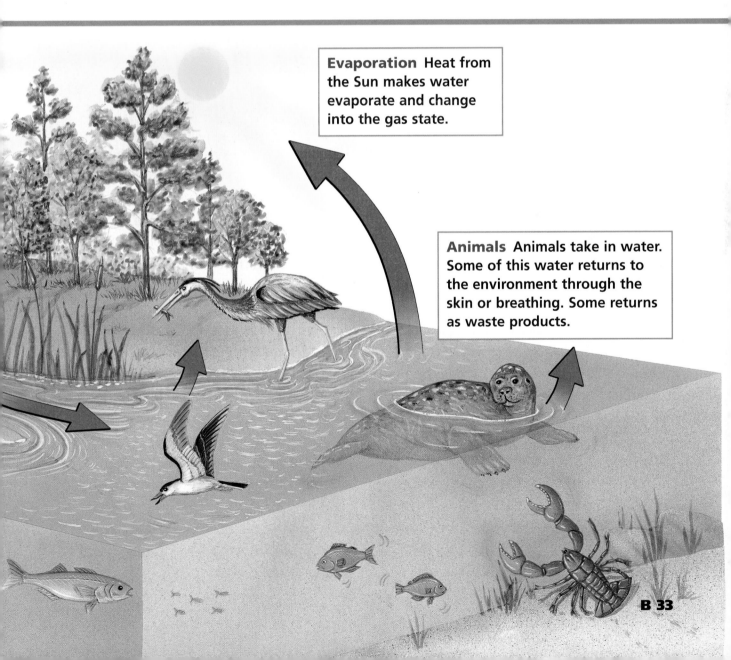

Evaporation Heat from the Sun makes water evaporate and change into the gas state.

Animals Animals take in water. Some of this water returns to the environment through the skin or breathing. Some returns as waste products.

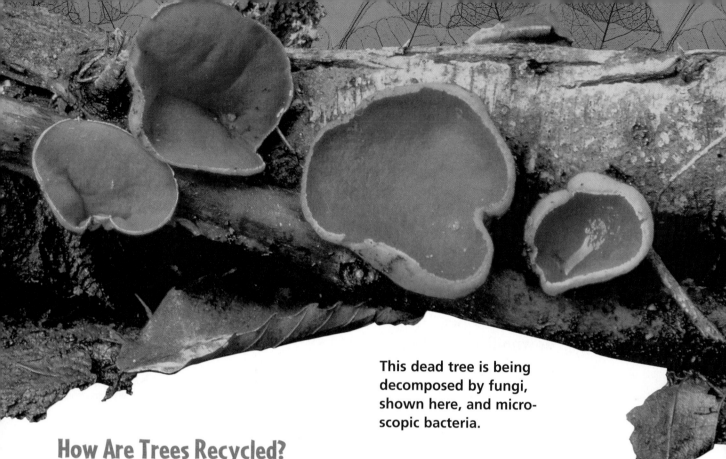

This dead tree is being decomposed by fungi, shown here, and microscopic bacteria.

How Are Trees Recycled?

How can a dead tree help living things? Even though the tree is dead, it is being turned into substances other organisms need to survive. Some of these organisms are other trees. The dead tree is providing elements for living trees. When these trees die, they will provide elements that other trees need. The cycling of matter is continuous. How does this happen?

An old, fallen tree is made of wood, bark, and other dead tree tissue. That tissue holds all sorts of complex chemical substances. Most of the chemicals are too complex to be used by other living things. They need to be broken down into simpler chemicals.

This is the job of the decomposers. They are organisms that recycle matter from dead organisms. Worms, crickets, cockroaches, bacteria, and fungi are decomposers. These organisms can break down dead wood and other dead plant parts into carbon dioxide and ammonia. All living plants need carbon dioxide in order to make sugars. Ammonia is a simple substance that contains the element nitrogen. Nitrogen is extremely important for plants. No plant can live or grow without nitrogen. All organisms need nitrogen in order to make proteins.

Nitrogen is a chemical found in plant *fertilizers*. Fertilizers are substances used to add minerals to the soil. Some fertilizers are natural. These are decaying plants and animals, and animal wastes. Other fertilizers are made in factories. Both natural and artificial fertilizers contain nitrogen. The next time you go to a store that sells fertilizers, read the labels. You're sure to find nitrogen as one of the ingredients.

Composting

You can help nature recycle plant material by composting. Gardeners use compost to make soil more fertile. A good mixture for compost is three parts dry leaves and plant material, one part fresh grass clippings, and one part food scraps. Earthworms, insects, fungi, and bacteria break down the leaves, grass, and food scraps into compost. The compost contains nitrogen, phosphorous, and potassium, which enrich the soil.

As you'll soon discover, like water, nitrogen and carbon have their own cycles in nature. Earth is a closed system. With the exception of energy, almost nothing gets out or gets in. It is recycled.

▷ **How do decomposers recycle nutrients?**

Fertilizers sold in stores contain nitrogen. Nitrogen is an element plants need to grow and stay healthy.

Guaranteed Analysis

Total Nitrogen (N) 10%
Available Phosphate (P_2O_5) 10%
Soluble Potash (K_2O) 10%
The Plant Foods used in   Garden Food are Ammonium Sulfate, Triple Superphosphate and Potash. Also contained in Garden Food is the natural mineral limestone.

...Food 10-10-10 is an agricultural...

QUICK LAB

FOR SCHOOL OR HOME

Soil Sample

BE CAREFUL! Do not touch the sharp edges of the can.

1. Go to a wooded area in a park or other location near your school. Find a patch of soft, moist soil.

2. Press a can, open side down, into the soil to get a core sample. You might have to gently rotate the can so it cuts into the soil.

3. **Observe** Carefully remove the core so it stays in one piece. Describe and draw the core.

4. **Infer** From top to bottom, what kind of matter does the core hold? In what order did the layers form?

5. **Infer** Which layer holds the most available nutrients? Explain.

What Is the Carbon Cycle?

Have you ever roasted marshmallows over a fire until the outsides turned black? Have you ever left bread in the toaster for so long that it burned? The "black" that you observe on burnt food is carbon.

Carbon is a very important element. It is one of the elements that make up all living things. It is found in the air as carbon dioxide and is used by plants in photosynthesis. It is found in many of the things we use every day, from fuel to chairs to nonstick pans.

The Carbon Cycle

Carbon enters the air when plants and animals decay. It enters the air when animals breathe out. It enters the air when fossil fuels such as coal, oil, gasoline, and natural gas are burned.

Plants During photosynthesis plants use the carbon from carbon dioxide to make sugars, starches, and proteins. They also give off oxygen, which is used by animals.

Car exhaust

Oil

Like water, carbon is recycled by nature. The process is called the **carbon cycle**. The carbon cycle shows the continuous transfer of carbon between the atmosphere and living things. Read the diagram to learn how nature does this.

▷ **What does the carbon cycle do?**

READING

Diagrams

1. When does carbon dioxide enter the air?

2. What happens to carbon when living things die?

Oxygen

Carbon

Death, Decay, Storage When living things die, the carbon in them goes into the air and ground. Some of it is turned into carbon dioxide by decomposers. Some is stored as fossil fuels. This is what happened to the carbon in certain organisms that died millions of years ago.

Animals Animals eat plant sugars, starches, proteins, and other substances. The animals use the carbon in these foods to make their own body chemicals.

Decaying matter

How Is Nitrogen Recycled?

What do you need nitrogen for? When you eat meat, fish, cereal, or vegetables, you are taking in the nutrients that your body needs to make *proteins*. Proteins are a part of your muscles and many cell structures.

Among other things, proteins are rich in the element nitrogen. You need nitrogen to make parts of your body, such as muscles, nerves, skin, bones, blood, and digestive juices.

Since air is 78 percent nitrogen, you might think that you do not need to eat protein to get nitrogen. However, animals and plants cannot use the nitrogen that is in the air. Animals get nitrogen by eating proteins. Plants get nitrogen by absorbing it from the soil. Some plants even get nitrogen with the help of a special group of bacteria.

The way nitrogen moves between the air, soil, plants, and animals is called the **nitrogen cycle**.

▷ **What organisms are involved in the nitrogen cycle?**

The Nitrogen Cycle

Air Air is made up of about 78 percent nitrogen gas.

Nitrogen-Fixing Bacteria Some bacteria that grow on pea and bean roots give those plants the nitrogen they need. The bacteria turn nitrogen gas in the air to nitrogen-containing substances the plants can use to make their proteins.

Decomposers When plants die, decomposers in the soil break down the plant proteins. One product is the nitrogen-containing substance ammonia. Soil bacteria change ammonia into nitrites.

Ammonia

Diagrams

1. Compare the different ways various kinds of bacteria help in the nitrogen cycle.

2. How do pea and bean plants get the nitrogen they need?

Denitrifying Bacteria Some soil bacteria turn nitrates back into nitrogen gas.

Plants Plants absorb nitrates dissolved in water through their roots. The nitrogen is then used by the plant to make proteins.

Animals Animals eat plant proteins, or they eat other animals that eat plant proteins. Animal wastes contain nitrogen compounds.

Nitrites

Nitrates

Nitrogen compounds

Nitrites and ammonia

Bacteria Certain bacteria can use nitrogen from the air to make nitrogen-containing substances called *nitrites*. Other bacteria can turn nitrites into *nitrates*—another group of nitrogen-containing substances.

Why Recycle?

Have you ever seen a paper bag with a symbol that says "Printed on recycled paper"? Why is this important?

The environment provides the materials people use to make products. Sunlight is an *inexhaustible resource*. The Sun will last for millions, if not billions, of years. Other resources, however, are not inexhaustible. The paper to make books, magazines, newspapers, and containers comes from the wood in trees. Metals mined from the ground are used to make cars, ships, pots and pans, appliances, and many other things. Glass is made from sand. Plastics are made from chemicals in oil found deep underground.

Wood, metals, sand, and oil are called *raw materials*. Raw materials are the building blocks of products.

Many raw materials, such as oil and metals, are *nonrenewable resources*. Earth's oil was formed millions of years ago. There's a limited amount of it. When it's gone, it's gone forever.

Certain other resources, such as wood, are *renewable resources*. If trees are cut down for lumber and paper, more can be planted to replace them. Even so, trees take years to grow. Recycling paper and other wood products can help keep forests from being destroyed. This can also help keep the animals in them from losing their homes and, perhaps, from facing extinction.

▷ **Why is it important to recycle both renewable and nonrenewable resources?**

Garbage Thrown Away Daily in the United States

This graph shows the percent of different materials in garbage thrown away each day by each person in the United States.

READING Graphs

Let's say there are 280,000,000 people in the United States. Each person throws away 1.8 kg (4 lb) of garbage each day. How much garbage is thrown away by all the people each day?

L·I·N·K·S

Why It Matters

Many people urge that we conserve raw materials by recycling them—just as nature recycles water, carbon, and nitrogen. Many communities have recycling programs. Glass products, metal, plastics and papers can all be recycled. Service stations can save oil that is drained from car engines.

The environment provides all the things we need. The environment will keep doing these things as long as we let it recycle the substances that make life possible and comfortable. People can either help or hinder the process.

Visit **www.mhscience02.com** to do a research project on recycling.

Think and Write

1. By what process does water move from oceans, lakes, rivers, and streams into the air?

2. What organisms turn a dead tree into substances that can be used by living trees?

3. Describe three ways that carbon dioxide gets into the air.

4. Name two substances that contain nitrogen.

5. **Critical Thinking** How can you and other people conserve trees?

MATH LINK

Make a circle graph. Use the data from page B40. Calculate (in kilograms) how much of each type of garbage Americans produce every day.

ART LINK

Make a collage. Weigh the amount of garbage you throw away each day. Estimate how much of it is paper, glass, plastic, and food scraps. Represent this in a collage.

WRITING LINK

Write a paragraph. Explain the importance of using recycled materials.

SOCIAL STUDIES LINK

Conduct research. The Carboniferous period happened about 300 million years ago. Research it by using the Internet or an encyclopedia.

TECHNOLOGY LINK

At the Computer Visit **www.mhscience02.com** for more links.

Coral Reefs

Rain Forests of the Sea

They're sometimes called "rain forests of the sea." That's because they're home for an amazing variety and number of creatures—up to a quarter of all the oceans' animals. They can take thousands of years to form. They grow in shallow, warm waters. Creatures smaller than your thumbnail build them, and they can be over a thousand miles long. What are they? Coral reefs!

A coral reef is built by millions of tiny animals called coral polyps. They live together in colonies, or groups. Coral polyps secrete a substance that hardens into skeletons. The hard skeletons build up reefs over time. Special algae live inside coral polyps. The algae produce food for the polyps. Coral reefs form only in shallow waters because the algae need sunlight to produce food.

A coral reef often looks like a sea garden because of its beautiful shades of orange, yellow, purple, and green. The colors come from the different algae and sea animals that live among the corals. Coral reefs provide food and shelter for thousands of ocean plants and animals, including hundreds of kinds of fish.

Some of the more unusual inhabitants of coral reefs include small fish and shrimp known as cleaners. Cleaners eat parasites from larger fish, such as barracudas and eels.

Coral reefs are endangered. As humans develop shorelines near the reefs, soil runs into coastal waters and smothers the fragile reefs. Pollution and destructive fishing practices also threaten reefs. Today many countries are trying to protect and save coral reefs.

What Did I Learn?

1. A coral reef is formed by

  A small pieces of rock
  B sea shells
  C tiny animals
  D sand particles

2. Coral reefs are endangered because of

  F severe storms
  G human development along shorelines
  H lack of sunlight
  J too many animals

Red and yellow soft coral

Cleaner shrimp at work

 AT THE COMPUTER Visit www.mhscience02.com for more amazing stories and facts about ecosystems.

Chapter 4 Review

Vocabulary

Fill each blank with the best word or words from the list.

abiotic factor, B6
community, B10
ecology, B6
evaporation, B32
food chain, B18
niche, B11
omnivore, B21
population, B10
precipitation, B32
predator, B21

1. A consumer that eats both plants and animals is called a(n) _____.

2. Water is an example of a(n) _____.

3. A(n) _____ includes all the members of a single species in a certain place.

4. Corn, elms, and armadillos are part of the _____ of the prairie ecosystem.

5. The study of how living and nonliving things interact in the same place is called _____.

6. All populations have a unique _____ in their habitat.

7. _____ is the process in which a liquid becomes a gas.

8. A(n) _____ is a consumer that hunts for its food.

9. _____ may include sleet and snow.

10. You can trace how energy moves in a community with a(n) _____.

Test Prep

11. All of the following are abiotic factors in an ecosystem EXCEPT
  A water
  B minerals
  C bacteria
  D soil

12. A vulture is an example of a
  F predator
  G scavenger
  H carnivore
  J all of the above

13. Plants absorb nitrogen
  A from the soil
  B from the atmosphere
  C from the Sun
  D from insects

14. In the carbon cycle, carbon is transferred between _____ and living things.
  F the ocean
  G the atmosphere
  H bacteria
  J minerals

15. As it absorbs heat energy from the Sun, water

  A soaks into the ground

  B flows into streams, lakes, and rivers

  C forms tiny ice crystals

  D evaporates into the air

Concepts and Skills

16. Process Skills: Use Variables
Study the table below. Suggest a reason for the change in the eagle population.

Population Size			
Year	Grasslands (mi^2)	Rabbits	Eagles
1960	10,200	101,000	1,050
1970	9,100	89,000	864
1980	8,200	78,000	782
1990	5,300	42,000	386
2000	5,140	41,900	378

17. Reading in Science Describe the sequence by which the Sun's energy is moved through a community.

18. Scientific Methods Conclude how plants take in nitrogen based on the data in the nitrogen cycle.

19. Critical Thinking What is the relationship between herbivores and carnivores? Explain your answer in a paragraph.

20. Decision Making Is it important to recycle the waste you produce? Why or why not?

Boost your test scores!

Be Smart!
Visit **www.mhscience02.com**

Populations and Ecosystems

Did You Ever Wonder?

Why do some animals—such as mallard ducks, humpback whales, and salmon—migrate, whereas others do not? In winter, these caribou leave their home on the tundra and migrate south, where they can find food and give birth to their young. What do you think they will do when summer comes?

How Populations Survive

Vocabulary

limiting factor, B50

adaptation, B52

symbiosis, B54

mutualism, B54

parasitism, B56

commensalism, B57

Get Ready

What affects the size of a population? Some forests are so thick with trees and shrubs that you would have a tough time hiking through them. However, hiking through other forests would be as easy as walking down a country road or the street in front of your house. What makes some areas crowded and others empty? What do organisms need in an environment in order to survive?

Process Skill

You communicate when you share information.

Explore Activity

What Controls the Growth of Populations?

Materials

4 small, clean milk cartons with the tops removed

40 pinto bean seeds that have been soaked overnight

soil

water

Procedure

1 Label the cartons 1 to 4. Fill cartons 1 and 2 with dry potting soil. Fill cartons 3 and 4 with moistened potting soil. Fill the cartons to within 2 cm of the top.

2 Plant ten seeds in each carton, and cover the seeds with 0.5 cm of soil.

3 **Use Variables** Place cartons 1 and 3 in a well-lighted area. Place cartons 2 and 4 in a dark place. Label the cartons to show if they are wet or dry and in the light or in the dark.

4 **Observe** Examine the cartons each day for four days. Keep the soil moist in cartons 3 and 4. Record your observations.

5 Observe the plants for two weeks after they sprout. Continue to keep the soil moist in cartons 3 and 4, and record your observations.

Drawing Conclusions

1 **Communicate** How many seeds sprouted in each carton?

2 **Observe** After two weeks how many plants in each carton were still living?

3 What factor is needed for seeds to sprout? What is needed for bean plants to grow? What evidence do you have to support your answers?

4 **Going Further: Infer** Why did some seeds sprout and then die?

What Controls the Growth of Populations?

How much do living things depend on conditions in their environment in order to survive? Certain factors control the growth and survival of living things. What do these factors include?

A dry wind howls across the prairie. The hot Sun bakes the ground below. No rain has fallen in days. Grasses have withered. Plant-eating insects have gone hungry.

High in the bright, cloudless sky, a hawk flies one way and then another. Its sharp eyes sweep over the barren land below. An unsuspecting deer mouse scurries along the ground in search of an insect.

The mouse's tan fur blends in with the dusty soil, but its movement gives it away. The hawk tucks in its wings and dives like a falling rock. In a flash its talons grab the mouse.

Hidden in this story are clues to how the size of a population is limited. Anything that controls the growth or survival of a population is called a **limiting factor**.

Some limiting factors are nonliving. In the story the sunlight, wind, water, and temperature were nonliving limiting factors. They controlled the population of grasses on the prairie.

The grasses, insects, deer mice, and hawks were living limiting factors. The grasses had withered. There was less food for plant-eating insects, so the number of insects living on the prairie decreased. That meant there was less food for the insect-eating deer mice. The deer mouse population was also limited by the hawks, which are predators.

Competition

The number of predators in an ecosystem affects the number of prey. The number of prey in an ecosystem

Organisms like coyotes (above) and raccoons (left) compete with each other for resources such as food, water, and territory.

can also determine how many predators the ecosystem can support. If there were few hawks, the deer mouse population might stay steady or even rise. More hawks, however, mean fewer deer mice.

Hawks compete with other predators, like coyotes and raccoons. Coyotes and raccoons hunt many animals, including small rodents like deer mice.

Coyotes and raccoons also compete with each other for food, water, and places to live. The population that wins such competitions is likely to grow.

However, even a growing population faces problems. Its size will soon limit its own growth. The organisms in the population will become crowded. They will have to compete with one another for food, water, and shelter. Some will die. Eventually there will be enough for the number of organisms that remain.

READING **Summarize** **What are six limiting factors that control population growth?**

Overcrowding, as in this group of walruses, limits the growth of any population.

QUICK LAB

FOR SCHOOL OR HOME

Playground Space

1. Measure Working in groups, use a meterstick to measure the length and width of your playground.

2. Use Numbers Multiply the length by the width to find the area in square meters.

3. Count the number of students in your class.

4. Use Numbers To find out how much space each student has, divide the area of the playground by the number of students.

5. Infer What would happen to the space each student had if the number of students doubled?

6. Infer Assume two other classes with the same number of students as yours used the playground at the same time as your class. What effect might this have on your class?

How Do Plants Adapt to Harsh Environments?

Plants live almost everywhere on Earth. They live in deserts, where rain seldom falls. They live in the icy northland, where there is little sunlight and winters are long and frigid. They live on the floor of rain forests, where the Sun rarely shines and the soil has few nutrients.

Plants can survive in these conditions because they have developed special characteristics. Characteristics that help an organism survive in its environment are called **adaptations**. Adaptations are inherited traits, not learned behaviors.

One of the harshest areas for plant growth is a desert. What adaptations do desert plants have that allow them to live where less than 5 cm (2 in.) of rain falls each year? Most people in the United States live where that much rain might fall in a few hours.

The Sonoran Desert stretches from southern California to western Arizona. If you were to visit there, you would see the barrel cactus. The barrel cactus is very well adapted to desert conditions.

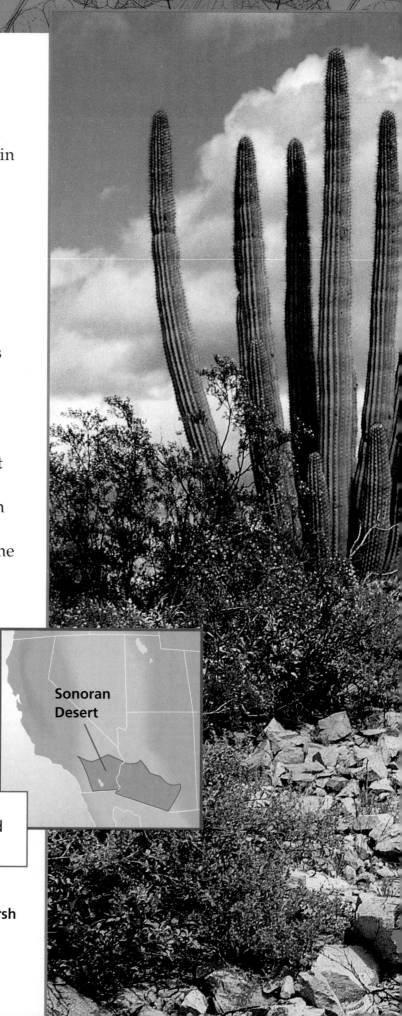

Sonoran Desert

READING
Maps

Describe where in the United States the Sonoran Desert is.

The barrel cactus is adapted to the harsh conditions of the Sonoran Desert.

The Barrel Cactus

The plant's roots are very shallow and grow only about 7.5 cm (3 in.) into the dry soil. There is an advantage to this. When rain does fall, the roots catch the rain and soak it up very quickly. However, during long dry spells, the fine ends of the roots fall off. What's the advantage? The lack of a fine network of root ends prevents water stored in the cactus from passing out into the soil.

The stem of the barrel cactus also helps it survive in the desert. It is folded and covered with needle-sharp spines. What are the advantages? The stem stores water. The folds, which are deepest during dry spells, protect moist parts of the stem from hot, dry desert winds. Otherwise these winds would draw away water from the stem's surface. The spines keep away birds and small animals that try to get water from the stems of plants. If you have a small spiny cactus plant at home, you've probably learned two things—you don't have to water it often, and it is better not to touch it.

▷ **What are three adaptations that help a barrel cactus to survive in a desert?**

What Is Symbiosis?

Organisms interact with each other in a number of different ways. You have already seen that some organisms hunt others. Some organisms are predators. Some organisms are prey. You have also seen that organisms may compete with each other for food or territory. Two different kinds of predators may hunt the same prey. However, there are also other kinds of relationships between different kinds of organisms. Some of these relationships are long lasting.

In nature a relationship between two kinds of organisms that lasts over a period of time is called **symbiosis**. There are different kinds of symbiosis. Sometimes both organisms benefit from the relationship. Sometimes one organism benefits while harming the other. Sometimes only one benefits, and the other is not affected. Let's take a closer look at each kind of symbiosis.

Mutualism

When a relationship between two kinds of organisms benefits both of them, it is called **mutualism**.

A strange-looking plant grows in the Mojave Desert of southern California. It's called a Joshua tree, or yucca plant.

When this tree's creamy flowers are in bloom, small gray shadows seem to dart from flower to flower. A more careful look reveals that the "shadows" are actually moths. These are yucca moths.

Yucca trees and yucca moths depend on each other for survival. Each helps the other reproduce.

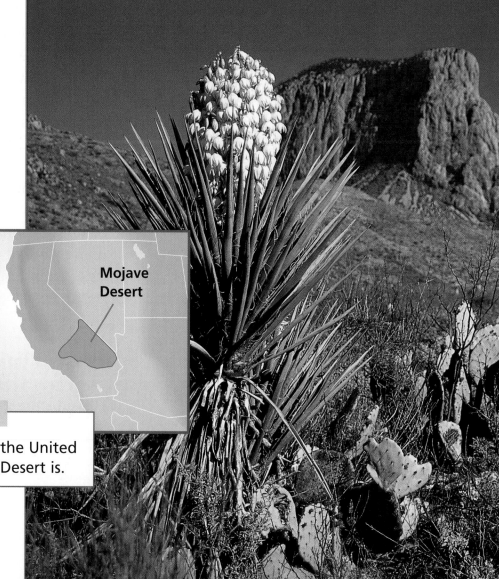

Mojave Desert

READING

Maps

Describe where in the United States the Mojave Desert is.

The Yucca Moth and the Yucca Tree

Yucca moths cannot survive without yucca trees. The yucca trees would also quickly become extinct if the moths vanished. The yucca moths and the yucca trees benefit from each other and share a relationship of mutualism. How does this work?

At night a female yucca moth visits a yucca flower. Inside the flower the moth picks up pollen and rolls it up into a ball, which it holds gently in its mouth. Then the moth flutters over to another flower. There it makes a hole in the flower's ovary. The moth injects its eggs through the hole. Finally, it packs the sticky ball of pollen onto the flower's stigma. The stigma and ovary are female reproductive parts of a flower. Pollen holds male sex cells.

In protecting its eggs, the moth has also pollinated the yucca flower. The pollinated flower can then make seeds. Eventually some of the seeds will sprout into new yucca plants. This means yucca plants will continue to grow in the desert.

The moth's eggs and the tree's seeds develop at the same time. When the eggs hatch into larvae, the larvae will feed on some of the seeds. All this is happening inside the protective ovary wall. The larvae are not only getting needed food, they are also safe from predators.

▷ **How is mutualism an example of symbiosis?**

Yucca moth

What Is Parasitism?

A relationship in which one kind of organism lives on or in another organism and may harm that organism is called **parasitism** (PAR·uh·sigh·tiz·uhm). The organisms that live on or in other organisms are called *parasites* (PAR·uh·sights). The organisms they feed on are called *hosts*. The parasites benefit from the relationship. The hosts are harmed by it.

Fleas are parasites of dogs and cats. The fleas live off the blood of these hosts and give nothing back but itching and irritation. Plants also have parasites, which often are other plants.

The bright orange dodder plant has little chlorophyll. This means that it can't make enough food to live on. Instead it winds around a plant that can make its own food. The dodder then sends tubes into the stem of the plant it is coiled around. Next, the dodder gets food from the plant through the tubes. Although the plant it lives on usually does not die, it is weakened, grows more slowly, and is not able to easily fight off diseases.

▷ **How does parasitism differ from mutualism?**

The coiling dodder plant, which can't make enough of its own food, draws food from other plants.

Mistletoe is another parasitic plant. It is an evergreen that grows on the trunk or branches of trees such as hawthorn, poplar, fir, or apple.

Flea

Some tropical fish are protected from predators by the poison in a sea anemone's tentacles.

Orchids benefit from their position on the trunks of trees.

What Is Commensalism?

Few plants can grow on the floor of a rain forest. One reason is that the thick canopy above keeps light from reaching the ground. Some plants, like orchids, attach themselves to the trunks of trees high above the rain forest floor. The orchids, which make their own food, don't take anything from the trees. They simply use the trees to get needed sunlight. This relationship, in which one organism benefits from another without harming or helping it, is called **commensalism** (kuh·MEN·suh·liz·uhm).

Many animals also have this kind of relationship. There are certain tropical fish that live unharmed among the poisonous tentacles of sea anemones. The anemones provide safety for the fish. However, the fish neither harm nor help the anemones.

▷ **What kind of relationship is commensalism?**

How Do Populations Survive Earth's Changes?

Earth is constantly changing. About 18,000 years ago, great sheets of ice moved deep into the heartland of what is now the United States. Vast ice sheets also covered much of Europe and parts of South America. Sea levels dropped as more and more water froze. New land was exposed. Earth was a cold place.

Slowly Earth began to warm up. The ice melted. Sea levels rose. Coastal land became flooded.

These kinds of changes have occurred no fewer than seven times during the past 700,000 years. Scientists call these cold periods *ice ages*.

Earth has also changed in other ways. Over millions of years, continents have moved north and south, east and west. Huge mountain-sized rocks have crashed into Earth. Volcanoes have poured gases and dust into the air.

Each of these events has had an effect on living things. Some organisms have survived these changes, while others have died out, or become extinct. Why have some of these organisms vanished while others survived?

To answer this, let's look at the age of the dinosaurs. Fossils from about 65 million years ago suggest that dinosaurs shared the land with many other animals. These animals included frogs, snails, insects, turtles, snakes, and some small furry mammals. Plants of all kinds grew everywhere. The seas were full of organisms like fish, sea urchins, clams, and algae.

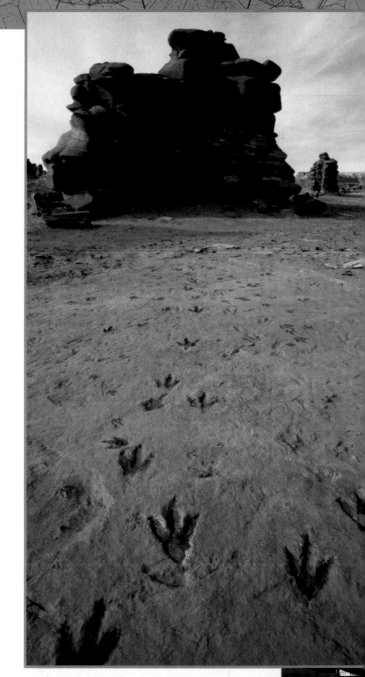

Dinosaur footprints

Scientific evidence suggests that a meteorite up to 10 km (6 mi) in diameter struck Earth from outer space. One theory states that the impact created a huge explosion. It gouged out a crater 64 km (40 mi) across and threw huge amounts of dust into the sky. The dust may have hung in the sky for months, even years. Sunlight was probably blocked from reaching the ground.

Plants needing lots of sunlight may have died out. That means that the large plant-eating dinosaurs could not get enough food. They would have died out. The large dinosaurs preying on plant eaters would have also died out. It may have been that every animal weighing more than about 121 kg (55 lb) became extinct.

However, many of the smaller animals could have survived. They needed less food to live. They could have moved more easily from habitat to habitat. They would no longer have been in competition with the dinosaurs. They would have been free to grow in size and variety. Possibly this is how a world once ruled by dinosaurs became ruled by mammals.

▷ **How do changes on Earth affect organisms?**

Dinosaurs became extinct about 65 million years ago. Scientists can study them today, however, by searching for fossils such as footprints and skeletons.

How Do People Change the Environment?

How do you affect your environment? About fifteen times a minute, you change the environment. That's the number of times you probably breathe in and out every 60 seconds. Each time you exhale, you add carbon dioxide and water to the air. Each time you inhale, you remove oxygen.

The amount of these substances you breathe in and out is small. However, they change the environment around you and far away. That's because air circulates around Earth. The carbon dioxide you exhaled might find its way into a local tree or a plant miles away. Oxygen that the plant gives off might be inhaled by an animal even farther from your home.

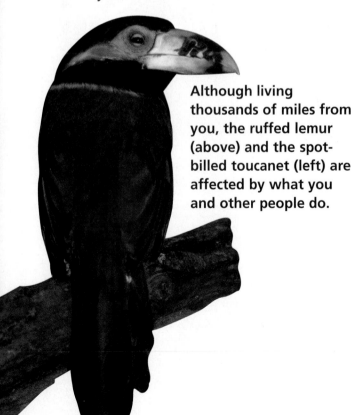

Although living thousands of miles from you, the ruffed lemur (above) and the spot-billed toucanet (left) are affected by what you and other people do.

Eventually some of the air you exhaled might go through several cycles. In the process that air might also travel around the world.

Some of that air might find its way into a *jaborandi* (zha·buh·ran·DEE) tree in northern Brazil. Some of it might wind up in a periwinkle shrub in Madagascar. Madagascar is an island in the Indian Ocean off the east coast of Africa.

The plants use the carbon to build their stems, leaves, roots, and other parts. Some of these parts will be eaten by animals. They might be Madagascar's big-eyed ruffed lemurs or Brazil's many-colored spot-billed toucanets. Each of these animals seeks food and shelter among the plants of its environment.

▷ **What is one way you affect the environment?**

Why It Matters

People interact with their environment. They can do good and bad things to the environment. They can interfere with an ecosystem by damming up rivers, using pesticides, and cutting down trees. They can also preserve an ecosystem by passing laws that protect its animals and plants.

The lives of all organisms are affected by other living things and by nonliving things. By understanding how living things interact with one another and with their environment, people can help preserve the treasures of nature.

Think and Write

1. Identify two biotic and two abiotic limiting factors.

2. How is mutualism like commensalism? How is it different?

3. Identify an organism and an adaptation that helps it survive in its environment.

4. Make a list of ways you and your community affect your environment.

5. **Critical Thinking** Several species of whales are threatened with extinction. Propose two hypotheses that might account for the threat.

L·I·N·K·S

HEALTH LINK

Investigate parasites. How do parasites affect humans? What do these organisms gain from their host? How do they harm it? Write a paragraph.

Human tapeworm

WRITING LINK

Write a poem. Write about a relationship in your life that is symbiotic. Explain what makes the relationship symbiotic. Who is helped? Who is the helper?

TECHNOLOGY LINK

Science Newsroom CD-ROM Choose *Keep Them Alive* to learn how sea turtles and other species get what they need to survive from their environment.

At the Computer Visit **www.mhscience02.com** for more links.

Biomes

Vocabulary

biome, B64

grasslands, B66

taiga, B67

tundra, B68

desert, B69

**deciduous
 forest,** B70

**tropical rain
 forest,** B71

Get Ready

What kinds of plants and animals live in
the tropical rain forest? Are they the same
as the ones that live in your community?
Why do certain plants live in some areas
and not others?

Soil varies greatly and is a distinctive
factor in each ecosystem. Soil content
can determine what plants and
animals can live there.

Process Skill

You observe when you use your senses
to learn about an object or event.

Explore Activity

Why Is Soil Important?

Materials

washed sand

soil

hydrogen peroxide

2 plastic cups

2 plastic spoons

dropper

goggles

apron

Procedure

BE CAREFUL! Wear goggles and an apron.

1 Place 1 tsp. of washed sand in a plastic cup.

2 **Observe** Using the dropper, add hydrogen peroxide to the sand, drop by drop. Count each drop. Bubbles will form as the hydrogen peroxide breaks down any decayed matter.

3 **Communicate** Record the number of drops you add until the bubbles stop forming.

4 **Experiment** Repeat steps 1–3 using the soil.

Drawing Conclusions

1 Which sample—soil or sand—gave off more bubbles?

2 **Infer** Why was the sand used?

3 **Infer** Decayed materials in soil release their nutrients to form humus. The amount of humus in soil depends on the rate of decay and the rate at which plants absorb the nutrients. Which sample had more humus?

4 **Going Further: Infer** In which sample could you grow larger, healthier plants? Why?

Read to Learn

Main Idea The world has a great number of ecosystems and biomes.

Taiga

What Is a Biome?

The land on Earth is divided into six major kinds of large ecosystems, called **biomes** (BIGH·ohmz). Each biome has its own kind of climate, soil, plants, and animals. Each biome can be found in different parts of the world. A desert biome is found in North America. Another is found in Africa. Still others are found in South America, Asia, and Australia. The map shows where Earth's six biomes are located around our planet.

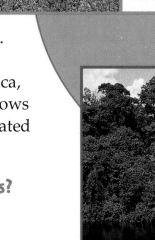

Deciduous forest

▷ **What are the six major biomes?**

Tropical rain forest

Taiga

Location: Mid- to high latitudes
Climate: Very cold winters, cool summers; about 50 cm (20 in.) of precipitation a year
Soil: Acidic, mineral-poor, decayed pine and spruce needles on surface
Plants: Mostly spruce, fir, and other evergreens
Animals: Rodents, snowshoe hares, lynx, sables, ermine, caribou, bears, wolves, birds in summer

Deciduous Forest

Location: Midlatitudes
Climate: Relatively mild summers and cold winters, 76–127 cm (30–50 in.) of precipitation a year
Soil: Rich topsoil over clay
Plants: Hardwoods such as oaks, beeches, hickories, maples
Animals: Wolves, deer, bears, and a wide variety of small mammals, birds, amphibians, reptiles, and insects

Tropical Rain Forest

Location: Near the equator
Climate: Hot all year round, 200–460 cm (80–180 in.) of rain a year
Soil: Nutrient-poor
Plants: Greatest diversity of any biome; vines, orchids, ferns, and a wide variety of trees.
Animals: More species of insects, reptiles, and amphibians than any place else; monkeys, other small and large mammals, including in some places elephants, all sorts of colorful birds

Desert

Tundra

Grassland

READING Maps

Which kind of biome is most abundant? Least abundant?

Desert

Location: Midlatitudes
Climate: Generally very hot days, cool nights; precipitation less than 4 cm (10 in.) a year
Soil: Poor in animal and plant decay products but often rich in minerals
Plants: None to cacti, yuccas, bunch grasses, shrubs, and a few trees
Animals: Rodents, snakes, lizards, tortoises, insects, and some birds. The Sahara in Africa is home to camels, gazelles, antelopes, small foxes, snakes, lizards, and gerbils.

Tundra

Location: High northern latitudes
Climate: Very cold, harsh, and long winters; short and cool summers; 10–25 cm (4–10 in.) of precipitation a year
Soil: Nutrient-poor, permafrost layer a few inches down
Plants: Grasses, wildflowers, mosses, small shrubs
Animals: Musk oxen, migrating caribou, arctic foxes, weasels, snowshoe hares, owls, hawks, various rodents, occasional polar bears

Grassland

Location: Midlatitudes, interiors of continents
Climate: Cool in winter, hot in summer; 25–75 cm (10–30 in.) of precipitation a year
Soil: Rich topsoil
Plants: Mostly grasses and small shrubs, some trees near sources of water
Animals: American grasslands include prairie dogs, foxes, small mammals, snakes, insects, various birds. African grasslands include elephants, lions, zebras, giraffes.

The lion lives on the savanna.

What Are Grasslands?

As the name tells you, **grasslands** are biomes where grasses are the main plant life. They are areas where rainfall is irregular and not usually plentiful.

Prairies, like the Blackland Prairie, are one kind of grassland. Called the "bread baskets" of the world, few temperate grasslands look as they did years ago. *Temperate* means "mild." It refers to grasslands such as those in the United States and Ukraine. Today many of these grasslands are covered with crops such as wheat, corn, and oats.

However, large parts of the world's tropical grasslands still look much as they have for hundreds of years. *Savannas* are grasslands that stay warm all year round. Their soil is not as fertile as that of temperate grasslands. However, they get more rain—about 86–152 cm (34–60 in.) a year.

The most famous savanna covers the middle third of Africa. Here the dust rises as countless hoofed animals thunder across the land. There are more hoofed animals in savannas than anywhere else on Earth. Graceful zebras and giraffes live here. Wildebeests travel in awesome herds of tens of thousands. Antelopes run from sprinting cheetahs. In the heat of the afternoon, lions rest in the shade of a thorny acacia tree. Nearby, hyenas prowl through the low grasses in search of dead or weak animals.

If you want to get a glimpse of a savanna while it still looks like this, you'd better do so soon. The land on savannas is being used more and more to graze domestic cattle. It won't be long until they replace the native animals, at least in unprotected parts of the savanna.

▷ **What are two types of grasslands? How are they different?**

What Is the Taiga Like?

Evidence indicates that about 15,000 years ago, huge fingers of ice, called glaciers, inched down from Earth's arctic regions. The ice was hundreds of feet thick. As it moved southward, it gouged great chunks of land out of northern Europe, Asia, and North America.

Some of the sediment carried by the glaciers dammed up streams, forming ponds and lakes. More lakes formed when the ice began to pull back. Holes dug by the glaciers filled with fresh water. These are the lakes and ponds of a cool, forested biome called the **taiga** (TIGH·guh).

Taigas are mostly conifer forests. They spread out over 11 percent of Earth's land. They are located in the upper latitudes of the Northern Hemisphere—in Alaska, Canada, Norway, Sweden, Finland, and Russia.

If you visit the taiga in the summer, you may hear the pleasant songs of birds. Many different kinds migrate to the taiga in summer. However, they head for warmer regions in the fall. You might also hear the whining sound of chain saws. That's because the taiga is a major source of lumber and pulpwood. Much of the lumber is used for making houses for the world's growing population. The pulpwood is turned into paper products of all kinds, such as the pages of this book.

READING Summarize

What are the main characteristics of the taiga?

Thousands of years ago, moving sheets of ice dug away the land of the taiga. The dug-out land would become some of its lakes and ponds. Today these bodies of water are guarded by great stands of evergreen trees.

The caribou, a member of the deer family, is among the large animals of the tundra.

What Is the Tundra?

Where is the ground frozen even in summer? Only 10–25 cm (4–10 in.) of precipitation fall here each year. Winters are long and icy cold. Summers are short and cool. Just a few inches below the surface, the ground is frozen all the time.

You can't find many plants taller than about 30 cm (12 in.). However, you have no trouble spotting weasels, arctic foxes, snowshoe hares, hawks, musk oxen, and caribou. Near the coast you see a polar bear. When warmer weather comes, mosquitoes by the millions buzz through the air. Where are you?

You are in the far north. You're between the taiga and the polar ice sheets. It could be northern Alaska or northern Canada. It could be Greenland or frigid parts of Europe or Asia. No matter which of these places you are in, you are in the same biome. This cold biome of the far north is the **tundra** .

Why is it so cold? Even in summer the Sun's rays only strike the tundra at a low, glancing angle. The Sun melts ice in the top layer of the soil. However, this water is kept from flowing downward by a layer of *permafrost*, or permanently frozen soil, underneath. The top layer of soil acts like a vast sponge for the melted ice.

Many tundra plants are wildflowers and grasses. The permafrost keeps large plants from developing the deep root systems they need. The growing season is very short—as little as 50 days in some places. The tundra soil is poor in nutrients, so the tundra cannot support large plants.

▷ **What are conditions in the tundra like?**

What Is the Desert Biome Like?

Sahara, Gobi and Atacama stir up thoughts of adventures in strange, dangerous places. These are among the world's greatest **deserts**. A desert is a sandy or rocky biome, with little precipitation and little plant life.

Every continent has at least one desert. Africa has an enormous desert called the Sahara. Its sands dip down to the Atlantic Ocean in the west, the Mediterranean Sea to the north, and the Red Sea to the east. It is the largest desert on Earth, with an area of about

9,000,000 km^2 (3,500,000 mi^2). It is so large that it could cover all of the United States south of Canada. Picture those 48 states covered with sand and you get an idea of the size of the Sahara.

The Gobi Desert in China and Mongolia is the world's second largest desert. It is about 1,300,000 km^2 (500,000 mi^2). That's about twice the size of Texas.

In South America the Atacama Desert runs 968 km (600 mi) from the southern tip of Peru down through Chile. It lies between the Andes Mountains to the east and the Pacific Ocean in the west. The driest place on Earth is found in Arica, Chile. It averages only about 0.08 cm (0.03 in.) of rain a year. That's about the depth of six sheets of paper.

Few animals and plants live in deserts. Those that do are very hardy. They are well adapted to living in the desert.

How is the desert similar to and different from the tundra?

To reach water, the roots of the mesquite plant (above) have been known to grow more than 79 m (260 ft) deep. That's the height of a 26-story building. Elf owls (left) build nests in cacti.

B 69

What Is a Deciduous Forest?

Have you ever seen leaves on trees change color in the fall? If you have, you have seen the **deciduous** (di·SIJ·ew·uhs) **forest** biome. This is a forest biome with many trees that lose their leaves each year.

This is where broad-leaved trees grow. Each autumn the leaves turn shades of yellow, orange, and red, giving the land beautiful colors. Then the leaves fall to the ground—which is what *deciduous* means—and decay. The dead leaves help make the soil rich and fertile.

Deciduous forests once covered most of the United States east of the Mississippi River and almost all of western Europe. Much has been cut down to make room for towns, cities, farms, and factories.

Many animals that once lived in deciduous forests still live on the land that was cleared for suburbs, farms, and towns. Chipmunks dart around bushes. Squirrels leap from branch to branch. Raccoons turn over trash cans. Skunks meander through the underbrush.

Birds like cardinals, robins, crows, and hawks, and insects such as bees still live in deciduous forests. Turn over a rock and you might discover a salamander or garter snake.

Many deciduous forests in the United States and Europe are now part of national parks or are in places where few people live. As long as they stay that way, people will be able to see the changing seasons.

▷ **What are the main characteristics of the deciduous forest?**

The trees of a deciduous forest shed their leaves each autumn, painting the land yellow, orange, and red.

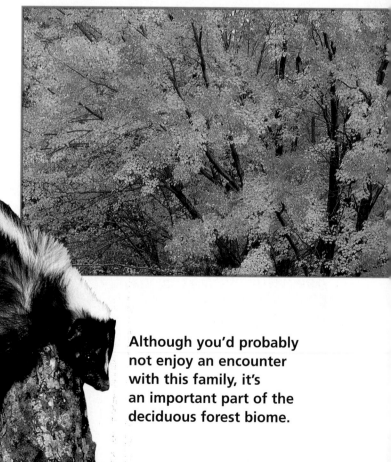

Although you'd probably not enjoy an encounter with this family, it's an important part of the deciduous forest biome.

What Are Tropical Rain Forests?

In areas along and near Earth's equator are **tropical rain forests**. These biomes are hot and humid, with much rainfall. They support a wide variety of life.

The canopy of a tropical rain forest spreads like a huge umbrella. It is so thick that little sunlight ever reaches the ground. With little light few plants can grow on the ground. Most of the life is up high in the branches, where howler monkeys and purple orchids cling.

There are no tropical rain forests in North America or Europe. They are too far from the tropics. However, Central America, South America, India, Africa, Southeast Asia, Australia, and many Pacific Islands have rain forests. Each has its own kinds of plants and animals.

Millions of species of animals live in the world's tropical rain forests. Many species have yet to be discovered.

In Africa you might see a silverback gorilla or a troop of playful chimpanzees.

On the island of Borneo, you might see a red-haired, long-armed orangutan (uh·RANG·oo·tan) swinging through the trees.

The anaconda is the largest snake on the planet.

The world's most colorful birds—such as toucans (TEW·kanz) and quetzals (ket·SAHLZ)—live in tropical rain forests. Giant snakes like the 9 m (30 ft), 136 kg (300 lb) South American anaconda also live in tropical rain forests.

The world's tropical rain forests have been victims of people's needs for lumber, farmland, and minerals. Fortunately, people are now replanting and restoring tropical rain forests. Still, some of their millions of undiscovered plant and animal species may become extinct before they are discovered.

▶ **What are some characteristics of the tropical rain forest?**

Some of the most colorful birds on Earth, like this toucan, live in tropical rain forests like those of South America.

QUICK LAB

FOR SCHOOL OR HOME

Freshwater Communities

1. Obtain from your teacher samples of pond, lake, or stream water taken at different locations. Use a different container for each sample. Record on the container the location each sample came from.

2. **Observe** Place a drop of water on a slide, and carefully place a coverslip over it. Examine the slide under a microscope.

3. **Communicate** Record the location of each sample and what you see. Use low and high power.

4. **Interpret Data** What does this tell you about aquatic ecosystems?

What Are Water Ecosystems Like?

Temperature and precipitation differ among ecosystems on land. For Earth's watery ecosystems, the main difference is saltiness.

Lakes, streams, rivers, ponds, and certain marshes, swamps, and bogs tend to have little salt in them. They're all freshwater ecosystems. Oceans and seas are saltwater ecosystems.

In fresh water or salt water, organisms can be divided into three main categories. *Plankton* (PLANGK·tuhn) are organisms that float on the water. *Nekton* (NEK·tahn) are organisms that swim through the water. *Benthos* (BEN·thahs) are bottom-dwelling organisms.

Freshwater Organisms

Many plants live in the shallow waters of lakes, ponds, and other bodies of fresh water. If you were to wade here, you might get your feet tangled in cattails, bur reeds, wild rice, and arrowheads. You might also spot a frog, a turtle, or maybe a crayfish.

Farther out, where the water gets deeper, are microscopic plankton like algae and protozoa.

Look beneath the surface, and nekton come into view. There might be large trout or other game fish. All the way to the bottom, an aquatic worm might be burrowing into the mud.

Saltwater Organisms

Like the freshwater ecosystem, the marine, or ocean, ecosystem is divided into several sections.

The shallowest is the *intertidal zone*. There the ocean floor is covered and uncovered as the tide goes in and out. Crabs burrow into the sand so they won't be washed away. Mussels and barnacles attach themselves to rocks.

The open ocean is divided into two regions. The first region is up to 200 m (656 ft) deep. In this upper region are many kinds of fish and whales. The world's largest animals—the 150-ton blue whales—live here.

The lower region goes from 200 m (656 ft) to the ocean bottom—perhaps 10.5 km (6.5 mi) down. At depths greater than about 1,000 m (3,281 ft), there is no sunlight. It is completely black!

Photosynthetic organisms, like algae, can only live where there is sunlight. They are found in the inter-tidal zone and in waters up to about 100 m (328 ft) deep. Many fantastic creatures live on the dark ocean bottom. Some of these fish "light up" like underwater fireflies. Other bottom-dwelling fish are blind. There are even bacteria that live in boiling water where fiery lava seeps out of the sea floor.

▷ **What are two water ecosystems? How do they differ?**

The types of animals you see in the ocean change as you go deeper.

Will the remaining whale populations survive? Will the eerie song of the humpback no longer be heard?

Can Humans Change Ecosystems?

People started hunting whales for their meat and oil at least 4,000 years ago. However, back then oceans held so many whales that hunting didn't have much effect on their populations.

As the centuries passed, however, whale hunting increased. So did the technology of finding and killing these gentle mammals. By 1850 American whalers alone accounted for the killing of 10,000 a year.

Over the next 100 years, new technologies made whale hunting easier and more efficient. In 1962 alone 66,000 whales were killed. The whales could not reproduce fast enough to replace those that were being killed. Many species, like blue whales, humpbacks,

bowheads, and right whales, became threatened with extinction.

The whales were being used for human and animal food, oil for lamps, and fertilizer. However, there were other sources of such products. Recognizing this and the danger to whale populations, the major whaling countries formed the International Whaling Commission (IWC) in 1946.

In 1971 the United States banned its citizens from whaling for profit or even buying products made from whales. By the 1990s the IWC had succeeded in getting whaling countries to reduce or stop hunting threatened whales.

▷ **How have humans affected the whale population?**

Why It Matters

The world's biomes remain constant as long as their climates and populations do not change greatly. However, human and natural activities can change biomes. Changes in a biome can affect the kinds of plants and animals that can live there. It can also affect people's lifestyles. It is important to know if, how, and why these factors are changing.

Think and Write

1. Describe the taiga biome in terms of its climate, soil, and inhabitants.

2. How do organisms found in desert and tundra biomes adapt to their environments?

3. Explain why few plants live on the floor of tropical rain forests.

4. Briefly describe the two types of aquatic ecosystems.

5. **Critical Thinking** Choose one biome, and explain how a change in its climate might affect its populations.

L·I·N·K·S

SOCIAL STUDIES LINK

Use a map. Choose a country, and identify its biomes. Find the major cities and other landmarks in each of the biomes. What plants and animals live in these areas? Construct a map. Draw each biome, and show which plants and animals live in it.

LITERATURE LINK

Read *Antarctica,* the story of the coldest continent on Earth. Try the activities at the end of the book.

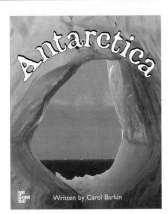

Written by Carol Barkin

WRITING LINK

Write a paragraph. Explain how your lifestyle would change if the biome where you live got warmer. What might happen if it got colder or if the precipitation decreased or increased? How would you have to adapt?

TECHNOLOGY LINK

At the Computer Visit www.mhscience02.com for more links.

Are Rain Forests Worth Saving?

Where might you be if you took a trip to one of the most famous ecosystems on Earth? You might be in a tropical rain forest!

Rain forests are full of secrets because they're hard to get through and you can't see everything in them. Although tropical rainforests cover only about 7 percent of all land, at least half of Earth's species live there.

Many plants and animals in the rain forests have never been seen or identified. Many could never survive outside the rain forests.

The largest of Earth's rain forests is in the Amazon River Basin of South America. Each year about 20,000 square kilometers (7,722 square miles) of this rain forest are destroyed by burning or cutting. The Amazon rain forest is thousands of years old, but is disappearing faster than ever before. New laws protect some areas, but the species of the Amazon will need even more protection to survive.

Why are people destroying the rain forests? The human population around the Amazon is growing fast, and people need a place to live. Some people want to replace part of the rain forest with farms.

Most minerals in a rain forest are in the plants, not the soil. After trees are cleared for farms, the soil is rich for only a few years. Then most of the nutrients are washed away by rain.

Parts of the rain forest are also rich in other minerals, like gold. Some people want to clear the trees and build mines. Do you think they should?

■ Cleared forest land
■ Frontier forest today

What Did I Learn?

1. Why are rain forests being destroyed?

A for mines
B for farms
C for homes
D all of the above

2. The minerals in a rain forest can be found mostly in

F organisms
G soil
H water
I plants

AT THE COMPUTER

Visit www.mhscience02.com to learn more about rain forests.

How Ecosystems Change

Get Ready

Before May 18, 1980, the area around Mount Saint Helens in the state of Washington was decorated with, wildflowers and beautiful groves of Douglas fir and western hemlock trees. Animals of many kinds made their home here. Then the mountain exploded. What happened to the community? How did this ecosystem change?

Process Skill

You predict when you state possible results of an event or experiment.

Explore Activity

How Do Ecosystems Change?

Procedure

1 **Observe** Examine the photograph.

2 **Communicate** Describe what you see.

Drawing Conclusions

1 **Infer** What happened to this farm after the owner left and moved to the city?

2 **Infer** Think about how this farm might have looked ten years ago. What kinds of plants lived there then?

3 **Interpret Data** How can one ecosystem be changed into another?

4 Compare what you think will happen to the abandoned farm with what happened at Mount Saint Helens. In what ways would the changes in ecosystems be similar? In what ways would they be different?

5 **Going Further: Predict** Think of another ecosystem that might be changed by nature. Think of an ecosystem that might be changed by humans. Describe how such ecosystems might continue to change over time.

Main Idea Ecosystems go through both slow and sudden changes.

How Do Ecosystems Change?

Changes happen everywhere on Earth. They can occur in your backyard. They can happen in an empty city lot or on one of its abandoned streets. If given a chance, nature has a way of changing an ecosystem or producing a new one. How does nature change an abandoned farm's field into a flourishing forest?

In the first year, a community of crabgrass, insects, and mice invades the field where corn or another crop once grew.

Abandoned cities of Angkor in Cambodia became covered by jungle.

Tall weeds, such as asters, ragweed, and goldenrod, and tall grasses grow among the crabgrass. The crabgrass can't easily survive in the shade cast by the taller weeds. It begins to die out in the second and third year. Rabbits and seed-eating birds move in.

The hot, dry field of tall weeds provides a perfect environment for

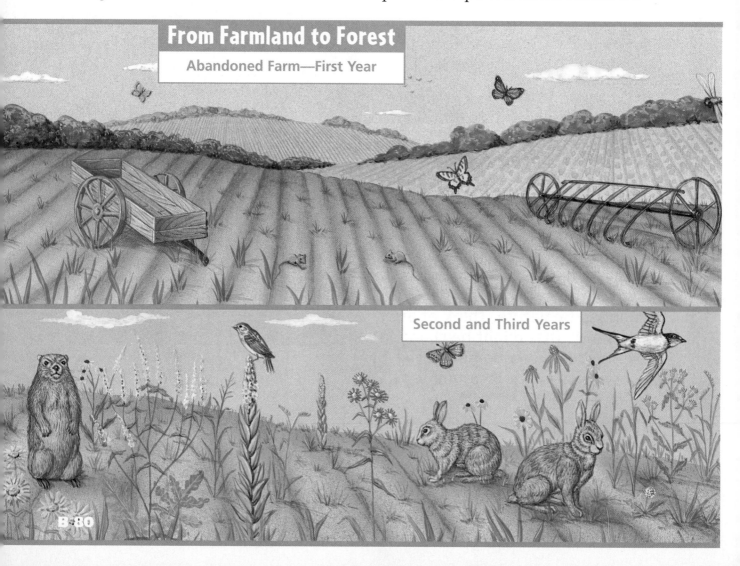

From Farmland to Forest

Abandoned Farm—First Year

Second and Third Years

pine seeds to sprout. By the fourth year, pine trees begin to grow and shade the weeds, which begin to die out. More birds join the community, as do small mammals like opossums and skunks.

A pine forest has replaced the old farm field within twenty-five years. The number of new pine seedlings drops, however, because they can't grow in the shade. Seeds of deciduous trees such as maple, hickory, and oak sprout and take root. Larger animals like raccoons and foxes begin to visit.

The forest is now mostly deciduous trees. These trees are the habitats of many different kinds of birds and small animals, such as squirrels. Deer, raccoons, and foxes also live in the forest.

▶ **How can an abandoned farm become a deciduous forest ecosystem?**

Four to Six Years Later

Twenty-Five Years Later

One Hundred Years Later

How Do Communities Change?

The abandoned farm field you just read about gave way to short crabgrass, then tall grasses and shrubs. Later, pine trees and, finally, deciduous trees grew there. Scientists call the gradual replacement of one community by another **ecological succession**.

Ecological succession can begin in two different kinds of places. It can begin where a community already exists—such as in an abandoned farm field. Ecological succession in a place where a community already exists is called *secondary succession*.

Ecological succession can also happen where there are few, if any, living things. This is called *primary succession*. Primary succession can begin where communities were wiped out. Such places would include land swept clean by a volcanic eruption or forest fire. It can also begin where communities never existed before, such as on a new island that rises out of the sea.

Mount Saint Helens

Explore what happened to Mount Saint Helens in the state of Washington shortly after May 18, 1980.

Mount Saint Helens had just erupted. The blast from the volcano knocked down thousands of trees. The whole area was covered knee-deep with hot volcanic ash and finely smashed up rock.

The landscape was different shades of gray as far as you could see. No spot of green greeted your eyes, not even a blade of grass. If you didn't

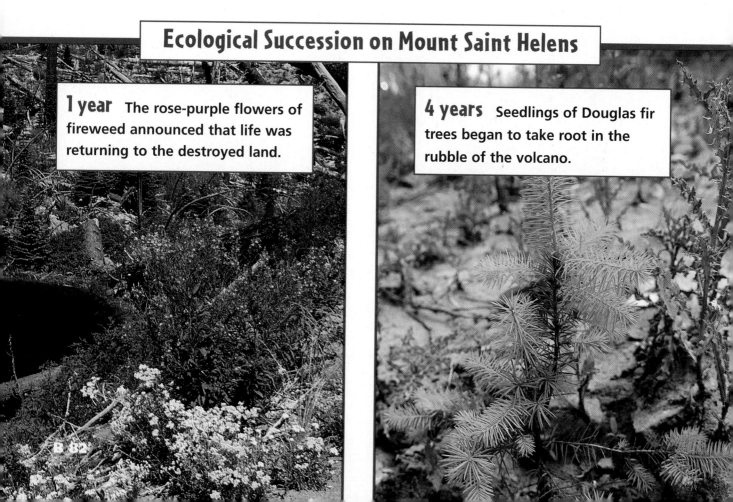

Ecological Succession on Mount Saint Helens

1 year The rose-purple flowers of fireweed announced that life was returning to the destroyed land.

4 years Seedlings of Douglas fir trees began to take root in the rubble of the volcano.

know better, you might have thought you were on the Moon.

A year passes. You return to the slopes of Mount Saint Helens expecting to see unbroken stretches of rock and stumps of dead trees. However, something has happened in the year you were gone. Wind and rain have cleared some of the ash and dust, especially from steep slopes. The wind has also blown in some seeds and fruits from nearby forests. You see a scattering of rose-purple objects among the charred and fallen tree trunks. They are the flowers of a plant called fireweed. It gets its name from the fact that it is often the first plant to grow after a forest fire.

Scientists would call the fireweed a **pioneer species**. That's because it is the first species to be living in an otherwise lifeless area. You notice that the blooming of fireweed has attracted animals such as insects and an occasional insect-eating bird. A new community, called a **pioneer community**, is beginning to thrive around Mount Saint Helens.

You return in 1984 and almost step on a little green shoot. You bend down and take a closer look. The shoot has little needlelike leaves. It is the sprout of a Douglas fir tree. Its seed was probably blown here from a forest miles away.

Now picture the land around Mount Saint Helens 100 or 200 years in the future. It is covered with a dense forest of evergreens. The forest is much like the one that spread around it before that explosive day in 1980.

▷ **How does ecological succession change communities?**

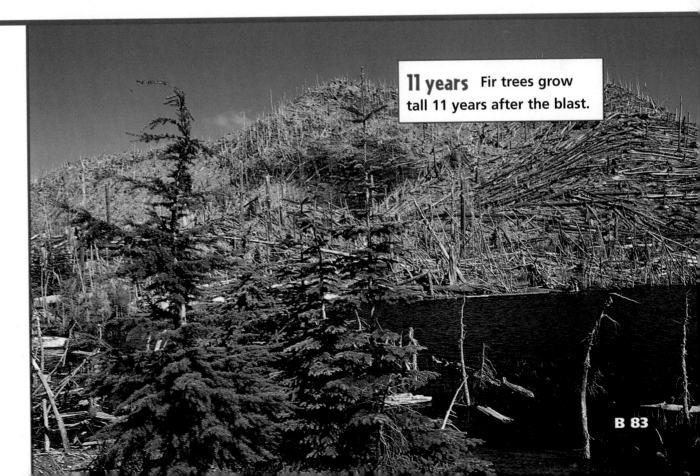

11 years Fir trees grow tall 11 years after the blast.

What Happens to Pioneer Communities?

Are the first organisms in a pioneer community always plants? In some places the answer is no. This is usually the case in newly formed, fiery volcanic islands that rise from the sea. Here the pioneer community is often made up of bacteria, fungi, and algae. Over many years these organisms slowly break down the volcanic rock into soil.

What happens when there is enough soil, and other conditions are right for plants to grow? A seed blown to the island by the wind or dropped by a passing bird will take root. The new plant, and others like it, will gradually spread over the land.

During their life cycles, plants will die and further enrich the soil.

Perhaps a coconut will drift ashore. When it germinates, its roots will find a good supply of nutrients. A coconut palm will spring up, and a new island paradise will be created.

Climax Communities

More years will pass—perhaps hundreds of them. The climate of the island will remain almost unchanged. Its community will grow. Its populations will become balanced and stable. Few new animals and plants will arrive. Few will leave. Ecological succession will slow down or stop altogether. This is a **climax community**, a final stage of succession. This community will stay largely unchanged unless some major event occurs.

Stages of Succession

Bare rock   Lichens/mosses   Grasses   Sedges   Aspens   Forest

READING Diagrams

Use the diagram to make a flowchart showing the changes from a pioneer community to a climax community.

What kind of event could change an entire ecosystem? A hurricane may sweep across the island. The volcano that created it might erupt again. People might come and build hotels or introduce new plants or animals. The climate might change. Then the processes of ecological succession would begin all over again. Another climax community would eventually develop. It might—or might not—be the same as the earlier climax community.

▶ **What is the difference between a pioneer community and a climax community?**

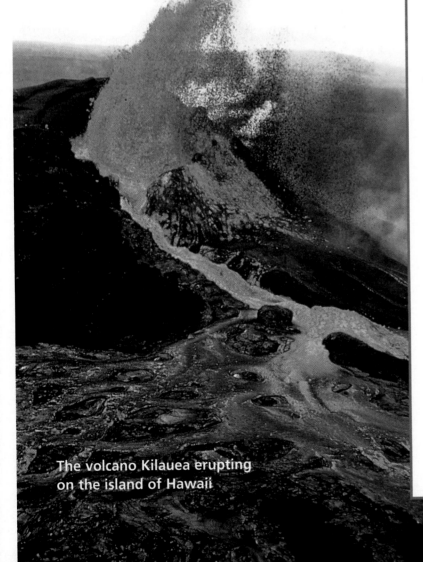
The volcano Kilauea erupting on the island of Hawaii

QUICK LAB

FOR SCHOOL OR HOME

Predicting Succession

1. **Observe** Identify an area near you where you think ecological succession is taking place.

2. **Communicate** Describe the area. List the evidence you have that indicates ecological succession is taking place.

3. **Infer** Do you think the succession will be primary or secondary? Explain.

4. **Predict** In what order do you think new species will colonize the area? Explain the reasons for your predictions.

5. **Communicate** Describe the climax community that you think will eventually live in the area. Give reasons for your conclusion.

What's Living on Surtsey?

In 1963 the island of Surtsey, near Iceland, was formed from a volcano. Between 1963 and 1996, at least 45 types of plants were seen growing there. Several kinds of birds, such as snow buntings, were also found raising their young on the island. Flying insects have also been found there. Scientists expect that more types of plants and birds will live on Surtsey in the future.

▶ **How is Surtsey an example of ecological succession?**

Surtsey, a volcanic island, rose from the sea near Iceland in 1963.

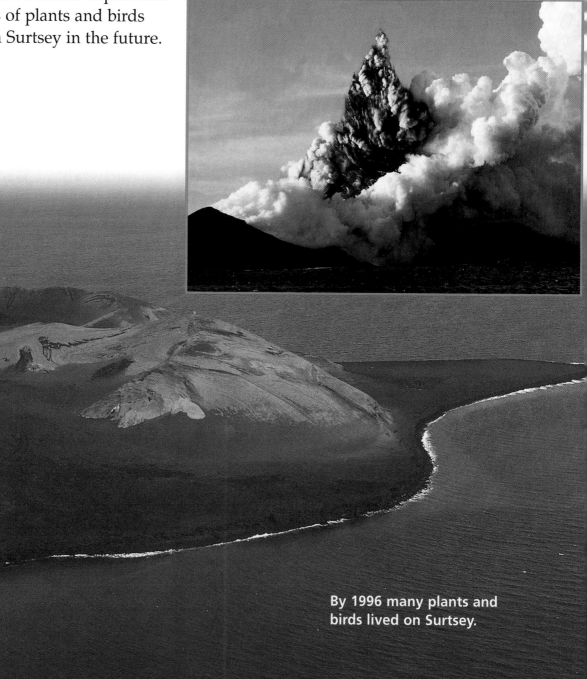

By 1996 many plants and birds lived on Surtsey.

Comparing Ecosystems in Volcanic Areas

In this activity you will collect data and infer about the ecosystems of two volcanic areas.

Data are different kinds of facts. They might include observations, measurements, calculations, and other kinds of information. Scientists collect data about an event to better understand what caused it, what it will cause, and how it will affect other events.

What do these data tell the scientist? The scientist first organizes the data in some way—perhaps a table, chart, or graph. The scientist then studies the organized data and makes inferences. To infer means to form an idea from facts or observations. In this case you will infer about which plants will return to a volcanic area.

Materials

research books

Internet

Procedure

1 Collect data on two volcanic areas, such as Mount Saint Helens and the Soufriere Hills volcano on the island of Montserrat or the active volcanoes of Hawaii. Organize the data.

2 **Communicate** Describe the sequence of events that has taken place.

3 **Interpret Data** Draw a conclusion about why certain plants return when they do.

Drawing Conclusions

1 In what ways is succession in the two areas alike? In what ways is it different?

2 **Infer** Why is the succession in these two areas similar or different?

3 **Infer** What abiotic factors must you consider when drawing conclusions? What biotic factors must you consider?

How Do Changes Affect Populations?

Our planet is changing all the time. Its continents move north and south, east and west. Climates change from hot to cold, cold to hot, wet to dry, or dry to wet. As these changes occur, populations and communities change with them.

Take, for example, the following mystery and its solution.

- Scientists gathering fossils in Italy make a discovery. About six million years ago, fish and other sea creatures disappeared from the Mediterranean Sea.

- Other fossils from a slightly later period reveal that horselike animals from Africa arrived in Europe.

- The fossil of an ancient African hippopotamus is found on an island in the middle of the Mediterranean.

- Fossil palm trees of the same age are dug up in Switzerland.

- Then there is another surprising discovery. Five-million-year-old fossils of fish turn up in the Mediterranean area.

What could have gone on back then to have these clues make sense? Scientists have developed hypotheses. One theory is called *plate tectonics*.

Scientists study fossils to discover how the Mediterranean area changed.

Earth's plates

Earth's crust is made up of moving plates—pieces of crust. About six million years ago, two plates—the African and the Eurasian—collided. The continents of Africa and Europe bumped into each other. This happened at what is now the Strait of Gibraltar. This collision created a natural dam between the Atlantic Ocean and the Mediterranean Sea.

Without a source of water from the ocean, the sea dried up in perhaps as little as 1,000 years. The Mediterranean Sea became a desert. The sea's fish and other marine life died out. Animals from Africa migrated across the desert to Europe. Palm trees sprouted in Switzerland.

Then about five million years ago, the dam began to crumble. A gigantic waterfall poured water into the desert. It carried many kinds of marine life from the Atlantic Ocean. The Mediterranean became a sea again.

6 million years ago

Present day

READING Summarize

How did changes in the Mediterranean affect populations?

Can Human Events Change Environments?

The soil under your feet looks brown. The rocks are mostly gray. However, both hold a treasure chest of glittering colorful metals—gold, silver, aluminum, iron, copper, and many more.

People use these metals in many ways. Gold is made into jewelry and coins. Silver is, too. Silver is also used in photographic film and tableware.

Fly in an airplane. Ride in an automobile. Open a soft drink can. Squeeze a toothpaste tube. Marvel at fireworks. For all these things, you can thank aluminum. It's in each of these products.

Every large building, bridge, ship, train, and piece of machinery has iron in it—usually as part of steel.

Turn on your TV, your home's lights, a CD player. Electricity flowing through copper wires gets them going.

Clearly metals play an important part in our modern society. However, we pay a price for them—and not only

The easiest way to mine metals that are near the surface is to scrape the surface away. However, this leaves the land barren and often covered with dangerous chemicals.

in money. Since metal-containing rocks are buried in the ground, we must change the ground to get at them. If the rocks are near the surface, we simply carve away huge areas of land. This is called surface mining, open-pit mining, or strip mining.

In the United States alone, about 2,331 km^2 (900 mi^2) of land has been cleared for mining. That's about three-fourths of the area of the entire state of Rhode Island.

Surface-mined land is loaded with substances that are harmful to living things. Rainwater flows easily over this kind of land and carries pollutants into nearby streams, rivers, and lakes. The wind picks up dust, which pollutes the air. In both cases, living things are harmed.

▷ **How does mining affect the environment?**

Why It Matters

The activities and health of all living things on Earth are interconnected. What happens to one living thing and one ecosystem usually affects other living things and other ecosystems. Human activities like strip mining can harm soil and the environment. Human actions can also help the environment, however. Composting, for example, can help restore soil. We can also help the environment by using only the things we need, and by not wasting materials.

Visit **www.mhscience02.com** to do a research project on conserving metals.

Think and Write

1. Describe how an abandoned farm field becomes a deciduous forest.

2. Give an example of a pioneer community and a climax community.

3. List the evidence that supports the conclusion that the Mediterranean Sea once dried up.

4. **Infer** How might a volcanic eruption affect an ecosystem?

5. **Critical Thinking** What things do you do every day that can affect the ecosystem you live in?

L·I·N·K·S

LITERATURE LINK

Read *Wildfire* to learn about the true story of a wildfire that destroyed 5,000 acres of land in New York. Try the activities in the back of the book.

SOCIAL STUDIES LINK

Conduct research. What happened to Angkor? What was the culture like? Why did the people leave their city? Use the Internet or an encyclopedia for your research.

TECHNOLOGY LINK

Science Newsroom CD-ROM Choose *From the Ground Up* to learn how ecosystems change over time.

At the Computer Visit **www.mhscience02.com** for more links.

Chapter 5 Review

Vocabulary

Fill each blank with the best word or words from the list.

adaptation, B52
biome, B64
climax community, B84
desert, B69
mutualism, B54
parasitism, B56
pioneer community, B83
symbiosis, B54
taiga, B67
tundra, B68

1. Part of the soil of the _____ is frozen all year round.

2. The relationship of _____ means that both populations benefit.

3. _____ is a relationship between two organisms in which one benefits while the other is harmed.

4. The _____ has many evergreen trees.

5. A(n) _____ is made up of the first organisms to colonize an area.

6. A characteristic that helps an organism survive is called a(n) _____.

7. When ecological succession slows down, a(n) _____ has formed.

8. A deciduous forest is an example of a(n) _____.

9. _____ describes relationships that last from one generation to the next.

10. The Gobi and Mojave are examples of the _____.

Test Prep

11. One example of a parasitic plant is _____.
   A mistletoe
   B an orchid
   C a fir tree
   D seaweed

12. Surface mining can harm the environment when _____.
   F trees are cut down to clear the land
   G dust from surface-mined land causes air pollution
   H rainwater washes pollutants into nearby streams
   J all of the above

13. A relationship in which one organism benefits from another without helping or harming it is called _____.
   A parasitism
   B mutualism
   C commensalism
   D symbiosis

14. _____ is an example of a biome.

   F A pond

   G Bacteria

   H A grassland

   J A mammal

15. The shallow roots of the barrel cactus help it survive in the desert by _____.

   A resisting flood damage

   B allowing the cactus to be blown to a wetter place

   C allowing the cactus to float

   D soaking up rain very quickly

Concepts and Skills

16. Process Skills: Infer

What can you infer from the data below?

Pond Populations and Acid Content				
Acid	**Yellow Perch**	**Brown Trout**	**Salamanders**	**Mayflies**
High	23	6	2	0
Medium	28	11	7	2
Low	36	18	10	14

17. Reading in Science Summarize how the structure of a cactus enables it to survive in the desert.

18. Critical Thinking How might a change in the biome you live in affect your way of life?

19. Scientific Methods You discover that there are no fossils of dinosaurs above a certain layer of rock, but there are below it. The rock in this layer has more in common with rocks from space than with Earth rocks. Hypothesize how these two discoveries may be linked.

20. Product Ads Advertisements for some products claim that the products are environmentally friendly. What does that mean? What are examples of products that are environmentally friendly and products that are not?

Boost your test scores!

Be Smart!

Visit www.mhscience02.com

MARINE BIOLOGIST

Dr. Lauren Mullineaux

Woods Hole Oceanographic Institution

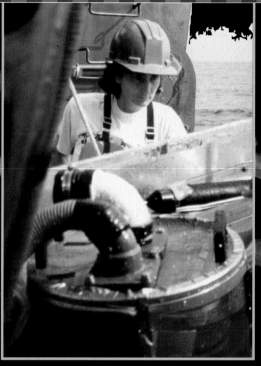

Earth's oceans are home to many populations of strange and unusual organisms. What different kinds of habitats exist on the ocean floor? What kinds of organisms live there, and how do they survive? How can we use new discoveries to benefit society? These are some of the questions inspiring today's oceanographers.

Dr. Lauren Mullineaux is a marine biologist at Woods Hole Oceanographic Institution in Massachusetts. She studies ocean ecosystems. One of the unanswered questions she is studying is how the animals of the ocean floor survive. These animals include tube worms, white crabs, and giant clams. Many live in hydrothermal vents created by volcanoes under the sea floor. The vents might seem to be too harsh an environment for living things, but these animals cannot survive anywhere else.

Sometimes the research of a marine biologist is not easy. To study the unique organisms of the ocean floor, Dr. Mullineaux has to dive in a submersible. A submersible is a special kind of submarine that can dive very deep. The vents are located thousands of meters beneath the ocean surface! Dr. Mullineaux sets up her experiments on the ocean floor.

Dr. Mullineaux grew up in Colorado, far from the ocean, but she's always had a love for nature and animals. She became interested in science as a way to understand nature. In college she studied ecology but soon realized that she wanted to study the mysteries of the ocean. After receiving her doctorate degree in biological oceanography, she was able to start her research career and begin unlocking the mysteries of the deep

Careers IN SCIENCE

Career Track

Here are some different types of careers related to the study of ecology and living things. Use the Internet or library resources to find out more about these and other careers.

- scuba diver
- aquarium worker
- fishery manager
- dolphin trainer
- ecologist
- microbiologist
- geneticist
- geophysicist

Hydrothermal vent

Write ABOUT IT

1. Why do you think many of the questions about ocean life remain unanswered?

2. Why is it important to understand how the organisms of the ocean floor survive?

AT THE COMPUTER

Visit **www.mhscience02.com** to learn more about careers.

Ecosystem Discovery

Your goal is to invent and describe a new ecosystem.

What to Do

1. Imagine you are an explorer. You have found the world's last unexplored ecosystem. Give your ecosystem a name.

2. Describe this new ecosystem. Write about the plants and animals there. Tell what each one needs to survive.

3. Draw a picture of your ecosystem.

Analyze Your Results

1. Tell how each plant and animal gets what it needs to survive in your ecosystem.

2. What nonliving things help plants and animals survive in your ecosystem?

3. Draw an energy pyramid to show how energy moves in your ecosystem. What belongs at the bottom of the pyramid? At the top?

Will Succession Succeed?

Your goal is to identify a place where ecological succession is taking place.

What to Do

1. Write a short paragraph describing what ecological succession is.

2. Think of an area you have visited where succession is taking place. If you can't think of an area near you, describe a place you have read about. Write down the name of the place or tell its location. Draw a picture.

Analyze Your Results

1. List evidence that succession is taking place in your area.

2. In what order will new species come to live in your area? Explain.

3. What could happen to prevent succession in your area?

UNIT

C Earth and Its Resources

NATIONAL GEOGRAPHIC

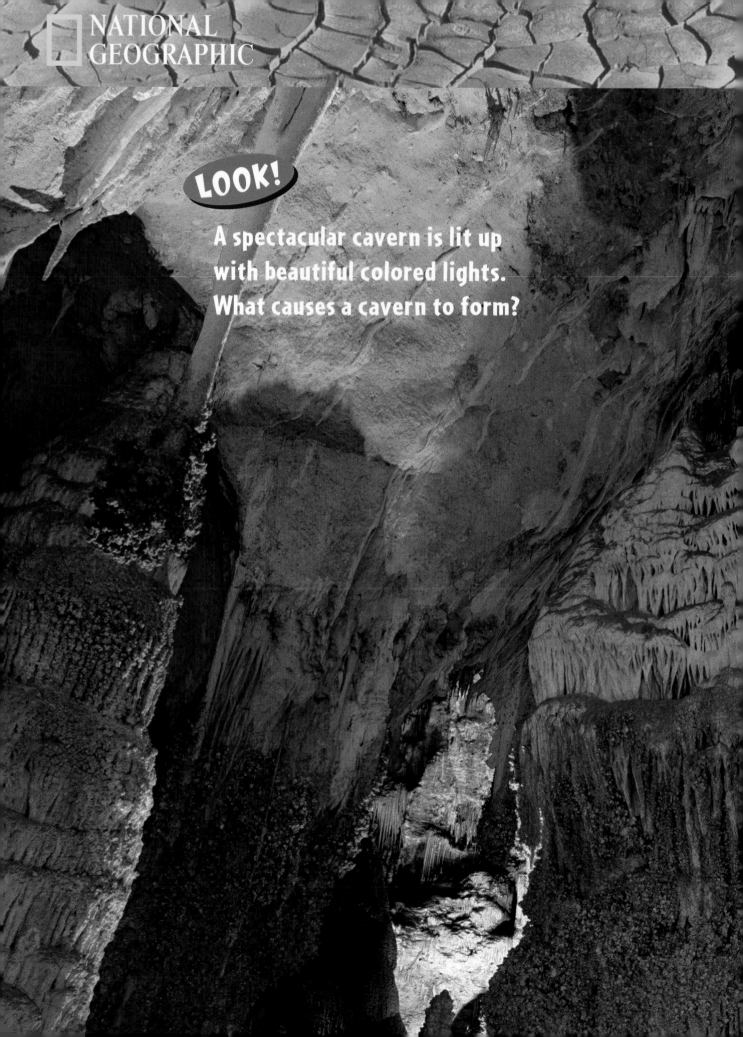

LOOK!

A spectacular cavern is lit up
with beautiful colored lights.
What causes a cavern to form?

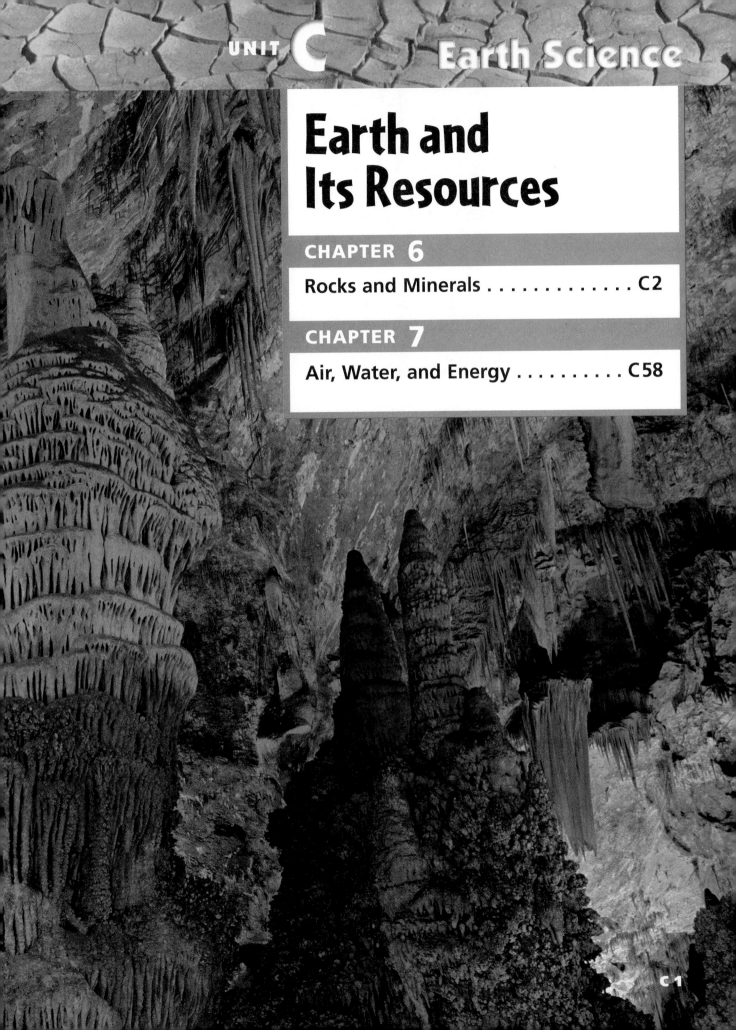

Earth and Its Resources

CHAPTER 6

Rocks and Minerals

Did You Ever Wonder?

What is this strange-looking rock formation? Did someone build it here in Zion National Park? No. This fantastic shape is a natural rock formation called a hoodoo. What natural processes could have produced a hoodoo and other unusual rock formations?

Earth and Its Neighbors

Vocabulary

solar system, C6

planet, C6

gravity, C8

inertia, C9

lithosphere, C12

crust, C12

hydrosphere, C12

atmosphere, C12

constellation, C14

Get Ready

Saturn is not standing still in one spot. It is moving around the Sun in an almost circular path. What holds Saturn, and all the other planets, near the Sun? What keeps each planet on its path?

Process Skill

You **use variables** when you identify and separate things in an experiment that can be changed or controlled.

Explore Activity

How Are Earth and the Sun Held Together?

Materials

clay

string

scissors

meterstick

goggles

Procedure

BE CAREFUL! Wear goggles. Twirl the model close to the ground.

1 **Make a Model** Cut a 40-cm length of string. Wrap it around a small, round lump of clay in several directions. Tie the ends to make a tight knot. Measure 60 cm of string, and tie it to the string around the ball.

2 **Observe** Spin the ball of clay slowly—just fast enough to keep the string tight and keep the ball off the ground. Keep the ball close to the ground. Describe the path of the ball.

3 **Experiment** At one point while spinning, let the string go. What happens? Describe the path of the ball of clay. Repeat until you get a clear picture of what happens.

Drawing Conclusions

1 How did your model represent Earth and the Sun? What represented Earth? Where was the Sun located? How did you represent the force between them?

2 **Infer** Explain what happened when you let the string go. Why do you think this happened?

3 **Going Further: Use Variables** How would your results change if the mass of the clay was doubled? Tripled? How does the mass affect the pull on the string? Make a prediction. Try it.

Read to Learn

Main Idea The solar system consists of nine planets, many moons, and many other bodies orbiting the Sun.

What Is the Solar System?

If you were traveling in a spaceship through space as fast as light, you would be passing stars. Perhaps in time you would approach one star in particular, the star you know as the Sun. If so, you would be approaching your home address, the **solar system**. The solar system is the Sun and the objects that are traveling around it.

Our Sun is a star similar to other stars in the night sky. It appears so large and bright to us because it is much closer to Earth. The Sun is composed mostly of hydrogen and helium. The formation of helium from hydrogen is what generates light and heat from the Sun.

The objects around the Sun include nine **planets**. Planets are objects that travel around a star in a path. That path is called an *orbit*. The planets are held in orbit around the Sun. The planets do not give off light, as stars do. They reflect light from their star, the Sun.

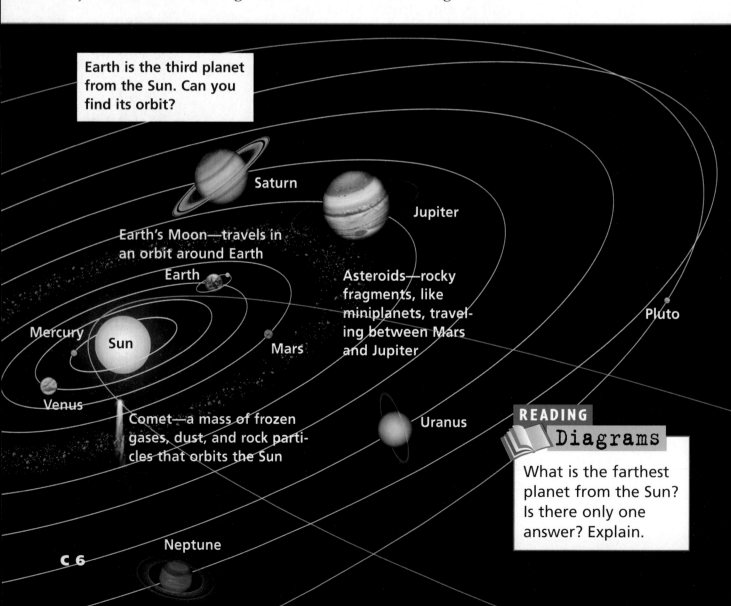

Earth is the third planet from the Sun. Can you find its orbit?

Saturn

Jupiter

Earth's Moon—travels in an orbit around Earth

Earth

Asteroids—rocky fragments, like miniplanets, traveling between Mars and Jupiter

Pluto

Mercury

Sun

Mars

Venus

Comet—a mass of frozen gases, dust, and rock particles that orbits the Sun

Uranus

READING Diagrams

What is the farthest planet from the Sun? Is there only one answer? Explain.

Neptune

C 6

Except for Pluto, the orbit of each planet is almost a circle. Each orbit is slightly oval. What effect does an orbit of this shape have on the distance from a planet to the Sun?

One complete trip of an object in its orbit around the Sun takes one *year*. A year is different from planet to planet. For Earth one year is 365.25 days. The table shows how long a year takes for each planet. The time is given in days as days are timed on Earth.

▷ **What are the parts of the solar system?**

FOR SCHOOL OR HOME

Orbit Times

1. **Communicate** Use graph paper. Draw a bar graph to compare the revolution times for the planets. The vertical axis of the graph represents time. Decide how much time each square on the paper represents. The horizontal axis represents the planets. How many pieces of graph paper will you need?

2. **Interpret Data** Based on your graph and the data table, what relationship can you find between the length of the year (time) and the planet's location in the solar system?

3. How could you change your graph to show the relationship even better? What might your new graph reveal?

4. **Use Variables** Draw a line graph. Let the vertical axis represent time for a complete orbit. Let the horizontal axis represent distance to the Sun. Label each point with the name of its planet.

Planet	Average Distance to the Sun (million km)	Year Time for complete orbit around the Sun (in Earth days)
Mercury	57.9	88 days
Venus	108.2	224 days
Earth	149.6	365 days
Mars	227.9	687 days
Jupiter	778.3	4,333 days
Saturn	1,427	10,759 days
Uranus	2,870	30,685 days
Neptune	4,497	60,188 days
Pluto	5,900	90,700 days

What Keeps the Planets in Orbit?

Earth travels around the Sun, but you won't find a string connecting them! What is it that holds Earth in its path around the Sun? What keeps Earth from flying off into space?

This question once puzzled scientists, too. They knew that everything in the solar system orbits the Sun. What holds it all together?

Gravity

One scientist who lived about 300 years ago, Sir Isaac Newton, had some ideas to explain this. He described an invisible force holding the Sun and a planet together. He called the invisible force **gravity**. He described gravity as a property of all matter. It is a force of attraction, or pull, between any object and any other objects around it.

Gravity depends on two measurements—mass and distance. The more matter, or mass, in an object, the greater the pull in the object's direction. The closer two objects are, the stronger the pull of gravity between them.

When Newton's ideas are applied to the world around us, we find that they can explain how most objects behave. In fact, Newton extended his ideas to include all objects on Earth, in the solar system, and beyond. His ideas are called the law of universal gravitation.

READING Diagrams

1. What are the differences between the objects in part A and part B?

2. Why is one arrow wider in part A? In part B?

A

Rocket 2

Rocket 1

Closer   Farther

B

Rocket 1   Rocket 2 (has much more mass than Rocket 1)

Gravity and inertia together make Earth follow this path.

Inertia alone would result in Earth following this path.

Gravity alone would pull Earth into the Sun.

According to Newton's law, there is a force of attraction between you and Earth. Earth pulls you. You pull Earth. When you stumble, why do you fall down? Why doesn't Earth fall up?

Compared with Earth, you have a very small amount of mass. As a result, your gravity is very weak. Earth's gravity, however, is very strong because Earth is so massive. Earth's pull is strong enough to make everything near it move in its direction, including you. That's why you fall "down" if you stumble.

The Sun has far more mass than Earth or any other planet. Since it is much more massive than Earth, its gravity is much stronger, too. The Sun's gravity holds all of the objects in the solar system together. Without gravity, Earth and all of the other objects orbiting the Sun would go flying off into space.

Sir Isaac Newton, 1642–1727, was an English mathematician and scientist. It is said that he thought of gravity when an apple dropped on his head.

Inertia

Gravity is not the only reason why the planets stay in their orbits. Gravity alone would pull Earth into the Sun, because the Sun is so massive. That doesn't happen because the planets are moving. The planets, as do all objects, have a property called **inertia** (i·NUR·shuh). Inertia is the tendency of a moving object to keep moving in a straight line.

The planets would move in straight lines without gravity because of their inertia. Gravity "steers" the planets in their oval paths around the Sun. It is gravity and inertia that keep the planets in their orbits.

▷ **How do gravity and inertia keep a planet in orbit?**

What Makes a Day?

The Sun does more than just hold the planets in their orbits in the solar system. It also provides them with light and warmth. The Sun is the reason for day and night. All planets spin, or *rotate*, like huge spinning tops.

READING
Tables

Make a list of planets in order from the shortest day to the longest day.

Length of Day

Planet	Day = time for complete spin (in Earth hours or days)
Mercury	59 days
Venus	243 days
Earth	24 hours
Mars	24 hours 30 minutes
Jupiter	9 hours 56 minutes
Saturn	10 hours 40 minutes
Uranus	17 hours 14 minutes
Neptune	16 hours 6 minutes
Pluto	6.39 days

At any point in time, half of a planet is facing the Sun—it has daylight on that half. At the same time, half is facing away from the Sun—that half is in darkness, night.

As a planet rotates, places that are in darkness eventually turn to face the Sun, and those in daylight eventually turn away. Each planet makes one complete spin in its day. Each planet has its own speed of turning. The length of a day (that is, one complete day-night cycle) is different for each planet.

How much light and warmth a planet receives depends on how far it is from the Sun. Light spreads out as it travels outward from the Sun. An area of one square meter on the planet Mercury receives much more energy than an area of one square meter on a farther planet—such as Pluto. That is why Mercury is much hotter than Pluto.

 What is a day?

Earth turns this way.

Dark side (night)

Sunrise

Noontime

Light side (day)

Axis

Sunlight

Summer in Northern Hemisphere
June 21 or 22

Northern Hemisphere

Direct ray

152 million kilometers

Southern Hemisphere

Fall, September 22 or 23

Equator

Spring, March 20 or 21

147 million kilometers

Direct ray

Winter in Northern Hemisphere December 21 or 22

What Causes Earth's Seasons?

As the third planet from the Sun, Earth is at a location where it receives just the right amount of energy to provide living things with the warmth and light they need.

Different animals and plants live in different temperatures, in different climates, and at different heights above sea level on Earth.

Why are places generally cooler in winter than in summer? Earth's orbit is like a slightly stretched circle—an oval. This shape brings Earth slightly closer to the Sun during part of the year and farther away during other parts of the year. In the Northern Hemisphere, Earth is actually slightly closer to the Sun during winter than during summer. Then what causes colder winters and warmer summers?

The answer is Earth's tilt as it travels around the Sun. During the winter the Northern Hemisphere is tilted away from the Sun. The winter Sun stays low in the sky in the Northern Hemisphere. Temperatures are cooler. During the summer, the Northern Hemisphere is tilted toward the Sun. The midday summer Sun is higher in the sky in the Northern Hemisphere. Temperatures are warmer.

The closer a place is to the equator, the less change there is in temperatures from season to season. Why? The midday Sun is high in the sky all year round.

Also, some surfaces warm up more than others when bathed in sunlight. Land heats up more than water. Dark soils heat up more than light-colored sands. As a result, Earth ends up with a whole range of temperatures, which can support the many different kinds of life on Earth.

▷ **How does Earth's tilt bring about the seasons?**

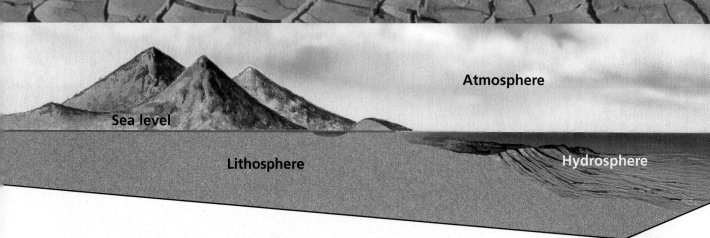

Atmosphere

Sea level

Lithosphere

Hydrosphere

What Is Planet Earth Like?

Earth

Is Earth a solid planet? Liquid? Gas? Earth is all of these. It has a solid surface layer, mostly covered by a layer of water, all surrounded by layers of gases. The Sun interacts with all of these layers of Earth.

- The **lithosphere** (LITH·uh·sfeer) is the hard, outer layer of Earth, about 100 km (62.14 mi) thick. The rocky surface that makes up the top of the lithosphere is the **crust** . The crust includes the continents and the ocean floors.

The crust includes the soil and many other *resources*. Earth's resources are materials that help support life on Earth. Earth has high mountains, like the Rockies. It also has low valleys, like those of the ocean bottoms.

- The **hydrosphere** (HIGH·druh· sfeer) is Earth's water—trillions of liters of water. Earth's waters are another valuable resource. There is so much water that it covers most of the lithosphere. Most of this water is called the ocean. It is salty because of minerals that have been washed into it over the ages. The

hydrosphere also includes all of Earth's lakes, rivers, streams, underground water, and ice. Most of this is fresh water, which we use for drinking, cooking, and bathing.

The hydrosphere acts as a big heat absorber. Water changes temperature slowly compared to land. The oceans keep temperatures on Earth from changing too drastically.

- Pictures of Earth taken from space show lots of white clouds swirling in the **atmosphere** . The atmosphere is many layers of gases that surround Earth. The atmosphere contains oxygen needed for living things on Earth. It also contains other gases that help protect Earth from forms of harmful energy from the Sun. These gases are more of Earth's precious resources.

READING **Sequence of Events**
What is the order of Earth's layers?

What Is the Moon Like?

With a telescope you can take a close look at Earth's nearest neighbor in the solar system. "Only" 384,000 km (240,000 mi) from Earth, the Moon's surface does not look at all like Earth's surface. You won't see clouds or oceans. There are no hills covered with forests—in fact there are no signs of life at all.

The Moon has no hydrosphere. It has no atmosphere to speak of. There is no water to drink, no air to breathe. There is no weather. Without the atmosphere to trap heat and the hydrosphere to circulate it, temperatures change greatly during a Moon day.

The Moon has a lithosphere, a rocky surface. With a telescope you can see features of the surface—such as dark-colored regions called *maria* (MAHR·ee·uh). *Maria* is Latin for "seas." In the past these areas were thought to be seas. They are really dry, flat land surrounded by mountains and ridges.

Earth's nearest neighbor looks nothing much like Earth.

Much of the Moon's surface is covered with huge dents, called craters. Trails of rock and dust extend out from them. They reflect sunlight and look like rays coming out of the crater.

The Moon is not a planet. It travels in an orbit around Earth. "Moon" light is actually "Sun" light. Your part of Earth is not facing the Sun at night. However, the Sun's light reaches the Moon and bounces into space. Some of this reflected light reaches Earth.

▷ **What are conditions on the Moon like?**

Astronauts landed in the Sea of Tranquility on their first visit to the Moon.

C 13

What Are Constellations?

When you look into the night sky, what else can you see besides the Moon? If the sky is dark enough, you can also see the stars. What are stars? A star is a large, hot ball of gas that is held together by gravity and gives off its own light. Stars look like points of light in the night sky. Unlike the Moon, stars are far outside the solar system.

In the past people looked at the stars and saw them arranged in groups that formed patterns in the sky. These patterns are called **constellations**. To these people the patterns looked like pictures of animals or people.

How can you find a star like Rigel in the night sky? The easiest way is by looking for its constellation. Rigel, for example, is a star in the constellation Orion, the hunter.

The pattern of stars in a constellation always looks the same even though the constellations appear to move across the sky. As Earth travels in its orbit around the Sun, its night side faces different

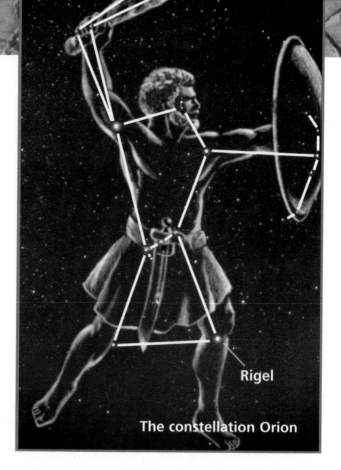

Rigel

The constellation Orion

directions. You see only the constellations that are in that direction. The constellation Orion, for example, is a winter constellation. We see it from the Northern Hemisphere in the winter months.

▷ **Why do constellations appear to move across the sky?**

Constellations seen from the Northern Hemisphere during different seasons

Pegasus

Corona Borealis

Fall Sky

Summer Sky

Winter Sky

Canis Major

Spring Sky

Leo

Aquila

Why It Matters

Earth is teaming with life and movement. The Sun's energy helps produce seasons, day-to-day weather, and climates.

When astronauts first visited the Moon in 1969, they faced a tough problem. How do you survive in such a place? They had to bring all of the things they needed to stay alive all the way from Earth.

Earth is the only member of the solar system that supports life as we know it.

Visit **www.mhscience02.com** to do a research project on the solar system.

Think and Write

1. How would you state your address in space? Explain your answer.

2. How is gravity important for Earth?

3. How does the Sun affect life on Earth?

4. Why is the Moon unlivable compared with Earth?

5. **Critical Thinking** Would you weigh the same on all of the planets? Explain your answer.

ART LINK

Construct a mobile. Make a model of the solar system. Use a hanger, string, and construction paper or clay. Be sure to include all the planets.

SOCIAL STUDIES LINK

Research the planets. Learn more about Earth's neighbors. Which planets have moons? Rings? Which planets are most likely to support life? Use the Internet or an encyclopedia.

LITERATURE LINK

Read *2061: Photographing Mars* to learn about a teacher's trip to Mars. Try the activities at the end of the book.

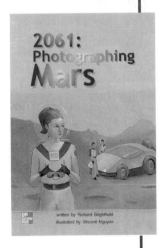

2061: Photographing **Mars**

written by Richard Brightfield
illustrated by Vincent Nguyen

TECHNOLOGY LINK

At the Computer Visit **www.mhscience02.com** for more links.

LESSON 2

Earth's Changing Crust

Vocabulary

fault, C18

geologist, C18

magma, C21

lava, C21

weathering, C22

erosion, C22

deposition, C25

meteorite, C26

Get Ready

What causes an earthquake? An earthquake seems to happen without warning. The ground shakes suddenly, often with enough power to damage objects on the surface.

Where do earthquakes happen? Earthquakes are common in places where the crust is "cracked." One such crack extends through much of the state of California. Why do you think earthquakes happen along this crack?

Process Skill

You experiment when you perform a test to support or disprove a hypothesis.

Explore Activity

What Makes the Crust Move?

Procedure: Design Your Own

Materials

4–6 matching books
(optional)

layers of clay or
modeling compound
(optional)

plastic knife

cubes

wax paper

1 **Make a Model** Work with a partner to model layers of rock. You may use books, clay, or other materials to represent rock layers. Build your model on wax paper. Include a "crack" down through the layers. Stack cubes on the top of the model to represent buildings and other surface features.

2 **Experiment** Find as many ways of moving the model as you can to show how the crust may move during an earthquake. What happens to the surface features as you move the model each way? Draw and describe each.

3 **Experiment** How can you show movement without causing any visible effect on the surface features?

Drawing Conclusions

1 How many different ways could you move your model? How were they different?

2 **Communicate** How did each way you moved the model affect the surface features? How did each way change the positions of the layers? Explain.

3 **Communicate** How did you move the model without moving the surface features? Did the model change in any way? Explain.

4 **Going Further: Experiment** How can you use your model to show how a mountain might rise up high above sea level? Explain and demonstrate.

What Makes the Crust Move?

Earth's crust is constantly moving,
if not in one place then in another.
Sometimes it moves quickly enough to
be seen and felt. People who have been
through an earthquake tell of seeing
the ground heave up and down like an
ocean wave.

Earthquakes are related to cracks in
the crust called **faults**. These faults
may have formed from earlier earthquakes. Sometimes they form while
the earthquake happens. During an
earthquake the crust on either side, or
on both sides, of a fault is in motion.

During an earthquake vibrations
travel through the crust. The farther
away people are from the earthquake,
the harder it is for them to feel the
vibrations. However, delicate devices
called *seismographs* (SIGHZ·muh·grafs)
can record this motion at locations all
around the crust.

Most of the time, however, the crust
moves very slowly. Rocks can move
slowly on either side of a fault over
centuries. People realize there is
movement only when something
visibly changes position. Not all
motion happens along faults, either.
Often, layers of the crust bend, as
shown in the picture below. Bending,
like motion along a fault, may happen
gradually over time.

To measure crust movement,
surveyors (suhr·VAY·uhrz) measure
elevation—how high a place is above
sea level. They leave plaques called
bench marks that tell the exact location
and elevation of a place. When some
bench marks are remeasured, they are
found to have risen or sunk.

Geologists (jee·AHL·uh·jists),
scientists who study Earth, place sensitive devices all along faults, such as the
San Andreas Fault in California. They
hope that records of tiny movements
can be used to predict an earthquake.

**Fossils in
mountain areas**

**Remains of
ancient sea life
are sometimes
found in rock
layers high up in
mountains.**

Plate

Sinking

Rising

Mantle

Core

Convection currents

Layers of Earth

Inner core

Outer core

Mantle

Crust

Plate Tectonics

The crust is Earth's hard surface. Compared with the distance to Earth's center, it is very thin. It is only about one-thousandth of Earth's thickness.

Under the crust is the mantle, Earth's thickest layer. The rock material here is solid. However, it can flow like a liquid—as putty can "flow" when you squeeze it between your hands. Below the mantle is Earth's core. It is in two parts, a liquid outer core and a solid inner core.

The rock material in the mantle is in motion, something like heated water in a pot. It rises and pushes against the bottom of the crust. This movement causes the thin, brittle crust at the surface to break into pieces, or *plates*. The plates themselves can move along Earth's surface. Earthquakes and the slow motions of the crust all result from moving plates.

▶ **How are earthquakes related to faults and plates in the crust?**

QUICK LAB

FOR SCHOOL OR HOME

Model of Earth

BE CAREFUL! Students who are allergic to peanuts should not do this activity.

graham crackers

PEANUT BUTTER
Smooth

1. **Infer** You will use four materials to make a model of Earth on wax paper. Each material is one of Earth's layers. Read step 2. Decide which material represents which layer. Decide how thick each layer needs to be.

2. **Make a Model** Wash your hands. Cover a hazelnut with a layer of peanut butter. Put the covered nut in a plastic bag of mashed banana so that banana covers it completely. Roll the result into graham cracker crumbs on wax paper.

3. **Draw Conclusions** How does each material represent a different layer?

4. How thick did you decide to make each layer? Explain your reasoning.

What Forces Act on the Crust?

As the plates of the crust move, they can collide. They can pull away from each other. They can also slide past each other. These movements cause three kinds of forces to act on the crust.

- *Tension* stretches or pulls apart the crust.

- *Compression* squeezes or pushes together the crust.

- *Shear* twists, tears, or pushes one part of the crust past another.

Each of these forces can cause a fault to form in the crust. Each can cause movement along a fault. These forces can also result in other kinds of motion in the crust.

As forces inside Earth cause the crust to move upward, the land is built up. Compression can crumple rock layers into wavy folds. Mountains can be formed when two pieces of crust crash together.

The impact squeezes the crust, causing it to crumple into huge folds. Mountains made of crumpled and folded layers of rock are called *fold mountains*. The Appalachians, the Alps, and the Himalayas are all ranges of fold mountains.

Tension and shear can also build up the crust. Mountains can be formed as the crust is pulled apart. How?

Forces in the Crust

Fold mountains

Layers of rock

Tension

Compression

Shear

Hot molten rock deep below Earth's surface, called **magma**, rises upward. If magma reaches the surface, it may flow out as **lava**.

Lava flows out or is hurled out when a volcano erupts. A volcano is building a new island off the coast of Iceland. Its lava is gushing up through a crack between two pieces of crust that are being pulled apart.

Tension and shear also cause great blocks of crust to break apart cleanly and move along faults. Blocks of crust moving along a fault can form *fault-block mountains*. A vast region of fault-block mountains known as the Basin and Range Province blankets several western states (see map).

Surtsey, an island near Iceland, is forming from an undersea volcano.

▷ **What are three forces that act on Earth's crust?**

Fault-block mountains

Basin and Range Province

What Other Forces Shape Earth's Surface?

While movements of the crust are building up Earth's surface, other forces are at work breaking it down. These processes are known as **weathering** (WETH·uhr·ing) and **erosion** (i·ROH·zhuhn). Weathering is the breaking down of the materials of Earth's crust into smaller pieces. Erosion is the picking up and carrying away of the pieces. Weathering and erosion have been going on for billions of years. They both happen in many ways.

Physical Weathering

Weathering happens when the crust is exposed to water, air, and changes in temperature. How do these break down rocks?

Water can break down the crust in many ways. Water can dissolve some minerals right out of the crust. Moving water can make pieces of rock bang into each other. Small chips can break

Rounded pebbles near a churning river

off the surface of the rock. This causes the rock to get smaller and rounder. The churning waters of a stream can wear down big pieces of rock into small rounded pebbles.

Wind is moving air. The wind blows sand and other broken bits of rock over Earth's surface. These particles also wear away rock.

If the temperature drops low enough, water can freeze. When water freezes it expands, or takes up more space. Water freezing in cracks in rocks expands against the rock. The force of the expanding water is so great that it can split the rock apart.

Limestone cavern

Rock formation carved by wind-blown sand

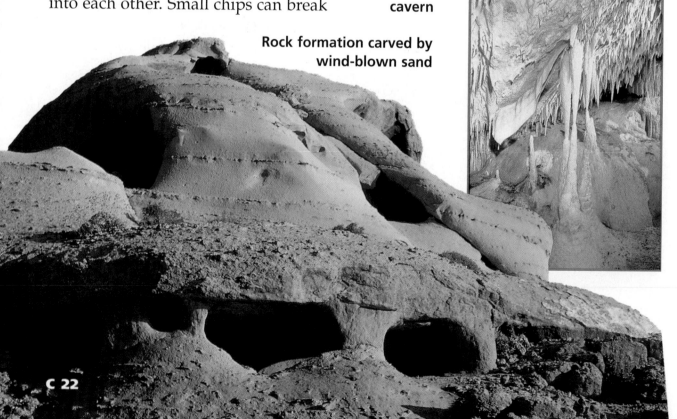

The action of plant roots also causes rocks to weather and erode.

Changes in temperature also cause rock to expand and contract. A rock may be made of a number of different materials. Sometimes one part of a rock expands or contracts more than another part. This difference can cause one part of the rock to push or pull against another part of the rock. Some geologists think that this eventually can cause the rock to break.

Chemical Weathering

Air contains gases that react chemically to form new substances. Oxygen in air reacts with iron to form rust. Carbon dioxide and sulfur dioxide in air react with rain to form acids. These acids eat away at limestone rocks. A limestone cavern was once solid rock. Acid rainwater seeping through the rock dissolved part of it. It "ate away" a huge hole—the cavern.

Erosion

Erosion is the carrying away of pieces of weathered rock by gravity, water, wind, and ice. Piece by piece erosion can carry away a boulder, a hill, or even a whole mountain range!

The greatest agent of erosion is water. From the moment a drop of water falling from the sky first hits the ground, it erodes the land.

It may not seem like much, but think of how many raindrops fall in a rainstorm. Altogether they can move a lot of soil.

Once water reaches the ground, it begins to flow downhill. Moving water can push and carry things along with it. Water running downhill picks up pieces of rock and carries them downhill. The faster the water is moving, the bigger the pieces of rock it can move.

Houses near the shore may be affected by erosion.

> ▶ **How do weathering and erosion work together to shape Earth's surface?**

How Can Wind and Ice Erode Rock?

Wind is moving air. Wind can push things along with it, just like moving water. Wind does not exert as hard a push as water moving at the same speed, however. Therefore, wind mostly erodes pieces of rock that are the size of sand particles or smaller.

Ice also causes a lot of erosion. The Margerie Glacier in Alaska is a moving river of ice. It may not move as quickly as water, but don't underestimate its power. When the ice of a glacier freezes onto rock and then the glacier moves downhill, the rock is torn right out of the ground. This glacier can carry chunks of rock bigger than your house with ease.

Glaciers also wear away the land as they flow over it. Place an ice cube in some sand for a minute or two. Then look at the bottom of the ice cube. What has become frozen into the bottom of the ice cube? Now rub the bottom of the ice cube on a bar of soap. What happens to the surface of the bar of soap?

Rocks of all sizes become frozen into the bottom of a glacier. As the glacier moves, the rock beneath it is scratched and worn down.

> **How do wind and ice cause erosion?**

The Margerie Glacier in Alaska

This satellite photo of the Mississippi River near New Orleans shows the deposition of sediment carried by the river.

Gulf of Mexico

As water stops flowing, pieces of rock are deposited.

Bedrock

Deposition

Layers of sediment

Where Do Eroded Rocks Go?

What happens to pieces of rock that are carried along by wind, moving ice, or moving water? A fast wind eventually slows down. A glacier stops moving and eventually melts at its front end and sides. All streams eventually slow down and end when they flow into a large body of water, such as a lake or ocean.

When water stops moving, it also stops carrying along bits and pieces of rock. The pieces of rock are dropped to the bottom of the stream, lake, or ocean. The dropping off of bits of eroded rock is called **deposition** (dep·uh·ZISH·uhn).

Deposition also takes place when glaciers melt and winds stop blowing. Layer by layer, pile after pile, bits and pieces of rock deposited by water, wind, and ice build up Earth's surface.

Very slowly deposition may fill up depressions, or basins, in Earth's surface. It can build up land along shorelines and at the end of rivers. Deposition does not seem as dramatic as colliding continents. However, the slow, steady work of deposition is one of the greatest constructive actions on Earth.

READING Sequence of Events
What happens to rocks after they break down?

C 25

What Forces Shape the Moon's Surface?

Earth's Moon, our nearest neighbor in space, is a far different place from Earth. There is no evidence of earthquake faults as on Earth's crust. There are no erupting volcanoes. In fact, there is no evidence of any of the kinds of motion that Earth's crust has.

Without air and water, there can be very little weathering or erosion. The Moon has almost no air or water. There are no streams, no glaciers, and no wind. The only weathering and erosion is due to the impact of rocks from space hitting the Moon's surface.

These rocks from space that strike a surface are called **meteorites**. Some craters formed by the impact of meteorites are big enough to be seen from Earth. Others are so tiny the entire crater is on a single mineral crystal.

Can meteorites also strike Earth's surface and produce craters? Yes. However, Earth's atmosphere protects its surface from many such impacts.

Meteorite impacts have been recorded on the Moon's surface.

Rocks from space "burn up" as they pass through Earth's atmosphere. The Moon has little atmosphere. How does that fact affect the Moon's surface?

Meteorite impacts shatter rocks on the Moon and also create a lot of heat. The heat melts the rock. Pieces of rock may melt together, and droplets and globs of molten rock can splatter outward. Over time continual meteorite impacts break down the rock. The end result is a mixture of shattered pieces of rock, rock droplets, and melted-together bits of rock.

▷ **How do meteorites shape the Moon's surface?**

Why It Matters

Natural forces change Earth and the other planets in our solar system. As the solar system has been explored, evidence of surface changes and erosion has been found on other worlds. There are perhaps thousands of volcanoes on Venus. The largest volcano in the solar system is Mars's Olympus Mons. It is 24 km (15 mi) high and 550 km (344 mi) across.

Some of Jupiter's moons also show evidence of constructive and destructive forces. The *Voyager* and *Galileo* spacecraft even sent back pictures showing some of Io's volcanoes erupting. The moons Ganymede, Callisto, and Europa have water and ice. The presence of water, organic compounds, and internal heat mean life may be possible on Europa.

Think and Write

1. What are some types of evidence that show Earth's crust has moved?

2. What are three types of forces acting on Earth's crust?

3. How are earthquakes measured?

4. What is the difference between weathering and erosion?

5. **Critical Thinking** How do fault-block mountains compare with fold mountains?

L·I·N·K·S

SOCIAL STUDIES LINK

Research earthquakes. Learn more about earthquakes in the United States. Where are they most common? What happened to the cities where they occurred? How did people overcome these disasters and plan for the future? Write a report to share what you have learned.

LITERATURE LINK

Read *Quinto's Volcano* to learn about a boy who overcomes his fear of the sea and saves his village. Try the activities at the end of the book.

Quinto's Volcano

WRITING LINK

Write a paragraph. How can people plan ahead to prepare for an earthquake or other force that can change the crust suddenly?

TECHNOLOGY LINK

At the Computer Visit **www.mhscience02.com** for more links.

Science, Technology,

Waves of Erosion

Have you ever stood by the ocean and felt a wave pull the sand from under your feet? Waves constantly carry sand away from a beach, bit by bit.

People who live by beaches can watch their "front yards" slowly disappear. Many beach homes are built on stilts. That puts the buildings above water during high tides and storms. However, if the sand supporting the stilts washes away, the houses fall!

If there are cliffs on a shoreline, the pounding waves can wear away the lowest parts. Eventually the cliffs collapse and fall into the water. Then waves slowly break the rocks into smaller pieces. In time the cliffs will become sand.

Stormy winter weather increases erosion. Fierce winds push the waves, giving them the strength to pick up and carry small stones. The stones pound cliffs along with the waves and help to break the rocks. The stronger wind also pushes waves farther inland.

Some towns truck in sand to replace what's lost. Other towns build breakwaters close to shore. The stone and concrete breakwaters reduce the force of the waves before they reach shore. An island or a sandbar close to shore serves as a natural breakwater.

Nearly all sand and rock removed by wave erosion is deposited elsewhere. Only a small percentage is carried out to sea.

Waves can wear away the sand that supports a beachfront home.

People sometimes build sea walls to try to protect the beaches from pounding waves.

What Did I Learn?

1. Beach homes may be protected from high tides by

A sea walls
B stilts
C breakwaters
D all of the above

2. The main idea of this story is that

F people should not live near the beach
G beaches are affected by erosion
H towns should build sea walls to protect beaches
J all of the above

AT THE COMPUTER Visit www.mhscience02.com to learn more about erosion.

Minerals of Earth's Crust

Get Ready

How many substances do you think make up Earth's solid surface, the crust? Would you believe about 2,000? The substances that make up Earth's crust are minerals. The formations you see here at Mono Lake in California are made entirely of a mineral called calcium carbonate. How can you tell one mineral from another?

Process Skill

You observe when you use one or more of the senses to identify or learn about an object or event.

Explore Activity

How Can You Identify a Mineral?

Materials

mineral samples

clear tape

red marker

copper penny or wire

porcelain tile

hand lens

nail

Procedure

1 **Communicate** Use tape and a marker to label each sample with a number. Make a table with the column headings shown. Fill in numbers under "Mineral" to match your samples.

2 **Observe** Use the table shown as a guide to collect data on each sample. Fill in the data in your table. Turn to the table on page C35 for more ideas to fill in "Other."

Drawing Conclusions

1 Use your data and the table below to identify your samples. Were you sure of all your samples? Explain.

2 Which observations were most helpful? Explain.

3 **Going Further: Experiment** How could you make a better Scratch (Hardness) test?

Color = color of surface

Porcelain Plate Test = the color you see when you rub the sample gently on porcelain

Shiny Like a Metal = reflects light like a metal, such as aluminum foil or metal coins

Scratch (Hardness): Does it scratch copper? A piece of glass?

Other: Is it very dense? (Is a small piece heavy?) Has it got flat surfaces?

	Mineral	Color	Shiny Like a Metal (Yes/No)	Porcelain Plate Test	Scratch (Hardness)	Other

Main Idea Earth's crust contains many types of minerals with important uses.

How Can You Identify a Mineral?

What do diamond rings, talcum powder, and aluminum foil have in common? They are made from minerals . So are copper wire, teeth fillings, china dishes, and table salt.

With so many differences in minerals, what can they have in common? Minerals are solid materials of Earth's crust. Like all matter they are made of elements. Some minerals, like gold, silver, copper, and carbon, are made of one element. Most minerals are chemical compounds, that is, two or more elements joined together.

Whether it is an element or a compound, each mineral has a definite chemical composition. Scientists can classify minerals by identifying the elements or compounds they are made of.

As minerals form, their atoms and molecules fall into fixed patterns. These patterns cause minerals to form geometric shapes, called *crystals*. Different patterns form different crystal shapes. You can see the six main crystal shapes on these pages.

No two minerals are exactly alike. Each mineral has a different composition. Each has its own set of properties

Crystal Shapes

Hexagonal

The "lead" in a lead pencil is not the metal element lead at all. It is the mineral graphite (GRAF·ight), which is a form of the element carbon.

Tetragonal

The mineral chalcopyrite (kal·kuh·PIGH·right) is a compound made of the elements copper, iron, and sulfur. It is where much of our copper comes from. Copper is used for wire, coins, pots, and pans.

Cubic

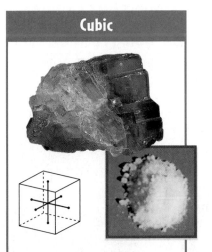

Rock salt, which is used to melt ice, is the mineral halite (HAL·ight). It is a compound made of the elements sodium and chlorine.

that you can use to tell them apart. Crystal shape is one property. However, telling the exact chemical composition of most minerals or their crystal shape isn't easy. This requires special instruments.

Here are some simpler properties to use.

- The color of the outer surface of the mineral is the first thing you see. However, if a mineral is exposed to weather, it can become discolored. Therefore, you should always observe color on a fresh surface. Color alone cannot be used to identify most minerals. Why not? Some minerals come in a variety of colors, and some colors are common to many minerals.

- **Luster** is the way light bounces off a mineral. Minerals with a metallic luster are shiny, like metals. Graphite has a metallic luster.

  Minerals with a nonmetallic luster may look shiny or dull. Nonmetallic luster can be described as glassy, waxy, pearly, earthy, oily, or silky. Talc has a nonmetallic luster often described as oily.

▷ **What are the characteristics of a mineral?**

Orthorhombic

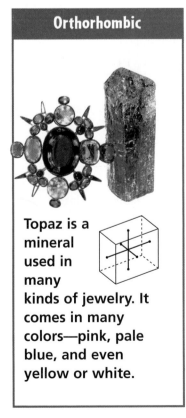

Topaz is a mineral used in many kinds of jewelry. It comes in many colors—pink, pale blue, and even yellow or white.

Monoclinic

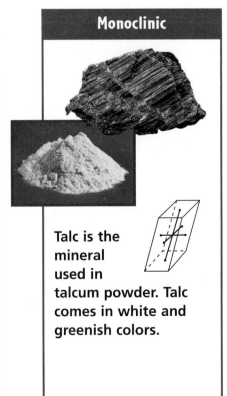

Talc is the mineral used in talcum powder. Talc comes in white and greenish colors.

Triclinic

The mineral kaolinite (KAY·uh·luh·night) is used in china plates and ceramic objects. It comes in many colors—red, white, reddish brown, and even black.

Galena has three cleavage planes. It breaks into cubes.

Mica has one cleavage plane. It breaks into sheets.

Hematite has a blackish color but a reddish streak.

How Else Can You Identify Minerals?

Here are three other ways to identify a mineral.

- **Streak** is the color of the powder left when a mineral is rubbed against a hard, rough surface. Rub it against a porcelain streak plate. The streak is always the same for a given mineral, even if the mineral varies in color.

   The streak may not be the color of the outer surface of the mineral. Fool's gold, pyrite, is brassy yellow, but it has a greenish black streak. Gold has a yellow streak. You would need a streak plate to identify real gold.

- **Hardness** is a measure of how well a mineral resists scratching. Soft minerals are easily scratched. Mohs' scale of hardness is a numbered list of minerals. Talc, number 1, is the softest mineral. It can be scratched with your fingernail. Any item on the list, including the tools, can scratch something above it. You can use the tools to help find the hardness.

- The way a mineral breaks is also helpful. Some minerals have **cleavage**. This property is the tendency of a mineral to break along flat surfaces. Cleavage is described by the number of directions, or planes, along which the mineral breaks.

READING

Tables

Which mineral does a fingernail scratch? Which does a glass plate scratch?

Mohs' Scale of Hardness		
Hardness	Sample Mineral	Tool
1 2	Talc Gypsum	
		Fingernail
3	Calcite	
		Copper penny/wire
4	Fluorite	
		Iron nail
5	Apatite	
		Glass plate
6	Feldspar	
		Steel file
7	Quartz	
		Streak plate
8 9 10	Topaz Corundum Diamond	

A form of calcite shows double image because it refracts light twice as you look through it.

READING
Tables

How is hornblende different from quartz? From feldspar? From mica?

Properties of Minerals

Mineral	Color(s)	Luster (Shiny as Metals)	Porcelain Plate Test (Streak)	Cleavage (Number)	Hardness (Tools Scratched By)	Density (Compared with Water)
Gypsum	colorless, gray, white, brown	no	white	varies	2 (all six tools)	2.3
Quartz	colorless, various colors	no	none	no	7 (streak plate)	2.6
Pyrite	brassy, yellow	yes	greenish black	no	6 (steel file, streak plate)	5.0
Calcite	colorless, white, pale blue	no	colorless, white	yes—3	3 (all but fingernail)	2.7
Galena	steel gray	yes	gray to black	yes—3 (cubes)	2.5 (all but fingernail)	7.5
Feldspar	gray, green, yellow, white	no	colorless	yes—2	6 (steel file, streak plate)	2.5
Mica	colorless, silvery, black	no	white	yes—1 (thin sheets)	2–3 (all but fingernail)	3.0
Hornblende	green to black	no	gray to white	yes—2	5–6 (steel file, streak plate)	3.4
Bauxite	gray, red, brown, white	no	gray	no	1–3 (all but fingernail)	2.0–2.5
Hematite	black, gray, red-brown	yes	red or red-brown	no	1–6 (all)	5.3

Many minerals do not break smoothly. They are said to have *fracture*. Quartz, for example, shows jagged edges when it breaks.

Some minerals have special properties that help you identify them. Magnetite, for example, is attracted by a magnet. Some minerals are more *dense* than others. That means they have a lot of mass packed into a given volume. *Density* makes a sample feel quite heavy. Gold, silver, and galena are examples of dense minerals.

▷ **How do tests for streak, hardness, and cleavage help you tell minerals apart?**

How Do Minerals Form?

Where do you find minerals? The answer is simple–in the ground. Minerals make up the rocks of the crust. If you examine rocks with a hand lens, you can often find some of the most common rock-forming minerals in the rock.

How do minerals form? Many form when hot liquid rock, or magma, cools and hardens into a solid. Magma is very hot, and its molecules move very fast. When magma cools, its molecules slow down and get closer together. Then they connect into a pattern, forming crystals. The longer it takes magma to cool, the more time the crystals have to grow, and the larger they get.

Some of the rarest minerals form deep within the Earth. The temperatures are high at great depths. The weight of rocks overhead presses down on rocks below, like a huge pressure cooker. The heat and pressure produce minerals such as diamonds. Movements of Earth's crust then bring the minerals near the surface, where they can be mined.

Diamond

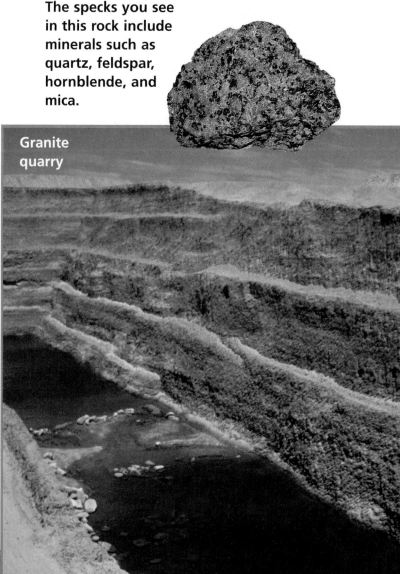

Crystals can form from the cooling of hot water. Water heated by magma inside the Earth is rich in dissolved minerals. Hot water can hold more dissolved minerals than cold water. As the water cools, it is able to hold less of the dissolved minerals. The minerals that can no longer stay dissolved form crystals. The huge quartz crystal shown below formed in this way.

The specks you see in this rock include minerals such as quartz, feldspar, hornblende, and mica.

Granite quarry

Quartz crystal

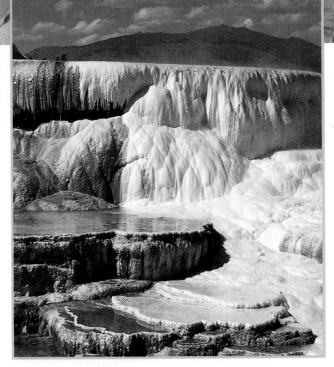

The piles of brightly colored minerals in this hot spring form when the heated water cools as it is exposed to the air.

These crystals then slowly settle to the bottom of the water.

Minerals can also form from evaporation. Ocean water contains many dissolved substances. As the ocean water evaporates, the substances that were dissolved form crystals. Common table salt is mined in areas that were once covered with salt water. The salt is a mineral, halite. It was left behind when an ancient sea evaporated.

READING Sequence of Events
In what ways do minerals form?

QUICK LAB

FOR SCHOOL OR HOME

Growing Crystals

Your teacher will put a cup of hot water onto a counter for you.

BE CAREFUL! Wear goggles. Use a kitchen mitt if you need to hold or move the cup. Don't touch the hot water.

1. Use a plastic spoon to gradually add small amounts of salt to the water. Stir. Keep adding and stirring until no more will dissolve.

2. Tie one end of a 15-cm piece of string to a crystal of rock salt. Tie the other end to a pencil. Lay the pencil across the cup so that the crystal hangs in the hot salt water without touching the sides or bottom.

3. **Observe** Observe the setup for several days. Record what you see.

4. Did any crystals grow? If so, did they have many shapes or just one? Explain your answer. If not, how would you change what you did if you tried again?

What Are Minerals Used For?

Can you find minerals being used at home or school? Minerals are used to make many products, from steel to electric light bulbs.

Some of the most useful minerals are called **ores** (AWRZ). An ore is a mineral that contains a useful substance. Ores contain enough useful substances to make them valuable to mine.

For example, iron comes from the mineral hematite (HEE·muh·tight). Iron is used to make nails, buildings, and even ships. Aluminum comes from the mineral bauxite. It is used for food-wrap foil, soft-drink cans, and pie tins, just to name a few uses.

The iron and aluminum that come from these two ores are *metals*. Metals

Gemstones mark special occasions— such as weddings and birthdays. What is your birthstone? Birthstones are gemstones.

Gypsum is used in drywall, or wall-board, for construction of buildings.

have many useful properties. Metals conduct electricity and can be stretched into wires. The metal copper, for example, comes from a mineral ore. It is used to make electrical wires.

Aluminum is lightweight and strong. It shares these properties with another metal that comes from an ore, magnesium. These metals are ideal for use in building jets and spacecraft.

If you look in a jewelry store window, you'll probably see some minerals called **gems**. Gems are minerals that are valued for being rare and beautiful. You may have seen diamond rings. Rubies and sapphires are other gemstones.

> **What are two types of useful minerals?**

Why It Matters

Minerals are nonrenewable resources. They cannot be replaced as trees can be, for example. They take so long to form that they cannot be replaced in your lifetime.

Because minerals are nonrenewable, they must be *conserved*. To *conserve* means to "use wisely or avoid waste." One way people can conserve minerals is by recycling them—finding ways to treat them or use them again. Researchers can also come up with substitutes to use in place of natural minerals. Many diamonds used in industry for cutting stone, for example, are not natural diamonds.

Think and Write

1. Which properties are most useful to identify a mineral? Explain your answer.

2. What if you had two white samples of talc and gypsum? How could you tell them apart in one step?

3. How does time affect crystals?

4. How useful are metallic ores? Give some ways you use them.

5. **Critical Thinking** How could you avoid the mistake that miners made, thinking fool's gold was real gold? What are all the observations you might make to tell them apart?

L·I·N·K·S

SOCIAL STUDIES LINK

Research minerals. Learn about ways to conserve and recycle minerals. Use the Internet or an encyclopedia.

ART LINK

Make a collage. Cut pictures from magazines of household items that are made from minerals. Paste your pictures on a board.

MATH LINK

Think about shapes. You have learned about the three-dimensional shapes of minerals. How many other regular 3-D shapes do you know? Make a poster illustrating different 3-D shapes.

TECHNOLOGY LINK

At the Computer Visit **www.mhscience02.com** for more links.

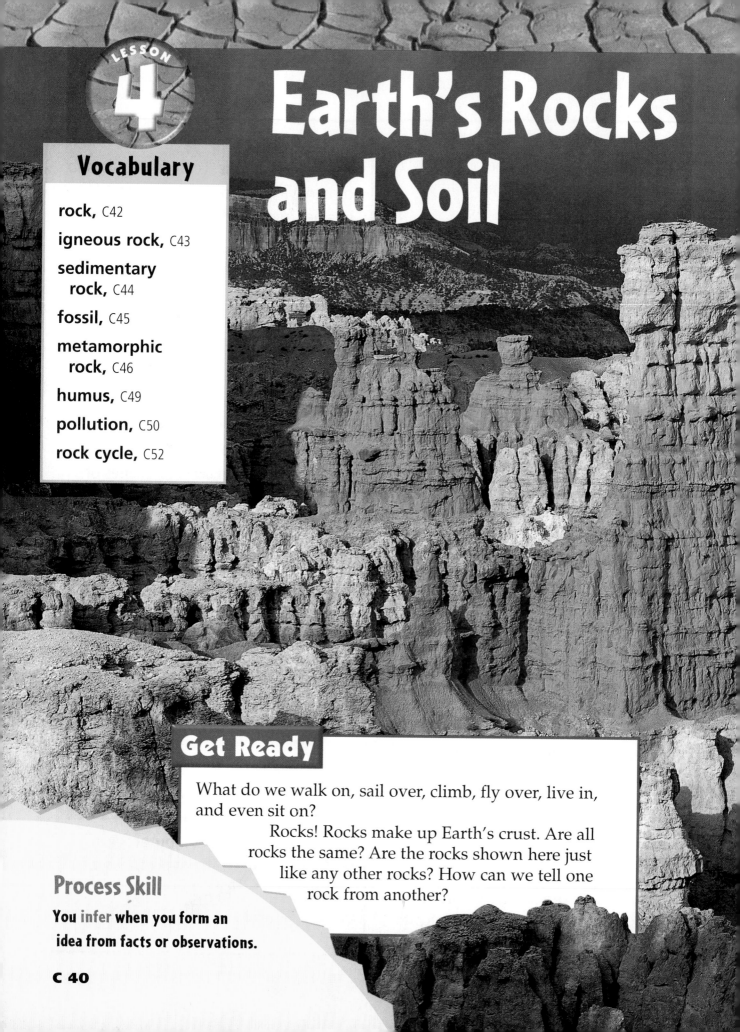

Earth's Rocks and Soil

Vocabulary

rock, C42

igneous rock, C43

sedimentary rock, C44

fossil, C45

metamorphic rock, C46

humus, C49

pollution, C50

rock cycle, C52

Get Ready

What do we walk on, sail over, climb, fly over, live in, and even sit on?

Rocks! Rocks make up Earth's crust. Are all rocks the same? Are the rocks shown here just like any other rocks? How can we tell one rock from another?

Process Skill

You infer when you form an idea from facts or observations.

Explore Activity

How Are Rocks Alike and Different?

Materials

samples of rocks

clear tape

red marker

hand lens

copper wire

streak plate

balance

metric ruler

calculator

Procedure: Design Your Own

1 Use the tape to number each sample in a group of rocks.

2 **Classify** Find a way to sort the group into smaller groups. Determine what properties you will use. Group the rocks that share one or more properties. Your fingernail, the copper wire, and the edge of a streak plate are tools you might use. Scratch gently. Record your results.

3 **Use Numbers** You might estimate the density of each sample. Use a balance to find the mass. Use a metric ruler to estimate the length, width, and height.
Length × width × height = volume
Density = mass ÷ volume

Drawing Conclusions

1 How were you able to make smaller groups? Give supporting details from the notes you recorded.

2 Could you find more than one way to sort the rocks into groups? Give examples of how rocks from two different smaller groups may have a property in common.

3 **Communicate** Share your results with others. Compare your systems for sorting the rocks.

4 **Going Further: Infer** How might a sample be useful based on the properties that you observed?

Main Idea Rocks can be classified according to their composition and properties.

How Are Rocks Alike and Different?

Rocks are mineral treasure chests. A **rock** is any naturally formed solid in the crust made up of one or more kinds of minerals. You can often see mineral crystals in a rock. Sometimes the crystals are too small to see easily.

Look with a hand lens at a piece of granite. You can often find crystals of quartz (whitish), feldspar (pink), mica (black), and even hornblende (black).

Each mineral in a rock has its own streak, hardness, or crystal shape. A rock with several minerals may have a mixture of properties. For example, it may have both hard and soft minerals. It may make both light and dark streaks.

The most exact way to identify a rock is to name the minerals it contains. However, color, density, and the way the rock's surface feels, or its *texture*, are also identifying features. The texture comes from the size, shape, and arrangement of the mineral crystals or grains in a rock. Are the grains large (coarse) or small (fine)? Do they interlock, or can you see each clearly? Are they soft edged or jagged?

A rock's color, density, and texture result from how the rock was formed. Rocks are grouped into three types according to how they were formed.

▷ **What are the characteristics of rocks?**

Igneous Rocks

Extrusive—Cooled Above Ground

Rhyolite (RIGH·uh·light) has a fine texture and is light colored.

Obsidian (uhb·SID·ee·uhn) has no mineral grains and is dark colored.

Basalt (buh·SAWLT) has a fine texture and is dark colored.

What Are Igneous Rocks?

All the rocks on these two pages were at one time deep below Earth's surface. There it is hot enough for some rocks to be melted, or molten. Molten rock material deep below the surface is called magma.

Magma is less dense than the material surrounding it, so it rises toward the surface. Before magma reaches the surface, however, it may cool and harden into solid rock. Rocks that form when melted rock material cools and hardens are called **igneous rocks**.

Often magma makes it to the surface before hardening. Magma reaching the surface is called *lava*. Exposed to the air above ground, lava, too, hardens and cools, forming igneous rocks.

Below ground magma cools slowly. Crystals take a long time to grow. They grow to large (coarse) sizes.

Above ground cooling is much quicker. Crystals are smaller. Lava may cool so quickly that no crystals have a chance to form. What results is obsidian, a solid piece of volcanic glass.

The granite and gabbro shown on this page formed below ground. They both have large mineral crystals. However, granite contains lighter-colored minerals than gabbro.

All the rocks on page C42 formed above ground. They have small crystals or no crystals at all. How do they differ in color?

The texture and color make a difference in how an igneous rock is used. If you were making a monument, which of these rocks might you choose?

 How are igneous rocks formed?

READING

Charts

How could you classify the rocks shown on these two pages? Show your results by making a table with two or three columns and rows. Use the properties as headings, and fill in the table with rock names.

Intrusive—Cooled Below Ground

Granite has a coarse texture. The crystals are large enough to be seen. It is a light-colored rock.

Gabbro (GAB·roh) has a coarse texture, but it is dark colored.

What Are Sedimentary Rocks?

How do the rocks here compare with igneous rocks? These rocks are **sedimentary rocks**. Sedimentary rocks are made of small bits of matter joined together. These bits of matter, or sediments, may be bits of weathered rocks. They may be shells or other remains of living things. Long ago water, wind, and ice picked up sediment and carried it. Eventually they dropped the sediment in places where it collected into layers.

Most common sedimentary rocks are formed when sediment is compacted or cemented together. The weight of layer upon layer of sediment on top of each other compacts or squeezes sediment together.

Coarser sediments are cemented by bits of minerals that "glue" the sediments together. Water that contains dissolved minerals seeps between the coarse pieces of sediment. The water evaporates, and mineral crystals form. These crystals hold together the coarse sediment, turning it into a solid rock.

You can see the pieces of sediment that make up these rocks. These rocks are named by the kind of sediment they contain.

Some sedimentary rocks are made of crystals of minerals that were once dissolved in water. The crystals were left behind when the water evaporated. Halite, the rock salt that is used to melt snow and ice, is formed this way.

A type of limestone consists mostly of a mineral called calcite. The mineral was dissolved in ocean water. As the water evaporated in certain areas, the calcite was left behind as solid limestone.

Some sedimentary rocks are made of substances that were once part of, or made by, living things. Cemented-together shells form *coquina* (koh·KEE·nuh). Coral skeletons form coral limestone.

▷ **How are sedimentary rocks formed?**

Coquina

Sediment (Small to Large)	Rock
Clay	Shale
Silt	Siltstone
Sand	Sandstone
Gravel	Conglomerate

How Are Sedimentary Rocks Useful?

They may be just clumps of bits and pieces, but sedimentary rocks are very useful. Sandstone, for example, is used for buildings and trim. Limestone is used for buildings, trim, monuments, and even park benches. Shale is often broken into pieces that are mixed with other materials to make concrete and cement.

Sedimentary rocks are very useful in helping to piece together Earth's history. They often contain clues, called **fossils**, to life long ago. Fossils are the remains or imprints of living things of the past.

The remains of dead organisms were often covered with mud, sand, or other sediment. Sometimes a living thing left an imprint, such as a footprint, in soft mud. Over centuries of time, the sediment and the remains or imprint hardened into rock. Almost all fossils are found in sedimentary rocks. Why do you think fossils could not be found in an igneous rock?

A type of coal is a sedimentary rock. This coal is called bituminous (bigh·TEW·muh·nuhs) coal, or soft coal. Earth's supplies of coal were formed millions of years ago from dead plants buried in ancient swamps and forests. Coal today is a source of energy, the energy that comes from those ancient forms of life.

▷ **What are some ways sedimentary rocks are used?**

Fossils

Limestone blocks

Bituminous coal lights quickly and provides much energy, but it burns with a lot of soot and yellow smoke.

What Are Metamorphic Rocks?

Deep below Earth's surface, rocks can undergo great change. They are heated by the high temperatures at great depths. They are under pressure from the rocks lying above.

Great heat and pressure can change one rock into another rock. A rock formed under heat and pressure from another kind of rock is called a **metamorphic** (met·uh·MAWR·fik) **rock**. In the process the original rock does not melt under heat and pressure. If it did, it would become an igneous rock. Instead the original rock remains solid, but

- the mineral grains in the original rock may flatten and line up

- the minerals may change their identity; substances in a mineral may be exchanged with substances in surrounding minerals

- the minerals in the original rock may separate into layers of different densities

In each case the result is a rock different from the original.

Original Rock	Metamorphic Rock
Granite (igneous rock)	gneiss (NIGHS)
Shale (sedimentary rock)	slate
Sandstone (sedimentary rock)	quartzite
Limestone (sedimentary rock)	marble
Slate (metamorphic rock)	schist

▷ **How are metamorphic rocks made from other rocks?**

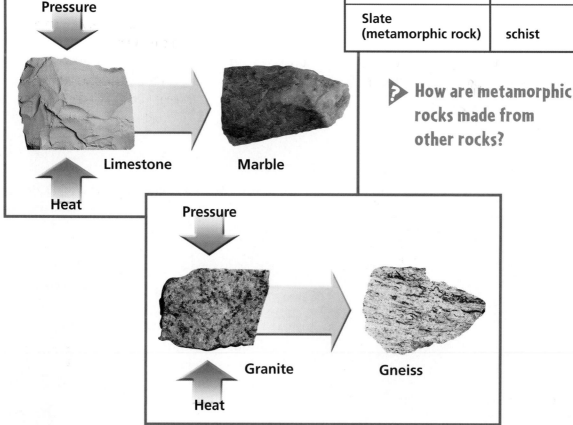

Pressure

Heat

Limestone   Marble

Pressure

Heat

Granite   Gneiss

How Are Metamorphic Rocks Used?

Metamorphic rocks are "rock makeovers." In their remade form, these rocks have new properties that are very useful.

Slate, for example, breaks into thin sheets. The minerals in slate are so tightly packed together that water cannot seep through this rock. This makes slate useful as roofing shingles as well as stepping stones and outdoor floors.

Marble is often shiny. It often contains minerals that give it brilliant colors, from greenish to red. It is easy to carve. It is often a first choice for making statues, floors, countertops, and monuments.

One kind of coal is a metamorphic rock. It is called anthracite, or hard coal. Anthracite is formed from soft coal.

> **Where might you find metamorphic rocks used in your community?**

Anthracite, hard coal, burns cleaner and longer than soft coal, but does not provide as much energy.

The Story of Coal

Millions of Years Ago					
300	280	220	150	10	Present
A forest swamp	Plants die and sink to the bottom.	A thick layer of peat, partly decayed plants, builds up.	The swamp dries up. Buried under layers of sediment, the peat changes to a sedimentary rock called lignite (LIG·night).	Buried by more and more layers of sediment, the lignite becomes more compacted. It forms bituminous coal.	Buried even deeper, bituminous coal is changed by great heat and pressure. It forms anthracite, a metamorphic rock.

Peat

Lignite

Bituminous (soft) coal (sedimentary rock)

Anthracite (hard) coal (metamorphic rock)

READING Diagrams

1. How is the position of the fuel layer changing from picture to picture?
2. How does this position affect what happens to the layer?

C 47

Process Skill BUILDER

SKILL Define Based on Observations

Defining Soil

Earth's crust is made up of rocks and minerals. However, to get to the rocks, you usually have to dig through layers of soil.

Soil looks different at different places. It has different properties. Soil can be sandy. It can be moist.

Just what is soil? Make some observations. Write a definition that fits your observations.

Materials

moist soil sample in plastic bag

sand sample in plastic bag

hand lens

2 cups

2 plastic spoons

Procedure

1 **Observe** Use a hand lens to examine a sample of moist soil. What materials can you find? How do their sizes compare? Write a description.

2 Some soils are more like sand. How does a sample of sand compare with your moist soil sample?

3 **Use Variables** Which sample absorbs water more quickly? Fill a cup halfway with sand and another with moist soil. Pour a spoonful of water in each at the same time.

4 **Experiment** Which absorbs more water? Make a prediction. Find a way to test your prediction.

5 **Experiment** Make any other observations. Look for other differences.

Drawing Conclusions

1 Based on your observations, what is soil made up of?

2 How may soils differ?

3 **Define** Write a definition for *soil*. Take into account all your observations.

Where Does Soil Come From?

Under a hand lens, you can see that any soil shows that it is a mixture of many things. The main ingredient in soil is weathered rock. Soil may also contain water, air, bacteria, and **humus**. Humus is decayed plant or animal material.

Where does soil come from? A layer of solid rock weathers into chunks. The chunks weather into smaller pieces. Living things die and decay and form humus.

Gradually layers of soil, or soil horizons, develop. If you dig down through soil, you can see many layers and the solid rock, bedrock, beneath it. How do the horizons differ?

Soils differ in different locations. In polar deserts there is no A horizon at the top. However, grassland and forest soils can have very thick A horizons. Why do you think this is so? Some soils are very sandy. Why? How would they differ from soils in many farms?

Sometimes the materials in soil match the bedrock below it. Sometimes they do not match. Can you explain why?

Soil is Earth's greatest treasure. Most plants need soil to grow. Therefore, almost all living things depend on soil for food—and survival. One of the most important uses of soil is farming. All of the food you eat depends on soil.

> **What is soil made up of?**

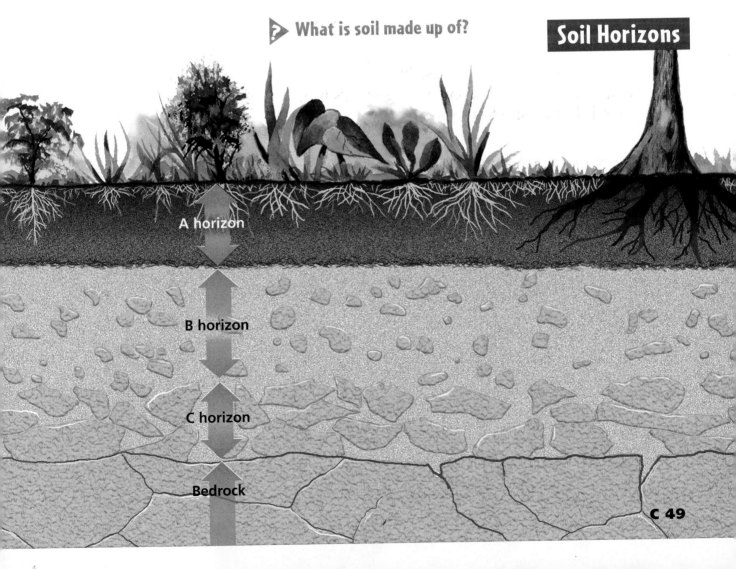

Soil Horizons

A horizon

B horizon

C horizon

Bedrock

How Can People Ruin Soil?

People depend on soil. Would you believe people ruin and waste soil? That might include you! It may be people in general or industries—such as factories or farms.

People often get rid of garbage and hazardous wastes by burying them in soil. Hazardous wastes are wastes that may be poisonous or cause diseases, such as cancer.

Spraying chemicals on soil to kill unwanted animals and plants also affects the soil. These chemicals become a part of the soil.

Tossing foam cups, plastic wrappers, and materials onto the ground, instead of using trash baskets, harms the soil. They do not decay. They remain as wastes in the soil. They may build up and make the soil unusable.

All these materials add up to **pollution**. *Pollution* means adding any harmful substances to Earth's land, water, or air. The substances are called *pollutants*. When people cause pollution, we say they *pollute* soil, water, or air.

Not only do people pollute soil, but they often waste it, too. For example, soil needs plants. When plants die and decay, they add valuable substances back into the soil. When a crop is harvested, the plants are removed. They do not decay and return nutrients back into the soil. Growing the same crop year after year uses up the nutrients in soil. Plants don't grow well in nutrient-poor soil.

Plant roots hold soil particles together. They protect soil from being blown away by wind or washed away by water. If plants are removed or if weak, sickly plants are growing in an area, the soil is exposed to erosion by wind and rain.

Letting cattle graze in the same area for a long time also exposes soil. Cutting down forests for lumber exposes soil, too. As a result of any of these practices, soil that took centuries to form may be removed in weeks.

▶ **How do people pollute and waste the soil?**

Each piece of garbage was thrown away by somebody. It takes people to make garbage. What are some ways to prevent this kind of pollution?

By building terraces people in Bali have been able to farm steep hillsides.

Contour means "shape." How does contour plowing prevent water from running downhill?

How Can People Protect the Soil?

People need to take care of soil. We have to protect it from being polluted and wasted. Farmers take care of soil by

- *adding fertilizers and humus.* After growing crops, farmers add these materials to replace minerals removed by crops.

- *using crop rotation.* Each year farmers grow different crops. In this way the soil does not use up the same kinds of minerals year after year. Crops from one year may help replace minerals in the soil that are used up another year.

- *strip farming.* Many crops have stems spaced far apart. Rainwater can run off between the stems and wash soil away. In strip farming strips of tightly growing grasses are grown between more widely spaced crops. The grasses trap runoff and the soil it carries. The next year the position of the strips is switched.

- *contour plowing.* Farmers plow furrows across a slope rather than up and down a slope. Each furrow traps rainwater and keeps it from eroding the soil.

- *terracing.* A hillside is shaped into a series of steps. Runoff water and eroded soil get trapped on the steps. Planting rows of trees to block the wind prevents soil from being blown away.

What can you do to prevent soil from being polluted or wasted? Think about what you toss away as garbage. Is there any way to throw it away to make sure it does not simply end up in the soil? Is there any way to keep from throwing as much garbage away each day as you might?

▶ **What are two ways people can protect the soil?**

What Is the Rock Cycle?

Where do rocks and soil come from? Igneous rocks come from magma or lava. However, where did the magma and lava come from?

Sedimentary rock is made of broken-up pieces of rock. However, where did the pieces of rock come from?

All rocks come from other rocks. Rocks are constantly changing from one rock into another. They change in a never-ending series of processes called the **rock cycle**. Part of this cycle is the weathering of rocks into bits and pieces—some of which may eventually become soil.

Rocks are constantly forming—one changing into another. However, any rock takes a really long time to form. When we dig up a deposit of sandstone or use up the coal in an area, it cannot be replaced. Rocks are a *nonrenewable* resource.

People get into the rock-making process, too. Concrete, porcelain, and brick are all artificial rocks.

READING **Sequence of Events**
What is the path of a rock through the rock cycle?

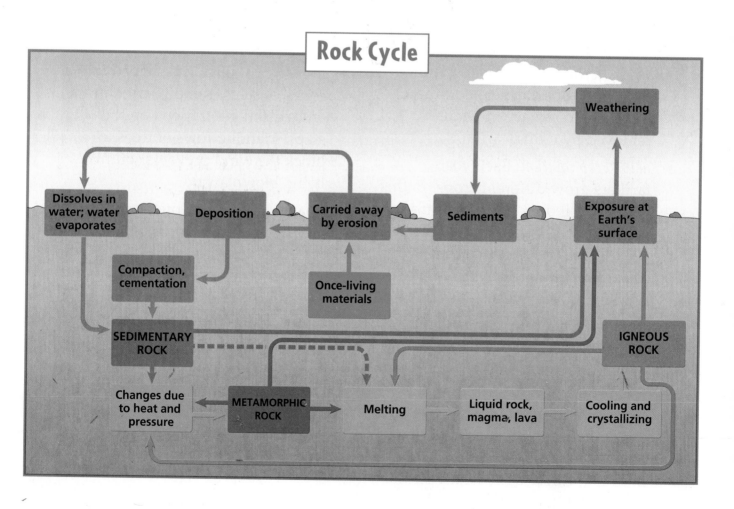

Rock Cycle

C 52

Why It Matters

It is important to be able to tell one type of rock from another. Just think of all the ways you use rocks. What would life be like without them? There would be no mountains to climb, no beaches to walk on. There would be no soil—so that means no food, or forests, or fields. There would be no metals, because metals come from mineral ores that are found in rocks. There would be no bricks, no concrete, no buildings, no . . .

Think and Write

1. How are soils alike? How are they different?

2. How can you tell igneous rocks apart?

3. You pick up a rock. How can you tell if it is a sedimentary rock?

4. **Define** How can you tell rocks apart? Why are they identified in a different way from minerals?

5. **Critical Thinking** How can an igneous rock become a metamorphic rock? Think of three different ways.

L·I·N·K·S

WRITING LINK

Write a paragraph. Even if you don't live anywhere near a farm, you depend on soil. Explain how soil is important to everyone.

SOCIAL STUDIES LINK

Investigate building materials. Observe the buildings and streets in your neighborhood. How many are constructed with the help of rocks? How many different rocks can you identify?

ART LINK

Make a diagram. Where do igneous rocks come from? Draw a picture to show how igneous rocks form.

TECHNOLOGY LINK

At the Computer Visit **www.mhscience02.com** for more links.

Silicon Rules!

It's the second most common element in Earth's crust after oxygen. It's found in almost all rocks, as well as in sand and clay. For centuries, it has been used to make glass. What element is it? It's silicon. Today, silicon is the most important material in computers and many other electronic devices.

Computers are made up of very small electronic circuits called chips. Almost all the chips are made from silicon. A computer chip is only the size of a fingernail but it can contain millions of pieces of information! Some chips carry instructions that tell the computer what to do. Other chips store data.

Silicon is used in computer chips for two reasons. First, it has excellent insulating properties that can endure high temperatures. Second, there's a huge supply of silicon!

Silicon chips are not just in computers. There are probably about 40 things in your home that contain chips! Chips control your video game and CD player. They make telephones and televisions work better.

Chips in some microwave ovens and washing machines "sense" when food is done or when clothes are clean. Your family car probably contains about 12 chips. One day, the car may drive itself using computer chips!

A silicon chip sits on a human fingertip to give an idea of its size.

In the future, chips may be implanted in the eyes of blind people to help them see. Special chips may help deaf people hear. Chips will control many devices around your home and may even respond to voice commands. If you want to turn a light off, for example, you will speak and your chip-controlled lamp will obey your command. If the telephone rings, you will just start talking!

Sometimes, it's hard to see how valuable Earth's resources can be. Desert sand doesn't look useful, but the silicon in it has changed our lives!

A typical computer chip

A CD player contains silicon chips.

What Did I Learn?

1. Which of the following devices use silicon chips?

  A video games
  B CD players
  C microwave ovens
  D all of the above

2. Silicon is the second most common element in Earth's crust after

  F carbon
  G oxygen
  H sulfur
  J hydrogen

AT THE COMPUTER

Visit www.mhscience02.com for more amazing stories and facts about silicon chip technology.

Chapter 6 Review

Vocabulary

Fill each blank with the best word or words from the list.

erosion, C22
fossil, C45
geologist, C18
hydrosphere, C12
igneous rock, C43
lithosphere, C12
metamorphic rock, C46
mineral, C32
ore, C38
planet, C6
sedimentary rock, C44
solar system, C6

1. Rock that changes due to heat and pressure is _____.

2. The oceans are part of Earth's _____.

3. The Sun and planets are part of the _____.

4. A scientist who studies Earth is called a(n) _____.

5. Earth is a(n) _____ that orbits the Sun.

6. A(n) _____ is the imprint of a living thing from the past.

7. _____ is made of small bits of matter joined together.

8. The _____ is the hard outer layer of Earth.

9. A solid material in Earth's crust is called a(n) _____.

10. _____ is a mineral containing a useful substance.

Test Prep

11. The Moon is unlivable compared with Earth because _____.

   A there is no air to breathe

   B there is no water to drink

   C the surface temperature can be hotter than boiling water

   D all of the above

12. Earth's thickest layer is called the _____.

   F mantle

   G crust

   H inner core

   J outer core

13. Fossils are most often found in _____.

   A sedimentary rock

   B lava

   C sand

   D igneous rock

14. Igneous rock is formed from
_____.

  F crystals left behind when water evaporated

  G meteorites that fell to Earth

  H melted rock material that cooled and hardened

  J layers of sediment that were squeezed together

15. The main ingredient in soil is
_____.

  A bacteria

  B weathered rock

  C decayed animal material

  D decayed plant material

Concepts and Skills

16. Process Skills: Define You find a rock that is made up of different-colored layers. It seems to be made of different-sized grains. Some of it looks as though it is made of tiny seashells glued together. What type of rock is it?

17. Critical Thinking Describe two tests you can use to determine what minerals a rock is made of.

18. Reading in Science Explain the sequence of events that would happen if the force that keeps the planets orbiting the Sun did not exist.

19. Scientific Methods Why is it unlikely we will find life on other planets in our solar system?

20. Decision Making What would you need to bring along on a space mission to another planet? Explain your choices.

Boost *your test scores!*

Be Smart!
Visit www.mhscience02.com

Air, Water, and Energy

Did You Ever Wonder?

Where does Earth's freshwater supply come from? When you look at the spectacular waterfalls of Iguazu in Argentina, you might think that there is an endless supply of fresh water on Earth. Is this true? Might we run out of clean drinking water? Where does your drinking water come from?

Earth's Atmosphere

Get Ready

From space Earth's atmosphere appears as a thin blue layer surrounding the planet. From the ground the air may appear different from day to day.

The air may seem clear and clean on some days. If you live in or near a big city, you may have days when the air seems smoky, or "hazy." Why? What kinds of pollutants are in the air that can make it look that way?

Process Skill

You **interpret data** when you use the information that has been gathered to answer questions or solve a problem.

Explore Activity

What Makes Air Dirty?

Materials

12 cardboard strips

petroleum jelly

plastic knife

transparent tape

string

hand lens

metric ruler

marker

Procedure

1 Make square "frames" by taping together the corners of four cardboard strips. Make three frames, and label them A, B, and C. Tie a 30-cm string to a corner of each frame.

2 Stretch and attach three strips of tape across each frame, with all sticky sides facing the same way. Use a plastic knife to spread a thin coat of petroleum jelly across each sticky side.

3 **Use Variables** Hang the frames in different places to try to collect pollutants. Decide on places indoors or outdoors. Be sure to tell a parent or teacher where.

4 **Observe** Observe each frame over four days. Record the weather and air condition each day.

5 **Measure** Collect the frames. Observe the sticky sides with a hand lens and a metric ruler to compare particles.

Drawing Conclusions

1 **Interpret Data** How did the frames change over time? How did the hand lens and ruler help you describe any pollution?

2 **Communicate** Present your data in a graph to show differences in amounts.

3 **Going Further: Use Variables** What kinds of pollutants would your frames not collect? How might you design a collector for them? How might you extend this activity over different periods of time?

Why Do Living Things Need the Atmosphere?

Why couldn't humans live on a planet that does not have an atmosphere as on Earth? Every minute of every day, you need air.

Air is a mixture of nitrogen, oxygen, and a few traces of other gases, including water vapor. This mixture is a vital resource. It supports and protects life on Earth in many ways.

Almost all organisms need air to live. Actually, they need oxygen, one of the gases that is in air. On land living things have structures that enable them to get oxygen directly from the air. Living things in water habitats take in oxygen that is dissolved in the water.

What is oxygen for? Living things take in oxygen for respiration. In this process oxygen is used to break down food so that energy can be gotten from it. As a result of this process, living things give off wastes, including the gas carbon dioxide.

Why doesn't the atmosphere fill up with carbon dioxide? Plants and other producers, living things that have the green substance chlorophyll, take in carbon dioxide. They use it for making food. In the presence of light, these organisms carry on the process called photosynthesis. In this process they make food and give off oxygen.

Producers range in size from green plants to one-celled algae. They replace oxygen in the atmosphere. This makes oxygen a naturally **renewable resource**. A renewable resource is one that can be replaced. It can be replaced in a short enough period of time, such as a human lifetime, to support life on Earth.

Protection

The atmosphere also acts as a protective shield. It shields Earth's surface from harmful energy that comes from

How Earth's Atmosphere Supports Life

One-celled algae of the oceans produce most of Earth's oxygen supply.

Producers take in carbon dioxide and produce food and oxygen.

Oxygen

Animals take in oxygen for respiration. They give off carbon dioxide.

Oxygen

Carbon dioxide

Carbon dioxide

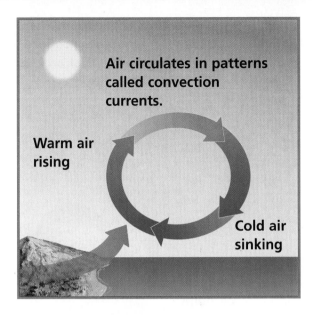

Air circulates in patterns called convection currents.

Warm air rising

Cold air sinking

the Sun. The atmosphere helps screen out harmful ultraviolet rays (UV rays) from the Sun. About 30 km (18.6 mi) above your head is a layer of gas called ozone (OH·zohn). This **ozone layer** screens out from 95 to 99 percent of the Sun's UV rays.

The atmosphere also shields Earth from rocks from space. The "shooting stars" you see on a clear night are not stars. They are rocks from space that burn up due to friction with the air as they speed through the atmosphere.

The atmosphere also protects life from extremes of temperature. Clouds block sunlight during the day. At night they keep much of the heat from escaping into space, so that the planet does not "cool off." Whenever one part of the atmosphere gets hotter than another, the air moves, or circulates, and spreads the heat around.

Most of the air, about 78 percent, is nitrogen. Nitrogen is an important ingredient in food,

namely proteins. How does it get into proteins? Nitrogen is taken from the air by certain kinds of bacteria. These bacteria change the nitrogen into a form that stays in the soil.

Plants use this nitrogen in the soil to make proteins. As living things eat the plants, nitrogen is passed along. It is returned to the soil when living things die.

> ❓ **What does the atmosphere provide for living things?**

READING

Diagrams

1. Do you see any cycles in this diagram? Cycles are continuous processes, where one thing happens after another over and over in the same order.

2. Explain any cycles you see.

Nitrogen in air

Nitrogen goes from air to plants to all living things. When living things die, nitrogen is returned to the soil.

Natural events can add to air pollution.

Industries produce wastes that add to air pollution.

Wearing a mask helps when smog is very heavy.

What Causes Pollution?

Many of the things humans do add pollution to the air. There are harmful solids, gases, and liquids in the air. Where do they come from?

Many pollutants get into the air from burning **fossil fuels**. These fuels were formed from the decay of ancient forms of life. Fossil fuels are **nonrenewable resources**. They cannot be replaced in your lifetime. Fossil fuels include coal, oil, and natural gas. Cars, buses, trucks, and planes burn these fuels, as do many homes and power plants. The wastes from burning these fuels add pollution to the air.

Burning trash adds smoke to the air. Dust comes from plowed fields. It comes from construction sites and from mines. Factories add chemical wastes to the air.

Other events also add to air pollution. Volcanoes erupt and shoot gases and particles into the air. Forest fires and grass fires can spread smoke over great distances.

All these pollutants can build up into thick clouds called **smog**. Smog is a mixture of smoke and fog. It forms when smoke and fumes collect in moist, calm air. Smog irritates the eyes, nose, and throat. People with breathing problems have died from heavy smog.

Smog hangs like a brown cloud over many cities. Why do you think it is most common in big coastal cities like Los Angeles?

Sometimes ozone can form in smog. High up in the atmosphere, remember, ozone protects Earth from UV radiation. However, at ground level this gas can make people sick.

 What are five sources of air pollution?

What Is Acid Rain?

What can destroy forests, kill animals and plants in lakes, and even eat away at buildings? Part of the answer comes from power plants that burn coal to produce energy. Another part comes from motor vehicles that burn gasoline.

Wastes that come from burning these fossil fuels travel into the air. In the air the wastes mix with moisture. They can form chemicals called acids in the moisture. The moisture with acids can eventually fall to Earth's surface as **acid rain** . This term includes all forms of precipitation—rain, snow, hail, and sleet.

Acid rain can harm soil and water supplies. Some trees sicken and die if there is too much acid in the soil. Fish die when water in lakes contains too much acid. The acid weathers away statues and buildings. It can cause metal surfaces on cars to crumble.

READING **Draw Conclusions**
Why is acid rain harmful?

Trees yellow and die due to acid rain.

FOR SCHOOL OR HOME

Acids

Your teacher will give you a stick of chalk and some rock samples.

BE CAREFUL! Wear goggles.

1. **Use Variables** Break a stick of chalk into smaller pieces. Place some small pieces in a plastic cup. Place each rock sample in its own cup. Slowly pour vinegar into each cup to cover each object.

2. Cover each cup using plastic wrap and a rubber band to help keep the vinegar from evaporating.

3. **Observe** Watch for any changes in the chalk and the rocks. Watch for several minutes and then at later times in the day. Record your observations.

4. Vinegar is a mild acid. How did it change the chalk?

5. Do all rocks change the same way? Explain based on your results.

How Can We Clean Up the Air?

Cleaning up the air is a job that takes all nations to work on. That is why the Congress of the United States passed laws to protect the air. It passed the Clean Air Act in 1967 and added more parts in 1970, 1977, and 1990.

As a result of these laws, cars now have lowered amounts of harmful wastes that are released. "Clean coal" methods were introduced to lower the amount of harmful wastes that result in acid rain. Power plants that burn coal can wash coal before burning it, to remove sulfur. Sulfur can result in acid rain when the coal burns.

In 1970 the first Earth Day was celebrated. People were becoming very concerned about the health of planet Earth. That year the Environmental Protection Agency (EPA) was formed. The EPA is part of the United States government. It has the job of checking that laws are being followed. It investigates new dangers and offers solutions and guidelines.

The photographs show "holes" in the ozone layer. The ozone layer, remember, is a layer high up in the atmosphere that protects Earth from harmful UV radiation. However, it seems humans have caused holes to form in this layer. The holes are letting UV radiation through.

How did the holes get there? Scientists are not totally sure. Much evidence points to substances that

Satellite photos of Earth's ozone layer

people have been using a lot. These substances are called CFCs, which is short for chlorofluorocarbons (klawr·oh·floor·oh·KAHR·buhnz). They are gases used in such things as refrigerators, freezers, and air conditioners. CFCs were also used in many aerosol spray cans. Spray paints, hair sprays, and even shaving foams released CFCs. When the CFCs leak out from these products, they rise into the atmosphere. There they can affect the ozone layer.

In 1990 a group of representatives from around the world met in London. They signed an agreement to ban the use of CFCs worldwide in just ten years.

Aerosol spray cans now use substitutes. Just read the label on a spray can, and you can see for yourself.

▷ **What are some ways we can reduce air pollution?**

L·I·N·K·S

Why It Matters

Air pollution harms trees, lakes, and buildings. It can also affect you directly. Air pollution can make people sick. It can make your eyes and nose feel like they are burning. It can make your throat feel itchy and irritated.

Laws help to protect the air. However, it takes people to save the air. The Clean Air Act can work only if people work together. For example, using less electricity can save fuel. Finding ways to cut down on using cars saves fuel, too. Cutting down on burning fuel lowers air pollution.

Visit **www.mhscience02.com** to do a research project on the EPA.

Think and Write

1. Why is air important to living things?
2. How does the atmosphere protect Earth?
3. How do people pollute the air?
4. What causes acid rain? How does acid rain affect land and water?
5. **Critical Thinking** How can using less electricity cut down on the use of fossil fuels?

MATH LINK

Make a graph. Air samples are graded according to how many parts per million (ppm) of various pollutants they contain. Watch the news or read the newspaper every night for one week. Note the air quality for each day. Show the range of air quality in your community with a bar graph.

Pollutants	Air Quality
0–50 ppm	good
50–100 ppm	moderate
100–200 ppm	unhealthy
200–300 ppm	very unhealthy
300–500 ppm	hazardous

WRITING LINK

Write a paragraph. How can you cut down on using electricity and fuel? Be specific. Think about things you, your family, and your friends can do.

SOCIAL STUDIES LINK

Conduct research. Learn more about the Clean Air Act. Use the Internet or an encyclopedia.

TECHNOLOGY LINK

At the Computer Visit **www.mhscience02.com** for more links.

PLANETARY WEATHER

What's the weather like on other planets? Knowing about the atmosphere on other planets tells us more about our entire solar system.

Over the years scientists have learned that Venus's atmosphere is 97 percent carbon dioxide. A greenhouse effect occurs when the layer of carbon dioxide traps the Sun's heat, making Venus's average temperature 460°C (860°F).

Like Earth, Jupiter has storms. The Sun heats our atmosphere which creates conditions that cause storms. But Jupiter receives less of the Sun's heat than Earth. Scientists believe that storms on Jupiter might originate with heat rising from the planet's own hot interior. When it rains on Jupiter it rains liquid helium!

Venus has yellow clouds of sulfuric acid. Precipitation from these clouds is like acid rain on Earth, only worse.

One of Jupiter's storms, the Great Red Spot, is about two times the size of Earth. It began before telescopes were invented.

Saturn has three cloud layers—water clouds, ammonia clouds, and ammonium hydrosulfide clouds. Together they form smog!

There is lightning on Venus, Jupiter, and Saturn. Uranus and Neptune are believed to have lightning as well. The lightning is from electrical discharges. Flashes on Jupiter may be 500 kilometers (310 miles) across.

Pluto has the greatest atmospheric changes of all the planets. That's because its orbit is irregular.

When Pluto is at its closest position to the Sun, the heat turns the frozen nitrogen on Pluto into a gas. This gives Pluto an atmosphere and weather to go with it. As Pluto moves farther from the Sun, the gas freezes.

Write
ABOUT IT

1. Why should the atmosphere on Venus be a warning to us on Earth?

2. What forms of weather do we share with other planets?

AT THE COMPUTER

Visit www.mhscience02.com **to learn more about weather on other planets.**

Earth's Fresh Water

Get Ready

Where do you get a drink when you are thirsty? Where does that water really come from?

Most of Earth's fresh water was once part of the ocean. How does salt water become fresh?

Process Skill

You **communicate** when you share information.

Explore Activity

Investigate How to Make Salt Water Usable

Materials

tea bag

deep pan

plastic cup

saucer (or petri dish)

large, clear bowl or container

water

Procedure

1 Make a Model Keep a tea bag in a cup of water until the water is orange.

2 Make a Model Place a pan where there is strong light (sunlight, if possible). Pour some tea water into the saucer. Put the saucer in the pan. Cover the saucer with a large bowl.

3 Observe Look at the bowl and pan several times during the day and the next day. Note any water you see on the bowl or in the pan. Record your observations.

Drawing Conclusions

1 How was the water that collected in the bowl or pan different from the tea water?

2 Infer What do you think caused the water to collect in the bowl and pan?

3 How does this model represent what might happen to salt water, the water of Earth's oceans?

4 Use Variables How long did it take for water to collect in the bowl and pan? How might this process be speeded up?

5 Going Further: Communicate Do you think this model shows a useful way of turning ocean water into fresh water? Explain.

Read to Learn

Main Idea Fresh water is constantly renewed by the water cycle.

How Do We Use Earth's Oceans?

If all the water in Earth's hydrosphere was represented by 100 cents, not even 3 cents would represent fresh water. Over 97 cents would be salt water. Salt water is water in the oceans as well as saltwater lakes and inland seas.

Much of the salt in salt water is halite, common rock salt. Salt water has seven times more salt than a person can stand. A person cannot survive drinking it. However, Earth's oceans and inland seas are still useful for the resources they contain.

- **Seafood** What kinds of seafood do you eat? Why are these foods healthful? The oceans support many forms of life. The water has dissolved gases, oxygen, and carbon dioxide, as well as minerals. Plants and other producers of the sea are able to get sunlight so that they can make food. They become food for other forms of sea life, which become food for us.

- **Minerals** Almost everything dissolves in water, at least a little. A pail of seawater contains almost every known element. It contains more minerals than just rock salt.

Hot water bubbling out of underwater volcanoes is especially mineral rich. It leaves rich deposits of minerals on the sea floor. Nodules, or lumps, of minerals can be picked up from the sea floor. They contain manganese and iron. Metals such as tin and gold are also found on the sea floor.

READING Graphs

1. Order the items in the bar graph from greatest to least.
2. Where is most of Earth's fresh water found?

Earth's Water Supply

Fresh water: 2.8%

Salt water: 97.2%

Lakes and streams: 0.01%

Surface water and groundwater: 0.6%

Ice caps and glaciers: 2.2%

Water vapor in atmosphere: 0.001%

Seawater

Condensing fresh water

Desalination plant

Heater

Boiling seawater

Evaporating fresh water

Fresh water

- **Fossil fuels** Offshore rigs pump oil and natural gas from beneath the ocean floor in many places around the globe. This fuel is worth more than all other resources taken from the oceans.

- **Fresh water** You can't drink seawater or use it to water plants. You need fresh water. Your fresh water comes mostly from freshwater lakes and rivers.

Some areas have very little fresh water available. The islands of Malta, for example, are surrounded by the Mediterranean Sea. However, they have no permanent lakes or rivers. Over two-thirds of the water used by the people comes from seawater.

Getting fresh water from seawater takes a process called **desalination** (dee·sal·uh·NAY·shuhn). Desalination helps to remove dissolved salts and materials from seawater to make it usable. A desalination plant aids in this process. Seawater entering the plant is heated. The boiling seawater is then pushed into another chamber. As water evaporates, it leaves the dissolved materials behind. The liquid water that collects at the end of the process is free of dissolved materials.

READING Draw Conclusions
Why are oceans a valuable resource?

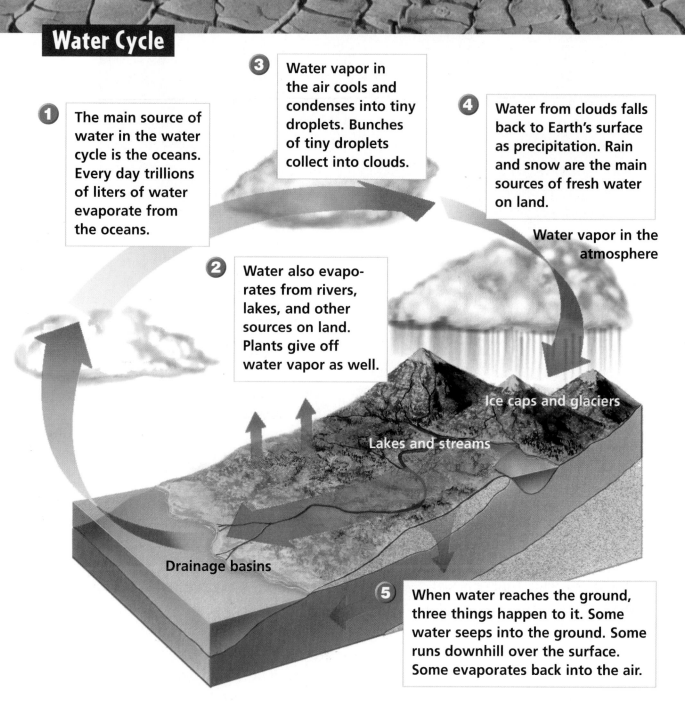

Water Cycle

1 The main source of water in the water cycle is the oceans. Every day trillions of liters of water evaporate from the oceans.

2 Water also evaporates from rivers, lakes, and other sources on land. Plants give off water vapor as well.

3 Water vapor in the air cools and condenses into tiny droplets. Bunches of tiny droplets collect into clouds.

4 Water from clouds falls back to Earth's surface as precipitation. Rain and snow are the main sources of fresh water on land.

Water vapor in the atmosphere

Ice caps and glaciers

Lakes and streams

Drainage basins

5 When water reaches the ground, three things happen to it. Some water seeps into the ground. Some runs downhill over the surface. Some evaporates back into the air.

Where Is Fresh Water From?

Only a tiny fraction of Earth's water is usable fresh water. People use so much fresh water each day, you might wonder why it doesn't run out. Fresh water doesn't run out because it is constantly renewed by the **water cycle**.

In the water cycle, water is on the move—as a liquid that changes to a gas (water vapor) and back to liquid.

When water evaporates, remember, it leaves behind the material it contained. The water vapor is not salt water.

When water falls back to Earth, where does it go? Some water seeps into the ground. It becomes **groundwater**. Groundwater seeps into the spaces between bits of rock and soil. It seeps downward until it is blocked by a kind of rock that is so tightly packed that it has few spaces.

Then the water starts to back up and fill the spaces in the soil and rocks above. The top of the water-filled spaces is called the **water table** . If the water table reaches above the surface, a pond, a lake, or a stream forms.

Ponds and lakes are still bodies of water. They form where water fills up low-lying places. Streams, however, flow downhill. As they flow, they join with other streams, becoming a river. Eventually rivers reach the oceans or other large bodies of water.

An underground layer of rock or soil that is filled with water is called an **aquifer** (AK·wuh·fuhr). Water can move through an aquifer for great distances.

Some groundwater seeps out of the ground in a **spring** . Springs occur where the water table meets the surface. They feed water into streams and lakes long after it stops raining.

Long ago people learned to tap into groundwater by digging **wells** . Wells are holes dug below the water table. The water seeps into the hole. In some wells people get the water out of the hole with pumps. Wells can also be dug deep into aquifers that are sandwiched between tightly packed layers of rock. Water spouts up in these wells because it is being squeezed by the rock layers.

Most supplies of fresh water for large towns and cities come from **reservoirs** (REZ·uhr·vwahrz). Reservoirs are storage areas for freshwater supplies. They may be human-made or natural lakes or ponds. Pipelines transport the water from reservoirs.

▷ **Why is groundwater an important part of the water cycle?**

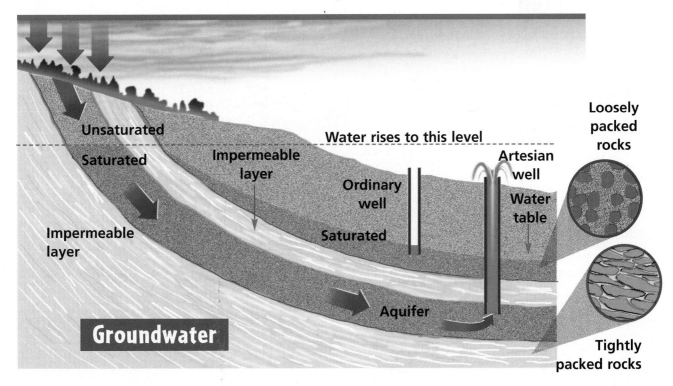

Unsaturated

Saturated

Impermeable layer

Water rises to this level

Loosely packed rocks

Artesian well

Ordinary well

Water table

Impermeable layer

Saturated

Aquifer

Groundwater

Tightly packed rocks

How Can Fresh Water Be Polluted?

Oceans are polluted by people dumping wastes and spilling chemicals. Fresh water can be polluted, too, in many ways.

- **Precipitation** Rain or snow may pick up pollutants from the air. Some chemicals in the air make the rain turn into an acid. Acid rain harms living things and property.

- **Runoff water** Fresh water also gets polluted as it runs off over the land. Water that runs over dumped garbage can end up in streams and lakes. In some cases garbage is dumped into rivers.

- **Groundwater** As water soaks down through the soil, it can pick up chemicals, such as pesticides.

- **Industry** Water used by industry gets polluted as it is used. For example, water that is used to help produce paper is filled with fibers and chemicals.

- **Household waste** You pollute water, too. Every time you flush the toilet, take a bath, brush your teeth, or wash dishes or clothes, water is polluted with wastes. Where do you think this water ends up?

Because of local pollution, many families use water-treatment devices in their faucets. Some families have to use bottled water for cooking and drinking.

▷ **What are four sources of water pollution?**

How Do Wastes from Land Get into Lakes and Rivers?

In seeking an answer to a question, the first thing you might do is find out as much as possible. You make observations. You might look up information.

Next, you would think of an explanation for these observations. That explanation is a hypothesis. It may be stated as an "If . . . then" sentence. "If water runs over land where garbage is dumped, then . . ." Sometimes you can test a hypothesis by making and observing a model.

Materials

soil

food color

foam bits

2 aluminum pans

water

2 textbooks

Procedure

1 **Hypothesize** Write a hypothesis to answer the question above.

2 **Make a Model** Pack moist soil to fill one-half (one side) of one aluminum pan. As you pack the soil, add 10–20 drops of food color to the soil just below the surface. Sprinkle crumbled bits of foam over the top.

3 **Experiment** Use two books to tilt the pan with the soil side up. Place the lower edge of the soil-filled pan in the other pan. Pour water over the uppermost edge of the pan. Describe what happens. Let your model stand for some time, and observe it again.

Drawing Conclusions

1 How does this model represent wastes on land?

2 Based on the model, how do wastes from land get into water? Does the model support your hypothesis? Explain.

3 **Hypothesize** How can some wastes be removed from water? Form a hypothesis, and test your ideas.

How Can We Purify Water?

Can polluted water be cleaned up? Yes, it can be—in many ways. For example, the water cycle helps clean water. Remember that when water evaporates, it leaves behind materials it contained. The water vapor and eventually the rain that forms no longer contain those materials.

When water seeps into the ground, the ground acts as a fine screen, or filter.

Most dirt particles in water are trapped, or filtered out, as water seeps down through the ground. As a result, a well that is dug down deep in the ground collects water that has been filtered.

Freshwater supplies for large areas can be cleaned on a large scale. Follow the steps in the process.

> **What are three ways that water is purified?**

The Water Purification Process

1 Water is often treated with chemicals that make particles in the water clump together. The big particles then sink to the bottom.

4 Chlorine is added to kill bacteria. Many cities also add fluoride, which helps prevent cavities in your teeth.

Pumps

Mixing basin

Settling basin

Offices

Factories

Homes

Raw water

Pumps

2 Then the water flows through layers of gravel and fine sand. The gravel and sand filter out smaller particles from the water.

3 Air may be bubbled through the water to improve the taste.

Why It Matters

The United States Congress has passed laws such as the Safe Drinking Water Act and the Clean Water Act. These laws set standards for water purity.

Laws are important. However, it takes people—like you—to help save water and keep it clean.

People waste fresh water more than they realize. Often water can be safely reused. At times when the rainfall is low, water supplies may be very low. You may live in a part of the country where water supplies are low much of the time. No matter where you live, saving and recycling water should be part of your daily routine.

Think and Write

1. How do you depend on the oceans, even if you don't live near one?

2. How can freshwater supplies be cleaned up?

3. How do wastes get into ocean water? Fresh water?

4. Hypothesize How does the Sun help provide you with freshwater supplies?

5. Critical Thinking How can you tell the amount of water wasted in a day by a leaky faucet? Find a way to tell without wasting any.

ART LINK

Make a collage. Cut out pictures from magazines showing the various ways people use water—swimming, doing laundry, washing a car or pet, or drinking.

MATH LINK

Make a graph. People use water every day. Show in a graph how much water is used in different tasks.

DAILY USES OF WATER	
Activity	**Amount of Water Used**
Flushing a toilet	16–24 liters
Washing dishes	32–80 liters
Taking a shower	80–120 liters
Taking a bath	120–160 liters

LITERATURE LINK

Read *Our Riverkeeper* to learn about cleaning up polluted waters. Try the activities at the end of the book.

TECHNOLOGY LINK

At the Computer Visit www.mhscience02.com for more links.

To Dam or Not to Dam

Have you ever stepped in a stream of water trickling down the driveway? If so, you built a dam. The small stream of water stopped flowing, and a small puddle formed behind your foot.

Dams block the flow of water in a river in the same way that your foot blocks the trickling stream. Dams are often built to generate clean, renewable energy. Some dams also help control flooding.

Dams in the United States provide about 10 percent of our electricity and about 50 percent of our renewable energy. The reservoirs that form behind dams are popular with fishers and boaters.

However, there's a downside to dams—they change rivers. In a river free of dams, water flows according to the seasons. The river may be high in the spring after the winter snows melt and low during a dry summer. After a river is dammed, the water flows only when the dam's gates are raised. These unnatural changes in water level can harm species that have adapted to the seasonal changes.

A dam also changes the water temperature. When a dam is built, a reservoir of water forms. Warmed by the Sun, the water at the top of a reservoir becomes warmer than normal. However, deep below, at the reservoir's bottom, the water becomes colder. These changes in temperature make dammed rivers less livable for some species and better for others.

Many salmon live their adult lives in the ocean. Then they return to the river where they were born to lay their eggs. If a dam blocks the salmons' path, they may die before producing the next generation.

and Society

The first dam on the Elwha River was finished in 1914. In 2000 the dam was bought by the United States government. It may soon be removed to restore the Elwha River.

Dams harm fish by blocking their path up and down the river. For example, consider the Elwha River in the Pacific Northwest. Before any dam was built on the river, about 380,000 adult salmon and trout returned each year to the Elwha to lay eggs. Today that number has fallen below 3,000.

What should we do? Should we keep the dams or get rid of them? The answer depends on which dam you're talking about.

On some rivers researchers are studying the advantages and disadvantages of the dams. Does the dam generate a large amount of clean energy? Does it cause great harm to the local ecosystem? Then the researchers weigh the good against the bad. If a dam does not provide much energy, or it harms the environment, it might be removed. The rest are left to control flooding and to make clean, renewable energy.

What Did I Learn?

1. Which fraction represents the renewable energy generated by dams in the United States?

   A $\frac{1}{4}$

   B $\frac{1}{3}$

   C $\frac{1}{2}$

   D $\frac{3}{4}$

2. Which of the following is a way that a dam benefits the environment?

   F A dam blocks fish from swimming up and down the river.

   G A dam generates clean, renewable energy.

   H A dam increases the chance of flooding.

   J A dam changes the temperature of the river's water.

AT THE COMPUTER

Visit www.mhscience02.com **to learn more about dams.**

Earth's Oceans

Vocabulary

basin, C84

current, C86

continental shelf, C90

continental slope, C90

continental rise, C90

abyssal plain, C90

seamount, C90

trench, C91

mid-ocean ridge, C91

Get Ready

Nearly three-fourths (71 percent) of Earth's surface is covered by water. In fact, you could call Earth a "water planet." Most of Earth's water is contained in the oceans that encircle our planet.

Process Skill

You **experiment** when you perform a test to support or disprove a hypothesis.

Explore Activity

How Do Ocean and Fresh Water Compare?

Materials

3 small plastic cups

"ocean water"

"fresh water"

clear-plastic straw

waterproof marking pen

wax paper

ruler

Procedure

1. Spread wax paper on your desk before you begin to work.

2. **Predict** What happens when you mix fresh and ocean water?

3. **Experiment** From the bottom of the straw, make a mark every 4 cm. Gently place the bottom of the straw 4 cm under the surface of the "ocean water." Seal the top of the straw with your finger. With your finger still sealing the straw, lift it out of the water. Keeping your finger on top of the straw, place the bottom of the straw 8 cm down in the "fresh water." Lift your finger off the straw, and then put it back again and lift the straw out of the water.

4. **Observe** What happened? Record the results. Now try it again, starting with "fresh water" first. Observe and record what happens.

Drawing Conclusions

1. **Communicate** Which liquid combinations mixed in the straw and which made layers?

2. **Going Further: Experiment** Make a third liquid by mixing equal parts of ocean water and fresh water. Experiment with the three liquids to see how many layers you can make.

Main Idea Ninety-seven percent of Earth's water comes from oceans. Oceans are an important natural resource.

What Are Oceans, Seas, and Basins?

Most of Earth's water is contained in large bodies of salt water called oceans. Examples include the Atlantic and Pacific Oceans.

If all the water evaporated from the oceans, a layer of salt about 60 m (200 ft) thick would be left on the ocean floor. Not all of the salt is table salt. There are many other forms of salt, too. Where does all this salt come from?

One source is the rocks on Earth's surface. Rocks break down through weathering. Their minerals flow into streams. Eventually, the minerals end up in the ocean—more than 2,500 million tons each year.

The other source is from deep inside Earth. When volcanoes erupt, they let out water vapor and other gases. The water vapor is the major source of Earth's water. The other gases include some of the salts that are found in the ocean.

Why doesn't the ocean get saltier and saltier? Because the salts are removed as fast as they are added. Plants and animals use them as they build shells and skeletons. Other minerals fall out of the water to become part of the ocean floor.

Although you may have heard the ocean called the "sea," a sea is actually a body of water much smaller than an ocean. Some seas are part of an ocean. The North Sea, for example, is

connected to the Atlantic Ocean and the Arctic Ocean, just north of Europe.

The ocean floor, or **basin**, is as varied as Earth's continents. It contains mountains, valleys, and plains.

Resources from the Ocean

As you saw in Lesson 6, the oceans are rich in natural resources. Seawater is an important source of minerals. To obtain these minerals, people use the heat of the Sun to evaporate water. The minerals left behind are then harvested.

Some resources, such as oil, natural gas, and coal, lie beneath the ocean floor. Drilling rigs such as the one shown are used to extract oil and natural gas from beneath the sea.

The ocean's living creatures are also a valuable resource. People use fish, crabs, and squid for food. They eat

From space it is easy to see that 71 percent of Earth's surface is covered by water. Oceans contain valuable resources such as fish and oil.

some kinds of seaweed. A product made from seaweed—called carrageenan—is used as an ingredient in everything from toothpaste to ice cream.

Other resources are too difficult for us to take from the ocean at this time. For example, certain parts of the ocean floor are covered with lumps called nodules. These nodules contain manganese, iron, and other useful minerals. Gold is an example of a mineral that is dissolved in ocean water. However, we do not yet know how to mine these minerals economically.

▷ **What are oceans like?**

Salt Water and Fresh Water

1. Fill a jar with fresh water to about 1 cm from the top. Carefully push a thumbtack into the center of the eraser of a pencil.

2. **Observe** Place the pencil, eraser side down, in the water. Let go. What happens?

3. **Measure** Using a waterproof marker, mark the pencil to show where the water line is. Use a ruler to measure the length of the pencil above the water mark. Record this measurement.

4. Fill the jar with salt water. Repeat steps 2–3.

5. How do your results for fresh water compare with your results for salt water?

6. **Predict** What do you think will happen if you add a tablespoon of salt to your salt water? Test your prediction.

What Causes Ocean Currents?

Ocean waters are constantly pushed around the planet by currents. A **current** is a stream of water that flows through the ocean like a river. Some currents are on the surface. Others move deep beneath the surface.

Surface currents are driven by the wind. As the winds blow steadily across the ocean, they cause the top layer of water to move in huge circular patterns. A current may move water hundreds of kilometers through the ocean.

Earth's rotation also affects surface currents. As Earth rotates, it pulls great masses of water on the surface along with it. This causes currents to bend to the right in the Northern Hemisphere and to the left in the Southern Hemisphere. The currents start flowing in huge circles.

Surface currents move at a speed of about 220 km (137 mi) a day. Some of these currents are huge. A surface current may move water hundreds of kilometers through the ocean and may carry more water than the Amazon River.

READING Maps

What if you enclosed a message in a bottle and dropped it in the ocean off the California coast? Where might the bottle be found?

The Gulf Stream is a surface current that begins near the equator and flows north past the United States, bringing warm waters to the eastern coast. What causes surface currents like the Gulf Stream?

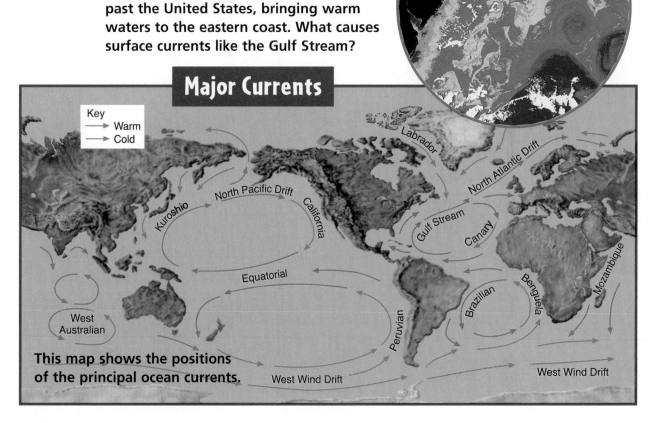

Major Currents

Key
→ Warm
→ Cold

Labrador
North Pacific Drift
North Atlantic Drift
Kuroshio
California
Gulf Stream
Canary
Equatorial
West Australian
Brazilian
Benguela
Mozambique
Peruvian
West Wind Drift
West Wind Drift

This map shows the positions of the principal ocean currents.

As ocean water freezes, the salts do not become part of the ice. The remaining water becomes saltier, causing it to become more dense. It begins to flow to the bottom of the ocean.

As ocean currents flow along the edges of continents, they affect the land's climate. The California current carries cold water along the West Coast of our country, helping it to stay cool there. On the East Coast, the Gulf Stream keeps the climate warm.

Deep-water currents move far beneath the ocean. They are set in motion by differences in the temperature and saltiness of water.

Near Earth's poles, water at the surface of the ocean loses heat to the atmosphere. It may also become saltier as water is removed by evaporation or freezing. This colder, saltier water is *denser* than the water below it. It slowly sinks toward the ocean bottom.

The less dense water below flows in to replace it closer to the surface.

In this way, a deep-water current is set up. The water in a deep-water current moves much slower than the water in a surface current—just a few meters a day.

Dense water forms mainly in Antarctica and in the North Atlantic Ocean. From there the water sinks and spreads slowly outward toward the equator. The water may not resurface for another 500 years.

▷ **What are three ways an ocean current may form?**

How Does the Water in a Wave Move?

Have you ever watched a toy boat bobbing on the surface of a lake or ocean? As the waves go by, the boat moves up, around, down, and then back. It returns to almost the same position where it started. This is exactly what happens to the water particles in waves—they move in circles.

All waves carry energy from place to place. In the ocean the winds blow across the surface, passing energy to the water. The energy of a wave moves forward across the water, but not the water particles themselves. As a wave passes through the ocean, each water particle moves in a circle, returning to almost its original position.

As the winds blow across the ocean, they also drag the water forward slightly, causing the surface currents you read about on page C86. However,

How Water Moves in a Wave

Wave movement

Water particle motion

most of the energy passes through the water as waves, as shown in the illustration above.

When a wave approaches the shore, it begins to slow down. At the same time, it gets higher. The tall wave reaches a point where it collapses, or breaks, against the shore.

The force of breaking waves can be very powerful. Each wave may hurl thousands of tons of water against the shore, breaking rocks apart and smoothing the fragments into pebbles and sand.

▶ **What is the motion of water particles as a wave passes through water?**

The Moon's gravitational pull causes water to bulge on the side of Earth nearest the Moon. At the same time, it causes high tide on the opposite side of Earth. As the Moon pulls solid Earth toward itself, the water seems to bulge.

What Causes the Tides?

People living along the coasts are familiar with the rise and fall of the ocean's surface, called the tide. Tides result from the pull of the Moon's and the Sun's gravity on Earth. Although the Moon is much smaller than the Sun, it is also much closer to Earth. It is the Moon that has the greatest effect on the tides.

The Sun also influences the tides. However, it is so far away that it has less than half the pull of the Moon. About twice a month, near the times of new and full Moons, the Sun and the Moon line up. Their combined pull causes the highest high tides and lowest low tides, called *spring tides*.

The tides with the smallest range, called *neap tides*, occur between spring tides. During a neap tide, the Moon and the Sun are at right angles to Earth, and their pulls partly cancel each other.

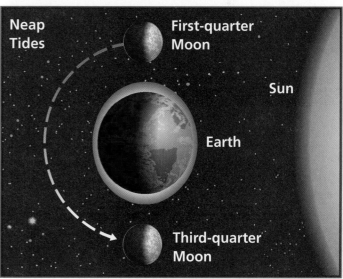

READING **Drawing Conclusions**
What are tides the result of?

C 89

What Is the Ocean Floor Like?

If you could ride in a submarine from the shore of the Atlantic Ocean out to its deepest part, you would see a varied landscape of mountains, valleys, and plains. As you left the shore, your trip would start above the **continental shelf**, the underwater edge of a continent. It extends from the shore to a depth of about 200 m (600 ft) and has a gentle slope.

About 80 km (50 mi) out from the shore, the land would slope steeply down. You would now be above the **continental slope**. The continental slope leads from the continental shelf toward the sea floor. It is steeper, deeper, and narrower than the shelf.

After traveling another 20 km (12.4 mi) out into the ocean, you would find yourself above the **continental rise**. The continental rise is a buildup of sediment on the sea floor at the bottom of the continental slope. It is a zone of sand and mud that stretches from the slope down to the deep-sea floor.

At the end of the continental rise, you would reach one of the flattest places on Earth—the **abyssal** (uh·BIS·uhl) **plain**. Most of the hills and valleys at the bottom of the ocean were buried under a layer of sand and mud long ago. This created the level abyssal plains. These vast, flat lands cover almost half of the deep ocean floor.

As your trip continued across the abyssal plain, you might come to a huge underwater mountain called a **seamount**. The peak of a seamount rises hundreds of kilometers above the ocean floor. A seamount is a volcano. It is formed in the same way as a volcano on land—hot molten rock from inside Earth rises to the surface and cools to a solid.

A seamount may never cross the surface of the ocean. However, if it

Ocean Floor

Abyssal plains

Continental slope

Continental shelf

Continental rise

grows large enough, it may emerge as an island. The Hawaiian Islands are an example of a chain of seamounts.

As your travels continued, your submarine might come to a long, narrow V-shaped valley known as a **trench**. Deep-sea trenches are the deepest points on Earth. They plunge as far down as 8,000–10,000 m (5–6 mi) below sea level. One is more than 11,000 m (7 mi) deep. If you could put the tallest mountain on Earth—Mount Everest—in the trench, its tip would still be about 2,000 m (1.25 mi) below the ocean surface.

The trenches are too deep beneath the ocean to ever see the sunlight. They are pitch black and freezing cold. Your submarine couldn't dive to the

bottom of a trench—the pressure of the water above is so great that it would crush a normal submarine.

As you reached the middle of the Atlantic Ocean, you would see a mountain range rising above the ocean floor. This is known as the mid-Atlantic ridge. It is part of the chain of mountains, called **mid-ocean ridges**, that winds its way through all the world's major oceans. The mid-Atlantic ridge runs the entire length of the Atlantic Ocean. Like seamounts, these mountain ranges were formed by molten rock that cooled and hardened.

▷ **What are some of the features of the ocean floor?**

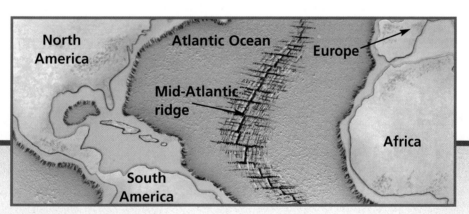

North America
Atlantic Ocean
Europe
Mid-Atlantic ridge
Africa
South America

Mid-ocean ridge
Trench
Seamounts

How Do We Explore the Oceans?

Today ocean scientists explore the oceans using a variety of techniques. One of the first breakthroughs in technology came in the 1920s, when sonar equipment was invented. Sonar helps scientists map the ocean floor. Sonar instruments give out sound waves that hit the ocean floor and send back echoes. The echoes are recorded. Their pattern is traced on paper to make a "sound map" of features like underwater mountains and trenches.

The ability of people to move about underwater was aided by the invention in the 1940s of scuba (*self-contained underwater breathing apparatus*). Scuba was invented by Jacques Cousteau and Emile Gagnan. For the first time, divers had their own air supply.

A diver wearing scuba gear can explore the ocean to about 50 m. After that, the water pressures are too great for the human body to handle safely.

Starting in the 1960s, scientists began using deep-diving research vessels called submersibles to explore the ocean. They can go much deeper than a diver can go. Using submersibles like *Alvin*, scientists have found a new world deep beneath the sea. They have studied new

The *Titanic*

animals like tube worms. Submersibles also helped locate and explore the ocean liner *Titanic*. The cruise ship lies on the Atlantic floor almost 4,000 m (2.5 mi) below the surface.

Satellites are yet another way to study the ocean. Satellites can measure surface temperature, wave height and direction, sea level, currents, sea ice, and levels of marine plant life. This information can be used in different ways. For example, patterns in ocean temperatures and currents can be used to predict the weather. Satellites can also monitor ocean pollution.

Deep-sea drilling is also used to study the ocean. Research vessels collect samples from beneath the sea floor. The sediment gathered allows scientists to understand how the oceans have changed over time.

Sea-Floor Vents

In 1977 scientists in a submersible traveled deep below the ocean to one of the mid-ocean ridges. They were there to study hot springs called *sea-floor vents*. These vents are formed when seawater trickles down into the hot, newly formed oceanic crust. The water becomes saturated with minerals. Eventually, it boils out of a vent in the crust.

To the scientists' amazement, large wormlike animals were waving in the water near some of the vents. They named the animals *tube worms*. Tube worms get nourishment from bacteria living inside them. The bacteria, in

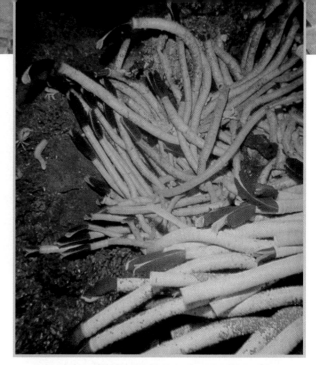

Tube worms are found deep beneath the ocean near vents in the ocean floor. How can tube worms get nutrients in these deep, dark waters?

turn, use the hydrogen sulfide and oxygen taken in by the worms to create nutrients through a process called *chemosynthesis* (kee·moh·SIN·thuh·sis).

Recall that photosynthesis is the food-making process in green plants that uses sunlight. Never before had scientists seen a food chain that did not rely on photosynthesis for energy and food. Instead, the bacteria–tube worm food chain gets its food and energy from the mineral-rich waters and the heat energy from the hot vents.

Since that first discovery, more than 400 species new to science have been found living in and around sea-floor vents.

▶ **What are some of the ways that today's scientists explore the oceans?**

People can help clean up polluted waters.

How Do People Affect the Oceans?

The oceans have a tremendous ability to absorb human waste. Unfortunately, at some point the pollution becomes too much for the water to handle. Marine pollution has become a serious problem for the world's oceans.

Each year sewage, waste from factories, and fertilizer and waste from farms are dumped into rivers that flow into the sea or into the ocean itself. Ships may spill oil or dump sewage overboard. Offshore drilling for oil and natural gas also harms the environment.

Ocean pollution can harm or kill marine animals and plants. It is also dangerous to people who eat seafood from the polluted waters.

Overfishing is another threat to marine animals. People around the world depend on fish and marine animals, such as crabs and lobsters, for food. According to the United Nations Food and Agriculture Organization, 70 percent of the fish species caught to be sold are being overfished. If this continues, entire species may die out.

> ▷ **What are some of the ways that people affect the ocean environment?**

A factory fishing boat is a huge boat where thousands of fish at a time can be caught, cleaned, and quick frozen. How might such a boat contribute to overfishing?

Why It Matters

Oceans provide many valuable resources. Most of the world's nations are now aware of the need to protect their coasts and water from pollution. They have begun to enforce laws to keep sewage, chemicals, and other waste out of the water.

Many countries have also agreed to prevent overfishing. They limit the number of fish that can be caught in their waters.

Many governments have also set aside protected areas in their waters where marine animals can live undisturbed. By the mid-1990s, 1,200 marine protected areas existed throughout the world.

Think and Write

1. What resources are found in oceans?

2. Where do the oceans' salts come from?

3. How does the water in waves move? In currents?

4. What does the ocean floor look like?

5. **Critical Thinking** In the Indian Ocean, there are seasonal wind shifts known as the summer and winter monsoons. What do you think happens to the surface currents when the winds change direction? Explain.

L·I·N·K·S

ART LINK

Make a diorama. Make a model of the ocean floor. Show the continental shelf, slope, and rise, and the abyssal plain. You may want to show a trench, a seamount, or sea-floor vents, too.

WRITING LINK

Write a paragraph. What are some of the ocean resources you use? Which ones do you use the most? Tell about them in a paragraph.

TECHNOLOGY LINK

Science Newsroom CD-ROM Choose *Sea to Shining Sea* to learn more about Earth's water and how it moves through the water cycle.

At the Computer Visit **www.mhscience02.com** for more links.

Science Magazine

Voyager to the Bottom of the Ocean

When Cindy Lee Van Dover was growing up, she thought that sea creatures were the most interesting animals. She liked finding weird animals on the beach.

Van Dover never imagined that in 1989 she would become the first female pilot of the submersible, *Alvin*. At the bottom of the ocean, she found lots of weird animals.

Van Dover was a submersible pilot until 1991. During this time she took *Alvin* as deep as 3,584 meters. That's more than 2 miles below the surface!

On a typical dive, *Alvin* might take $1\frac{1}{2}$ hours to reach the bottom of the ocean. Then the pilot uses the sub's manipulators to gather samples of sea-floor creatures for the scientists. She also takes readings of the water pressures and temperatures outside the submersible. After about five hours on the bottom, the pilot releases weights from the sub, and it floats back to the surface.

During one of Van Dover's trips, *Alvin* got stuck in the mud deep below the ocean. How did this happen? *Alvin* is taken completely apart and then rebuilt every three years. During the rebuilding process, some metal flaps were accidentally left off *Alvin*'s "belly." The openings allowed mud to fill the bottom.

When Van Dover tried to move the submersible off the ocean bottom, it was stuck. After discussing the problem with engineers on the ship at the surface, Van Dover dropped *Alvin*'s weights and waited. Luckily, *Alvin* was now light enough to slowly float back to the surface.

Today Van Dover is an ocean-ographer who studies the ecology of sea-floor vents. She still dives to the ocean floor about three times a year, but these days she goes as a scientist, not a pilot. Van Dover studies the communities of mussels that live near the vents. When she's not out on a dive gathering samples to study in her laboratory, Professor Van Dover teaches at a university in Virginia.

What Did I Learn?

1. As pilot of the submersible *Alvin*, Cindy Lee Van Dover might

  A take readings of water pressure

  B measure water temperature

  C gather samples of sea creatures

  D all of the above

2. How does *Alvin* get back to the surface?

  F It drops weights and floats back to the surface.

  G It uses its engines.

  H A surface ship pulls it to the surface.

  J Metal flaps on its belly are closed.

Like tube worms, these mussels depend on chemosynthesis for food. Each mussel may be 20–25 centimeters across. Professor Van Dover studies the ecology of deep-ocean mussel beds. There may be 30–70 species found at each vent—including shellfish, worms, and snails. Van Dover studies how the different species interact with each other.

AT THE COMPUTER

Visit www.mhscience02.com
to learn more about oceans.

Energy Resources

Vocabulary

alternative energy source, C104

geothermal energy, C104

biomass, C106

Get Ready

How many hours a day do you use energy? What kinds do you use, and what do you use them for? You use energy all the time. How is that possible? How many different ways is energy being used in this picture?

Process Skill

You **hypothesize** when you make a statement that can be tested to answer a question.

Explore Activity

How Do People Use Energy?

Procedure

1 **Communicate** Make a list of all the different ways you use energy.

2 Make a table listing all the kinds of energy you use in a day, how you use that energy, and how many hours you use each kind.

Drawing Conclusions

1 How many different ways do you use electricity each day? How many hours a day do you use electricity? What other sources of energy do you use? How many hours a day do you use each?

2 **Infer** Make a log to keep track of your energy use at home and at school. How can you use that information to help you make a plan to save energy?

3 **Use Numbers** If it costs you an average of ten cents an hour for the energy you use, how much would the energy you use cost each week? About how much would it cost each month?

4 **Going Further: Hypothesize** How can you use less electricity? How much money do you think you could save on energy use in a month? How would you go about testing your hypothesis?

Main Idea Some energy sources will last forever, while others will run out eventually.

How Are Fossil Fuels Turned into Energy?

You use a number of different energy sources each day. Where does the energy you use come from? Try tracing it back to its source. Many homes, schools, and businesses get heat by burning oil or natural gas. Some older buildings still burn coal for heat. Some homes burn wood for heat.

The heat in many other homes and businesses comes from electricity. So does the energy to run many common devices, such as lights, computers, radios, TVs, and washers. Some small devices such as flashlights and portable CD players get their electricity from batteries. Most of the other devices use electricity from a wall outlet. That electricity comes from a power plant. Electricity from that plant reaches your home through wires. However, the power plant makes electricity by using energy from burning fuels such as coal, oil, and natural gas.

It takes a lot of energy to move a car, bus, or train. Public and private transportation is one of the greatest uses of energy in today's world. Most vehicles get their energy from burning fuels such as gasoline or diesel oil. Others run on electricity, propane, or liquefied natural gas.

Electricity from a power plant goes to your home.

Batteries provide energy for an electric car.

Energy is used to heat your home.

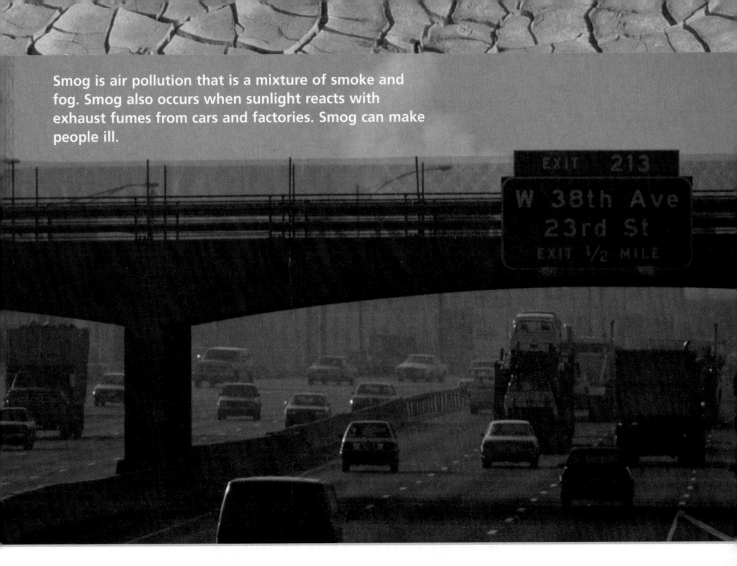

Smog is air pollution that is a mixture of smoke and fog. Smog also occurs when sunlight reacts with exhaust fumes from cars and factories. Smog can make people ill.

As you can see, most of the energy you use can be traced back to fossil fuels—coal, oil, or natural gas. The energy in fossil fuels, in turn, can be traced back to the Sun.

Heat from burning fossil fuels can be used directly to heat homes, schools, businesses, and factories.

The heat can also be used to generate electricity. The heat is used to boil water and turn it into steam. The steam is trapped, and pressure builds up. Then the steam is released. The steam is directed at a big, pinwheel-like turbine. When the steam hits the turbine, it causes it to spin. The spinning turbine turns a generator to make electricity.

All fuels have advantages and disadvantages. The advantage of using fossil fuels is that they contain a lot of energy. However, fossil fuels take millions of years to form. Once used they cannot be replaced fast enough for future use. Therefore, they are nonrenewable.

Burning a fossil fuel also gives off smoke, gases, and other by-products. These pollute the environment. That is why the search is on for other, cleaner fuels.

▷ **What are some energy sources that come from fossil fuels?**

Where Do Fossil Fuels Come From?

Fossil fuels are the remains of once-living things. Coal formed from the remains of dead plants buried in ancient swamps and forests. Natural gas and oil formed from the remains of tiny ocean plants and animals. These sea creatures died and fell to the bottom of the ocean. There their bodies were buried by layers of sand and mud. As more and more layers covered these remains, pressure on them built up. Eventually, the layers of sediments turned into sedimentary rock. Over millions of years, the plant and animal remains changed into oil and natural gas. Plants and animals get their energy from the Sun. Therefore, the source of energy in fossil fuels can be traced back to the Sun.

Our supplies of fossil fuels are limited, and fossil fuels are not a renewable energy source.

With the growth of industry, the demand for and use of energy also grows. The United States is the world's largest consumer of energy. The energy we use makes our lives easier.

How Fossil Fuels Are Formed

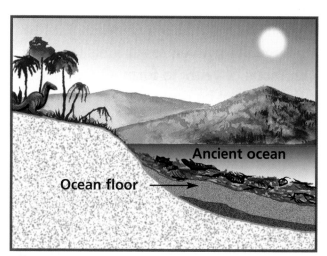

1 Dead plants and animals fall to the ocean floor.

2 Dead plants and animals are covered with layers of sand and mud.

However, energy use pollutes the environment. It also speeds up the rate at which Earth's energy resources are used up.

If we continue to use fossil fuels at our present rate, we will run out of them. There are two possible solutions to this problem. One is to conserve our energy resources so that they will last longer. Another is to search for other sources of energy.

> **How do fossil fuels form?**

READING
 Diagrams

What were oil and natural gas made from?

Gas
Oil

3 Over millions of years, pressure and heat help to turn the dead plant and animal remains into oil and natural gas.

FOR SCHOOL OR HOME

Fuel Supply

This table shows how fast we are using up oil and natural gas.

World Supply of Oil and Natural Gas (as of January 1, 1996)	
Oil	1,007 billion barrels (1,007,000,000,000)
Natural gas	4,900 trillion cubic feet
World Use of Oil and Natural Gas for 1995	
Oil	about 70 million barrels a day (70,000,000)
Natural gas	about 78 trillion cubic feet

1. **Observe** Examine the data in the table.

2. **Communicate** Draw a graph showing how long the fossil fuels we know about will last, based on the data in the table.

3. **Infer** How long will it be until we run out of each type of fossil fuel? Assume that the rate of use remains the same.

What Other Sources of Energy Are There?

Sources of energy other than the burning of fossil fuels are called **alternative energy sources**. Here are some alternative energy sources.

Water

Any whitewater rafter can tell you that running water has a lot of energy. That energy can be harnessed to do work using waterwheels. Running or falling water turns the wheel. The turning wheel spins an axle, which is attached to various machines to do work.

In a mill the axle turns a big stone that grinds up grain. In a sawmill it spins a blade to cut wood. In a *hydroelectric* (high·droh·i·LEK·trik) *plant*, running or falling water spins a generator to make electricity.

Wind

Wind, or moving air, can also spin a wheel. Windmills generate electricity in the same way waterwheels do.

Internal Heat

The Earth's interior is very hot. The most common evidence of that heat is simply hot water or steam coming out of the ground. The water is heated below the surface in places where magma collects. Earth's internal heat is called **geothermal** (jee·oh·THUR·muhl) **energy**. Geothermal energy can be used to heat homes and produce electricity.

- Homes in Boise, Idaho, have been heated by hot springs since the 1890s.

- At The Geysers in California, steam drives turbines that generate electricity. The steam comes from underground water heated by geothermal energy.

Geothermal energy helps keep the country of Iceland warm.

Hydroelectric Plant

Solar houses use solar cells for electric energy and solar collectors for heat.

The Sun

Every day the Sun bathes Earth in energy. We usually think of that solar energy simply as sunlight. Plants harness the Sun's energy through photosynthesis to make chemical compounds rich in energy. When you burn wood, you are releasing energy that a tree absorbed from the Sun.

Sunlight also gives water the energy to evaporate and rise into the atmosphere. In this way the energy of running water can also be traced back to sunlight.

Today people are using new ways to harness the power of sunlight. One way is to trap or concentrate sunlight with the use of solar panels, or collectors. The trapped sunlight can be used to heat water or entire homes. Another way to use it is with solar cells. Solar cells are devices that convert sunlight into electric energy.

Tides

Every day the tide causes the water level to rise and drop along the world's coastlines. Now imagine a big tank built just below the high-water level. The tide rises, and water fills the tank. When the tide drops, the water flows out of the tank. Add a waterwheel so the water flowing out of the tank spins the wheel. Now you have a spinning axle that can be used to do work. That's the idea behind tidal power plants.

 What are five alternative energy sources?

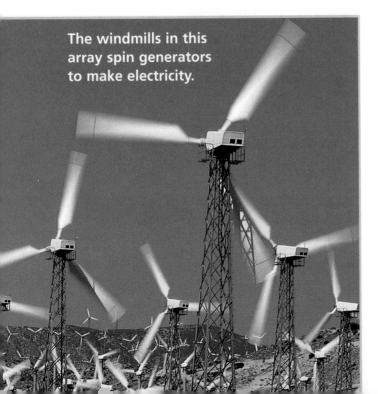

The windmills in this array spin generators to make electricity.

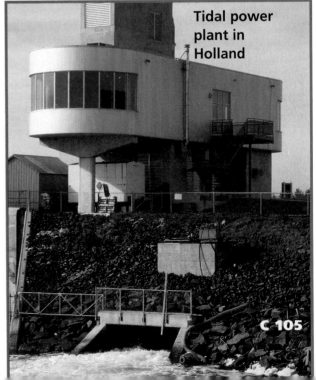

Tidal power plant in Holland

C 105

Cars can be powered by a special mixture that combines alcohol from biomass with gasoline.

How Can We Conserve Energy?

Unfortunately, alternative energy sources are not fully replacing fossil fuels. Therefore, we need to conserve these nonrenewable resources.

What does it mean to conserve our resources? It means we don't waste what we have and we use as little of what we have as possible. Take a typical house as an example. Better insulation of homes has cut United States' consumption of fuel oil almost in half. Newly designed bodies and engines have doubled the gasoline mileage of most cars. If we could cut our present consumption in half, our oil reserves would last twice as long! How can we do that?

One way is to use alternative energy sources such as water, wind, and solar energy. Every watt of electricity we get from a solar cell is one less watt we have to get by burning oil or coal.

You have learned that fossil fuels are the stored energy that came from once-living plants and animals. Fossil fuels are nonrenewable. However, plant matter and animal wastes or other remains—called **biomass**—can be used as a renewable energy source. Plant material and animal wastes that might wind up as garbage can be processed to form fuel. This is done in waste-treatment plants. The treated wastes can then be burned. Special devices called scrubbers help prevent pollutants from entering the air when these wastes are burned. Solid wastes can also be digested by bacteria. The bacteria produce methane gas in the process. Methane gas can be used as fuel.

Corn and other grains, and even sugarcane, can also be turned into fuel. This fuel can be used to heat foods. It can also be mixed with gasoline to help run cars while saving gasoline supplies.

READING Draw Conclusions
How can biomass help conserve energy?

L·I·N·K·S

Why It Matters

You probably look forward to driving a car someday. Won't it be great to get around on your own? Well, think about this: Cars run on gasoline, and gasoline comes from oil. Remember the graph you did comparing known oil reserves with our current rate of use? If we don't conserve, will there be enough gas for your children's cars? Will there be enough gas for their children?

Think and Write

1. How do you use energy each day?

2. Why are coal, oil, and natural gas called "fossil" fuels?

3. How does the burning of fossil fuels pollute the environment?

4. List five ways people can help to conserve fossil fuels. Which of these suggestions do you think would conserve the most fuel? Which of these suggestions do you think more people would be willing to try?

5. **Critical Thinking** What alternatives do we have to using fossil fuels for energy? What are some of the advantages and disadvantages to using these energy sources?

ART LINK

Design an advertisement. There are many alternative energy sources. Develop an ad trying to convince people to use an alternative energy source.

MATH LINK

Calculate percents. A barrel of crude oil contains 42 gallons. When refined, it produces 21 gallons of gasoline, 9 gallons of fuel oils, 5 gallons of jet fuel, 4 gallons of lubricants, and 3 gallons of asphalt. Convert these numbers to percents and make a circle graph with your results.

TECHNOLOGY LINK

Science Newsroom CD-ROM Choose *Fuels Rush In* to learn how fossil fuels are formed and used.

At the Computer Visit **www.mhscience02.com** for more links.

Chapter 7 Review

Vocabulary

Fill each blank with the best word or words from the list.

acid rain, C65
biomass, C106
continental shelf, C90
continental slope, C90
fossil fuel, C64
geothermal energy, C104
ozone layer, C63
reservoir, C75
smog, C64
water table, C75

1. The _____ screens out much of the Sun's UV rays.

2. The top of the water-filled spaces in the ground is the _____.

3. Dangerous air pollution is called _____.

4. A(n) _____ is a storage area for fresh water.

5. A type of precipitation caused by air pollution is _____.

The **6.** _____ of the ocean floor is steeper and deeper than the **7.** _____.

8. _____ and **9.** _____ are alternative energy sources to **10.** _____.

Test Prep

11. Most of Earth's oxygen supply is produced by _____.

   A bacteria in the soil
   B one-celled algae of the ocean
   C green plants
   D the ozone layer

12. All of the following are examples of nonrenewable resources EXCEPT _____.

   F oil
   G coal
   H oxygen
   J natural gas

13. Geothermal energy comes from _____.

   A the Sun
   B falling water
   C fossil fuels
   D Earth's internal heat

14. Fossil fuels are stored energy that came from _____.

   F sedimentary rocks
   G wind and water
   H once-living plants and animals
   J waste-treatment plants

15. An underground layer of rock or soil that is filled with water is _____.

A a reservoir

B an aquifer

C a lake

D groundwater

Concepts and Skills

16. Process Skills: Hypothesize Does rain remove pollutant particles from the air? Form a hypothesis. What could you do to test your hypothesis?

17. Reading in Science All electricity is made by burning fossil fuels. Is this true or false? Explain your answer.

18. Making Decisions Solar energy is considered "too expensive" to use in the Northeast. However, sunlight is a renewable resource. Is it better to use solar energy or depend on fossil fuels? What are the benefits and disadvantages to both?

19. Scientific Methods How can salt water be turned into drinkable water?

20. Critical Thinking Does filtering water remove all impurities? Explain your answer. How would you prove your answer?

Boost *your test scores!*

Be Smart!

Visit www.mhscience02.com

Volcanologist
Randy White

U.S. Geological Survey

When a volcano starts to rumble, most people in the area think about leaving. However, some scientists, called volcanologists, head right for the action! It is their job to predict what a volcano is going to do. Randy White is a volcanologist and a member of the Volcano Disaster Assistance Program, a division of the United States Geological Survey (USGS).

White's interest in volcanoes started in high school, when he was a foreign exchange student in Japan. He lived near an erupting volcano called Mount Sakurajima. He was so fascinated by the eruption that he decided to become a volcanologist. After receiving his graduate degree in geophysics from Stanford University in 1974, he went to work for the USGS.

Speed is vital when a volcano is showing signs of waking. White and his team must always be ready to reach a site within 24 hours. When they reach the volcano, they have to answer three important questions. Is the volcano going to erupt? How big an eruption will it be? When will it erupt?

White uses many special instruments in his work. One of the most important is a seismometer. A seismometer measures ground movement and is used to predict earthquake activity. Earthquakes often signal volcanic eruptions. White also takes samples of the atmosphere to check the levels of carbon dioxide and sulfur dioxide. If levels of these gases are high, the volcano might be ready to blow!

In 1991, White and his team were sent to Mount Pinatubo in the Philippines. Using their equipment, they

Careers IN SCIENCE

Career Track

Here are some different types of careers related to the study of volcanology. You can use the Internet or library resources to find out more about these careers.

- seismologist
- geologist
- geochemist
- meteorologist
- physicist

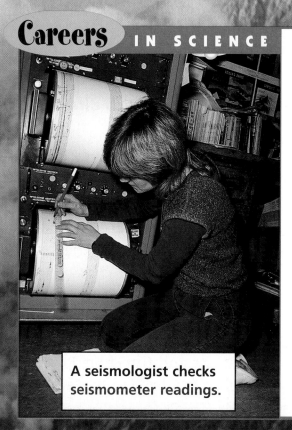

A seismologist checks seismometer readings.

were able to predict the time and size of the eruption. Pinatubo turned out to be the largest volcanic eruption in the world in 80 years. Thanks to the team's predictions, the area was evacuated before the eruption. About 20,000 lives were saved!

Write ABOUT IT

1. What are three important things White needs to find out about a volcano?

2. What two measurements help predict a volcanic eruption?

AT THE COMPUTER Visit www.mhscience02.com to learn more about careers.

Name That MINERAL

Your goal is to test properties of minerals to determine their identity.

What to Do

1. Make a table with the column headings shown below.

2. Do the following tests to determine properties. Record data in your table for each sample.

   Color(s): What color is its surface?

   Luster: How shiny is the sample?

   Porcelain plate test: What color is the powder when the mineral streaks?

Cleavage: How many directions does it break into?

Hardness: How well does the mineral resist scratching?

Density: How heavy does the sample feel compared with a sample of water with the same volume?

Analyze Your Results

Complete the table. Use the results of your tests and the chart Properties of Minerals (page C35) to name each mineral.

SPOT the SOURCE

Your goal is to make a brochure to educate people about air pollution.

What to Do

1. Look at pictures in a newspaper or magazine. Which of the pictures show things that cause air pollution?

2. Create a brochure about air pollution. Your brochure should do three things:

   a. explain what air pollution is

   b. name the sources of air pollution in the pictures

   c. describe how those sources pollute

Analyze Your Results

1. Name one way that people use energy that causes air pollution.

2. How are air pollution and water pollution alike?

UNIT D

Weather and Climate

NATIONAL GEOGRAPHIC

Weather and Climate

LOOK!

A powerful hurricane swirls
over the Atlantic Ocean. What
causes such severe storms?

CHAPTER

8

Weather

Did You Ever Wonder?

What is frost? What causes frost to form? Frost forms when the air is cold enough that water vapor in the air changes from gas to ice crystals on trees, grass, and other objects. In warmer weather dew would form instead of frost. Is the weather always the same where you live, or does it change from day to day and season to season?

D 3

Atmosphere and Air Temperature

Vocabulary

insolation, D6
atmosphere, D10
troposphere, D10
air pressure, D11
weather, D12
barometer, D12

Get Ready

If it's summer, is it always hot? These animals may find it warmer in summer than in winter. However, it isn't exactly hot here on this beautiful summer day. How can summer be hot in some places and so cold in others?

How does the angle at which the Sun's energy hits Earth affect the warming of Earth?

Process Skill

You experiment when you perform a test to support or disprove a hypothesis.

Explore Activity

Does the Sun's Angle Matter?

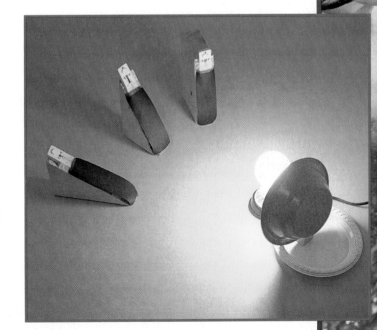

Materials

3 thermometers

triangular blocks

black paper

white paper

centimeter ruler

scissors

tape

150-W clear-bulb lamp

stopwatch

foam bowl

clay

Procedure

BE CAREFUL! Do not look into the lamplight.

1 Place a thermometer onto each of the three blocks, as shown. Cover each with black paper. Put the blocks 20 cm from the light bulb, level with its filament (curly wire).

2 **Observe** Measure the starting temperature at each block. Record the temperatures.

3 **Predict** What will happen when the lamp is turned on? Turn the lamp on. Record the temperature at each block every two minutes for ten minutes.

4 **Communicate** Make a line graph showing the change in temperature at each block over time.

5 **Use Variables** Repeat the activity with white paper.

Drawing Conclusions

1 **Communicate** Which block's surface was warmed most by the lamplight? Which block's surface was warmed the least?

2 **Infer** How does the angle at which light hits a surface affect how much the surface is heated? How does the surface color affect how much it is heated?

3 **Going Further: Experiment** What other factors might affect how much a surface is warmed by sunlight? How would you test your ideas?

Main Idea The Sun warms Earth's surface, which transmits heat to the air above it.

Does the Sun's Angle Matter?

Where do you think you might find warm temperatures all year long? Where would you find very cold weather? That depends a lot on the angle at which sunlight hits a region. Angles make a difference in how much the Sun warms an area. The areas around the equator are hottest. That's because the Sun's path is high overhead at midday. In those areas the Sun's rays hit Earth at their strongest.

The areas around the North and South Poles are coldest. In those areas the Sun is much lower at midday.

The Sun's rays hit Earth's surface at a low angle. The strength of the rays is much weaker at this angle.

The angle at which sunlight strikes Earth's surface is called the angle of **insolation**. *Insolation* is short for *incoming solar radiation*. It means the amount of the Sun's energy that reaches Earth at a given place and time.

The diagram shows how sunlight warms Earth in summer and winter. The amount of warming depends on the angle of insolation. The greater the angle, the warmer it gets. The angle of insolation is always smaller near the poles than near the equator. That means while it's freezing cold in one part of the world, it's hot in another.

▷ **How do differing angles of insolation cause differences in warming?**

How Sunlight Warms Earth

The Sun's rays strike the surface at different angles as Earth travels around the Sun.

June
(summer in Northern Hemisphere)

December
(winter in Northern Hemisphere)

North Pole

Concentrated

Earth

Spread out

South Pole

Sun

Spread out

North Pole

Earth

Concentrated

South Pole

Charts

1. Which location on the graph has the biggest change between winter and summer? Which has the smallest change?

2. How can you describe the pattern of temperatures using what you know about the Sun's rays?

Williston, ND

Del Rio, TX

Maracaibo, Venezuela

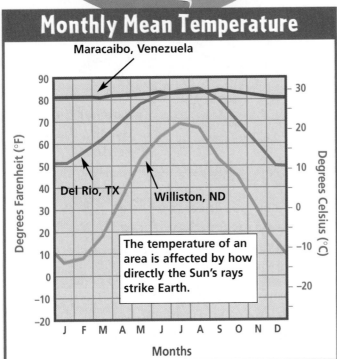

Monthly Mean Temperature

Maracaibo, Venezuela

Del Rio, TX

Williston, ND

The temperature of an area is affected by how directly the Sun's rays strike Earth.

Degrees Farenheit (°F)

Degrees Celsius (°C)

Months

QUICK LAB

FOR SCHOOL OR HOME

Investigating Angles

1. Fold a sheet of graph paper lengthwise in three equal parts. Put a small lump of clay in the middle of each part. Stand a toothpick straight up in each lump of clay.

2. Hold a flashlight directly over the first toothpick. Have a partner trace a line around the circle of light and trace the toothpick shadow.

3. **Use Variables** Repeat step 2 for the other two toothpicks, changing only the angle of the flashlight.

4. **Measure** Count the number of boxes in each circle. Measure the lengths of the toothpick shadows. Record your results.

5. **Infer** How is the length of the shadows related to the angle?

6. **Infer** How is the number of boxes in the circle related to the angle?

What Affects Insolation?

In the morning the Sun is close to the horizon. What happens as time goes by? At midday the Sun is high up in the sky, as high as it gets during the day. After midday the Sun is lower and lower in the sky.

How does this affect the angle of insolation? How do we measure it? In an earlier illustration, you saw that both location and time of year affect this angle. This illustration shows how the time of day affects the angle of insolation.

Measuring the angle of insolation is a challenge. It is not easy to see individual light rays. How can you find the angle at which they hit the surface?

Look at the shadows cast by objects they strike! The lower the angle of the light rays, the longer the shadows. As you can see in the diagram, the angle of insolation is the same as the angle between the ground and the line from the tip of the shadow to the top of the wall.

▷ **How does the time of day affect the angle of insolation?**

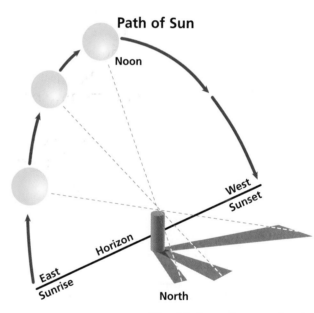

The higher the Sun is in the sky, the shorter the shadow.

Angle of Insolation

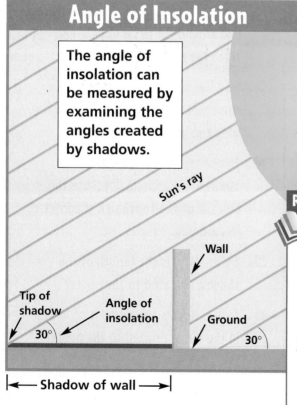

The angle of insolation can be measured by examining the angles created by shadows.

Sun's ray

Wall

Tip of shadow

Angle of insolation

Ground

30°

30°

← Shadow of wall →

READING

Diagrams

1. How can you measure the angle of insolation without being able to see the Sun's rays individually?

2. What will happen to the angle as the Sun gets higher in the sky? How will this affect the temperature?

Why Do Some Things Get Hotter than Others?

As you may know, dark colors get hotter than light colors in the same light. This is why black asphalt roads get so hot in the sunlight. Dark soils and rocks also get very hot. White sand and light-colored soils do not get as hot in sunlight. Plants can also help keep an area cooler in sunlight than surrounding rocks and soil, or black asphalt.

Texture is how smooth or rough a surface is. Rough textures cause light to bounce around at many angles. Each time a little more energy is absorbed by the surface. Rough surfaces tend to get hotter in sunlight than smooth surfaces.

Why do you go swimming when it is hot and you want to cool off? You go

Rough texture
More impacts = more heat energy absorbed

Smooth texture
Fewer impacts = less heat energy absorbed

swimming because the water is cooler than the air. The air above the land is warmed by the land. Although the water and the land next to it are both being warmed by the Sun, the water is cooler. Why? The same amount of light energy will heat land to a higher temperature than it will heat water.

> **How do color and texture affect the amount of heat absorbed?**

READING
Charts

1. Which material is warmer after being placed near the light?

2. How can you use the graph to tell which substance heats faster?

Heating Rate

90°F

SOIL

Degrees Fahrenheit (°F)
100 90 80 70 60 50

Degrees Celsius (°C)
40 30 20 10

0 1 2 3 4 5 6 7 8 9 10
Time

60°F

WATER

Degrees Fahrenheit (°F)
100 90 80 70 60 50

Degrees Celsius (°C)
40 30 20 10

0 1 2 3 4 5 6 7 8 9 10
Time

The graphs show how soil and water react when heated.

Why Do You Cool Down As You Go Up?

Did you ever climb a high mountain? As you go higher and higher above sea level, air temperatures drop. The natural drop in air temperature with altitude is about 2°C (3.6°F) for every 305 meters (1,000 ft).

Climbing up a mountain is really a journey up into the **atmosphere**, the air that surrounds Earth. The atmosphere reaches from Earth's surface to the edge of space. What if you could travel to the top part of the atmosphere? The diagram of the atmosphere shows what you would find.

You would find that the temperature does not fall steadily with altitude. It changes abruptly several times. These changes mark the boundaries of four main layers. These layers surround Earth like huge shells.

The layer closest to Earth's surface is the **troposphere** (TROP·uh·sfeer). It's the narrowest layer—between 8 and 18 kilometers (5–11 miles) thick—but it contains most of the air in the atmosphere. All life on Earth exists here. In this layer all moisture is found and all clouds, rain, snow, and thunderstorms form. Above this layer the air gradually thins out to the near-emptiness of space, with no exact upper boundary.

READING Diagrams

Describe how the temperature changes in each layer of the atmosphere.

▷ **What is the relationship between altitude and temperature?**

Layers of the Atmosphere

Thermosphere
80 km
Mesosphere
50 km
Ozone
Stratosphere
8–18 km
Troposphere
0 km

Ionized gas
Radio waves
Mt. Everest

−100°C −50°C 0°C 50°C
Low   Temperature   High

Most weather occurs in the troposphere. The ozone layer in the stratosphere helps shield us from the Sun's ultraviolet light. *Auroras* (the northern and southern lights) may form in the *ionized* (electrically charged) gas in the thermosphere.

Composition of Dry Air by Volume

Argon, carbon dioxide, and other trace gases 1%

Oxygen 21%

Nitrogen 78%

10,000 m

2,000 m

Sea level

Air in the Atmosphere

Lower altitudes have a larger air column above them, which creates greater air pressure.

READING Charts

1. What is meant by *trace*?
2. Which gas is the most abundant in the atmosphere?

What Happens to the Air Pressure?

As you go higher in altitude, **air pressure** decreases steadily. Air pressure is the force put on a given area by the weight of the air above it. Air is a mixture of gases. It is made up mostly of *molecules* of nitrogen and oxygen. Molecules are the smallest pieces that a substance can be broken into without changing what the substance is.

The molecules have mass. They are attracted to Earth by gravity, so they have weight.

Normal air pressure is greatest at sea level. There the column of air extending above the surface to the top of the atmosphere is tallest. Sea level air pressure is about 1.04 kilograms per square centimeter (14.7 pounds per square inch). As you go higher in altitude, the height of the air column above you becomes shorter. Therefore the weight of that column—or air pressure—becomes less.

In the lower atmosphere, the composition of air varies very little. Up to an altitude of about 100 km (62 mi), air consists of a mixture of gases, water vapor, and dust particles. Nitrogen and oxygen make up 99 percent of the gases in dry air.

Water vapor is a gas. It should not be confused with clouds or fog, which are made of liquid or solid water. The amount of water vapor in air varies from $\frac{1}{10,000}$ of air in dry arctic regions to $\frac{1}{25}$ of air in moist equatorial regions.

The dust in air is made of particles so tiny that 100,000 lined up would only form a row 1 cm (0.4 in.) long. Some of it comes from Earth's surface, from fires and volcanic eruptions, or from tiny crystals of salt.

▷ **How does air pressure change with altitude?**

What Is Weather?

When you say, "It sure is hot today!" the *it* is the air. You really mean that the air around you is hot. The same is true if you say, "It is windy, " or "It is cloudy," or give any other similar description of the weather . The weather is simply what the lower atmosphere, or troposphere, is like at any given place and time.

The conditions that make up weather are the characteristics that change. They are air temperature, air pressure, amount of moisture in the air, wind, clouds, and rain or snow.

Measuring Temperature

You can measure temperature with a thermometer. Thermometers can use two different temperature scales. The Celsius scale is marked with the letter *C*. The Fahrenheit scale is shown by the letter *F*.

Measuring Air Pressure

Air pressure is measured with a barometer (buh·ROM·i·tuhr). Two common types of barometers are the mercury barometer and the aneroid barometer.

Mercury barometers use a mercury-filled glass tube with one closed end. The open end is submerged in liquid mercury. Air pressure on the mercury pushes it up into the tube. When the weight of the mercury column equals the air pressure, the mercury stops rising.

Aneroid barometer

Two common types of barometers

Mercury barometer

An *aneroid* (AN·uh·royd) barometer is an accordion-like metal can with most of the air removed. Inside, a spring balances the outside air pressure. When outside air pressure increases, the can squeezes the spring. When air pressure decreases, the spring pushes outward. A needle inside indicates changes in pressure.

You can monitor and record weather conditions for your own weather station. Measure and record air temperature several times a day. Record daily air pressure by using a barometer or by getting air pressure readings from the weather reports.

READING Main Idea
What conditions make up weather?

L·I·N·K·S

Why It Matters

Have you ever heard a day called a "scorcher"? That means a really hot day. On really hot days, your body can lose a lot of moisture. Your body gives off sweat gradually most of the time. On a hot day, your body tends to give off more and more. That's why it's important to have plenty of drinking water handy on a hot day.

On really cold days, many people have other problems—such as frostbite. You have to cover your face, ears, and hands to avoid contact with air at extremely low temperatures.

Visit **www.mhscience02.com** to do a research project on the atmosphere.

Think and Write

1. How do temperatures on Earth depend on angles?

2. List factors that affect temperatures of places on Earth.

3. What is air pressure? How does it change in the atmosphere?

4. What is the troposphere? What happens there?

5. **Critical Thinking** Is the weather one or more than just one thing? Defend your answer.

MATH LINK

Solve this problem. The sunniest place on Earth is in the eastern Sahara Desert, where sunlight shines an average of 4,300 hours per year. Calculate the percentage of possible sunlight hours a year this number represents. (Assume 12 hours of daylight per day.)

WRITING LINK

Write a story. How do you depend on the weather? Write a story explaining how the weather affects your life.

SOCIAL STUDIES LINK

Research the history of the thermometer. The maximum-and-minimum thermometer was invented in 1780 by Cambridge scientist James Six. A column of mercury moves up and down a U-shaped tube. An index moves with it, recording the highest and lowest temperatures. Research the history of the thermometer, and write a report for the class.

TECHNOLOGY LINK

At the Computer Visit **www.mhscience02.com** for more links.

Water Vapor and Humidity

Get Ready

What if you were walking on this bridge? What would you see and feel all around you? It's fog. What is fog made of? Here's a hint. What if you put a cold glass of lemonade outside on a table on a hot, humid day? What would you see and feel on the outside of the glass?

What is a humid day like? Where is the moisture on a humid day?

Process Skill

You use variables when you identify and separate things in an experiment that can be changed or controlled.

Explore Activity

Where Does the Puddle Come From?

Materials

plastic cups

ice

paper towels

food coloring

thermometer

goggles

Procedure: Design Your Own

BE CAREFUL! Wear goggles.

1 **Form a Hypothesis** Write down your idea about why a puddle forms around a frosty drink. Where do you think the puddle came from?

2 **Experiment** Describe what you would do to test your idea. How would your test support or reject your idea?

3 **Communicate** Draw a diagram showing how you would use the materials. Keep a record of your observations.

Drawing Conclusions

1 **Communicate** Describe the results of your investigation.

2 **Communicate** What evidence did you gather? Explain what happened.

3 **Infer** How does this evidence support or reject your explanation?

4 **Going Further: Use Variables** Do you get the same results on a cool day as on a warm day? Do you get the same results on a humid day as on a dry day? How might you test your ideas?

Main Idea Water on Earth's surface and in the atmosphere changes form and affects the weather.

Where Does Water Vapor Come From?

Put a frosty glass of lemonade on a table on a hot day. What happens? A puddle forms on the table. Where does the puddle come from? The water level in the glass does not drop as the puddle forms. The water in the puddle isn't lemonade.

The water in the puddle comes from the air around the glass. When the warm air touches the cold glass, the air cools. Droplets of water form, run down the side of the glass, and make a puddle on the table.

The water in the air is **water vapor**. Water vapor is water in the form of a gas. Water vapor is invisible, colorless, odorless, and tasteless. The amount of water vapor in the air is called **humidity**. Do not confuse humidity with droplets of liquid water you see in rain, fog, or clouds.

How does water vapor get into the air in the first place? More than two-thirds of planet Earth is covered with liquid water—oceans, rivers, and lakes. There is also water in the ground and in plants. To get into the air, this liquid water must be changed into water vapor.

The changing of a liquid into a gas is called **evaporation**. This takes lots of energy. The main energy source for Earth is the Sun. Each day the Sun turns trillions of tons of ocean water into water vapor.

Water molecules absorb the Sun's energy and speed up. "Speedy" water

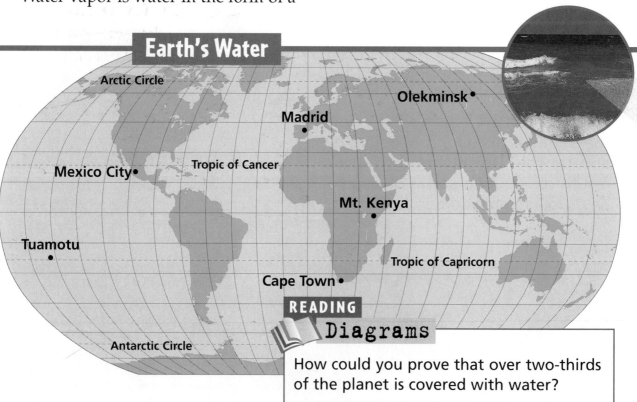

Earth's Water

Arctic Circle

Olekminsk •

Madrid

Mexico City •

Tropic of Cancer

Mt. Kenya

Tuamotu

Tropic of Capricorn

Cape Town •

Antarctic Circle

READING
Diagrams

How could you prove that over two-thirds of the planet is covered with water?

molecules near the surface of the liquid "escape" or evaporate into the atmosphere as water vapor. Some hit other molecules and return to the liquid. When air is cooled, molecules in the air slow down. The molecules of water vapor in the air also slow down. If they slow enough, water vapor molecules that collide stick together and change to liquid droplets on cool surfaces. **Condensation** is the changing of a gas into a liquid. You see condensation on shower doors, on cold drink glasses, and as dew on grass in the early morning.

Plants' roots absorb water that has seeped into the ground. Plants transport the liquid water through their roots and stems to their leaves.

The leaves then give off water in the process called transpiration. This is the second-largest source of water vapor in the atmosphere.

▷ **How does water get into the air?**

Some water molecules "escape" into the air. Some water molecules are knocked back into the liquid.

FOR SCHOOL OR HOME

Transpiration

1. Place a clear-plastic bag completely over a houseplant. Tie the bag tightly around the base of the stem. Do not put the soil-filled pot in the bag.

2. **Observe** Place the plant in a sunny location. Observe it several times a day. When you are done, remove the plastic bag from the plant.

3. **Communicate** Describe what you see on the inside of the bag. How can you explain what happened?

4. **Draw Conclusions** *Transpiration* sounds like *perspiration*—sweating. How might the two processes be alike?

5. **Predict** How would your results vary if you put the plant in the shade?

What Is Relative Humidity?

Humidity and relative humidity both describe the amount of water vapor in the air. Do they mean the same thing, or are they different? Think of a "box" of air that is one cubic meter in volume. Humidity is the actual amount or mass of water vapor in that "box." Humidity is measured in grams per cubic meter.

Two factors determine the amount of humidity in the air. First, there has to be water available to evaporate. Second, the warmer the temperature, the faster the water evaporates. This means that if water is available, warm air will take on more water vapor than cold air.

Weather forecasters often use temperature readings from a wet bulb/dry bulb thermometer—or *hygrometer*—along with a chart to find the relative humidity.

Is there a limit to how much water vapor air can hold? Yes. Air at any temperature has a water vapor capacity or limit. When it becomes full, we say it is saturated. If there is very little water vapor in the air, we say the air is dry.

Relative humidity is a comparison between how much water vapor is in the air and how much the air could hold—at a given temperature—if it were full or saturated. Relative humidity is given in percents (%). Therefore, 50% relative humidity means that air is holding half of what it could if it were full.

On a very humid day, the relative humidity of the air might be 70% or 80%. If the relative humidity is just 25% or 30%, we say the air is dry. The relative humidity of your air may change from day to day. It depends upon changes in your weather.

READING
Graphs

How does the amount of water vapor per cubic centimeter compare at 25°C and 40°C?

Relative Humidity

Water Vapor at 100% Humidity and Various Temperatures

Grams of Water Vapor per Cubic Meter of Air vs *Temperature (°C)*

Relative humidity can be used to predict how the air will feel to a person. The higher the relative humidity, the less water can evaporate into the air. The less water, such as sweat, can evaporate from our skin, the wetter and "stickier" the air feels.

Relative humidity can also be used to predict when condensation will occur. Remember that condensation, like the drops of water on the lemonade glass, is the changing of a gas into a liquid. In the atmosphere condensation is usually the result of warm air being cooled. That is, when warm air is cooled, water vapor in it condenses.

Condensation explains what happened to the glass of lemonade. The cold glass cooled the air that touched it. Water vapor condensed, forming liquid droplets on the outside of the glass.

Can you see condensation happening? Have you ever seen frozen food held over hot water? What do you notice? You see a mist forming. When this happens in the air, a cloud forms. The greater the relative humidity, the more likely condensation will occur, and the greater the chance of clouds—and rain.

You may have heard people complain on a hot day, "It's not the heat, it's the humidity." Why do you think humidity is so important, especially when the weather is hot? Why doesn't a cold day with 70% relative humidity feel as uncomfortable as a hot day with 70% relative humidity?

READING Main Idea
How does temperature affect relative humidity?

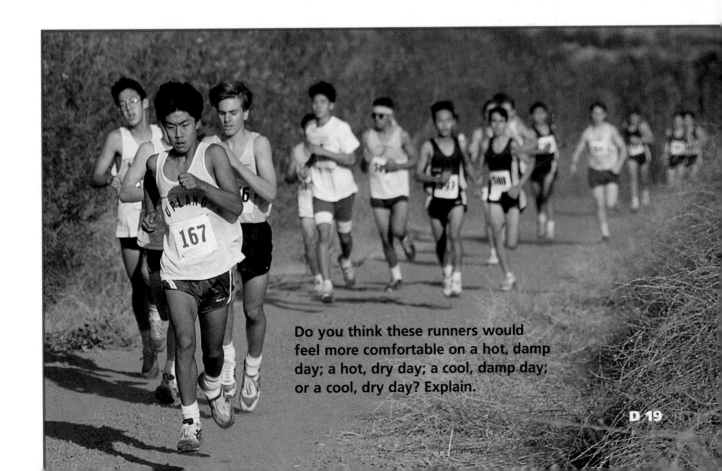

Do you think these runners would feel more comfortable on a hot, damp day; a hot, dry day; a cool, damp day; or a cool, dry day? Explain.

D 19

What Happens When Warm, Moist Air Cools?

How can warm, moist air cool off? In the lower atmosphere, the air gets colder with increasing altitude.

- Air can cool by being pushed upward over mountains by winds.

- Heating the air also causes it to rise. When the Sun heats the ground, air above the ground warms and rises. As it rises, it expands and cools.

- Air can also be pushed upward when cooler air and warmer air meet. When the two meet, they don't mix. The lighter, warm air is pushed up over the heavier, cold air. The result is the warm air, pushed higher into the atmosphere, cools.

In each case the end result is the same. As the air rises and cools, the water vapor in it condenses into tiny water droplets, forming clouds.

If the temperature is below the freezing point of water, its water vapor will form a cloud of tiny ice crystals.

In order for water vapor to condense, it must have a surface on which the liquid droplet or ice crystal will form. This surface is provided by tiny dust particles in the air. You will learn more about clouds in the next lesson.

▷ **How can warm air rise and cool?**

How Clouds Form

1 Cloud forms

Warm air

2 Cloud forms

Warm air

3 Cloud forms

Warm air

Cool air

READING Diagrams

1. What can cause air to rise?

2. What happens to the air temperature as air rises?

L·I·N·K·S

Why It Matters

Have you ever had sweat trickle down your face on a hot day? People sweat every day. Sweating is a way our bodies release wastes. We don't always feel the sweat because we sweat gradually, and it evaporates.

As sweat evaporates, the water droplets absorb heat from the skin's surface, cooling it. It is a way your body controls surface temperature.

On very hot days and when you are physically active, you may sweat a lot. The sweat builds up, does not evaporate fast, and collects. On a high-humidity day, you feel even "stickier." On a low-humidity day, the sweat evaporates more quickly. You might think you're not sweating—but you are.

Think and Write

1. Where does water vapor in the air come from? What process produces it?

2. How is relative humidity different from humidity? How are the two terms alike?

3. What causes water vapor to change into droplets of liquid water?

4. How does water vapor get cooled in the atmosphere?

5. **Critical Thinking** Would you say that the Sun is a cause of clouds? Defend your answer.

WRITING LINK

Write an essay. Why are you more comfortable in lower relative humidity? Write an essay explaining how relative humidity can affect you.

MATH LINK

Find the heat index. Use an almanac to find a heat index prepared by the weather service. This chart tells how warm a person feels at a particular temperature and humidity level. Using the chart, find the heat index for each of the days in the table below. Then use newspaper weather reports for one week last summer. Find the heat index for each of those days.

	Mon	Tues	Wed	Thurs	Fri
High temp.	25°C	35°C	30°C	35°C	25°C
Relative humidity	90%	97%	89%	48%	45%

ART LINK

Make a poster. Very hot, humid weather can be dangerous. Make a poster warning about the dangers of very hot, humid weather. Include a list of safety tips.

TECHNOLOGY LINK

At the Computer Visit **www.mhscience02.com** for more links.

Clouds and Precipitation

Get Ready

How can you predict the weather without using the instruments weather forecasters use? Look at the sky. There are clues up there. They're called clouds. Different kinds of clouds bring different kinds of weather. What is a cloud? What makes a cloud form? What do evaporation and condensation have to do with it?

Process Skill

You infer when you form an idea from facts or observations.

Explore Activity

How Do Clouds Form?

Materials

hot tap water

2 identical clear containers

mug

3 ice cubes

food coloring

Procedure

BE CAREFUL! Be careful handling the hot water.

1. Chill container 1 by putting it in a refrigerator or on ice for about ten minutes.

2. Fill a mug with hot water.

3. **Make a Model** Fill container 2 with hot water. Place empty cold container 1 upside down on top of container 2 with the water. Fit the mouths together carefully. Place the ice cubes on top of container 1.

4. **Observe** Record your observations.

Drawing Conclusions

1. **Communicate** What did you observe?

2. **Communicate** Where did this take place?

3. **Infer** Where did the water come from? Explain what made it happen.

4. **Going Further: Infer** Where would you expect to find more clouds—over the ocean or over a desert? Why?

Read to Learn

Main Idea Water vapor and ice form clouds that produce precipitation.

How Do Clouds Form?

What has to happen for a cloud to form? Clouds are made up of tiny water droplets or ice crystals. The air is filled with water vapor. When the air is cooled, the water vapor condenses. That is, the water molecules clump together around dust and other particles in the air. They form droplets of water.

Clouds look different depending on what they are made of. Water-droplet clouds tend to have sharp, well-defined edges. If the cloud is very thick, it may look gray, or even black. That's because sunlight is unable to pass through. Ice-crystal clouds tend to have fuzzy, less distinct edges. They also look whiter.

All clouds form in the troposphere. There are three basic cloud forms. **Stratus clouds** form in blanketlike layers. **Cumulus clouds** are puffy clouds that appear to rise up from a flat bottom. **Cirrus clouds** form at very high altitudes out of ice crystals and have a wispy, featherlike shape. If rain or snow falls from a cloud, the term *nimbo* or *nimbus*—for "rain"—is added to the cloud's name.

Clouds are further grouped into families by height and form. They are low clouds, middle clouds, high clouds, and clouds that develop upward—clouds of vertical development. Cumulonimbus clouds develop upward. These clouds bring thunderstorms.

Stratus clouds

Cumulus clouds

Cirrus clouds

They can start as low clouds and reach up to the highest clouds. If moist air at ground level cools, a cloud can form right there. A cloud at ground level is called **fog**.

▶ **What are three basic cloud forms?**

Types of Clouds

Cirrus

Anvil top

Cirrocumulus

High clouds

Altocumulus

Cirrostratus

5 km

Clouds of vertical development

Altostratus

Middle clouds

Cumulonimbus
(vertical development)

Stratus

2 km

Low clouds

Nimbostratus

Stratocumulus

Cumulus

0 km

Fog

READING Diagrams

1. How are low, middle, and high clouds different?

2. Why are clouds of vertical development not grouped together with any of the other cloud families?

What Is Precipitation?

How do rain and snow form and fall? **Precipitation** is any form of water particles that falls from the atmosphere and reaches the ground. Precipitation can be liquid (rain) or solid (such as snow).

Clouds are made up of tiny water droplets or ice crystals—only about $\frac{1}{50}$ of a millimeter across. These tiny particles are so light that they remain "hanging" in the air. This is why many clouds do not form precipitation.

Precipitation occurs when cloud droplets or ice crystals join together and become heavy enough to fall. They clump around particles of dust in the air. Each particle is like a *nucleus* that the water molecules condense around. The chart shows the different types of precipitation and how they form.

> **When does precipitation occur?**

READING
Diagrams

1. Classify the types of precipitation into two groups—solids and liquids.
2. Which types of precipitation form in similar ways?

Types of Precipitation

Condensation around nucleus	Condensation around nucleus	Condensation around ice nucleus	Condensation around nucleus
○	○	○	○ Cloud droplet
		Supercooled water freezes around ice nucleus, or water vapor changes to ice crystals.	Freezing
Cloud droplets collect. ◎	Cloud droplets collect. ◎	Ice crystals grow larger.	Cloud droplets collect around ice crystal. Freezing
	Raindrop ○	Snowflakes	Repeats over and over
Fall through warm air	Fall through air at freezing temperature	Cold ground temperature	Warm ground temperature
Rain	**Sleet**	**Snow**	**Hail**

Are Cloud Type and Precipitation Related?

Do certain kinds of clouds give certain kinds of precipitation? Yes.

- In tall clouds there is more chance for droplets to run into one another and combine, making larger raindrops.

- Precipitation from large cumulus clouds is often heavy rain or snow showers that don't last too long.

- Precipitation from stratus clouds is usually long lasting, with smaller drops of rain or snowflakes.

- Clouds with great vertical development hold a lot of water. These clouds are very *turbulent*, or violent. Their tops often reach heights where it is below freezing. They often produce great downpours. They also sometimes produce *hail*. Hail is pellets or lumps of ice.

These clouds have updrafts—strong winds that move up inside. Hail forms when updrafts in these huge clouds hurl ice pellets upward again and again. As the pellets fall, they become coated with water. As they rise, the water freezes into an icy outer shell. This process usually happens over and over, adding more and more layers to the hailstones. The more violent the updrafts, the bigger the hailstone can get before it falls to the ground.

READING Main Idea

What kind of cloud can produce hail? Why?

Path of Growing Hailstone

Strong winds in cloud

Strong winds

Hailstones form in layers and can sometimes grow very large. Hailstorms can be very dangerous.

What Is the Water Cycle?

When precipitation reaches Earth's surface, it doesn't just disappear. Some of it evaporates right back into the atmosphere. Some of it runs off the surface into rivers and streams. We call this water *runoff*.

Much of it seeps into the ground. We call this water *groundwater*. Groundwater collects in tiny holes, or pores, in soil and rocks. Groundwater can often seep down through soil and rocks when the pores are interconnected. It can fill up all the pores in a layer of rock below the surface. Much of this water eventually moves back to the rivers and then to lakes or oceans.

Earth's water moves from place to place through the processes of evaporation, condensation, and precipitation. Condensation and precipitation take water out of Earth's atmosphere.

READING
Diagrams

What happens to precipitation once it reaches Earth's surface?

The Water Cycle

Condensation the process in which a gas is changed to a liquid

Transpiration the process by which plant leaves release water into the air

Evaporation the process in which a liquid changes directly to a gas

Evaporation puts water back into the atmosphere. This complex web of changes is called the **water cycle**.

The water cycle is the continuous movement of water between Earth's surface and the air, changing from liquid to gas to liquid. The diagram shows the many different paths water can take into and out of the atmosphere in the water cycle.

▷ **What are the main processes of the water cycle?**

Precipitation any form of water particles that falls to Earth's surface

Groundwater water that seeps into pores in soil and rocks

Runoff water that runs off Earth's solid surface

QUICK LAB

FOR SCHOOL OR HOME

Feel the Humidity

1. **Observe** Use a thermometer to record the air temperature.

2. Put the thermometer in cold water. Slowly add warm water until the water temperature matches the air temperature.

3. Wrap a 5-cm-square piece of old cotton cloth around the bulb of the thermometer. Gently hold it with a rubber band. Dampen the cloth in the water.

4. **Observe** Gently wave the thermometer in the air. Record temperatures every 30 seconds for 3 minutes.

5. **Infer** What happened to the temperature of the wet cloth? How does the cloth feel? Explain.

6. **Infer** If you try this experiment on a day that is humid and on a day that is dry will you get the same results? Explain.

How Do You Record How Cloudy It Is?

As you observe the weather each day, you might wish to record the types of clouds you see in the sky. You can use the charts in this lesson to indicate the cloud family and the types of clouds.

Try to estimate the cloud cover— that is, the amount of the sky covered by clouds. Use the terms *clear*, *scattered clouds*, *partly cloudy*, *mostly cloudy*, or *overcast* to describe cloud cover.

One way to record cloud cover is to make a weather station model. Start by drawing a circle for each day. An empty circle means "clear skies." A fully shaded circle means "completely overcast." Portions of a circle are shaded to show different amounts of cloud cover.

Precipitation is measured with a rain gauge. You can make a simple rain gauge from an empty coffee can. Place it outside, open end up, away from buildings or trees. When the precipitation stops, measure its depth in the can. Keep track of the type of precipitation and how much falls.

▷ **What are the terms used to record cloud cover?**

○	Clear
●	Overcast
◔	Scattered clouds
◑	Partly cloudy
◕	Mostly cloudy

Symbols are used to show cloud cover on a weather station model.

Why It Matters

If you ever had a baseball game rained out, you know how rain can ruin your day.

Rain may ruin your plans for a day, and flooding can sometimes cause disasters. However, rain is vital for life on Earth. Rain helps crops grow. That means food for you and others. Rain helps build the amount of water in wells and water-collecting areas, such as reservoirs. If you ever had a drought in your area, a time when there is little or no precipitation, you know how scarce water can be.

Hail, on the other hand, can ruin entire crops. It can also damage cars and buildings.

Think and Write

1. How do clouds form?

2. What are some different types of precipitation? Why are there different types?

3. What are the main processes that show how liquid water changes in the water cycle? List them in order.

4. How can you measure and describe the amount of precipitation and cloud cover on a given day?

5. **Critical Thinking** "Sun showers" are sudden rainfalls on a sunny day. How can a sun shower happen?

L·I·N·K·S

LITERATURE LINK

Read *The Great Johnstown Flood*, the story of the storm that destroyed a town. When you finish reading, think about how you would prepare for a flood. Try the activities at the end of the book.

The Great Johnstown Flood

by Lisa Sorley

MATH LINK

Calculate your accuracy. Observe the clouds in your area each day for a week. Predict the weather based on the precipitation those clouds are likely to produce. Keep a record of how accurate your predictions are. At the end of the week, calculate—in percent—your accuracy.

SOCIAL STUDIES LINK

Research Inuit words. The Inuit have more than 20 different words for snow. Research and write a report on why you think they use so many.

TECHNOLOGY LINK

Science Newsroom CD-ROM Choose *On the Vapor Trail* to learn more about how warm, moist air reacts when it cools.

At the Computer Visit **www.mhscience02.com** for more links.

Flood: Good News or Bad?

Can you imagine a flood being good news? It was to many ancient Egyptians living near the Nile River. They looked forward to its annual summer flood. Land that was flooded was better for crops!

No one knew for sure why the flood came. Some people believed that great rains fell near the source of the Nile to start the flood. Much of the water actually comes from rains that fall in the mountains of Ethiopia.

Ethiopia has many mountains over 4,000 meters (13,000 feet) tall. In June the monsoons blow from the South Atlantic over the rain forests of Africa. When the winds reach the mountains of Ethiopia, giant rain clouds let loose their water in great thunderstorms. Rain-filled mountain streams join to form a great river. The river carries the water to the Nile. By July the water reaches Egypt and produces the flood.

Summer winds

MEDITERRANEAN SEA

EGYPT

SAUDI ARABIA

NILE RIVER

RED SEA

SUDAN

ETHIOPIA

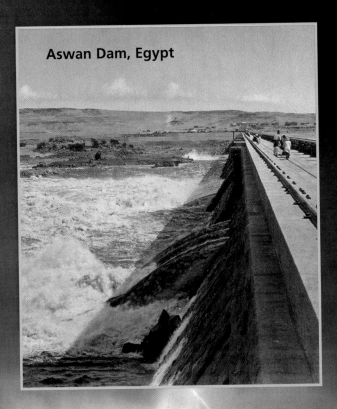
Aswan Dam, Egypt

Today the flood waters are stopped soon after they reach Egypt. A high dam holds back the water to form a great lake. The good news is that buildings on the shore are no longer swept away. Farmers no longer depend on floods to plant one crop each year. Now they have water to plant during summer and winter.

Stopping the flood has changed the environment, and that's bad news. The flood kept the fields fertile; but now farmers must use fertilizer. The Mediterranean Sea was nourished by mud from the Nile. Now fish that were common are gone, and a serious disease is spread by snails thriving in the Nile's slow waters.

What Did I Learn?

1. Where did the Nile flooding start?

A in the Red Sea
B in the Mediterranean Sea
C in the mountains of Ethiopia
D in Saudi Arabia

2. Stopping the Nile flooding

F kept the fields fertile
G increased the fish population
H killed off the snails
J changed the environment

AT THE COMPUTER

Visit www.mhscience02.com
to learn more about floods

Air Pressure and Wind

Vocabulary

wind, D38

convection cell, D38

sea breeze, D39

land breeze, D39

Coriolis effect, D40

isobar, D42

weather vane, D44

anemometer, D44

Get Ready

What makes the air move? What causes wind? Winds make these kites fly. Some winds move so fast and powerfully, they can knock down trees or even lift trucks into the air. Some winds can be so gentle, they hardly ruffle your hair. Air moves from one place to another because of differences in air pressure. What causes these differences?

Process Skill

You **use variables** when you identify and separate things in an experiment that can be changed or controlled.

Explore Activity

What Can Change Air Pressure?

Materials

plastic jar with hole in bottom

plastic sandwich bag

rubber band

masking tape

Procedure

1 **Make a Model** Set up a jar-and-bag system as shown. Make sure the masking tape covers the hole in the jar. Have a partner place both hands on the jar and hold it firmly. Reach in and slowly pull up on the bottom of the bag. Describe what happens.

2 **Experiment** Pull the small piece of tape off the hole in the bottom of the jar. Repeat step 1. Push in on the bag. Record your results.

3 **Observe** Place some small bits of paper on the table. Hold the jar close to the table. Point the hole toward the bits of paper. Pull up on the bag, and observe and record what happens.

4 **Experiment** Do just the opposite. Push the bag back into the jar. What happened?

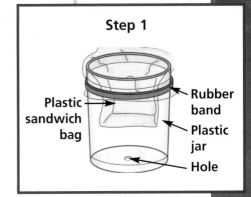

Step 1

Plastic sandwich bag

Rubber band

Plastic jar

Hole

Drawing Conclusions

1 **Observe** What differences did you observe with the hole taped and with the tape removed?

2 **Infer** Explain what happened each time you pushed the bag back into the jar. How does this model show air pressure changes?

3 **Going Further: Use Variables** Will the model work the same with paper clips? Bits of cotton? Make a prediction, and test it.

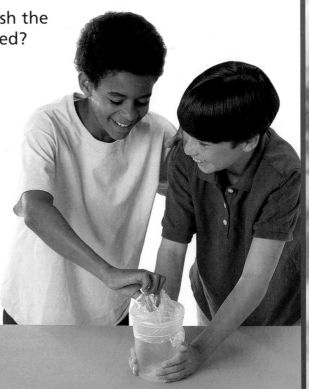

Main Idea Differences in air pressure on Earth's surface cause wind.

How Can Air Pressure Change?

Many factors can affect the air pressure of a region. Here are some of those factors.

Volume

Pulling up on the bag in the diagram below increases the volume inside the bag-jar system. The amount of air inside stays the same. The air inside the jar spreads out into the larger volume. The air pressure inside the bag-jar becomes less. The outside air pushes in harder than the inside air pushes out. That extra force pushing in is what you pull against as you pull up on the bag.

Height Above Earth's Surface

Air pressure depends on the weight of its molecules pressing down on a given area. Molecules are closer together, or more dense, at sea level than high in the atmosphere. Denser air weighs more than an equal volume of less dense air and pushes down harder. That is why air pressure is higher at sea level than high in the atmosphere.

Temperature

Air pressure also depends on temperature. When air is heated, its molecules speed up. The faster-moving molecules move around more. They

An Air Pressure Model

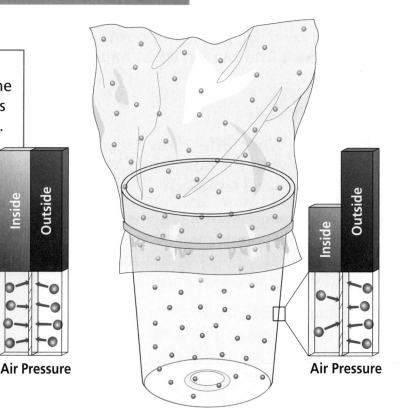

READING Diagrams

Explain what happens to the air pressure inside the jar as you push down on the bag.

Inside Outside

Air Pressure

Inside Outside

Air Pressure

Cold Air **Warm Air**

Even though the molecules are moving slower and collide with less force, the cold air on the left exerts more pressure because its closely spaced molecules collide much more frequently.

Oxygen molecule

Nitrogen molecule

READING
Diagrams

What differences do you see between the pictures for cold air and warm air?

spread out into a larger space. The same volume of air weighs less, and the pressure decreases. What do you think happens when air is cooled?

Amount of Water Vapor

Air is a mixture of nitrogen, oxygen, and other gases. Adding water vapor to air also affects air pressure. Molecules of oxygen or nitrogen are heavier than molecules of water vapor. Light molecules exert less pressure because they weigh less. In moist air lighter water vapor molecules take the place of heavier oxygen and nitrogen molecules. Moist air exerts less pressure than dry air.

You can now enter two more bits of information on your weather station model. To the upper right, place the air pressure reading in millibars. Right below this number, you may wish to put a short line. This line tells how air pressure is changing at that station.

- A line slanting to the upper right indicates the air pressure is rising (a rising barometer). A rising barometer may indicate fair weather approaching.

- A line slanting to the lower right indicates the air pressure is falling (a falling barometer). A falling barometer may be a sign that a storm is on its way.

- A horizontal line indicates the air pressure is not changing. In the station model, the air pressure is 980 millibars and is rising.

▷ **How would an increase in temperature affect air pressure?**

Showing Air Pressure on a Station Model

980 ← Air pressure (in millibars, mb)

Line showing change in air pressure

Why Do Winds Blow?

Think of what happens if you put a blob of soft clay on a table and push down on it, using a flat hand. The clay squishes out from under your fingers, where the pressure is high. It moves to the spaces between your fingers, where the pressure is lower.

Air acts in a similar way. Denser air exerts a higher pressure than less dense air. Like the clay, denser air flows toward less dense air. This flow of air is wind. Air that moves horizontally is called **wind**. Air that rises or sinks is an *updraft* or a *downdraft*.

Convection Cells

How can air become more or less dense? As the Sun's rays hit an area, they transfer energy to the air. The air heats up. Because it is warmer, the heated air is less dense. Then, just like a cork in water, the warm air rises above the surrounding cooler, denser air. On the other hand, if a region of air is cooled, it becomes denser and sinks.

This unequal heating and cooling of the air often makes a pattern of rising air, sinking air, and winds, called a **convection** (kuhn·VEK·shuhn) **cell**. A convection cell is a part of the atmosphere where air moves in a circular pattern because of unequal heating and cooling.

The drawing shows how a convection cell forms. Cities A and B have the same air pressure. Then direct sunlight heats city A. The air above it warms and expands. It becomes less dense and rises, forming an updraft. The air pressure goes down. The unheated air on either side has a higher pressure. This air moves in toward the low-pressure area, making a surface wind.

▶ **How are winds produced?**

READING Diagrams

Use the diagram to explain what happens to city B during the formation of the convection cell.

Updraft

Warm air rising

Cool air sinking

Downdraft

Wind

CITY A

CITY B

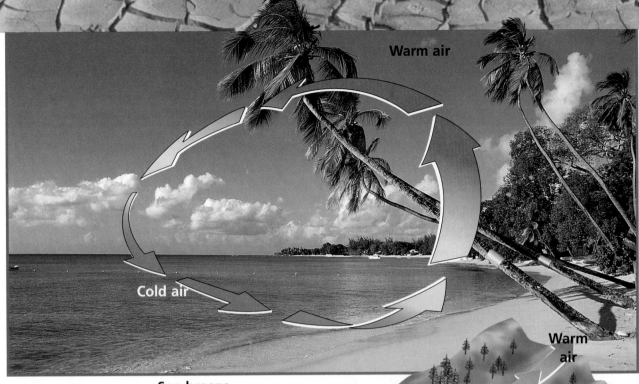

Warm air

Cold air

Sea breeze

Warm air

Cold air

Valley breeze

What Are Sea and Land Breezes?

An example of convection is a breeze that occurs along a coastline.

In Lesson 1 you learned that land warms faster than water. On sunny days air over land warms faster than air next to it over the sea. The warm air expands and rises. Cooler air from over the ocean replaces the rising warm air. A wind blows onto the land. A wind that blows from the sea toward the land is called a **sea breeze**.

At night the reverse happens. The air over the land cools more rapidly than the air over the water. A **land breeze** blows from land toward the water.

Convection cells also occur along mountains. As the Sun shines on a mountain during the day, the slope heats up faster than the valley below.

READING
Diagrams

These pictures show what happens during the day. How would you show what happens at night?

Air over the slope warms and rises. Cooler air over the valley replaces the rising warm air, creating a *valley breeze* that blows up the slope. At night the mountain slope cools rapidly. This causes a *mountain breeze* to blow down the slope.

▷ **How are sea and land breezes produced?**

What Is the Coriolis Effect?

Earth's rotation affects winds blowing across its surface. As Earth rotates, every spot on its surface moves with it. However, in the same 24-hour period, places near the poles travel a shorter distance than places near the equator. This means that places near the poles are moving slower!

Now what if you are in an airplane flying in a straight line from the North Pole to Chicago? While you are in the air, Earth is *rotating*, or spinning, underneath you. Earth rotates counterclockwise as seen from the North Pole. As Earth rotates, Chicago is moving west to east. To someone in Chicago, though, the plane's flight path seems to curve to the southwest.

The same thing happens with winds blowing from the North Pole. Because Earth rotates, the winds seem to curve to the right as they head southward.

No matter which way the wind blows, it will curve to the right in the Northern Hemisphere. This curving is called the **Coriolis effect**. In the Southern Hemisphere, the Coriolis effect causes winds to curve to the left. This is because, as viewed from the South Pole, Earth rotates clockwise. The effect works on other moving objects as well, such as missiles and rockets.

 What causes the Coriolis effect?

Coriolis Effect

If you were standing at the North Pole looking south, this arrow would appear to curve to the right.

Rotation

If you were standing at the South Pole looking north, this arrow would appear to curve to the left.

How Are Global Wind Patterns Produced?

Year round the equator is heated strongly by sunlight. The air becomes very warm. Heat also causes evaporation, so the air becomes moist. Warm, moist air over the equator creates a zone of low pressure around the globe.

As the air at the equator warms, it becomes less dense and rises. It rises to the top of the troposphere and spreads out, moving north and south. As the air moves away from the equator, it cools and becomes denser. At about 30° north and south latitudes, the cold air begins to sink toward the surface. This sinking air creates a high-pressure zone on both sides of the equator at these latitudes. A belt of winds is set in motion around Earth by air moving from these high-pressure zones toward the low pressure at the equator. These are the *trade winds*. The Coriolis effect curves these winds, as you see in the diagram.

The poles get very low-angle sunlight, and the air there is very cold. Cold, dense air can hold very little water vapor. Cold, dry air over the poles has high pressure. Air at the poles moves toward 60° latitude, forming winds. Because of the Coriolis effect, the winds curve. These are the polar *easterly winds*. *Easterly* means the wind blows "from the east."

Other winds occur between 60° latitude and the poles as well as between 30° and 60° latitudes. Between 30° and 60° latitudes is the zone of *westerly winds*. The continental United States is in the zone of westerly winds.

▷ **What causes the global trade winds?**

Global Wind Zones

90°N

Polar easterlies

60°N

Prevailing westerlies

30°N

Trade winds

0° equator

Trade winds

30°S

Prevailing westerlies

60°S

Polar easterlies

90°S

READING

Diagrams

Make a table listing different global wind zones and a description of the directions in which winds move in each zone.

What Are Isobars?

Why is it important to know about air pressure? Knowing where the air pressure is high or low allows you to predict which way air will move. This is why weather scientists make maps showing air pressure. They start by plotting the air pressure at many different locations on a map. Then they connect all places with the same air pressure with a line. A line on a map connecting places with equal air pressure is called an **isobar**. Isobars make pressure patterns easier to see.

Find the series of circular isobars in the west, surrounding a region of high pressure (H). This pattern is called a *high-pressure system*. Since the center has higher pressure than its surroundings, winds blow outward from the center in a clockwise pattern.

A similar set of isobars in the east marks a *low-pressure system* (L). In a low-pressure system, the central region is surrounded by higher pressure. The winds blow in toward the center in a counterclockwise pattern.

The pressure on each isobar is in millibars (mb).

Isobars also help scientists predict how fast air will move. Big differences in air pressure over short distances cause strong winds. This is shown on a map by drawing closely spaced isobars. Small differences in air pressure cause gentle winds. This is shown by widely spaced isobars.

You show wind on a station model by a straight line touching the circle. The line tells where the wind is blowing from. "Feathers" are used to show speed.

READING Main Idea
How do isobars help scientists predict how air will move?

How Winds Blow

Clockwise direction

A   High pressure

B   Low pressure

Showing Wind on a Station Model

NE

NE = Northeast wind

Full feather = 14–22 km/h (8–12 knots)

Half feather = 5–13 km/h (3–7 knots)

A Weather Station Model

A weather station model includes temperature, cloud cover, air pressure, pressure tendency, wind speed, and wind direction. The circle is at the location of the station. You will interpret the data—use the information—from the weather station models to answer questions and solve problems.

Wind direction (from north)

Wind speed (knots or km/h)

Air temperature (°C) (It may also be recorded in °F.) → **13** | **1014**

Air pressure (mb)

Pressure change

Cloud cover

34 ○ 1004 — **Dallas**

28 — 980 **Charlotte**

14 ◔ 1012 **Oakland**

30 ◑ 996 **Tampa**

Procedure

1. **Use Numbers** Look carefully at the Dallas weather station model. How fast is the wind blowing? What is the wind direction? Record your answers.

2. **Interpret Data** What other information does this weather station model give you?

3. Look at the other weather station models. Make a table recording weather conditions for each city.

Drawing Conclusions

1. Compare the information in the table you made with these station models. Which way is the information easier to interpret?

2. **Interpret Data** Where was wind fastest? Slowest? Which tells you this information more quickly, the table or the models?

3. **Communicate** Compare and contrast other weather conditions in the cities.

Anemometer

weather vane

Wind speed is measured with a device called an **anemometer** (an·uh·MAHM·i·tuhr). An anemometer is a series of cups mounted on a shaft that can spin freely. When the wind blows against the cups, they spin like a pinwheel. The faster the wind blows, the faster the cups spin the shaft. A speedometer is attached to the shaft to measure wind speed.

How Do We Study the Wind?

What is that curious-looking device on the roof? It is a **weather vane**. It is used to tell wind direction. A weather vane has a pointer that blows around in the wind. The pointer is mounted so it can point to the different compass markings.

The tail of the pointer has a larger surface area than the tip. When a wind blows, it exerts more pressure on the tail than the tip. This causes the tail to swing around so that the tip points in the direction the wind is blowing from.

The Beaufort Scale

Strong winds create high waves. That is why sailors have always been concerned about wind speed. In 1805, Sir Francis Beaufort of the British Navy devised a system for measuring wind speed by observing its effect on the surface of the sea. He assigned a number from 0 to 12 to each effect. This is the Beaufort scale.

 What devices are used to find wind speed and direction?

Beaufort Wind Scale

Type of Wind	Kilometers per Hour	Miles per Hour	Observations
0 Calm	less than 1	less than 0.6	Calm; smoke rises straight up
1 Light air	1–5	0.6–3	Weather vanes don't move
2 Light breeze	6–11	4–7	Weather vanes move slightly
3 Gentle breeze	12–19	8–12	Leaves move; flags stretch out
4 Moderate breeze	20–29	13–18	Small branches sway
5 Fresh breeze	30–38	19–24	Trees sway; white caps on ponds
6 Strong breeze	39–50	25–31	Large branches sway
7 Moderate gale	51–61	32–38	Hard to walk into the wind
8 Fresh gale	62–74	39–46	Branches break off trees
9 Strong gale	75–87	47–54	Shingles blow off roofs
10 Whole gale	88–101	55–63	Trees are uprooted
11 Storm	102–117	64–73	Extensive damage
12 Hurricane	118+	74+	Violent destruction

Why It Matters

Wind can be very useful. It is often used as a source of power. Winds turn special machinery— windmills— that produce electricity. They run the machinery that grinds grain. Windmills are still used today to pump water.

Wind also carries pollen to flowers. Seeds form as a result. Many kinds of seeds, in turn, are carried by wind to new places.

Think and Write

1. What makes air pressure change?

2. What causes wind to blow in a particular direction?

3. Why are there zones of winds around the world?

4. **Interpret Data** On a weather map, how can you compare the speed and direction of winds in different locations?

5. **Critical Thinking** How might you make a simple device to tell wind direction?

L·I·N·K·S

LITERATURE LINK

Read *The Sky-Watchers,* the story of how two students maintained a weather station. When you finish reading, think about how you would build a weather station. Try the activities at the end of the book.

WRITING LINK

Write a story. List all the ways you can think of that people can make use of the wind. Write a story about them.

MATH LINK

Calculate weather factors. Collect a week's worth of national weather maps from a newspaper. Select a region of the country, such as the Midwest or Southeast. Calculate its average temperature, wind speed, and air pressure.

SOCIAL STUDIES LINK

Write a report. Research the origin of the term "trade winds," and write a report on your findings.

TECHNOLOGY LINK

At the Computer Visit **www.mhscience02.com** for more links.

Hurricane Hunters

Winds are blowing at 200 kilometers per hour (125 miles per hour). There's so much rain, city streets look like rivers. Huge waves pound the shores, flooding coastal areas. This is not your average storm. It's a hurricane. It's time to stay indoors and protect yourself, right? Not if you're a hurricane hunter. For hurricane hunters, it's time to get in an airplane and fly into the middle of the storm.

Hurricanes are powerful storms. They form over warm oceans and sometimes move onto land. It's important to know where a hurricane will hit land. Meteorologists measure air pressure, temperature, and wind speeds to try to predict a hurricane's path. They track the storm with satellites and radar, but these efforts are often not enough. The most helpful measurements are taken inside the storm.

People who fly specially equipped airplanes into hurricanes are called hurricane hunters. Their planes can withstand wind speeds up to 483 km/h (300 mph). As the plane enters the hurricane, it passes through bands of howling winds, blinding rain, and thunderstorms. The ride gets very bumpy. Often the crew cannot read instruments because the plane is shaking so much. The rain is so loud, they cannot hear each other speak, and the plane is often hit by lightning!

Hurricane winds swirl around the "eye"—a calm area in the center of the storm. As the airplane flies through the eye, a crew member drops a device called a dropsonde from the plane. A dropsonde is a small tube with an attached parachute. The tube contains measuring instruments and a radio transmitter. As the dropsonde falls toward the sea, it

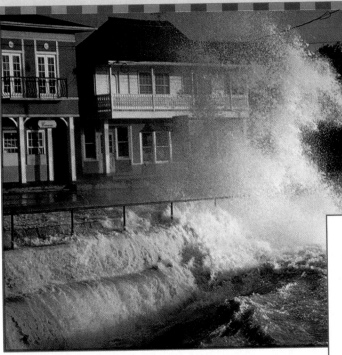

What Did I Learn?

1. Hurricane hunters

A track storms from their offices in Florida

B parachute through hurricanes

C watch for hurricanes from the seashore

D fly special planes into hurricanes

2. A dropsonde is

F what the hurricane hunters call their airplanes

G a parachute carried into a hurricane

H a small tube with special instruments that is dropped from a plane

J the radio hurricane hunters use to call the National Weather Service

transmits weather data up to the airplane. Crew members send these data to the National Hurricane Center in Miami, Florida. There, scientists use the weather data to determine the strength of the hurricane, and predict the direction it is heading. Sometimes they alert people to move from their homes near the coast to safer buildings inland.

Hurricane hunters brave some of Earth's roughest weather. To get all the information needed, a crew may make several passes through a storm. Flights may last 11 hours or more, but hurricane hunters know their efforts may save many lives.

AT THE COMPUTER

Visit **www.mhscience02.com** for more amazing stories and facts about storms.

Chapter 8 Review

Vocabulary

Fill each blank with the best word or words from the list.

barometer, D12
cirrus cloud, D24
condensation, D17
Coriolis effect, D40
evaporation, D16
humidity, D16
land breeze, D39
precipitation, D26
sea breeze, D39
stratus cloud, D24

1. Rain, snow, and sleet are kinds of _____.

2. The _____ causes winds to follow a curved path over Earth's surface.

3. A(n) _____ forms in blanketlike layers.

4. Liquid changes directly to a gas by the process called _____.

5. The amount of water vapor in the air is called _____.

6. Wind blowing from the ocean toward the land is called a(n) _____.

7. Wind blowing from the land toward the ocean is called a(n) _____.

8. The process that turns water vapor into raindrops is called _____.

9. A high, wispy cloud made of ice crystals is a(n) _____.

10. A(n) _____ measures air pressure.

Test Prep

11. The water cycle describes how water _____.
    A flows upstream
    B spins in a tornado
    C changes form
    D heats up the atmosphere

12. Weather takes place in the _____.
    F thermosphere
    G mesosphere
    H troposphere
    J stratosphere

13. Water drops that collect on a cold glass of lemonade come from _____.
    A the lemonade
    B the air
    C a puddle
    D the glass itself

14. Isobars indicate _____.
    F humidity
    G temperature
    H air pressure
    J cloud cover

15. On a hot day, a lake is likely to be _____.

   A cooler than nearby land

   B hotter than nearby land

   C the same temperature as the land

   D the cause of the heat

Concepts and Skills

16. Reading in Science Write a paragraph explaining why north winds blow to the southwest.

17. Safety Why do you need to be careful on hot days when the relative humidity is high? Write a paragraph explaining your answer.

18. Scientific Methods How much does humidity change over a day? Write up a design for an experiment that would test this.

19. Process Skills: Interpret Data You are given this information on a weather map: What kind of weather is city A having? What kind of weather is city B having? Write a paragraph explaining your answer.

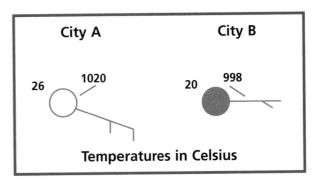

20. Critical Thinking What if there were no plants? Do you think Earth would still get as much rain as it does now? Write your ideas. Describe how you might test them.

Boost your test scores!

Be Smart!

Visit www.mhscience02.com

Weather Patterns and Climate

Did You Ever Wonder?

Why is a desert hot and dry? Conditions in the Mojave Desert
in California are partly caused by the mountains you see in the
background. Rain falls on the other side of the mountains before
it can reach the Mojave. Why does one side of a mountain get a lot
of rain while the other side gets very little?

Air Masses and Fronts

Get Ready

Have you ever watched a "wall" of clouds heading toward you? Did the clouds bring gentle, steady rain or heavy downpours? Knowing what kind of weather is on the way can help you make plans.

Part of what weather forecasters need to watch for is approaching air masses and fronts. Why might your weather today depend on what someone else's weather was like yesterday?

Process Skill

You interpret data when you use the information that has been gathered to answer questions or solve a problem.

Explore Activity

How Can You Compare Weather?

Materials

station model key

newspaper weather map (optional)

pencil

crayons

Procedure

Communicate Think of the country in large regions—the Northeast, the Southwest, and so on. Think of regions like the Pacific Coast, the Atlantic Coast, and the Gulf Coast. Write a report for the weather in each region based on the map you see here.

Drawing Conclusions

1 **Infer** Which areas are having warm, rainy weather?

2 **Infer** Where is the weather cool and dry?

3 **Predict** How do you think weather in any part of the country may change, based on the data in this map? Give reasons for your answer. How would you check your predictions?

4 **Going Further: Interpret Data** Using weather maps in a newspaper, or the one on this page, describe the weather.

W   E

San Francisco

Lines are drawn to show wind direction, not speed. This is a wind coming from the east, going west—an east wind.

55 1014 Seattle

47 1020 Butte

CANADA

30 1013 Bismarck

Minneapolis 34 1010

Buffalo 40 1008

Boston 39 1014

57 1025 Salt Lake City

Detroit 44® 1039

60 1014 San Francisco

51 1020 Denver

Chicago 40 1004

42® 1011 New York

62 1015 Los Angeles

Kansas City 50 1011

Cincinnati 60® 1001

Richmond 45® 1008

68 1017 Phoenix

54 1013 Oklahoma City

57 1016 Roswell

58 1014 Fort Worth

71 1009 Atlanta

N

NW   NE

W   E

SW   SE

S

Jacksonville 72 1016

60® 1011 Galveston

76® 1010 New Orleans

Temperatures here are given in Fahrenheit degrees.

MEXICO

Miami 80 1020

® = rain

D 53

Main Idea Weather changes often occur at fronts, where different air masses meet.

How Do Air Masses Affect Weather?

Weather maps show that cities across a large region can share the same weather. They also show how the weather in different areas can differ.

Why are weather conditions in one part of a country different from those in another part? Look back at the map on page D53. Some of the cities are having clear, cool weather. The air throughout this region is cool and dry. Other cities are having warmer, cloudy weather. The air throughout this region is warm and moist. A large region of the atmosphere where the air has similar properties throughout is called an **air mass**.

An air mass gets its properties from the region where it forms. Air over the Gulf of Mexico is above very warm water. The water warms the air, and evaporation from the Gulf adds water vapor. The air becomes warm and moist. Air masses are named for the region they come from.

As air masses move, they bring these conditions with them. What happens if a cool, moist air mass moves over an area that has warm, dry weather? The warm, dry weather will change.

Air Masses

Continental polar (cP)
cold, dry air

Maritime polar (mP)
cool, moist air

Maritime polar (mP)
cool, moist air

Pacific Ocean

Atlantic Ocean

Maritime tropical (mT)
warm, moist air

Continental tropical (cT)
hot, dry air

Maritime tropical (mT)
warm, moist air

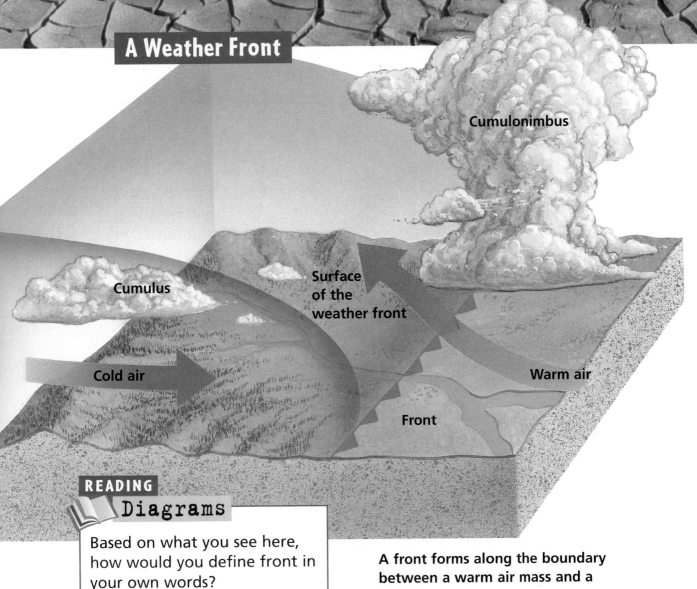

A Weather Front

Cumulonimbus

Cumulus

Surface
of the
weather front

Cold air

Warm air

Front

READING Diagrams

Based on what you see here, how would you define front in your own words?

A front forms along the boundary between a warm air mass and a cold air mass.

Once an air mass is formed, it is moved by global winds. In the United States, global winds tend to move air masses from west to east.

Air masses with different conditions can "meet." That is, one runs into another. What happens when air masses with different temperatures meet? They don't mix together. Instead, a narrow boundary forms between them. This boundary is called a **front**. It marks the leading edge, or front, of an air mass that is moving into an area where another air mass is moving out. Weather changes rapidly at fronts. That's because you pass from one kind of air mass into another. Fronts often cause rainy, unsettled weather. There are several types of fronts that can form.

READING Sequence of Events
What happens when a cold air mass meets with a warm air mass?

How Do Fronts Affect Weather?

- In a **cold front**, cold air moves in under a warm air mass. Cold fronts often bring brief, heavy storms. There may be thunderstorms and strong winds. After the storm the skies are usually clearer, and the weather is usually cooler and drier.

- In a **warm front**, warm air moves in over a cold air mass. Warm fronts often bring light, steady rain or snow. The precipitation may last for days. Winds are usually light.

Warm fronts may also bring fog—stratus clouds that form near the ground. Afterward the weather is usually warmer and more humid.

- An **occluded** (uh·KLEWD·uhd) **front** occurs when a cold front and a warm front meet. A fast-moving cold front moves in on a warm front. There are two ways this can happen:

    In a cold-front occlusion, the air behind the front is cold. The air ahead of the warm front is cool. What is happening is that cold air is

Weather Produced by Fronts

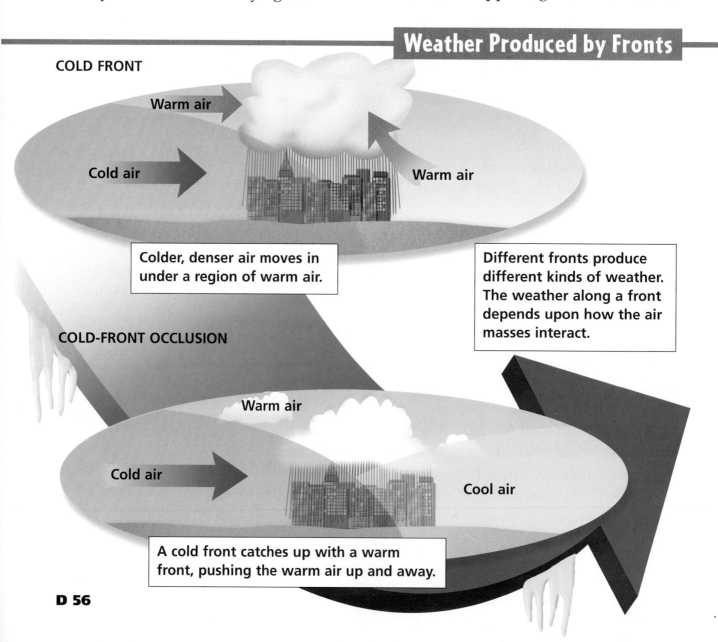

COLD FRONT

Warm air

Cold air

Warm air

Colder, denser air moves in under a region of warm air.

Different fronts produce different kinds of weather. The weather along a front depends upon how the air masses interact.

COLD-FRONT OCCLUSION

Warm air

Cold air

Cool air

A cold front catches up with a warm front, pushing the warm air up and away.

moving in on cool air and warm air is pushed up between them. The weather along this front will be like that produced by a cold front.

In a warm-front occlusion, the air behind the incoming cold front is just cool, not cold. The air in front of the warm front, however, might be cold. Then the weather will be more like that produced by a warm front.

- A cold air mass and a warm air mass may meet and remain over an area for days without moving. This is called a **stationary front**. Stationary fronts usually have calm weather.

▷ **What kind of weather does a cold front usually produce?**

READING Diagrams

1. Write a paragraph comparing a warm front with a cold front.

2. Write an explanation of what an occluded front is.

WARM FRONT

Warm air

Cold air

Warm air moves into a region, rising up and over the colder air mass already there.

WARM-FRONT OCCLUSION

Warm air

Cool air

Cold air

A cold front catches up with a warm front, pushing the warm air up and away.

Why Are Weather Satellites Important?

Pictures taken from space are great tools for seeing large weather patterns, such as fronts and storms. Scientists send up satellites in orbit around Earth. Some of these satellites are equipped to take pictures of weather patterns. These satellites move in orbit in a way that allows them to follow a weather pattern as it moves slowly across Earth's surface.

To find fronts on a satellite map, look for swirling lines of clouds. The curved lines often mark the movement of fronts.

Fronts are an important clue to how weather will change. As a front moves, areas just ahead of the front are about to have a change in weather.

Weather satellites are located above the equator. They are more than 36,000 km (22,000 mi) above Earth's surface. Several of these satellites work together to produce a nearly complete picture of the globe every half-hour.

The weather may be cool and dry before a front approaches. The weather then becomes rainy and warmer as the front passes by.

When fronts collide, scientists can locate places where the weather may change quickly, even dangerously. Sudden storms may break out. Knowing about fronts helps scientists to stay on the alert!

▷ **How do scientists use weather satellites?**

READING
Maps

1. Where do you see low pressure systems in the satellite picture? What do the clouds appear to be doing?

2. What kind of weather is happening in different parts of the country in each map? Explain.

Front Symbols

Warm front

Cold front

Occluded front

Stationary front

QUICK LAB

Weather Prediction

1. The map shows weather across the United States at 6 P.M. on October 29. Describe the weather in Washington, D.C. The temperatures are in degrees Celsius.

2. Describe the weather in the northwest part of the country and in the southeast.

3. Infer Weather patterns move from west to east across the United States. How do you think the weather just east of the cold front will change in the next day or so? Explain.

The temperatures here are given in Celsius degrees.

Why Use Weather Records?

Scientists usually forecast the weather using a *synoptic weather map*. It shows a summary of the weather using station models. By comparing maps made every six hours, scientists can tell how weather systems are moving and use this information to predict the weather.

If you look at weather records to see what happened in the past, you can find patterns. *Statistical forecasting* is based on finding patterns.

What if the wind has just started blowing from the west? Past records show that 75 out of the last 100 times the wind blew from the west, your weather became clearer and colder. What weather prediction would you make?

▷ **How do scientists use weather records to forecast weather?**

L·I·N·K·S

Why It Matters

Weather forecasting is hard. Knowing how the atmosphere is moving lets you predict the weather. The problem is that the atmosphere is huge and complex. A weather forecaster might predict clear weather for tomorrow. However, another air mass might move in. Everything can change.

Computers do high-speed calculations to predict the atmosphere's motion. Predictions are compared with forecasts to account for any differences. Two-day forecasts are calculated every 12 hours. A five-day forecast is calculated daily.

Think and Write

1. What are four different kinds of air masses? How are they different?

2. What kind of weather is produced by a cold front? A warm front?

3. How can satellites help predict the weather?

4. How can you use weather maps to predict weather?

5. **Critical Thinking** How can you tell what kind of front is passing by just by observing the weather?

WRITING LINK

Write a story. Explain how changes in the weather affected the way three different people spent their day.

SOCIAL STUDIES LINK

Research the history of weather prediction. Use encyclopedias or other reference books to learn about the *Book of Signs*. The *Book of Signs* is a book of 200 weather indicators. It was written in 300 B.C. by Theophrastus. Pick one of the signs dealing with weather fronts. Do you think that sign might be helpful in predicting the weather? Write a paragraph explaining why or why not.

TECHNOLOGY LINK

Science Newsroom CD-ROM Choose *It's Up in the Air* to learn more about how air masses affect weather conditions.

At the Computer Visit **www.mhscience02.com** for more links.

Weather Watch: Then and Now

The barometer is invented. Changes in air pressure help modern scientists predict the weather.

The telegraph is invented. Forecasters begin talking to one another and sharing information.

350 B.C.   A.D. 1643   1732   1837   1869

Aristotle writes one of the first books about weather. He tries to explain rain, snow, and other "meteors" from the sky!

Benjamin Franklin writes *Poor Richard's Almanac,* in which he predicts the next year's weather. He bases his forecasts on what he sees and a few measurements.

A telegraph system is set up across the nation. The system is used to collect weather data and warn people about storms.

AT THE COMPUTER

Visit www.mhscience02.com to learn more about weather.

Poor Richard, 1733.

AN

Almanack

For the Year of Chrift

1733,

Being the Firft after LEAP YEAR.

	Years
And makes fince the Creation	7241
By the Account of the Eaftern Greeks	6932
By the Latin Church, when ☉ ent. ♈	5742
By the Computation of W.W.	5682
By the Roman Chronology	5494

Scientists in Norway use math and physics to explain weather and identify weather patterns.

Doppler radar is developed. It compares radio waves sent out with those that bounce back. The greater the difference, the faster a storm is moving.

Two kinds of satellites track weather patterns. One orbits about 36,000 kilometers (22,000 miles) above Earth, monitoring changes in storm systems. The other orbits only 850 kilometers (530 miles) above Earth to provide details about cloud systems.

| 1918 | 1942 | 1954 | 1960 | Today |

During World War II, radar is used to locate storms by bouncing radio waves off raindrops in clouds.

NASA sends up its first weather satellite.

Write ABOUT IT

How do you think computers have helped make weather predictions more accurate?

Severe Storms

Vocabulary

thunderstorm, D66

tornado, D68

hurricane, D70

storm surge, D72

Get Ready

What's it like to be in the path of a tornado?
People have reported a sound like the rumble of
an approaching freight train. Tornadoes are the
most powerful storms on Earth. Although most
tornadoes are not very wide and they don't last
too long, when they touch down watch out! Like
deadly whirling brooms, they can sweep away
anything in their path. Tornadoes strike all parts
of the United States, but they are more frequent
in some regions than in others. Where in
the U.S. is "tornado country"?

Process Skill

**You use numbers when you use
ordering, counting, adding, subtracting,
multiplying, and dividing to explain data.**

Explore Activity

Where Do Tornadoes Occur?

Materials

map of U.S., including Alaska and Hawaii

blue marker

red marker

Procedure

1 **Infer** The table shown here lists how many tornadoes occurred in each state over a 30-year period. It also shows about how many tornadoes occur in each state each year. Look at the data in the table for two minutes. Now write what part of the country you think gets the most tornadoes.

2 Use the red marker to record on the map the number of tornadoes that occurred in each state over the 30-year period. Use the blue marker to record the average number of tornadoes that occurred in a year in each state.

Drawing Conclusions

1 **Use Numbers** Which states had fewer than 10 tornadoes a year? Which states had more than 20 tornadoes a year?

2 **Interpret Data** Which six states had the most tornadoes during the 30-year period?

3 **Interpret Data** Which part of the country had the most tornadoes?

4 **Going Further: Communicate** Many people refer to a certain part of the country as "Tornado Alley." Which part of the country do you think that is? Why do you think people call it that? What else might these states have in common? Describe how you would go about finding the answer to that question.

State	Total	Average per year
AL	668	22
AK	0	0
AZ	106	4
AR	596	20
CA	148	5
CO	781	26
CT	37	1
DE	31	1
FL	1,590	53
GA	615	21
HI	25	1
ID	80	3
IL	798	27
IN	604	20
IA	1,079	36
KS	1,198	40
KY	296	10
LA	831	28
ME	50	2
MD	86	3
MA	89	3
MI	567	19
MN	607	20
MS	775	26
MO	781	26
MT	175	6
NE	1,118	37
NV	41	1
NH	56	2
NJ	78	3
NM	276	9
NY	169	6
NC	435	15
ND	621	21
OH	463	15
OK	1,412	47
OR	34	1
PA	310	10
RI	7	0
SC	307	10
SD	864	29
TN	360	12
TX	4,174	139
UT	58	2
VT	21	1
VA	188	6
WA	45	2
WV	69	2
WI	625	21
WY	356	12

Main Idea Thunderstorms, tornadoes, and hurricanes are severe storms that can cause great damage.

What Are Thunderstorms?

A tornado is a violent kind of storm that forms under special conditions. Often such storms grow out of another, more common kind of storm—a **thunderstorm**.

Thunderstorms are the most common kind of severe storm. They form in clouds called *thunderheads*—cumulonimbus clouds. The storms cause huge electric sparks called *lightning*. The lightning heats the air and causes the noise called *thunder*. Thunderstorms usually have heavy rains and strong winds. Some thunderstorms also produce hail.

First Stage

A thunderstorm starts when intense heating causes air to rise very quickly. A cloud forms where there is an upward rush of heated air, an *updraft*. As more and more warm, moist air is carried upward, the cloud grows larger and larger. Strong updrafts keep droplets of water and ice crystals in the cloud, so they grow in size, too. When the updrafts can't support them anymore, they fall as heavy rain or even hail.

Second Stage

Once the rain falls, it causes downdrafts in the cloud. That is, air moves downward. When the air going up rubs against air going down, static electricity builds up. When enough builds up, there's a huge spark—lightning.

How a Thunderstorm Forms

Warm air rises.

1 Strong updrafts form inside the cloud.

Heavy rain

+++

+ = Positive electric charge

− = Negative electric charge

2 Electric charges build up inside the cloud.

Thunderstorms form in cumulonimbus clouds. Thunderstorms often produce strong winds and heavy downpours along with the lightning and thunder.

Lightning is unpredictable. It may jump from the cloud to the ground or from the ground to the cloud. It may jump between two thunderclouds. It may also jump from one spot to another within the cloud. Lightning superheats the air so the air suddenly expands. It slams into the air around it with such force that it makes a mighty sound—thunder.

Third Stage

The storm dies when a downdraft becomes stronger than the updraft. Heavy rain lightens up and stops.

Thunderstorms usually form in the warm air just ahead of a cold front. The cold, dense air wedges under the warm, moist air and causes the warm air to rise rapidly. Be on the lookout for thunderstorms. They are likely when the weather is hot and humid and a cold front is approaching.

▷ **Where do thunderstorms usually form?**

READING Diagrams

Write a description of how a thunderstorm forms. Identify what happens during each stage of formation.

Light rain

3 A thunderstorm dies when a downdraft becomes stronger than the updraft.

QUICK LAB

FOR SCHOOL OR HOME

Tornado in a Bottle

1. **Make a Model** Fill a 2-L plastic bottle one-third full of water. Dry the neck of the bottle, and tape over the top with duct tape. Use a pencil to poke a hole in the tape.

2. Place another 2-L plastic bottle upside down over the mouth of the first bottle. Tape the two bottles together.

3. **Observe** Hold the bottles by the necks so the one with the water is on top. Swirl them around while your partner gently squeezes on the empty bottle. Then place the bottles on a desk with the water bottle on top. Describe what you see.

4. **Infer** How is this like what happens when a tornado forms? Explain.

How and Where Do Tornadoes Happen?

The most violent thunderstorms often spin off even more dangerous storms—**tornadoes**. A tornado is a violent whirling wind that moves across the ground in a narrow path.

How They Happen

Late in the day, when Earth's surface is very warm, convection can get very strong. This can lead to a tornado. A tornado is a sort of runaway convection cell.

- When the updraft in a convection cell is really strong, the air rushes in from all sides at high speeds.

- The air curves into a spin. This lowers the pressure even more. Air rushes in even faster, and the pressure gets even lower, and so on. Like a spinning skater who pulls her arms in close to her sides, the spinning tornado gets faster and faster.

- As the tornado gets stronger, a funnel forms that eventually touches the ground. In the center of a tornado, winds can reach speeds of 500 km per hour (about 300 mi per hour) or more. At such high speeds, winds can destroy anything in their path.

The speed of the wind in the tornado is not the speed with which the tornado moves across the ground. It moves across the ground very fast but can change its direction continually.

Where They Happen

Most tornadoes in the United States seem to occur in the Midwest and in the South.

Tornadoes form where dry, cold air masses mix with warm, moist air masses. In the United States, this is most likely to happen in the Great Plains region and the Mississippi Valley. Florida also gets lots of tornadoes.

Tornadoes are most likely to occur when there are big differences in the air masses. This happens most often in early spring and summer. Tornadoes can also form over water. Such tornadoes are called *waterspouts*.

Maps

What states are in Tornado Alley?

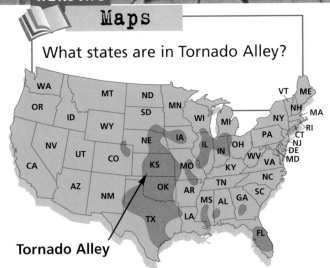

Tornado Alley

More tornadoes occur in the United States than in any other country, especially in the area known as Tornado Alley.

▷ **When are tornadoes likely to form?**

Warm air rising in strong updraft

Low-pressure spot

Diagrams

1. Where is the pressure lowest in the tornado?

2. In what direction is the wind spinning—clockwise (like the hands of a clock) or counterclockwise (the opposite direction)?

Tornadoes that form over water are called waterspouts.

How Do Hurricanes Form?

If you live near an ocean or the Gulf Coast, you may have experienced a **hurricane** . Hurricanes are very large, swirling storms with very low pressure at their center. They form over tropical oceans—near the equator.

Air masses near the equator tend to be very much alike. They don't form the fronts that you learned about in Lesson 5. Instead, they form lots of thunderstorms.

- Strong heating and lots of evaporation over the ocean can cause a large low-pressure center to form. If this happens, winds begin to blow in toward the low. As this rushing air nears the center, it moves upward and forms a ring of tall thunderstorms.

- The Coriolis effect causes winds to spiral counterclockwise in the Northern Hemisphere. Clusters of thunderstorms are pulled into the spiral. The thunderstorms merge, forming a single large storm.

- As water vapor in the storms condenses, heat is released. The air

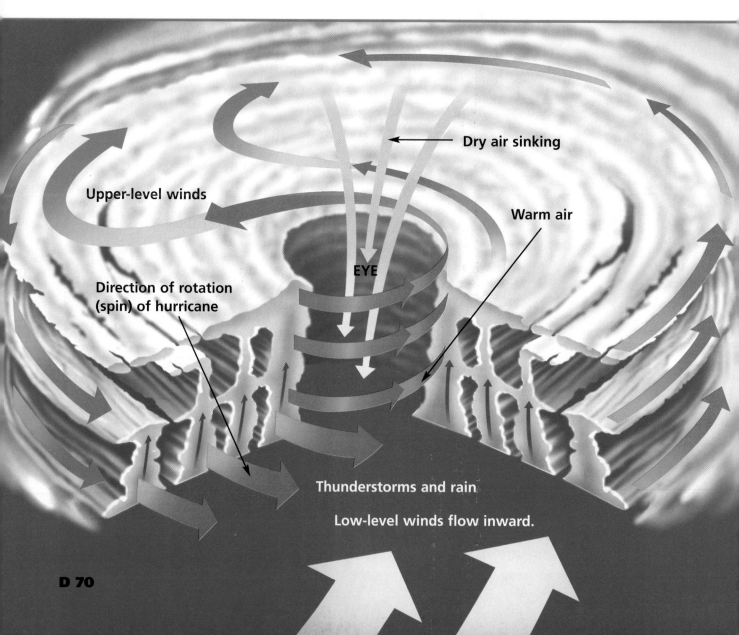

Dry air sinking

Upper-level winds

Warm air

EYE

Direction of rotation (spin) of hurricane

Thunderstorms and rain

Low-level winds flow inward.

is warmed. This decreases the air's density and pressure. Moisture evaporating into the air decreases the air's density and pressure even more. Low air pressure favors more evaporation. This lowers the pressure even more.

- The lower the air pressure, the faster are the winds that blow in toward the center of the storm. When the winds reach speeds of 120 km per hour (about 75 mi per hour) or higher, the storm is a hurricane.

- As the moist air in the storm rises and cools, condensation takes place. The clouds thicken. Heavy rains fall through the high winds. When fully formed, a hurricane has an eye at its center. The eye is an area of light winds and skies that are nearly clear.

Hurricanes can easily grow to more than 700 km (about 400 mi) in diameter. For example, Hurricane Fran was almost as large as the entire state of Florida!

READING Sequence of Events
How does lower and lower air pressure lead to the formation of a hurricane?

This satellite photograph shows a hurricane and its eye. Hurricanes can pick up about 20 billion tons of water a day from the oceans. Much of this water falls as rain over land areas.

Direction of wind

How Do Hurricanes Affect Ocean Waves?

Just north of the equator, gentle global winds move hurricanes west to northwest at 10 to 20 km per hour (6 to 12 mi per hour). As they move north, away from the equator, their speed tends to increase.

Hurricane winds whip up large waves in the ocean. These waves move outward from the storm and pound against a shore for days before the storm arrives. However, it is the **storm surge** that causes the most destruction. Storm surge is a great rise of the sea along a shore. Its main cause is low air pressure.

Air pressure normally presses down on the surface of the sea like a giant hand. When the pressure drops in a hurricane, it is like lifting the hand slightly. The surface of the sea rises, forming a bulge beneath a hurricane.

When the hurricane moves over a coast, the bulge can cause water levels to suddenly rise several feet, or surge.

Hurricane winds also push water ahead of the storm, forcing water onshore and adding to the storm surge. If the storm surge comes at high tide, it is even worse. Great storms have surges that raise the water level by 7 meters (about 20 feet) or more.

During a great storm, the surge, large waves, high winds, and torrential rain of the storm all happen at the same time. Low-lying coastal areas are flooded. Beachfront homes are destroyed. Beaches can get worn away.

A Real Hurricane–Fran

On August 22, 1996, a storm formed off the coast of Africa and began moving west-northwest at about 16 km per hour (10 mi per hour). By August 29 it had become more concentrated. Winds reached hurricane strength. Hurricane Fran was born. Fran continued moving

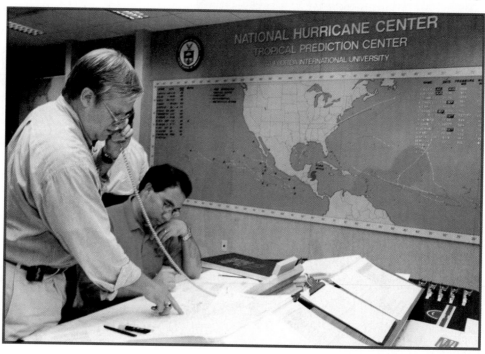

Scientists from the National Hurricane Center in Florida keep an eye on dangerous hurricanes.

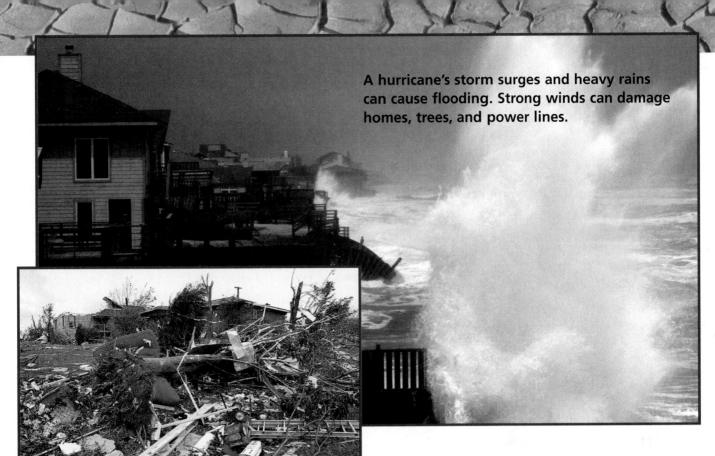

A hurricane's storm surges and heavy rains can cause flooding. Strong winds can damage homes, trees, and power lines.

west and was even stronger by the time it skirted the Bahamas. By September 5, 1996, Fran had 105-knot winds and was 400 km (250 mi) off the Florida coast.

A large low-pressure system over Tennessee steered it westward, and it struck North Carolina and Virginia on September 6. Winds of 120 knots were clocked off Cape Fear as Fran came ashore. Sea level surged to 3.6 m (12 ft) above normal. As much as 40 cm (16 in.) of rain fell in parts of North Carolina. Thirty-four people died. Flash flooding caused most deaths. A storm surge on the North Carolina coast destroyed many beachfront houses.

High winds damaged trees and roofs. They also downed power lines, leaving 4.5 million people without power. Nearly half a million people were ordered to evacuate the coast. Altogether it is estimated that Fran caused 3.2 billion dollars of damage.

Hurricanes begin to die out when they move over land. Cut off from the warm ocean, the hurricane has no water to replace what falls as rain. Friction between the winds and the land decreases wind speed. When it has been over land long enough, it will completely die out.

Once Hurricane Fran moved ashore, it steadily weakened. By the time it reached central North Carolina, it was no longer a hurricane. By the time it reached the Great Lakes on September 9, it was no longer even a storm. The remains of Fran disappeared on September 10.

 What do hurricanes do to ocean waves?

What Can You Do to Be Safe in a Storm?

Thunderstorms, tornadoes, and hurricanes can be very dangerous. In order to stay safe in these storms, you need to follow certain safety rules.

A storm watch means that conditions are right for a storm to form. A storm warning means that a storm has been spotted and is heading your way.

Tornadoes happen fast. If a tornado is spotted, a tornado warning is given. Take action immediately. If you hear storm watches or warnings on TV or radio, follow their directions carefully!

▷ **What are three thunderstorm safety rules?**

Thunderstorm Safety Rules

Go inside a house or large building, but don't go into a small building that stands off by itself. It is also safe to stay inside a closed car or truck (not a convertible!). Be sure the doors and windows are closed. Do not touch any metal inside the car.

Stay away from pipes, faucets, electrical outlets, and open windows.

Don't use the telephone, except in an emergency. Electricity can travel through phone lines.

Stay away from the water. If you are in the water, GET OUT. Do not go out in a boat. Lightning is attracted to water.

If you are outside, be sure you are not the tallest thing around. Be sure, also, that you are not standing near or under the tallest thing around. Do not stand up on a beach, in an open field, or on a hilltop. Do not stand under a tree. Do not stand under an object that is standing alone in an open area.

If you are stuck in an open area, crouch down. Stay away from metal objects, including bicycles, motorcycles, farm equipment, golf clubs, and golf carts.

If your hair feels like it's standing on end, lightning may be about to strike. Crouch down. Lean forward, and put your hands on your knees. Try to make yourself as low to the ground as possible while touching as little of the ground as you can.

Hurricane Safety Rules

People living in coastal areas may be warned to board up their homes and head for safer, inland areas. If you live in an area connected to the mainland by a bridge, be sure you allow plenty of time to leave. Traffic on the bridge may be very heavy. People who live in low-lying areas that flood in heavy rains may also be warned to go to shelters.

Board or tape up windows and glass doors. Bring outdoor objects—such as furniture, bikes, potted plants—indoors.

Be sure you stock up on bottled water, canned and packaged foods, and first-aid supplies and medicines for the family and pets. Don't forget flashlights and fresh batteries. Test the flashlights ahead of time to be sure the bulbs are working. You may be without power for several days. Be sure the food you have can be eaten without cooking.

If your home is on sturdy, high ground, stay there. Otherwise go to a shelter.

Don't be fooled by the eye of the hurricane. Everything may be calm. Skies may be fair for a short time, but the rest of the hurricane's fury is right behind the eye.

Tornado Safety Rules

At home open the windows slightly, then seek shelter. Stay away from windows and doors.

The safest place is in a storm cellar. The next safest is a basement. Stay under a table, staircase, or mattress. If you have no storm cellar or basement, seek shelter in a strong building. Stay on the ground floor. Stay under a table or bed, or in a closet.

Do not stay in a mobile home.

Outdoors lie facedown in a ditch. Cover your head to protect yourself from flying debris.

At school go to an inside hallway on the lowest floor. If your school has a tornado shelter, go there. Follow your teacher's or principal's directions.

How Can Radar Track Storms?

Storms are hard to predict because they form so quickly. Scientists use the best methods possible to try to identify conditions long before a storm occurs. They look for clues, like the movement of fronts and the formation of very low pressure areas. Once these conditions are located, scientists keep a "weather eye" on them to see how they develop.

Special methods are used to find storms as they form. One such method is Doppler radar. The word *radar* stands for *r*adio *d*etection *a*nd *r*anging. Radar works by sending out radio waves and recording their echo. The change in the radio signal from the original to the echo tells us something about where it reflected.

Doppler radar looks at how the echoes have changed in frequency from the original signals. This information gives clues about the movement of the reflective surface. Doppler radar is a very good tool for scientists to track storms. The radio waves reflect off storm clouds and are picked back up again at the radar stations.

With Doppler radar scientists can tell if rain is moving toward or away from them. Doppler radar can also spot spinning motions of clouds. These motions help warn scientists that tornadoes or hurricanes may be forming. Scientists use Doppler radar to find and track thunderstorms, tornadoes, and hurricanes. Doppler radar helps forecasters predict which way the storms will travel.

▶ **How can Doppler radar help in predicting severe storms?**

Radar helps forecasters watch how storms form and move.

Why It Matters

Scientists have used radar systems to track storms since the 1950s. NEXRAD—"NEXt generation of weather RADar"—is a newer form of Doppler radar that is replacing older radar systems. NEXRAD can spot small particles such as blowing dust, very light snow, and even drizzle. NEXRAD is more accurate than conventional radar at predicting floods and flash floods. It can show the exact locations of different fronts. It also shows changes in wind speed and direction. This helps scientists make more accurate weather predictions.

Visit **www.mhscience02.com** to do a research project on storms.

Think and Write

1. How does a thunderstorm form?

2. How is a tornado related to a thunderstorm?

3. What causes a hurricane to form? What moves it in a certain direction?

4. Why can hurricanes cause so much damage?

5. **Critical Thinking** Why do you think predicting a severe storm is so difficult?

L·I·N·K·S

LITERATURE LINK

Read *Trouble at Forest Park*, the story of a family surviving getting lost in the woods. When you finish reading, think about how you would stay safe in the woods. Try the activities at the end of the book.

ART LINK

Make a poster. Let others know what to do in a storm. Make a poster illustrating important storm safety rules.

MATH LINK

Find the number of tornadoes. Research how many tornadoes hit your state in the past year. Compare that number with the average number listed for your state in the chart on page D65. Were the number of tornadoes in your state last year higher, lower, or the same as the listed average?

TECHNOLOGY LINK

At the Computer Visit **www.mhscience02.com** for more links.

Science, Technology,

Storm Tracking

It's easy for meteorologists to predict a storm that's part of a giant weather system; it's been reported by people experiencing it! Wind direction and changes in air pressure also signal a storm is near.

Smaller storm systems are harder to predict, but computers help. They are fed data about a storm's present location; current wind direction, air pressure, and rainfall; and how similar storms have behaved. The computer plots the path the storm will likely follow.

The use of radar has advanced hurricane prediction. Radar bounces radio waves off raindrops to discover where the storm is heading. Today, thanks to radar tracking, damage from hurricanes has been greatly reduced.

Tornadoes, or twisters, are the most violent windstorms. Because the right conditions for developing tornadoes occur quite often, they're hard to predict. The United States had more "killer tornadoes" during the first half of 1998 than in all of 1996 or 1997! Doppler radar helps meteorologists predict tornadoes. It doesn't just spot a tornado's heavy rains, it tells the speed and direction of the funnel. With Doppler, people can be warned to seek cover before a twister hits!

There will be heavy rain all up the West coast. Ships in the Pacific report storm conditions.

A tornado warning is in effect for Mills county. A tornado watch covers the rest of the region.

What Did I Learn?

1. Radar systems track storms using

  A sound waves
  B radio waves
  C anemometers
  D wind vanes

2. Doppler radar helps meteorologists predict tornadoes by

  F telling their speed and direction
  G observing lightning patterns
  H photographing storm clouds
  J measuring rainfall

Hurricane Clyde is predicted to make landfall before dawn. People in coastal regions should secure their homes and head inland.

AT THE COMPUTER

Visit www.mhscience02.com to learn more about weather forecasting.

Climate

Vocabulary

climate, D82

radiative balance, D86

greenhouse effect, D87

Get Ready

What if you lived here, in this desert? What would summers be like? What would winters be like?

Think about what factors are used to describe the average weather pattern of a region. How might you use graphs of year-round weather in different places to test your ideas?

Process Skill

You communicate when you share information.

Explore Activity

What Do Weather Patterns Tell You?

Procedure

1 **Use Numbers** Look at the graph for city 1. The bottom is labeled with the months of the year. The left side is labeled with the temperature in degrees Celsius. Use this scale to read the temperature line. What is the average temperature in city 1 during July?

2 **Use Numbers** The right side of the graph is labeled with millimeters of precipitation. Use this scale when reading the precipitation bars. What is the average precipitation in city 1 during July?

3 Repeat steps 1 and 2 for city 2.

Drawing Conclusions

1 **Use Numbers** How do the annual amounts of precipitation compare for the two cities? Record your answer.

2 **Interpret Data** When is the average temperature highest for each city? Lowest? When does each city receive the greatest amount of precipitation?

3 **Interpret Data** Describe the average weather pattern for each city. Be sure to include temperature and precipitation, and their relationship to the seasons.

4 **Going Further: Communicate** How would you go about making a graph of the weather patterns for your town?

City 1

City 2

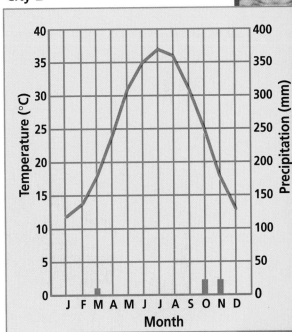

— Temperature (in Celsius)
■ Precipitation (in millimeters)

Read to Learn

Main Idea Long-term weather patterns determine climates, which can change over time.

What Is Climate?

Weather changes from day to day. However, the weather in any area tends to follow a pattern throughout the year. For example, Fairbanks, Alaska, tends to have long, cold winters and short, cool summers. Miami, Florida, tends to have long, hot summers and short, cool winters.

When you make descriptions such as these, you are describing the **climate** (KLIGH·mit) of a region. Climate is the average weather pattern of a region. One way to describe a region's climate is with a temperature-precipitation graph.

The climate of a region can also be described by some other factors, such as winds, distance from a coast, mountain ranges, and ocean currents. The *climate zones* shown here take all these factors into account.

Another way to describe the climate of a region is by the plants that grow there, such as grasslands or coniferous forests. Each kind of plant requires its own conditions for growth, such as amount of sunlight, precipitation, and temperature.

▷ **What factors describe climate?**

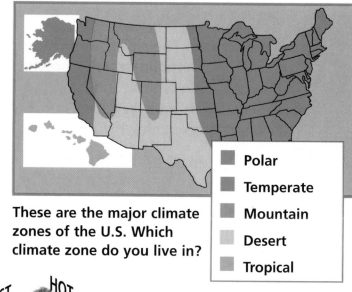

These are the major climate zones of the U.S. Which climate zone do you live in?

- Polar
- Temperate
- Mountain
- Desert
- Tropical

Modeling Climates

In this activity you will make a model of the soil conditions in two cities. Use the information in the graphs on page D81. The soil conditions you set up will model—or represent—the climates of the two cities. To do this, you will need to measure the amount of water you use and the amount of time you use the lamp.

Materials

stick-on notepaper

marking pencil or pen

2 trays of dry soil

spray bottle of water

lamp

thermometer

Procedure

1 **Measure** Put 3 cm of dry soil into each tray. Label one tray City 1 and the other tray City 2.

2 **Use Numbers** What do the bars on each graph represent?

3 **Measure** Model the yearly precipitation and temperature like this: Let 5 minutes equal 1 month. One squeeze of water sprayed on the tray equals 10 millimeters of precipitation. Every minute the lamp is on equals 20 degrees of temperature. That means that from 0 to 5 minutes is January. During January the City 2 tray gets no water and the lamp shines on it for $\frac{3}{4}$ minute. The City 1 tray gets 12 squeezes of water and the lamp shines on it for $1\frac{1}{4}$ minutes.

4 **Make a Model** Model the two cities for all 12 months. Record your observations.

Drawing Conclusions

1 **Observe** Examine the soil in the trays. Compare them for the same months. How do they differ?

2 **Communicate** How did measuring help you model climates?

What Affects Climate?

Several things affect temperature and precipitation over a long period of time.

Latitude

One way to describe location is to tell the latitude of a place. Latitude is a measure of how far north or south a place is from the equator. The angle of insolation is different at different latitudes. As a result, the temperatures are different at different latitudes.

- **Tropical Zone** Near the equator temperatures are high all year. Rainfall is plentiful. At about 30° latitude in each hemisphere are deserts, areas of high temperatures and low precipitation.

- **Temperate Zones** In the middle latitudes, summers are warm and winters are cool or cold. Precipitation may be plentiful.

- **Polar Zones** At high latitudes winters are long and cold. Summers are short and warm. Precipitation all year is low.

Bodies of Water

A glance at any globe shows that land and water are not evenly distributed. Most of the globe is covered with water. However, some places on a continent can be more than 1,600 km (1,000 mi) from any large body of water. Land and water heat and cool at different rates. Land heats up faster in the sunlight than water does. Land also cools off faster than water. As a result, air temperatures over land are warmer in summer and cooler in winter than they are over oceans at the same latitude.

Winds and Ocean Currents

In Lesson 4 you learned that wind patterns circle the globe. These patterns are not the day-to-day winds. Instead they are winds that blow continually above Earth's surface.

- **Wind Patterns** For example, just above and below the equator, the trade winds blow continually. In the middle latitudes are the westerlies. In the polar areas are the easterlies. Westerlies blow across the continental United States from west (the Pacific) to east (the Atlantic). They bring warm, moist air to the west coast. They push air masses and fronts across the country.

North Pole

Polar zone — Sparse precipitation

Temperate zone — Ample precipitation

Tropical zone — Abundant rainfall

Temperate zone — Ample precipitation

Polar zone — Sparse precipitation

South Pole

- **Currents** These winds also move water across the surface of the ocean. As ocean water moves, it moves warm or cool air with it. A warm current, the Gulf Stream, flows up along the east coast. The California Current, a cool current, moves down along the west coast.

Altitude

Altitude is a measure of how high above sea level a place is. The higher a place is above sea level, the cooler its climate is.

- **Mountains** Along the base of a high mountain, you may find tropical plants growing. Halfway up you may find pine forests. At the mountain peaks, you will find permanent ice and snow. Mountain ranges affect climate, too. The Alps protect the Mediterranean coast from cold polar air. The Himalayas protect the lowlands of India from cold Siberian air. Mountain ranges also affect rain patterns. Often one side of the mountain gets lots of rain while the other side gets very little.

Air passing over a mountain cools. Rain clouds may form and drop their moisture on that side of the mountain. Air reaching the other side is often dry.

- **Rain Shadow** Global wind patterns can force air up along the side of a mountain. For example, warm, moist air from the Pacific Ocean is blown up the side of the Sierra Nevada and the Cascades. As the air moves up, there is precipitation on the windward side. Having lost the moisture, dry air descends down the leeward side of the mountain. This side is said to be in a *rain shadow*.

▶ **How does latitude affect climate?**

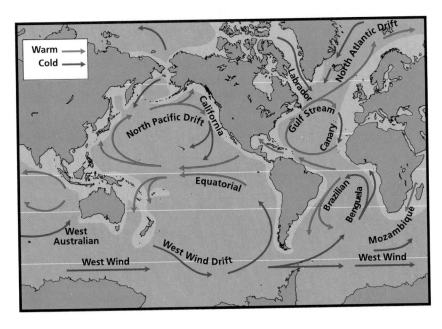

Ocean currents move surface water in huge circular patterns. As ocean currents flow past land areas, they affect the land's climate.

How Does Earth Gain and Lose Energy?

Earth's climates depend a great deal on the Sun's energy. Earth absorbs heat from sunlight. It also gives off, or *radiates*, heat into space. Earth gains and loses energy.

If the amount of energy gained balances the energy lost, Earth is in **radiative** (RAY·dee·uh·tiv) **balance**. Then Earth's average temperature remains about the same. Earth's average temperature is about 14°C (59°F). A tip of the balance will cause Earth's average temperature to rise or fall.

The atmosphere plays an important role in Earth's radiative balance. If Earth had no atmosphere, it would be a lot like the Moon, which has no atmosphere. Daytime temperatures on the Moon soar to more than 100°C (212°F). Nighttime temperatures drop to 115°C (240°F) below zero.

Earth's atmosphere acts as a protective blanket. Clouds and dust in the atmosphere reflect about 30 percent of incoming sunlight back out into space. The atmosphere absorbs another 15–20 percent. Only about half of incoming sunlight reaches Earth's surface. This keeps surface temperatures from rising much higher during the day.

At night Earth's surface radiates heat. If there are lots of clouds in the atmosphere, they absorb most of this

Earth's Energy Budget

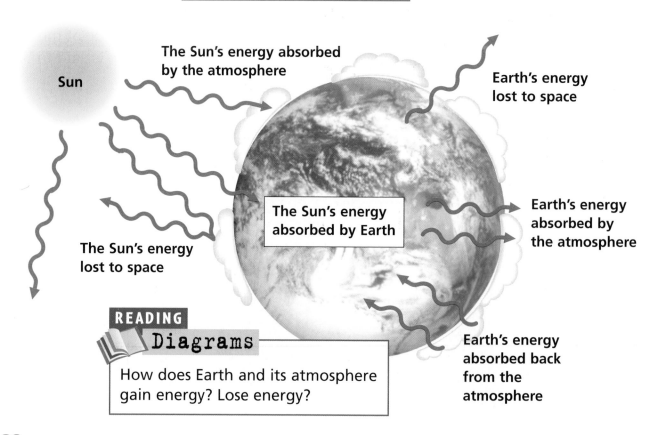

Sun

The Sun's energy absorbed by the atmosphere

Earth's energy lost to space

The Sun's energy absorbed by Earth

Earth's energy absorbed by the atmosphere

The Sun's energy lost to space

Earth's energy absorbed back from the atmosphere

READING Diagrams

How does Earth and its atmosphere gain energy? Lose energy?

Glass of greenhouse

Sun

Incoming solar energy

Heat

Sun

Incoming solar energy

Heat

Cutting down forests

Cows

Industry

Greenhouse gases

Vehicle exhaust

Rice paddies

READING
Diagrams

Write a description from this diagram of what causes the greenhouse effect.

heat. This keeps the night from getting too cold. If there are few clouds, less heat is absorbed, and the night is cooler.

The Greenhouse Effect

Why doesn't all of Earth's heat just go out into space? The atmosphere keeps Earth warmer than it would otherwise be. This is called the **greenhouse effect**. Earth's atmosphere acts somewhat like the glass in a greenhouse. In a greenhouse the glass lets sunlight in but does not let heat escape. This helps create a warm environment in which plants can flourish.

Earth's greenhouse effect is caused by just a few gases. These greenhouse gases make up only a tiny part of the air. The main greenhouse gases are water vapor and carbon dioxide. Other gases also have less of an effect. These

gases are methane, nitrous oxide, and chlorofluorocarbons (CFCs).

Human activities are putting more and more greenhouse gases into the atmosphere. Many scientists are worried that these gases may change Earth's climate. Even a small increase in these gases adds to the greenhouse effect, making our planet warmer.

Scientists are still examining and interpreting data in order to understand the greenhouse effect better.

▷ **How does the greenhouse effect keep Earth from losing energy?**

What Causes Climate Change?

There is much evidence that over long periods of time, Earth goes through warming and cooling trends. Warming and cooling are signs that Earth's radiative balance has shifted. What causes such shifts?

The shifts are caused by changes in sunlight. They are also caused by changes in the movements of air, water, landmasses, and Earth itself.

The Sun's Output

The amount of energy the Sun sends out changes. One clue to how the Sun's output may be changing comes from sunspots. Sunspots are dark areas that appear on the surface of the Sun. They appear dark because they are cooler than the surrounding regions. They appear to be "storms" on the Sun.

Sunspots have been observed for centuries. However, they are not permanent. They appear and disappear over several days or several months.

At times there are many large sunspots. Such a high count is called a sunspot maximum. The last sunspot maximum was in 2000.

A sunspot maximum appears to happen about every 11 years. Scientists also record changes in Earth's temperatures about the same times. Around the time of a sunspot maximum, Earth's average temperature has gone up. The pattern is not exact or complete. However, it has led some scientists to suggest that droughts, rainfall, and very cold winters might be related to times when sunspots are very numerous or very few.

The Sun's Surface

Sunspot

This false-color image of the Sun shows temperature differences on the sun's surface. Why do sunspots appear dark?

Currents and Landmasses

How do the oceans help move Earth's heat around? Ocean currents act like huge conveyor belts, carrying heat from the equator to the poles. Changes in the speed and direction of these currents could explain sudden and long-term climate changes.

The continents have changed their positions over time. In fact, the continents are still moving very gradually. Their climates are likely to change with their locations.

Volcanoes

When volcanoes erupt, they send dust and gases into the atmosphere. Atmospheric dust can block sunlight, causing cooling. In the past eruptions were more frequent. The dust from all of those eruptions may have caused enough cooling to trigger ice ages. Volcanic eruptions are not as common today as they were in the past. While eruptions still cause cooling, they probably don't affect long-term climate as much as in the past.

300 Million Years Ago

Present

Do you think the ocean currents were the same 300 million years ago as they are today? Changes in ocean currents would profoundly affect climates.

READING **Sequence of Events**

How might frequent volcanic eruptions change the climate?

Some currents affecting the Western Hemisphere today.

How Can Climate Affect You?

How do you deal with cold weather? Cold weather cools the surface of the body. The body responds by circulating warm blood faster to counteract the cooling. The heart pumps faster. Blood pressure increases and puts a strain on the heart.

Cold Climates

How can you stay warm in cold weather? Use proper clothing and shelter. Clothing traps body heat to warm the air close to your body. Cold-weather clothes are often made with materials that trap air between loose fibers. Your body heats the trapped air, and soon a thin, warm layer of air surrounds you.

Hot Climates

In hot, dry climates, the main health problem is water loss. Heating the body triggers sweating. When sweat evaporates, it cools the skin. However, if you don't drink enough water, your body eventually stops sweating. No sweat, no cooling. Body temperature rises. This can cause *hyperthermia* (overheating), which can be fatal.

Clothing can help you deal with the heat. Light-colored fabric protects the skin and reflects a lot of the sunlight. Loose clothing lets air circulate so sweat can evaporate and cool the body.

▷ What is the main health problem in hot, dry climates?

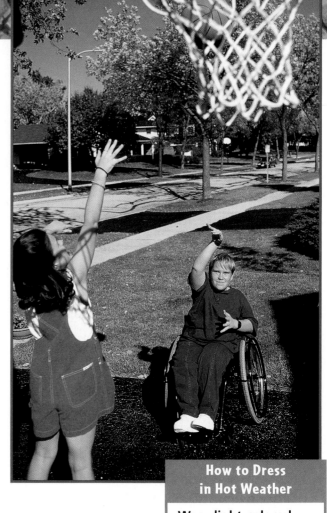

How to Dress in Hot Weather

Wear light-colored, loose clothing that protects you from the Sun and lets your skin breathe.

Wear a sun hat.

Use sunscreen.

How to Dress in Cold Weather

Protect nose and ears on blustery, cold days.

Keep hands, head, and feet warm.

Dress in layers to trap body heat.

Why It Matters

Since 1900, Earth's average temperature has increased by about 0.5°C (1°F). Most of the warming has come in two periods—from 1920 to 1940 and since the mid-1970s. A drought during the 1920s–1940s led to the Dust Bowl days. Millions of acres of United States farmland dried out. Crops failed. Farmers went broke trying to pay their bills. Many families lost their homes and farms.

Today the warming trend continues. Cutting down on the use of greenhouse gases and preserving forests may help slow the trend.

Think and Write

1. What is climate? What are the main factors that are used to describe the climate of an area?

2. What is the greenhouse effect?

3. Why are climates different at different places on Earth?

4. **Measure** What variables do you have to measure to describe the average weather pattern, or climate, of a region?

5. **Critical Thinking** Do you think people can live in all climates? Explain your answer.

WRITING LINK

Write an essay. Choose a climate different from your own. Write an essay on how the climate affects the lives of the people who live there.

SOCIAL STUDIES LINK

Write a report about changing climates. The illustration shows a winter fair held on the Thames River in England during the Little Ice Age. Research how Earth's climate has changed since farming began. Write a report for the class.

MATH LINK

Make a pie graph. Find out what proportions of greenhouse gases exist in the atmosphere. Make a pie graph.

TECHNOLOGY LINK

At the Computer Visit www.mhscience02.com for more links.

Chapter 9 Review

Vocabulary

Fill each blank with the best word or words from the list.

air mass, D54
climate, D82
cold front, D56
front, D55
greenhouse effect, D87
hurricane, D70
storm surge, D72
thunderstorm, D66
tornado, D68
warm front, D56

1. A boundary between air masses of different temperatures is called a(n) _____.

2. A storm often created in thunderstorms is a(n) _____.

3. A(n) _____ may bring fog.

4. A storm that produces lightning is a(n) _____.

5. A great rise of sea level at a shore due to a hurricane is a(n) _____.

6. The _____ may be making Earth warmer.

7. A large region of the atmosphere in which the air has similar properties is a(n) _____.

8. A dangerous storm that forms over warm ocean waters is a(n) _____.

9. A(n) _____ forms when cold air moves in under a warm air mass.

10. The average weather pattern of a region is its _____.

Test Prep

11. Statistical weather forecasts are based on _____.

  A the kinds of fronts moving out of an area

  B severe storms

  C the chance of a weather pattern repeating itself

  D weather station symbols

12. Earth gets its heat from _____.

  F trees

  G convection

  H greenhouses

  J the Sun

13. When a cool air mass and a warm air mass meet and stay over an area for days without moving, this is called a(n) _____.

  A warm front

  B occluded front

  C stationary front

  D cold front

14. A balance between energy lost and energy gained is called _____.

F the greenhouse effect

G climate

H solar energy

J radiative balance

15. A hurricane can cause sea level to rise because the air pressure under the hurricane _____.

A is higher than normal

B is lower than normal

C is the same as usual

D does not affect why a hurricane makes the sea level rise

Concepts and Skills

16. Reading in Science Write a paragraph explaining how a thunderstorm forms.

17. Safety Write a paragraph explaining safety rules to follow in a thunderstorm.

18. Product Ads What products are advertised to protect you from the weather in the winter? In the summer? What is each product supposed to do? Are the products as good as the ads say? Write a paragraph explaining your answer.

19. Process Skills: Measure What if your area were to get twice as much rain as usual for the next ten years? Write a paragraph explaining how you would make a model of your climate as it is now. How would you adjust it to study the effect of extra rainfall?

20. Critical Thinking Do you think that Earth is getting warmer? Write a paragraph explaining your hypothesis. Describe what you might do to test your ideas.

Boost *your test scores!*

Be Smart!

Visit www.mhscience02.com

Climatologist

Dr. Henry Diaz

National Oceanic and Atmospheric Administration

■s it going to rain tomorrow? Will it be warm enough to go swimming? Sometimes it's important to know what the weather is going to be. The weather reporter on TV is usually good at forecasting the weather. Some meteorologists, however, do more than just predict tomorrow's weather.

These meteorologists conduct research. They use tools like radar, satellites, computers, and special aircraft. They might study the chemical properties of the atmosphere. They might study how energy is transferred. Some meteorologists are climatologists. A climatologist studies past records of weather. These records may help to predict future changes that could affect human life.

Dr. Henry Diaz is a climatologist. He works for the National Oceanic and Atmospheric Administration (NOAA). Dr. Diaz was born and raised in Cuba, an island in the Caribbean Sea. Cuba is part of the "Hurricane Belt." As a teenager living in Florida, he experienced some violent hurricanes. These storms fueled his interest in weather. He decided to become a meteorologist.

This radar image of the western Pacific Ocean shows temperature differences that might help explain El Niño.

Dr. Diaz received his doctorate in climatology from the University of Colorado in 1985. He was hired by the NOAA and conducted research projects. One project was on how climate affects the water resources of the western United States.

Dr. Diaz has also become an expert on El Niño. El Niño is the largest single weather influence on Earth. El Niño occurs every few years when areas of high-pressure and low-pressure air suddenly switch places along the equator in the South Pacific. The shift causes huge climate changes around the world. The result is floods, droughts, cyclones, and even fire damage.

Dr. Diaz is working with other scientists to try to predict when future El Niños will occur. This will give people around the world a chance to prepare for the El Niños. If their research is successful, many lives will be saved!

Careers IN SCIENCE

Physicist

If you're interested in meteorology, you may want to be a physicist. A physicist studies the laws of nature. He or she applies these laws to everyday life. Physicists study matter and energy. Some physicists study atoms. Some study the stars.

Most physicists work for colleges and universities. Some work for the government. Wherever a physicist works, his or her office is the laboratory. Physicists need to be familiar with tools like computers, telescopes, and lasers.

A career in physics starts with four years of college. Almost all physicists study to get doctorates in physics. Many teach college physics while still doing their research.

Write
ABOUT IT

1. What is the difference between a TV weather reporter and a climatologist?

2. Where does El Niño begin? How does it begin?

AT THE COMPUTER Visit **www.mhscience02.com** to learn more about careers.

Part of Highway 1 near Half Moon Bay was washed out by **El Niño.**

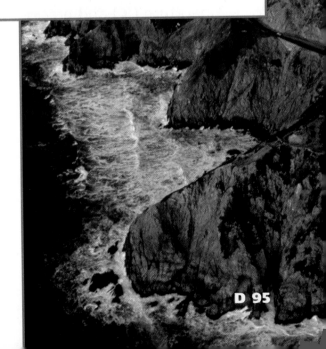

Where's the WATER?

Your goal is to determine why water droplets form from the air.

What to Do

1. Place five ice cubes in a clear bowl. Add a drop of food coloring. Stir. Wait three minutes. Observe the outside of the bowl. Record your observations.

2. Carefully pour hot water into an identical bowl. Empty the first bowl and place it on top to form a sphere. Put three ice cubes on top. Record your observations.

Analyze Your Results

1. In Step 1, where did the water on the outside of the bowl come from? Explain.

2. Where did water droplets form in Step 2? Where did the water come from? Explain.

3. How is what you observed in Step 2 similar to how a cloud forms over the ocean?

CLIMATE on a CHART

Your goal is to make a climate chart of your local area.

What to Do

A climate chart shows average values for temperature (°C) and precipitation (mm). Use local data to make a climate chart for your area.

Analyze Your Results

1. What is the rainiest month where you live? The least rainy month?

2. What is the hottest month where you live? The coldest?

3. Describe your local climate in words based on your climate chart.

UNIT E

Properties of Matter and Energy

Properties of Matter and Energy

LOOK!

With a mighty roar, the
space shuttle blasts off.
What kind of energy powers
the space shuttle's engines?

Properties and Structure of Matter

Did You Ever Wonder?

How can potters use their talent and creativity to turn clay and water into beautiful vases? When wet, clay has certain physical properties that allow potters to shape it into different forms. What happens to the clay when the vases are dried in a hot kiln, or oven?

Physical Properties

Get Ready

When you say something is "bigger" than something else, what does "bigger" mean? What is bigger than a hot air balloon? What is smaller?

If the balloon is empty and folded up, are the same things bigger or smaller?

Bigger or smaller. More or less. In what ways can things be "more" or "less" than other things? Are there different ways something can be "more" than other things?

Process Skill

You experiment when you perform a test to support or disprove a hypothesis.

Explore Activity

Which Is More?

Materials

golf ball or wooden block

blown-up balloon

equal-pan balance

ruler

string

box, such as a shoe box

pail of water

Procedure: Design Your Own

1 **Observe** Look at the golf ball (or wooden block) and blown-up balloon. Which is "more"? Think of how one object could be "more":
- more when you use a balance
- more when you put it in water and see how much the water level goes up, and so on

Record your observations.

2 Use the equipment to verify one way that one object is more than another. Decide which of the two objects is "more" and which one is "less."

3 Repeat your measurements to verify your answer.

4 Now use different equipment to compare the two objects. Is the same object still "more"? Explain.

5 Repeat your measurements to verify your answer.

Drawing Conclusions

1 **Communicate** Identify the equipment you used. Report your results.

2 For each test, which object was more? In what way was it more than the other object?

3 **Going Further: Experiment** What if you were given a large box of puffed oats and a small box of oatmeal? Which do you think would be more? Design an experiment to test your hypothesis. Tell what equipment you would use.

Main Idea Matter is anything that has mass and occupies space.

What Is Matter?

All of the gases, liquids, and solids in the world around you—the air you breathe, the water you drink, and the chair you sit on—are made of **matter** . Testing to see whether a golf ball or a balloon is "more" measures *properties* of the matter in these objects.

A golf ball has more **mass** because it tips the balance more. However, a balloon has more **volume** because it fills up a greater amount of space.

Mass is a measure of the amount of matter in an object. The photo shows how a balance is used to measure mass. Mass is often measured in kilograms.

Volume describes how much space a sample of matter takes up. Volumes are often measured in milliliters (mL). As the photo shows, the volume of a liquid may be measured using a graduated cylinder, a beaker, or a measuring cup. The volume of a solid may be measured by multiplying its height times its length times its width. Solids don't always have regular shapes, however. We can also measure the volume of a solid by seeing how much water it displaces from a container. A solid with a volume of 1 cm³ will make the water rise 1 mL, for example. A volume of 1 cm³ equals 1 mL.

Matter is defined using the properties of mass and volume. Matter is anything that has mass and takes up space.

Measuring Mass and Volume

We determine the mass of an object by comparing it with known masses. The mass of this block is 25 g.

Graduated cylinder

Beaker

height

length width

Equal-pan balance

Measuring cup

Weight

What if you find the mass of a certain book to be 1 kilogram? You might be tempted to say, "This book weighs 1 kilogram." However, this is incorrect. The book's **weight** is actually the force of gravity between Earth and the book. The book's mass, on the other hand, is a measure of the amount of matter in the book compared with known masses.

As you know, we can use kilograms to measure an object's mass. However, to measure weight, we must use a quantity that describes the force of gravity between two masses. Scientists prefer to use a quantity called the *newton* (N) to measure force. One

newton is the same as 0.22 pound. (One pound is 4.45 newtons.) Newtons and pounds both describe the amount of pull or push a force produces. In this case the force is the pull of gravity.

An object's weight depends on its location in the universe. If you were to travel to the Moon, for example, you would have less weight. The Moon has less mass than Earth, so the force of gravity between your body and the Moon would be less. However, your mass would remain unchanged, as shown in the diagram.

▷ **What are two properties of matter?**

On Earth

1,200 N

120 kg

WEIGHT   MASS

200 N

WEIGHT

On the Moon

120 kg

MASS

READING Diagrams

1. What stays the same as the astronauts go from Earth to the Moon? What changes?

2. How does the astronaut's weight on the Moon compare with the astronaut's weight on Earth?

What Is Density?

As you learned on page E6, mass and volume are two properties of matter. Can we use these properties to tell us more about matter? How can these two measurements tell us something new?

If we divide the mass of a sample by its volume, we get a new measurement of matter. This property is called density . The density of an object tells us how massive something is for its size. It compares an object's mass with its volume.

Let's look at an example. If 2 mL of water has a mass of 2 g, then 2 g divided by 2 mL equals 1 g per mL.

The density is 1 g per mL. If we combined that water sample with another 2 mL sample, we would have 4 mL and 4 g of water. The density would still be 1 g per mL.

As long as conditions such as temperature do not change, the density of a substance does not change. The size of the sample does not matter. Density can be used to help identify materials because of this. If you had a piece of metal with a density of 11.3 g per mL, it would probably be lead. A similar-looking piece with a density of 2.7 g per mL, however, would probably be aluminum. Each material has its own density.

▷ **How can density be measured?**

Calculating Density

190 g → ← 190 g

← 150 mL

← 170 mL

An object's density is calculated by dividing its mass by its volume. The mass of this rock is 190 g. Its volume can be determined by calculating how much water it displaces from the beaker. If you subtract the volume of the water from the volume of the water plus the rock, you get the volume of the rock. (170 mL – 150 mL = 20 mL). The volume of this rock is 20 mL. The density of this rock is: 190 g ÷ 20 mL = 9.5 g per mL.

How Metal Boats Float

Think about objects that have more matter packed into the space they take up than water does. Will such objects sink or float in water? You have probably seen how a metal object like a nail or a spoon sinks in water. However, huge ships made of similar metal float even when they carry large cargoes. How is this possible? In this activity you will make a model of a metal boat. Scientists use models to help them understand properties of matter. Working with a model makes experimenting easier. Experiment to see how boats are designed so that they can carry heavy cargo.

Materials

aluminum foil

large paper clips

pan of water

Procedure

1 **Make a Model** Make a boat out of a 10-cm by 10-cm (4-in. by 4-in.) piece of aluminum foil. Then float it on water.

2 **Predict** Write down what you think will happen when you place more and more matter in the empty space of the boat. What steps should you follow to test your prediction? Be sure to use only the materials listed above.

3 **Experiment** Carry out your procedure, keeping a written record of what you observe.

Drawing Conclusions

1 **Communicate** How well did your results agree with your prediction?

2 Compare your model with those of your classmates. Which boat held the most clips? Why?

3 **Make a Model** The aluminum foil boat is a model of a steel ship. Use the way your boat floats to explain how a steel ship floats. Why was using a model of a large ship helpful?

4 **Communicate** What changed as more and more matter was added to the empty space of the boat? What happened as a result of this change?

How Dense Are Solids, Liquids, and Gases?

Imagine cutting a piece of aluminum foil into smaller and smaller pieces until the pieces are tinier than specks of dust. All matter—solids, liquids, and gases—is made of similar tiny particles. An object's mass is related to the number and type of particles it has.

Density describes how tightly these particles are packed together. A high density means that many particles are packed tightly into a given space. A low density means that only a few particles fill the same amount of space.

The particles of a solid tend to be packed very tightly together. They don't have a lot of room to move around. However, the particles of a gas usually spread out. In general, matter in the solid state is more dense than in the liquid state. Likewise, matter in the liquid state tends to be more dense than in the gaseous state.

READING Main Idea
How do the densities of solids, liquids, and gases compare?

Water is special! Solid water, ice, is less dense than liquid water. The particles in ice are more spread out than the particles in liquid water.

Solid (ice)

Liquid (water)

Gas (steam)

Densities of Common Substances

State	Substance		Density (g/cm³)
Solid	Aluminum	Gold	Aluminum, 2.7 Gold, 18.9
Liquid	Water	Mercury	Water, 1.0 Mercury, 13.5
Gas	Helium 	Air	Helium, 0.00018 Air at sea level, 0.0012

READING Charts

1. Which is denser—aluminum or gold? Mercury or gold?

2. Organize the substances in the chart from the least dense to the most dense. Make a bar graph with the densities of these substances.

How Does Density Make Things Sink or Float?

Have you ever observed a beach ball floating in a pool? Have you ever dropped your towel in the water, only to see it sink to the bottom? What makes some things float, while others sink?

Density determines an object's ability to sink or float. An object floats in a liquid when its density is less than the liquid's density. A beach ball is filled with air. Air is less dense than water, so the beach ball floats. We describe an object's ability to float as its *buoyancy* (BOY·uhn·see).

Ice cube
D = 0.9 g/cm³

Cork
D = 0.4 g/cm³

Copper cylinder
D = 8.9 g/cm³

Liquid water
D = 1.0 g/cm³

Copper cylinder
D = 8.9 g/cm³

Alcohol
D = 0.8 g/cm³

Ice cube
D = 0.9 g/cm³

Liquid mercury
D = 13.5 g/cm³

Why does ice float in water? Why does it sink in alcohol? The copper cylinder floats in mercury but sinks in water. Do you think it will sink or float in alcohol?

Submarine

Hatch

Propeller

Rudder

Aft ballast tanks

Machinery rooms

Nuclear reactor

Helium balloons can float, too. However, they float in air instead of water. Helium is less dense than air, so helium balloons rise into the sky.

As you know, not all objects float. An object sinks in a liquid when it is more dense than the liquid. The copper cylinder shown in the diagram sinks in water. The ice cube sinks in alcohol.

It's easy to float in Utah's Great Salt Lake. That's because salt water is denser than fresh water. The lake has six billion tons of salt! Swimmers float higher in the lake than in ocean water.

Sailors pump seawater into ballast tanks on a submarine to bring its average density close to the density of the surrounding water. This makes the sub have little tendency to rise or sink.

▷ **How does density determine an object's ability to float in water?**

Periscope

Antenna

Crew's quarters

Forward ballast tanks

28
7
6
5

Forward machinery room

Batteries

READING
Diagrams

1. Why do you think the ballast tanks aren't put in just one part of the submarine?

2. What would adding more water to the ballast tanks do? What would letting water out of the ballast tanks do?

What Are Conductors and Insulators?

Matter has many important properties besides density. For example, some materials **conduct** energy very well. These materials allow energy to flow through them easily. However, other materials **insulate** against the passage of energy. They do not readily permit energy to flow. Look carefully at the photographs to learn about materials that conduct or insulate.

Cooking pots and pans are made of metal because metal conducts heat well. However, they should have wooden or ceramic handles. Such handles insulate against heat so you don't get burned when you touch the handles.

Metals like the copper in the wire are also good conductors of electricity.

Which material in this pan is a conductor? Which is an insulator?

The electricity flows from the battery to the light bulb through the wire, producing light and heat. The plastic that coats the wire is an insulator. Anyone who touches the plastic coating will not be shocked, because the electricity cannot pass through it.

Sound booths are made of materials that insulate the room from outside noise. This property is important for musicians who are recording a new CD.

The walls of this room are made of a material that insulates sound. Why might this property be useful?

The wire is a good conductor of electricity. The plastic that coats the wire is an insulator. Why must electrical wire be insulated?

 What do *insulate* and *conduct* mean?

Individual iron particles | Small regions of magnetism

Magnetized iron bar

Demagnetized iron bar

When iron particles in small areas of the metal line up, a permanent magnet is formed.

▷ What makes a material magnetic?

What Is Magnetism?

Certain objects push or pull on each other because they are *magnetic*. Magnetism is another property of some kinds of matter. A magnet has a north pole and a south pole. North poles and south poles of magnets attract, but two poles that are alike repel. Magnets can also attract certain materials that are made of a metal like iron.

Like density, magnetism results from the combined effect of the properties of tiny particles. In iron, for example, each tiny particle of iron is itself a magnet.

Look at the diagram above. Each particle has a north and a south pole. When the particles line up, the material is magnetic. When the particles do not line up pole to pole, however, the material is not magnetic.

Earth acts like a huge magnet. A compass uses this property of matter to help you find your way home.

How Do We Use Properties of Matter?

Engineers and scientists use properties of matter when they design and build new things.

Aerogels are new materials with very low density and relatively great strength. They are made of tiny pockets of air surrounded by thin walls of silica. Silica is the same material found in sand and in window glass.

Aerogels are very good insulators of heat. Insulated windows containing aerogel would be from 10 to 20 times better at holding in heat than ordinary glass windows.

Scientists have discovered that some materials become perfect conductors of electricity when they are very cold. The photo shows a ceramic, glasslike material that conducts perfectly when cooled to $-196°C$ ($-320.8°F$).

This white aerogel has such a low density that it can float on top of soap bubbles.

▷ **How are properties of matter used?**

A magnetic cube floats above a disk made of a "superconducting" ceramic material. This effect can lift trains above the rails so that they can travel faster.

Why It Matters

You use many different properties of matter every day. Matter that conducts electricity lets you use a reading lamp at night or listen to your favorite CDs. Density allows you to float in a boat on a lake or float through the sky in a hot air balloon. Magnets help you find your way home with a compass.

Think and Write

1. List four properties of matter.

2. If a rock were taken from Earth to the Moon, how would its mass and weight be affected?

3. What if you had paper clips, rubber bands, wood chips, straight pins, strips of aluminum foil, and glass beads? Using a property of matter you've learned, classify these objects. Show your results in a table.

4. **Make a Model** How does the density of warm water compare with the density of cold water? How would you design a model to test your ideas?

5. **Critical Thinking** Think of the properties of matter you use every day. In what ways are they important to you?

L·I·N·K·S

WRITING LINK

Write a paragraph. Tell about a typical day from the time you wake up until the time you go to sleep. What properties of matter do you rely on to get to school, do your homework, and play with your friends?

MATH LINK

Calculate density. Find some small objects around your classroom or house—a seashell, a rock, or even a piece of fruit. Measure its mass and its volume. Use its mass and volume to find its density.

LITERATURE LINK

Read *Moon Landing That Never Was* to learn about the spacecraft *Apollo 13*. Try the activities at the end of the book.

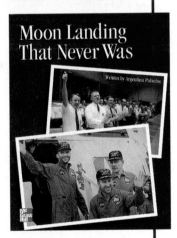

Moon Landing That Never Was

Written by Argentina Palacios

TECHNOLOGY LINK

At the Computer Visit **www.mhscience02.com** for more links.

ANIMALS: icy SURVIVAL

Water molecules

Ice molecules

Imagine a world where water's like most other substances—it becomes denser as it freezes. Ice, now heavier than water, sinks to the bottoms of ponds. The water quickly freezes from the bottom up into solid blocks of ice. Fish in the ponds freeze, too. That's the end of most freshwater fish.

In summer the ice near the top of the ponds melts, but not the ice at the bottom. That ice never melts. Each summer things get worse. Before long there's no liquid water left on Earth!

Luckily that scenario is science fiction, but real water is stranger than science fiction! Why doesn't it become denser when it turns solid? The answer lies in what happens when water molecules get cold enough to freeze.

As you know, water molecules are made of two hydrogen atoms and one oxygen atom. When water freezes, the molecules are kept farther apart than they are in liquid water.

Ice is only nine-tenths as dense as

liquid water, so when water freezes, it expands. A given volume of ice weighs less than the same volume of water. That's why ice floats in your lemonade!

Ice forms a protective covering for ponds. Under the ice the water stays liquid, allowing plants and animals to survive the winter. Because ice floats, oceans have icebergs. They can mean trouble for ships, because most of an iceberg is underwater. Look at the ice cube in your next drink. How much of it is under the surface?

What Did I Learn?

1. Water is different from other substances because

   A it is less dense as a solid than as a liquid
   B it is more dense as a solid than as a liquid
   C its molecules are packed more tightly as a solid
   D none of the above

2. Ice helps plants and animals in ponds survive by

   F preserving their habitat
   G providing more molecules of water
   H keeping the temperature low
   J forming a protective covering

AT THE COMPUTER **Visit www.mhscience02.com to learn more about survival in cold.**

Elements and Compounds

Get Ready

How is Jupiter like Earth? How are they alike on the outside?

Both planets have atmospheres. What are the atmospheres made of? Are they similar? What are the planets made of "beneath" the atmospheres?

Here's a similar question. What is matter made of? If you cannot "look inside" something—a planet or a piece of matter—how can scientists tell what a planet or any piece of matter is made of?

Process Skill

You communicate when you share information.

Explore Activity

Materials

3 identical, sealed, opaque boxes

How Do We Know What's "Inside" Matter?

Procedure

1 **Observe** Examine the three boxes, but do not open them. You can lift them, shake them, listen to the noises they make, feel the way their contents shift as you move them, and so on. Record your observations.

2 **Infer** Try to determine what is in each box.

Drawing Conclusions

1 **Communicate** Describe what you think is in each box.

2 How did you make your decision?

3 Do these boxes have anything in common? In what ways are they similar? In what ways are they different?

4 **Going Further: Experiment** What if you have a can of peanuts and a can of stewed tomatoes? The cans look the same except for the labels. Now what if your baby brother takes the labels off? You want the peanuts, but you don't want to open the tomatoes by mistake. What experiments can you do to find out what is inside—before you open the cans?

Main Idea All matter is made of elements.

What Is Matter Made Of?

In studying matter scientists face a challenge. The basic particles that make up matter are too small to be seen directly. In the past the tests scientists performed on matter gave only hints about how matter is put together. That's because particles of matter cannot be observed.

People have experimented with matter for thousands of years. In ancient times the goal was often a practical product like a colorful dye, a metal sword, or a plow. In recent centuries matter has also been studied with carefully planned scientific experiments.

The ancient Greek philosopher Aristotle believed that all matter was composed of four elements—earth, air, fire, and water. However, during the last three centuries, scientists have identified the true chemical **elements**. These substances are the basic building blocks of all matter. One of the most interesting elements is shown in the photograph at the bottom of the page. It expands very evenly when warmed and makes a good liquid for thermometers. What is it?

This bronze coin was made about 2,500 years ago. Bronze is made by mixing the metals copper and tin.

The element mercury is also known as liquid silver. It is beautiful but highly poisonous. Mercury is often used in thermometers. Why?

The Elements

Elements are pure substances that cannot be broken down into any simpler substances. You are probably familiar with many of them. Several are shown in the photographs. How many do you recognize?

Many elements have been known since ancient times but were not truly recognized as elements until the last few centuries. Other elements were found for the first time only recently. For example, germanium was not discovered until 1885. Also, some elements are not even found in nature. They have been made by scientists in nuclear reactors and huge machines called particle accelerators. Even though there are many different elements, living organisms and most materials are made up of just a few elements.

Each element is given a special symbol of one or two letters. The first letter is always a capital. The second letter is never a capital. Sometimes the letters match the English name, such as Ni for nickel or Zn for zinc. In other cases the symbol comes from an ancient name. Gold, for instance, is given the symbol Au from its Latin name, *aurum*.

Gold
Au

Aluminum
Al

Carbon
C

Sulfur
S

Copper
Cu

Oxygen
O

A few elements are pictured here. How many other elements can you name?

READING Main Idea

What are the building blocks of matter?

What Are Compounds?

Imagine looking at pure water through a microscope. It would look the same everywhere. Water has this appearance because it is a single substance. However, the photograph below shows how passing electricity through water breaks it apart into two elements, hydrogen and oxygen. If water is a single substance, how could it contain the elements hydrogen and oxygen?

Actually, the hydrogen and oxygen in water are chemically combined. This makes them act like a single substance. Any substance that is formed by the chemical combination of two or more elements is called a **compound**.

All compounds are single substances that can only be broken apart into simpler substances by chemical reactions. Compounds have different properties than the elements that make them up, as the lower photographs show.

▷ **How is a compound different from an element?**

Water is made of hydrogen and oxygen, as this experiment shows.

The compound sodium chloride is a solid at room temperature. We use it on our foods to give them more flavor. It belongs to a group of compounds called salts. Salts are always made up of a metal and a nonmetal.

Sodium and chlorine combine to make sodium chloride. Sodium is a soft, reactive metal that can explode on contact with water. Chlorine is a very poisonous gas.

Sodium   Chlorine

Sodium chloride (table salt)

1 When sulfuric acid is added to sugar, it breaks the compound apart into its elements.

2 The gas you observe is oxygen and hydrogen.

3 The black solid left behind is carbon.

How Do You Write a Compound's Name?

As you know, each element has a one or two letter symbol. Scientists also write symbols for compounds, which are called *chemical formulas*. A compound's chemical formula contains the symbols for the elements that make it up.

The formula also contains numbers below the element symbols called *subscripts*. The table shows chemical formulas for some familiar compounds.

The subscripts in a chemical formula tell us the number of particles that combine in a compound. For example, water is made up of two elements—hydrogen and oxygen. For every oxygen particle, there are two hydrogen particles. The formula for water is written H_2O.

Table sugar is made up of the elements carbon, hydrogen, and oxygen.

Common Compounds	
Compound	**Chemical Formula**
Water	H_2O
Carbon dioxide	CO_2
Baking soda	$NaHCO_3$
Table salt	$NaCl$
Table sugar	$C_{12}H_{22}O_{11}$
Glucose (a sugar)	$C_6H_{12}O_6$

For every 12 carbon particles, there are 22 hydrogen particles and 11 oxygen particles. We write $C_{12}H_{22}O_{11}$ for table sugar's chemical formula.

The photo shows what happens to table sugar when it is treated with strong sulfuric acid. **(Warning: Sulfuric acid is a dangerous substance.)** The acid takes out all the hydrogen and oxygen, leaving a black mass, carbon.

▷ **What is a chemical formula?**

What Are Elements Made Of?

In 1803 an English scientist named John Dalton stated an important theory: Matter is made up of tiny particles that cannot be cut apart into smaller pieces. Today we call Dalton's tiny particles **atoms**.

According to Dalton, the atoms of one element were all alike. Each element was made up of one kind of atom. However, the atoms of one element were different from the atoms of any other element. While many parts of Dalton's theory have been improved since 1803, the basic idea of atoms is correct. An atom is the smallest unit of an element that retains the properties of the element.

Individual carbon atoms

Dalton drew the symbols above for atoms. He believed that each element's atoms weighed a different amount from the atoms of other elements.

Many experiments since Dalton's day have shown us what atoms are like. Atoms are so small that we cannot see them directly, even through a microscope. Scientists have had to observe atoms indirectly. A special microscope called a *scanning tunneling microscope* uses a very sharp needle that can trace the bumps in a surface made by individual atoms. The photograph above shows some of what such special microscopes can "see."

Images made by these microscopes show that atoms are discrete and often occur in well-ordered arrays. For example, the carbon atoms in the photo are arranged in rings of six atoms each.

 What is an atom?

What Is Inside Atoms?

John Dalton imagined that atoms were like tiny steel marbles—solid and unbreakable. However, we now know that atoms are made of still smaller particles. Atoms are far from being solid—they are mostly empty space!

Atoms contain three kinds of particles called **protons** (PROH·tahnz), **neutrons** (NEW·trahnz), and **electrons** (i·LEK·trahnz). The protons and neutrons are located in a tiny, very dense body in the atom's center, called the atomic **nucleus** (NEW·klee·uhs). The electrons are in the space outside the nucleus.

Protons and neutrons have nearly the same mass, but electrons are about 2,000 times less massive than protons and neutrons.

Protons carry one unit of positive electric charge, while electrons carry one unit of negative electric charge.

Neutrons have no electric charge. All atoms have equal numbers of electrons and protons, so they have no overall electric charge.

The number of protons in an atom determines what element it is. For example, any atom with six protons is a carbon atom. Any atom with eight protons is an oxygen atom.

Look carefully at the diagrams on this page to see how atoms are put together.

▷ **What are the three particles that make up an atom?**

Atoms are made of protons, neutrons, and electrons. The number of protons an atom has determines what element it is.

Hydrogen

Electron
Proton
Neutron

Helium

Carbon

What Properties Do Elements Have?

We now know of 112 elements. These substances have many different properties. There are patterns in the properties of the elements. Study the photographs on this page to learn about properties that can demonstrate these patterns.

Chemical Reactivity

Some elements take part in chemical reactions much more easily than others. The magnesium reacts rapidly with the acid, but the copper hardly reacts at all. Reactive elements, like magnesium, are usually combined with other elements when found in nature.

Metal Versus Nonmetal

About three-fourths of the elements are metallic, like copper, gold, silver, aluminum, iron, and nickel. Metals conduct electricity and heat well. Metals are also shiny when freshly polished, and many can be worked into thin sheets or different shapes. In contrast nonmetals, like iodine, phosphorus, and carbon, are often poor conductors of heat and electricity. They are not reflective like metals.

States at Room Temperature

The elements shown are all at room temperature, about 22°C (71.6°F). Copper, aluminum, and iodine are solids at 22°C. Bromine, though, is a liquid at 22°C. Neon is a gas at 22°C.

 How can elements be classified?

Property: Chemical Reactivity

Magnesium

Copper   Hydrochloric acid

Magnesium takes part in chemical reactions much more easily than copper. Here the magnesium reacts rapidly with the acid. The copper hardly reacts at all.

Property: Metal Versus Nonmetal

Metals

Goldleaf   Copper

Aluminum

Nonmetals

Neon   Bromine   Iodine

Metals, like copper, gold, silver, aluminum, iron, and nickel, are good conductors of heat and electricity. Nonmetals are often poor conductors of heat and electricity.

How Can the Elements Be Grouped?

In 1869 a Russian scientist named Dmitry Mendeleyev found that the properties of the elements went through repeating cycles. Mendeleyev created a table of elements based on these cycles. Each group in his table contains elements with similar chemical properties. For example, one group contains lithium (Li), sodium (Na), potassium (K), rubidium (Rb), and cesium (Cs). All of these elements combine with chlorine in the same way. The formulas for their chlorine compounds are LiCl, NaCl, KCl, RbCl, and CsCl.

We call Mendeleyev's table the periodic table after the "periodic" changes he found in the elements' properties.

The metals lie on the left, and the nonmetals lie mainly on the right, with elements called metalloids in between.

Most of the elements are solids at room temperature, and all metals are solids except mercury.

The most reactive metals are at the left, and the most reactive nonmetals are in the second column from the right.

> **What is the periodic table? How is it organized?**

READING
Charts

1. Is sodium a metal or a nonmetal? Is chlorine a metal or a nonmetal?

2. Which elements are liquid at 20°C?

The Modern Periodic Table

The number in each box is the number of protons an atom of that element has.

Metallic Properties
Li Metal
B Metalloid
C Nonmetal

Phase at 20°C
C Solid
Br Liquid
H Gas

H 1																	He 2
Li 3	Be 4											B 5	C 6	N 7	O 8	F 9	Ne 10
Na 11	Mg 12											Al 13	Si 14	P 15	S 16	Cl 17	Ar 18
K 19	Ca 20	Sc 21	Ti 22	V 23	Cr 24	Mn 25	Fe 26	Co 27	Ni 28	Cu 29	Zn 30	Ga 31	Ge 32	As 33	Se 34	Br 35	Kr 36
Rb 37	Sr 38	Y 39	Zr 40	Nb 41	Mo 42	Tc 43	Ru 44	Rh 45	Pd 46	Ag 47	Cd 48	In 49	Sn 50	Sb 51	Te 52	I 53	Xe 54
Cs 55	Ba 56	Lu 71	Hf 72	Ta 73	W 74	Re 75	Os 76	Ir 77	Pt 78	Au 79	Hg 80	Tl 81	Pb 82	Bi 83	Po 84	At 85	Rn 86
Fr 87	Ra 88	Lr 103	Rf 104	Db 105	Sg 106	Bh 107	Hs 108	Mt 109	110	111	112		114		116		118

La 57	Ce 58	Pr 59	Nd 60	Pm 61	Sm 62	Eu 63	Gd 64	Tb 65	Dy 66	Ho 67	Er 68	Tm 69	Yb 70
Ac 89	Th 90	Pa 91	U 92	Np 93	Pu 94	Am 95	Cm 96	Bk 97	Cf 98	Es 99	Fm 100	Md 101	No 102

Nitrogen
N_2

Oxygen
O_2 and O_3

Neon
Ne

Compounds

Carbon dioxide
CO_2

Water
H_2O

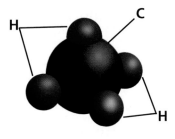

Methane
CH_4
(natural gas)

What Are Molecules?

Some elements, such as neon, are made up of single atoms that do not attach to any other atoms. Other elements have atoms that attach to one or more additional atoms. Particles that contain more than one atom joined together are called **molecules** .

Nitrogen is an example of an element that is made up of molecules. Its molecules are made up of two nitrogen atoms. Some elements even exist in more than one form, such as oxygen. Oxygen is usually made up of two-atom

molecules, much like nitrogen, but oxygen can also exist as three-atom molecules. The three-atom form of oxygen is known as ozone. The three-atom ozone has properties different from the two-atom oxygen.

Molecules of elements always contain only one kind of atom. Compounds are made up of molecules that have different kinds of atoms joined together, as the lower diagram shows.

Note how the chemical formulas in both diagrams tell you the number of atoms in the molecules.

When a compound forms from elements, changes occur in the way that atoms are linked together. This causes the compound to have properties different from the elements. For example, water is a liquid, yet it is formed from two gases, hydrogen and oxygen. The diagram shows why water has properties different from hydrogen and oxygen gas—the atoms are linked in a new way when water forms.

▷ **What is the difference between a molecule of oxygen and a molecule of methane?**

Hydrogen
H_2

+

Oxygen
O_2

=

Water
H_2O

Hydrogen plus oxygen makes water.

Modeling Molecules

1. Using small marshmallows for hydrogen atoms and large marshmallows for oxygen atoms, make two H_2 molecules and one O_2 molecule. Join the atoms with toothpicks.

2. **Use Numbers** Count the number of atoms of each type you have in your molecules. Record these numbers. Take this many more marshmallows and make as many water molecules as you can, using toothpicks to join the atoms.

3. **Observe** How many water molecules did you make?

4. **Infer** Why would real water molecules have properties different from real hydrogen and oxygen molecules?

How Do We Use Compounds?

By studying matter scientists have learned how to prepare compounds that are very useful. Many things are made from the atoms of just a small number of elements. The photographs on this page show several compounds that we depend on a great deal in modern life.

Take petroleum, for example. Petroleum is a complex mixture of *hydrocarbons*—compounds made of hydrogen and carbon atoms. Gasoline comes from petroleum. Its molecules usually have from 5 to 12 carbon atoms in chains. Gasoline gives off a lot of energy when it is burned, so we use it as a fuel in cars.

Many kinds of plastics are also made from hydrocarbons in petroleum or natural gas.

▷ **What are some useful compounds?**

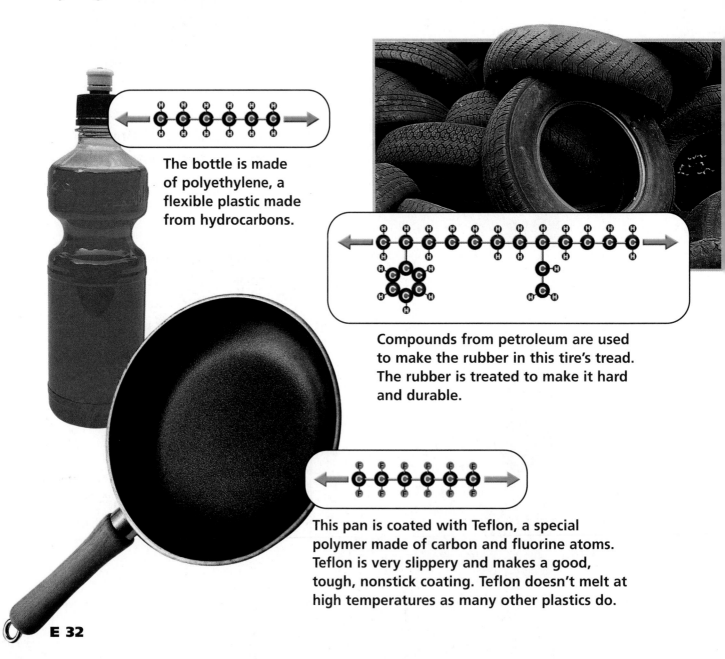

The bottle is made of polyethylene, a flexible plastic made from hydrocarbons.

Compounds from petroleum are used to make the rubber in this tire's tread. The rubber is treated to make it hard and durable.

This pan is coated with Teflon, a special polymer made of carbon and fluorine atoms. Teflon is very slippery and makes a good, tough, nonstick coating. Teflon doesn't melt at high temperatures as many other plastics do.

Why It Matters

Imagine what the world would be like if there were no compounds. There wouldn't be any plants. There wouldn't be any water or food or animals or things people build. In fact, there wouldn't be any people either.

New compounds are discovered in nature every day. Scientists also develop new compounds in labs. Many compounds are used to help make life better.

Visit **www.mhscience02.com** to do a research project on the uses of new compounds.

Think and Write

1. Why must some element symbols have two letters instead of just one?

2. A beryllium atom is made of four protons, five neutrons, and four electrons. Draw a model of this type of atom.

3. Give an example of a compound whose properties are much different from the elements it is made of. Describe how it is different.

4. Why do scientists use models to study atoms and molecules?

5. **Critical Thinking** Are all molecules compounds? Explain.

L·I·N·K·S

SOCIAL STUDIES LINK

Write a biography. John Dalton was the scientist who defined atoms. Learn more about his life by doing research. Use the Internet or an encyclopedia.

HEALTH LINK

Research calcium. Calcium is an important element. You need to have calcium-rich foods in your diet. Why does your body need calcium? What foods are a good source of calcium?

ART LINK

Make a model. What is your favorite element? Helium? Oxygen? Copper or iron? Draw a picture or make a model of this element. Include its protons, electrons, and neutrons.

TECHNOLOGY LINK

At the Computer Visit **www.mhscience02.com** for more links.

Solids, Liquids, and Gases

Vocabulary

state of matter, E36
melting point, E37
boiling point, E37
freezing point, E37

Get Ready

How many different kinds of matter do you see here? How are they changing?

Glaciers are huge sheets of moving ice and snow. At a shoreline chunks of ice fall off and float away as icebergs.

Ice is solid water. You are looking at solid and liquid water. What does it take for solid ice to become liquid—to melt?

Process Skill

You predict when you state possible results of an event or experiment.

Explore Activity

What Happens When Ice Melts?

Materials

ice cubes

water

graduated cylinder

plastic or paper cup

thermometer

heat source (lamp or sunlight)

watch or clock

Procedure

1️⃣ **Measure** Put ice cubes in the cup. Add 50 mL of water to the cup. Swirl the ice-and-water mixture together for 15 seconds.

2️⃣ **Measure** Place the thermometer in the cup. Wait 15 seconds. Then read the temperature. Record your observation.

3️⃣ **Measure** Put the cup under a heat source (lamp or sunlight). Take temperature readings every 3 minutes as the ice melts.

4️⃣ **Measure** After all the ice has melted, continue taking temperature readings every 3 minutes for another 15 minutes.

Drawing Conclusions

1️⃣ **Observe** What happened to the temperature as the ice melted?

2️⃣ **Hypothesize** Why do you think you got the results described in question 1?

3️⃣ **Going Further: Predict** What do you think would happen if you didn't add any water to the ice? What do you think would happen if you added more water to the ice? Design an experiment to test each of your predictions. What do you think happens as you freeze water? How would you design an experiment to test your prediction?

Main Idea Matter exists as a solid, a liquid, or a gas.

What Are the States of Matter?

Water turns from a solid to a liquid when it absorbs enough heat. If even more heat is supplied, the water will turn to a gas called steam. Most substances exist in one of three **states of matter**—*solid, liquid, or gas.* Adding or removing heat can make substances change from one state to another.

When a change of state occurs, the identity of the substance remains the same. However, the substance gains new properties because the molecules are arranged in a different way.

The molecules of any substance are attracted to each other. The attraction is just a weaker form of the force that links the atoms in each of the molecules. When the molecules are arranged in organized positions, a solid results.

When heat is absorbed by a solid, the molecules vibrate faster and faster. At some point the molecules separate from one another. This causes the solid to become a liquid. When even more

Change of State

As heat is absorbed, molecules move faster and become less organized.

Melt

Boil

Freeze

Condense

The "cloud" is liquid water, not gas. The invisible gas—water vapor—is in the air.

Solid

Liquid

Gas

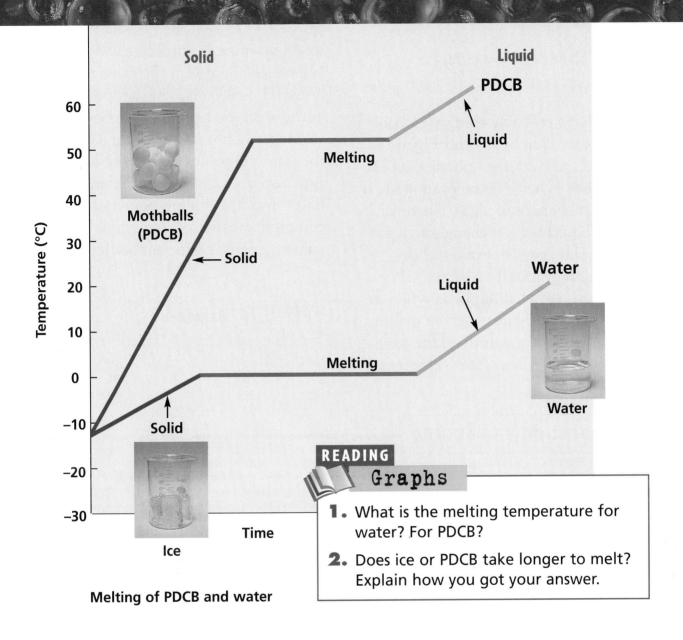

Melting of PDCB and water

READING

Graphs

1. What is the melting temperature for water? For PDCB?

2. Does ice or PDCB take longer to melt? Explain how you got your answer.

heat is absorbed, the molecules move faster and form a gas.

The graph shows how the temperatures of two different compounds change as they are being heated. As you can see, these substances melt at different temperatures. In fact, each different pure substance has its own particular **melting point**. Each different substance also has its own boiling temperature, called the **boiling point**.

While a substance is melting or boiling, its temperature stays the same.

It warms up only before or after the change of state.

What happens when heat is removed from the substance? It *condenses*—turns from a gas to a liquid—at the boiling temperature. It freezes—turns from a liquid to a solid—at the melting temperature. For this reason the melting point is also known as the **freezing point**.

▷ **What are melting and boiling points?**

E 37

How Can Matter Change to a Gas?

You have probably seen water boiling on the stove. You have probably also observed that water evaporates out of wet clothes. When a liquid evaporates, it gradually changes to a gas. However, when a liquid boils, it changes to a gas rapidly. The diagram explains how boiling and evaporation occur.

Remember what happens when ice melts? The temperature of the melting ice does not change until all the ice has turned to water. Then the water begins to get warmer. In the same way, a substance remains at the same temperature while it boils. This happens because all the heat energy goes into turning the liquid into steam. Once all the liquid becomes steam, the temperature also goes up. The graph on page E39 shows the boiling points of common substances. Note how each substance has a different boiling point.

READING Main Idea

How is evaporation different from boiling?

Evaporation and Boiling

① A few molecules escape into the air, causing evaporation at room temperature.

② When the liquid is heated, more molecules escape. The liquid evaporates faster.

③ As more heat is absorbed over time, the liquid reaches its boiling temperature. Boiling begins at the boiling point.

1. Is butane a liquid or a gas at 10°C?

2. Which boils at a lower temperature, rubbing alcohol or oxygen?

3. Which state of matter is lead at 80°C?

Solid and Liquid Ranges of Common Substances (in degrees Celsius)

Name	Formula	Melting Point	Boiling Point
Oxygen	O_2	–218°	–183°
Nitrogen	N_2	–210°	–196°
Butane	C_4H_{10}	–138°	–0.5°
Rubbing alcohol	C_3H_8O	–90°	82.4°
Water	H_2O	0°	100°
Mercury	Hg	–39°	357°
Lead	Pb	327°	1,740°

The table lists the melting points and boiling points of some common substances.

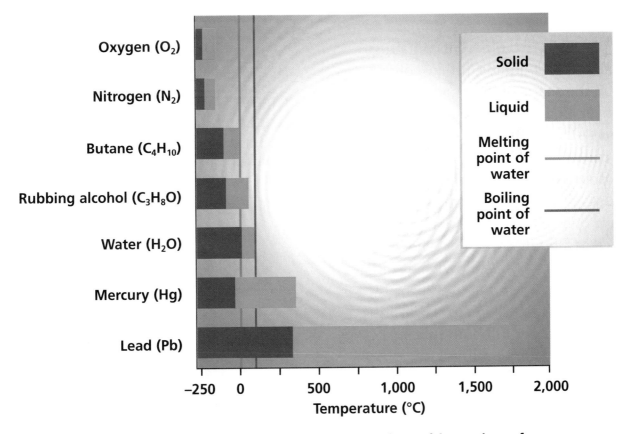

Use this graph to compare the melting points of the substances listed in the table.

What Are the Properties of Solids, Liquids, and Gases?

The aluminum cube in the first photo is a typical solid. It shows that solids retain their shape. Solids have the same volume no matter what container they are placed in. Also, solids cannot be poured, so they are not fluid.

Many solids form crystals, as in the second photograph. A gemlike crystal of alum is shown. The shape of such crystals results from the way the particles are arranged. The particles link together in an organized pattern.

Liquids have different properties from solids. Compare the first and third photographs. In the third photograph, the same volume of a colored liquid has been placed in two different containers. This shows that liquids, unlike solids, take on the shape of their containers. However, liquids do have a definite volume—they settle to the bottom of their containers. Also, as you know from pouring water, liquids are fluid.

Gases do not have a fixed volume of their own. The volume of a gas is determined by its container. The last photograph shows a yellowish gas in a tube separated from a second tube by a glass plate. When the plate is removed, the gas expands to fill both tubes. Gases always fill the full volume of their containers. Also, gases are fluid—they can be pumped through pipelines just like liquids.

Solids keep their shape.

Many solids form crystals.

Liquids take the shape of their containers.

Gases fill the volume of their containers.

Expansion and Contraction

When the temperature of a material increases, its particles move faster. On average these particles tend to spread out more. This causes materials to *expand*—spread out—as they get hotter. The opposite happens when the temperature of a material decreases. Cool materials tend to *contract*—shrink. The material's particles tend to slow down and stay closer together. Gases expand or contract the most with changing temperature, but liquids and solids are also affected by temperature.

You have probably observed expansion and contraction in your everyday life. This property of matter makes bicycle tires and basketballs flat on cold days and your classroom door stick and be difficult to open on hot days. Can you think of other examples?

▶ **How are solids, liquids, and gases different?**

QUICK LAB

FOR SCHOOL OR HOME

Collapsing Bottles

1. **Predict** How does heat affect an empty plastic bottle? What do you think will happen to the bottle when it is warmed? What do you think will happen to it when it is cooled? Record your predictions.

2. With the cap off, hold the bottle for a minute or two in a pail of hot tap water. Then screw the cap on tightly while the bottle is still sitting in the hot water.

3. **Experiment** Now hold the bottle in a pail of ice water for a few minutes.

4. **Communicate** Record your observations.

5. **Infer** Write out an explanation of why the bottle changed as it did. Be sure to use the idea of how molecules move at different temperatures.

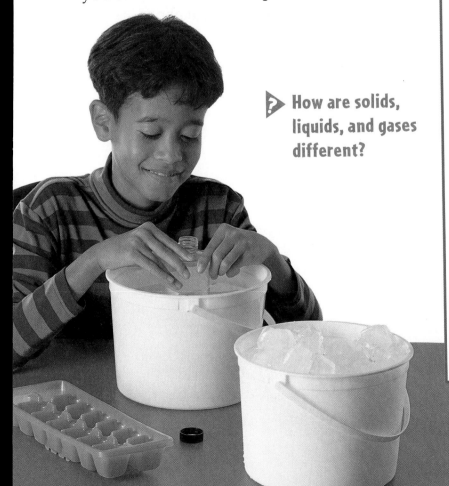

E 41

How Can Expansion and Contraction Be Used?

You have probably had your temperature taken with a thermometer. Thermometers have liquid mercury or colored alcohol in a bulb connected to a very thin tube. The liquid expands or contracts with changes in temperature and moves up or down in the tube. The position of the liquid in the tube gives the temperature.

In the cylinders of a car's engine, burning fuel produces hot, expanding gases. The expanded gas pushes on the pistons in the cylinders. The pistons in turn provide the power that drives the car forward.

The solid materials that make up a bridge or sidewalk expand when

Expansion joints keep roads and bridges from cracking on hot days when the road expands.

warmed. If the sections are assembled tightly on a normal day, they will expand against each other on very hot days. This expansion can cause cracks to form. To guard against this problem, engineers leave some space between the sections and fill it with a flexible material. Look for these "expansion joints" in the photograph above.

Spark plug

Combustion cylinder

Piston

▷ How does a thermometer use expansion and contraction?

E 42

L·I·N·K·S

Why It Matters

You sit, write, and climb on solids. Liquids allow you to bathe, swim, and drink. Gases are what you breathe every day. They are what allow you to smell odors at a distance. You learned that gases always fill the full volume of their containers. Did you realize that you notice this property of gases every time you are in your room and smell food cooking in the kitchen?

Think and Write

1. Explain what happens to the temperature of ice as it melts.

2. Acetone freezes at 95.35° below 0°C and boils at 56.2°C. At 42°C what state of matter would acetone be in? At 84°C?

3. Gases can be easily squeezed into a smaller volume. Why is this so?

4. On a hot, damp summer day, drops of water will form on the outside of a glass containing an ice cold drink. Explain how this happens.

5. **Critical Thinking** Water boils at 100°C at sea level. High up in the mountains, water boils at a lower temperature. Why does it take longer to cook potatoes high up in the mountains than it does to cook potatoes at sea level?

LITERATURE LINK

Read *Chilled to the Bone* to learn about icy places. Try the activities in the end of the book.

ART LINK

Draw a chart. Make a list of all the things you do before you go to bed at night. How many of these things involve solids? Liquids? Organize the things you use according to the three states of matter. Draw a chart showing how you use matter in its different states.

MATH LINK

Use conversions. Scientists use the Celsius scale to measure temperature. Most people in America, however, measure temperature in Fahrenheit. You can change Celsius into Fahrenheit by multiplying the temperature in Celsius by 9, dividing that number by 5, and then adding 32. Using this method, try to calculate the melting and boiling temperatures of water in Fahrenheit.

TECHNOLOGY LINK

At the Computer Visit www.mhscience02.com for more links.

Neon

Neon is a colorless, odorless gas. But something magical happens when electrical current passes through neon. The gas and electricity create brightly colored light.

French chemist Georges Claude discovered neon light around 1910. It wasn't long before glassmakers made fanciful signs using neon. The signs were so beautiful, businesses started using them. Theaters, diners, car dealerships and other businesses used neon signs to advertise. Some signs were huge. One sign for chewing gum was eight stories high and one block long! Some signs had moving tubes to create animated scenes.

To make neon signs, glassblowers heat glass tubes and bend the softened glass into different shapes or letters. Then, neon gas is pumped into the tubes, and they are sealed shut. Wires conduct electrical current into the tubes through electrodes. Electricity speeds back and forth between electrodes at both ends of the tubes. The electrons in the neon start to vibrate. As they vibrate, they release excess energy as light.

Neon light glows bright red. Gases similar to neon create different colors. Argon gas, for example, makes bright green light. With different combinations of gases, certain chemicals, and colored glass, neon artists can create more than a hundred colors. Though different materials are used, they're all called "neon signs."

Bright neon lights have another important use. Airplane pilots use lights on land to guide them to safe landings. The lights are often neon lights because they can penetrate fog. Pilots can see neon lights from far away!

What Did I Learn?

1. What is the first step in making a neon light?

A Neon gas is pumped in a glass tube.
B A glassblower heats a glass tube over a flame.
C The inside of a glass tube is coated with colored powder.
D A glass tube is bent into a certain shape.

2. What color light does neon gas make?

F red
G green
H blue
J yellow

AT THE COMPUTER

Visit www.mhscience02.com to learn more about neon and other elements.

Chapter 10 Review

Vocabulary

Fill each blank with the best word or words from the list.

> **atom,** E26
> **boiling point,** E37
> **density,** E8
> **electron,** E27
> **insulate,** E14
> **mass,** E6
> **molecule,** E30
> **nucleus,** E27
> **proton,** E27
> **state of matter,** E36
> **weight,** E7

1. An atomic particle that has a positive charge is called a(n) _____.

2. A substance made of different atoms linked together is called a(n) _____.

3. _____ is a measure of the force of gravity between Earth and an object.

4. A(n) _____ is the smallest unit of an element.

When a compound reaches its **5.** _____, its **6.** _____ changes.

A(n) **7.** _____ is a negatively charged particle in the space outside an atom's **8.** _____.

9. _____ is a measure of matter's **10.** _____ divided by its volume.

11. An object's ability to float depends on its _____.

   A size

   B temperature

   C insulation

   D density

12. Water can turn from liquid to gas by evaporating or _____.

   F condensing

   G pouring

   H boiling

   J freezing

13. Mass is the measure of the _____.

   A amount of material in an object

   B weight of an object

   C space an object takes up

   D density of an object

14. The molecules of a _____ tend to be packed tightly in an organized way.

   F gas

   G solid

   H liquid

   J neutron

15. The number of _____ an atom has determines what element it is.

A electrons

B neutrons

C protons

D charges

Concepts and Skills

16. Process Skills: Make a Model Scientists use a variety of models to understand and explain the natural world. A formula such as H_2O is a model for water. Tell what the formula means. Give another example of a chemical formula, and tell what it means.

17. Reading in Science What is the main difference between mass and weight? Support your answers with any facts or details necessary.

18. Scientific Methods Which do you think would evaporate faster— pure water or salt water? Why? Describe an experiment that would test your idea.

19. Critical Thinking Are all molecules compounds? Explain your answer.

20. Product Ads Teflon is an artificial compound. It is a "nonstick" plastic. What products might advertise the use of this material?

Boost *your test scores!*

Be Smart!
Visit www.mhscience02.com

CHAPTER 11

Forms of Matter and Energy

Did You Ever Wonder?

Where does the steel used to build bridges and skyscrapers come from? Steel is a mixture of several different elements, including iron, carbon, and nickel. Is the process of making steel a physical change or a chemical change? How are the properties of steel different from the properties of the metals that make it up?

Mixtures and Solutions

Get Ready

Why do people call the Mississippi River the "muddy Mississippi"? What happens when the muddy Mississippi flows into the Gulf of Mexico?

The flowing water of the river joins with standing water in the gulf. The river drops much of what it is carrying.

The Mississippi is made of things mixed together. How many other examples can you give of things that are mixed together?

Process Skill

You **observe** when you use one or more of the senses to identify or learn about an object or event.

E 50

Explore Activity

How Can You Take Apart Things That Are Mixed Together?

Materials

sample of substances mixed together

hand lens

toothpicks

magnet

paper (coffee) filters

2 cups or beakers

water

goggles

Procedure: Design Your Own

BE CAREFUL! Wear goggles. Do not taste your sample.

1. **Observe** Examine the sample your teacher gives you. It is made of different substances. One of the substances is table salt. What else does it seem to be made of? Record your observations.

2. **Experiment** Design and carry out an experiment to separate the various ingredients in your sample.

Drawing Conclusions

1. **Infer** How many parts or substances were mixed into your sample? How did you reach that conclusion?

2. You knew one substance was salt. What properties of salt might help you separate it from the rest? Could you separate salt first? Why or why not?

3. How did you separate out the substances? How did you use the properties of these substances to separate them?

4. **Going Further: Experiment** What if you were given white sand and sugar mixed together? How would you separate the two ingredients?

Main Idea Substances can combine to form mixtures.

What Is a Mixture?

The iron filings and yellow sulfur powder in the first photo have been stirred together. The two materials were *physically* combined. The result is a **mixture** .

The substance shown in the second photograph, iron disulfide, also contains both iron and sulfur. However, now the iron and sulfur are *chemically* combined, and a new substance is formed, a compound.

How do mixtures and compounds differ? Compounds are produced by chemically combining substances. Mixtures are produced by a physical combination of substances. In mixtures the parts simply blend together without forming new substances. Differences in chemical and physical properties of substances are used to separate mixtures and identify compounds.

A compound has different properties from the substances it contains. For example, iron disulfide is not magnetic, while pure iron is. In contrast, the parts of a mixture keep their original properties. Even though the iron has been mixed with sulfur in the first picture, it remains magnetic. You could use a magnet to remove the iron filings from the mixture.

Iron filings　　　Sulfur powder

When iron filings and yellow sulfur powder are stirred together to make a *mixture*, the substances keep their original properties. The iron remains magnetic. You could use a magnet to remove the iron filings.

This is *iron disulfide*, a mineral known as iron pyrite, or "fool's gold." Iron disulfide is a compound of iron and sulfur. When a *compound* forms, it has different properties from the substances it contains. Unlike iron, iron disulfide is not magnetic.

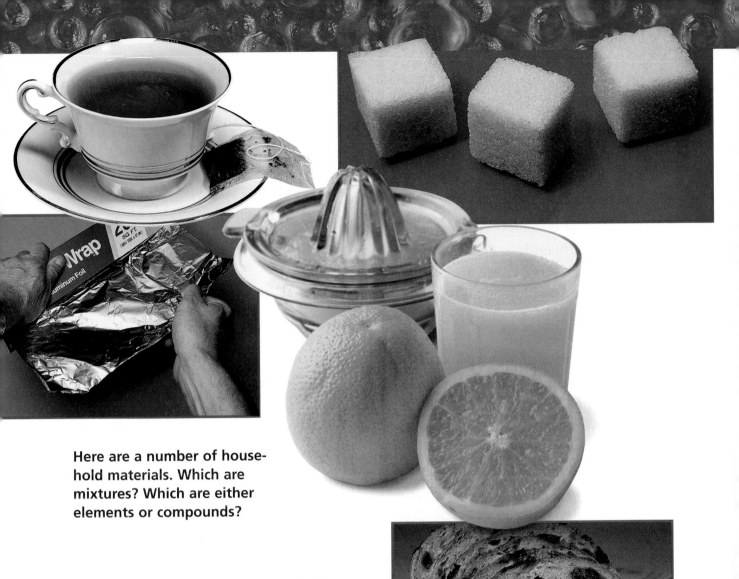

Here are a number of household materials. Which are mixtures? Which are either elements or compounds?

What if you stir one spoonful of sugar into a glass of water to make a sugar-water mixture? A friend could stir two spoonfuls of sugar into the same amount of water. You would both have the same kind of mixture. However, your friend's drink would have a much sweeter taste.

Like the sugar water, any type of mixture can contain varying amounts of the parts that make it up. Salt water could be barely salty or very salty. Granola cereal could have many or few raisins. Tea could be strong or weak, and so on.

On the other hand, compounds are always made up in the same way. For example, about two-fifths of the mass of any sample of table salt is sodium, and three-fifths is chlorine.

▶ **What is the difference between compounds and mixtures?**

How Can Mixtures Be Classified?

Mixtures are not pure substances because they contain more than one element or compound. If the substances in a mixture are blended completely, the mixture looks the same everywhere, or is *homogeneous* (hoh·muh·JEE·nee·uhs). We call such mixtures **solutions**. There are many different types of solutions. Look at the table on page E55 for examples of some common solutions.

On the other hand, the parts of a mixture may be only partly blended. The mixture may look "speckled," either to your eye or through a microscope. This type of mixture is said to be *heterogeneous* (het·uhr·uh·JEE·nee·uhs). Most mixtures are heterogeneous. Rivers contain a mixture of water, rock, and soil. Stones are heterogeneous, too.

Some mixtures are neither solutions nor heterogeneous mixtures. These mixtures are called **colloids**. Colloids have properties in between those of solutions and heterogeneous mixtures. Like solutions, there are many types of colloids. The chart on page E55 shows some of these.

▷ **What are three types of mixtures?**

A lunch of a chicken salad sandwich, tea, and gelatin dessert with whipped cream contains each type of mixture. Can you tell which one is which?

Types of Solutions

Substance	Dissolved In	Examples
Liquid	liquid gas solid	cranberry juice in water water dissolved in air mercury in silver (dental fillings)
Gas	liquid gas	carbon dioxide in soda oxygen and nitrogen in air
Solid	liquid solid gas	salt in water copper and zinc mixed in brass mothballs

Types of Colloids

Substance	Mixed In	Examples
Liquid	liquid gas solid	mayonnaise clouds jam
Gas	liquid solid	shaving cream marshmallows
Solid	liquid gas	toothpaste smog

What Kinds of Solutions Are There?

You are already familiar with many solutions. In fact, you are surrounded by them all the time. The atmosphere contains a very important solution—air. Seawater is another type of solution.

Solutions are usually transparent or are evenly colored. They never settle into layers. They are the same all the way through.

Solutions come in many different forms. Air is an example of a gaseous solution. Nitrogen, oxygen, and a small amount of other gases mix evenly together. One breath of air is always made up of 78 percent nitrogen and 20 percent oxygen gas.

Seawater is an example of a liquid solution. Tea and your favorite fruit punch are other examples. These solutions are all made from solids that dissolve in a liquid—water. Liquid solutions can also be made by mixing two liquids together, as in nail polish

Not all solutions are liquid. The flask contains a solution of two gaseous compounds, NO_2 and N_2O_4. NO_2 is red-brown, while N_2O_4 is colorless.

remover. Mixing a liquid with a gas, as in a bottle of soda, is another way to form a liquid solution.

Solutions may also be solid. Alloys are solid solutions. They are made by mixing two or more metals together. Bronze, steel, and brass are all alloys.

The properties of an alloy can be varied by changing the amounts of pure metals it contains. The stainless steel used in silverware uses only a slightly different mixture of elements than the

This bridge is made of an alloy, steel.

Heat is released when calcium chloride dissolves in water. Hot packs can be used to warm your hands on a cold day for this reason.

high-strength steel you might find in construction.

Solutes and Solvents

Solutions may form in many different ways. However, no matter how they form, all solutions have two parts. The substance that makes up the smaller part of a solution is called the *solute*. The substance that makes up the larger amount is the *solvent*. The solute dissolves in the solvent to form a homogeneous mixture. All solutions consist of at least one solute and one solvent.

Think about the examples on page E56. What is the solvent in fruit punch? What is the solute in seawater? Think about which of the substances is in the greater amount.

Water is an important solvent. Many different kinds of compounds can dissolve in water, such as salts, minerals, proteins, and sugars. Nutrients from food dissolve and are carried through your body because of the water in blood.

Some solute and solvent pairs give off or absorb heat when they are combined. Hot and cold packs use this property of solutions. Calcium chloride is a salt that releases a great deal of heat when it is mixed with water. A hot pack often contains a small pouch of this salt in a sealed package of water. When the package is struck, the pouch of salt breaks open. This allows the salt to dissolve. Heat is then released.

▷ **What are five types of solutions?**

QUICK LAB

FOR SCHOOL OR HOME

Solubility

1. **Measure** Add 100 mL of water to each of three cups. Place a sugar cube in one of the cups, and stir until the cube is dissolved. Record the time it took to dissolve.

2. **Predict** Carefully break a second sugar cube into two pieces. How long do you think it will take to dissolve? Place the two pieces in a second cup of water, and stir until they dissolve. Record the time they took to dissolve.

3. **Use Variables** Fold a piece of paper around a sugar cube, and carefully break the cube into many pieces. Pour the pieces into the third cup of water, and stir until dissolved. Record the dissolving time.

4. **Interpret Data** Construct a graph that illustrates your findings. Which sugar cube dissolved the fastest?

5. What conclusion can you make regarding dissolving time based on the experiment?

What Is Solubility?

Have you ever tried making fruit punch from a mix? How easy is it to get all of the mix to dissolve? Solutes act differently in different solvents. This property describes *solubility*. Solubility explains the ability of a solute to dissolve in a solvent.

Many things affect solubility. Temperature is an example. Most solutes dissolve more quickly when a solvent is hot. Sugar is more soluble in hot tea than in cold, iced tea.

The amount and type of solute and solvent also affect solubility. Some substances do not dissolve in others. Oil does not dissolve in water. It is *insoluble* in water. It does dissolve in other substances, like dish detergent, however. The structure of a substance determines its solubility in different solvents.

Most solute-solvent combinations have a limit of how much solute will dissolve in a volume of solvent. After that limit is reached, no more solute will dissolve. You may observe this when you add sugar to a glass of lemonade. After a few teaspoons, the sugar settles to the bottom of the glass, and no more sugar will dissolve.

▷ **What are some factors that affect solubility?**

What Are Heterogeneous Mixtures Like?

Rocks are an example of heterogeneous mixtures. Tomato sauce, casseroles, and taco salads are also familiar examples.

Heterogeneous mixtures are even more common than solutions. Heterogeneous mixtures, unlike solutions, settle into layers in a fluid. Oil-and-vinegar salad dressing separates when it is left alone, for example.

Heterogeneous mixtures are either cloudy or opaque. They are not evenly mixed. Think of a pot of chicken soup. One ladle may have a lot of carrots. The next may have few carrots and a lot of rice. One part of a mixture may have more of one substance than another.

Mixtures like clay and water, with particles that are easily seen, are called

Rocks are heterogeneous mixtures. They are composed of pieces or layers of different minerals.

suspensions. Suspensions form when one substance is insoluble, or does not dissolve in a solvent.

▷ **What are the characteristics of heterogeneous mixtures?**

Heterogeneous Mixtures Can Settle into Layers

Clay and water   Oil and water

Freshly shaken mixtures of clay and water, and oil and water

Water
Clay

Oil

Water

The mixtures after they were allowed to stand for a length of time

E 59

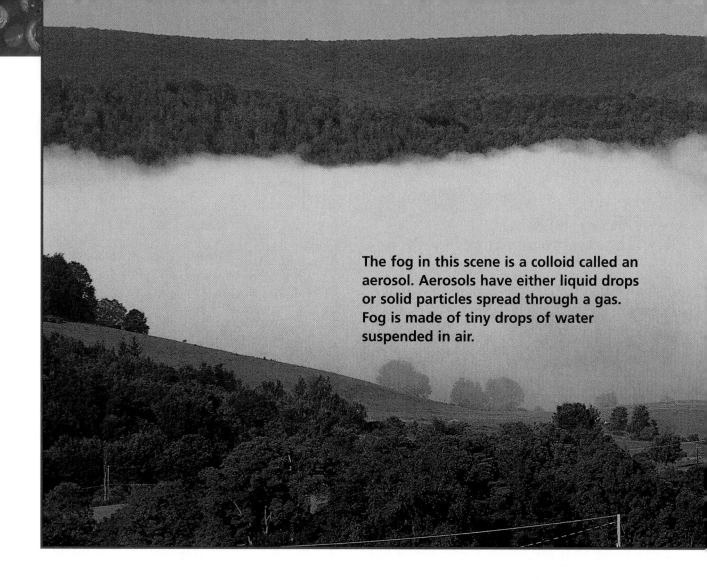

The fog in this scene is a colloid called an aerosol. Aerosols have either liquid drops or solid particles spread through a gas. Fog is made of tiny drops of water suspended in air.

What Types of Colloids Are There?

Milk is not transparent, so it cannot be a solution. It does not settle out into layers, so it is not a heterogeneous mixture. Milk is a colloid. Like milk, all colloids have properties between those of solutions and heterogeneous mixtures.

The photograph on page E61 shows what milk looks like under a microscope—droplets of fat spread throughout water. Other colloids are similar. They have particles of one material scattered through another. The particles are big enough to block or scatter light but not big enough to settle out.

There are many types of colloids. Milk is an example of an **emulsion**, a liquid (fat) spread through another liquid (water).

Another type of colloid is called an **aerosol**. Aerosols have either liquid drops or solid particles spread through a gas. Fog is made of tiny drops of water suspended in air.

Many food products are colloids. Gelatin dessert is a **gel**. A gel is a solid spread through a liquid. The solid in the gelatin is protein. The liquid in the gelatin is water.

Whipped cream is a **foam**. A foam is a gas spread through a liquid. The gas in the whipped cream is air. The

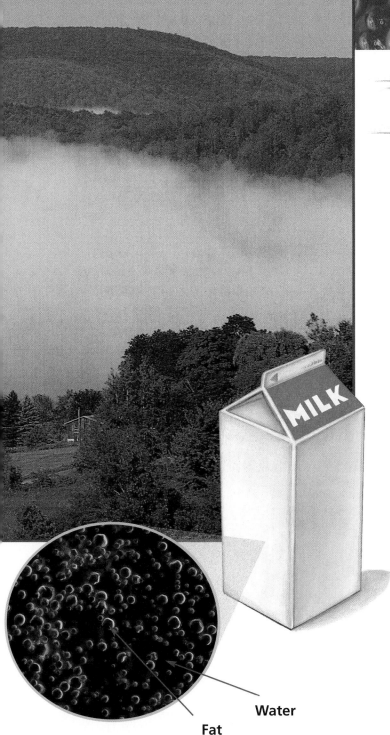

Water

Fat

liquid in the whipped cream is water and fat. Marshmallows are a solid foam—a gas spread through a solid. The gas in the marshmallows is air. The solid in the marshmallows is a sweetened gelatin.

▷ **What are four types of colloids?**

FOR SCHOOL OR HOME

Kitchen Colloids

1. Pour some whipping cream into a bowl. Set this bowl in a bed of ice in another bowl. Let the cream and bowl chill.

2. **Experiment** Use a whisk to whip the cream until it becomes a fluffy texture.

3. **Observe** Let the cream warm, and continue beating it. Observe how it changes. Record your observations.

4. **Define** What kind of colloid is the whipped cream in step 2?

5. **Interpret Data** What is it made of?

6. **Infer** In step 3 you made a colloid. What is this colloid commonly known as? What do you think it is made of?

How Can Mixtures Be Separated?

We can separate the parts of mixtures using methods called physical separations. A physical separation gets the parts of a mixture away from one another without changing their identities.

We can use the different properties of matter to separate mixtures. Density, magnetism, and boiling and melting temperatures are all helpful tools.

The illustrations on these pages show examples of physical separation methods. Study them to see the steps and equipment needed.

▷ **What properties might you use to separate mixtures?**

The mud particles cannot pass through the pores in the paper, but the water molecules can. The mud collects in the paper, while the water drips through.

Muddy water

Filter
Funnel
Mud particles

Water

① To separate a mixture of sand and salt, pour in water and stir. The salt dissolves, but the sand doesn't.

② Use a filter to separate the sand from the salt water.

③ Then let the water evaporate to get back the salt.

Separating Sand and Wood Chips

To separate sand and wood chips, first pour in water. Stir briefly.

The wood chips float to the top, while the sand settles to the bottom. The wood chips can be skimmed off and dried. The water can be poured off, and the sand dried.

Separating Alcohol and Water

You could separate alcohol and water by heating them in this apparatus.

Alcohol and water are heated. Alcohol boils at a lower temperature than water, so at the beginning, more of the vapor will be alcohol than water.

Vapor

The vapors cool and condense.

Alcohol and water mixture

Cold water

Waste water

The condensed liquid has more alcohol than water.

To sink

READING Diagrams

1. What is one way to separate two substances in a mixture?

2. Could you separate sand and wood chips the same way you separate sand and salt? Explain.

3. Make a list of three ways to separate parts of a mixture.

Which Resources Come from Mixtures?

Many of Earth's resources exist as mixtures. Ores are mixtures that provide us with metals and minerals. Seawater is a mixture that can be used as a resource for fresh water, thanks to desalination—another separation process.

Crude oil, our major energy source, is a mixture, too. The diagram below shows a process called *distillation*. We use this process to separate important chemicals out of crude oil.

First, the crude oil is heated until it becomes a gas. Then, the vapors are sent to the tower. There they rise and cool. As they cool, they condense to form liquids.

The substances with large molecules and high boiling points quickly cool into a liquid. The substances with small molecules and low boiling points rise higher in the tower before condensing. The condensed liquids are drawn off as shown.

READING **Cause and Effect** How can we get resources from mixtures?

Distillation

Crude oil is heated until it becomes a gas. The vapors are sent to the tower. There they rise, cool, and condense to form liquids. Substances with smaller molecules and lower boiling points rise higher in the tower before condensing.

Distillation tower

Gasoline

Vapors rise and cool in tower

Kerosene

Crude oil vapors

Diesel fuel

Liquid crude oil

Lubricating oil

Asphalt

Why It Matters

Many things you use every day—from the air you breathe to the milk you drink to the steel in your bicycle—are mixtures. Some mixtures need to have just the right amounts of their ingredients each time. For example, you need a certain amount of oxygen in the air you breathe. The amount of iron, carbon, and other metals in steel determines its properties, such as hardness and resistance to rusting.

As you go through your day, think of all the mixtures you use and why they are important to you.

Think and Write

1. How do the properties of sugar and water alone compare with the properties of a sugar-water solution?

2. How are mixtures different from compounds?

3. Air is a mixture of oxygen and nitrogen gas. What type of mixture is air? Why?

4. Oil paints are made of colored particles spread through an oil. Are oil paints solutions, heterogeneous mixtures, or colloids? How do you know?

5. **Critical Thinking** Describe the steps you could follow to separate a mixture of sawdust and salt.

L·I·N·K·S

ART LINK

Make a collage. Cut pictures of mixtures from magazines. Paste them on a board. Tell your classmates which are solutions, colloids, and heterogeneous mixtures.

MATH LINK

Make a graph. Air is a solution of gases. Research what the gases are and how much of each gas is in air. Show the results in a graph.

WRITING LINK

Write a poem. Many meals are made from a mixture of foods, like salad, casserole, and pizza. Sometimes the mixture tastes better than the ingredients by themselves. Write a poem about a dish like this. Tell about all the ingredients that are part of this mixture.

TECHNOLOGY LINK

Science Newsroom CD-ROM Choose *Here's the Solution* to learn how the three types of mixtures are similar.

At the Computer Visit www.mhscience02.com for more links.

Got Milk?
Got Butter?

The success of mammals on Earth is helped by what they feed their newborns: milk produced by their mothers. Humans also raise other large mammals to produce milk for them.

A mammal's milk is seven-eighths water, but the other eighth has nearly everything needed for good health! Some food value comes from the lactose, or milk sugar, dissolved in it.

Milk has a lot of fat globs. Because they're lighter than water, the globs rise to the top of a container. Gravity pulls the heavier liquid down. The fat globs merge to become cream. Milk with little or no fat is skim milk.

Many people prefer skim or low-fat milk. The fat in milk contributes to weight problems, heart disease, and possibly other diseases.

Cream
Milk

Milk you buy has vitamins D and A added to make it more nutritious. It's been pasteurized—heated to kill disease-causing bacteria. The heating also makes some milk proteins inactive and slows down the spoiling.

Milk is homogenized by putting it through a fine screen to break fat globs into tiny specks. They're so small that the movement of the other molecules in milk keeps them from rising. For that reason cream doesn't form at the top of homogenized milk.

By constantly moving cream in a closed container, you cause the fat globs to merge. Drain off the thin, watery stuff and you've got . . . butter!

Automatic Milking Machine

Milk

Butter

Write
ABOUT IT

1. What other foods are vitamins added to? Why do you think that is done?

2. Fat is used to make cells' outer membranes. How does this explain why mammals' milk is high in fat?

AT THE
COMPUTER

Visit www.mhscience02.com to learn more about milk products.

An old-fashioned churn stirs up milk to form butter.

Chemical Changes

Get Ready

How can you tell changes occur?
Metal rusts. Milk sours. Bread dough
rises when baking powder is mixed
into it. A runny egg hardens when it
is cooked. What are other changes
going on around you?

Process Skill

You **infer** when you form an idea
from facts or observations.

Explore Activity

How Can You Recognize a Change?

Materials

baking soda

baking powder

cornstarch

salt

iodine solution

vinegar

water

wax paper

permanent marker

4 toothpicks

3 droppers

4 plastic spoons

7 small cups

goggles

Procedure

BE CAREFUL! Wear goggles.

1. Copy this grid on wax paper with a marking pen. Using a spoon, put a pea-sized amount of cornstarch in each of the three boxes in the first row.

2. **Observe** Use a dropper to add five drops of water to the cornstarch in the first column. Stir with a toothpick. Record your observations.

3. **Experiment** Using a different dropper, add five drops of vinegar to the cornstarch in the second column. Stir with a new toothpick. Record your observations.

4. **Observe** Use a third dropper to add five drops of iodine solution to the cornstarch in the third column. Record your observations.
   CAUTION: Iodine can stain and is poisonous.

5. **Experiment** Repeat steps 1–4 for baking powder, baking soda, and salt.

Drawing Conclusions

1. **Infer** In which boxes of the grid do you think substances changed into new substances? Explain your answers.

2. **Going Further: Infer** Your teacher will give you samples of two unknown powders. Use what you have learned to identify these powders. Report on your findings.

	Water	Vinegar	Iodine Solution
Cornstarch			
Baking powder			
Baking soda			
Salt			

Read to Learn

Main Idea Matter can undergo chemical as well as physical changes.

What Are Physical and Chemical Changes?

Different kinds of changes are going on all the time. In a **physical change**, matter changes in size, shape, or state without also changing identity.

In Lesson 3 you learned about the states of matter. Change of state is an example of a physical change. A substance can change from solid to liquid to gas. The substance does not change its chemical identity in this process. Its state simply changes. The photograph below shows why a change of state is a physical change.

You also learned in Lesson 4 about mixtures. Combining two substances to form a solution is another example of physical change. The two substances do not lose their identities. They can be physically separated from each other to give back the original substances. The photograph above shows this kind of physical change.

Baking soda

Baking soda and water mixture

When baking soda mixes with water, the baking soda seems to disappear. However, when the water evaporates, baking soda is left behind. This is a physical change.

A change of state is a physical change. When the steam—gaseous water—hits the dish, it cools and turns back into liquid water.

Steam condenses to form liquid water.

The photo on page E68 shows a **chemical change**. Chemical changes occur when atoms link together in new ways. The changes cause new compounds to form. The new compounds have properties different from the original substances from which they were formed.

The reaction between vinegar and baking soda is an example of a chemical change. When these two materials are mixed, gas bubbles form. A change in the linking pattern of the atoms in the vinegar and baking soda causes a new substance—carbon dioxide—to form. Other new substances form, too. However, you cannot see them because they remain in the liquid.

Chemical changes are often referred to as **chemical reactions**. The original substances are called the **reactants**. The new substances produced by the chemical reaction are called the **products**. During chemical reactions the atoms in the reactants rearrange to form products with different properties. In the reaction between baking soda and vinegar, the baking soda and the vinegar are the reactants. The carbon dioxide, water, and a chemical called sodium acetate are the products.

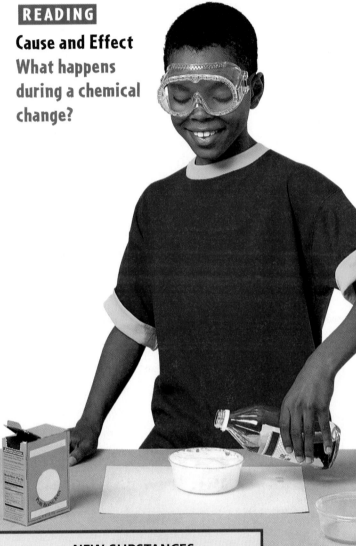

READING

Cause and Effect
What happens during a chemical change?

What happens when baking soda and vinegar mix?

STARTING SUBSTANCES		NEW SUBSTANCES
$NaHCO_3$ + CH_3COOH	→	H_2O + CO_2 + $NaC_2H_3O_2$
Baking soda + Acetic acid (part of vinegar)	→	Water + Carbon dioxide + Sodium acetate

E 71

What Are the Signs of a Chemical Change?

Chemical reactions often show one or more signs that a chemical change has occurred. These signs include a color change, formation of a gas, and formation of light and heat. The reactions on these pages show some of these signs.

Does a chemical reaction occur when reddish brown iodine is placed on a potato? The iodine reacts with starch in the potato. The white starch and iodine change to a bluish black color.

When reddish blueberry juice is mixed with a solution of baking soda, it turns to a greenish color. The green color results from a chemical change in the molecules of the blueberry juice.

The bubbles you see when lemon juice is added to a solution of baking soda are a sign of a chemical change. Carbon dioxide gas forms by the reaction between acid in the lemon juice and the sodium bicarbonate in the baking soda.

Have you ever put hydrogen peroxide on a cut to kill germs? The bubbles tell you that a chemical change is occurring.

What happens when propane gas is released from a tank? It reacts with oxygen in the air. The light and heat produced are signs of this chemical reaction.

▷ **What are three signs of a chemical change?**

Color Change

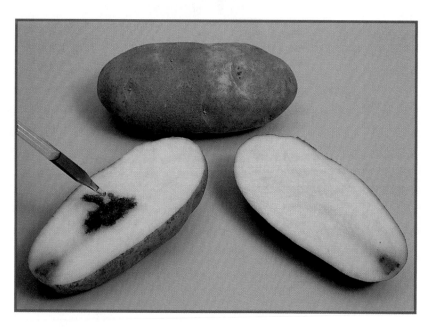

When iodine is dropped onto a potato, a color change is observed.

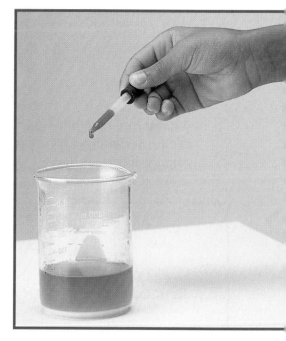

The reaction of blueberry juice and baking soda shows a change of color.

Formation of a Gas

Carbon dioxide gas forms when lemon juice is added to a baking soda solution.

When hydrogen peroxide comes into contact with bodily fluids, it reacts and gives off pure oxygen gas. The oxygen gas, in turn, kills germs in the cut and guards against infection.

Formation of Light and Heat

When you light a match, it gives off light and heat all on its own. This tells you that a chemical change is occurring.

When propane mixes with oxygen, a chemical reaction occurs.

What Are Some Familiar Chemical Changes?

As a cake bakes, several chemical changes occur. Heat turns the baking soda (sodium bicarbonate) in the cake dough into sodium carbonate, steam, and carbon dioxide gas. The sodium carbonate is a harmless solid that remains in the cake. The steam helps make the cake moist. The bubbles of carbon dioxide help the dough expand and make the cake light and fluffy. The heat of the oven also triggers other chemical reactions in the cake batter. These strengthen the cake and keep it from collapsing after it is baked.

The red powder covering the wheelbarrow above is iron oxide. Iron oxide is commonly known as rust. Rust forms when iron atoms in steel react with oxygen from the air. The reaction is very complex and needs moisture to occur. Steel objects are most likely to rust if they get wet and are not dried right away.

Rocket engines use chemical reactions that produce lots of heat. This space shuttle's main engines are powered by liquid hydrogen and liquid oxygen. When the two react together, they make water vapor and the energy the shuttle needs. The shuttle is also equipped with launch boosters that use a solid fuel. When the solid fuel burns, aluminum powder is converted to aluminum oxide.

Rust

Tarnish

The silver spoon in the photo is partly covered with a tarnish of silver sulfide. The silver sulfide forms when silver reacts with sulfur or hydrogen sulfide in foods or the air. You can even tarnish silver by wrapping it with a rubber band. Sulfur added to strengthen the rubber causes the tarnish to form. Polishes can be used to remove the tarnish and restore the silver's shiny appearance.

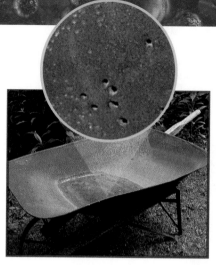

▷ **What are three examples of chemical changes?**

Preventing Rust

You've learned that steel forms rust when exposed to oxygen and moisture. Rusting can ruin metal objects. Can you find a way to stop or slow rusting? In this activity you will experiment to try to find the answer. In order to experiment, you need to do the following things. Form a hypothesis. Design a control. Carry out your experiment. Analyze and communicate your results.

Materials

steel nails and sand-paper

paper cups

dilute salt water

goggles

Procedure

BE CAREFUL! Wear goggles.

1. **Hypothesize** The photograph shows a method for making a steel nail rust. Think of a way to protect a steel nail from rusting under such conditions. Write down an explanation of why you think your method will work.

2. **Experiment** To test your method of rust protection, you need a control nail kept under normal conditions. Each experimental nail will have just one condition (variable) change. For example, what if you wanted to make a nail rust? You might leave one nail in a clean, empty jar (the control). You might put another in water. You might put a third in lemon juice. The amount of rusting that occurs is called the *dependent variable*. Write out how you will set up the experimental and control nails for your experiment.

3. **Experiment** Carry out your experiment, and record your observations.

Drawing Conclusions

1. **Infer** Write out a description of how well your hypothesis agreed with your results. Be sure to compare the experimental nail with the control nail.

2. **Communicate** Why did you need a control in this experiment?

Which Are Easier to Reverse – Chemical or Physical Changes?

You would probably agree that turning carbon dioxide gas, water, and sodium acetate back into baking soda and vinegar would be difficult. Simply stirring the three ingredients together would not give you baking soda and vinegar. In general, chemical changes are difficult to reverse. Imagine trying to "unburn" toast or "unspoil" milk!

On the other hand, physical changes can sometimes be easily reversed. Although this is not always true. For example, melting an ice cube can easily be reversed by cooling it until it freezes again. Stirring sugar into water can be reversed by letting the water evaporate.

What changes occur when toast burns? What happens when a candle burns?

However, it would not be so easy to put pieces of paper back together after cutting them from a single page. Still, if a change seems very easy to reverse, it is more likely to be a physical change.

The photograph of a burning candle shows that many changes are happening. Wax melts, runs down the side, and turns solid again. However, some of the wax turns into carbon dioxide gas and steam when it combines with oxygen in the air. This change releases enough heat to make the candle flame you see.

▷ **Why are chemical changes more difficult to reverse than physical changes?**

L·I·N·K·S

Why It Matters

Chemical changes bake your cakes and let your bread rise. They turn fuels into heat to warm your home. Chemical changes even turn the food you eat into energy to keep you going. In what other ways are chemical changes important to you?

Visit **www.mhscience02.com** to do a research project on chemical changes.

Think and Write

1. Is the rusting of a nail a chemical or a physical change?

2. Is the melting of ice a chemical or a physical change? Why?

3. When a match burns, what evidence is there that a chemical change is occurring?

4. **Experiment** What if you wanted to find out if a cake bakes better with baking soda or baking powder? Design an experiment to test your ideas. Why might you want to use a control?

5. **Critical Thinking** What could you do to protect a bike from rusting?

LITERATURE LINK

Read *Let's Go Spelunking!* to learn about a trip to Howe Caverns. Try the activities at the end of the book.

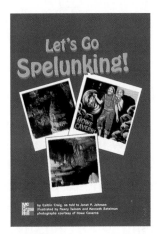

Let's Go Spelunking!

SOCIAL STUDIES LINK

Research the Statue of Liberty. The Statue of Liberty is a famous statue in New York Harbor. What does it look like today? What did it look like 100 years ago? What is the statue made of? What could have happened to make the statue appear the way it does today?

TECHNOLOGY LINK

Science Newsroom CD-ROM Choose *The Action of Reaction* to learn more about physical and chemical changes.

At the Computer Visit **www.mhscience02.com** for more links.

Can Chemical Reactions Make Food Safe or Unsafe?

Why do mold and bacteria grow in foods and spoil them? Are the foods unsafe to eat? What can be done to prevent microorganisms like molds and bacteria from spoiling foods? All the answers involve chemical reactions.

Like all living organisms, molds and bacteria require food. They can "eat" the same foods we eat and multiply in the food. They cause chemical reactions to occur in food, making it spoil.

In some cases, molds and bacteria can be harmful, perhaps even deadly, to people who eat foods in which these microorganisms have grown. Bacteria from contaminated food can multiply in the digestive tract of a person, causing vomiting, diarrhea, and intestinal bleeding. Hamburger, for example, may be contaminated with a bacterium known as *E. coli* O157:H7. Each year, *E. coli* O157:H7 causes about 73,000 illnesses and about 60 deaths in the United States.

To help prevent bacteria and molds from spoiling foods, food manufacturers may add chemicals to kill microorganisms. Sodium propionate, for example, is a chemical often added to cheeses and baked goods to keep molds from growing. Manufacturers also package foods in airtight containers and bags to prevent spoiling.

While food manufacturers take steps to keep the foods you eat safe, what can you do at home? Chemical reactions slow down as the temperature is lowered. Keeping foods in the refrigerator or freezer is a primary means of preventing the growth of bacteria and molds. The cold temperatures slow down the chemical reactions that make food spoil. Foods such as lunch meats and potato salads should not be kept out of the refrigerator for a long time.

The cheese in the photograph has spots of mold growing on it.

AT THE COMPUTER

Visit www.mhscience07.com to learn more about bacteria and mold.

Vacuum-sealed containers prevent bacteria from contaminating food.

Write ABOUT IT

1. How can molds and bacteria cause food to spoil?

2. What are some harmful effects of eating food contaminated with bacteria such as *E. coli*?

Acids and Bases

Get Ready

Have you ever tried to suck on a lemon? It might have made your cheeks pucker! Lemons taste very sour. Why is this?

Have you ever seen ammonia being used to mop the floor? Why is it a good cleaning agent?

The answer to these questions is that these substances are either acids or bases. What are acids and bases? Are there any other substances in your house that contain an acid or base? How can you find out?

Process Skill

You observe when you use one or more of the senses to identify or learn about an object.

Explore Activity

Which Are Acids and Which Are Bases?

Materials

red and blue litmus paper

wide-range pH paper

plastic cups

labels

goggles

gloves

apron

household solutions

Procedure

BE CAREFUL! Wear goggles, gloves, and an apron.

1 **Predict** Which solutions do you think are acids and which are bases? Write your predictions in a chart like the one shown below.

2 **Observe** Vinegar is an acid. Put a small amount in a cup, and mark the cup with a label. Test by dipping a piece of red litmus paper into the vinegar. Record the result in your table. Repeat with a piece of blue litmus paper. Litmus paper is a material that allows you to tell which solutions are acids and which are bases.

3 **Classify** Test all of your other solutions in the same way, and record your results.

Sample	Predict: Acid or Base?	Affect on Red Litmus	Affect on Blue Litmus	Result: Acid or Base?
Vinegar	ACID			ACID
Baking soda				
Lemon juice				

Drawing Conclusions

1 Which samples are acids? How do you know?

2 Which samples are bases? How do you know?

3 **Measure** Now test each sample with a small strip of pH paper. Match the color of the paper to the color scale on the holder, and find the pH.

4 **Going Further: Interpret Data** Look at your data. Do acids have higher or lower pH values than bases? Which sample is most acidic? Which is most basic? How do you know?

Main Idea Many important substances in our lives are acids or bases.

What Are Acids and Bases?

How do you know whether something is an **acid** or a **base**? Vinegar, orange juice, and lemon juice are acids. An acid tastes sour and turns blue litmus paper red. Bases, like ammonia and baking soda, taste bitter and turn red litmus paper blue. (You should never test acids and bases by tasting them, however.)

In Lesson 5 you learned about chemical reactions. When you mixed vinegar, an acid, with baking soda, a base, a chemical reaction occurred. Acids and bases can react with each other to form water and a salt.

In a reaction acids "give away" hydrogen particles, or *hydronium ions*. Bases give off *hydroxide ions*.

This is a simplified hydronium ion. Acids release them in solution.

Bases release hydroxide ions, such as this, in solution.

Hydroxide ions are particles that are made up of one oxygen atom and one hydrogen atom linked together. Hydronium and hydroxide ions combine to make water. What is left of the acid and base also combines to make a new substance—a salt.

If you place a blue and a red strip of litmus paper in a glass of water, both strips will stay the same color. This tells you that water is neither acidic nor basic. A solution that is neither acidic nor basic is **neutral**. Water is a neutral substance.

When hydrochloric acid is added to a base, sodium hydroxide, a chemical reaction occurs to produce water and sodium chloride (table salt).

HCl + $NaOH$ → $NaCl$ + H_2O

You can make an acid neutral by mixing it with a base. Likewise, you can make a base neutral by mixing it with an acid. Acids and bases react to form neutral compounds.

The chemical properties, or reactivity, of acids and bases are what make them useful and important. You may know not to add lemon to hot tea with milk. This is because the acid in the lemon can react with the milk, causing it to sour. Acids react strongly with metals, as well. Statues can corrode from the acid found in rain and the atmosphere. The acid in rain is also harmful to plant and animal life.

Acids aren't only harmful, however. Acids are used in batteries to help make electricity. They are used in industry to produce plastics, metals, explosives, textiles, and dyes. They are also used for many functions in your body. All living things use amino acids, for example, to build proteins. All of an organism's muscles and tissues are made up mostly of proteins.

Bases can also be reactive. You may have experienced a bloody nose from smelling ammonia. Ammonia is a strong base that can be corrosive. Bases are often used in cleansers. They can break down grease and oil. Soap is a base you use every day.

Baking soda and baking powder are bases used in cooking. They are often used in baking to make cakes rise. When these bases mix with an acid, carbon dioxide gas is produced. The carbon dioxide gas that is released helps to make cakes become airy and rise.

This statue of George Washington has been corroded by acid in rain.

READING Cause and Effect

What happens when an acid is added to a base?

How Can You Tell if Something Is an Acid or a Base?

Litmus paper has a different color in acids than it does in bases. Litmus is an example of an **indicator**. An indicator is a substance whose color changes when it is mixed with an acid or a base. You can use litmus paper to tell which household materials are acids and which are bases.

Many indicators come from plants. Litmus, for example, is made from certain lichens. Another common vegetable indicator is phenolphthalein (fee·nawl·THAL·ee·in). Phenolphthalein is colorless in acid and pink in base.

Red cabbage juice is another indicator. Add acid to red cabbage juice, and the juice turns maroon. If there is a lot of acid, the juice turns pink. A neutral substance does not change the color. A base turns it green. A very basic substance turns it yellow.

Many household materials can act as indicators. These materials include blueberry juice, beet juice, carrot juice, grape juice, red cabbage, purple hollyhock flowers, and blue iris flowers. Each has one color in an acid and another color in a base.

▷ **What is an indicator?**

Hydrangeas have pink flowers in basic soil and blue flowers in acidic soil. Are these flowers indicators?

Cabbage juice is an indicator because it changes color in acids and bases. Litmus paper can also be used as an indicator.

Slightly acidic

Slightly basic

Very acidic

Neutral

Very basic

How Can Indicators Be Useful?

The photograph shows a test kit that can be used to find how acidic the soil is. Doing so is important because certain plants grow well only when soil is slightly acidic. The test kit has paper strips that are soaked with an indicator. When a strip is placed in moist soil, it turns a certain color. Matching the color of the strip against the colored scale on the container reveals how acidic the soil is.

Indicators are important in many situations other than gardening. For example, swimming pool water must be routinely checked with a test kit. Aquarium owners or pond owners periodically have to check how acidic the water is to make sure it is healthy for the fish and plants.

▷ **What are some ways indicators are used?**

Mystery Writing with a Base

1. Using a cotton swab, write a short message to your partner on a piece of paper with a baking soda solution.

2. Put the paper aside, and allow it to completely dry. After it is dry, give it to your partner.

3. Can you read the message your partner gave you? You probably cannot. Use another cotton swab and gently "paint" the paper with grape juice.

4. **Observe** What happened when you painted the paper with the grape juice?

5. **Infer** Is the grape juice an indicator? Why or why not?

Are All Acids and Bases the Same?

Are all acids equally acidic? Are all bases equally basic? No. Acids and bases have different strengths. The strength of an acid is called its **acidity**. The strength of a base is called its **alkalinity**.

Hydrochloric acid, a laboratory chemical, is much more acidic than citric acid, the acid found in citrus fruits like oranges and lemons. Hydrochloric acid, therefore, has a higher acidity.

Acidity and alkalinity depend on how many hydronium and hydroxide ions are in a solution. The diagram below compares the solution of a strong acid with a weak acid, and a strong base with a weak base.

A scientist named Soren Sorenson developed a scale in 1909 to compare acidic and basic solutions. This scale is called the *pH scale*. The **pH** of a solution tells how acidic or basic the solution is. It measures acidity and alkalinity. Scientists still use this scale today.

The pH of most solutions lies between pH 1 and pH 14. A pH of 1 means that there are a lot of hydronium ions in a solution. The solution is very acidic. A pH of 14 means that there are a lot of hydroxide ions in a

The first solution is a stronger acid than the second because it has more hydronium ions. The third solution is a weaker base than the fourth solution because it has fewer hydroxide ions. Alkalinity increases as the pH increases from 7 to 14. Acidity increases as the pH decreases from 7 to 0.

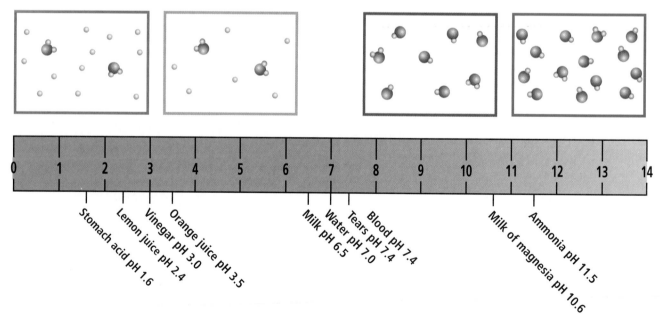

0 1 2 3 4 5 6 7 8 9 10 11 12 13 14

Stomach acid pH 1.6
Lemon juice pH 2.4
Vinegar pH 3.0
Orange juice pH 3.5
Milk pH 6.5
Water pH 7.0
Tears pH 7.4
Blood pH 7.4
Milk of magnesia pH 10.6
Ammonia pH 11.5

pH meter

solution. The solution is very basic. A pH of 7 means that the solution is neutral.

Scientists often use a pH meter to determine the acidity or alkalinity of a solution. Strips of paper called pH paper are also commonly used. This paper changes to a different color depending on the exact pH of a solution.

Your blood has a pH of 7.4. Doctors can use this pH to diagnose certain diseases. The blood of a person with diabetes, for example, has a pH that is lower than normal.

▷ **How can acidity and alkalinity be measured?**

The color match indicates that the solution has a pH of 2, which means that it is acidic.

How Can Acids and Bases Be Used?

Acids and bases are used in many different ways every day. They can be used in your home as cleaning agents. Bleach contains acids, for example. Ammonia, drain cleaners, and window cleaning solutions all contain bases. Bases are good cleaning agents because they dissolve grease, fats, and oils.

Many foods get their flavor from acids. Tomatoes, grapefruit, lemons, and limes all contain acids.

Acids and bases are used in scientific laboratories and in industry to make plastics and textiles. Cotton is often treated with a base to make it look shiny.

The reaction of acids and bases is very useful. You have learned that acids and bases react to make neutral compounds. You may have even experienced this kind of reaction in your own body! Have you ever taken an antacid or milk of magnesia for an upset stomach? Your stomach contains acids to help you digest food. In fact, the pH of your stomach is usually between 1 and 2.

Sometimes there is too much acid in your stomach, causing the pH to go even lower. This may happen when you eat foods that are very acidic or when you are very nervous. The decrease in pH can cause a stomachache.

Products like antacids are basic. When you take them, they react with the extra acid in your stomach. They help increase the pH of your stomach back to its normal level and make you feel better.

▷ **How can acids and bases be useful?**

Why It Matters

Acids and bases make up many of the compounds around you. They clean your clothes and help you to digest food. Oranges are acidic. Eating oranges is obviously not dangerous. However, there are other acids and bases that must be treated with care. Use these materials safely. Wear protective eyewear and cover your skin when working with these acids and bases. Understanding pH lets you know how strong these substances are.

Think and Write

1. What kind of particles do acids produce?

2. What are the properties of a base?

3. Your friend wonders if a cleanser is an acid or a base. What test could you do to help him answer the question?

4. What numerical scale describes acidity? How does this scale work?

5. **Critical Thinking** A friend calls you and says he accidentally spilled some acid. Describe what you would tell him to do to clean up the spill safely.

L·I·N·K·S

MATH LINK

Solve a problem. An acid with a pH of 3 is 10 times more acidic than an acid with a pH of 4. How much more acidic is an acid with a pH of 1 than an acid with a pH of 3? With a pH of 4?

ART LINK

Draw a picture. Use lemon juice to paint a picture. Let the lemon juice dry, and then "develop" your picture with grape juice.

HEALTH LINK

Research swimming pools. You learned that swimming pools are checked for their acidity level. Why is this? Use the Internet or an encyclopedia to learn more.

TECHNOLOGY LINK

At the Computer Visit **www.mhscience02.com** for more links.

Matter and Energy

Vocabulary

kinetic energy, E95

potential energy, E95

conduction, E97

convection, E97

radiation, E97

Get Ready

If you were scuba diving and saw this animal, what would you do? Swim the other way! It is an electric ray. It produces enough electricity to power a small motor.

Luckily, you don't need an electric ray to run appliances for you. Batteries let you carry electricity with you wherever you go. Rays don't run out of electricity, however. Do batteries run out?

Process Skill

You interpret data when you use the information that has been gathered to answer questions or solve a problem.

Explore Activity

How Well Do Batteries Provide Energy?

Materials

battery

flashlight bulb

2 wires

Procedure

1. **Experiment** Connect one end of a wire to the light bulb. Connect the other end of the wire to the battery. Do the same for the other wire. Record what time the light bulb went on. Record the type, size, and brand of battery you used.

2. **Observe** Examine the light bulb every 15 minutes to see if it is still lit. Record the time the light bulb goes off.

3. Repeat the experiment using another type or brand of battery.

Drawing Conclusions

1. **Use Numbers** Divide the time each battery lasted by the cost of that type of battery. Share your results with your classmates.

2. Make a graph of the class's results. Which batteries lasted the longest? Which batteries cost the least per hour of use? Were some brands longer lasting? Were some brands cheaper to use than others?

3. **Infer** Are the cheapest batteries the best buy? Are the longest lasting batteries the best buy?

4. **Going Further: Interpret Data** When might you choose the longest lasting batteries? The least expensive batteries? The batteries that cost the least per hour of use? Explain.

Main Idea Energy has different forms.

What Is Electrical Energy?

You know that a battery can produce enough power to light up a light bulb. How does it do this? What is the "power" in a battery? Where does it come from?

A battery provides electrical energy. Chemicals inside the battery react. These reactions produce electrons. As you learned in Lesson 2, an electron is one of the particles that make up an atom. Each electron carries energy, giving the battery its "power".

When a battery is connected to a light bulb with wires, a closed circuit is formed. A closed circuit means that there is a continuous path for electrons to travel through. The diagram below shows a closed circuit.

In some cases the amount of electrical energy in a circuit may not be great enough to light certain bulbs. For example, a flashlight battery could not light up a 60-watt light bulb from a lamp. Electrical energy can be measured by the size of the bulb it can light.

Electrons flow from the battery to the light bulb through wires. Some of the energy is given up to the wire in the light bulb, called the *filament*. The filament gets hot enough to glow and give off light. The electrical energy is changed into light and heat.

The rest of the electrons flow back into the battery. They can be sent through the circuit again.

Electrical Energy

READING
Diagrams

Describe the path electrons take in a closed circuit.

Hot filament

Electrons

BATTERY

Electrons

After a time the chemicals in a battery have all reacted, and no more electrons can be produced. This causes the battery to go dead.

Measuring Electrical Energy

Electrical energy can be measured in a number of ways. The circuit with two batteries has twice as many electrons flowing as the circuit with one battery. The bulb is brighter when two batteries are present. The brightness of a bulb can measure electrical energy.

We can also use different kinds of meters to measure electrical energy. An *ammeter* measures *amperes*, or *amps*. It tells us how many electrons flow each second. The *voltmeter* measures *volts*. Volts are another measure of electrical energy.

READING Cause and Effect
How does a battery produce electrical charge?

QUICK LAB

FOR SCHOOL OR HOME

Measuring Electricity

1. Wrap fine varnished wire around a compass. Use sandpaper to remove the coating from the ends of the wire.

2. Turn the compass until the needle is lined up with the coils of wire.

3. Keeping the compass this way, connect the ends of the wire to a circuit of a battery and small light bulb. See the photograph.

4. Observe What happens to the compass needle as you connect and disconnect the circuit? Record your observations.

5. How did you know when electricity was flowing in the circuit?

6. Observe When electricity was flowing, what did the compass needle do?

7. Infer How do you think the needle would move if you used a less powerful battery?

What Are Other Forms of Energy?

You've seen how chemical changes in a battery can produce electrical energy. You've also seen how that electrical energy can produce light and heat. All of these things are forms of energy. What exactly is energy? We know energy has many forms, but defining energy can be a little difficult.

A good place to start in talking about energy is to look at what energy can do. Energy is a measure of how much work something can produce.

To scientists work means using a force—a push or a pull—to move an object. Energy is the ability to do work.

Energy is not a type of matter. Matter is something you can often touch or see—solids, liquids, gases. Energy may be thought of as the ability to move matter around.

We can describe energy by its source or by how it is carried. For example, the energy produced by a chemical reaction is called chemical energy. Some typical forms of energy are shown in the table on page E95.

ELECTRICAL ENERGY
Electrons flowing through circuits

Electric motor

Gears and axle

MECHANICAL ENERGY
Moving gears, axles, wheels

READING Diagrams

List the energy changes that take place in the toy car.

Kinetic and Potential Energy

Look at the toy car in the diagram. Electrical energy is being used by the headlights. Electrons are being produced by the battery and are moved through a circuit. When something moves, its energy is called **kinetic energy**. Electrical energy is an example of kinetic energy. Any object that is in motion has kinetic energy.

When the headlights are turned off, the battery stops working. Electrons stop moving, and no new electrons are produced. No energy is being used. However, energy is stored in the chemicals in the battery. This energy is waiting to be used. We refer to stored energy as **potential energy**. Chemical energy is an example of potential energy.

Matter always has at least one of these energy forms.

▶ **What are the two main forms of energy?**

Energy Forms	
Form of Energy	**Description**
Chemical	stored in links between atoms
Mechanical	sum of the kinetic and potential energy of a system
Electrical	movement of electrons
Thermal	motion of atoms and molecules
Radiant	the energy of light

CHEMICAL ENERGY
Chemicals changing in battery

Battery

THERMAL ENERGY
Heat produced by filament

Light bulb

RADIANT ENERGY
Light from filament in bulb

How Can We Describe Thermal Energy?

Have you ever used a thermometer to measure temperature? You have learned that thermal energy is a form of energy that describes the motion of atoms and molecules. Temperature tells us how fast the particles in matter are moving. High temperatures mean the molecules are moving fast and have a lot of energy. Lower temperatures mean the molecules are moving more slowly and have less energy. The movement of molecules is what makes things feel hot or cold.

Heat is the transfer of thermal energy from one object to another.

Heat flows when an object is warmer than its surroundings. Heat always flows from hotter materials to cooler materials, never the other way. Heat flows until objects and their surroundings have the same temperature.

When you hold your hands around a mug of hot chocolate, your body gets warmed. This happens because heat flows from the hot mug into your skin. Thermal energy is transferred from the cup to your hands. Your body gains energy, and your temperature rises as a result. Energy is lost from the mug, however. Its temperature decreases.

> **How are temperature and heat related?**

The Sun is the most important source of heat for life on our planet.

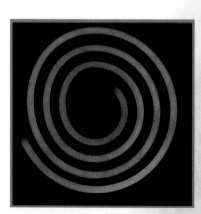

These heating coils in an oven are warmed by an electric current. The space inside the oven is warmed by heat flowing from the hot coils.

Heating just started

After a few minutes

After many minutes

How Does Heat Move?

When heat flows, it can move in three ways—conduction, convection, and radiation. In **conduction** thermal energy flows through objects without the movement of any matter. Conduction is the way your hand is warmed by a mug of hot chocolate. It usually occurs in solids and between objects that are touching.

In **convection** thermal energy is transferred by the movement of matter. Convection occurs in liquids and gases. In convection hot parts of a material rise, while cooler parts sink. There is a flow of material and heat.

A pot of water is heated by convection, for example. As water is heated on a stove, the water near the burner gets hot and rises to the top of the pan. The cooler water near the top then sinks and gets warmed. Thermal energy is transferred by a cycle of rising and sinking matter.

In **radiation** heat is transferred through electromagnetic rays. Matter is not needed at all in this energy transfer. All objects around us give off radiation. Radiation can travel through space. Radiation from the Sun warms Earth, for example.

▷ **What are three ways that heat can move?**

In convection, cooler materials sink while warmer materials rise in a cycle of motion.

What Materials Conduct Heat Well?

The photograph shows very hot tea in a foam cup. A metal spoon has been sitting in the tea for some time. The outside of the cup is slightly warm. However, the spoon's handle is almost too hot to hold. Why has more heat flowed into the handle of the spoon than into the walls of the cup?

As you learned in Lesson 1, some materials are better at conducting heat than others. The metal spoon is a good conductor of heat. However, the foam cup is a poor conductor of heat. As a result, heat flows quickly from the hot bowl of the spoon to its handle. However, heat flows very slowly from the tea into the foam.

Metals are the best conductors of heat. Why do metals conduct heat so well?

Heat is carried through a material by the motion of molecules. When a metal is heated at one end, the molecules move about rapidly. They collide with their neighbors, spreading the motion through the material. The spreading of the motion warms up other parts of the material.

The molecules in solids are packed very closely together. This makes transferring energy easier.

In Chapter 10 you learned that the molecules in gases are spread apart. They cannot transfer heat between one

| How Materials Conduct Heat | |
Material	How Many Times Better than Air It Conducts Heat
Wood	5
Water	23
Brick	25
Glass	42
Rock	67
Aluminum	8,300
Copper	15,300

another as easily as in liquids and solids. This explains why air is such a poor conductor of heat. Gases are the poorest thermal conductors of all. Look at the table to see how well common materials conduct heat.

 What materials are the best conductors?

Why It Matters

Energy comes in many forms. The air in your home is warmed by convection of thermal energy. There is energy stored in batteries and energy stored in the food you eat. The Sun gives us light and heat as well. You depend on various forms of energy to live, move, and have a comfortable life.

Think and Write

1. Describe how a battery makes a light bulb glow. Identify the different forms energy takes.

2. Why is energy not a form of matter?

3. How does thermal energy get from place to place?

4. Insulating windows have two layers of glass with air sealed in between. Why is this layer of air important?

5. **Critical Thinking** Two flashlights have the same kind of bulb. One glows more dimly than the other. Why do you think this is so?

L·I·N·K·S

SOCIAL STUDIES LINK

Research electricity. Who discovered electricity? When was this important discovery made? What was used to light and heat houses before electrical energy? Use the Internet or an encyclopedia for your research. Write a report.

ART LINK

Make a collage. Cut pictures of different types of energy from a magazine. Identify the source of energy being used. Paste your pictures onto a poster. Present your poster to the class.

WRITING LINK

Write a poem. Make up a poem to explain how you use different types of energy every day.

TECHNOLOGY LINK

At the Computer Visit **www.mhscience02.com** for more links.

Chapter 11 Review

Vocabulary

Fill each blank with the best word or words from the list.

acid, E82
alkalinity, E86
base, E82
chemical change, E71
colloid, E54
conduction, E97
convection, E97
kinetic energy, E95
mixture, E52
potential energy, E95
radiation, E97
solution, E54

1. A(n) _____ is a mixture that looks the same everywhere, even under a microscope.

2. A(n) _____ turns blue litmus paper red.

3. In a(n) _____ two chemicals react to form a new substance.

4. The Sun's energy is transferred to Earth by _____.

5. An object that is moving has _____.

6. In _____ energy is transferred without the movement of matter.

7. A(n) _____ has properties between a solution and heterogeneous mixture.

8. Stored energy is called _____.

9. Energy is usually transferred by _____ in liquids and gases.

10. The strength of a base is called its _____.

Test Prep

11. In a chemical reaction, there may be a _____.

A color change
B formation of a gas
C heat change
D all of the above

12. All of the following are poor conductors of heat EXCEPT _____.

F wood
G glass
H copper
J air

13. An example of a physical change is _____.

A ice melting
B bread baking
C a match burning
D a nail rusting

14. Heat always flows _____.

    F from lighter materials to heavier materials

    G from heavier materials to lighter materials

    H from cooler materials to hotter materials

    J from hotter materials to cooler materials

15. _____ may be used as an indicator.

    A cabbage juice

    B litmus paper

    C a pH meter

    D all of the above

Concepts and Skills

16. Reading in Science What signs are there that baking bread is a chemical change?

17. Process Skills: Experiment A friend says he removed tarnish from a silver spoon by putting it in the bottom of an aluminum pot containing a hot baking-soda solution. What really removed the tarnish? Describe how you would perform experiments to find out.

18. Critical Thinking A certain material can be separated by physical changes. Can it be a single compound? Why or why not?

19. Scientific Methods What are two things you might see during a chemical change?

20. Safety Whenever you use a cleaning material, you should read the label carefully. Some kinds of cleaning materials should never be used together. What may be one reason for this?

Boost your test scores!

Be Smart!
Visit www.mhscience02.com

Chemist
Dr. Mario Molina

Massachusetts Institute of Technology

The rise of pollution in our world has led to the need for new kinds of scientists. Environmental chemists like Dr. Mario Molina study the effects of chemicals on the environment. Dr. Molina has been especially interested in the effect of pollution on Earth's ozone layer.

When he received his first toy microscope and chemistry set as a child, Dr. Molina turned his family's bathroom into a laboratory! He knew then that he wanted to become a research chemist. Dr. Molina received his doctorate in chemistry from the University of California in 1972.

Dr. Molina decided to study a group of chemicals called chlorofluorocarbons, or CFCs. CFCs are compounds that were used in aerosol sprays, refrigerators, and air conditioners.

When exposed to radiation, CFCs break down into chlorine, fluorine, and carbon atoms. The chlorine atom is very reactive. It breaks down ozone. A single chlorine atom can destroy as many as 100,000 ozone molecules! This is especially destructive because the amount of ozone in the atmosphere is very limited and because ozone provides us with needed protection from the Sun.

More research showed that enough ozone had been destroyed by CFCs to create a "hole" in the ozone layer over Antarctica. Almost all the nations of the world agreed to a ban on the production of CFCs starting in 1996. Thanks to Dr. Molina, people around the world are working to ensure that the ozone layer continues to help protect life on Earth.

Careers IN SCIENCE

Environmental Engineer

If you're interested in chemistry, you may want to be an environmental engineer. An environmental engineer studies ways to eliminate, control, or prevent pollution in our environment. Some try to clean polluted lakes and rivers. Environmental engineers usually split their time between the laboratory and the field.

To become an environmental engineer, you need a college degree, usually in environmental engineering. An advanced degree is required for research and teaching. A license is also required for engineers working in the area of public health and safety.

Computer-enhanced images of ozone hole over Antarctica

Write ABOUT IT

1. What three elements make up CFCs?

2. How is chlorine especially destructive to ozone?

AT THE COMPUTER

Visit www.mhscience02.com to learn more about careers.

PROBiNG the PROPERTiES

Your goal is to describe objects in a collection in terms of their properties.

What to Do

1. List each object in your collection. Leave space next to each name where you can list the object's properties.

2. List as many properties as you can observe for each object.

3. Measure the mass of each object, and record it on your list.

Analyze Your Results

What are all of the objects in your collection made of?

- -

TESTING FOR pH

Your goal is to put eight unknown solutions in order from most acidic to most basic.

What to Do

1. Use eight unknown solutions, pH paper, a pH scale, a pencil, and paper. Dip a piece of pH paper into each solution. Compare the color of the pH paper with the pH scale. Record each pH in a table.

2. Make a new table that shows the order of the solutions from most acidic to most basic. Include the pH of each solution.

Analyze Your Results

1. Which solutions are acids? Which solutions are bases?

2. If you have an upset stomach, it might be because you have too much acid in your stomach. Why are medicines taken for a stomachache usually bases?

UNIT
F

Motion and Energy

192

NATIONAL
GEOGRAPHIC

Motion and Energy

LOOK!

Runners race past in a blur
of motion. How could you
measure how fast these
runners are moving?

Newton's Laws of Motion

Did You Ever Wonder?

Is it true that what goes up must come down? How can these skydivers appear to float in the air? The skydivers are actually in free fall until their parachutes open. What force pulls them, and all objects, toward Earth? Do all objects fall at the same rate?

Newton's First Law

Vocabulary

force, F6

inertia, F7

friction, F8

speed, F11

velocity, F12

acceleration, F13

Get Ready

What if a car ran out of gas and you had to help push it to the side of the road? Would you rather push a small compact car or a large minivan? How would the bulk of a car affect how difficult it is to push?

How would the amount of matter in an object affect how fast a spring can set it in motion? Would a spring move a large mass faster? Would it move a small mass faster? Might the mass have no effect on the motion?

Process Skill

You infer when you form an idea from facts or observations.

Explore Activity

How Fast Does a Spring Move Objects?

Materials

3 masses (washers or AAA batteries)

metal ruler

rubber bands

clock with second hand

graph paper

goggles

Procedure

BE CAREFUL! Wear goggles.

1. Attach a mass to the end of a metal ruler with a rubber band. Hold the ruler tightly against the edge of a table as shown so it can act like a spring.

2. **Use Numbers** Pull the mass back 5 cm (2 in.), and release it crisply. Count and record how many swings the mass completes in ten seconds.

3. **Predict** How will adding more mass to the end of the ruler affect how fast it swings back and forth? Record your predictions.

4. Add a second mass, and repeat the procedure. Repeat again with a third mass.

Drawing Conclusions

1. **Infer** Why does the ruler move the attached mass when it is pulled back and released?

2. **Observe** What effect did increasing the mass have on how fast the mass was swung back and forth by the ruler?

3. **Hypothesize** Why do you think the increase in mass had this effect?

4. **Interpret Data** Make a graph of your results. What two variables should you plot?

5. **Going Further: Predict** Use your graph to estimate how many swings would be observed in ten seconds when four masses are attached to the ruler.

Main Idea Objects that contain more matter are harder to set in motion.

What Does it Take to Make an Object Move?

The students below are investigating how easily objects of different masses are set into motion. First, one student uses a spring scale to pull a toy car from rest through a distance of one meter (39.37 inches). As she pulls, she keeps the reading on the spring scale constant. Her teammate times how long it takes the toy car to travel one meter. Next, the students repeat the experiment using a toy truck that has three times the mass of the toy car.

The results of the experiment show that the toy car traveled the one-meter distance in a shorter time than the toy truck. The amount of pull was kept the same, so why did the car travel faster than the truck? The car traveled faster because objects with more mass are harder to set in motion with a certain push or pull than objects with less mass. The car has less mass, so the pull of the spring scale set it into more rapid motion.

A pull or push that acts on an object is called a **force**. The students' experiment shows you how forces are needed to set objects in motion. As you've seen, objects with more mass move more slowly when acted on by a certain force.

Average Time to Travel 1 Meter with a Steady Pull

An Object's Natural Motion

The mass of an object tends to make the object resist being set into motion. That's why objects with more mass are set into less rapid motion by a certain amount of force. The tendency of an object to resist a change in its state of motion is called the object's **inertia**.

Several centuries ago the famous Italian scientist Galileo began to understand how inertia affects the motion of objects. Galileo imagined rolling a ball down a fixed *incline* (ramp) and then back up ramps of varying steepness, as in the diagram. Galileo had observed that pendulums swing back and forth to the same height. He reasoned that the ball would roll to the same height on any ramp. He realized that if the ramp were less steep, the ball would roll a greater distance and slow down more gradually.

Thinking further, Galileo inferred that if the second ramp were flat, the ball would roll forever at a steady rate (assuming no force is acting on the ball).

Galileo had observed that pendulums swing back and forth to the same height. He reasoned that a ball rolling down one ramp and up another would roll to the same height on any ramp.

To Galileo this meant that the ball's natural state of motion was coasting. Just as it takes a force to set an object in motion, it also takes a force to slow or stop a coasting object. Without any such force, the object will coast forever in a straight line.

▷ **What does it take to change an object's state of motion?**

The ball is released from A. It rolls down the incline, then back up one of the facing inclines. If there is no force acting on the ball, it slows and comes to a stop just as it reaches the starting height.

Incline C is not as steep as incline B, so the ball takes longer to slow down. Galileo reasoned that if there were no incline for the ball to climb, it would not slow down at all—as in D.

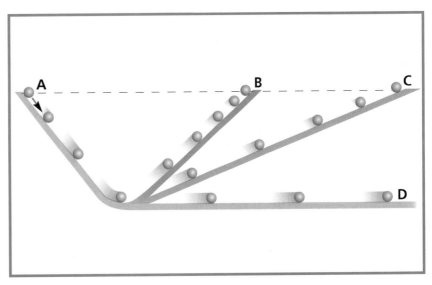

Is Force Needed to Maintain Motion?

The sailboat in the picture is traveling at a steady rate in a straight line. The wind has filled its sails and is pushing the boat forward. Until just a few centuries ago, most people believed that a force was necessary to keep an object traveling at a steady rate, just like the wind pushing the boat.

Galileo realized that this idea was incorrect. He understood that a force called **friction** acts against moving objects. Friction opposes the motion of one object moving past another. If the friction is taken away, no force is needed to maintain motion at a steady rate. An object's inertia is all that is needed to keep it moving.

Forty-five years after Galileo died, Sir Isaac Newton published a complete description of the concept of inertia. This is *Newton's first law of motion*: Objects at rest remain at rest and objects traveling at a steady rate in a straight line continue that way until a force acts on them.

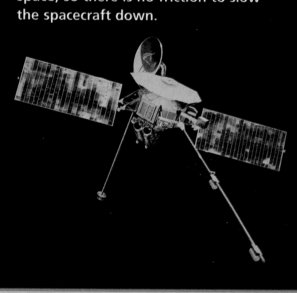

A spacecraft far from any star or planet can continue traveling in a straight line at a steady speed. There is no air in space, so there is no friction to slow the spacecraft down.

The sailboat needs the force of the wind to keep it moving. That is because the friction between the boat and the water tends to slow the boat down.

How Inertia Works

Newton's first law of motion—the law of inertia—tells us that the state of motion of an object does not change until a force is applied to it. That means, if an object is traveling at a steady rate in a straight line, it will continue to do so until a force is applied to it. Newton's law also means that if the object is sitting at rest, it will continue to be at rest until a force is applied to it. Each of the photographs shows an example of Newton's first law of motion.

It takes the force of the engines to get the rockets moving from rest on the launch pad. The force of a big rocket's engines must be much greater than the force of a small rocket because a big rocket has so much more mass than a small rocket.

▷ Is a force needed to keep a moving spacecraft moving in a straight line?

These race cars could not change their direction of travel without the force of the road surface pushing sideways against the tires.

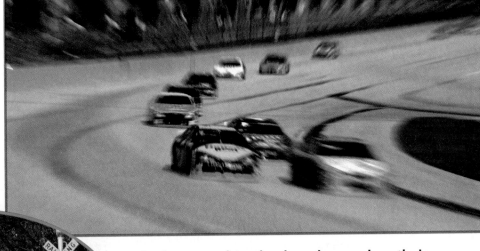

Both cars and trucks slow down when their drivers use their brakes. The force produced by the brakes slows the vehicles down. A truck has much more mass than a car, so its brakes must provide more force than the car's brakes in order to slow down or stop.

QUICK LAB

FOR SCHOOL OR HOME

Using a Position Grid

1. Make a grid. A grid has rows and columns labeled with letters and numbers. Each box in the grid has a particular position. The position of any box is given by a number and a letter, such as box A5 or box F2. Make a grid that goes from 1 to 29 across and from A to G down. You may wish to use graph paper. Follow the directions below to find out with your grid why the snail didn't want to move!

2. Find each box, and shade it in with a colored pencil.

E27, B8, F24, D15, B29, C20, D5, F14, D29, B3, D11, B16, F3, D7, B27, B2, B11, F27, B20, F12, B23, D8, E17, F20, F23, C6, E2, E24, B10, B1, F10, C29, C2, F17, D24, E8, B15, E14, F1, B12, F5, D16, B21, B24, D27, C5, C10, E29, E7, B5, C14, C24, C16, E20, D2, C27, D10, C8, D17, E28, E10, D6, F25, D20, D14, F8, F29, B19, B14, F11, E5, B25, F2, B28

The snail didn't want to move because he had _____.

Where Is It?

How do you know when you are moving? You are moving when you are changing position. Position is the location of an object. Your position might be in front of, behind, to the right or to the left of some object. Cities or landmarks can be located on a map. The position of each object can be found by using a grid. The position of any object on a map is a comparison of the object's location to other things on the map. We can describe positions of things with a grid like the one covering the map. For example, the location of Atlanta can be described as box J16. You can find the number of Atlanta's position along the top or bottom and the letter along either side.

Find the city in each location.
a. K10   b. H11

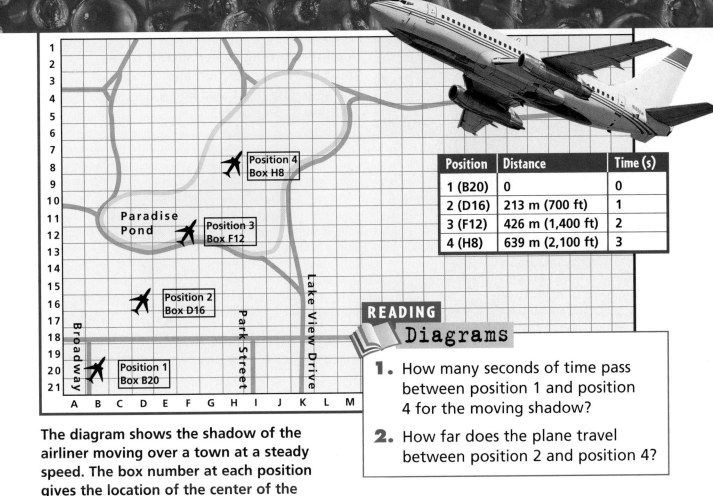

Position	Distance	Time (s)
1 (B20)	0	0
2 (D16)	213 m (700 ft)	1
3 (F12)	426 m (1,400 ft)	2
4 (H8)	639 m (2,100 ft)	3

The diagram shows the shadow of the airliner moving over a town at a steady speed. The box number at each position gives the location of the center of the plane. One second passes between each position.

READING Diagrams

1. How many seconds of time pass between position 1 and position 4 for the moving shadow?

2. How far does the plane travel between position 2 and position 4?

What Speed Is

The airliner in the photo is moving rapidly through the air. How can we tell that it is moving? Think about watching the shadow of the airliner on the ground below, as in the diagram. We can see the shadow sweeping past fixed objects like ponds, homes, or streets. The change in the position of the shadow compared with the surrounding objects reveals its motion as well as the motion of the airliner.

The table describes the motion of the airliner by giving the position of the airliner's shadow at various times. The position can be measured as the box number of the center of the shadow.

The position can also be measured as the distance traveled past position 1.

As for any moving object, the **speed** of the airliner is how fast its position is changing with time at any moment. When the distance traveled by an object in a given time is known, the speed is found by dividing the distance by the time. The airliner, for example, travels 213 meters (700 feet) in 1 second. Therefore, the airliner's speed is 213 meters per second (700 feet per second) or 213 meters/second (700 feet/second).

▷ **What tells you how fast the plane is moving?**

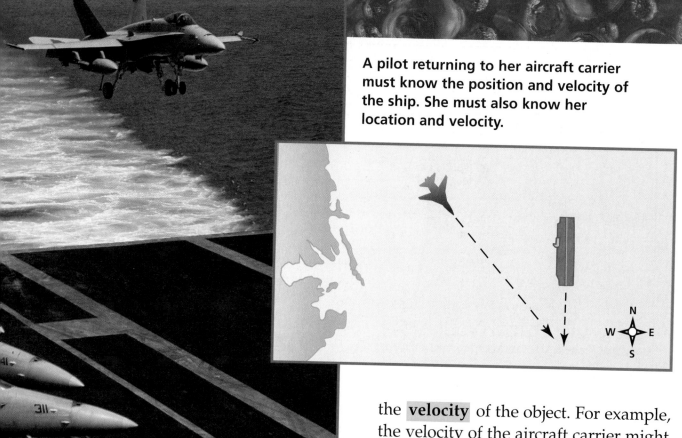

A pilot returning to her aircraft carrier must know the position and velocity of the ship. She must also know her location and velocity.

What Is Velocity?

The pilot of the navy jet is out on a mission. She needs to return to her aircraft carrier before she runs low on fuel. Her position and the position of the aircraft carrier are shown on the map. To get back safely, what information must she obtain from the ship to know in what direction to fly her plane?

First, she must know the position of the ship. She will also need to know the speed and the direction in which the ship is traveling. With this information, plus a knowledge of her own speed, the pilot can decide which direction she must travel in to meet up with the carrier, as shown by the dotted lines.

The speed of a moving object taken together with its direction of travel gives the **velocity** of the object. For example, the velocity of the aircraft carrier might be 40 kilometers/hour (40 km/h) due south, or the velocity of the plane might be 600 km/h to the southeast.

How can you tell the velocity of a car you are riding in? You need to know your speed. The car's speedometer will give you that information. You also need to know the direction you are traveling in. For that, you may need to use a map or road signs.

Two objects can have the same speed but different velocities if they are traveling in different directions. They may also have different velocities if they are traveling in the same direction but with different speeds. The only way two objects can have the same velocity is for the objects to both be traveling in the same direction at the same speed.

> **How is velocity different from speed?**

What Is Acceleration?

As long as an object travels in a straight line at a steady speed, its velocity is constant. Newton's first law tells us that an object's velocity will remain constant unless a force is applied to it. What if such a force is applied? How could the force affect the velocity of a moving object?

Both of the photographs on this page show how the velocity of an object can change when a force is applied. The force may change the object's speed, its direction of travel, or both. Any of these changes will change the velocity.

A change in velocity is called **acceleration**. Isaac Newton realized that applying a force to an object would overcome its inertia and change its velocity, causing it to accelerate. A special case of acceleration—*deceleration*—occurs when a force causes the speed of an object to decrease. Look at the photographs. Each photograph

A motor drives these riders in a circle. Even when the riders' speed is constant, their direction of travel is always changing. Therefore, they are accelerating.

shows acceleration due to changing velocity. Which photograph shows a change in direction? Which photograph shows a deceleration?

▷ **How is acceleration related to velocity?**

With the help of its brakes and this parachute, this race car will decelerate—change its velocity and come to a stop.

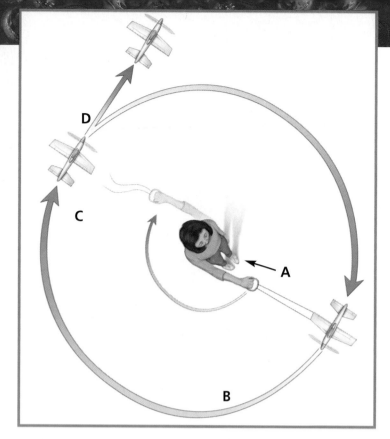

D

C

A

B

The inward force of the strings (A) keeps the plane on a circular path (B). If the strings were to break (C), the plane would fly off in a straight line (D) at a constant speed due to inertia.

What Keeps Things Moving in a Circle?

A gas-powered model airplane can be tied to a handle with strings. This allows the plane to be flown in a circle. Without strings, the plane tends to fly in a straight line at constant speed—a constant velocity. When it is tied with strings, however, the strings provide a force that pulls on the plane. This force steadily changes the plane's direction of travel, keeping it on a circular path.

Even though the plane's speed remains constant as it flies in a circle, its steadily changing direction of travel means that its velocity is changing and that it is accelerating. Note how the force causing the acceleration—the pull of the strings—is always directed toward the center of the circle.

If the strings tethering the plane were to break suddenly, it would fly off in a straight line at a constant speed. There would no longer be any force to overcome its inertia, and it would travel with constant velocity.

Although Earth and the Sun are much bigger than model airplanes, all of these objects obey the laws of motion in the same way. The pull of *gravity* between Earth and the Sun acts like the strings on the model plane. Gravity is the force that keeps Earth moving in a circular path about the Sun. If the force of gravity were somehow to disappear, Earth would fly off in a straight line into deep space! (You'll learn more about gravity in Lesson 3.)

READING Draw Conclusions

Why is a force needed to keep an object moving in a circle?

L·I·N·K·S

Why It Matters

In outer space, spacecraft are not slowed by air resistance. When a pilot tries to dock one spacecraft with another, she sets her craft in motion with a burst of gas from a thruster. To slow her craft, she applies a force from a burst of gas in the opposite direction. With too little force, her craft may strike the other. With too much force, she may start going backward. It takes great skill to guide a spacecraft.

Think and Write

1. A boat's motor dies when it is traveling at high speed. The boat gradually slows to a stop. Why?

2. On a rainy day, a car heads into a turn at high speed. Instead of making the turn, the car slides straight out into a field. Explain why.

3. What do you need to know to find a car's velocity?

4. What is happening when a mass on a spring swings back and forth?

5. **Critical Thinking** If you tie a thread to the middle of a water-filled plastic bottle and pull slowly, the bottle moves. If you pull very rapidly, the thread breaks before the bottle can move. Why?

MATH LINK

Solve a problem. The distance between Atlanta, GA and Richmond, VA is about 750 km. How long will it take an airplane traveling from Atlanta at a speed of 700 km/h to reach Richmond? How long will it take a car traveling at 75 km/h? Select other modes of transportation and other speeds to calculate how long it will take to travel between the two cities.

WRITING LINK

Write a story. On a trip to the Moon and back, when would the astronauts be accelerating? When would they be traveling at a constant velocity? What forces would they experience? Write a story including all the details.

ART LINK

Make a poster. A weather satellite circles Earth at a steady speed. Make a poster that shows its orbit and illustrates why it is accelerating.

TECHNOLOGY LINK

At the Computer Visit www.mhscience02.com for more links.

Newton's Second and Third Laws

Get Ready

Have you ever been in a hurry on a bicycle? To get moving faster, you pedal harder. The extra force you apply to the pedals makes you reach a greater speed. However, what happens if you are wearing a heavy backpack or carrying a lot of books in your back baskets? Is it just as easy to get up to speed, or do you have to pedal harder to reach the same speed?

How does the amount of force applied to an object affect how fast its velocity changes? What if you kept the force the same but increased the mass of the object? How fast would the velocity change?

Process Skill

You observe when you use one or more of the senses to identify or learn about an object or event.

Explore Activity

How Does Force Affect an Object's Motion?

Materials

toy car

2 boards with hooks for rubber bands

rubber bands

meterstick

masking tape

goggles

Procedure

BE CAREFUL! Wear goggles

1 Place a 15-cm (6-in.) strip of masking tape on the floor for a starting line. Hold two boards on either side of the starting line with a rubber band stretched between them.

2 **Measure** Launch a toy car along the floor as shown. The car should be pulled back against the rubber band exactly 5 cm (2 in.) prior to its release. Measure how far the car travels.

3 **Observe** Repeat step 2 twice more, and average the three distances.

4 **Predict** What will happen when you use one, then two more rubber bands to launch the toy car? Test your prediction. Record your findings.

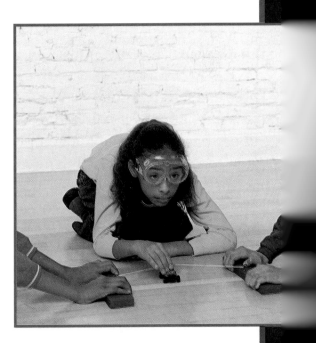

Drawing Conclusions

1 **Interpret Data** When did the car move farthest on average—when one, two, or three rubber bands were used?

2 **Infer** How is the distance traveled by the car in any trial related to the speed it was given by the rubber band? Why?

3 **Going Further: Predict** If you taped a second toy car on top of the first and launched them with two rubber bands, how far would the cars travel? Test your prediction. Explain your observations.

Main Idea As the net force acting on an object increases, the object accelerates more.

What Affects Acceleration?

What if you use a rubber band to launch a toy car along the floor? The rubber band will apply a force to the car, and the force will cause the car to speed up. Once the rear of the car passes the starting line, however, the rubber band no longer is applying force. At this point the car will begin coasting until friction brings it to a stop. The farther the car travels before stopping, the faster it must have been going at the start.

Force and Acceleration

What happens if you add extra rubber bands? Then you are applying more force to the car. As the force increases, the distance the car travels also increases. This, in turn, tells you that the car reaches its greatest starting speed when the force applied to it is greatest.

Sir Isaac Newton realized that forces produce acceleration. In other words, if we apply a force to an object, the object's velocity will change. The object might speed up, slow down, or change direction. It could even change both speed and direction.

Newton reasoned this way: If we multiply the force by a certain amount, we will change the acceleration by the same amount. (This assumes that no other changes are made.) For example, if we triple the force, the acceleration will also be tripled. What if you tried launching your toy car first using one rubber band, then using three rubber bands of the same size? You should see that as the force on the car is increased, the speed it reaches increases by about the same amount. The graph shows an example of how the car's acceleration would be related to the force acting on it, according to Newton's ideas.

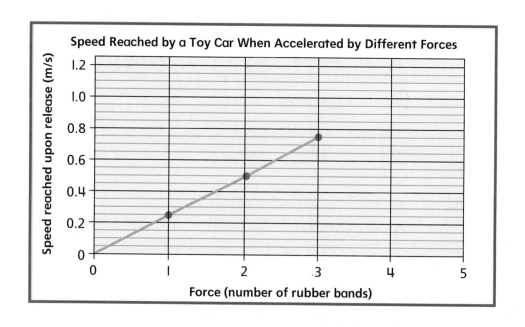

Speed Reached by a Toy Car When Accelerated by Different Forces

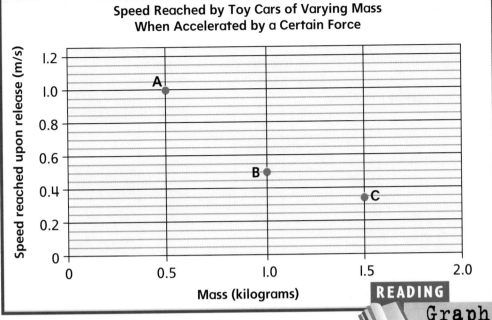

Speed Reached by Toy Cars of Varying Mass When Accelerated by a Certain Force

Mass (kilograms)

Speed reached upon release (m/s)

Using the same amount of force, it is easier to accelerate a less massive object than a more massive object.

READING

Graphs

What would the speed reached be for a mass of 2 kilograms?

Mass and Acceleration

What happens if you tape a second car on top of the first? You double the mass being accelerated by the force from the rubber bands. Now the two cars together will travel only about half as far as one car would alone when launched by the same number of rubber bands. This tells you that doubling the mass resulted in about half the acceleration.

Isaac Newton understood that changing the force isn't the only thing that affects acceleration. He also understood that mass affects acceleration. However, while increasing the force increases the acceleration, increasing the mass decreases the acceleration.

When the mass is multiplied by a certain factor, the new acceleration is obtained by dividing the old acceleration by that factor. (Again, this assumes that nothing else has changed.) For example, what if the mass of an object being accelerated by a certain force is doubled? The new acceleration would then be the previous acceleration divided by 2. Put another way, if the mass is doubled, the acceleration is reduced to one-half of its previous value.

The relationship between acceleration and force is said to be direct— when one is increased, the other increases. The relationship between acceleration and mass, on the other hand, is inverse—when one goes up, the other goes down. The graph shows an example of how the acceleration of a toy car is inversely related to its mass.

▷ **What two factors determine how great an object's acceleration is?**

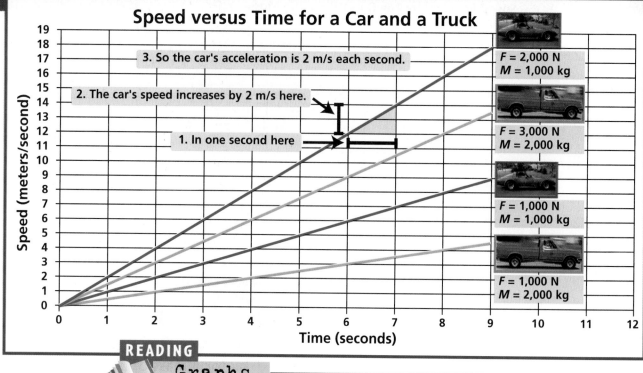

Speed versus Time for a Car and a Truck

3. So the car's acceleration is 2 m/s each second.

F = 2,000 N
M = 1,000 kg

2. The car's speed increases by 2 m/s here.

F = 3,000 N
M = 2,000 kg

1. In one second here

F = 1,000 N
M = 1,000 kg

F = 1,000 N
M = 2,000 kg

Speed (meters/second)

Time (seconds)

READING

Graphs

Describe two ways you could use the information on the graph to calculate the acceleration of the truck when a force of 3,000 N acts on it.

How Is Acceleration Calculated?

You learned in Lesson 1 that acceleration is a change in velocity. Recall that velocity describes both the speed and direction of a moving object. To calculate the acceleration of an object moving in a straight line you first must know three things—the object's starting speed, its new speed, and the amount of time it took for the change to occur.

Look at the lowest blue line on the graph above. In one second, the speed of the car has gone from zero to 1 meter per second. For each second that passes, the car's speed increases by another meter per second. The car is accelerating at 1 meter per second each second. Now look at the top blue line for the same

1,000-kg car. In one second the car's speed now increases by 2 meters per second. That means its acceleration is 2 meters per second each second.

What was changed to make the car's acceleration double? The force acting on the car was changed.

We can write an equation to show how acceleration is related to force and mass: $a = F \div m$. This equation says the acceleration is found by dividing the force by the mass. In the examples shown, forces are in units called newtons (N). A force of 1 newton makes the speed of a 1 kg mass change by 1 meter per second each second.

▶ **What do you need to know to calculate the acceleration an object will have?**

What Are Balanced and Unbalanced Forces?

The plane in the photograph below is flying at a constant speed in a constant direction. Its speed is not changing, nor is its direction of travel, so the plane cannot be accelerating. However, the pilot is using the throttle to make the plane's motor apply a forward force to it. How can the motor apply force to the plane without causing the plane to accelerate?

The explanation is that the force of the plane's motor is exactly offset by other forces acting in the opposite direction, as the diagram shows. In fact, there are a number of forces acting on the plane, but for each one there are others that cancel it out. When all of the forces on an object cancel one another out, the forces are said to be **balanced forces**.

In cases where a certain force is either only partially canceled or not canceled at all by other forces, the force is said to be an **unbalanced force**. For example, what if a plane's motor applies more forward force than the amount of friction and air resistance apply against its forward motion? The friction and air resistance will cancel some, but not all, of the forward force. This will leave an unbalanced forward force acting on the plane.

When we use the equation $a = F/m$ to find acceleration, F always stands for the unbalanced force. This equation

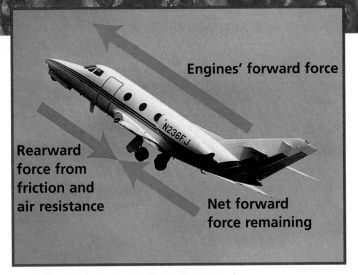

Engines' forward force

Rearward force from friction and air resistance

Net forward force remaining

Are the forces acting on this plane balanced or unbalanced?

Force of engines

Weight of plane

Air resistance

Lift

Are the forces acting on this plane balanced or unbalanced?

is actually one possible way of stating *Newton's second law of motion*: When an unbalanced force acts on an object, the object's acceleration equals the force divided by the object's mass.

READING Draw Conclusions
What happens to an object's motion when the forces acting on it are unbalanced?

QUICK LAB

FOR SCHOOL OR HOME

Racing Balloon Rockets

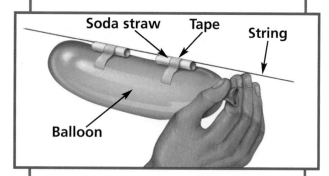

Soda straw   Tape   String

Balloon

1. Look at the picture of how to construct a balloon rocket. Thread several pieces of soda straw onto the string. Then stretch the string tightly between two chairs.

2. **Observe** Blow up a balloon. Hold the neck closed with your fingers while your partner tapes two straw pieces to the balloon. Let go of the balloon, and watch what it does!

3. **Observe** How does the direction in which the balloon moves compare with the direction in which the air is forced out?

4. **Infer** Is there an unbalanced force on the balloon? In which direction does it push?

F 22

Where Does the Force Come From?

The rocket in the picture is accelerating upward due to the force provided by its engine. Fuel has been burned into hot gases in the engine's combustion chamber. The hot gases rush out of the engine nozzle in a downward direction. How is it that gases rushing down can cause the rocket to accelerate up?

If the rocket is accelerating, it must have an unbalanced force acting on it. Clearly, this force comes from the hot gases in its engines. Knowing the unbalanced force and the rocket's mass, we could calculate the acceleration of the rocket with Newton's second law of motion, $a = F/m$. However, as you will see, it takes another law of motion to explain how gases rushing one way can accelerate the rocket in the opposite direction.

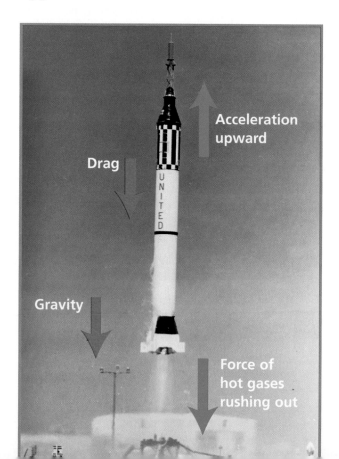

Acceleration upward

Drag

Gravity

Force of hot gases rushing out

Push of stretched rubber on air
Return push of air on rubber

All the way around the balloon, the inward push of the stretched rubber is balanced by the return outward push of the air. The balloon neither expands nor contracts, and it is not moved in any direction.

Force A pushes the balloon forward. When the balloon is opened, there are no longer any forces at the opening to offset forces A and B. Force B makes air rush out of the balloon, as shown by arrow B.

Making a Rocket Go

When you blow up a balloon and then release it without tying it closed, it flies through the air. You can take advantage of this behavior to make a balloon rocket. You know that air rushes out one end of the balloon, while the balloon itself moves in the opposite direction. Where do the forces come from that move the balloon and the air?

The air inside the balloon is "squeezed" by the stretched rubber. At the same time, the air resists being squeezed and pushes back on the rubber. When the balloon is inflated and tied off, these pushes are in balance and the balloon neither changes in size nor moves.

What happens if we leave the neck of the blown-up balloon open, instead?

At the point of the opening, there is no stretched rubber squeezing the air. However, there *is* stretched rubber squeezing the air at a point opposite the opening. As a result, there is a net force on the air that pushes it out through the opening.

At the same time, the air pushes forward on the balloon opposite the opening. There is no such push at the opening itself, because there is no rubber surface on which the air can push. Since the push of the air forward on the balloon is not offset by any rearward push, an unbalanced force results that pushes the balloon forward.

▷ **What force makes a balloon rocket go forward?**

How Do Forces Act Between Objects?

In a balloon the air returns the push of the stretched rubber that squeezes it inward. Sir Isaac Newton understood that one object pushing on another will always receive a push in return. In the same way, the stretched rubber of a balloon receives a return push from the air it is squeezing. The same reasoning also applies to pulling forces.

When one object applies a force to a second, we call this force the **action**. The force the second object returns to the first is called the **reaction**. Think about what happens when a 50-kg student on ice skates pushes forward on another 50-kg student on ice skates. Both of them wind up moving at the same speed, but in opposite directions. Newton realized that while the action and reaction act in opposite directions, they have the same strength. These ideas are summarized in *Newton's third law of motion*: For every action, there is an equal but opposite reaction.

An accelerating race car demonstrates Newton's third law. The car's tires push to the rear on the road surface. At the same time, the road pushes back on the tires in a forward direction. This reaction force is what propels the car ahead.

Now you can see how gas rushing out of a rocket engine could propel the rocket in the opposite direction. The hot gas tends to expand, so it applies an action force to the walls of the combustion chamber. The walls of the

Force of hot gases on walls of combustion chamber

Force of walls of combustion chamber on gases

Action A is an unbalanced force that propels the rocket ahead. Reaction B is an unbalanced force that pushes the hot gases out through the nozzle.

combustion chamber apply a reaction force to the gas. The result is similar to what happened to the balloon rocket racer. The gas pushes the rocket ahead, while the walls of the combustion chamber push the gas to the rear, out through the nozzle.

When one object applies a force to another, both objects feel force. The second object feels the action force, while the first object feels the reaction force. If these forces are not balanced by other forces, *both* objects will accelerate.

100 kg cart and crate

50 kg wagon and girl

Reaction   Action

1. The girl is preparing to pull the wagon with the crate toward her.

0   1   2   3   4   5   6   7   8

2. The girl and crate both move, and the girl moves faster.

0   1   2   3   4   5   6   7   8

The girl in the wagon is trying to pull another wagon with a crate on it toward her. When she tightens her grip and pulls on the rope, she applies an action force to the other wagon. This force causes the wagon with the crate to accelerate toward her. At the same time, the wagon with the crate applies a reaction force back on the girl in the wagon, and she accelerates toward the crate.

The girl and the crate are obeying Newton's third law. They are also obeying the second law. Both are acted on by forces of the same strength. The girl-plus-wagon, however, has less mass than the crate-plus-wagon, so she gains speed faster. When the girl and the crate meet, the girl has traveled farther!

The effects of a reaction force are sometimes hidden. The girl, for instance, could put on tennis shoes and stand securely on the floor. In this case, the reaction force would have to overcome the friction that helps her stay firmly on the floor. Now the girl would have an easier time pulling the crate-plus-wagon all the way toward herself.

▷ **What happens when one object exerts a force on another?**

How Can You Tell When Forces Are Acting?

You are a passenger in a car. It is traveling at 96 km/h (60 mi/h) on a smooth, straight road. The windows are closed, and your eyes are shut. Do you feel the car's motion? Surprisingly, you would no more sense your speed than if you were sitting in your living room. If the driver presses harder on the gas pedal and accelerates the car, however, the situation changes.

Once the car begins accelerating, you feel pressed back into your car seat. Your tummy might even feel strange if the car accelerates very rapidly. If you had a glass of water in your hands, the water would be "piled up" at the edge of the glass nearest the rear of the car. Similar things would happen if the driver applied the brakes or drove around a corner—either of which would also cause acceleration.

When we sense that we are accelerating, we know that an unbalanced force is acting. Unbalanced forces reveal their action by causing acceleration. The acceleration could be a change in speed, a change in direction, or both. Look at the diagrams to see an illustration of the effects that tell us when an unbalanced force is acting.

READING

Diagrams

How can you tell that cart 2 is accelerating?

1 In this experiment the spring scale is applying just enough force to offset the friction in the wheels of the cart. The cart is moving at a constant speed.

2 Now the spring scale applies more than enough force to offset friction in the wheels of the cart. There is extra force left over, and this unbalanced force accelerates the cart.

As you saw in Lesson 1, it takes a force to keep an object moving in a circle. What happens to the water in a cup when the cup is spun in a circle? The water piles up on the far side of the cup. This tells us that the cup must be accelerating.

If the cup is accelerating when it is swung in a circle, there must be an unbalanced force acting on it. Indeed, all objects traveling at constant speed in a circle experience such an unbalanced force. It is directed toward the center of the circle and acts constantly to change the direction of the circling object.

In the experiment shown, a spring scale is attached to a beanbag and a rope. A student is whirling the beanbag around overhead. The spring scale shows that a force is acting, because the reading is greater than zero. If the student shortens the rope or swings the beanbag around faster, the force reading on the spring scale increases.

How do we know a force is acting on the beanbag?

Someday scientists may use the force felt by an object traveling in a circle to produce artificial gravity in space stations. If the walkways were built around the rim and the space station were made to spin, the floor would push on the passengers. The passengers would feel this push as weight.

▷ **How can you tell if an unbalanced force is acting on a car?**

Someday, perhaps, spinning space stations will give passengers a feeling of weight.

Direction of artificial gravity

Direction of rotation

How Do Forces Affect Us?

Everywhere around us, forces act. Newton's laws of motion give us a useful picture of the way forces work. They also tell us how to predict what will happen when forces are applied to objects. Look at the examples of forces on this page. Think about how Newton's laws explain what is occurring in each case.

The bat applied a force to the ball and sent it flying to the outfield. At the same time, the ball applied a force to the bat, in this case enough to break it!

The water coming from this hose is under very high pressure. The water applies a large force back on the hose. The firemen have to use great strength to keep the hose from getting loose and flying around dangerously.

The hot gases in the jet engines push it forward, while the engines force the hot gases rearward.

▷ **How are forces affecting the racing boat?**

The crew on this racing craft push on the water with their oars. The water, in turn, pushes back on the oars and moves the boat forward.

Why It Matters

In the weightlessness of outer space, it is important to be aware of even small accelerations. While weight seems to disappear in orbit, small accelerations remain, such as gradual slowing due to tiny amounts of air resistance. Measuring these accelerations is important in studying things such as crystal growth and fluid flow in space.

Think and Write

1. How could you find an object's acceleration if you knew the object's mass and the force acting on it?

2. How could a boat travel with constant velocity even though its propeller is steadily applying a force to it?

3. A 1-kg magnet and a 0.5-kg piece of steel are placed 25 cm apart on hockey pucks on ice. When released, how will the objects move?

4. If an object is observed to accelerate, what does that tell you?

5. **Critical Thinking** If you hold a helium-filled balloon in a car with the windows up, the balloon moves forward when the car speeds up and backward when it slows down. Why do you think this happens?

L·I·N·K·S

LITERATURE LINK

Read *The Rise and Fall of Galloping Gertie,* to learn about a bridge that was destroyed by wind. When you finish reading, think about how you would design a safer bridge. Try the activities at the end of the book.

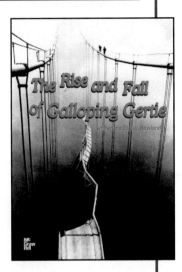

WRITING LINK

Write a story. You are a sports reporter interviewing a race driver about the forces and accelerations she feels during a race. Write about your interview.

MATH LINK

Solve this problem. Examine the equation $a = F/m$. Without using numbers, explain what happens to the acceleration if the force increases. Prove it using the equation. What happens to acceleration if mass increases?

TECHNOLOGY LINK

At the Computer Visit **www.mhscience02.com** for more links.

Planet Hunting

In July 1976, the Viking Orbiter I spacecraft took an image of the surface of Mars that seemed to show a face. Scientists, however, believed that the face was formed by natural processes. Their belief was confirmed in 1998 when the Mars Global Surveyor spacecraft took a detailed image of the "face," showing it to be a rocky hill.

People have long wondered if we are alone in the universe. Are there intelligent beings out there somewhere? Presently, there is no evidence that intelligent life exists anywhere but on Earth. There is also little evidence that any kind of life exists elsewhere.

Still, there are countless hundreds of billions of stars in the universe. Many may have planets orbiting them.

Perhaps there is life on these planets, possibly even intelligent creatures. How can we look for such planets? They are too faint to be seen with any telescope, so other means of detection are needed.

When starlight is passed through an instrument called a spectroscope, the colors that make up the light are spread out into a rainbow called a spectrum. Either bright or dark lines on the spectrum, caused by various gases in the star's composition, are used by scientists to determine the star's chemical make-up. They also indicate whether the star is moving toward or away from Earth: if the line is toward the blue end of the spectrum the star is moving toward us, and if the line is toward the red end of the spectrum the star is moving away from us. If a fairly large planet is orbiting a star, the planet's gravity will cause a

Scientists measure a change in the wavelength of light coming from a star over the course of days, months, and years.

Planet

This changing wavelength is the Doppler shift of the light, resulting from the star orbiting a common center of mass with a companion planet.

slight wobble in the star's movement. As the star wobbles, the lines in the star's spectrum repeatedly shift toward the red and the blue. Astronomers can keep track of these tiny spectral line shifts and use them to calculate the planet's mass and the shape and size of its orbit. As of January 2001, over 50 new planets have been discovered using this technique.

Just finding planets, however, does not prove they have life. All of the planets found so far are much larger than Earth, with masses from about one-fifth the mass of Jupiter to many times Jupiter's mass. Their orbital paths are often quite oval, and can bring them very close to their companion stars. It does not seem likely that life as we know it could exist on such worlds. Still, as our measuring techniques improve, we should be able to detect smaller and smaller planets. One day, we might even find a world like Earth orbiting a star like the Sun!

What Did I Learn?

1. The *Viking Orbiter I* spacecraft orbited which planet?

   A Earth
   B Venus
   C Mars
   D Jupiter

2. So far, all the planets found orbiting other stars are

   F much smaller than Earth
   G much larger than Earth
   H the same size as Earth
   J the same size as Jupiter

AT THE COMPUTER

Visit www.mhscience02.com to learn more about planets.

Newton's Law of Gravitation

Vocabulary

gravity, F35

weight, F36

Get Ready

Think about what happens when you drop two objects with very different weights. Does one fall faster than the other? Thanks to scientists such as Galileo and Newton, we now have a good answer to this question.

About 400 years ago, Galileo described a special experiment. Two objects with different weights were dropped at the same time from a tall tower known as the Leaning Tower of Pisa. What do you think happened to the objects in Galileo's experiment?

You drop a golf ball and a table tennis ball side-by-side from the same height. Which do you think will land first?

Process Skill

You hypothesize when you make a statement that can be tested to answer a question.

Explore Activity

Does Weight Affect How Fast an Object Falls?

Materials

table tennis ball

golf ball

pencil

eraser

goggles

Procedure

BE CAREFUL! Wear goggles.

1 **Predict** Do heavy objects fall faster than lighter objects? Record your prediction and your reasons for making it.

2 **Observe** Stretch out your arms in front of you at shoulder height. Hold the two different balls—one in each hand—at the same height, and drop them at exactly the same time. Listen for them to hit the floor. Which one hit the floor first? Record your results.

3 **Experiment** Repeat step 2 several more times to be sure your observations are accurate. Try dropping a pencil or an eraser at the same time as one of the balls. Record your observations.

Drawing Conclusions

1 **Observe** Which ball hit the ground first?

2 **Observe** When you dropped different objects, which hit first, the heavier or the lighter?

3 **Hypothesize** Suggest an explanation for what you observed.

4 **Going Further: Experiment** Take two pieces of paper. Wad one into a tight ball. Leave the other alone. When you drop the two pieces of paper as you did the golf ball and table tennis ball, which will hit the ground first? Test your prediction. Explain your results.

Main Idea **We are pulled to the ground by the same force that keeps the Moon orbiting Earth, and the planets orbiting the Sun.**

Why Would Air Make a Difference?

The student in the diagram has just dropped a solid rubber ball and a feather from the same height at the same time. The ball has covered a greater distance than the feather in the same amount of time. This means that the ball has fallen at a greater rate. Should we conclude that heavier objects fall faster than lighter objects?

It is important to realize that when the ball and feather are falling, they both must pass through air. Air offers resistance to the motion of objects through it. In the case of the ball and feather, air resistance acts against the feather's motion more than it does

against the ball's motion. As a result, the air slows the feather more than it does the ball, and the ball falls farther during the same amount of time.

What would happen, though, if the air were removed so that air resistance disappeared? There is no air on the Moon. If you were to drop a hammer and a feather at the same time on the Moon, would they still fall at different rates? No. Since there is no air resistance, the ball and the feather would fall at the same rate!

Scientists have learned that when the effects of air resistance are removed, objects of different weights do, indeed, fall at the same rate. In addition, air resistance may be too small to matter for objects that are fairly compact. Over short distances such objects fall at the same rate even in air.

▷ **How does air affect how a feather falls to the ground?**

Do the ball and feather fall at the same rate on Earth as they do on the Moon? Explain.

Before the parachutes open, these skydivers are in *free fall*— falling toward Earth with the acceleration caused by gravity.

What Makes Objects Fall at the Same Rate?

Aristotle was a philosopher who lived in ancient Greece nearly 2,400 years ago. He believed that heavy things fall faster than lighter things. Aristotle's teachings were accepted for nearly 2,000 years after his death.

In the early 1600s, however, Galileo challenged Aristotle's ideas. Galileo reasoned that objects fall at the same rate (ignoring air resistance). To test his ideas about falling objects, Galileo carried out experiments that involved rolling marbles down ramps. He also talked about dropping two objects with different weights off a tall tower to show that they would hit the ground at the same time. Galileo concluded that objects accelerate steadily as they fall and that an object's weight (or mass) does not affect how fast it accelerates when falling.

We know today that Galileo was right. An object is pulled to Earth by gravity, an attraction between the mass of Earth and the mass of the object. Objects with a large mass are pulled on by gravity with more force,

but they also have more inertia. (Remember that an object's inertia is its resistance to a change in motion.) This extra resistance to motion exactly offsets the greater pull of gravity on them. Therefore, objects with greater mass fall with the same acceleration as less massive objects!

> ## What force pulls falling objects toward the ground at the same rate?

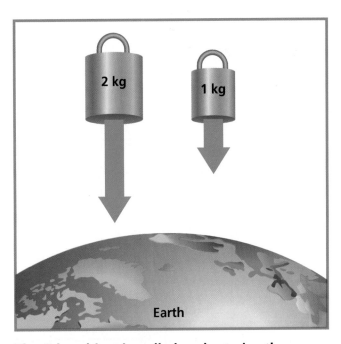

The 2-kg object is pulled on by twice the force, but its mass is also twice as great, so it has the same acceleration as the 1-kg object.

What Is the Acceleration of Falling Objects?

There is a story that says that a falling apple may have set Isaac Newton to thinking about gravity. In the late 1660s, there was a plague (very bad illness that spread very easily) in Cambridge, England, where Newton had gone to college. To avoid the plague, he went home to the countryside. The legend says Newton was sitting under an apple tree one day when an apple hit him on the head. The legend may or may not be true. However, an idea did hit Newton. That idea was that the force that pulls an apple to the ground is the same force that keeps the Moon in its orbit around Earth.

The graph shows how an apple's speed changes as it falls from a tree. Since the apple's speed changes, it must be accelerating. This, in turn, means that it is acted on by an unbalanced force. The force acting on the falling apple is gravity. We give the force of gravity on any object a special name—**weight**. It is the weight of the apple that makes it accelerate to the ground. You can find

Speed Versus Time for a Falling Apple	
Time (s)	Speed (m/s)
0.0	0.00
0.2	1.96
0.4	3.92
0.6	5.88
0.8	7.84
1.0	9.80

READING

Graphs

What if the apple fell for a full two seconds? Ignoring air resistance, what speed would it reach?

Speed versus Time for a Falling Apple

In one second on the time axis, the speed of the apple has increased by 9.8 m/s. This means the apple accelerates at 9.8 m/s each second.

the weight in newtons of any object by multiplying its mass in kilograms by 9.8. If the apple has a mass of 0.4 kg for example, its weight is 0.4 x 9.8 = 3.92 N.

The weight or mass of an object does not affect how fast it accelerates when falling (if we ignore air resistance). This means that all objects accelerate to the ground at 9.8 meters per second each second. Put another way, the speed of any object falling to the ground increases by 9.8 meters per second each second. However, as you will shortly learn, this value is only true for objects falling near the surface of Earth.

Isaac Newton once wrote, "I began to think of gravity extending to the orb [orbit] of the Moon." He wondered if the gravity of Earth could be the force that holds the Moon in its orbit. Just as there is a force between an apple and Earth, there is a force between the Moon and Earth. The force is stronger if the objects are more massive, but it is weaker the farther they are apart. The Moon is much more massive than an apple. However, the Moon is also much farther from Earth's surface than an apple hanging on a tree is. Even so, the same force that pulls the apple to the ground keeps the Moon from flying off into outer space. A combination of the Moon's inertia and the force of gravity between Earth and Moon keeps the Moon orbiting Earth.

▷ **How fast do falling objects on Earth fall toward the ground?**

The Moon's Acceleration

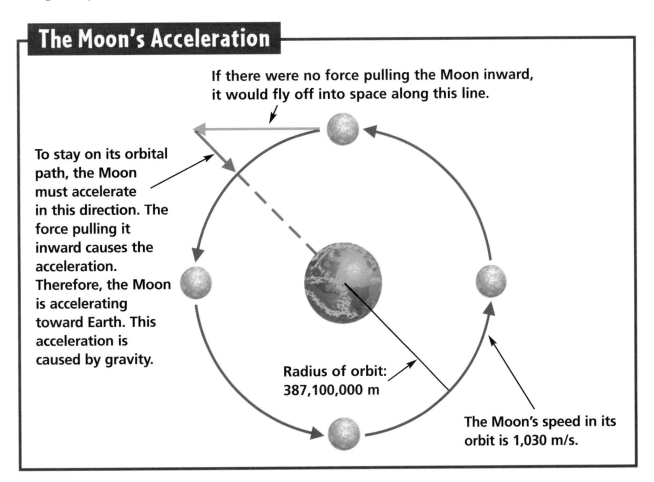

If there were no force pulling the Moon inward, it would fly off into space along this line.

To stay on its orbital path, the Moon must accelerate in this direction. The force pulling it inward causes the acceleration. Therefore, the Moon is accelerating toward Earth. This acceleration is caused by gravity.

Radius of orbit: 387,100,000 m

The Moon's speed in its orbit is 1,030 m/s.

How Can Gravity Be Universal?

When Isaac Newton discovered that Earth's gravity held the Moon in orbit, he next applied his ideas to the planets in the solar system. Could the Sun's gravity hold the planets in their orbits? First, Newton had to work out how the strength of the force depends on the mass of the Sun and each planet.

Newton decided that as mass increases, the force of gravity also increases. From his third law of motion, he knew that two objects pull on each other due to gravity. Then he reasoned that increasing the mass of either object will increase the force of gravity.

In thinking about the Moon, Newton had already inferred how gravity would change with distance. Putting all of his ideas together, he arrived at another law. This is *Newton's law of universal gravitation:* The force of gravity between two objects increases with the mass of the objects and decreases with the distance between them squared.

Newton's law of gravity is "universal" because it applies to any objects, not just moons, planets, and stars. We could find, for example, the force of gravity between two cars in a parking lot. For light objects the force of gravity is quite weak—it will not pull two parked cars together. For massive objects like moons, planets, and stars, though, the masses are so large that the force of gravity becomes very large also.

> **What does it mean to say that the law of gravity is universal?**

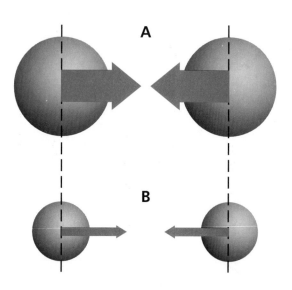

The force of gravity between two objects increases as their masses increase.

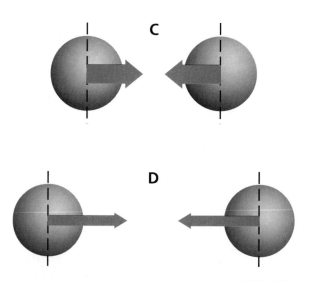

The force of gravity between two objects decreases as the distance between them increases.

What Do I Weigh on Other Worlds?

The Sun, planets, and moons in the solar system have different masses and radii. This causes the force of gravity at their surfaces to vary from world to world (for a gaseous planet, the "surface" is the top of its atmosphere). As the mass of any world increases, surface gravity tends to be stronger. However, as the radius increases, surface gravity tends to weaken. How would your weight change from one world to the next?

Table 1 lists gravity multipliers for solar system bodies. These values show the combined effect of the objects' different masses and radii on surface gravity compared with Earth. You can use the gravity multipliers to find your weight on other worlds. Just multiply your weight on Earth by the gravity multiplier for the new world. On Neptune, for example, your weight would be your weight on Earth multiplied by 1.1.

Mass   Mass   Radius

Procedure

1. **Analyze** Study Tables 1 and 2. Look carefully to see how numbers were used in the examples in Table 2.

2. **Use Numbers** Copy and complete Table 2.

Drawing Conclusions

1. **Predict** A student who weighs 95 pounds on Earth has a mass of about 43 kg. What would the student's mass be on each world above?

2. **Infer** Saturn has much more mass than Earth, but your weight on Saturn is about the same as on Earth. How is this possible?

Table 1

Object	Gravity (Earth = 1)
Sun	28
Moon	0.16
Mars	0.38
Jupiter	2.6
Saturn	1.07
Neptune	1.1
Venus	0.91
Mercury	0.38
Uranus	0.91

Table 2

World	Weight of a 250-Pound Astronaut	Your Weight in Pounds
Sun	7,000 lb	
Moon		
Mars	95 lb	
Jupiter		
Saturn		
Neptune		
Venus		
Mercury		
Uranus	227.5 lb	

Weight = 50 lb

Older Bicycle

Weight = 30 lb

Newer Bicycle

When Is Added Weight Helpful?

We are accustomed to gravity giving things on Earth weight, including our own bodies. Sometimes, though, weight causes problems. How would it feel to ride up a hill on an old bicycle like the one on the left? Compared with the newer one on the right, the older bike is so much more massive that it would take a lot more force to accelerate it. Which would you rather ride?

Older bicycles were made with steel frames. While steel is strong, it is also very heavy. Some modern bicycle frames are made with steel alloys, titanium, aluminum, or carbon fiber.

These materials are a great deal lighter than plain steel, and bikes made with them are much easier to pedal. Of course, the lightweight materials are also much more expensive than steel!

In cycling, weight does offer certain advantages. The weight of the rider and bicycle presses the tires against the ground. This downward force creates increased friction between the tires and the road, giving the tires traction. If it were not for the friction, the tires could not push on the road surface to drive the rider forward.

Bicycle racers often travel on a circular path at high speed. There must be a force acting inward on them to change their direction of travel. The banked track they are riding on uses their weight to help provide this force. The weight of each bike and rider presses into the track through the tires. The track, in turn, pushes back through the tires on each bike and rider. Due to the tilt of the track surface, some of this return push is directed inward and can act as the force that changes each bike's direction of travel.

The banked surface makes it easier to go around the turn.

READING Draw Conclusions
How is added weight helpful in cycling?

Why It Matters

On a flat road, the only force available for making cars go around a turn is the friction between the tires and the road surface. In wet or icy weather, the friction may not be strong enough, and the cars can slide off and crash on the turn. If the road is banked like the bicycle race track, though, the inward push of the road surface helps cars to make the turn. The same sort of banking is also done when making auto racetracks.

Visit **www.mhscience02.com** to do a research project on gravity.

Think and Write

1. What causes objects to fall?

2. Ignoring air resistance, why do objects with different masses fall at the same rate?

3. A rubber ball is dropped off a tall tower. After one second, how fast will it be traveling?

4. **Use Numbers** Two planets in a distant solar system have the same radius but different masses. On which world would you weigh more? Why?

5. **Critical Thinking** How could you carry out a demonstration on Earth of a feather falling at the same rate as a bowling ball?

L·I·N·K·S

MATH LINK

Solve a problem. Look at the tables on page F39. How much would the astronaut weigh on a planet with 1.5 times as much gravity as Neptune?

WRITING LINK

Write a radio play. You are a passenger on a space shuttle flight. You're in orbit. For the first time ever, you can't feel your weight. Write a dialogue of a radio conversation with a friend on the ground describing what it's like to not feel your weight.

MUSIC LINK

Write a song. Think about what it might be like to live on a world where you weigh half as much as you do now. Write a song describing your experiences on such a world.

TECHNOLOGY LINK

At the Computer Visit **www.mhscience02.com** for more links.

RiDE THE "VOMiT COMET"

It's called the "Vomit Comet," and students can't wait to go on it! It's not an amusement park ride, but it can feel like one. The Vomit Comet is a special NASA aircraft used to train astronauts in weightlessness. Two weeks out of the year, NASA also allows college students aboard. The students conduct research on how weightlessness can affect things, and they learn firsthand what zero gravity feels like.

After testing and training on the ground, it's time for the students to fly. Onboard they help bolt their equipment to the floor. Padding covers the floor, walls, and ceiling. All the seats have been removed except for a few rows in the rear. A deep roar of the engines means the first climb has begun. Weightlessness will begin in a few seconds.

The Vomit Comet flies up and down fast like a roller coaster ride. It levels off at 7,315 m (24,000 ft), and the pilot tells passengers to get ready. First, the plane climbs another 3,048 m (10,000 ft) at high speed. At the top of the climb, passengers experience weightlessness for about 25 seconds. Then, the plane dives 3,048 m (10,000 ft) at high speed. Each climb and dive is called a parabola. Every flight has about 32 parabolas, so passengers have about 13 minutes of weightlessness!

At first, weightlessness is scary. That's because you feel like you're falling. Then, you feel excited because you realize you're floating in space! The hardest part for the students is concentrating on what's happening with their experiments. They have only 25 seconds before the dive!

The dive feels very different. Your body feels much heavier than usual. You can hardly lift your arms. Any movement can make you feel very dizzy. That's because the force you feel pulling down on you is twice the force of gravity.

By the ninth or tenth parabola, some students suffer from motion sickness. They head for the seats in the rear and strap themselves in. It's up to the others to finish the experiments. When it's over, even the sick students say it was the ride of a lifetime. For a short time, they felt just like an astronaut!

Astronauts in training experience several minutes of weightlessness on the Vomit Comet.

What Did I Learn?

1. The Vomit Comet is

   A an amusement park ride
   B a NASA aircraft used to train astronauts in weightlessness
   C a special section for student experiments on the space shuttle
   D a strange object from outer space

2. About how long are the students weightless on a Vomit Comet flight?

   F about 13 minutes
   G about 25 seconds
   H about a day
   J about 30 minutes

AT THE COMPUTER

Visit www.mhscience02.com for more amazing stories and facts about gravity.

Vocabulary

Fill each blank with the best word or words from the list.

acceleration, F13
balanced forces, F21
force, F6
gravity, F35
inertia, F7
reaction, F24
speed, F11
unbalanced force, F21
velocity, F12
weight, F36

1. How fast the position of an object changes is its _____.

2. An object's speed in a certain direction is its _____.

3. A change in a velocity in a certain amount of time is called _____.

4. How much an object weighs depends on its mass and the force of _____.

5. An object's tendency to resist a change in motion is its _____.

6. An astronaut on the moon has the same mass as she did on Earth, but has less _____.

7. For every action, there is an equal but opposite _____.

8. Pushes or pulls which completely cancel one another out are called _____.

9. A push or pull that acts on an object is called a(n) _____.

10. Pushes or pulls which are not cancelled by other pushes or pulls are called _____.

Test Prep

11. Gravity is a _____.
    A velocity
    B speed
    C force
    D weight

12. When object A exerts a force on object B, object B _____.
    F doesn't move
    G exerts a reaction force on object A
    H doesn't affect object A
    J exerts an action force on object A

13. A mass accelerates because _____.
    A it has inertia
    B it is moving
    C it isn't moving
    D a force is acting on it

14. An object is accelerated when it is acted on by _____.
    F an unbalanced force
    G a balanced force
    H inertia
    J velocity

15. A baseball and a sheet of paper are dropped at the same time from the same height. If there is no air resistance _____.

  A the baseball will land first

  B the paper will float slowly through the air

  C the baseball will float slowly through the air

  D the baseball and the paper will land at the same time

Concepts and Skills

16. Reading in Science How did Newton conclude that the same force that pulls an apple to the ground also keeps the moon orbiting Earth? Write a paragraph explaining your answer.

17. Safety Why do seat belts help protect passengers when a car stops quickly? Write a paragraph explaining your answer.

18. Scientific Methods How could you find out how much an object moving in a circle is accelerating? Write up a design for an experiment that would test this.

19. Process Skills: Use Numbers What would a 100-kg astronaut weigh on a planet with five times the gravity of Uranus? Write a paragraph explaining how you would find the answer.

20. Critical Thinking You are sitting on a playground merry-go-round holding a cup of water. What happens to the water in the cup as the merry-go-round spins faster and faster? Write your ideas. Describe how you might test them.

Sound Energy

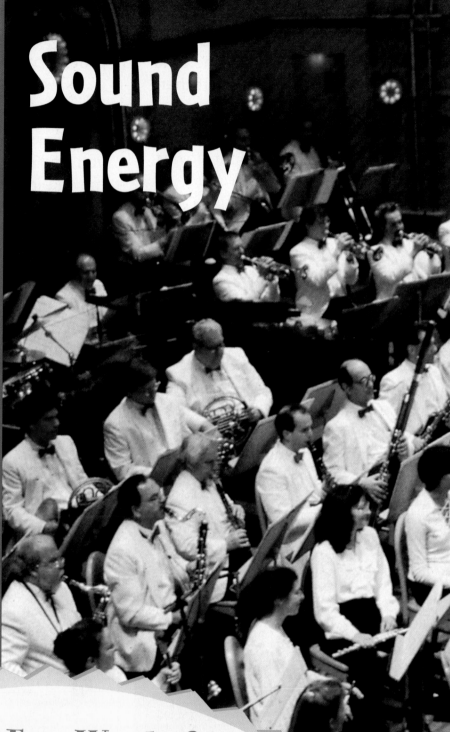

Did You Ever Wonder?

How do the instruments in an orchestra, such as the Boston
Pops, produce such beautiful sounds? Each instrument—violin,
tuba, drum, clarinet—has its own way of producing sound.
Together, the sounds of the instruments combine to make beautiful
music. Noise is also sound. What makes noise different from music?

Sound Waves

Vocabulary

vibration, F50

matter, F51

sound wave, F51

compression, F51

rarefaction, F51

Get Ready

Do you know that without earphones you could not hear your radio on the Moon? Why do you think this is true? If you place your hand over the speaker of a radio, you can feel the sound. Try it. Why does it happen? Would you be able to feel the sound on the Moon?

What causes sound? Keep in mind that sounds can be different. How could you build an instrument to test your ideas?

Process Skill

You predict when you state possible results of an event or experiment.

Explore Activity

What Makes Sound?

Materials

wood or plastic ruler

long rubber band

plastic or foam cup

clear tape

ballpoint pen

scissors

goggles

Procedure

BE CAREFUL! Wear goggles.

1 Use a pen point to poke a hole in the bottom of the cup. Cut the rubber band. Insert one end into the hole. Tie two or three knots to keep the rubber band in place.

2 Tape the cup to the end of the ruler. Stretch the rubber band to the other end of the ruler. Tape it securely.

3 **Observe** Hold the cup next to your ear. Pluck the rubber band. Watch a partner do the same thing. Record what you hear and see.

4 **Experiment** Put one finger on the rubber band, hold it against the ruler, and then pluck it again. What happens to the sound?

Drawing Conclusions

1 **Infer** What did you observe that made your instrument work? How can you explain what makes sound?

2 What happened to the sound when you changed the rubber band with your finger? Explain why, based on your observations.

3 **Going Further: Predict** What do you think will happen to the sound if you stretch the rubber band tighter? Untape the end of the rubber band and pull it a bit tighter. Retape the end to the ruler. Repeat steps 3 and 4. How do the results compare with your prediction? Give reasons for what happened.

Main Idea Sound is provided by the vibrations of objects.

What Makes Sound?

Sound is provided by making something move back and forth. You can't produce a sound without making something move. If you pluck a rubber band, the rubber band moving back and forth produces twanging sounds. This back-and-forth motion is called a **vibration**. Unless something vibrates, there can be no sound. Many vibrations are too fast for you to see. You may not see the bat vibrating when the ball hits it, but you can still feel it.

Energy Transfer

If you pluck a guitar string, you can see it moving back and forth. You provide the energy necessary for this vibration when you pluck it. This energy is transferred to the rubber band and causes it to vibrate. When you touch the rubber band, you can feel it vibrating.

What can you notice if you place your fingers gently against your throat while you talk or hum? You can feel a vibration. You feel the vibration of your vocal cords. Vocal cords in your throat vibrate when air moves past them, allowing you to speak.

What vibrates when you play a guitar? When the strings of a guitar or violin are bowed or plucked, they begin to vibrate. They produce sounds. However, not all instruments rely on strings. Sounds can also be produced by vibrating surfaces and by vibrating columns of air. The instruments in each section of the orchestra have their own characteristic ways of producing sounds. In each section different materials vibrate.

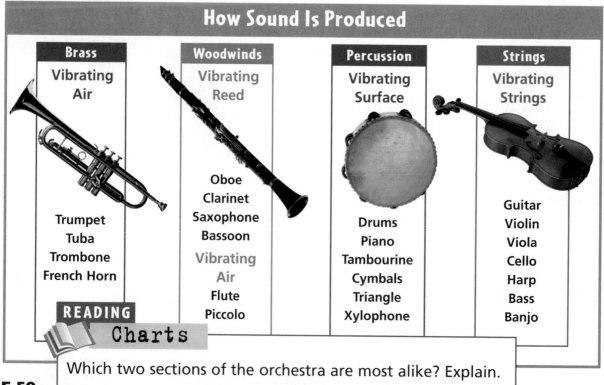

How Sound Is Produced

Brass	Woodwinds	Percussion	Strings
Vibrating Air	Vibrating Reed	Vibrating Surface	Vibrating Strings
Trumpet	Oboe	Drums	Guitar
Tuba	Clarinet	Piano	Violin
Trombone	Saxophone	Tambourine	Viola
French Horn	Bassoon	Cymbals	Cello
	Vibrating Air	Triangle	Harp
	Flute	Xylophone	Bass
	Piccolo		Banjo

READING Charts

Which two sections of the orchestra are most alike? Explain.

Sound Waves

Sound is a vibration that travels through **matter**. Matter is anything that has mass and takes up space. Matter can be a solid, liquid, or gas. Some types of matter are made of pieces too small to be seen, called *molecules*. Molecules are the smallest pieces that matter can be broken into without changing the kind of matter.

How does the sound made by a vibrating string travel? When a string vibrates, it makes molecules of gases in the air next to it vibrate. The molecules squeeze together, then spread apart. The vibrating molecules near the string then make the molecules next to them start to vibrate.

The vibration continues to spread. A vibration that spreads away from a vibrating object is a **sound wave**. It carries the energy from the vibrating object outward in all directions.

READING **Cause and Effect**

What has to happen to make sounds travel?

Sound Waves

Vibrating string

Sound waves

compression
(kuhm·PRESH·uhn) the part of a sound wave where molecules are crowded together

rarefaction
(rayr·uh·FAK·shuhn) the part of a sound wave where molecules are spread apart

F 51

QUICK LAB

FOR SCHOOL OR HOME

Sound Carriers

1. **Observe** Put a wind-up clock on a wooden table. Put your ear against the table. Listen to the ticking. Lift your head. How well can you hear the ticking now? Record your observations.

2. **Use Variables** Fill a sealable pint-size plastic bag with water. Seal the bag. Hold it against your ear. Hold the clock against the bag. How well can you hear the ticking? Move your ear away from the bag. How well can you hear the ticking now?

3. **Interpret Data** Rate wood, air, and water in order from best sound carrier to worst.

4. **Experiment** How would you test other materials, like sand?

What Else Can Sound Go Through?

When you hear sounds, what is usually around you? Air! You can hear sounds in the air. When sound waves reach your ear, they make parts inside the ear vibrate. Since air is a mixture of gases, you may conclude that sound can travel through gases. It travels as sound waves.

Solids

Can sound also travel through solids and liquids? You can tell that sound travels through solids just by putting your ear onto a tabletop. If someone taps the table at the other end, you can hear the tapping louder than if you lift your head away from the table.

Liquids

If you do any underwater swimming, you probably can tell that you can hear sounds in water. You can hear someone calling you from above the surface. You can also hear sounds in the water around you.

▷ **How can you tell that sound travels through liquids and solids?**

Why It Matters

Sound waves can travel through all forms of matter. In fact, sound waves depend on matter in order to travel away from the vibrating object that produces them. Without matter, sound waves could not travel. Can you hear sounds in a vacuum? No. A vaccum is a place where there is no matter.

HEALTH LINK

Write an essay. Research what causes hearing loss. Find out what can be done to help prevent it. Then write about it.

LANGUAGE ARTS LINK

Send a message. Study the sign language chart. Try signing sentences with a partner.

Think and Write

1. What is needed to make sound?
2. What can sounds travel through?
3. How does a vibrating guitar string make sound?
4. How does a drum make sound?
5. **Critical Thinking** What if you put a ticking clock in a box and pump all the air out? The clock is on a thin string so that it is not touching the walls of the box. Would you hear the clock ticking?

LITERATURE LINK

Read *Making Sounds*, to learn how a sound effects studio makes sounds for the movies. When you finish reading, think about how you would make sound effects for a school play. Try the activities at the end of the book.

Making Sounds
by Elaine Israel

TECHNOLOGY LINK

At the Computer Visit www.mhscience02.com for more links.

Pitch and Loudness

Get Ready

How have people made music since ancient times? Shepherds have used instruments like this simple one for centuries. They use the instruments to call their flocks or keep them quiet.

Each musical instrument has a sound all its own. As you play an instrument, you make the sound change. What causes the sound to change? Test it by building a homemade instrument from simple items like straws.

Process Skill

You **experiment** when you perform a test to support or disprove a hypothesis.

Explore Activity

How Can You Change a Sound?

Materials

12 plastic drinking straws

scissors

metric ruler

masking tape

Procedure: Design Your Own

1. **Predict** Work in pairs to make a homemade instrument. Start with straws. Blow over one end of a straw. Will there be a difference if you seal the other end with tape? Record your prediction.

2. **Observe** Tape one end, and blow over the open end. Describe what you hear. Does it work better with or without one end taped?

3. **Classify** Repeat with different lengths cut from a straw. Try at least four lengths. How are the sounds different? Arrange the straws in order to hear the difference.

4. **Experiment** Flatten one end of a straw. Cut the end to a point. Wet it. With your lips stretched across your teeth, blow into that end of the straw. Try to make different sounds with the straw. How might you modify the instrument the girl is using?

Drawing Conclusions

1. **Infer** Why do you think the sounds changed when you cut different lengths of straw? Hint: What is inside a straw—even if it looks empty?

2. **Communicate** Write a description of your instruments for a partner to build them exactly as you did. Include measurements taken with a ruler.

3. **Going Further: Experiment** Try other materials to make other instruments. Try such things as bottles with water, craft sticks, and so forth. Tell what causes the sound to change in each case.

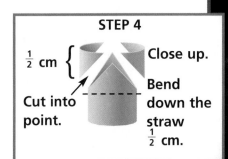

STEP 4

$\frac{1}{2}$ cm

Cut into point.

Close up.

Bend down the straw $\frac{1}{2}$ cm.

Main Idea Pitch and loudness are two characteristics of sound.

What Is Pitch?

Some sounds are "higher" than others; some sounds are "lower." *High* and *low* are words that describe the pitch of a sound. In the sixth century B.C., the Greek mathematician Pythagoras (pi·THAG·uhr·uhs) observed that a longer string produces a sound with a lower pitch than a shorter string.

Changes in Pitch

What can you do to a rubber band to make different sounds? If you pluck a rubber band to make sounds, you can change the pitch by shortening the rubber band. You make it shorter by pressing a thumb over part of it so less of it vibrates. A shorter string vibrates faster and produces a higher pitch.

A second way you can change the pitch is to stretch the rubber band tighter. This causes the rubber band to vibrate faster and, therefore, to produce a higher-pitched sound. The pitch of a vibrating string is also related to its thickness. Compare the strings of this guitar.

Did you know that the length and thickness of your vocal cords, and how you tighten or relax them, affects the pitch of your voice?

Singers can sing a range from high to lower notes by tightening and relaxing their vocal cords. Men usually have longer and thicker vocal cords than women, so men's voices tend to be lower pitched than women's voices.

Tuning pegs are turned to tighten or loosen the strings.

When you press the frets, you change the length of the vibrating portions of the strings.

A thinner string vibrates faster and produces a higher-pitched sound than a thicker string.

A thicker string vibrates slower and produces a lower-pitched sound than a thinner string.

Sound Waves

You can't see sound waves, but scientists study them with an oscilloscope. This device makes a "picture" of sound waves. An oscilloscope allows you to compare the waves of sounds that have different pitches.

Oscilloscope

Length of a sound wave produced by low-pitched sounds

Length of a sound wave produced by higher-pitched sounds

Frequency

The higher the pitch, the more "squeezed together" the waves are. Higher-pitched waves have a greater **frequency** . Frequency is the number of times an object vibrates per second.

Frequency describes vibrations and sound waves. Pitch describes how your brain interprets a sound. A flute has a high pitch. A bass guitar has a low pitch. Frequency and pitch are related: the higher the frequency, the higher the pitch; the lower the frequency, the lower the pitch.

Frequency is measured in units called **hertz** . A frequency of one vibration per second is one hertz (Hz). *Hertz* comes from the name of Heinrich Hertz (1857–1894), a German physicist who studied sound and radio waves.

Humans hear from about 20 Hz to about 20,000 Hz. Sounds with a frequency higher than 20,000 Hz are *ultrasonic*—too high to be heard by humans, but not by some animals.

▶ **How are frequency and pitch related?**

Frequencies of Sounds Heard by Some Organisms

Frequency (in hertz)

Organism	Low	High
Human	20	20,000
Bat	1,000	120,000
Dog	15	50,000
Dolphin	150	150,000

READING Graphs

A range graph shows differences between highest and lowest.

1. Arrange organisms in order of range of hearing, from greatest to least.

2. Put organisms in order of the highest frequencies they hear.

What Is Volume?

A sound wave makes the molecules of gases in air vibrate. The back-and-forth distance they vibrate is based on how much energy the sound wave carries. The more the energy, the greater the distance. The more the energy, the greater the height of the wave as it appears on an oscilloscope. Which of the waves below is carrying more energy?

What is the difference between a yell and a whisper? A sound's **volume**—how loud or soft it is— depends on the amount of energy in a sound wave. To make a louder sound with a rubber band, pluck it harder. A loud sound has more energy than a soft sound and produces a taller wave on an oscilloscope.

You can also make a sound louder by increasing the amount of surface that vibrates. For example, when a cup is attached to a rubber band, the cup and rubber band vibrate together.

Another way to communicate is by using Morse code—a series of long and short taps sent out by telegraph.

Together they make a louder sound than just a rubber band alone.

Volume is measured in units called **decibels** (dB) with an instrument called a decibel meter. On the decibel scale, a sound that measures 50 dB is 10 times louder than one that measures 40 dB. The same 50-dB sound is 100 times louder than a 30-dB sound—that is, 10 x 10 times louder. The 50-dB sound is 1,000 times louder than a 20-dB sound—10 x 10 x 10 times louder.

READING Cause and Effect
Why do sounds differ in volume?

Today's telephones date back to Alexander Graham Bell, who invented the telephone in 1875. Where do you think the word *decibel* came from?

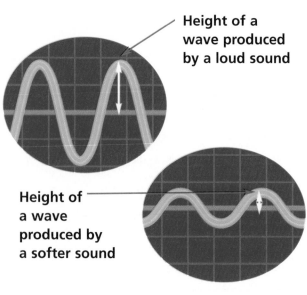

Height of a wave produced by a loud sound

Height of a wave produced by a softer sound

Making Tables and Graphs

In this activity you will interpret data, classify sounds, and create your own table. Tables are helpful tools that organize inform- ation. The table shown gives the loudness of some common sounds in decibels (dB). Sounds below 30 dB can barely be heard. Quiet sounds are between 30 dB and 50 dB. Moderate sounds begin at 50 dB. At 70 dB, sounds are considered noisy. At 110 dB and above, sounds are unbearable.

Procedure

1. **Classify** Determine which sounds are barely audible (can barely be heard), quiet, moderate, noisy, or unbearable.

2. **Communicate** Make your own table to show how you classified the sounds.

3. **Communicate** Make a data table to record how many quiet, moderate, noisy, or unbearable sounds you hear in one hour. Make a graph to show your results. "Number" is the vertical axis. "Kind of Sound" is the horizontal axis.

Drawing Conclusions

1. **Interpret Data** How much louder is a soft radio than your house at night? A classroom than a house at night?

2. **Interpret Data** How much softer is normal conversation than thunder?

3. **Communicate** Make a chart listing loud sounds in the environment. What can you do to protect your ears from harm done by each loud noise?

Loudness of Some Sounds

Sound	Loudness (in decibels)
Hearing limit	0
Rustling leaves	10
Whisper	20
Nighttime noises in house	30
Soft radio	40
Classroom/office	50
Normal conversation	60
Inside car on highway	70
Busy city street	80
Subway	90
Siren (30 meters away)	100
Thunder	110
Pain threshold	120
Loud indoor rock concert	120
Jet plane (30 meters away)	140

How Is Sound Recorded?

What if there were no favorite recordings of music? Fortunately, Thomas Alva Edison first recorded sound back in 1877. Today sound is recorded like this.

A microphone includes a diaphragm, a coil of fine wire, and a magnet. When you sing, speak, or play music into the microphone, sound waves make the diaphragm vibrate. The pitch of the sound determines how fast the diaphragm vibrates. The loudness of the sound determines how far the diaphragm moves with each vibration.

The vibration of the diaphragm makes the coil of wire vibrate near the magnet. Each vibration produces a tiny current of electricity. The coil sends this electric pattern to an amplifier.

The tiny pulses of electricity coming from the coil are very weak. The amplifier makes them up to 50,000 times stronger.

Blank tapes are coated with scrambled magnetic particles. During recording, the electric current from the

Microphone

amplifier arranges the particles on the tape into a pattern—a "code" for the sounds.

When you push "play," the process reverses. The magnetic particles on the tape create a current in the coil. This current vibrates a stiff paper cone in the speaker. This creates the sound waves you hear.

Compact discs do not store sound in magnetic patterns. Instead, a computer in CD-recording equipment translates the sound waves into a code. The code is a combination of 1s and 0s.

Then a laser beam uses the code to cut millions of tiny pits into a blank compact disc. About 85,000 pits cover only one inch of the disc.

When you play a CD, a laser beam shines on it. The flat parts of the CD reflect light back to a small computer. The computer changes the pattern of these reflections back into sound.

▶ **What steps are involved in recording and playing a CD?**

Sound waves **Diaphragm** **Magnet** **Wire coil** **Electric current**

How does a microphone work? Sound waves make the diaphragm in the microphone vibrate. That makes the coil of wire vibrate, sending an electric pattern to an amplifier.

Why It Matters

Next time you strum a guitar, pound a drum, or sing a tune, keep in mind what you learned in this lesson. The different musical sounds you make on an instrument or when you sing are different pitches. You can play an instrument at different volumes—to make the sounds louder or softer. You sing louder when you take a deeper breath and breathe out harder. You use loudness and pitch to express different emotions, too.

Think and Write

1. On a stringed instrument, why are some sounds higher than others?

2. How is pitch related to frequency?

3. How can sounds be changed into an electric current?

4. **Communicate** How is loudness measured? How would you set up a table showing the loudness of different sounds?

5. **Critical Thinking** Why do the notes of a musical instrument have different sounds?

L·I·N·K·S

HEALTH LINK

Make a poster. Research ways people can protect their ears from loud sounds. Make a safety poster illustrating what you found.

SOCIAL STUDIES LINK

Investigate the history of the telegraph. Write a report telling why this invention has been so important.

ART LINK

Make a poster. Illustrate how CDs are made and played, and make a poster for the class.

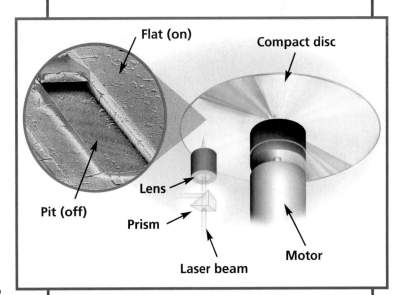

Flat (on)

Compact disc

Pit (off)

Lens

Prism

Laser beam

Motor

TECHNOLOGY LINK

At the Computer Visit **www.mhscience02.com** for more links.

Hit That Note!

Ever think of yourself as a musician? Well you are one. When you sing you play an instrument—your voice!

Musical instruments vary in the pitches, or tones, they can produce. It all depends on the frequencies of vibrating parts. Singers produce different tones, too.

You've probably noticed differences in the sounds of some of your favorite singers. The tones they use depend on the vibrations of their vocal cords. Thicker, longer cords vibrate more slowly and have lower tones. Ever wonder why your voice sounds lower when you have a sore throat? It's because your vocal cords are swollen, so they vibrate more slowly!

Here are pitch categories for most human singing voices. Try classifying some of your favorite singers.

	FEMALE	MALE
High pitch	Soprano	Tenor
Medium pitch	Mezzo-soprano	Baritone
Low pitch	Alto (contralto)	Bass

A baritone usually can't hit the high notes a tenor can because of the size and shape of his vocal cords. Likewise a tenor usually can't hit the low notes a baritone can.

When composers write music, they think about the notes that each instrument and voice can produce.

AT THE COMPUTER

Visit www.mhscience02.com to learn more about music.

Pitch ranges of some musical instruments

Violin

Flute

Clarinet

Trumpet

Trombone

Cello

100 Hz   200 Hz   500 Hz   1,000 Hz   2,000 Hz

Soprano

Mezzo-soprano

Alto

Tenor

Baritone

Bass

Pitch ranges of the human singing voice

This diagram shows the lowest to the highest notes for each instrument and singing voice. The difference between the highest and lowest is called a range.

Write
ABOUT IT

1. Which instrument shown can reach the highest pitch? About what frequency is that?

2. Which instrument has the greatest range? The smallest range?

Reflection and Absorption

Vocabulary

reflection, F66

absorption, F66

echo, F68

echolocation, F70

Doppler effect, F71

quality, F72

fundamental frequency, F72

overtone, F72

resonance, F72

Get Ready

What makes a car race at a racetrack so exciting? Is it the speed, the swerves? Is it the roar of the crowd? What would the race be like if it were totally quiet? Would it still be as exciting?

What makes the race so noisy? Describe the racetrack from the photograph. How does the way the racetrack is built contribute to the loud sounds?

What happens when sound "hits" a surface? Does the kind of surface make a difference?

Process Skill

You make a model when you make something to represent an object or event.

Explore Activity

Do Sounds Bounce?

Procedure

1 Collect a variety of hard, smooth materials and soft, textured materials. Place one of the objects on a table. Set up your tubes in a V-shaped pattern on a table, as shown. The V should meet at the object you are testing. Record the name of the object.

2 **Observe** Place a sound maker (clicker or timer) at one end of the V. Listen for ticking at the other end of the V. Rank the loudness of the ticking on a scale of 1 (lowest) to 5 (highest). Record the number.

3 **Experiment** Repeat steps 1 and 2 with the different materials you collected.

Drawing Conclusions

1 **Classify** What kinds of materials are the best reflectors—hard, smooth materials or soft, textured materials? What kinds of materials are the best absorbers?

2 **Make a Model** Draw a diagram of the path of sound from the sound maker to your ear. On your diagram, mark the point in the path where the sound wave bounced.

3 **Going Further: Infer** Theaters often have soft velvet curtains, thick carpets, and cushioned seats. How do you think these objects affect the sound in a theater?

Main Idea Sounds vary because objects reflect, absorb, or transmit sound differently.

Do Sounds Bounce?

A sound hitting a towel will sound different from the same sound hitting a metal sheet. Why? A sound wave does not act the same way when it hits a hard, smooth surface as when it hits a soft, textured surface.

The pictures below show what happens when sound waves come into contact with a surface. When a sound wave hits a surface, some of its energy bounces off the surface. The bouncing of a sound wave off a surface is called **reflection**. However, not all of the sound wave reflects off the surface. Some of the wave's energy enters the surface, and part of the sound disappears. The disappearance of a sound wave into a surface is called **absorption**.

When a sound wave is absorbed, its energy is changed into heat energy. Sometimes not all of the energy that enters a surface is absorbed. Part of the energy of the sound wave may also travel through a surface and come out the other side—when you hear a sound through a wall.

How much of the sound wave's energy is reflected or absorbed depends on the kind of material of the surface. When sound waves hit a hard, smooth surface such as the wall around the racetrack, much of the sound wave's energy is reflected. However, when sound waves hit a soft, textured surface such as a towel, less of the sound wave's energy is reflected and more is absorbed.

Compare the crack of the bat when the ball and bat meet with the sound when the ball hits the glove.

How Reflection and Absorption Affect Concert Halls

Designing concert halls has always been a tricky business. To get the "right" sound, engineers try to get a good balance of reflection and absorption. Too much reflection results in an empty, hollow sound. Too much absorption deadens the music.

When the London Music Hall was built in 1871, the hall was considered to be one of the great places in the world to hear music. By the 1930s listeners complained that the music did not sound good anymore. Sound engineers were baffled. Nothing in the concert hall had changed since it was built, over 60 years earlier.

Finally, an explanation was found. The concert hall may have stayed the same, but its audience had changed. Most importantly, women were no longer wearing the billowing, layered, sound-absorbing gowns that had been popular earlier. The new styles were shorter and simpler, and didn't absorb sound as well. Overall they changed the balance of reflection and absorption of sound in the room.

▷ Do more sound waves bounce from hard, smooth surfaces or soft, textured surfaces?

The group below is dressed in a style common in the mid- to late 1800s. The billowy gowns and long coats had an effect on sound in a concert hall.

QUICK LAB

FOR SCHOOL OR HOME

Clap! Clap!

1. **Observe** Stand about 8 m away from a large wall, such as the side of your school building. Make sure there is plenty of open space between you and the wall. Clap your hands, and listen for an echo. Notice how much time there is between your clap and the echo.

2. **Observe** Move closer to the wall, and clap again. Listen for an echo. Try this several times.

3. **Observe** As you got closer to the wall, how did the time between the clap and the echo change? Did you always hear an echo? Explain.

4. **Experiment** Repeat at different distances. What happens?

What Is an Echo?

Have you ever made an echo? When you yell "hello!" your vocal cords make sound waves that travel away from you in all directions. If the sound wave hits a surface, some of the sound wave's energy will reflect off the surface and travel back to you. A reflected sound wave is called an **echo**. If the echo is strong enough, you will hear yourself yelling "hello!" after you said it! If there is more than one reflecting surface near you, you may hear "hello!" several more times.

If you sing in the shower, you may notice how rich your voice sounds. The hard, smooth walls of the bathroom are often great for making echoes. The echoes reflect back and forth off the walls many times. They make your voice sound rich and mellow, as if background singers were repeating each note you sing.

READING Cause and Effect
How are echoes made?

You hear sound as soon as you make it. After it reaches a reflecting surface, you hear the echo when the waves return.

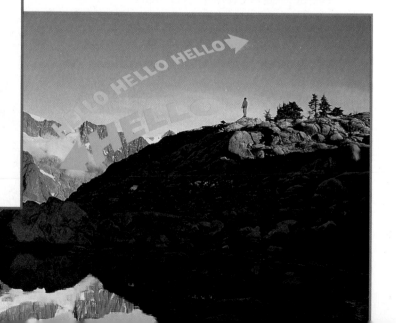

How Fast Is Sound?

It takes almost no time for an echo to bounce back to you after you yell "hello!" Sound waves travel fast. In air at room temperature (20°C), sound waves travel 343 meters per second, faster than most jet planes. In general, sound waves have a greater speed in a solid than in a liquid, and a greater speed in a liquid than in a gas.

The speed of sound waves depends largely on the molecules of the material—on how tightly packed molecules are and how easily they spread apart and move together. Temperature affects the speed of sound. In general, temperature affects the speed of sound more in gases than in liquids and solids.

▷ **Will sound travel faster through air or steel?**

Speed of Sound Through Common Materials

Sound travels through air at 25°C at 346 m/s.

One Second

Sound travels through an aluminum boat at 5,000 m/s.

Sound travels through seawater at 25°C at 1,531 m/s.

stone   5,971 m/s

aluminum   5,000 m/s

seawater at 25°C   1,531 m/s

water at 25°C   1,498 m/s

air at 25°C   346 m/s

air at 0°C   331 m/s

rubber   60 m/s

READING Graphs

1. In which material does sound travel slowest?

2. Would you hear the same sound from the same distance faster in winter or in summer?

What Can Echoes Do?

Sonar, or *so*und *na*vigation and *r*anging, uses sound waves to detect objects far away. A sonar technician sends out sound waves and then times how long those sound waves take to bounce off distant objects and return.

What if a sonar technician on a ship sends out a sound wave toward the ocean bottom? Sound waves travel about 1,500 meters per second in water.

What if the sound wave takes two seconds to return to the ship? The technician will know that the sound wave took one second to reach the ocean floor and then one second more to bounce back to the surface. He or she will conclude that the ocean is 1,500 meters deep.

Many animals find things around them with a form of sonar called **echolocation**. Whales and dolphins bounce sound waves off objects to find out how far away they are.

Bats are able to live in dark caves because they use a form of echolocation rather than sight to navigate. Bats send out high-pitched squeals and clicks into the air at their prey. Their large, forward-pointing ears pick up the echoes. Using this information, bats can close in on their prey.

▷ **How does sonar use echoes to locate objects?**

Sonar

The two-way travel time of the wave varies at different locations. The different times indicate that the ocean bottom gets deeper as the ship goes away from the coast and eventually becomes a flat plain.

How Do Moving Sounds Change?

An echo is a copy of the original sound. Both the original sound and the echo have the same pitch. However, have you ever heard a siren blaring as a police car sped past you? If you listened carefully, you may have noticed that the pitch of the siren changed as the police car sped by. As the car came toward you, the siren was higher in pitch. As it sped away from you, the pitch was lower.

Approaching Sound

As the blaring siren approaches, its sound waves crowd together. There are more sound waves reaching your ear each second than there would be if the police car were standing still. The frequency of the sound increases. The pitch is higher.

Sound waves from the moving police car bunch together (1) as the car approaches the listener. They spread apart (2) as the police car moves away from the listener.

Departing Sound

As the siren moves away from you, its sound waves spread apart. There are fewer sound waves reaching your ear each second than there would be if the police car were standing still. The frequency of the sound decreases. The pitch of the siren moving away from you is lower.

Change of Frequency

This change in frequency (and pitch) as a source of sound moves toward or away from you is known as the **Doppler effect**. It is named for the 19th century Austrian scientist Christian Johann Doppler, who first described it.

Many radar (radio detection and ranging) devices use the effect to find the speed of objects. Patrol cars detect changes in frequency as a way of detecting speeding vehicles.

> How does a sound that is moving away from you change in pitch?

Whales and dolphins use a form of sonar to locate things in their environment.

What Is Fundamental Frequency?

Saxophone

How can you tell the difference in voices? What if two people sing the same note—the same pitch—at the same loudness? You can still hear a difference between the two voices. The **quality** of a sound is what makes it different from another sound of the same loudness and pitch. Quality makes a sound unique.

The quality of a sound depends on the vibrations that produce the sound. When a string vibrates, for example, it vibrates at more than one frequency at a time. The whole string vibrates at the **fundamental frequency**, the lowest frequency at which it vibrates.

At the same time, sections of the string are vibrating at higher frequencies, called **overtones**. Each overtone is a different pitch. It is the blend of the fundamental frequencies and the overtones produced that gives each sound its own quality.

Each sound—whether it's a voice or musical instrument, whether produced by a vibrating string or

column of air—is different from all other sounds. Each sound has its own blend of fundamental frequency and overtones that allows you to identify it.

What do buildings and bridges have in common with musical instruments? Each has its own natural frequency of vibration. If a vibrating force shakes them at their natural frequency, the vibration builds up. This buildup results in a condition called **resonance**. Resonance can make a violin or trumpet sound louder. However, resonance can also cause great damage to buildings and bridges, making them rattle and sway. Bridges have collapsed as a result of resonance.

? Why is fundamental frequency important in designing buildings?

If the saxophone and the trumpet play the same note at the same loudness, the sound waves differ because the blend of overtones differs.

Wynton Marsalis

Trumpet

L·I·N·K·S

Why It Matters

Knowing how different materials reflect and absorb sound waves can be helpful at school or home. Your school library probably has stacks of books and other sound-absorbing materials. They help keep the library quiet so you can read and study. Whether you are a student deciding what furniture to put in a room to make it quiet or an architect deciding how to design a building, you must know how different materials affect sound waves.

Visit **www.mhscience02.com** to do a research project on sound.

Think and Write

1. What is an echo? What is necessary in order to hear an echo?

2. How can sound be used to find the depth of the ocean?

3. Why does the same note played on two different instruments at about the same loudness sound different?

4. What kinds of materials reflect sound best? What kinds of materials absorb sound best?

5. **Critical Thinking** Does sound travel with the same speed through all materials? Write a paragraph explaining your answer.

WRITING LINK

Write an essay. Research the importance of "tuning" a car's suspension and why a Monster Car's suspension is so important. Write an essay on what you discovered.

MATH LINK

Solve this problem. Sound waves travel about 1,500 meters per second in water. A ship sends out a sound wave toward the ocean floor. If the echo takes four seconds to return to the ship, how deep is the ocean at that point?

TECHNOLOGY LINK

Science Newsroom CD-ROM Choose *Sounds Good to Me* to learn how sound waves move through matter.

At the Computer Visit **www.mhscience02.com** for more links.

The Sounds of Earthquakes

The ground begins vibrating wildly. Rising from Earth are seismic (SIGHZ·mik) waves—they're like huge sound waves. It's an earthquake!

This simple seismograph has a pen held delicately against a rolling drum with graph paper on it. The pen records the seismic waves.

As soon as an earthquake begins, seismic waves travel out in all directions from the focus—where the quake began. They also travel inside Earth. Scientists used seismic waves to piece together a model of the inside of Earth.

Surface waves

Fault

FOCUS

Secondary waves

Primary waves

Seismic waves get weaker the farther they get from the focus. Even so they can still be detected by very sensitive devices called seismographs (SIGHZ·muh·grafs).

The fastest, or primary, waves are recorded soon after an earthquake occurs. Slower, secondary waves come later. Surface waves, the slowest, come even later.

Scientists found that seismic waves change speeds at certain depths below Earth's surface. They speed up when they reach about 30–60 kilometers (19–37 miles) below the surface. Why? This depth, called the Moho (after its discoverer), is a boundary between two of Earth's layers—the outer layer, or thin crust, and the next layer, or thick mantle.

The primary waves slow down when they reach Earth's outer core, a layer of thick liquid. Secondary waves completely stop there. The primary waves speed up again as they reach Earth's solid, inner core.

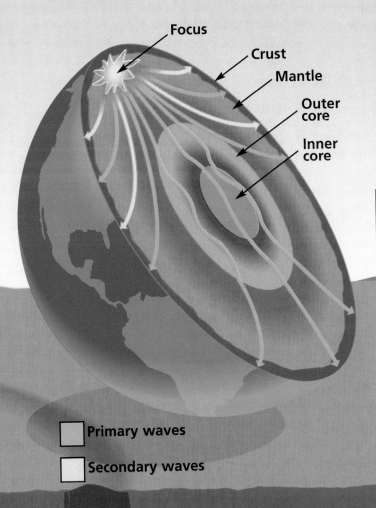

Focus

Crust

Mantle

Outer core

Inner core

Primary waves

Secondary waves

What Did I Learn?

1. An instrument that detects earthquakes is a

A mantle
B seismic wave
C seismograph
D Moho

2. The boundary between Earth's crust and mantle is called the

F outer core
G inner core
H secondary core
J Moho

AT THE COMPUTER

Visit www.mhscience02.com to learn more about earthquakes.

Chapter 13 Review

Vocabulary

Fill each blank with the best word or words from the list.

absorption, F66
compression, F51
decibel, F58
echo, F68
hertz, F57
quality, F72
rarefaction, F51
reflection, F66
sound wave, F51
vibration, F50

1. The unit for measuring frequency is a(n) _____.

2. An echo is caused by a(n) _____.

3. A sound starts with a(n) _____.

4. Loudness is measured in a unit called a(n) _____.

5. Overtones affect the _____ of a sound.

6. A sound travels as a(n) _____.

7. A reflected sound is called a(n) _____.

8. Sound tends not to bounce off carpets because of _____.

9. When molecules bunch together, that's the _____ stage of a sound wave.

10. When molecules spread apart, that's the _____ stage of a sound wave.

Test Prep

11. If the frequency of a musical note is increased, _____.
  A the note gets louder
  B the note gets softer
  C the note gets higher
  D the note gets lower

12. Echoes are the result of _____.
  F the Doppler effect
  G reflection
  H absorption
  J quality

13. The two parts of a sound wave are _____.
  A compression and rarefaction
  B pitch and quality
  C overtone and resonance
  D absorption and reflection

14. The changing pitch of a moving siren is caused by _____.
  F the Doppler effect
  G reflection
  H absorption
  J quality

15. Two differences we hear in sounds are _____.

   A compression and rarefaction

   B absorption and rarefaction

   C pitch and quality

   D absorption and reflection

Concepts and Skills

16. Reading in Science Write a paragraph explaining how a sound reaches your ear.

17. Decision Making You are organizing a band. Some of the band members want to play their music as loud as possible all the time. Some of them say it is safer for everyone's hearing to play much more softly. How loud would you tell everyone to play? Write a paragraph explaining your answer.

18. Scientific Methods Do people learn better if they listen to Mozart's music than if they listen to rock music? Write up a design for an experiment that would test this.

19. Process Skills: Communicate Write a paragraph explaining how the instruments below were built to make different sounds.

20. Critical Thinking Do you think louder sounds travel faster than softer ones? Write and explain a hypothesis. Describe how you might test your idea.

Boost *your test scores!*

Be Smart!

Visit www.mhscience02.com

CHAPTER

14

Light Energy

Did You Ever Wonder?

How does a lighthouse work? This lighthouse on the coast uses powerful lenses to focus a beam of light so it can be seen far out at sea. How are lenses able to focus light? Are the lenses in a lighthouse the same as the lenses in a pair of eyeglasses?

Light and Mirrors

Vocabulary

light ray, F85
law of reflection, F87
concave mirror, F88
convex mirror, F88

Get Ready

What happens in any city or town when the Sun sets? What if you were in a plane as the Sun was setting and you could look down at a big city? What would you notice as time goes by?

What if you are in a room, sitting near a window and reading? The Sun sets. How does everything in the room seem to change? What do you need to do if you want to keep reading? Is it possible to see objects if there is no light?

Process Skill

You **predict** when you state possible results of an event or experiment.

Explore Activity

Can You See Without Light?

Materials

small cardboard box with lid

small object to put inside box, such as an eraser, crayon, or coin

scissors

flashlight

Procedure

BE CAREFUL! Handle scissors carefully. Do not put any sharp objects in the box.

1. Cut a hole about the size of a dime in the box as shown. Put an object inside the box. Close the lid.

2. **Observe** Look in the box through the hole. What do you see? Write a description of it.

3. Now cut a small hole in the top of the box.

4. **Experiment** Shine the flashlight through the top hole while you look into the box again. Can you see the object this time?

Drawing Conclusions

1. **Communicate** Could you see the object inside the box in step 2? In step 4? Explain any difference in your answers.

2. **Infer** Is it possible to see an object in the dark? Explain.

3. **Predict** Do any characteristics of the object in the box affect the results? Try different kinds of objects. Predict any differences in your results. Test your ideas.

4. **Going Further: Predict** How much extra lighting would you need on a dark, cloudy day in order to safely walk around your classroom or your room at home? Would a night-light work? How would you test your ideas safely?

Main Idea Light is a form of energy that is reflected from some objects.

Can You See Without Light?

The Moon looks very bright in the evening sky. However, the Moon does not give off any light of its own.

We are able to see the Moon only because sunlight bounces off the Moon's surface and into our eyes. The dark half of the Moon in the photo is actually a part of the side of the Moon that is not being lit by the Sun. Since sunlight does not reach the Moon there, we cannot see this part of the Moon's surface.

What is light? Scientists know that light, like sound, is not matter. We

You see the Moon because it is lit by the Sun.

could never observe a "piece" of light at rest, taking up space and having mass. Light and sound are both means of transferring energy between points.

The photograph below clearly shows that light carries energy. In fact, light is a form of energy.

A beam of light from a laser carries enough energy to melt the hardest metals.

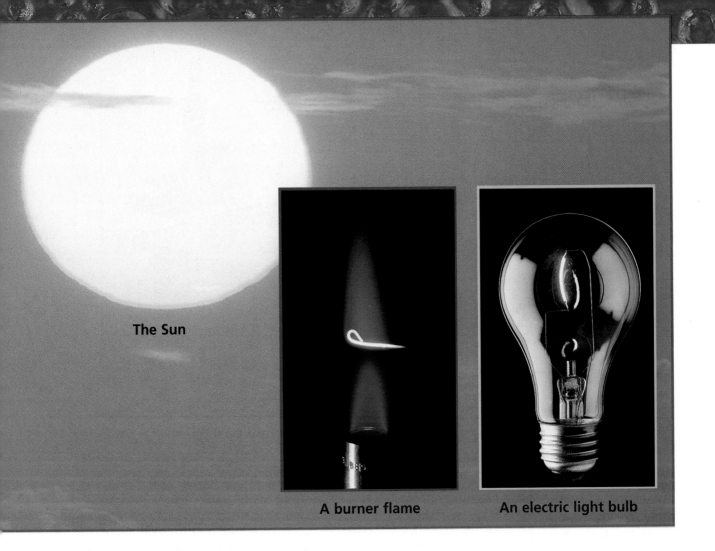

The Sun

A burner flame

An electric light bulb

How Light Is Produced

All the objects we can see either give off their own light or, more often, reflect the light from a source such as a light bulb or the Sun. The photos show objects that produce light. As you can see, heat is involved in all three cases. Nuclear reactions heat the Sun. Chemical reactions heat the burner flame. Electricity heats the glowing wire of the light bulb.

In a very hot material, the molecules move swiftly. At times when these molecules collide, some energy from the collision may be given off as light.

At other times the molecules themselves vibrate and give off light waves.

Any light source converts energy of one kind into light energy. For example, the Sun makes light from nuclear energy, a burner makes light from chemical energy, and an electric light bulb makes light from electrical energy. The light waves given off by these sources carry the energy away at great speed.

▷ **What can you see in a room that is totally dark?**

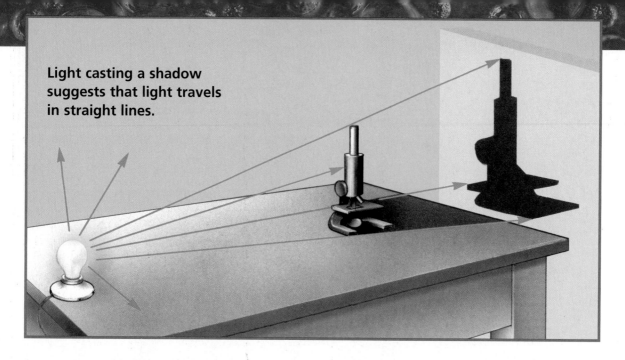

Light casting a shadow suggests that light travels in straight lines.

How Does Light Travel?

Take a look at the drawings below. Which path do you think shows how light travels to your eyes?

In the illustration above, a light bulb casts the shadow of a microscope on a wall. If we draw a straight line from the light bulb to any part of the microscope, we can follow the line directly to that part of the microscope's shadow. This might suggest that light always travels in straight lines. However, this is true only when a substance like air or water remains the same along the whole pathway of light.

Path A

Path B

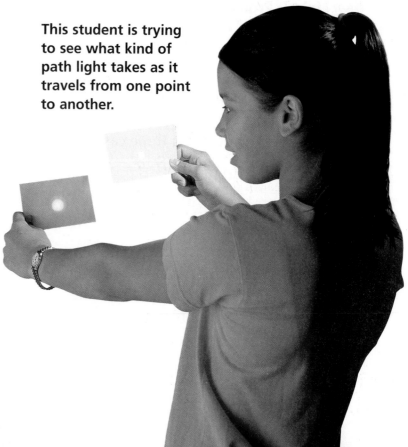

This student is trying to see what kind of path light takes as it travels from one point to another.

In fact, light usually changes direction when it passes from one substance into another. Otherwise, as long as light travels through air or water, it follows a straight line.

Actually, light travels as a series of waves. These waves can be disturbed or bent when they travel past the edge of a thin object or flow through a very narrow opening.

When free of snags, however, light waves move as shown below. If we could follow a point on a light wave as it ripples outward from its source, we would trace a straight line. This beam of light is called a **light ray**.

This model uses water waves to show how light waves bend as they travel past very thin objects or pass through very tiny holes.

❓ How does light travel when it passes from one substance into another?

Switch

Off | On

Metal strip

Spring

Batteries

Light bulb

Each small section of a light wave follows a straight path, creating a ray of light.

When the flashlight is on, electric current from the batteries flows through the metal strip and lights the bulb.

QUICK LAB

FOR SCHOOL OR HOME

Follow the Bouncing Light

1. Hold a small pocket mirror as shown. Adjust it so your partner can see your face in the middle of the mirror.

2. Have your partner run a piece of string from the tip of his or her nose to the reflection of your nose in the mirror. Leave a length of string dangling at the mirror. Then run the extra string from the mirror to the tip of your nose. Be sure the string is taut. Note the angles formed between string and mirror.

3. **Observe** Move a little farther apart. How does the mirror have to be moved for your partner to see your face?

4. **Interpret Data** Were both of you able to see each other in the mirror? What did you observe about the angles the string made with the mirror?

How Does Light Bounce Off Objects?

Review how any visible object must either give off its own light or reflect light from another light source. We can picture how light reflects (bounces) off objects using light rays as in the diagram.

How is light reflected by a mirror? When a ray of light reaches your eye from a mirror, where did the light come from before it struck the mirror?

Light rays reflecting off flat, polished surfaces create mirror images.

Light rays reflecting off rough surfaces scatter in all directions.

The Law of Reflection

The angle between an incoming light ray and a surface equals the angle between the reflected light ray and the surface. This is called the **law of reflection**. The illustration below helps to demonstrate this idea.

Light rays that bounce off polished, shiny surfaces can reflect a "picture" of the light source, called an *image*. The things you see when you look in a flat mirror, for example, look very real, almost as if they existed on the other side of a window. However, your experience tells you they are not real—they are just images of the real things in your world. The picture shows how flat mirrors form images.

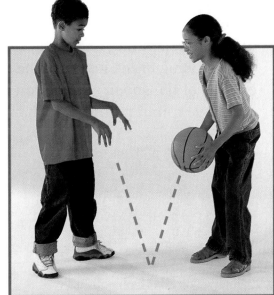

Ambulance signs are often done in "mirror writing" so that they read correctly when seen in a rearview mirror.

Whom does each student see when he or she looks in the mirror?

The path taken by the basketball shows what a light ray does when it reflects off a surface. The angles between the path of the ball and the floor are equal on either side of the bounce.

▶ **How does light bounce off a mirror?**

How Do Curved Mirrors Form Images?

Mirrors that curve in on the shiny side are **concave mirrors**, while mirrors that curve out on the shiny side are **convex mirrors**. Curved mirrors form images that are different from those formed by flat mirrors.

How do you think the images formed by concave and convex mirrors will differ from one another? From the image formed by a flat mirror?

Have you ever looked at your reflection in a soupspoon? You may have found that your image looked different depending on whether you were looking at the inside or the outside of the spoon's bowl. You may also have found your image changed,

Inside of spoon

Back of spoon

depending on how far away you held the spoon.

The inside of the soupspoon behaves like a concave mirror. The outside of the spoon behaves like a convex mirror.

Curved mirrors create a variety of images that can be of practical use. Convex mirrors always form reduced, upright images. However, concave mirrors can form many different types of images, depending on the position of the object in relation to the mirror.

The illustrations on the next two pages demonstrate how different kinds of mirrors form images.

Concave mirrors are often used in telescopes. The images they form can be cast on film or light detectors for study.

Concave Mirrors

Images formed by a concave mirror depend on how far the object is from the mirror. Objects very close to the mirror produce enlarged, right-side-up images. Objects a bit farther back produce enlarged, upside-down images. As the object moves back even farther from the mirror, the image remains upside-down but gets smaller and smaller.

Flat Mirrors

Light rays coming from the candle bounce off the flat mirror and create an image on the other side of the mirror. The image in a flat mirror is always upright, life sized, and left-to-right reversed.

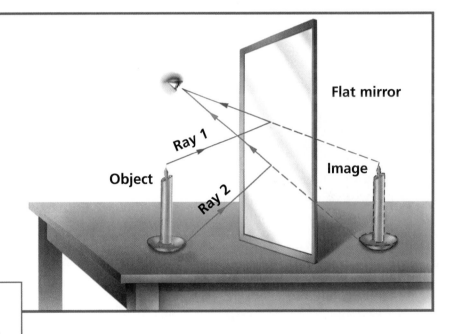

READING Diagrams

1. What happens to the light rays reflected by the concave mirror?

2. Look at the image produced by the concave mirror. How do the image and object compare?

READING **Compare and Contrast**
How are images formed by curved mirrors different from those of flat mirrors?

How Do Convex Mirrors Work?

A convex mirror is curved like part of the outside of a sphere. It produces an image that is right-side up and much smaller than the object. Convex mirrors are used as side rearview mirrors in cars. They give a wide-angle view. However, the cars seem to be farther away than they really are. Convex mirrors are also used in stores as security mirrors to give a wide view of what's going on in the store.

▷ **Why is a convex mirror useful for store security?**

READING
Diagrams

Examine the ray diagram, and explain how images are formed by convex mirrors.

Convex mirrors provide a wide-angle view.

Convex Mirrors

The image lies behind the mirror and is smaller than the object. Note how ray 2 reflects back upon itself.

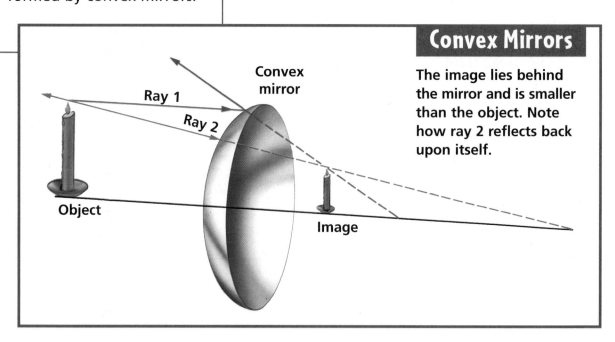

Ray 1

Ray 2

Convex mirror

Object

Image

Why It Matters

Have you ever gone to a parade and missed almost everything because the people in front of you were taller than you? A simple periscope might have helped. Simple periscopes are tall tubes with mirrors inside that help you see over things that would other-wise block your view. Periscopes are also used in submarines to allow the subs to stay underwater while getting a look at what's going on above the water's surface.

Think and Write

1. Is it possible to see in the dark? Explain.

2. What evidence can you give that light travels in straight lines?

3. How are the images formed by concave mirrors different from those formed by convex mirrors?

4. The rearview mirror on the right side of a car is usually a convex mirror. Explain why a convex mirror is best for this purpose.

5. **Critical Thinking** Describe a demonstration that would show how light carries energy.

L·I·N·K·S

WRITING LINK

Write an essay. You own an amusement park and want to make a "fun house" of mirrors. Write an essay telling what sorts of mirrors you would use and why.

ART LINK

Make a kaleidoscope. Cover one end of a toilet paper tube with plastic wrap. Tape together three small rectangular mirrors (all the same size) to form a triangle. Be sure the mirrors are facing out. Slide your triangle of mirrors into the tube. Place bits of colored paper in the tube. Cover the open end with a round piece of cardboard that has a hole cut in the center. Tape it securely. Hold the kaleidoscope up to the light while turning it to see the patterns that form. Describe what you see.

TECHNOLOGY LINK

At the Computer Visit www.mhscience02.com for more links.

BULBS: The Bright Idea!

This has been the typical light bulb for more than 60 years. It has a tightly coiled tungsten filament in a bulb that's filled with a special gas.

Filament

Glass

Whose bright idea was the light bulb? No one person can take all the credit because you need electricity to light the bulb!

It began in 1800, when Alessandro Volta produced the first steady electric current. In 1820 an inventor put a current through a metal wire, saw a glow, and put it in a closed glass container, creating the first light bulb.

In 1841 someone built the first light with glowing carbon. Other inventors used other kinds of filaments—thin materials that glow when electrified.

The first popular light bulb in the United States was a carbon-filament bulb invented by Thomas Edison in 1879. Two years later Lewis Howard Latimer patented an improved bulb with a carbon filament he invented. Latimer was later hired by Edison.

By 1902 metal-filament light bulbs were for sale, but they were very expensive. The General Electric Corporation set up a laboratory to create new bulbs. By 1910 lab workers discovered how to make inexpensive, bright bulbs with tungsten filaments. Sadly, black material coated the inside of the bulbs, dimming the light.

Lab scientist Irving Langmuir found that by filling the bulbs with a special gas, they didn't turn black. By 1934 he'd learned that coiling the filament made the light brighter. Our modern light bulb had arrived!

In the 1980s small fluorescent bulbs that screw into ordinary sockets were introduced. These use much less electricity than ordinary light bulbs.

Fluorescent light bulbs were also produced in the 1930s. They use light from a glowing gas to make a coating inside the bulbs glow. Fluorescent lights use less electricity and are cooler than ordinary bulbs.

Write ABOUT IT

1. What's the difference between an ordinary light bulb and a fluorescent light bulb?

2. How has the invention of the light bulb affected the space shuttle? The camera? The automobile?

Lewis Howard Latimer

Irving Langmuir

AT THE COMPUTER

Visit www.mhscience02.com **to** learn more about electricity.

Light and Lenses

Get Ready

What are shadows? What kinds of materials cast shadows? Can a window glass cast a shadow? Are shadows always black?

What if you turn off the lights in your room? Then you flick on a flashlight on various objects in the room. You look for shadows. Do the shadows differ? Are some sharper than others? If so, why? How do objects cast shadows? Do all objects cast shadows the same way? Are all shadows alike? If light passes through an object, does the object cast a shadow?

Process Skill

You experiment when you perform a test to support or disprove a hypothesis.

Explore Activity

What Can Light Pass Through?

Materials

plastic sandwich bag

paper

waxed paper

aluminum foil

other assorted materials to test

flashlight

clear-plastic cup

water (other liquids, optional)

food dye

Procedure

1. **Classify** Sort the test materials into those that you think light can pass through and those that light cannot pass through.

2. **Experiment** Use the flashlight to test if light can pass through each of the solid materials. Record your observations. Test if light will pass through water. What about water colored with food dye?

3. **Infer** How can you test if light passes through gases? Explain. What materials would you need?

Drawing Conclusions

1. **Interpret Data** Can light pass through all the materials equally well?

2. **Interpret Data** Can light pass through solids, liquids, and gases?

3. **Predict** What else might you add to water to see if light gets through—sand, ink, instant coffee? Predict if each lets light through. How would you test your ideas?

4. **Going Further: Experiment** Design a room from window coverings to lighting, where shadows of objects are always soft and fuzzy, never sharp. What sorts of materials would you use?

Read to Learn

Main Idea Light is blocked by some objects and passes through others.

What Can Light Pass Through?

Sometimes when light strikes matter, almost all the light gets through. Sometimes only some light gets through. Sometimes none of it gets through.

- **Opaque** materials completely block light from passing through.

- **Transparent** materials allow light to pass through with almost no disturbance. Transparent materials may or may not color the light, but you can see objects clearly through them.

- **Translucent** materials allow only part of the light to pass through, while also bouncing it in many new directions. Since translucent materials give only a blurry view, they are often used in shower doors. They let some light in, but provide privacy.

Light from celestial objects, such as this galaxy, passes through empty space to reach us.

You might think empty space is opaque to light. After all, light and sound are both waves, and sound waves do need some kind of matter to travel through. However, as the starry night sky shows, light *can* travel through empty space. We'll learn why in Lesson 10.

Kaleidoscopes use mirrors to turn reflected light into changing patterns. Translucent pieces of colored glass or plastic are often used to create various designs inside.

Which objects in this scene are transparent? Translucent? Opaque?

Controlling Light

In our daily lives, we use many products to control light. You may be familiar with some of the products shown here.

One of the most interesting ways for controlling light depends on **polarization** (poh·luhr·uh·ZAY·shuhn). Light travels in waves. Normally these waves vibrate in all directions. However, light can be *polarized* by some materials. That is, only one direction of light vibrations can pass through them.

Polarized sunglasses use one kind of polarizing material to help us see better on a bright day. On bright days much of the glare we see comes from light reflecting off water and other surfaces.

This reflected light is often naturally polarized to vibrate sideways. Polarizing materials in sunglasses, however, let through only the light that is vibrating up and down. This blocks glare and all other kinds of light that vibrates sideways.

Scientists have also developed sunglasses that change color by themselves! They turn dark in the sunlight but lighten indoors. The lenses

Thin plastic films can be applied to car windows to give them a darker tint. This cuts down on the brightness of the light coming through.

of self-tinting glasses contain very small amounts of a transparent, silver-containing chemical. When struck by bright light, this chemical turns into tiny silver particles. These particles block light and darken the glass.

When taken indoors, the silver particles become transparent again, so the lenses automatically lighten.

READING Compare and Contrast
Compare how light passes through opaque, transparent, and translucent materials.

Self-tinting glasses indoors

Outside in bright light

How Can Light Rays Be Bent?

The pencil in the photograph certainly appears to be bent. However, the bend is actually just a "trick" that light rays play on our eyes. The illusion is caused when light rays from the lower part of the pencil change direction as they go from water into air. The bending of light rays as they pass from one substance into another is called **refraction** (ri·FRAK·shuhn). The photograph on page F99 illustrates the refraction of a light beam.

How does light affect what you see when it passes through water?

You've seen that light rays may bend as they move from one substance into another. Can light rays move from one substance into another without bending?

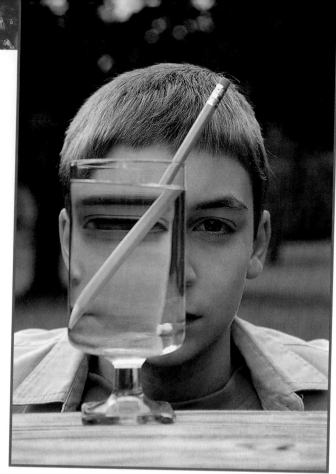

Light rays bend as they go from water into air, making the pencil appear to be bent.

How Refraction Works

Imagine skating onto grass from a sidewalk. If you skate straight onto the grass at a 90° angle, you will slow down, but your direction will remain the same. If you skate onto the grass at any other angle, though, one skate will slow before the other. This will cause you to turn in a new direction. The shallower the angle between your original path and the grass, the more your direction will change.

Put a penny in each cup. Add a little water to one cup. Stand away from the table. Can you see both pennies? What would you have to do so that you could see both coins at the same time?

Like a skater, light traveling from one substance into a denser substance slows down. (The denser substance is made of material that is packed together more tightly than the material that makes up the less-dense substance.)

If light strikes the new material head-on, its direction is unchanged. However, if it strikes at any other angle, it gets refracted into a new direction. The amount of refraction increases as the incoming angle gets shallower.

Look at the photos of the skaters. The first skater skates onto the grass at a 90° angle. Both skates hit the grass at the same time. The second skater's skates don't hit the grass at the same time. Why not? How will the path the second skater takes differ from the path the first skater takes? How do the paths the skaters take compare with the paths the light beams take?

? **When do light rays bend?**

READING
Charts

1. What happens as the light beams enter the glass? Compare the paths of the two light beams. Why are they different?

2. How do the paths the light beams take compare with the paths the skaters take? Why do you think this is so?

QUICK LAB

FOR SCHOOL OR HOME

Seeing Through a Lens

1. Observe Hold a convex lens about a foot from your eye. View the image of the room around you. Record what you see. Repeat with the lens quite close to the page of a book.

2. Experiment Aim the lens at a light bulb or window. Move an index card back and forth on the other side of the lens until you see an image of the light source cast sharply on the card. Record what you see.

3. Observe When the image was upright, was it enlarged or reduced?

4. Observe When you cast an image on the card, was it upright or inverted?

5. Classify Summarize your observations in a table.

How Do Lenses Work?

Lenses are pieces of transparent materials with curved surfaces that use the refraction of light to make images. **Convex lenses** curve outward, while **concave lenses** curve inward. The diagrams show how these lenses form images.

Lens

Object

Image

Convex lenses form images by refracting light rays together. The size and position of the image depend on how far the object is from the lens.

Concave lenses form images by refracting light rays apart. These images are always right-side up and smaller than the object.

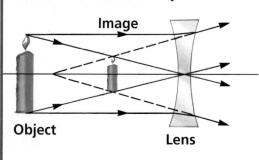

Image

Object

Lens

▶ **How do convex and concave lenses work?**

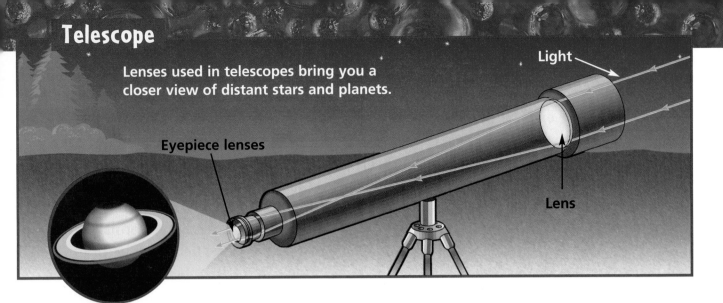

Telescope

Lenses used in telescopes bring you a closer view of distant stars and planets.

Light

Eyepiece lenses

Lens

Binoculars

Binoculars work like a pair of small telescopes—one for each eye. They are used for viewing distant objects. Unlike most telescopes, binoculars give an enlarged, right-side-up view.

Focusing wheels

Light

Eyepiece lenses

Prisms (bend light)

Lens

Microscope

Lenses used in microscopes help you see a tiny world that is invisible to your unaided eye.

Lenses

Eyepiece lenses

Light

Microscope lamp

READING
Diagrams

Why does the telescope pictured give an upside-down view of the planets?

How Does the Eye Work?

Each of your eyes has a convex lens that casts an image onto the back of the eye. Here a sheet of tissue called the retina converts the light into signals that nerves carry to the brain. Your brain then turns the nerve signals into your view of the world.

The diagram shows how your eyes work. Light from an object reaches the eye and is refracted by the cornea. The refracted light then enters the eye through the pupil and travels to the lens.

The lens of the eye bends the light even more, so that it forms an image on the retina.

Images that form on the retina are sent on by the optic nerve to the brain. The brain then turns these images into your view of the world.

How the Eye Works

Normal Eye

1 Object
2 Cornea
3 Pupil
4 Lens
5 Image
6 Retina
7 Optic nerve

> How can lenses help nearsighted eyes work better?

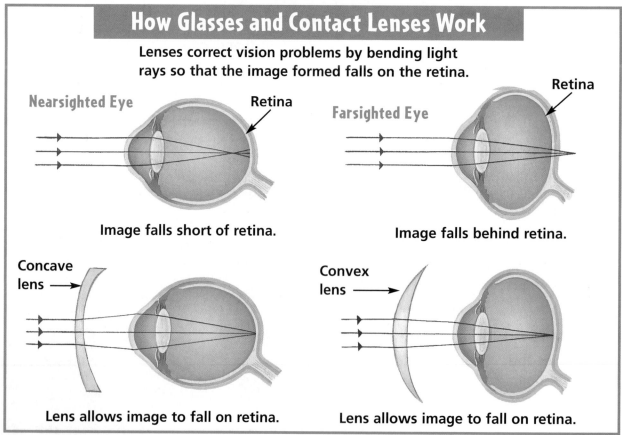

How Glasses and Contact Lenses Work

Lenses correct vision problems by bending light rays so that the image formed falls on the retina.

Nearsighted Eye

Retina

Image falls short of retina.

Concave lens →

Lens allows image to fall on retina.

Farsighted Eye

Retina

Image falls behind retina.

Convex lens →

Lens allows image to fall on retina.

Why It Matters

Light bends as it travels from one kind of substance to another. You can use lenses to focus light and form various kinds of images. The cornea and lens of your eye act as lenses to focus light rays on the retina of your eye. Without this focusing ability, you would not be able to see things clearly.

Braille alphabet

Think and Write

1. Give two examples each of
   a. an opaque material
   b. a transparent material
   c. a translucent material

2. How can light rays enter a new material without being refracted?

3. Why are lenses curved?

4. If it weren't for your brain, you might see the world upside down. Why?

5. **Critical Thinking** The Sun is visible at sunrise a few minutes before its disk actually rises above the horizon. How is this possible?

L·I·N·K·S

WRITING LINK

Write an essay. What are some of the ways lenses are important to you? Write an essay that tells about these lenses and their uses.

ART LINK

Make a poster. Research the types of aids available to visually impaired people, and make a poster describing them.

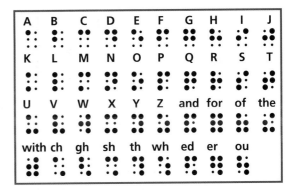

A	B	C	D	E	F	G	H	I	J
K	L	M	N	O	P	Q	R	S	T
U	V	W	X	Y	Z	and	for	of	the
with	ch	gh	sh	th	wh	ed	er	ou	

HEALTH LINK

Make a health poster. Use encyclopedias or other references to learn about astigmatism. Draw diagrams showing how light travels through an astigmatic eye. Then draw diagrams showing how cylindrical lenses are used to correct this condition. Make a poster for the class.

TECHNOLOGY LINK

At the Computer Visit **www.mhscience02.com** for more links.

History of Science

Cameras — Say "Cheese"!

Even in ancient times, people knew how to make glass. Later they found that curved-glass lenses made an object appear larger or smaller.

One of the earliest devices with a lens was the *camera obscura*. (That's Latin for "dark room.") It was a closed box with a lens on the front, a tilted mirror inside, and glass on the top. The lens allowed light from an object into the box. The light hit the mirror and reflected an image of the object onto the glass.

A "bull's-eye" lantern was also an enclosed box with a lens. When a light was placed inside the box, a narrow, bright beam shone through the lens. The lantern was used in lighthouses.

CAMERA OBSCURA

Reflected image

Glass

Light from scene

Scene

Lens

Mirror

Like the bull's-eye lantern, lenses have also been used in light-houses. They create beams of light that can even cut through fog.

Someone placed an image on a transparent sheet and placed it between the light and the lens of a bull's-eye lantern. The image was projected outside the box! The device became known as the "magic lantern," and many people attended magic-lantern shows!

The lens and chamber of the eye are like a small camera obscura. Sometimes an image is formed either too far in front or too far in back of the eye. This can be corrected by adding other lenses in front of the eyes—glasses or contacts!

Some chemicals change color when light shines on them. Inventors put a surface coated with such chemicals at the back of a camera obscura. After many improvements this became the most common way of taking pictures. No one called it a camera obscura anymore. They just called it a "camera"!

MAGIC LANTERN

CAMERA

Light Source

Lens   Shutter   Film

What Did I Learn?

1. The word *camera* comes from the Latin phrase for

   A dark room
   B image taker
   C picture
   D image maker

2. Which one of these was used to produce a lighthouse's beam of light?

   F bull's-eye lantern
   G camera obscura
   H magic lantern
   J camera shutter

AT THE COMPUTER

Visit www.mhscience02.com to learn more about lenses.

Light and Color

Get Ready

Does a red object always look red? Stage lights can be used to change the color an object appears to be. Why does an object that is one color in normal light look different in certain colors of light, but not in others? Why do you see a color at all? What color will a blue object appear to be if you look at it under a blue light? Under a red light? How could you test your ideas even if you did not have a red or blue light bulb?

Process Skill

You **predict** when you state possible results of an event or experiment.

Explore Activity

What Is Color?

Materials

red, yellow, blue, and green cellophane sheets

white paper

crayons

red, yellow, blue, green, and black squares of construction paper

flashlight

Procedure

1. **Observe** Instead of using colored light bulbs, shine a flashlight at a sheet of white paper through each of the cellophane sheets. Record what you see.

2. **Predict** Is there a difference if you observe the paper by looking through colored cellophane instead? What color will each of the colored squares appear to be through each of the cellophane sheets? Check your predictions.

3. **Make a Model** Use the crayons to make additional colored squares to view through the cellophane sheets.

4. **Communicate** Make a table that shows what color each square appears to be through each of the cellophane sheets.

Drawing Conclusions

1. **Communicate** What color does the red square appear to be when viewed through the red cellophane sheet? Why? What color does the blue square appear to be when viewed through the red cellophane sheet? Why?

2. **Going Further: Predict** What do you think would happen if you looked at the red square through both the red and blue cellophane sheets at the same time? Try it to test your prediction.

Main Idea White light is a combination of all colors.

How Do You Get Color from White Light?

When Sir Isaac Newton passed a beam of white sunlight through a **prism**—a triangular piece of cut and polished glass—in a dark room, he was startled to see a band of rainbow colors. He called the color band a **spectrum** after a word meaning "ghostly vision."

Newton wanted to know more about the colors cast by the prism. Where did they come from? He believed that white sunlight was actually a mixture of all the colors. The prism simply spread the colors out by refracting each one at a different angle. Red is refracted the least, violet the most.

Later, Newton predicted that if the spectral colors cast by one prism were passed through a second prism, the colors would recombine into white light.

The result proved his prediction was right. White light is really made up of many colors, including red, orange, yellow, green, blue, and violet.

Rainbows

The rainbow colors you see after a storm result from water drops that act

READING
Diagrams

How do raindrops break up the Sun's light into different colors?

How Rainbows Form

Rain

Sunlight

Rainbow

Observer

both as prisms and mirrors. The drops bend rays of sunlight at different angles, causing the colors to spread out. Then the various colors reflect off the back of the drops into your eye. As the drawing shows, that is how rainbows form in the sky.

Can you make a rainbow with a garden hose? If you've stood with your back to the Sun and looked at the fine mist from a hose, fountain, or waterfall, you've probably seen a rainbow form.

You can also make a rainbow indoors, as this student (top right) is doing. Fill a clear-plastic cup about halfway with water. Carefully place it on the edge of a table. A third of it should extend over the edge. Hold a piece of white paper directly behind the cup. Shine a flashlight vertically through the bottom of the cup. You should see a rainbow on the paper.

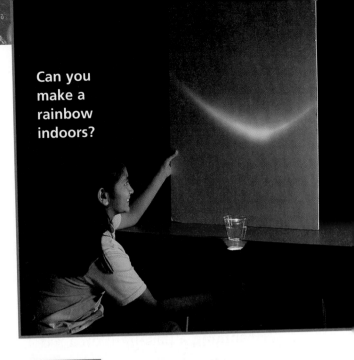

Can you make a rainbow indoors?

READING Compare and Contrast

How do raindrops and prisms produce rainbow colors from white light?

A Recipe for White Light

You've learned that white light is a mixture of an entire spectrum of colors. In the picture at right, the girl is using a color spinner she made from cardboard. She pushed a pencil through the center so that when she twirls it between her palms, others can see the colors mix. She is trying to make the right mix of colors so that others will see white light when she spins the spinner.

What colors would you put on your spinner to try to produce white light?

When the spinner is twirled at the right speed, you can see all the colors turn into white.

How Do Colors Look in Colored Light?

A color filter is a material that absorbs certain colors of light and allows others to pass through. The color of an object depends on the color of the light hitting it. What if you looked through colored cellophane sheets as color filters? For example, the red cellophane allows red light to pass through it but blocks other colors.

Try shining a flashlight on a red tomato. Use a sheet of red cellophane as your filter. The tomato still looks red. Now try a green sheet as your filter. Since the tomato can only reflect red light, it now looks black. Try other filters to see how they work.

If you mixed equal amounts of red, green, and blue light, you would get white light, and the tomato would look red. In fact, all of the colors of the spectrum can be created by mixing proper amounts of red, green, and blue light. For this reason we call red, green, and blue the **primary colors** of light.

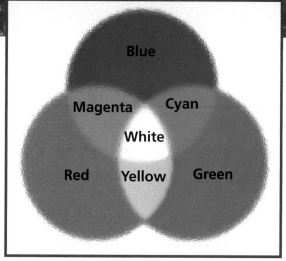

Mixing red, green, and blue light. Note that white is formed in the middle.

Our eyes have cells in the retina that react to colors of light. Some cells react only to red, others only to green, and still others only to blue. If the retina is struck with equal amounts of red, green, and blue light, we see white.

However, if the retina is struck with only red and green light, we see yellow. The drawing above shows some of the different colors that various mixtures of red, green, and blue light can cause us to see.

▷ **How does a red object look in green light?**

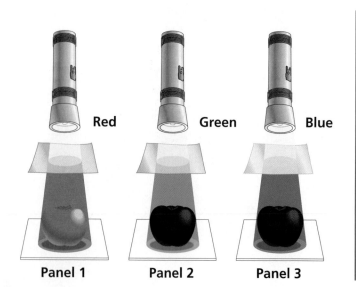

Red   Green   Blue

Panel 1   Panel 2   Panel 3

Stare steadily at the blue square above. This tires the cells in your eye that react to blue light. After a full minute, quickly look at a piece of white paper. What color do you see? Why?

Mixing Colors

You will use pigments—colored substances—in this activity to see the way pigments blend to make other colors.

In this activity you will make a prediction before you do the activity. That is, you will make a reasonable guess about what you expect the results to be. Predict what colors will result when you mix certain colors of food dyes together.

Procedure

BE CAREFUL! Wear goggles.

1 Place four cups on a piece of paper. Add enough water to each cup to cover the bottom.

2 **Predict** What color will be made by mixing one drop of red food dye and one drop of yellow food dye in the water? Mix well. Record the result.

3 **Experiment** Do step 2 with red and blue dyes. Be sure to make a prediction before you mix the colors.

4 **Experiment** Do step 2 again with yellow and blue, and then with all four colors. Again, be sure to make your predictions before you mix the colors.

Drawing Conclusions

1 **Communicate** What color resulted when you mixed red and yellow?

2 **Communicate** What color resulted when you mixed red and blue? Blue and yellow? When you mixed all four colors?

3 **Infer** What would happen if you used different amounts of each dye? Experiment to find out. Make predictions about the final color before you mix the dyes.

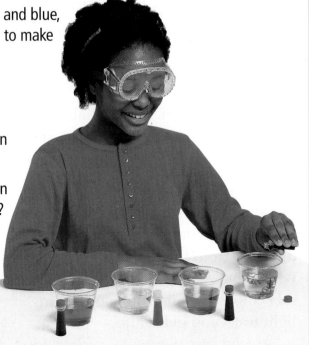

Materials

red, yellow, blue, and green food dyes

water

plastic cups

goggles

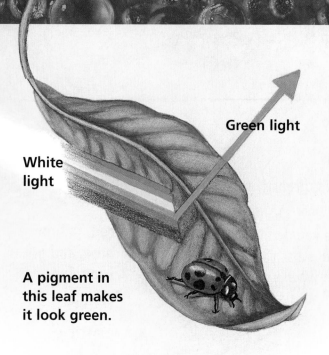

White light

Green light

A pigment in this leaf makes it look green.

What Happens When Color Is Reflected?

When light strikes an object, pigments—colored substances—in the object reflect some colors but absorb other colors. The absorbed colors are missing in the reflected light. The reflected colors mix to produce the color of the object, as shown above.

The leaf in the drawing looks green because it has a pigment that absorbs red and blue light but reflects green light. Some materials reflect all colors and so appear white. Other materials absorb all colors and so appear black.

Colors Made by Blending Paints

Remember that the colors that result when you blend paints are different from the colors that result when you blend colored lights. As you mix colored lights, you keep adding light until you get white.

As you mix pigments, such as food dyes or markers or paints, you keep

subtracting colors until you get black. That is how black is formed at the center of the color wheel below.

Magenta, cyan, and yellow are called the **primary pigments**. Each absorbs one primary color of light and reflects the other two. When properly mixed, these pigments can create any desired color by reflecting a blend of primary colors of light.

Under white light, for example, equal amounts of magenta and cyan would produce the color blue. The cyan would absorb the red out of the white light and the magenta would absorb the green out of the light. Only blue would be reflected.

▷ **What happens when an object absorbs red and green light and reflects blue light?**

READING

Diagrams

What colors would you see if you mixed equal amounts of magenta and yellow? Cyan and yellow?

The Color Wheel

Cyan

Magenta

Black

Yellow

Why It Matters

The four-color printing process uses yellow, magenta, cyan, and black plates to make four-color photos. The red in the final print is a combination of different amounts of yellow and magenta. The blue is a mixture of cyan and magenta. Green is a mixture of cyan and yellow. Darker colors also mix in a little black. Other colors are formed by mixing various amounts of three or all four color plates.

Think and Write

1. Why do objects appear to be different colors when seen under different-colored lights? When seen through different-colored filters?

2. What happens when white light passes through a prism?

3. What are the primary colors of light? The primary colors of pigments? Why are they different?

4. **Predict** What color would be created by mixing red and green light? What color would be created by mixing cyan and yellow pigments?

5. **Critical Thinking** Where in nature can you see a spectrum? Explain.

L·I·N·K·S

WRITING LINK

Write an essay. What are some of the ways color is important to your life? Write an essay describing what you think life would be like if you could not see in color.

HEALTH LINK

Make a health poster. Some people are color-blind. They cannot tell the difference between certain colors, or certain colors may appear gray to them. Research color blindness and make a poster about it. Include illustrations of how certain things, such as the design of traffic lights, can help people who are color-blind.

TECHNOLOGY LINK

At the Computer Visit **www.mhscience02.com** for more links.

Invisible Light

Vocabulary

electromagnetism, F118

electromagnetic spectrum, F119

laser, F122

Get Ready

How long does it take to see light when you turn on a lamp in a darkened room? How long does it take for light from a lamp at the end of a long hallway to reach the other end?

It takes about eight minutes for light from the Sun to reach Earth. It can take hundreds, thousands, millions or billions of years for the light from distant stars to reach us.

How does light travel? Sound travels in waves. If light travels in waves, could they be different from sound waves? Explain.

Process Skill

You experiment when you perform a test to support or disprove a hypothesis.

Explore Activity

How Do Waves Move?

Materials

two 1-m strips of tape

20 straws

meterstick

20 paper clips

stopwatch or digital watch

Procedure

1 Work in groups of four. Starting 10 cm from one end, press 20 straws onto the sticky surface of a strip of tape. Be sure the straws are 4 cm apart, centered, and parallel. Secure them with the second strip.

2 **Observe** Have two members of your group take one end of the model each, so it spreads out lengthwise. Have a third person tap a straw at one end. Have the fourth person time how long the wave takes to travel across from one end of the model to the other. Record the time it takes.

3 **Experiment** Repeat step 2 several times, sometimes with the model tightly stretched, other times with it loosely stretched. Record your results.

Drawing Conclusions

1 **Observe** In what direction does the wave move? In what direction do the straws move?

2 **Interpret Data** How does holding it tighter or looser change how the wave moves?

3 **Going Further: Experiment** Place paper clips at the ends of the first ten straws. Repeat steps 2 and 3 of the procedure. What happens? Try other combinations of paper clips. What happens?

Main Idea Waves that produce visible light are part of the electromagnetic spectrum.

How Do Waves Move?

All waves carry energy from place to place. The way a wave carries energy depends on the kind of wave motion.

Remember that sound waves are produced by vibrations. As a string or bar or some other object vibrates, it causes molecules of gas in the air to move back and forth. The energy of the vibration is carried through the air to your ear. In a similar way, sound waves travel through solids, liquids, and gases.

The wave in the spring below moves from left to right. Notice that the particles of matter also vibrate back and forth along the *same* direction—from left to right.

Without particles vibrating back and forth in the direction the sound is traveling, the energy of the sound vibration could not travel. Sound waves cannot travel in a *vacuum*, a space where there is no matter.

By vibrating one end of a spring toy in and out, you can see waves travel much as sound waves do.

As the wave moves from left to right, how do the water and the ball move?

If you toss a pebble into a quiet pond, you can see waves travel across the surface. How does a particle of matter move in the water as the wave moves past it from left to right? Each particle moves in a circle. So does the ball floating on the water.

The waves shown below also move from left to right. How does a particle in the string or the spring move when a wave passes through it? It does not move back and forth as in a sound wave. It does not move in a circle as in a water wave. It moves up and down.

▶ **Do all waves move the same way?**

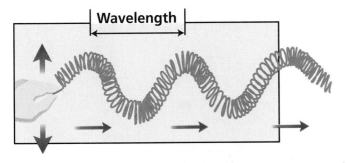

By vibrating one end of a spring toy up and down, you can see waves travel much as waves do on a watery surface.

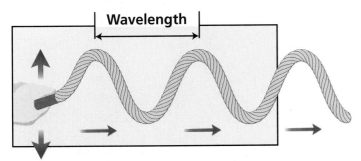

How do the waves made by a jump rope behave?

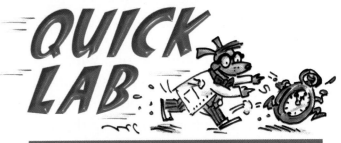

FOR SCHOOL OR HOME

Water Waves

1. **Fill a shallow pan or tray (20 cm by 28 cm) half full of water. Fold small squares of foil (1 cm by 1 cm) into tiny "boats." Place several of these boats on the surface of the water.**

2. **At one end of the tray, make waves on the water's surface. Do this by moving a pencil horizontally up and down in the water.**

3. **Predict** What do you think will happen to the boats after 30 seconds? After one minute?

4. **Observe** What happened to the boats? How did they move? How far did they move? Were your predictions correct?

5. **Experiment** What happens if you change how fast you make the waves? What happens if you change the number of boats you use?

How Do Light Waves Travel?

Connect both ends of a wire to a battery, then put a compass near the wire. The compass needle moves. The electric charges flowing through the wire create a magnetic field that affects the compass. This is an example of **electromagnetism** (i·lek·troh·MAG·ni·tiz·uhm).

Electromagnetism refers to forces that come from electricity and magnetism. When an electric charge moves in a magnetic field, it produces electromagnetic energy.

In the 1850s, James Clerk Maxwell concluded from his work that light is electromagnetic energy. The electrical and magnetic parts of the energy can carry themselves as a wave moving through space. Electromagnetic waves can travel without matter or through matter.

Electromagnetic waves vibrate back and forth across (*perpendicular to*) the direction in which light travels. Water waves are usually used as models for light waves. The wavelength is the distance from crest to crest. However, light is not just one wavelength. It is many wavelengths. The colors of light are different wavelengths. A prism refracts the different wavelengths different amounts.

However, all the wavelengths of light travel through empty space at the same speed—over 300 million meters per second. Light slows down when it travels through matter. However, it always travels much, much faster than sound. That's why you see a lightning flash before you hear the thunder.

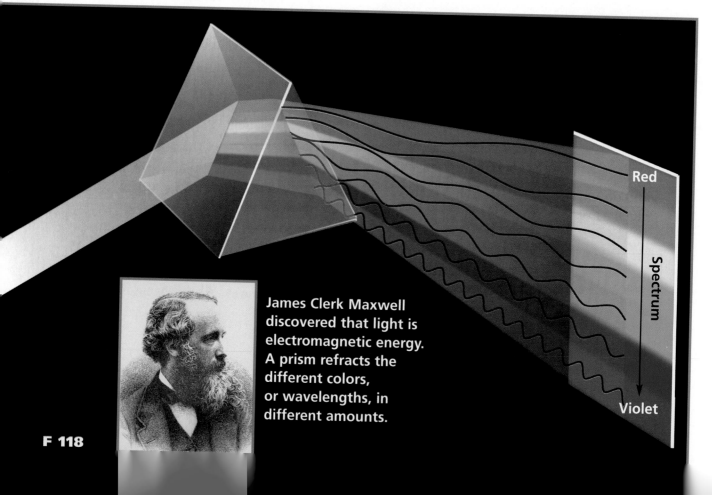

Red

Spectrum

Violet

James Clerk Maxwell discovered that light is electromagnetic energy. A prism refracts the different colors, or wavelengths, in different amounts.

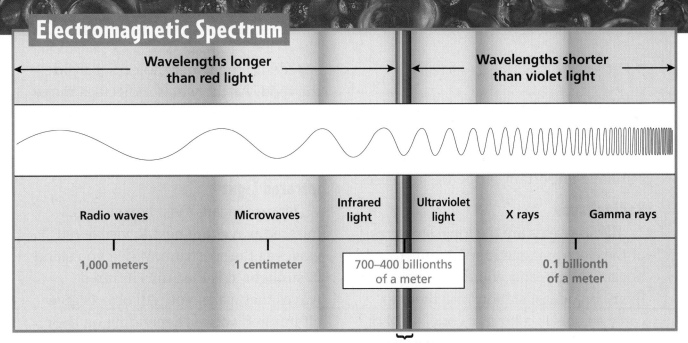

Electromagnetic Spectrum

Wavelengths longer than red light			Wavelengths shorter than violet light		
Radio waves	Microwaves	Infrared light	Ultraviolet light	X rays	Gamma rays
1,000 meters	1 centimeter	700–400 billionths of a meter		0.1 billionth of a meter	

Visible light

Which kind of wave is the shortest? The longest?

Since Maxwell's work, scientists have formed another idea of how light travels. Rather than as a smooth vibrating wave, perhaps light travels as tiny bundles of energy. Scientists call the bundles *photons*.

Waves or photons? Scientists use both models to explain light. For example, your eye picks up only so many photons of light at any instant. We can see the wavelengths of light that make up the colors of light.

However, there are wavelengths longer than red light and shorter than violet. We cannot see these wavelengths. Together all these wavelengths of light, the ones we see and the ones we cannot see, are called the **electromagnetic spectrum**.

Although we cannot see wavelengths longer than red or shorter than violet, we can detect them, and we can use them in many ways. One way to detect some of this "invisible light" is by using a spectroscope.

READING **Compare and Contrast**
What is one difference between the ways light waves travel and sound waves travel?

Instruments such as this spectroscope (above) allow us to detect forms of light we can't see. This image (right), taken by the spectroscope, analyzes the light coming from an object.

Which Wavelengths Are Longer than Red Light?

The wavelengths of light listed here are longer than red. They are invisible but have important properties and uses.

Radio Waves

Radio waves are the longest waves of the electromagnetic spectrum. You do not see them—and you do not hear them. Broadcast stations use them to carry signals in a kind of code—AM or FM. In AM the height of the waves is changed to carry the signal. In FM the frequency changes. The number of your favorite radio station represents the frequency at which the station sends out radio waves. When these signals are picked up by a radio or television, they produce the sounds and sights that you hear and see.

Radar

Some animals, such as bats and whales, send out sound waves with a high frequency. The echo of the waves helps the animals locate things. Radar works in a similar way. *Radar* stands for "**ra**dio **d**etecting **an**d **r**anging." Radar uses radio waves that reflect off many objects. The waves can help weather forecasters detect rain and thick fog.

Microwaves

A microwave oven uses electromagnetic waves, too. Microwaves are shortwave radio waves. Water in foods absorbs microwaves very readily. The energy from the absorbed microwaves speeds up the water molecules inside the food. As the water molecules move faster, the food gets hotter. Microwave ovens can heat many foods faster, using less energy than a regular oven.

Infrared Light

Infrared means "just beyond red." Infrared waves are next to visible red waves in the spectrum. When you stand in sunlight, it is the Sun's infrared waves that warm you. All objects give off infrared waves, depending on their temperature. Warmer objects give off more infrared waves than cooler objects do. Special photographic film and electronic sensors can detect infrared light.

> ▷ **What kinds of electromagnetic energy have longer wavelengths than visible light?**

This photograph was taken with film that picks up infrared light.

Which Wavelengths Are Shorter than Violet Light?

The wavelengths of light listed here are shorter than violet light. They are invisible but have important properties and uses.

Ultraviolet Light

Ultraviolet (UV) light is made up of waves just shorter than visible violet light on the spectrum. UV light causes chemical changes. It can produce vitamin D in your body. You need vitamin D for healthy bones and teeth. Ultraviolet light produces vitamin D in milk. Hospitals use ultraviolet light to kill harmful bacteria in equipment used in operating rooms. However, UV light can cause harm. UV light from the Sun can cause a sunburn. Scientists have found that UV light can also cause some forms of cancer on the skin. Cancer is a disease in which cells multiply rapidly with harmful effects.

Earth is protected from much of the Sun's UV light by the ozone layer. The ozone layer is a part of the upper atmosphere that screens out UV light. However, some chemicals produced by factories are eating away at the ozone layer. Thus more of the Sun's UV light will pass through to Earth's surface. Care is being taken to prohibit the chemicals from being manufactured.

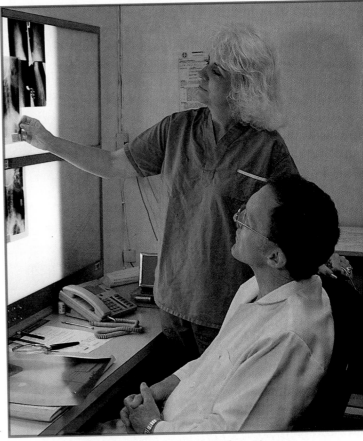

Doctors use light boxes to examine X rays.

X Rays and Gamma Rays

The shortest wavelengths of the spectrum—X rays and gamma rays—have great penetrating power. X rays can pass right through most objects. Thicker or denser objects tend to absorb X rays. This means that X rays can produce a picture when they pass through an arm or leg, or your jaw. The denser objects, such as bones and teeth, can show up very clearly on the finished picture.

▷ **What kinds of electromagnetic energy have shorter wavelengths than visible light?**

What Are Lasers?

You've seen **lasers** in many places—such as at music events and even the checkout counter at the supermarket. Lasers are devices that produce thin streams of light. What makes light from a laser special?

Regular light from a bulb or a candle has many wavelengths all mixed together. As the light travels away from the bulb or candle, it spreads out and gets less noticeable. It gets weaker and weaker the farther it travels.

Lasers produce light that does not spread out or become weaker. Lasers, such as this device using a red ruby, produce light by absorbing flashes of light from a coiled tube. Inside the ruby the absorbed light bounces back and forth between mirrors at the ends of the ruby. As a result, the ruby gives off a light of just a few close wavelengths. The wavelengths are all one color and line up "in step." The beam that comes out of the ruby is narrow and direct.

▷ **What is special about laser light?**

Lasers are used in astronomy.

Flash tube   Ruby crystal

Ruby Laser

Mirror   Partial mirror

Laser light does not spread out.

Regular light spreads out as it travels away from a source.

Flashlight

READING
Diagrams

How does laser light compare to light from a flashlight?

Why It Matters

Light has many wavelengths. Only some are visible. Radar waves help forecasters predict the weather. X rays help dentists and doctors check for cavities and broken bones. Every time you turn on a radio or TV, you are picking up invisible waves of "light."

Some laser beams can be used to melt metals and "crack open" granite. Doctors can use other kinds of lasers to perform delicate surgery. There are even weak laser beams in CD players.

Visit **www.mhscience02.com** to do a research project on light.

Think and Write

1. How does light travel? Does it travel the same way as sound?

2. What is radar? How is it used in weather forecasting?

3. How is ultraviolet light harmful? How is it helpful?

4. If a spacecraft were 900 million meters from Earth, how long would it take to send a radio signal from Earth to the spacecraft?

5. Critical Thinking What's the difference between a beam of light from a flashlight and a beam of light from a laser?

L·I·N·K·S

LITERATURE LINK

Read *Light Up the Sky with Lasers*, to learn how scientists and artists create laser light shows for planetariums and special events. When you finish reading, think about what you would like to see in a laser light show. Try the activities at the end of the book.

MATH LINK

Make a graph. Use encyclopedias or other reference books to find the wavelengths of the different colors of light. Also research the wavelengths for invisible light in the electromagnetic spectrum. Prepare a color-coded bar graph comparing the wavelengths.

SOCIAL STUDIES LINK

Research the history of lasers. Write a report for the class.

TECHNOLOGY LINK

Science Newsroom CD-ROM Choose *Out of Sight* to learn how infrared and ultraviolet light differ from visible light.

At the Computer Visit **www.mhscience02.com** for more links.

Vocabulary

Fill each blank with the best word or words from the list.

concave mirror, F88
convex lens, F100
convex mirror, F88
electromagnetic spectrum, F119
light ray, F85
opaque, F96
primary color, F110
prism, F108
translucent, F96
transparent, F96

1. A straight-line narrow beam of light traveling out from its source is a(n) _____.

2. A mirror that curves in on its shiny side is a(n) _____.

3. A lens that curves outward is a(n) _____.

4. White light is broken up into a rainbow of colors by a(n) _____.

5. A kind of material that allows some light to pass through but may give a blurry view is called _____.

6. Red, blue, or green—each is a _____ of light.

7. A material that light cannot pass through is called _____.

8. A material that light can easily pass through is called _____.

9. Microwaves and X rays are part of the _____.

10. A security mirror used in a store is a(n) _____.

Test Prep

11. Light is a form of _____.
  A heat
  B electricity
  C energy
  D sound

12. Which of the following is translucent?
  F a car windshield
  G a convex mirror
  H a frosted light bulb
  J a concrete block

13. Which is NOT found in the electromagnetic spectrum?
  A X rays
  B infrared light
  C FM radio waves
  D sound waves

14. Sunglasses that reduce glare are _____.
  F transparent
  G translucent
  H cloudy
  J polarized

15. Objects that light can easily pass through are called _____.

   A translucent

   B transparent

   C opaque

   D cloudy

Concepts and Skills

16. Scientific Methods Copy and complete the diagram to show what happens to a light ray as it passes through the lens. Write a paragraph explaining your diagram.

17. Product Ads How does TV advertising use light and color to capture your attention? Write a paragraph giving three examples.

18. Reading in Science What is the difference between the primary colors of light and the primary colors of pigments? Why won't combining colors of paints give you the same results as combining colors of light? Write a paragraph explaining your answer.

19. Process Skills: Predicts How many different colors do you think you could make using two flashlights, a piece of white paper, and one piece of red and one piece of green cellophane? What if you placed the two pieces of cellophane on top of each other and looked through them. Do you think you would get the same result? Write a paragraph explaining your answer.

20. Critical Thinking Cameras let you take pictures by using lenses to focus light onto film. What if you wanted to make a simple camera but didn't have any lenses. Would you be able to use a mirror instead? What kind of mirror might you try? State and explain a hypothesis. Write a paragraph describing how you would test your idea.

NUCLEAR PHYSICIST

Dr. Shirley Jackson

Rensselaer Polytechnic Institute

The young girl went to her family's rose bushes with 30 jars. In each jar she collected one bumblebee, one yellow jacket, and one wasp. She studied how different foods affected the insects and how the different insects got along with each other.

The young scientist was Shirley Jackson. She would become one of the great nuclear physicists of her time. In 1973, Dr. Jackson became the first African-American woman to receive a doctorate from the Massachusetts Institute of Technology. She studied particles that are smaller than atoms and the forces that bind these particles together.

In 1948, scientists learned that the atoms in silicon and a few other materials could be used to transmit electricity very effectively. These materials are called semiconductors. The discovery of semiconductors eventually led to the invention of the computer. Dr. Jackson's later research on semiconductors helped develop a semiconductor laser. Every time you play your CD player, you use a semiconductor laser.

In 1995, Dr. Jackson became the first African-American woman to head the Nuclear Regulatory Commission (NRC). It became her job to make sure that our nuclear plants were safe and to find safe ways to store nuclear wastes. When she found out that some plants were ignoring NRC safety rules, she shut them down. She also increased plant inspections so that problems could be found more quickly.

Dr. Jackson is currently the President of Rensselaer Polytechnic Institute. She is the first African-American woman to lead a national research university. She hopes that all her "firsts" will inspire other African-American students to become scientists.

Write ABOUT IT

1. What discovery led to the invention of the computer?

2. What were Dr. Jackson's two duties as head of the Nuclear Regulatory Commission?

Careers IN SCIENCE

Nuclear Engineer

If you're interested in physics, you may want to be a nuclear engineer. A nuclear engineer works with nuclear power, the strongest source of energy known. Nuclear power can be used to produce weapons and generate electricity. It can also be used for medical purposes such as taking X-rays.

Many nuclear engineers work at nuclear power plants, making sure the plant is running safely. Some work in laboratories conducting research on atomic particles and how to use the energy contained in the atom.

A student interested in becoming a nuclear engineer should enroll in an accredited engineering school after high school. A graduate degree is needed for most jobs, with a doctorate usually required for research jobs.

As Chair of the NRC, Dr. Jackson discusses energy with Senator Joseph Lieberman.

AT THE COMPUTER

Visit www.mhscience02.com to learn more about careers.

It's the LAW!

Your goal is to show how Newton's laws of motion work.

What to Do

1. Place a ball in a shoe box open at one end. Facing the open end, slowly push the box forward. Suddenly stop it. What happens?

2. Push against a wall. What do you feel? Record your observations.

Analyze **Your Results**

Relate your observations to Newton's laws.

Good VIBRATIONS

Your goal is to make and use an instrument to detect sound vibrations.

What to Do

1. Stretch plastic wrap over one end of a tube. Secure it with a rubber band. Tape a straw to the plastic wrap.

2. Hold the detector still. Talk into the open end while you gently touch the straw. Use a low voice then a high voice. Record your observations.

Analyze **Your Results**

Draw a diagram of your detector showing how energy is transmitted from you to the straw.

COLOR VISION

Your goal is to explain what happens when you look at colored objects through different color filters.

What to Do

1. Predict which color cellophane you need to look through to make an object look the same color or appear black.

2. Test your predictions. Record your observations.

Analyze **Your Results**

Which color cellophane made both a red and a green object appear black? Explain.

For Your Reference

Science Handbook

Health Handbook

Glossary

Index

Units of Measurement

The temperature is 77 degrees Fahrenheit.

That is the same as 25 degrees Celsius.

Water boils at 212 degrees Fahrenheit.

Water freezes at 0 degrees Celsius.

I weigh 85 pounds.

That baseball bat weighs 32 ounces.

32 ounces is the same as 2 pounds.

The mass of the bat is 907 grams.

This classroom is 10 meters wide and 20 meters long.

That means the area is 200 square meters.

Units of Measurement

This bottle of juice has a volume of 1 liter.

That is a little more than 1 quart.

She can walk 20 meters in 5 seconds.

That means her speed is 4 meters per second.

Table of Measurements

International System of Units (SI)	English System of Units
Temperature	**Temperature**
Water freezes at 0°C and boils at 100°C.	Water freezes at 32°F and boils at 212°F.
Length and Distance	**Length and Distance**
1,000 meters (m) = 1 kilometer (km)	5,280 feet = 1 mile
100 centimeters (cm) = 1 meter	3 feet = 1 yard
10 millimeters (mm) = 1 centimeter	12 inches = 1 foot
Volume	**Volume of Fluids**
1,000 milliliters (mL) = 1 liter (L)	4 quarts = 1 gallon
1 cubic centimeter (cm³) = 1 milliliter	2 pints = 1 quart
	2 cups = 1 pint
Mass	8 fluid ounces = 1 cup
1,000 grams (g) = 1 kilogram (kg)	**Weight**
	2,000 pounds = 1 ton
	16 ounces = 1 pound

Use a Hand Lens

You use a hand lens to magnify an object, or make the object look larger. With a hand lens, you can see details that would be hard to see without the hand lens.

Magnify a Piece of Cereal

1. Place a piece of your favorite cereal on a flat surface. Look at the cereal carefully. Draw a picture of it.
2. Look at the cereal through the large lens of a hand lens. Move the lens toward or away from the cereal until it looks larger and in focus. Draw a picture of the cereal as you see it through the hand lens. Fill in details that you did not see before.
3. Look at the cereal through the smaller lens, which will magnify the cereal even more. If you notice more details, add them to your drawing.
4. Repeat this activity using objects you are studying in science. It might be a rock, some soil, or a seed.

Observe Seeds in a Petri Dish

Can you observe a seed as it sprouts? You can if it's in a petri dish. A petri dish is a shallow, clear, round dish with a cover.

1. Line the sides and bottom of a petri dish with a double layer of filter paper or paper towel. You may have to cut the paper to make it fit.
2. Sprinkle water on the paper to wet it.
3. Place three or four radish seeds on the wet paper in different areas of the dish. Put the lid on the dish, and keep it in a warm place.
4. Observe the seeds every day for a week. Use a hand lens to look for a tiny root pushing through the seed. Record how long it takes each seed to sprout.

Collect Data

Use a Microscope

Hand lenses make objects look several times larger. A microscope, however, can magnify an object to look hundreds of times larger.

Examine Salt Grains

1. Look at the photograph to learn the different parts of your microscope.
2. Place the microscope on a flat surface. Always carry a microscope with both hands. Hold the arm with one hand, and put your other hand beneath the base.
3. Move the mirror so that it reflects light up toward the stage. Never point the mirror directly at the Sun or a bright light. Bright light can cause permanent eye damage.
4. Place a few grains of salt on the slide. Put the slide under the stage clips. Be sure that the salt grains you are going to examine are over the hole in the stage.
5. Look through the eyepiece. Turn the focusing knob slowly until the salt grains come into focus.
6. Draw what the grains look like through the microscope.
7. Look at other objects through the microscope. Try a piece of leaf, a human hair, or a pencil mark.

Eyepiece

Arm

Stage clip

Stage

Focusing knob

Mirror

Base

Measure Time

You use timing devices to measure how long something takes to happen. Some timing devices you use in science are a clock with a second hand and a stopwatch. Which one is more accurate?

Comparing a Clock and Stopwatch

1. Look at a clock with a second hand. The second hand is the hand that you can see moving. It measures seconds.
2. Get an egg timer with falling sand or some device like a wind-up toy that runs down after a certain length of time. When the second hand of the clock points to 12, tell your partner to start the egg timer. Watch the clock while the sand in the egg timer is falling.
3. When the sand stops falling, count how many seconds it took. Record this measurement. Repeat the activity, and compare the two measurements.
4. Switch roles with your partner.
5. Look at a stopwatch. Click the button on the top right. This starts the time. Click the button again. This stops the time. Click the button on the top left. This sets the stopwatch back to zero. Notice that the stopwatch tells time in minutes, seconds, and hundredths of a second.
6. Repeat the activity in steps 1–3, using the stopwatch instead of a clock. Make sure the stopwatch is set to zero. Click the top right button to start timing the reading. Click it again when the sand stops falling. Make sure you and your partner time each other twice.

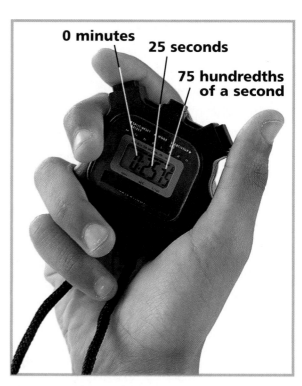

0 minutes
25 seconds
75 hundredths of a second

More About Time

1. Use the stopwatch to time how long it takes an ice cube to melt under cold running water. How long does an ice cube take to melt under warm running water?
2. Match each of these times with the action you think took that amount of time.

   a. 0:00:14:55
   b. 0:24:39:45
   c. 2:10:23:00

   1. A Little League baseball game
   2. Saying the Pledge of Allegiance
   3. Recess

Measure Length

Find Length with a Ruler

1. Look at this section of a ruler. Each centimeter is divided into 10 millimeters. How long is the paper clip?
2. The length of the paper clip is 3 centimeters plus 2 millimeters. You can write this length as 3.2 centimeters.
3. Place the ruler on your desk. Lay a pencil against the ruler so that one end of the pencil lines up with the left edge of the ruler. Record the length of the pencil.
4. Trade your pencil with a classmate. Measure and record the length of each other's pencil. Compare your answers.

1 centimeter = 10 millimeters

Measuring Area

Area is the amount of surface something covers. To find the area of a rectangle, multiply the rectangle's length by its width. For example, the rectangle here is 3 centimeters long and 2 centimeters wide. Its area is 3 cm x 2 cm = 6 square centimeters. You write the area as 6 cm^2.

2 cm

3 cm

1. Find the area of your science book. Measure the book's length to the nearest centimeter. Measure its width.
2. Multiply the book's length by its width. Remember to put the answer in cm^2.

Find Length with a Meterstick

1. Line up the meterstick with the left edge of the chalkboard. Make a chalk mark on the board at the right end of the meterstick.
2. Move the meterstick so that the left edge lines up with the chalk mark. Keep the stick level. Make another mark on the board at the right end of the meterstick.
3. Continue to move the meterstick and make chalk marks until the meterstick meets or overlaps the right edge of the board.
4. Record the length of the chalkboard in centimeters by adding all the measurements you've made. Remember, a meterstick has 100 centimeters.

Estimating Length

Try estimating the length of objects in the room. Then measure the length, and compare the estimation with the measurement.

Measure Mass

Mass is the amount of matter an object has. You use a balance to measure mass. To find the mass of an object, you balance it with objects whose masses you know. Let's find the mass of a box of crayons.

Measure the Mass of a Box of Crayons

1. Place the balance on a flat, level surface. Check that the two pans are empty and clean.
2. Make sure the empty pans are balanced with each other. The pointer should point to the middle mark. If it does not, move the slider a little to the right or left to balance the pans.
3. Gently place a box of crayons on the left pan. This pan will drop lower.
4. Add masses to the right pan until the pans are balanced.
5. Add the numbers on the masses that are in the right pan. The total is the mass of the box of crayons, in grams. Record this number. After the number write a *g* for "grams."

Estimating Mass

Once you become familiar with the mass of objects, you can try estimating the masses of objects. Then you can compare the estimation with the actual mass.

More About Mass

The mass of your crayons was probably less than 100 grams. You may not have enough masses to balance a pineapple. It has a mass of about 1,000 grams. That's the same as 1 kilogram, because *kilo* means "1,000."

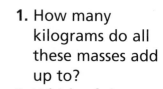

50   500   100   100   20   20   5   2 2   1

1. How many kilograms do all these masses add up to?
2. Which of these objects have a mass greater than 1 kilogram?

Measure Volume

Volume is the amount of space something takes up. In science you usually measure the volume of liquids by using beakers and graduated cylinders. These containers are marked in milliliters (mL).

Measure the Volume of a Liquid

1. Look at the beaker and at the graduated cylinder. The beaker has marks for each 25 mL up to 200 mL. The graduated cylinder has marks for each 1 mL up to 100 mL.
2. The surface of the water in the graduated cylinder curves up at the sides. You measure the volume by reading the height of the water at the flat part. What is the volume of water in the graduated cylinder? How much water is in the beaker? They both contain 75 mL of water.
3. Pour 50 mL of water from a pitcher into a beaker.
4. Now pour the 50 mL of water into a graduated cylinder.

Find the Volume of a Solid

Here's a way to find the volume of a solid, such as a rock.

1. Start with 50 mL of water in a graduated cylinder.
2. Place a small rock in the water. The water level rises.
3. Measure the new water level. Subtract 50 mL from the new reading. The difference is the volume of the rock. Record the volume in cm^3.

Estimating Volume

Once you become familiar with the volumes of liquids and solids, you can estimate volumes. Estimate the amount of liquid in a glass or can. Estimate the volume of an eraser.

Measure Weight/Force

You use a spring scale to measure weight. An object has weight because the force of gravity pulls down on the object. Therefore, weight is a force. Weight is measured in newtons (N) like all forces.

Measure the Weight of an Object

1. Look at your spring scale to see how many newtons it measures. See how the measurements are divided. The spring scale shown here measures up to 5 N. It has a mark for every 0.1 N.

2. Hold the spring scale by the top loop. Put the object to be measured on the bottom hook. If the object will not stay on the hook, place it in a net bag. Then hang the bag from the hook.

3. Let go of the object slowly. It will pull down on a spring inside the scale. The spring is connected to a pointer. The pointer on the spring scale shown here is a small bar.

4. Wait for the pointer to stop moving. Read the number of newtons next to the pointer. This is the object's weight. The mug in the picture weighs 4 N.

More About Spring Scales

You probably weigh yourself by standing on a bathroom scale. This is a spring scale. The force of your body stretches a spring inside the scale. The dial on the scale is probably marked in pounds—the English unit of weight. One pound is equal to about 4.5 newtons.

A bathroom scale, a grocery scale, and a kitchen scale are some other spring scales you may have seen.

Measure Temperature

You use a thermometer to measure temperature—how hot or cold something is. A thermometer is made of a thin tube with colored liquid inside. When the liquid gets warmer, it expands and moves up the tube. When the liquid gets cooler, it contracts and moves down the tube. You may have seen most temperatures measured in degrees Fahrenheit (°F). Scientists measure temperature in degrees Celsius (°C).

°F °C

Water boils

Water freezes

Room temperature

Read a Thermometer

1. Look at the thermometer shown here. It has two scales—a Fahrenheit scale and a Celsius scale.
2. What is the temperature shown on the thermometer? At what temperature does water freeze?

What Is Convection?

1. Fill a large beaker about two-thirds full of cool water. Find the temperature of the water by holding a thermometer in the water. Do not let the bulb at the bottom of the thermometer touch the sides or bottom of the beaker.
2. Keep the thermometer in the water until the liquid in the tube stops moving—about 1 minute. Read and record the temperature in °C.
3. Sprinkle a little fish food on the surface of the water in the beaker. Do not knock the beaker, and most of the food will stay on top.
4. Carefully place the beaker on a hot plate. A hot plate is a small electric stove. Plug in the hot plate, and turn the control knob to a middle setting.
5. After 1 minute measure the temperature of water near the bottom of the beaker. At the same time, a classmate should measure the temperature of water near the top of the beaker. Record these temperatures. Is water near the bottom of the beaker heating up faster than near the top?
6. As the water heats up, notice what happens to the fish food. How do you know that warmer water at the bottom of the beaker rises and cooler water at the top sinks?

R 11

Use Calculators

Sometimes after you make measurements, you have to analyze your data to see what it means. This might involve doing calculations with your data. A calculator helps you do time-consuming calculations.

Find an Average

After you collect a set of measurements, you may want to get an idea of a typical measurement in that set. What if, for example, you are doing a weather project? As part of the project, you are studying rainfall data of a nearby town. The table shows how much rain fell in that town each week during the summer.

Week	Rain (cm)
1	2.0
2	1.4
3	0.0
4	0.5
5	1.2
6	2.5
7	1.8
8	1.4
9	2.4
10	8.6
11	7.5

What if you want to get an idea of how much rain fell during a typical week in the summer? In other words, you want to find the average for the set of data. There are three kinds of averages—mean, median, and mode. Does it matter which one you use?

Find the Mean

The mean is what most people think of when they hear the word *average*. You can use a calculator to find the mean.

1. Make sure the calculator is on.
2. Add the numbers. To add a series of numbers, enter the first number and press ⊞. Repeat until you enter the last number. See the hints below. After your last number, press ⊟. Your total should be 29.3.
3. While entering so many numbers, it's easy to make a mistake and hit the wrong key. If you make a mistake, correct it by pressing the clear entry key, CE. Then continue entering the rest of the numbers.
4. Find the mean by dividing your total by the number of weeks. If 29.3 is displayed, press ÷ ① ① =. Rounded up to one decimal point, your mean should be 2.7.

Hints:

- If the only number to the right of the decimal point is 0, you don't have to enter it into the calculator. To enter 2.0, just press ②.
- If the only number to the left of the decimal point is 0, you don't have to enter it into the calculator. To enter 0.5, just press . ⑤.

Use Technology

Find the Median

The median is the middle number when the numbers are arranged in order of size. When the rainfall measurements are arranged in order of size, they look like this.

0.0
0.5
1.2
1.4   The median is 1.8.
1.4   This number is in
1.8 ———   the middle; there
2.0   are five numbers
2.4   above it and five
2.5   numbers below it.
7.5
8.6

Find the Mode

The mode is the number that occurs most frequently. From the ranked set of data above, you can see that the most frequent number is 1.4. It occurs twice. Here are your three different averages from the same set of data.

Average Weekly Rainfall (cm)

Mean	2.7
Median	1.8
Mode	1.4

Why is the mean so much higher than the median or mode? The mean is affected greatly by the last two weeks when it rained a lot. A typical week for that summer was much drier than either of those last two weeks. The median or mode gives a better idea of rainfall for a typical week.

Find the Mean, Median, and Mode

The table shows the length of 15 peanuts. Find the mean, median, and mode for this set of data. Which do you think best represents a typical peanut?

Peanut	Length (mm)
1	32
2	29
3	30
4	31
5	33
6	26
7	28
8	27
9	29
10	29
11	32
12	31
13	23
14	36
15	31

Find the Percent

Sometimes numbers are given as percents (%). *Percent* literally means "per hundred." For example, 28% means 28 out of 100. What if there are about 14,000 trees in the forest and 28% are over 50 years old? How many of them are over 50 years old? Use your calculator. You want to find 28% of 14,000. Press ⓵④⓪⓪⓪ ⓧ ②⑧%. The answer should be 3,920.

Use Computers

A computer has many uses. The Internet connects your computer to many other computers around the world, so you can collect all kinds of information. You can use a computer to show this information and write reports. Best of all you can use a computer to explore, discover, and learn.

You can also get information from CD-ROMs. They are computer disks that can hold large amounts of information. You can fit a whole encyclopedia on one CD-ROM.

Use Computers for a Project

Here is how one group of students uses computers as they work on a weather project.

1. The students use instruments to measure temperature, wind speed, wind direction, and other parts of the weather. They input this information, or data, into the computer. The students keep the data in a table. This helps them compare the data from one day to the next.

Use Technology

2. The teacher finds out that another group of students in a town 200 kilometers to the west is also doing a weather project. The two groups use the Internet to talk to each other and share data. When a storm happens in the town to the west, that group tells the other group that it's coming their way.

3. The students want to find out more. They decide to stay on the Internet and send questions to a local TV weather forecaster. She has a Web site and answers questions from students every day.

4. Meanwhile some students go to the library to gather more information from a CD-ROM. The CD-ROM has an encyclopedia that includes movie clips. The clips give examples of different kinds of storms.

5. The students have kept all their information in a folder called Weather Project. Now they use that information to write a report about the weather. On the computer they can move around paragraphs, add words, take out words, put in diagrams, and draw weather maps. Then they print the report in color.

Represent Data

Make Graphs to Organize Data

When you do an experiment in science, you collect information. To find out what your information means, you can organize it into graphs. There are many kinds of graphs.

Bar Graphs

A bar graph uses bars to show information. For example, what if you do an experiment by wrapping wire around a nail and connecting the ends of the wire to a battery? The nail then becomes a magnet that can pick up paper clips. The graph shows that the more you wrap the wire around the nail, the more paper clips it picks up. How many paper clips did the nail with 20 coils pick up? With 50 coils?

Pictographs

A pictograph uses symbols, or pictures, to show information. What if you collect information about how much water your family uses each day? The table shows what you find.

You can organize this information into the pictograph shown here. The pictograph has to explain what the symbol on the graph means. In this case each bottle means 20 liters of water. A half bottle means half of 20, or 10 liters of water.

1. Which activity uses the most water?
2. Which activity uses the least water?

Activity	Water Used Each Day (L)
Drinking	10
Showering	180
Bathing	240
Brushing teeth	80
Washing dishes	140
Washing hands	30
Washing clothes	280
Flushing toilet	90

A Family's Daily Use of Water

Drinking	
Showering	
Bathing	
Brushing teeth	
Washing dishes	
Washing hands	
Washing clothes	
Flushing toilet	

= 20 liters of water

Represent Data

Circle Graphs

A circle graph is helpful to show how a complete set of data is divided into parts. The circle graph here shows how water is used in the United States. What is the single largest use of water?

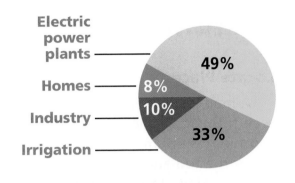

Line Graphs

A line graph shows information by connecting dots plotted on the graph. It shows change over time. For example, what if you measure the temperature out of doors every hour starting at 6 A.M.? The table shows what you find.

Time	Temperature (°C)
6 A.M.	10
7 A.M.	12
8 A.M.	14
9 A.M.	16
10 A.M.	18
11 A.M.	20

You can organize this information into a line graph. Follow these steps.

1. Make a scale along the bottom and side of the graph. The scales should include all the numbers in the chart. Label the scales.

2. Plot points on the graph. For example, place your finger at the "6 A.M." on the bottom line. Place a finger from your other hand on the "10" on the left line. Move your "6 A.M." finger up and your "10" finger to the right until they meet, and make a pencil point. Plot the other points in this way.

3. Connect the points with a line.

The line graph to the right organizes measurements you collected so that you can easily compare them.

1. Between which two weeks did the plant grow most?

2. When did plant growth begin to level off?

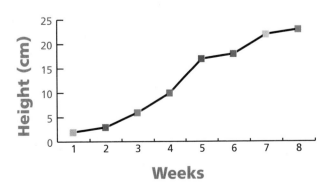

R 17

Represent Data

Make Maps to Show Information

Locate Places

A map is a drawing that shows an area from above. Most maps have coordinates—numbers and letters along the top and side. Coordinates help you find places easily. For example, what if you wanted to find the library on the map? It is located at B4. Place a finger on the letter B along the side of the map, and another finger on the number 4 at the top. Then move your fingers straight across and down the map until they meet. The library is located where the coordinates B and 4 meet, or very nearby.

1. What color building is located at F6?
2. The hospital is located three blocks north and two blocks east of the library. What are its coordinates?
3. Make a map of an area in your community. It might be a park or the area between your home and school. Include coordinates. Use a compass to find north, and mark north on your map. Exchange maps with class-mates, and answer each other's questions.

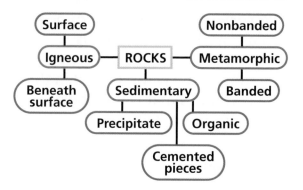

Idea Maps

The map below shows how places are connected to each other. Idea maps, on the other hand, show how ideas are connected to each other. Idea maps help you organize information about a topic.

The idea map above connects ideas about rocks. This map shows that there are three major types of rock—igneous, sedimentary, and metamorphic. Connections to each rock type provide further information. For example, this map reminds you that igneous rocks are classified into those that form at Earth's surface and far beneath it.

Make an idea map about a topic you are learning in science. Your map can include words, phrases, or even sentences. Arrange your map in a way that makes sense to you and helps you understand the ideas.

Make Tables and Charts to Organize Information

Tables help you organize data during experiments. Most tables have columns that run up and down, and rows that run across. The columns and rows have headings that tell you what kind of data goes in each part of the table.

A Sample Table

What if you are going to do an experiment to find out how long different kinds of seeds take to sprout? Before you begin the experiment, you should set up your table. Follow these steps.

1. In this experiment you will plant 20 radish seeds, 20 bean seeds, and 20 corn seeds. Your table must show how many radish seeds, bean seeds, and corn seeds sprouted on days 1, 2, 3, 4, and 5.

2. Make your table with columns, rows, and headings. You might use a computer to make a table. Some computer programs let you build a table with just the click of a mouse. You can delete or add columns and rows if you need to.
3. Give your table a title. Your table could look like the one here.

Make a Table

Now what if you are going to do an experiment to find out how temperature affects the sprouting of seeds? You will plant 20 bean seeds in each of two trays. You will keep each tray at a different temperature, as shown below, and observe the trays for seven days. Make a table you can use for this experiment.

Make a Chart

A chart is simply a table with pictures as well as words to label the rows or columns.

The Skeletal System

The body has a supporting frame, called a skeleton, which is made up of bones. The skeleton has several jobs.

- It gives the body its shape.
- It protects organs in the body.
- It works with muscles to move the body.

Each of the 206 bones of the skeleton is the size and shape best fitted to do its job. For example, long and strong leg bones support the body's weight.

CARE!

- Exercise to keep your skeletal system in good shape.

- Don't overextend your joints.

- Eat foods rich in vitamins and minerals. Your bones need the minerals calcium and phosphorus to grow strong.

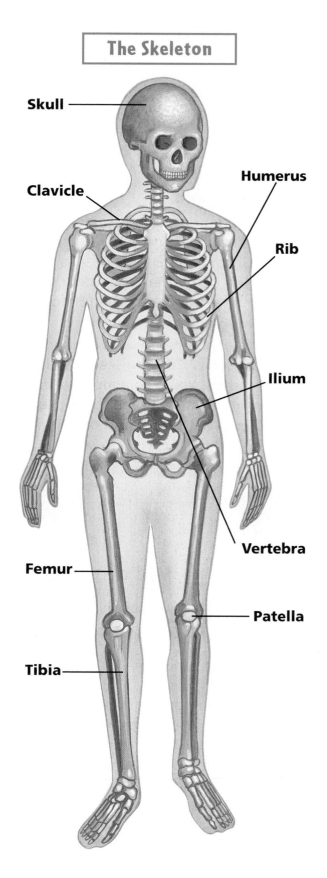

The Skeleton

Skull

Clavicle

Humerus

Rib

Ilium

Vertebra

Femur

Patella

Tibia

Joints

The skeleton has different types of joints. A joint is a place where two or more bones meet. Joints can be classified into three major groups—immovable joints, partly movable joints, and movable joints.

Types of Joints

Immovable Joints

Head

Immovable joints are places where bones fit together too tightly to move. Nearly all the 29 bones in the skull meet at immovable joints. Only the lower jaw can move.

Partly Movable Joints

Partly movable joints are places where bones can move only a little. Ribs are connected to the breastbone with these joints.

Ribs

Breastbone

Movable Joints

Movable joints are places where bones can move easily.

Gliding joint

Hand and wrist

Small bones in the wrists and ankles meet at gliding joints. The bones can slide against one another. These joints allow some movement in all directions.

The hips are examples of ball-and-socket joints. The ball of one bone fits into the socket, or cup, of another bone. These joints allow bones to move back and forth, in a circle, and side to side.

Ball-and-socket joint

Hip

Hinge joint

Knee

The knees are hinge joints. A hinge joint is similar to a door hinge. It allows bones to move back and forth in one direction.

The joint between the skull and neck is a pivot joint. It allows the head to move up and down, and side to side.

Pivot joint

Neck

The Muscular System

Three types of muscles make up the body—skeletal muscle, cardiac muscle, and smooth muscle.

The muscles that are attached to and move bones are called skeletal muscles. These muscles are attached to bones by a tough cord called a tendon. Skeletal muscles pull bones to move them. Muscles do not push bones.

Cardiac muscles are found in only one place in the body—the heart. The walls of the heart are made of strong cardiac muscles. When cardiac muscles contract, they squeeze blood out of the heart. When cardiac muscles relax, the heart fills with more blood.

Smooth muscles make up internal organs and blood vessels. Smooth muscles in the lungs help a person breathe. Those in the blood vessels help control blood flow around the body.

CARE!

- Exercise to strengthen your muscles.
- Eat the right foods.
- Get plenty of rest.
- Never take steroids unless your doctor tells you to.

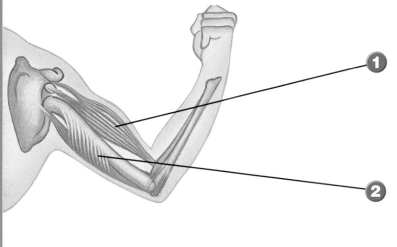

1 A message from you brain causes this muscle, called the biceps (BIGH·seps), to contract. When a muscle contracts, it becomes shorter and thicker. As the biceps contacts, it pulls on the arm bone it is attached to.

2 Most muscles work in pairs to move bones. This muscle, called the triceps (TRIGH·seps), relaxes when the biceps contacts. When a muscle relaxes, it becomes longer and thinner.

3 To straighten your arm, a message from your brain causes the triceps to contract. When the triceps contracts, it pulls on the bone it is attached to.

4 As the triceps contracts, the biceps relaxes. Your arm straightens.

The Circulatory System

The circulatory system consists of the heart, blood vessels, and blood. Circulation is the flow of blood through the body. Blood is a liquid that contains red blood cells, white blood cells, and platelets. Red blood cells carry oxygen and nutrients to cells. White blood cells work to fight germs that enter the body. Platelets are cell fragments that make the blood clot.

The heart is a muscular organ about the size of a fist. It beats about 70 to 90 times a minute, pumping blood through the blood vessels. Arteries carry blood away from the heart. Some arteries carry blood to the lungs, where the cells pick up oxygen. Other arteries carry oxygen-rich blood from the lungs to all other parts of the body. Veins carry blood from other parts of the body back to the heart. Blood in most veins carries the wastes released by cells and has little oxygen. Blood flows from arteries to veins through narrow vessels called capillaries.

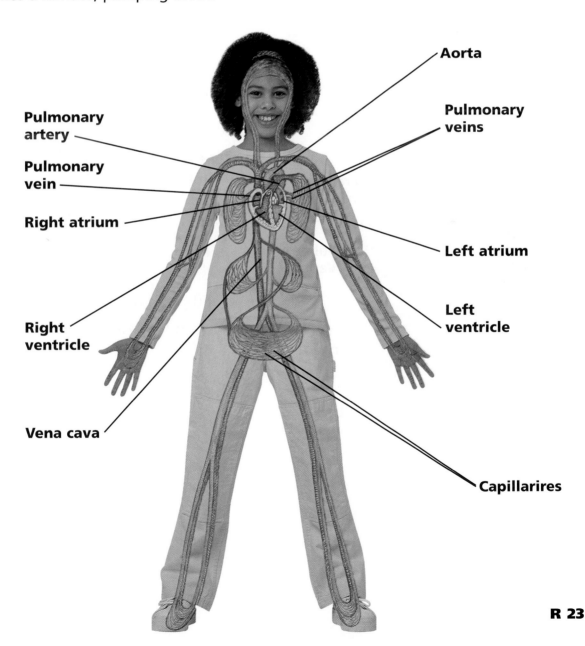

Aorta

Pulmonary artery

Pulmonary veins

Pulmonary vein

Right atrium

Left atrium

Right ventricle

Left ventricle

Vena cava

Capillarires

R 23

The Heart

The heart has two sides, right and left, separated by a thick muscular wall. Each side has two chambers for blood. The upper chamber is the atrium. The lower chamber is the ventricle. Blood enters the heart through the vena cava. It leaves the heart through the aorta.

The pulmonary artery carries blood from the body into the lungs. Here carbon dioxide leaves the blood to be exhaled by the lungs. Fresh oxygen enters the blood to be carried to every cell in the body. Blood returns from the lungs to the heart through the pulmonary veins.

CARE!

- Don't smoke. The nicotine in tobacco makes the heart beat faster and work harder to pump blood.

- Never take illegal drugs, such as cocaine or heroin. They can damage the heart and cause heart failure.

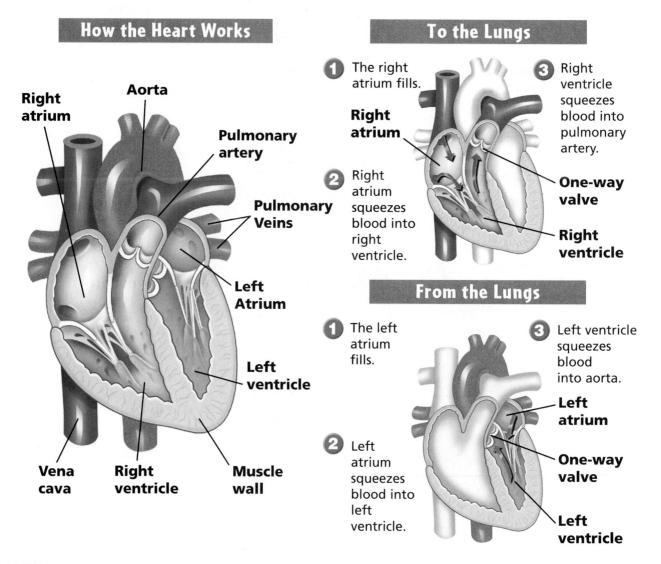

How the Heart Works

Right atrium
Aorta
Pulmonary artery
Pulmonary Veins
Left Atrium
Left ventricle
Vena cava
Right ventricle
Muscle wall

To the Lungs

1 The right atrium fills.

Right atrium

2 Right atrium squeezes blood into right ventricle.

3 Right ventricle squeezes blood into pulmonary artery.

One-way valve

Right ventricle

From the Lungs

1 The left atrium fills.

3 Left ventricle squeezes blood into aorta.

Left atrium

2 Left atrium squeezes blood into left ventricle.

One-way valve

Left ventricle

The Respiratory System

The process of getting and using oxygen in the body is called respiration. When a person inhales, air is pulled into the nose or mouth. The air travels down into the trachea. In the chest the trachea divides into two bronchial tubes. One bronchial tube enters each lung. Each bronchial tube branches into smaller tubes called bronchioles.

At the end of each bronchiole are tiny air sacs called alveoli. The alveoli exchange carbon dioxide for oxygen.

Oxygen comes from the air a person breathes. Two main muscles control breathing. One is located between the ribs. The other is a dome-shaped sheet of muscle called the diaphragm.

To inhale, the diaphragm contracts and pulls down. Other muscles pull the ribs up and out. This makes more room in the chest. Air rushes into the lungs and fills the space.

To exhale, the diaphragm relaxes and returns to its dome shape. The lungs get smaller and force the air out.

CARE!

- **Don't smoke. Smoking damages your respiratory system.**

- **Exercise to strengthen your breathing muscles.**

- **If you ever have trouble breathing, tell an adult at once.**

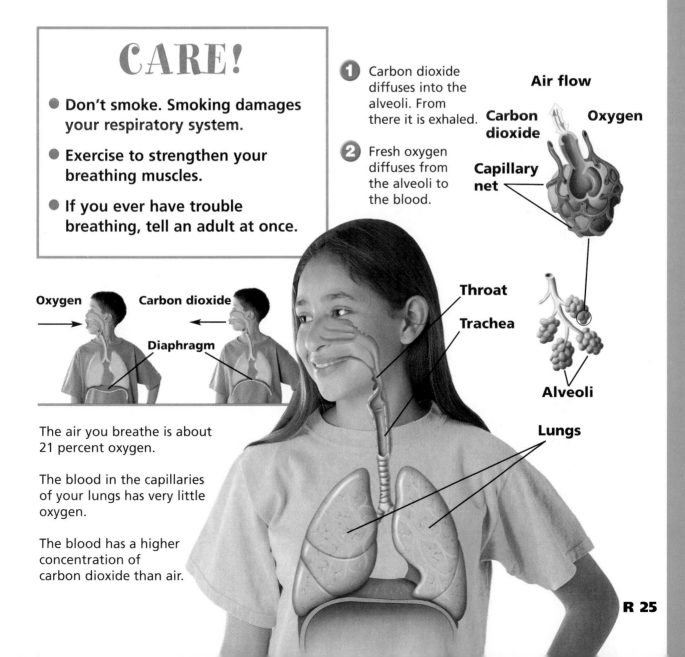

① Carbon dioxide diffuses into the alveoli. From there it is exhaled.

② Fresh oxygen diffuses from the alveoli to the blood.

Air flow

Carbon dioxide   **Oxygen**

Capillary net

Oxygen   **Carbon dioxide**

Diaphragm

Throat

Trachea

Alveoli

Lungs

The air you breathe is about 21 percent oxygen.

The blood in the capillaries of your lungs has very little oxygen.

The blood has a higher concentration of carbon dioxide than air.

Activity Pyramid

Physical fitness is the condition in which the body is healthy and works the best it can. It involves working the skeletal muscles, bones, joints, heart, and respiratory system.

Occasionally
Inactive pastimes such as watching TV, playing board games, talking on the phone

2–3 times a week Leisure activities such as gardening, golf, softball

3–5 times a week Aerobic activities such as swimming, biking, climbing; sports activities such as basketball, handball

Daily Substitute activity for inactivity—take the stairs, walk instead of riding, bike instead of taking the bus

The activity pyramid shows you the kinds of exercises and other activities you should be doing to make your body more physically fit.

CARE!

- Stay active every day.
- Eat a balanced diet.
- Drink plenty of water—6 to 8 large glasses a day.

Food Guide Pyramid

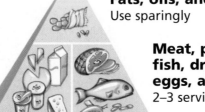

Fats, oils, and sweets
Use sparingly

Milk, yogurt, and cheese group
2–3 servings

Meat, poultry, fish, dry beans, eggs, and nuts group
2–3 servings

Vegetable group
3–5 servings

Fruit group
2–4 servings

Bread, cereal, rice, and pasta group
6–11 servings

The Digestive System

Digestion is the process of breaking down food into simple substances the body can use. Digestion begins when a person chews food. Chewing breaks the food down into smaller pieces and moistens it with saliva. Saliva is produced by the salivary glands.

Digested food is absorbed in the small intestine. The walls of the small intestine are lined with villi. Villi are tiny fingerlike projections that absorb digested food. From the villi the blood transports nutrients to every part of the body.

CARE!

● Chew your food well.

● Drink plenty of water to help move food through your digestive system.

The shape of the small intestine's villi increases the amount of nutrients that can be absorbed from the food.

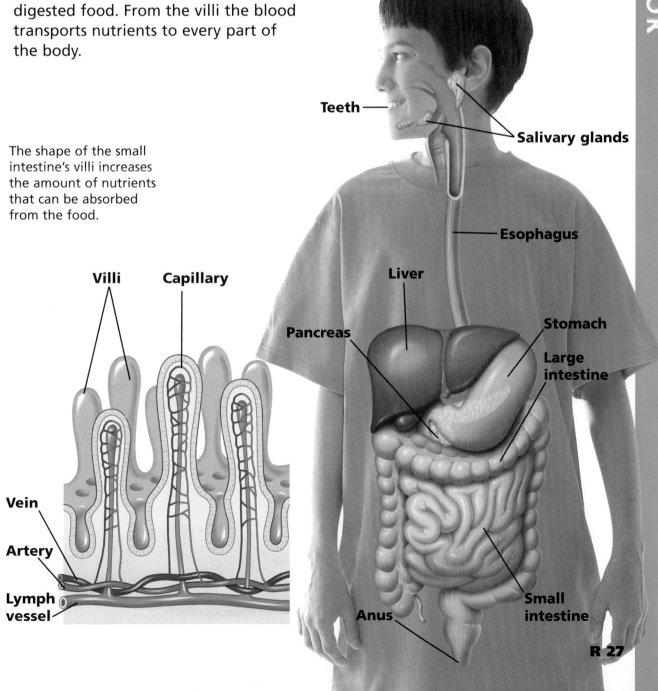

Villi   Capillary

Vein

Artery

Lymph vessel

Teeth

Salivary glands

Esophagus

Liver

Pancreas

Stomach

Large intestine

Anus

Small intestine

The Excretory System

Excretion is the process of removing waste products from the body. The liver filters wastes from the blood and converts them into urea. Urea is then carried to the kidneys for excretion. Each kidney contains more than a million nephrons. Nephrons are structures in the kidneys that filter blood.

The skin takes part in excretion when a person sweats. Glands in the inner layer of the skin produce sweat. Sweat is mostly water. Sweat tastes salty because it contains mineral salts the body doesn't need. There is also a tiny amount of urea in sweat.

Sweat is excreted by the sweat glands onto the outer layer of the skin. There it evaporates into the air. Evaporation takes place in part because of body heat. When sweat evaporates, a person feels cooler. On hot days or when exercising, a person sweats more to keep the body from overheating.

How You Sweat

Glands under your skin push sweat up to the surface, where it collects.

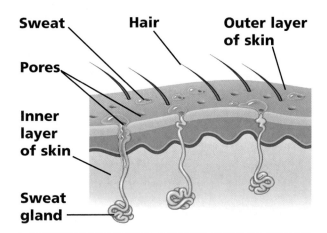

Sweat · Hair · Outer layer of skin · Pores · Inner layer of skin · Sweat gland

How Your Kidneys Work

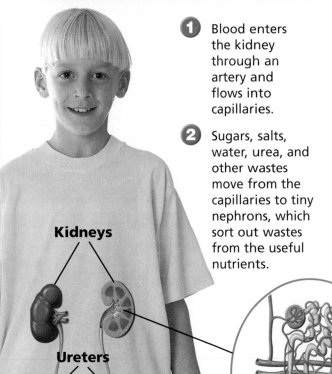

Kidneys · Ureters · Bladder · Urethra · Artery · Vein · Capillaries

1. Blood enters the kidney through an artery and flows into capillaries.

2. Sugars, salts, water, urea, and other wastes move from the capillaries to tiny nephrons, which sort out wastes from the useful nutrients.

3. The nutrients return to the blood and flow back out through veins.

4. Urea and other wastes become urine, which flows down the ureters.

5. Urine is stored in the bladder and excreted through the urethra.

CARE!

- Drink plenty of water to help the kidneys do their job and to replace water loss from sweating.

- Wash regularly to avoid body odor, clogged pores, and skin irritation.

The Nervous System

The nervous system has two parts. The brain and the spinal cord are the central nervous system. All other nerves are the outer, or peripheral, nervous system.

The largest part of the brain is the cerebrum. A deep groove separates the right half, or hemisphere, of the cerebrum from the left half. Both the right and left hemispheres of the cerebrum contain control centers for the senses.

The cerebellum lies below the cerebrum. It coordinates the skeletal muscles so they work smoothly together. It also helps in keeping balance.

The brain stem connects to the spinal cord. The lowest part of the brain stem is the medulla. It controls heartbeat, breathing, blood pressure, and the muscles in the digestive system.

Cerebrum — Movement, Reason, Touch, Speech, Hearing, Taste, Smell, Vision, Balance
Heartbeat, Breathing
Cerebellum
Medulla

Parts of a Neuron

The nerves in the nervous system are made up of nerve cells called neurons. Each neuron has three main parts—a cell body, dendrites, and an axon. Dendrites are branching nerve fibers that carry impulses, or electrical signals, toward the cell body. An axon is a nerve fiber that carries impulses away from the cell body.

When an impulse reaches the tip of an axon, it must cross a tiny gap to reach the next neuron. This gap between neurons is called a synapse.

Cell body   Dendrites   Axon
Fatty covering   Synapse   Impulse

Brain
Skull
Spinal cord
Nerves
Vertebral column
Spinal cord

CARE!

- Wear protective headgear when you play sports or exercise.

- Stay away from drugs, such as stimulants, which can speed up the nervous system.

- Stay away from alcohol, which is a depressant and slows down the nervous system.

R 29

The Senses

Seeing

Retina **Cornea** **Pupil** **Lens** **Iris** **Optic nerve**

Light reflected from an object enters the eye and falls on the retina. Receptor cells change the light into electrical signals, or impulses. These impulses travel along the optic nerve to the vision center of the brain.

1 Light reflects off the tree and into your eyes.

4 Receptor cells on your retina change the light into electrical signals.

2 The light passes through your cornea and the pupil in your iris.

3 Your eye bends the light so it hits your retina.

5 The impulses travel along neurons in your optic nerve to the seeing center of your brain.

Hearing

Sound waves enter the ear and cause the eardrum to vibrate. Receptor cells in the ear change the sound waves into impulses that travel along the auditory nerve to the hearing center of the brain.

1 Your outer ear collects sound waves.

Hammer **Anvil**

6 Receptor cells inside your cochlea change.

Stirrup **Cochlea** **Auditory nerve**

Semicircular canals

2 They are funneled down your ear canal.

3 The eardrum vibrates.

4 Three tiny ear bones vibrate.

5 The cochlea vibrates.

Hearing center

7 The impulses travel along your auditory nerve to the brain's hearing center.

CARE!

- **To avoid straining your eye muscles, don't sit too close to the TV screen or computer monitor.**

- **Avoid loud music. Turn down the volume when wearing headphones.**

The Senses

Smelling

The sense of smell is really the ability to detect chemicals in the air. When a person breathes, chemicals dissolve in mucus in the upper part of the nose. When the chemicals come in contact with receptor cells, the cells send impulses along the olfactory nerve to the smelling center of the brain.

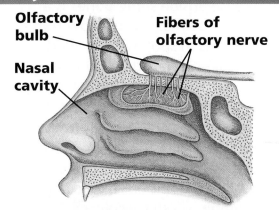

Olfactory bulb

Fibers of olfactory nerve

Nasal cavity

Tasting

When a person eats, chemicals in food dissolve in saliva. Saliva carries the chemicals to taste buds on the tongue. Inside each taste bud are receptors that can sense the four main tastes—sweet, sour, salty, and bitter. The receptors send impulses along a nerve to the taste center of the brain. The brain identifies the taste of the food, which is usually a combination of the four main tastes.

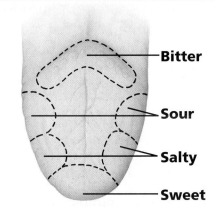

Bitter

Sour

Salty

Sweet

Touching

Receptor cells in the skin help a person tell hot from cold, wet from dry, and the light touch of a feather from the pressure of stepping on a stone. Each receptor cell sends impulses along sensory nerves to the spinal cord. The spinal cord then sends the impulses to the touch center of the brain.

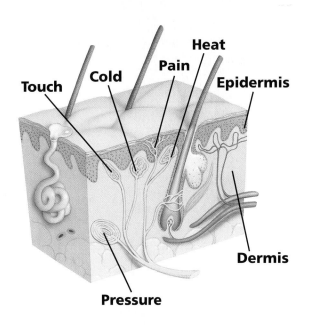

Touch   Cold   Pain   Heat   Epidermis

Dermis

Pressure

CARE!

- To prevent the spread of germs, always cover your mouth and nose when you cough or sneeze.

The Immune System

The immune system helps the body fight disease. Inside some bones is a soft tissue known as red marrow that fills the spaces in spongy bone. Red marrow makes new red blood cells, platelets that stop a cut from bleeding, and germ-fighting white blood cells.

There are white blood cells in the blood vessels and in the lymph vessels. Lymph vessels are similar to blood vessels. Instead of blood, they carry lymph. Lymph is a straw-colored fluid surrounding body cells.

Lymph nodes filter out harmful materials in lymph. Like red marrow, they also produce white blood cells to fight infections. Swollen lymph nodes in the neck are a clue that the body is fighting germs.

Lymph vessels

Lymph nodes

Lymph node

Lymph vessels

CARE!

● Be sure to get immunized against common diseases.

● Keep cuts clean to prevent infection.

1 A bone is covered with a tough but thin membrane that has many small blood vessels. The blood vessels bring nutrients and oxygen to the living parts of the bone and remove wastes.

2 Inside some bones is a soft tissue known as marrow. Yellow marrow is made mostly of fat cells and is one of the body's energy reserves. It is usually found in the long, hollow spaces of long bones.

3 Part of the bone is compact, or solid. It is made up of living bone cells and nonliving materials. The nonliving part is made up of layers of hardened minerals such as calcium and phosphorus. In between the mineral layers are living bone cells.

4 Red marrow fills the spaces in spongy bone. Red marrow makes new red blood cells, germ-fighting white blood cells, and cell fragments that stop a cut from bleeding.

5 Part of the bone is made of bone tissue that looks like a dry sponge. It is made of strong, hard tubes. It is also found in the middle of short, flat bones.

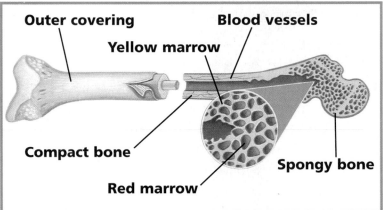

Outer covering　　**Blood vessels**

Yellow marrow

Compact bone

Red marrow

Spongy bone

The Endocrine System

Hormones are chemicals that control body functions. A gland that produces hormones is called an endocrine gland. Sweat from sweat glands flows out of tubes called ducts. Endocrine glands have no ducts.

The endocrine glands are scattered around the body. Each gland makes one or more hormones. Every hormone seeks out a target organ, the place in the body where the hormone acts.

CARE!

● Doctors can treat many diseases, such as diabetes, caused by endocrine glands that produce too little or too much of a hormone.

Some Glands in the Endocrine System

- Hypothalamus
- Pituitary gland
- Parathyroid gland
- Thyroid gland
- Adrenal glands
- Pancreas
- Ovaries
- Testes

The Reproductive System

The testes are the male reproductive organs. At puberty the testes begin to produce sperm. Sperm move through sperm ducts, where they mix with fluid from endocrine glands.

The ovaries are the female reproductive organs, which contain eggs. After puberty one mature egg is released about once every 28 days. The egg moves to the oviduct, a narrow tube leading from the ovary.

CARE!

- **Abstinence is the only sure way to avoid sexually transmitted diseases.**

The Male Reproductive System

Sperm move from the testes through sperm ducts, where they mix with fluid from the glands. The sperm and fluid move through the urethra, a tube that leads out through the penis.

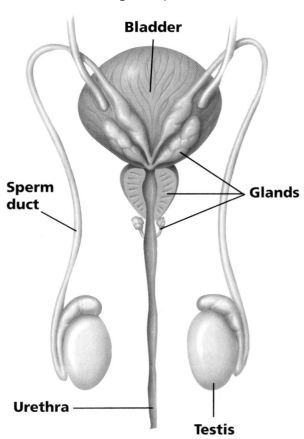

Bladder

Sperm duct

Glands

Urethra

Testis

The Female Reproductive System

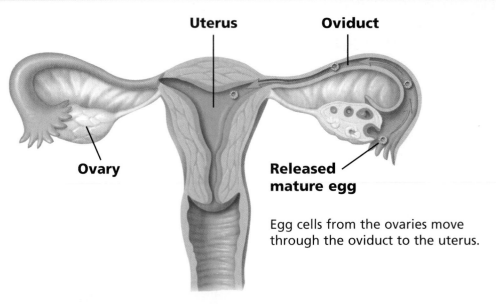

Uterus

Oviduct

Ovary

Released mature egg

Egg cells from the ovaries move through the oviduct to the uterus.

Glossary

This Glossary will help you to pronounce and understand the meanings of the Science Words introduced in this book. The page number at the end of the definition tells where the word appears.

A

abiotic factor (ā′bī ot′ik fak′tər) A nonliving part of an ecosystem. (p. B6)

absorption (əb sôrp′shən) The disappearance of a sound wave into a surface. (p. F66)

abyssal plain (ə bis′əl plān) The vast flat lands beyond the continental shelf that cover almost half of the deep ocean floor. (p. C90)

acceleration (ak sel′ə rā′shən) Change in velocity with respect to time. (pp. F13, F22)

acid (as′id) A substance that tastes sour and turns blue litmus paper red. (p. E82)

acid rain (as′id rān) Moisture that falls to Earth after being mixed with wastes from burned fossil fuels. (p. C65)

acidity (ə sid′ə tē) The strength of an acid. (p. E86)

action (ak′shən) The force one object applies to a second, as in Newton's third law of motion, which states, "For every action, there is an equal but opposite reaction." *See* **reaction**. (p. F24)

adaptation (ad′əp tā′shən) A characteristic that enables a living thing to survive in its environment. (pp. A82, A106, B52)

aerial root (âr′ē əl rüt) A root that never touches the ground but can take in moisture from the air. (p. A21)

aerosol (âr′ə sōl′) A type of colloid in which liquid drops or solid particles are spread throughout a gas. (p. E60)

air mass (âr mas) A large region of the atmosphere where the air has similar properties throughout. (p. D54)

air pressure (âr presh′ər) The force put on a given area by the weight of the air above it. (p. D11)

alkalinity (al′kə lin′i tē) The strength of a base. (p. E86)

alternation of generations (ôl′tər nā′shən uv jen′ə rā′shənz) The process in which offspring are reproduced sexually, their offspring are reproduced asexually, and so on. (p. A53)

alternative energy source (ōl tûr′nə tiv en′ər jē sôrs) A source of energy other than the burning of a fossil fuel. (p. C104)

PRONUNCIATION KEY

The following symbols are used throughout the McGraw-Hill Science 2002 Glossaries.

a	at	e	end	o	hot	u	up	hw	white	ə	about
ā	ape	ē	me	ō	old	ū	use	ng	song		taken
ä	far	i	it	ôr	fork	ü	rule	th	thin		pencil
âr	care	ī	ice	oi	oil	ù	pull	th	this		lemon
ô	law	îr	pierce	ou	out	ûr	turn	zh	measure		circus

′ = primary accent; shows which syllable takes the main stress, such as **kil** in **kilogram** (kil′ə gram′).

′ = secondary accent; shows which syllables take lighter stresses, such as **gram** in **kilogram**.

ammonia (ə mōn'yə) A compound that contains the element nitrogen and is used as a fertilizer. (p. B34)

anemometer (an'ə mom'i tər) A device that measures wind speed. (p. D44)

aneroid barometer (an'ə roid bə rom'i tər) A spring enclosed in a pleated metal can that expands or contracts to indicate changes in air pressure. (p. D12)

angiosperm (an'jē ə spûrm') A seed plant that produces flowers. *See* **gymnosperm**. (p. A58)

aquifer (ak'wə fər) An underground layer of rock or soil filled with water. (p. C75)

asexual reproduction (a sek'shü əl rē'prō duk'shən) The production of a new organism from only one cell. (p. A52)

atmosphere (at'məs fîr') The blanket of gases that surrounds Earth. (pp. C12, D10)

atom (at'əm) The smallest unit of an element that retains the properties of that element. *See* **molecule**. (p. E26)

aurora (ə rôr'ə) The northern or southern lights that appear in the night sky, especially in polar regions. (p. D10)

aurum (ôr'əm) The Latin word for *gold*. (p. E23)

B

bacterium (bak tîr'ē əm) *sing., n. pl.* **bacteria** (-ē ə) A member of either of two kingdoms of one-celled living things that have no nucleus, or center, in their cell body. (p. A15)

balanced forces (bal'ənst fôrs'əz) Forces that cancel each other out when acting together on a single object. (p. F21)

barometer (bə rom'i tər) A device for measuring air pressure. (p. D12)

base (bās) A substance that tastes bitter and turns red litmus paper blue. (p. E82)

basin (bās'in) The floor of an ocean, containing mountains, valleys, and plains. (p. C84)

Beaufort scale (bō'fərt skāl) A system for measuring wind speed by observing its effect on the surface of the sea, using a scale of 0 (low) to 12 (high) for each effect. (p. D44)

bench mark (bench'märk') A plaque left by surveyors to tell the exact location and elevation of a place. (p. C18)

benthos (ben'thos) Organisms that live on the bottom in aquatic ecosystems. (p. B72)

biomass (bī'ō mas') Energy from plant matter or animal waste. (p. C106)

biome (bī'ōm) One of Earth's large ecosystems, with its own kind of climate, soil, plants, and animals. (p. B64)

biotic factor (bī ot'ik fak'tər) A living part of an ecosystem. (p. B7)

boiling point (boil'ing point) The particular temperature for each substance at which it changes state from a liquid to a gas. (p. E37)

buoyancy (boi'ən sē) The upward push of a liquid on an object placed in it. (p. E12)

C

cambium (kam'bē əm) The layer in plants that separates the xylem from the phloem. (p. A21)

camouflage (kam'ə fläzh') An adaptation in which an animal protects itself against predators by blending in with the environment. (p. A108)

carbon cycle (kär'bən sī'kəl) The continuous exchange of carbon dioxide and oxygen among living things. (p. B37)

carnivore (kär'nə vôr') An animal that eats another animal. (p. B20)

chemical change (kem'i kəl chānj) A change of matter that occurs when atoms link together in a new way, creating a new substance different from the original substances. (p. E71)

chemical formula (kəm'i kəl fôr'myə lə) A way to write a compound's name using symbols. The letters tell what elements are in the compound, and the subscripts tell the number of particles in the compound. (p. E25)

chemical reaction (kem'i kəl rē ak'shən) Another name for chemical change. (p. E71)

chemosynthesis (kē'mō sin'thə sis) In tube worms the process by which bacteria create nutrients from hydrogen sulfide and oxygen, using chemical reactions rather than light. (p. C93)

chlorophyll (klôr'ə fil') A green chemical in plant cells that allows plants to use the Sun's energy for making food. (pp. A6, A32)

chloroplast (klôr'ə plast') The part of a plant cell containing chlorophyll, the green substance that enables the plant to produce food. (p. A24)

cirrus cloud (sir'əs kloud) A high-altitude cloud with a featherlike shape, made of ice crystals. (p. D24)

classification (klas'ə fi kā'shən) The science of finding patterns among living things. (p. A8)

classification key (klas'ə fi kā'shən kē) A series of paired choices describing organisms that is arranged in a way that leads to the identity of a given organism. (p. A100)

classify (klas'ə fi) To place things that share properties together in groups. (p. S7)

cleavage (klē'vij) The tendency of a mineral to break along flat surfaces. (p. C34)

climate (klī'mit) The average weather pattern of a region. (p. D82)

climate zone (klī mat' zōn) A region that has similar weather patterns based on temperature, precipitation, wind, distance from a coast, mountain ranges, ocean currents, and vegetation. (p. D82)

climax community (klī'maks kə mū'ni tē) The final stage of succession in an area, unless a major change happens. (p. B84)

cold front (kōld frunt) A front where cold air moves in under a warm air mass. (p. D56)

colloid (kol'oid) A special type of mixture in which the particles of one material are scattered through another and block the passage of light without settling out. (pp. E54, E60)

commensalism (kə men'sə liz'əm) A relationship between two kinds of organisms that benefits one without harming the other. (p. B57)

communicate (kə mü'ni kāt') To share information. (p. S7)

community (kə mü'ni tē) All the living things in an ecosystem. (p. B10)

complete flower (kəm plēt' flou'ər) A flower that has sepals, petals, stamens, and pistils. (p. A70)

compound (kom'pound) Any substance that is formed by the chemical combination of two or more elements and acts like a single substance. (p. E24)

compression (kəm presh'ən) **1.** The part of a sound wave where molecules are crowded together. (p. F51) **2.** A movement of plates that presses together or squeezes Earth's crust. (p. C20)

concave lens (kon kāv' lenz) A lens that is thicker at the edges than at the middle. As it curves inward, it spreads light rays apart, making images appear smaller. (p. F100)

PRONUNCIATION KEY

a **a**t; ā **a**pe; ä **f**ar; âr **c**are; ô **l**aw; e **e**nd; ē **m**e; i **i**t; ī **i**ce; îr **pi**erce; o **h**ot; ō **o**ld; ôr **f**ork; oi **oi**l; ou **ou**t; u **u**p; ū **u**se; ü **r**ule; ů **p**ull; ûr **t**urn; hw **wh**ite; ng so**ng**; th **th**in; th **th**is; zh mea**s**ure; ə **a**bout, tak**e**n, penc**i**l, lem**o**n, circ**u**s

concave mirror (kon kāv′ mir′ər) A mirror that curves in on the shiny side. (p. F88)

condensation (kon′den sā′shən) *n.* The changing of a gas into a liquid. (pp. B32, D17) —**condense** (kən dens′) *v.* (p. E37)

conduction (kən duk′shən) *n.* The passing of heat through a material while the material itself stays in place. (p. E97) —**conduct** (kən dukt′) *v.* (p. E14)

conifer (kon′ə fər) Any of a group of gymnosperms that produce seeds in cones and have needlelike leaves. (p. A59)

conserve (kən′sûrv′) To save, protect, or use resources wisely. (p. C39)

constellation (kon′stə lā′shən) Any of the patterns formed by groups of stars in the night sky. To people in the past, these patterns looked like pictures of animals or people. (p. C14)

consumer (kən sü′mər) Any animal that eats plants or eats other plant-eating animals. (pp. B7, B20)

continental rise (kon′tə nen′təl rīz) A buildup of sediment on the sea floor at the bottom of the continental slope. It is a zone of sand and mud that stretches from the slope down to the deep-sea floor. (p. C90)

continental shelf (kon′tə nen′təl shelf) The underwater edge of a continent. (p. C90)

continental slope (kon′tə nen′təl slōp) The steep slope leading down from the continental shelf toward the sea floor. (p. C90)

contour plowing (kon′tür plou′ing) Preventing erosion by plowing across rather than up and down a slope. (p. C51)

contract (*v.,* kən trakt′) To shrink, as when a material gets colder. (p. E41)

convection (kən vek′shən) The flow of heat through a liquid or a gas, causing hot parts to rise and cooler parts to sink. (p. E97)

convection cell (kən vek′shən sel) A circular pattern of air rising, air sinking, and wind. (p. D38)

convex lens (kon veks′ lenz) A lens that is thicker at the middle than at the edges. As it curves outward, it brings light together, making images appear larger. (p. F100)

convex mirror (kon veks′ mir′ər) A mirror that curves out on the shiny side. (p. F88)

coquina (kō kē′nə) A sedimentary rock formed from seashell fragments. (p. C44)

Coriolis effect (kôr′ē ō′lis i fekt′) The curving of the path of a moving object caused by Earth's rotation. (p. D40)

cortex (kôr′teks) The layer of tissue just inside the epidermis of a plant's roots and stems. (p. A20)

cotyledon (ko′tə lē′dən) A tiny leaflike structure, also called a seedleaf, inside the seed of an angiosperm. (p. A62)

crop rotation (krop rō tā′shən) Growing different crops each year so that the soil does not use up the same kinds of minerals year after year. (p. C51)

crossbreeding (krôs′brēd′ing) Producing offspring by mating individuals from two distinct breeds or varieties of the same species. (p. A112)

cross-pollination (krôs′pol′ə nā′shən) The transfer of pollen from one flower to another. (p. A72)

crust (krust) The rocky surface that makes up the top of the lithosphere and includes the continents and the ocean floor. (p. C12)

crystal (kris′təl) The geometric shape a mineral forms when its atoms and molecules get into fixed patterns. (p. C32)

cumulus cloud (kū′myə ləs kloud) A puffy cloud that appears to rise up from a flat bottom. (p. D24)

current (kûr′ənt) An ocean movement; a large stream of water that flows in the ocean. (p. C86)

cycad (sī′kad) One of the evergreen gymnosperms that resemble palms and have seed-bearing cones. (p. A59)

decibel (dB) (des′ə bel′) A unit that measures loudness. (p. F58)

deciduous (di sij′ü əs) Said of a plant that loses its leaves each fall. *See* **evergreen.** (pp. A59, B70)

deciduous forest (di si′jə wəs fôr′ist) A forest biome with many kinds of trees that lose their leaves each autumn. (p. B70)

decomposer (dē′kəm pōz′ər) Any of the fungi or bacteria that break down dead plants and animals into useful things like minerals and rich soil. (pp. B7, B21, B34)

define based on observations (di fīn′ bāst ôn ob′zər vā′shənz) To put together a description that relies on examination and experience. (p. S7)

density (den′si tē) A measure of how tightly packed the matter in an object is. (pp. C35, E8)

deposition (dep′ə zish′ən) The dropping off of bits of eroded rock. (p. C25)

desalination (dē sal′ə nā′shən) Getting fresh water from seawater. (p. C73)

desert (dez′ərt) A sandy or rocky biome, with little precipitation and little plant life. (p. B69)

dicot (dī′kot′) An angiosperm with two cotyledons in each seed. *See* **monocot.** (p. A62)

dinoflagellate (din′ə flaj′ə lāt′) A protist containing chlorophyll that has two flagella for motion. When they overreproduce, they can cause "red tides." (p. A14)

distillation (dis′tə lā′shən) The process of separating the parts of a mixture by evaporation and condensation. (p. E64)

diversity (di vûr′si tē) A wide variety of traits in individuals from the same population. (p. A114)

Doppler effect (dop′lər i fekt′) The change in frequency (and pitch) as a source of sound moves toward or away from you. (p. F71)

downdraft (doun′draft′) A downward rush of air caused by the falling of rain during a thunderstorm. (pp. D38, D67)

echo (e′kō) A reflected sound wave. (p. F68)

echolocation (ek′ō lō kā′shən) Finding an object by using reflected sound. (p. F70)

ecological succession (ek′ə loj′i kəl sək sesh′ən) The gradual replacement of one community by another. (p. B82)

ecology (ē kol′ə jē) The study of how living and nonliving things interact. (p. B6)

ecosystem (ek′ō sis′təm) All the living and nonliving things in an environment, including their interactions with each other. (p. B6)

electromagnetic spectrum (i lek′trō mag net′ik spek′trəm) All the wavelengths of visible and invisible light in order, from short (gamma rays) to long (radio). (p. F119)

electromagnetism (i lek′trō mag′ni tiz′əm) The production of magnetism by electricity (and the production of electricity by magnets). (p. F118)

electron (i lek′tron) A particle in the space outside the nucleus of an atom that carries one unit of negative electric charge. (p. E27)

element (el′ə mənt) A pure substance that cannot be broken down into any simpler substances. (p. E22)

PRONUNCIATION KEY

a at; ā ape; ä far; âr care; ô law; e end; ē me; i it; ī ice; îr pierce; o hot; ō old; ôr fork; oi oil; ou out; u up; ū use; ü rule; ù pull; ûr turn; hw white; ng song; th thin; <u>th</u> this; zh measure; ə about, taken, pencil, lemon, circus

elevation (el′ə vā′shən) The height of a place above sea level. (p. C18)

embryo (em′brē ō′) The immature plant inside a seed. (p. A74)

emulsion (i mul′shən) A type of colloid in which one liquid is spread throughout another. (p. E60)

epidermis (ep′i dûr′mis) An outermost layer of such plant parts as roots and leaves. (p. A20)

erosion (i rō′zhən) The picking up and carrying away of pieces of rocks. (p. C22)

evaporation (i vap′ə rā′shən) The slow changing of a liquid into a gas. (pp. B32, D16, E38)

evergreen (ev′ər grēn′) Said of a gymnosperm that keeps its leaves for at least a few years. See **deciduous**. (p. A59)

expand (ek spand′) To spread out, as when a material gets hotter. (p. E41)

experiment (ek sper′ə ment′) To perform a test to support or disprove a hypothesis. (p. S7)

F

fault (fôlt) A crack in Earth's crust whose sides show evidence of motion. (p. C18)

fault-block mountain (fôlt blok moun′tən) A mountain formed by blocks of Earth's crust moving along a fault. (p. C21)

fertilization (fûr′tə lə zā′shən) The joining of a sperm cell with an egg cell to make one new cell, a fertilized egg. (pp. A52, A73)

fertilizer (fûr′tə lī′zər) A substance used to add minerals to the soil. (p. B34)

fibrous root (fī′brəs rüt) One of the many hairy branching roots that some plants have. (p. A21)

filament (fil′ə mənt) The wire in a light bulb that gives off light and heat. (p. E92)

foam (fōm) A type of colloid in which a gas is spread throughout a liquid. (p. E60)

fog (fôg) A cloud that forms at ground level. (p. D24)

fold mountain (fōld moun′tən) A mountain made up mostly of rock layers folded by being squeezed together. (p. C20)

food chain (füd chān) The path of the energy in food from one organism to another. (p. B18)

food web (füd web) The overlapping food chains in an ecosystem. (p. B20)

force (fôrs) A push or pull exerted by one object on another, causing a change in motion. (p. F6)

form a hypothesis (fôrm ə hī poth′ə sis) To make a statement that can be tested to answer a question. (p. S7)

fossil (fos′əl) Any remains or imprint of living things of the past. (p. C45)

fossil fuel (fos′əl fū′əl) A fuel formed from the decay of ancient forms of life. (p. C64)

fracture (frak′chər) The characteristic way some minerals break in uneven patterns. (p. C35)

freezing point (frēz′ing point) Another name for *melting point*, that temperature at which a substance changes state, either from a liquid to a solid or from solid to liquid. (p. E37)

frequency (frē′kwən sē) The number of times an object vibrates per second. (p. F57)

friction (frik′ shen′) A force that opposes the motion of one object moving past another. (p. F8)

frond (frond) The leaf of a fern. (p. A51)

front (frunt) A boundary between air masses with different temperatures. (p. D55)

fruit (früt) The ripened ovary of a flowering seed plant. (p. A75)

fundamental frequency (fun′də men′təl frē′kwən sē) The lowest frequency at which an object vibrates. (p. F72)

fungus (fung′gəs) *n.,* **fungi** (fun′jī) *pl.* Members of a kingdom that contains one-celled and many-celled living things that absorb food from their environment. (p. A13)

G

gas (gas) A form of matter that does not take up a definite amount of space and has no definite shape. (p. E36)

gel (jel) A type of colloid in which a solid is spread throughout a liquid. (p. E60)

gem (jem) A mineral valued for being rare and beautiful. (p. C38)

geologist (jē ol′ə jist) A scientist who studies rocks to tell how they formed and to predict when an earthquake may occur. (p. C18)

geothermal energy (jē′ō thûr′məl en′ər jē) Earth's internal energy. (p. C104)

germination (jûr′mə nā′shən) The sprouting of a seed into a new plant. (p. A75)

ginkgo (ging′kō) *n., pl.* **ginkgoes** A large gymnosperm with fan-shaped leaves. (p. A59)

gnetophyte (ne′tō fīt′) One of the gymnosperms that are closely related to flowering plants and live in both deserts and the tropics. (p. A59)

grassland (gras′land′) A biome where grasses, not trees, are the main plant life. Prairies are one kind of grassland region. (p. B66)

gravitropism (grav′ī trō′pi′zəm) The response of a plant to gravity. (p. A80)

gravity (grav′i tē) A force of attraction, or pull, between any object and any other objects around it. Gravity is a property of all matter. (pp. C8, F35)

greenhouse effect (grēn′hous′ i fekt′) The ability of the atmosphere to let in sunlight but not to let heat escape. (p. D87)

groundwater (ground wô′tər) Precipitation that seeps into the ground and is stored in tiny holes, or pores, in soil and rocks. (pp. B33, C74, D28)

gymnosperm (jim′nə spûrm′) A seed plant that does not produce flowers. *See* **angiosperm**. (p. A58)

H

habitat (hab′i tat) The place where a plant or animal naturally lives and grows. (p. B11)

hail (hāl) Pellets made of ice and snow. (p. D27)

hardness (härd′nis) How well a mineral resists scratching. (p. C34)

herbivore (hûr′bə vôr′) An animal that eats plants, algae, and other producers. (p. B20)

heredity (hə red′i tē) The passing down of inherited traits from parents to offspring. (p. A110)

hertz (Hz) (hûrts) A unit for measuring frequency. One hertz equals a frequency of one vibration per second. (p. F57)

heterogeneous (het′ər ə jē′nē əs) Differing in kind or nature; dissimilar; not homogeneous. (p. E54)

high-pressure system (hī′presh′ər sis′təm) A pattern surrounding a high pressure center, from which winds blow outward. In the Northern Hemisphere these winds curve to the right in a clockwise pattern. (p. D42)

host (hōst) The organism a parasite lives in or on and is harmed by. (p. B56)

humidity (hū mid′i tē) The amount of water vapor in the air. (p. D16)

humus (hū′məs) Decayed plant or animal material in soil. (pp. B14, C49)

hurricane (hûr′i kān′) A very large, swirling storm with very low pressure at the center. (p. D70)

PRONUNCIATION KEY

a at; ā ape; ä far; âr care; ô law; e end; ē me; i it; ī ice; îr pierce; o hot; ō old; ôr fork; oi oil; ou out; u up; ū use; ü rule; u̇ pull; ûr turn; hw white; ng song; th thin; <u>th</u> this; zh measure; ə about, taken, pencil, lemon, circus

hybrid (hī′brid) An organism produced by the crossing of parents that have different forms of the same trait. (p. A112)

hydrocarbon (hī′drə kär′bən) Any of the large group of compounds made solely from hydrogen and carbon atoms. (p. E32)

hydroelectric plant (hī′drō i lek′trik plant) A factory where running or falling water spins a generator to make electricity. (p. C104)

hydrosphere (hī′drə sfîr′) Earth's water, found in continents and oceans, including the fresh water in ice, lakes, rivers, and underground water. (p. C12)

hydrotropism (hī drot′rə piz′əm) The response of a plant to a nearby source of water. (p. A81)

hyperthermia (hī′pər thûr′mē ə) The overheating of the body that can be caused by overexposure in a hot, dry climate. (p. D90)

hypothesis (hī poth′ə sis) A guess or *if . . . then* statement that can be answered clearly in an experiment. (p. A35)

I

ice age (īs āj) Any period when glaciers and ice sheets covered much of Earth's surface. (p. B58)

igneous rock (ig′nē əs rok) A rock formed when melted rock material cools and hardens (p. C43)

image (im′ij) A "picture" of the light source that light rays make in bouncing off a polished, shiny surface. (p. F89)

imperfect flower (im pûr′fikt flou′ər) A flower with either a stamen or a pistil, but not both. (p. A70)

incomplete flower (in′kəm plēt′ flou′ər) A flower that lacks sepals, petals, stamens or pistils. (p. A70)

indicator (in′di kā′tər) A substance such as litmus paper whose color changes when it is mixed with an acid or a base. (p. E84)

inertia (i nûr′shə) The tendency of a moving object to keep moving in a straight line or of any object to resist a change in motion. (pp. C9, F7)

inexhaustible resource (in′eg zôs′tə bəl rē′sôrs′) A resource that cannot be depleted or used up easily. (p. B40)

infer (in fûr′) To form an idea from facts or observations. (p. S7)

inherited trait (in her′i təd trāt) A characteristic that is passed from parents to offspring. (p. A110)

insolation (in′sə lā′shən) The amount of the Sun's energy that reaches Earth at a given time and place. *Insolation* is short for *in*coming *sol*ar radi*ation*. (p. D6)

instinct (in′stingkt′) An inherited behavior, one that is not learned but is done automatically. (p. A110)

insulate (in′sə lāt′) To prevent heat from passing through. (p. E14)

interpret data (in tûr′prit dā′tə) To use the information that has been gathered to answer questions or solve a problem. (p. S7)

intertidal zone (in′tər tī′dəl zōn) The shallowest section of the marine, or ocean, ecosystem, where the ocean floor is covered and uncovered as the tide goes in and out. (p. B73)

invertebrate (in vûr′tə brit) An animal that does not have a backbone. (p. A95)

ionized (ī′ə nīzd′) Electrically charged by radiation, as gas particles of auroras in the night sky. (p. D10)

isobar (ī′sə bär′) A line on a weather map connecting places with equal air pressure. (p. D42)

K

kinetic energy (ki net′ik en′ər jē) The energy of any moving object. (p. E95)

L

land breeze (land brēz) Wind that blows from land to sea. (p. D39)

laser (lā'zər) A device that produces a thin stream of light of just a few close wavelengths. (p. F122)

lava (lä'və) Magma that reaches Earth's surface. (pp. C21, C43)

law of reflection (lô uv ri flek'shən) The angle between an incoming light ray and a surface equals the angle between the reflected light ray and the surface. (p. F87)

light ray (līt rā) A straight-line beam of light as it travels outward from its source. (p. F85)

lightning (līt'ning) One of the huge electric sparks that leap from clouds to the ground in thunderstorms. (p. D66)

limiting factor (lim'ə ting fak'tər) Anything that controls the growth or survival of a population. (p. B50)

liquid (lik'wid) A form of matter that takes up a definite amount of space and has no definite shape. (p. E36)

lithosphere (lith'ə sfîr') The hard outer layer of Earth, about 100 km thick. (p. C12)

long-day plant (lông'dā plant) A plant that blooms when there is much more daylight than darkness. (p. A82)

low-pressure system (lō'presh'ər sis'təm) A pattern surrounding a low-pressure center, in which winds blow in toward the center. In the Northern Hemisphere, these winds blow to the right in a counterclockwise pattern. (p. D42)

luster (lus'tər) The way light bounces off a mineral's surface. (p. C33)

M

magma (mag'mə) Hot, molten rock deep below Earth's surface. (p. C21)

magnetic (mag net'ik) The property of a material like iron in which the particles line up pole to pole, causing it to be attracted or repelled by a magnet. (p. E15)

make a model (māk ə mod'əl) To make something to represent an object or event. (p. S7)

mare (mär'ā) *n., pl.* **maria** (mär'ē ə) Dark-colored land on the Moon that is dry and flat and is surrounded by mountains and ridges. (p. C13)

mass (mas) A measure of the amount of matter in an object. (p. E6)

matter (ma'tər) Anything that has mass and takes up space. (pp. E6, F51)

measure (mezh'ər) To find the size, volume, area, mass, weight, or temperature of an object, or how long an event occurs. (p. S7)

melting point (melt'ing point) The particular temperature for each substance at which it changes state from a solid to a liquid. (p. E37)

membrane (mem'brān) A thin envelope surrounding the nucleus of a cell. (p. A14)

metal (met'əl) Any of a group of elements found in the ground that conducts heat and electricity. (p. C38)

metamorphic rock (met'ə môr'fik rok) A rock formed under heat and pressure from another kind of rock. (p. C46)

meteorite (mē'tē ə rīt') A chunk of rock from space that strikes the surface of Earth or the Moon. (p. C26)

mid-ocean ridge (mid ō'shun rij) Chain of mountains that wind along all the world's major oceans. (p. C91)

PRONUNCIATION KEY

a at; ā ape; ä far; âr care; ô law; e end; ē me; i it; ī ice; îr pierce; o hot; ō old; ôr fork; oi oil; ou out; u up; ū use; ü rule; ù pull; ûr turn; hw white; ng song; th thin; th this; zh measure; ə about, taken, pencil, lemon, circus

mimicry (mim′i krē) An adaptation in which an animal is protected against predators by its resemblance to another, unpleasant animal. (p. A106)

mineral (min′ə rəl) A solid material of Earth's crust with a definite composition. (p. C32)

mixture (miks′chər) A physical combination of two or more substances that are blended together without forming new substances. (p. E52)

molecule (mol′ə kūl′) A particle that contains more than one atom joined together. (p. E30) *See* **atom**. (p. E26)

monocot (mon′ə kot′) An angiosperm with one cotyledon in each seed. *See* **dicot**. (p. A62)

mountain breeze (moun′tən brēz) A cool night wind that blows down a mountain slope to replace the warmer air in the valley. (p. D39)

mutualism (mū′chü ə liz′əm) A relationship between two kinds of organisms that benefits both. (p. B54)

N

neap tide (nēp tīd) The slightest changes from high to low tide that occur when the Sun, the Moon, and Earth form a right angle or are perpendicular to each other. (p. C89)

nekton (nek′tən) Organisms that swim through the water in aquatic ecosystems. (p. B72)

neutral (nü′trəl) Neither acid nor base. (p. E82)

neutron (nü′tron) A particle in the nucleus of an atom that has no net electric charge. (p. E27)

newton (nü′tən) A basic unit measuring the amount of pull or push a force such as gravity produces between two masses. (pp. E7, F20)

NEXRAD (neks′rad′) A new form of Doppler radar that is used to track storms. The word stands for *NEXt generation of weather RADar.* (p. D77)

niche (nich) The role of an organism in a community. (p. B11)

nitrogen cycle (nī′trə jən sī′kəl) The continuous trapping of nitrogen gas into compounds in the soil and its return to the air. (p. B38)

nonrenewable resource (non′ri nü′ə bəl rē′sôrs′) A resource that cannot be replaced within a short period of time or at all. (pp. B40, C64)

nonvascular (non vas′kyə lər) Containing no plant tissue through which water and food move. (p. A9)

nucleus (nü′klē əs) **1.** A dense structure inside the cell. (p. A14) **2.** One of the airborne dust particles around which water condenses as droplets or ice crystals before falling as precipitation. (p. D26) **3.** An atom's dense center, where most of its mass is. (p. E27)

O

observe (əb sûrv′) To use one or more of the senses to identify or learn about an object or event. (p. S7)

occluded front (ə klüd′id frunt) A front formed where a warm front and a cold front meet. (p. D56)

omnivore (om′nə vôr′) An animal that eats both plants and animals. (p. B21)

opaque (ō pāk′) Completely blocking light from passing through it. (p. F96)

orbit (ôr′bit) The path of a planet traveling around a star. (p. C6)

ore (ôr) A mineral containing a useful substance. (p. C38)

organ (ôr′gən) A group of tissues that work together to do a certain job. (p. A94)

organism (ôr′gə niz′əm) Any living thing that can carry out its life on its own. (p. B6)

ovary (ō′və rē) A structure containing egg cells; the base of a pistil in a flower. (p. A70)

overtone (ō′vər tōn′) One of a series of pitches that blend to give a sound its quality. (p. F72)

ozone layer (ō′zōn lā′ər) A layer of ozone gas in the atmosphere that screens out much of the Sun's UV (ultraviolet) rays. (p. C63)

P

parasitism (par′ə sī tiz′əm) A relationship in which one organism lives in or on another organism and benefits from that relationship while the other organism may be harmed by it. (p. B56) —**parasite** (par′ə sīt′) (p. A61)

perfect flower (pûr′fikt flou′ər) A flower with both male and female parts, that is, both a stamen and a pistil. (p. A70)

permafrost (pûr′mə frôst′) A layer of permanently frozen soil found in arctic and antarctic regions. (p. B68)

pH (pē′aitch′) The scale that tells how acidic or basic a solution is. (p. E86)

phloem (flō′em) The tissue through which food from the leaves moves down through the rest of a plant. (p. A21)

photon (fō′ton) The tiny bundles of energy by means of which light travels. (p. F119)

photoperiodism (fō′tō pîr′ē ə diz′əm) The flowering response of a plant to changing periods of daylight and darkness. (p. A82)

photosynthesis (fō′tə sin′thə sis) The food-making process in green plants that uses sunlight. (p. A32)

phototropism (fō tot′rə piz′əm) The response of a plant to changes in light. (p. A80)

phylum (fī′ləm) *n., pl.* **phyla** (-lə) One of the large groups in the animal kingdom. (p. A12)

physical change (fiz′i kəl chānj) A change of matter in size, shape, or state without any change in identity. (p. E70)

pioneer community (pī′ə nîr′ kə mū′ni tē) The first community thriving in a once lifeless area. (p. B83)

pioneer species (pī′ə nîr′ spē′shēz) The first species living in an otherwise lifeless area. (p. B83)

pitch (pich) How high or low a sound is. (p. F56)

planet (plan′it) Any of the nine objects that travel around the Sun and shine by reflecting its light. (p. C6)

plankton (plangk′tən) Organisms that float on the water in aquatic ecosystems. (p. B72)

plate (plāt) One of the moving pieces of Earth's crust that has been broken by upward pressure from the mantle. (p. C19)

plate tectonics (plāt tek ton′iks) A scientific theory that Earth's crust is made of moving plates. (p. C19)

polarization (pō′lər ə zā′shən) Allowing light vibrations to pass through in only one direction. (p. F97)

pollen (pol′ən) Dustlike grains in the flower of a plant that contain its male sex cells. (p. A64)

pollination (pol′ə nā′shən) The transfer of a pollen grain to the egg-producing part of a plant. (p. A72)

pollute (pə lüt′) *v.* To add unnatural substances to Earth's land, water, or air. (p. C50) —**pollutant** (pə lü′tənt) *n.* Something that pollutes. (p. C50) —**pollution** (pə lü′shən) *n.* A polluted condition. (p. C50)

PRONUNCIATION KEY

a at; ā ape; ä far; âr care; ô law; e end; ē me; i it; ī ice; îr pierce; o hot; ō old; ôr fork; oi oil; ou out; u up; ū use; ü rule; u̇ pull; ûr turn; hw white; ng song; th thin; th this; zh measure; ə about, taken, pencil, lemon, circus

population (pop′yə lā′shən) All the members of one species in an area. (p. B10)

potential energy (pə ten′shəl en′ər jē) Stored energy. (p. E95)

precipitation (pri sip′i tā′shən) Any form of water particles that falls from the atmosphere and reaches the ground. (pp. B33, D26)

predator (pred′ə tər) An animal that hunts other anmals for food. (pp. A106, B21)

predict (pri dikt′) To state possible results of an event or experiment. (p. S7)

prey (prā) A living thing that is hunted for food. (p. B21)

primary color (prī′mer′ē kul′ər) Red, green, or blue. Mixing these colors can produce all the colors of the spectrum. (p. F110)

primary pigment (prī′mer′ē pig′mənt) Magenta, cyan, or yellow. Materials with any of these colors absorb one primary color of light and reflect the other two. (p. F112)

primary succession (prī′mer′ē sək sesh′ən) The beginning of a community where few, if any, living things exist, or where earlier communities were wiped out. (p. B82)

prism (priz′əm) A cut piece of clear glass (or plastic) with two opposite sides in the shape of a triangle or other geometric shape. (p. F108)

producer (prə dü′sər) Any of the plants and algae that produce oxygen and food that animals need. (p. B7)

product (prod′ukt) A new substance produced by a chemical change. (p. E71)

prop root (prop rüt) One of the roots that grow out of a plant's stemlike main roots and help prop up the plant. (p. A21)

property (prop′ər tē) A characteristic of matter that can be observed, such as mass, volume, weight, or density. (pp. E6, E24)

protective coloration (prə tek′tiv kul′ə rā′shən) A type of camouflage in which the color of an animal blends in with its background, protecting it against predators. (p. A109)

protein (prō′tēn) A substance rich in nitrogen that the body uses for growth and the repair of cells. (p. B38)

protist (prō′tist) A member of a kingdom that contains one-celled and many-celled living things, some that make food and some that hunt for food. (p. A14)

proton (prō′ton) A particle in the nucleus of an atom that carries one unit of positive electric charge. (p. E27)

Q

quality (kwol′i tē) The difference you hear between two sounds of the same loudness and pitch. (p. F72)

R

radar (rā′där) A device for tracking the position and path of a distant moving object. It works by sending out radio waves and recording their echoes. The word stands for *RAdio Detecting And Ranging.* (p. D76)

radiation (rā′dē a′shən) The transfer of heat through electromagnetic rays. (p. E97)

radiative balance (rā′dē a′tiv bal′əns) A balance between energy lost and energy gained. (p. D86)

rarefaction (râr′ə fak′shən) The part of a sound wave where molecules are spread apart. (p. F51)

raw material (râ mə tîr′ē əl) Material not yet refined, manufactured, or processed. (p. B40)

reactant (rē ak′tənt) An original substance at the beginning of a chemical reaction. (p. E71)

reaction (rē ak′shən) The force with which an object responds to an action, as in Newton's third law of motion, which states, "For every action, there is an equal but opposite reaction." *See* **action**. (p. F24)

reflection (ri flek′shən) The bouncing of a sound wave off a surface. (p. F66)

refraction (ri frak'shən) The bending of light rays as they pass from one substance into another. (p. F98)

relative humidity (rel'ə tiv hū mid'i tē) A comparison between how much water vapor is in the air and how much the air could hold at a given temperature if it were full, or saturated. (p. D18)

renewable resource (ri nü'ə bəl rē'sôrs') A resource that can be replaced in a short period of time. (pp. B40, C62)

reservoir (rez'ər vwär') A storage area for fresh water supplies. (p. C75)

resonance (rez'ə nəns) In an instrument or object, a unique blend of the fundamental frequency and its overtones. When an external force vibrates at the same frequency, a buildup of that resonance can occur. (p. F72)

resource (rē'sôrs') Any material that helps support life on Earth. (p. C12)

respiration (res'pə rā'shən) The release of energy in plants and animals from food (sugar). (p. A33)

response (ri spons') What a living thing does as a result of a stimulus. (p. A80)

rhizoid (rī'zoid) One of the hairlike fibers that anchor a moss to the soil and take in water from the soil. (p. A48)

rhizome (rī'zōm) The underground stem of a fern. (p. A51)

rock (rok) A naturally formed solid in the crust made up of one or more minerals. (p. C42)

rock cycle (rok sī'kəl) Rocks changing from one into another in a never-ending series of processes. (p. C52)

root cap (rüt kap) A thin covering made up of cells that protect the root tip of a plant as it grows into the soil. (p. A20)

root hair (rüt hâr) Any of the threadlike projections from a plant root that absorb water and dissolved minerals from the soil. (p. A20)

rotate (rō'tāt) To make a complete spin on an axis, causing one day on a planet. A day differs in length from planet to planet. (p. C10)

runoff (run'ôf) Precipitation that flows across the land's surface or falls into rivers and streams. (pp. B33, D28)

savanna (sə van'ə) A tropical grassland with some trees and shrubs. (p. B66)

scanning tunneling microscope (scan'ing tun'əl ing mī'krə skōp') A device that uses electric current flowing through a needle to trace the contours of atoms and magnify them as much as 30 million times. (p. E26)

scavenger (skav'ən jər) A meat-eating animal that feeds on the remains of dead animals. (p. B21)

sea breeze (sē brēz) Wind that blows from sea to land. (p. D39)

sea-floor vent (sē'flôr' vent) An opening in a mid-ocean ridge where mineral-saturated water boils up from the seafloor crust. (p. C93)

seamount (sē'mount') A huge underwater volcanic mountain that may emerge from the ocean surface as an island. (p. C90)

secondary succession (sek'ən der'ē sək sesh'ən) The beginning of a new community where an earlier community already exists. (p. B82)

sedimentary rock (sed'ə men'tə rē rok) A rock made of bits of matter joined together. (p. C44)

PRONUNCIATION KEY

a **at**; ā **ape**; ä **far**; âr **care**; ô **law**; e **end**; ē **me**; i **it**; ī **ice**; îr **pierce**; o **hot**; ō **old**; ôr **fork**; oi **oil**; ou **out**; u **up**; ū **use**; ü **rule**; ù **pull**; ûr **turn**; hw **white**; ng **song**; th **thin**; th **this**; zh measure; ə about, taken, pencil, lemon, circus

seed (sēd) An undeveloped plant with stored food sealed in a protective covering. (p. A58)

seed coat (sēd kōt) The outer covering of a seed. (p. A74)

seed dispersal (sēd di spûr'səl) The movement of a seed from the flower to a place where it can sprout. (p. A75)

self-pollination (self'pol'ə nā'shən) The transfer of pollen from an anther to a stigma in the same plant. (p. A72)

sexual reproduction (sek'shü əl rē'prō duk'shən) The production of a new organism from a female sex cell and a male sex cell. (p. A52)

shear (shîr) A movement of plates that twists, tears, or pushes one part of Earth's crust past another. (p. C20)

short-day plant (shôrt'dā plant) A plant that blooms when there is more darkness and less daylight. (p. A82)

smog (smog) A mixture of smoke and fog. (p. C64)

solar system (sō'lər sis'təm) The Sun and the objects that are traveling around it. (p. C6)

solid (sol'id) A form of matter that has a definite shape and takes up a definite amount of space. (p. E36)

solubility (sol'yə bil'i tē) The ability of a substance to be dissolved by another substance. (p. E58)

solute (sol'ūt) A substance that is dissolved by another substance to form a solution. (p. E57)

solution (sə lü'shən) A mixture of substances that are blended so completely that the mixture looks the same everywhere. (p. E54)

solvent (sol'vənt) A substance that dissolves one or more other substances to form a solution. (p. E57)

sound wave (sound wāv) A vibration that spreads away from a vibrating object. (p. F51)

spectrum (spek'trəm) A band of colors produced when light goes through a prism. (p. F108)

speed (spēd) How fast an object's position changes with time at any given moment. (p. F11)

spore (spôr) Cells in seedless plants that grow into new organisms. (p. A48)

spring (spring) A place where groundwater seeps out of the ground. (p. C75)

spring tide (spring tīd) The greatest changes from high to low tide that occur when the Sun, the Moon, and Earth are lined up. (p. C89)

state of matter (stāt uv mat'ər) One of the three forms that matter can take—solid, liquid, or gas. (p. E36)

stationary front (stā'shə ner ē frunt) An unmoving front where a cold air mass and a warm air mass meet. (p. D57)

statistical forecasting (stə tis'ti kəl fôr'kas'ting) Predicting weather by using past weather records, based on the chances of a pattern repeating itself. (p. D60)

stimulus (stim'yə ləs), *n., pl.* **stimuli (-lī)** Something in the environment that causes a living thing to react. (p. A80)

stomata (stō'mə tə) *pl. n., sing.* **stoma** Pores in the bottom of leaves that open and close to let in air or give off water vapor. (p. A24)

storm surge (stôrm sûrj) A great rise of the sea along a shore caused by low pressure clouds. (p. D72)

stratus cloud (strā'təs kloud) A cloud that forms in a blanketlike layer. (p. D24)

streak (strēk) The color of the powder left when a mineral is rubbed against a hard, rough surface. (p. C34)

strip farming (strip fär'ming) Trapping runoff by alternating tightly growing grasses with more widely spaced plants. (p. C51)

subscript (sub'skript') A number in a chemical formula that tells the number of atoms in the compound. (p. E25)

surveyor (sər vā′ər) A specialist who makes accurate measurements of Earth's crust. (p. C18)

suspension (sə spen′shən) A mixture in which suspended particles can easily be seen. (p. E59)

symbiosis (sim′bē ō′sis) A relationship between two kinds of organisms that lasts over time. (p. B54)

synoptic weather map (si nop′tik weth′ər map) A type of map showing a summary of the weather using station models. (p. D60)

system (sis′təm) A group of organs that work together to carry on life functions. (p. A94)

T

taiga (tī′gə) A cool forest biome of conifers in the upper Northern Hemisphere. (p. B67)

taproot (tap′rüt′) A root that has few hairy branches and grows deep into the ground. (p. A21)

temperate (tem′pər it) Free from extremes of temperature. (p. B66)

tension (ten′shən) A movement of plates that stretches or pulls apart Earth's crust. (p. C20)

terracing (ter′is ing) Shaping hillsides into steps so that runoff and eroded soil get trapped on the steps. (p. C51)

texture (teks′chər) An identifying quality of a rock based on how coarse, fine, or glassy it is and on how angular or rounded it is. (p. C42)

thunder (thun′dər) The noise caused by lightning-heated air during a thunderstorm. (p. D66)

thunderhead (thun′dər hed′) A cumulonimbus cloud in which a thunderstorm forms. (p. D66)

thunderstorm (thun′dər stôrm′) The most common severe storm, formed in cumulonimbus clouds. (p. D66)

tissue (tish′ü) A group of similar cells that work together at the same job. (pp. A7, A94)

topsoil (top′soil′) The dark, top layer of soil, rich in humus and minerals, in which many tiny organisms live and most plants grow. (p. B14)

tornado (tôr nā′dō) A violent whirling wind that moves across the ground in a narrow path. (p. D68)

trade wind (trād wind) A belt of winds around Earth moving from high pressure zones toward the low pressure at the equator. (p. D41)

translucent (trans lü′sənt) Letting only some light through, so that objects on the other side appear blurry. (p. F96)

transparent (trans pâr′ənt) Letting all light through, so that objects on the other side can be seen clearly. (p. F96)

transpiration (tran′spə rā′shən) The loss of water through a plant's leaves, which draws water up through the plant to replace it. (pp. A25, D17)

trench (trench) A deep valley in the sea floor. (p. C91)

tropical rain forest (trop′i kəl rān fôr′ist) A hot, humid biome near the equator, with much rainfall and a wide variety of life. (p. B71)

tropism (trō′piz′əm) A growth response of a plant toward or away from a stimulus. (p. A80)

troposphere (trop′ə sfîr′) The layer of the atmosphere closest to Earth's surface. (p. D10)

PRONUNCIATION KEY

a at; ā ape; ä far; âr care; ô law; e end; ē me; i it; ī ice; îr pierce; o hot; ō old; ôr fork; oi oil; ou out; u up; ū use; ü rule; ù pull; ûr turn; hw white; ng song; th thin; th this; zh measure; ə about, taken, pencil, lemon, circus

tube worm (tüb wûrm) Large wormlike animals that live near sea floor vents and obtain their food through bacterial chemosynthesis. (p. C93)

tundra (tun′dra) Large, treeless plain in the arctic regions, where the ground is frozen all year. (p. B68)

U

ultrasonic (ul′trə son′ik) Said of a sound with a frequency too high to be heard by humans. (p. F57)

unbalanced forces (un bal′ənst fôrs′əz) Forces that do not cancel each other out when acting together on a single object. (p. F21)

updraft (up′draft′) An upward rush of heated air during a thunderstorm. (pp. D38, D66)

use numbers (ūz num′bərz) To order, count, add, subtract, multiply, and divide to explain data. (p. S7)

use variables (ūz vâr′ē ə bəlz) To identify and separate things in an experiment that can be changed or controlled. (p. S7)

V

vacuum (vak′ū əm) A space through which sound waves cannot travel because it contains no matter. (p. F116)

valley breeze (val′ē brēz) A cool wind that blows up a mountain slope and replaces the slope's rising Sun-warmed air. (p. D39)

variable (vâr′ē ə bəl) One of the changes in a situation that may affect the outcome of an experiment. (p. A35)

vascular (vas′kyə lər) Containing plant tissue through which water moves up and food moves down. (p. A9)

velocity (və los′i tē) The speed and direction of a moving object. (p. F12)

vertebrate (vûr′tə brit) An animal that has a backbone. (p. A95)

vibration (vī brā′shən) A back-and-forth motion. (p. F50)

volume (vol′ūm) **1.** A measure of how much space an object takes up. (p. E6) **2.** The loudness or softness of a sound. (p. F58)

W

warm front (wôrm frunt) A front where warm air moves in over a cold air mass. (p. D56)

water cycle (wô′tər sī′kəl) The continuous movement of water between Earth's surface and the air, changing from liquid to gas to liquid. (pp. B33, C74, D29)

water table (wô′tər tā′bəl) The top of the water-filled spaces in the ground. (p. C75)

water vapor (wô′tər vā′pər) Water in the form of a gas. (pp. B32, D16)

waterspout (wô′tər spout′) A tornado that forms over water. (p. D69)

weather (weth′ər) What the lower atmosphere is like at any given place and time. (p. D12)

weather vane (weth′ər vān) A device that indicates wind direction. (p. D44)

weathering (weth′ər ing) Breaking down rocks into smaller pieces. (p. C22)

weight (wāt) The force of gravity between Earth and an object. (pp. E7, F36)

well (wel) A hole dug below the water table that water seeps into. (p. C75)

wind (wind) Air that moves horizontally. (p. D38)

X

xylem (zī′ləm) The tissue through which water and minerals move up through a plant. (p. A20)

Y

year (yîr) The time it takes a planet to orbit the Sun. A *year* is different from planet to planet. (p. C7)

Index

A

Abiotic factors, B6–7
Absorption, of sound, F66–67
Abyssal plain, C90
Acceleration, F13, F18, F26–27
    calculation of, F20
    force and, F18
    mass and, F19, F20
    of falling objects, F36
    of the Moon, F37
Acidity, E86
Acid rain, C23, C65
Acids, C65*
    identifying, E81*–82, E84–85
    reactivity of, E83
    strength of, E86–87
    uses of, E88
Action, F24
Adaptation, A78–89, A104–109
    camouflage as, A108–109
    chemical, A84
    competition as, A83*, B23
    in sow bugs, A105*
    in taste, A107
    mimicry as, A106
    root growth as, A79*
    thorns as, A107
    to harsh environments, B52–53
    tropisms, A80–81
Aerial roots, A21
Aerogels, E16
Aerosol, E60
Agnatha, A98
Air, C62–63
    as solution, E56
    cleaning up, C66
    composition of, D11
    cooling of, D20
    dirty, C61*
    dust in, D11
    nitrogen in, B38
    pollution of, C64, C67
Air masses, D54–55
Air pressure
    altitude and, D11

changes in, D35*–37
convection cells and, D38
isobars, D42
measuring, D12
storm surges and, D72
Air resistance, F34
Air sac (swim bladder), A98
Air temperature
    altitude and, D10
    mean, D6
    measuring, D12
    relative humidity and, D19
    Sun's angle and, D5*–7*
Algae, B24, B73
    as producers, B7
    blooms, B26
    green, A14, A54
Alkalinity, E86
Alloys, E56
Alternation of generations, A53
Alternative energy sources,
    C104–105, C106
Altitude
    air pressure and, D11, D36
    air temperature and, D10
    climate and, D85
Aluminum, C38, E23
Alvin (submersible), C92, C96–97
AM, F120
Amazon rain forest, B76–77
Ammeter, E93
Ammonia, B34, B38, B39, E83
Amphibia, A98
Amphibians, A12
Amplifier, F60
"Ancient" bacteria kingdom, A15
Anemometer, D44
Anemones, A12, A96, B57
Aneroid barometer, D12
Angiosperms, A11, A54, A58,
    A59, A60–61, A60–65
    aromatic flowers, A64
    cotyledons, A62–63*, A74
Animals, A12, A92–120. *See also*
    Populations.
    adaptation of, A104–109
        camouflage, A108–109

        mimicry, A106
        sow bugs, A105*
        taste, A107
        thorns, A107
    as consumers, B7
    carbon cycle and, B37
    classification of, A93*–101
        invertebrates, A95–97
        traits used for, A94–95
        vertebrates, A95, A98–99
    crossbreeds, A112–113
    diversity among, A114–15
    habitat change and, B12
    hoofed, B66
    hybrids, A112, A113*
    in deciduous forests, B70
    inherited vs. learned traits in,
        A110–111
    in nitrogen cycle, B39
    in prairie ecosystem, B8–9
    in tropical rain forests, B71
    plants vs., A12
    water cycle and, B33
Annelida (segmented worms),
    A97
Antacids, E88
Anther, A70, A72
Anthracite (hard coal), C47
Aquifer, C75
Arica, Chile, B69
Aristotle, D62, E22, F35
Armadillo, B9
Arthropoda, A12, A97
Asexual reproduction, A52
Atacama Desert, B69
Atmosphere, C12, C60–67, D10
    acid rain and, C65
    greenhouse effect and, D87
    living things' need for,
        C62–63
    of other planets, C68–69
    radiative balance and, D86
    weather and, D12
Atoms, E26–27
Auroras, D10
Auxin, A81
Aves (birds), A12, A99

---

* Indicates an activity related to this topic.

*Indicates an activity related to this topic.

*Indicates an activity related to this topic.

*Indicates an activity related to this topic.

*Indicates an activity related to this topic.

*Indicates an activity related to this topic.

*Indicates an activity related to this topic.

Credits

Page placement key: (t) top, (tr) top right, (tl) top left, (tc) top center, (m) middle, (l) left, (r) right, (b) bottom, (br) bottom right,(bl) bottom left, (bc) bottom center, (bg) background, (i) inset

Cover Design and Illustration: Robert Brook Allen

Cover Photos: ©Tim Flach/Stone; (bg) ©Darrell Gulin/Natural Selection; (i) ©PhotoSpin 2000.

Illustrations: Kenneth Batelman: pp. C9, C89, F24, F35, F37, F39; Tom Bean: p. S2; Denny Bond: p. B36; Ka Botzis: pp. B20, B21; Drew-Brook-Cormack: p. D20; Susan Carlson: p. A12; Andrea Champlin: pp. F31, C10, C11, D6, D42, D70, D82, D84, E12, E62, E63, E64; Barbara Cousins: pp. R24, R26, R27, R28; Marie Dauenheimer: pp. A6, A7; John Edwards: pp. C6, E7, E10, E12, F70, F84, F85, F89, F90, F100; Peter Fasolino: pp. E43, E60; Robert Frank: p. B38; Function Thru Form: pp. A32, A62, A117, B18, B20, B21, B24, B25, B27, B40, B51, C8, C31, C33, C37, C39, C46, C50, C65, C72, C76, C103, D6, D7, D8, D10, D11, D16, D17, D25, D26, D30, D35, D39, D41, D43, D51, D53, D81, D85, D86, D89, D93, E15, E26, E27, E29, E30, E31, E32, E36, E37, E39, E46, E69, E82, ,E86, E92, E97, F6, F7, F10, F11, F12, F18, F19, F20, F21, F22, F23, F36, F38, F51, F55, F57, F59, F60, F61, F66, F69, F71, F76, F108, F112, F117, F119, F124, F125; Thomas Gagliano: pp. D36, D37, D39; Peter Gunther: p. F30; Greg Harris: pp. B73, D55; Carlyn Iverson: pp. B32, B80, B81; Sidney Jablonski: p. C86; John Karapelou: pp. R29, R30, R31; Virge Kask: pp. A12, A70, A72, A73, A74, A76, B18, B24, B25; George Kelvin: pp. A24, A32, A35, A52, A53, A54, A79, A81, A82, A88, C12, C14, C19, C20, C25, C47, C49, C62, C63, C74, C75, C88, C90, C91, C102, C103, F27, F85, F101, F118; Katie Lee: pp. B6, B7, B84; Tom Leonard: pp. F102, R20, R21, R22, R32; Rebecca Merrilees: pp. A20, A21, A22, A37, A38, A51; Dave Merrill: pp. B9, B52, B54, C21, D85; Mowry Graphics: pp. D28, D54, D89; Steve Oh: pp. A95, F3, F14, D22, F25, F26, F27, F34, R27, R28, R29, R32, R33, R34,; Chris Porter: pp. B6, C14; Saul Rosenbaum: pp. D8, D9, D27, D38, D56, D57, D66, D67, D87, F99, F116, F117; Wendy Smith: pp. A8, A10, A11, A60, A62, F112; Steve Stankiewicz: pp. B64, B89, C32, C52, C73, C78, C100, D18, D40, D53, D60, D69, D89, E38, E42, E92, E94, F74, F86, F93, F101, F104, F105, F110, F122, R8, R9, R13; Patricia Wynne: pp. R23, R31.

Photography Credits: All photographs are by the Macmillan/McGraw-Hill School Division (MMSD) and Dan Howell for MMSD except as noted below.

Contents: iv: ©Norbert Wu. v: ©Tim Flach/Stone. vi: l ©Jules Cowan/Index Stock Imagery; b ©Joyce Photographics/Photo Researchers, Inc; r ©A.J. Copley/VU. vii: l ©NOAA, colored by John Wells/Science Photo Library/Photo Researchers, Inc; r ©Runk/Schoenberger/Grant Heilman. viii: l ©Roger Ressmeyer/Corbis; b ©Science/VU; ix: ©Duomo/Corbis.

National Geographic Invitation to Science: S1: ©Gianni Tortoli/Photo Researchers, Inc. S2: ©Tom Bean/Tom & Susan Bean Photography Inc. S3: ©Chris Hondros/Liaison Agency Inc. S4: ©Carlos Munoz-Yague/ Eurelios/Science Photo Library/Photo Researchers, Inc. S5: ©Mark Pilkington/Geological Survey of Canada/Science Photo Library/Photo Researchers, Inc. S7: ©Richard Hutchings.

National Geographic Unit Opener A: A0 ©Kelvin Aitken/Peter Arnold,Inc;A1 ©Norbert Wu; A1 ©Kelvin Aitken/Peter Arnold,Inc. **Unit A:** A2: ©William Waterfall/The Stock Market. A4: ©Ted Levin/Animals Animals/Earth Scenes. A5: ©Richard Hutchings. A6: ©Peter Miller/Photo Researchers, Inc. A7: ©Dick Thomas/VU. A9: ©Rob Hadlow/Bruce Coleman, Inc. A13: (tr) ©Doug Sokell/VU; (br) ©R.M. Meadows/Peter Arnold, Inc.; (bl) ©Veronika Burmeister/VU. A14: (br) ©Cabisco/VU; (bl) ©Gilbert S. Grant/Photo Researchers, Inc.; (bl) ©Patrick W. Grace/Science Source/Photo Researchers, Inc.; (br) ©R. Kessel-G. Shih/VU; (bl) ©Veronika Burmeister/VU. A15: (br) ©A. & F. Michler/Peter Arnold, Inc.; (bl) ©Telegraph Colour Library/FPG. A16: (b) ©Adam Jones/Dembinsky Photo Associates; (br) ©Arthur R. Hill/VU. A17: ©Manfred Kage/Peter Arnold, Inc. A18: ©Dominique Braud/Dembinsky Photo Associates. A19: ©Richard Hutchings. A23: (tl) ©George Bernard/Animals Animals/Earth Scenes; (tr) ©Robert Maier/Animals Animals/Earth Scenes; (tr) ©Willard Clay/Dembinsky Photo Associates. A25: ©G.Buttner/OKAPIA/Photo Researchers, Inc. A26: (tr) ©David S. Addison/VU; (m) ©Tim Hauf/VU. A27: ©James R. Holland/National Geographic Society. A 28: (bl) ©Michael J. Balick/Peter Arnold, Inc.; (br) ©Ray Pfortner/Peter Arnold, Inc. A29: ©J.C. Teyssier/Publiphoto/Photo Researchers, Inc. A30: ©Robert Maier/Animals Animals/Earth Scenes. A31: ©Richard Hutchings. A32: ©PHOTODISC/Gettyone. A34: ©Willard Clay/Dembinsky Photo Associates. A36: (t) ©Gerry Ellis/ENP Images; (bl, br) ©Jack M. Bostrack/VU. A37: ©Phil Degginger/Color-Pic. A40: ©Jim Olive/Pictor/Uniphoto. A41: (tl) ©courtesy of Katherine Banks/Prof. K. Banks; (tr) ©Hans Reinhard/Bruce Coleman, Inc.; (r) ©WHM

Bildarchiv/Peter Arnold, Inc. A42: ©1998 PhotoDisc, Inc. A43: ©Hans Reinhard/Bruce Coleman, Inc. A44: ©Bob Krist/Corbis. A46: ©Michael Fogden/Bruce Coleman, Inc. A47: ©Richard Hutchings. A48: (br) ©David Sieren/VU; (bl) ©Doug Sokell/VU; (bl) ©John Trager/VU. A49: (bc) ©E.F.Anderson/VU; (bl) ©Ed Reschke/Peter Arnold, Inc.; (bl) ©Mike Perry/Pictor/Uniphoto. A50: (tl) ©Dan Suzio/Photo Researchers, Inc.; (br, tr) ©Richard Hutchings. A51: ©David Dennis/Animals Animals/Earth Scenes. A54: ©Dick Keen/VU. A55: ©Ed Degginger/Color-Pic, Inc. A56: ©Michael Gadomski/Animals Animals/Earth Scenes. A57: ©Richard Hutchings. A58: (bl) ©Jim Hughes/VU; (br) ©V.P. Weinland/Photo Researchers, Inc.; (br) ©W. Ormerod/VU. A59: (m) ©Ed Degginger/Bruce Coleman, Inc.; (br) ©E. Webber/VU; (bl) ©Gerald & Buff Corsi/VU;(bl) ©Jan Taylor/Bruce Coleman, Inc.; (b) ©John N. Trager/VU. A60: (b) ©Dick Keen/VU; (tr) ©V. McMillan/VU. A61: (br) ©Bud Nielsen/VU; (t) ©E.F. Anderson/VU. A63: (br) ©Arthur R. Hill/VU; (br) ©Mark S. Skalny/VU. A64: (tr) ©Jerome Wexler/Photo Researchers, Inc.; (tl) ©John Gerlach/VU. A66: (tl) ©Jeff Greenberg/VU; (tr) ©Larry Lefever/Grant Heilman Photography, Inc. A67: ©Jim Sugar Photography/Bettmann/CORBIS. A68: ©Robert P. Carr/Bruce Coleman, Inc. A69: ©Richard Hutchings. A71: (b) ©Adam Jones/Photo Researchers, Inc.; (tl) ©Derrick Ditchburn/VU; (m) ©Doug Sokell/VU. A74: ©Henry T. Kaiser/Pictor/Uniphoto. A75: (tl) ©Inga Spence/VU; (m) ©Ken Wagner/VU; (tr) ©Stephen J. Lang/VU. A76: ©Scott T. Smith. A78: ©Mack Henley/VU. A80: ©David Newman/VU. A81: ©R. Calentine/VU. A83: (m) ©Dick Keen/VU; (br) ©Richard Hutchings. A84: (b) ©Bill Beatty/VU; (tr) ©Parke H. John, Jr./VU. A85: ©Runk/Schoenberger/Grant Heilman Photography, Inc. A86: (bg) ©Brock May/Photo Researchers, Inc.; (tr) ©Joel Sartore/Grant Heilman Photography, Inc. A87: ©Catherine Karnow/CORBIS. A88: (bl) ©Hans Reinhard/Bruce Coleman, Inc.; (bl) ©John McAnulty/CORBIS. A90: ©R&V Taylor/Bruce Coleman, Inc. A92: ©Frank Krahmer/Bruce Coleman, Inc. A95: (bl) ©BIOS Klein/Hubert/Peter Arnold, Inc.; (m) ©Joe McDonald/Bruce Coleman, Inc.; (tr) ©John Hyde/Bruce Coleman, Inc. A96: (m) ©Ed Degginger/Bruce Coleman, Inc.; (br) ©Ed Degginger/Color-Pic; (tr) ©Jeff Mondragon/Mondragon Photography; (bl) ©Scott Johnson/Animals Animals/Earth Scenes; (tl) ©Susan Blanchet/Dembinsky Photo Associates; (tl) ©Tom E. Adams/Peter Arnold, Inc. A97: (bl) © Breck P. Kent/Animals Animals/Earth Scenes; (tr, br) ©Fred Bavendam/Peter Arnold, Inc.; (tl) ©Hans Pfletschinger/Peter Arnold, Inc.; (bl) ©Jeff J. Daly/Stock Boston; (br) ©Pictor/Uniphoto; (m) ©Robert Lubeck/Animals Animals/Earth Scenes. A98: (br) ©Gary Meszaroa/Bruce Coleman, Inc.; (m) ©Marilyn Kazmers/Dembinsky Photo Associates; (m) ©Norbert Wu/Peter Arnold, Inc.; (bl) ©Skip Moody/Dembinsky Photo Associates; (m) ©Pictor/Uniphoto; (tl) ©Zig Leszczynski/Animals Animals/Earth Scenes. A99: (br) ©Bob Cranston/Animals Animals/Earth Scenes; (tl) ©Darrell Gulin/CORBIS; (m) ©Des & Jen Bartlett/Bruce Coleman, Inc.; (m) ©Ed Degginger/Color-Pic; (tl) ©Michael Newman/PhotoEdit; (tl) ©Rob Simpson/Pictor/Uniphoto; (tl) ©Pictor/Uniphoto. A100: (m) ©Ed Degginger/Color-Pic; (br) ©Jim Roetzel/Dembinsky Photo Associates; (m) ©John Cancalosi/Peter Arnold, Inc.; (br) ©John Shaw/Bruce Coleman, Inc.; (bc) ©Skip Moody/Dembinsky Photo Associates. A101: ©Graham Pizzey/Bruce Coleman, Inc. A104: (bg) ©John Gerlach/Dembinsky Photo Associates; (m) ©Rolf Kopfle/Bruce Coleman, Inc. A106: (bl) ©L. West/Bruce Coleman, Inc.; (br) ©Stan W. Elems/VU. A107: (bl) ©Ed Degginger/Color-Pic; (m) ©Rod Planck/Dembinsky Photo Associates; (tl, br) ©Stan W. Elems/VU. A108: ©Steve Kaufman/Peter Arnold, Inc. A109: ©Kim Taylor/Bruce Coleman, Inc. A110: ©Ed Degginger/Color-Pic. A111: (b) ©D. Robert Franz/Bruce Coleman, Inc.; (br) ©Erwin & Peggy Bauer/Bruce Coleman, Inc.; (m) ©John Shaw/Bruce Coleman, Inc.; (tl) ©John Snyder/Bruce Coleman, Inc.; (tr) ©Skip Moody/Dembinsky Photo Associates. A112: (tl, tr) ©Ed Degginger/Color-Pic; (tl) ©Randa Bishop/Pictor/Uniphoto. A113: (br) ©Fritz Prenzel/Animals Animals/Earth Scenes; (br, m) ©Hans Reinhard/Bruce Coleman, Inc. A114: ©Stan Osolinski/Dembinsky Photo Associates. A115: ©Gerard Lacz/Animals Animals/Earth Scenes. A118: ©Courtesy of HSWRI. A119: ©Courtesy of HSWRI.

National Geographic Unit Opener B: B0 ©Tim Flach/Stone; B1 ©Art Wolfe/Stone; B1 ©Tim Flach/Stone. **Unit B:** B2: ©Lee Rentz/Bruce Coleman, Inc. B4: ©Zig Leszczynski/Animals Animals/Earth Scenes. B5: ©Richard Hutchings. B8: (t) ©John Shaw/Bruce Coleman, Inc.; (br) ©John Shaw/Bruce Coleman, Inc. B9: (tc) ©David J. Sams/Stock, Boston; (tr) ©Joe McDonald/CORBIS; (m) ©John Giustina/Bruce Coleman, Inc. B10: ©Lee Rentz/Bruce Coleman, Inc. B11: (tr) ©Laura Riley/Bruce Coleman, Inc.; (br) ©Robert M. Balou/Animals Animals/Earth Scenes. B12: (br) ©Bruce Coleman, Inc.; (tr) ©N.E. Swedsberg/Bruce Coleman, Inc. B13: ©Joe McDonald/Animals Animals/Earth Scenes.B14: ©John Shaw/Bruce Coleman, Inc. B16: ©Beverly Joubert/National Geographic Collection/GettyOne Images. B19: ©1998 PhotoDisc, Inc. B22: (m) ©Gary Braasch/Tony Stone Images; (b) ©Joe McDonald/Bruce Coleman, Inc.; (m) ©Larry West/Bruce Coleman Inc. B23: (tr) ©Doug Wechsler/Animals Animals;

R 65

(bl) ©Scott Smith/Animals Animals. B26: (tr) ©Jeff Foote/Bruce Coleman, Inc.; (m) ©John Pontier/Animals Animals. B27: ©Zig Leszczynski/Animals Animals. B28: (bl) ©Artville/PictureQuest, Burke/Triolo PictureQuest. B29: (bl) ©Artville/PictureQuest, Burke/Triolo PictureQuest; (tl) ©B. Daemmrich/Stock Boston. B30: ©John Shaw/Bruce Coleman, Inc. B31: ©Richard Hutchings. B34: ©Ed Degginger/Earth Scenes. B35: ©Cesar Llacuna.B41: ©Peter Beck/The Stock Market. B42: (bg) ©Joe Sroka/Dembinsky Photo Associates; (t) ©Lynn Funkhouser/Peter Arnold, Inc. B43: (br) ©Fred Bavendam/Peter Arnold, Inc.; (bl) ©Kelvin Aitken/Peter Arnold, Inc. B45: ©N.E. Swedberg/Bruce Coleman, Inc. B46: ©Kennan Ward/The Stock Market. B48: ©James Randklev/Tony Stone Images. B49: ©Richard Hutchings. B50: (br) ©B&C Calhoun/Bruce Coleman, Inc.; (bl) ©John Shaw/Bruce Coleman, Inc. B51: (b) ©Jeff Foott/Bruce Coleman, Inc. B52: ©Patti Murray/Earth Scenes. B53: ©Linda Bailey/Earth Scenes. B56: (tr) ©David Overcash/Bruce Coleman, Inc.; (br) ©John Shaw/Bruce Coleman, Inc. B57: (t) ©Gregory Brown/Animals Animals; (bl) ©Patty Murray/Earth Scenes. B58: (b) ©Bob Burch/Bruce Coleman, Inc.; (tr) ©Tom Bean/CORBIS. B60: (bl) ©Kevin Schafer/Bettmann/CORBIS; (tr) ©Rod Williams/Bruce Coleman, Inc. B61: ©David Burder/Tony Stone Images. B62: ©Pictor/Uniphoto. B63: ©Richard Hutchings. B64: (tr) ©Breck P. Kent/Earth Scenes; (m) ©Lee Rentz/Rentl/Bruce Coleman, Inc.; (m) ©Nigel J.H. Smith/Earth Scenes. B65: (tr) ©Eastcott/Momatiuk/Earth Scenes; (tl) ©J.C. Carton/Bruce Coleman, Inc.; (m) ©M. Timothy O'Keefe/Bruce Coleman, Inc. B66: ©A.&M. Shah/Animals Animals. B67: ©Eastcott/Momatiuk/Earth Scenes. B68: ©Joe McDonald/Bruce Coleman, Inc. B69: (bl) ©Jen & Des Bartlett/Bruce Coleman, Inc.; (m) ©Joy Spurr/Bruce Coleman, Inc. B70: (bl) ©Jeff Foott/Bruce Coleman, Inc.; (m) ©John Shaw/Bruce Coleman, Inc. B71: (br) ©E&P Bauer/Bruce Coleman, Inc.; (tr) ©Joe McDonald/CORBIS. B72: ©1998 PhotoDisc, Inc. B74: ©M. Newman/Bruce Coleman, Inc. B75: ©N. Devore III/Bruce Coleman, Inc. B76: (bg) ©Danny Lehman/CORBIS; (l) ©John D. Cunningham/Visuals Unlimited. B78: ©Gary Braasch/CORBIS. B79: ©John Shaw/Bruce Coleman, Inc. B80: ©John Elk III/Bruce Coleman, Inc. B82: (r) ©David Falconer/Bruce Coleman, Inc.; (bl) ©Patti Murray/Earth Scenes. B83: ©John Lemker/Earth Scenes. B85: (bl) ©Ed Degginger/Earth Scenes; (m) images copyright ©1998 PhotoDisc, Inc. B86: (m) ©Ed Degginger/Earth Scenes; (tr) ©S. Jonasson/Bruce Coleman, Inc. B87: ©Richard Hutchings. B88: ©1998 PhotoDisc, Inc. B90: ©John H. Hoffman/Bruce Coleman, Inc. B91: ©John Elk III/Bruce Coleman, Inc. B94: ©Craig Dickson/Woods Hole Oceanographic Institute. B94: (bg) ©Jeffrey L. Rotman/Peter Arnold, Inc. B95: (r) ©Ralph White/CORBIS.

National Geographic Unit Opener C: C0, C1 ©Jules Cowan/Index Stock Imagery. **Unit C:** C2: ©Peter French/Bruce Coleman, Inc. C5: ©Richard Hutchings. C7: ©Richard Hutchings. C8: (t) ©Blocker CollectionsUT Medical Bank. C13: (bl, br) ©NASA; (bg) ©Science/VU; (t) ©World Perspectives/Explorer/Photo Researchers, Inc. C14: ©Pekka Parviainen/Dembinsky Photo Associates. C15: ©E.Karkoschka/UA/NASA. C16: ©AFB/CORBIS. C17: ©Richard Hutchings. C18: (r) ©John D. Cunningham/VU; (l) ©Sinclair Stammers/Science Photo Library/Photo Researchers, Inc. C21: ©Dr. Ed Degginger/Color-Pic. C21: (r) ©Stella Snead/Bruce Coleman, Inc. C22: (l) ©Jerry Schad/Photo Researchers, Inc.; (r) ©Jim Steinberg/Photo Researchers, Inc.; (m) ©Robert Godwin/National Audubon Society/Photo Researchers, Inc. C23: (tr) ©David Austin/Stock Boston; (bl) ©Gilbert Grant/Photo Researchers, Inc. C24: ©Renee Lynn/Photo Researchers, Inc. C25: ©Terranova International/Photo Researchers, Inc. C26: (tr) ©Bruce Coleman, Inc.; (tr) ©David Scharf/Peter Arnold, Inc.; (t) ©NASA/PhotoTake. C28: (bg) ©Dave Bartruff/Stock Boston; (b) ©Mark Mellett//Stock Boston. C29: (l) ©Annie Griffiths Belt/Bettmann/CORBIS; (bg) ©Dave Bartruff/Stock Boston; (r) ©Morton Beebe,S.F./Bettmann/CORBIS. C30: ©George Lepp/CORBIS. C32: (bl) ©Cesar Llacuna; (bc) ©Charles D. Winters/Timeframe Photography, Inc./Photo Researchers, Inc.; (bl) ©E. R. Degginger/Photo Researchers, Inc.; (br) ©George Whiteley/Photo Researchers, Inc.; (bc) ©Joyce Photographics/Photo Researchers, Inc. C33: (bc, br) ©Cesar Llacuna; (bl) ©David Lees/CORBIS; (br) ©J.H. Robinson/Photo Researchers, Inc.; (bc) ©Kaj R. Svensson/Science Photo Library/Photo Researchers, Inc.; (bl) ©Roberto De Gugliemo/Science Photo Library/Photo Researchers, Inc. C34: (tl) ©John D. Cunningham/VU; (tc) ©Mark A. Schneider/VU; (tr) ©Tom Pantages/PhotoTake. C35: (tc) ©A.J. Cunningham/VU. C36: (tr) ©A.J.Copley/VU; (m) ©Joyce Photographics/Photo Researchers, Inc.; (bl) ©Ross Frid/Korner Gems, Traverse City, MI/VU. C37: ©Peter Aitken/Photo Researchers, Inc. C38: (b) ©A.J. Copley/VU; (bl) ©David Young-Wolf PhotoEdit/PictureQuest; (tr) ©Richard T. Nowitz/Photo Researchers, Inc.; (tr) ©Zale Corporation/Zales. C40: ©Lee Rentz/Bruce Coleman, Inc. C41: (bc) ©Doug Sokell/VU; (br) ©Richard Hutchings. C42: (br) ©Andrew J. Martinez/Photo Researchers, Inc.; (bl) ©Andrew J. Martinez/Photo Researchers, Inc. C43: (br) ©Biophoto Associates/Photo Researchers, Inc. C44: (bl) ©A.J. Copley/VU; (bl) ©Andrew J. Martinez/Photo Researchers, Inc.; (bl) ©Joyce Photographics/Photo Researchers, Inc.; (bl) ©Martin G. Miller/VU.

C45: (b) ©John D. Cunningham/VU; (bl) Joyce Photographics/Photo Researchers, Inc.; (bl) ©Kjell B. Sandved/Photo Researchers, Inc. C46: (m) ©Arthur R. Hill/VU; (br) ©Charles R. Belinky /Photo Researchers, Inc.; (bl) ©Ed Degginger/Photo Researchers, Inc.; (m) ©L.S. Stepanowicz/VU. C47: ©Michael P. Gadomski/Photo Researchers, Inc. C48: ©Joyce Photographics/Photo Researchers, Inc. C50: ©G. Büttner/Naturbild/OKAPIA/Photo Researchers, Inc. C51: (tr) ©Christian Grzimek/OKAPIA/Photo Researchers, Inc.; (t) ©Ron Spomer/VU. C53: (m) ©John Elk III/Stock Boston. C54: (br) ©G. I. Bernard/Animals Animals/Earth Scenes; (m) ©Michael Newman/PhotoEdit. C55: ©W. Geiersperger/Stock Boston. C57: (tr) ©NASA/JPL/Caltech/NASA. C58: ©Paul Steel/THE STOCK MARKET. C60: ©NASA. C61: ©Richard Hutchings. C64: (t) ©Gary Withey/Bruce Coleman, Inc.; (tr) ©Hattie Young/Science Photo Library/Photo Researchers, Inc.; (tl) ©Phil Degginger/Color-Pic. C65: ©Simon Fraser/Science Photo Library/Photo Researchers, Inc. C67: (b) ©Chase Swift/CORBIS; (bl) ©Tom McHugh/Photo Researchers, Inc. C68: ©JPL/NASA. C69: (tr) ©Photo Researchers, Inc.; (tl) ©NASA. C70: ©IFA/Peter Arnold, Inc. C71: ©Richard Hutchings. C73: ©Calvin Larsen/Photo Researchers, Inc. C76: ©Simon Fraser/Science Photo Library/Photo Researchers, Inc.; C77: ©Richard Hutchings. C80: ©Victoria McCormick/Animals Animals/Earth Scenes. C81: ©Kevin Schafer/Peter Arnold, Inc. C82: ©Dave G. Houser/Pictor/Uniphoto. C84: (tr) ©L.Lipsky/Bruce Coleman, Inc.; (m) ©VCG/FPG. C85: ©Jan Stromme/Bruce Coleman, Inc. C86: ©NASA/Tom Pantages. C87: ©Ira Rubin/Dembinsky Photo Associates. C88: ©Jeff Greenberg/Stock Boston/PhotoEdit. C92: (br) ©Emory Kristof/National Geographic/Gettyone; (tr) ©R&V Taylor/Bruce Coleman, Inc. C93: ©Norbert Wu/Norbert Wu Productions. C94: (t) ©Chinch Gryniewicz/Ecoscene/CORBIS; (br) ©Fulvio Eccardi/Bruce Coleman, Inc. C95: ©L.Lipsky/Bruce Coleman, Inc. C96: ©Rod Catanach/Woods Hole Oceanographic Institute. C97: ©Woods Hole Oceanographic Institute. C98: ©Ron Sherman/Stock Boston. C99: ©Richard Hutchings. C100: (br) ©Joseph Nettis/Photo Researchers, Inc.; (bl) ©Phil Degginger/Color-Pic. C101: ©Ted Speigel/Bettmann CORBIS. C104: (bl) ©Phil Degginger/Color-Pic; (b) ©Russell D. Curtis/Photo Researchers, Inc.; (m) ©Simon Fraser/Science Photo Library/Photo Researchers, Inc. C105: (tl) ©John Keating/Photo Researchers, Inc.; (br) ©Kevin Schafer/Peter Arnold, Inc. C106: ©Patrick Grace/Photo Researchers, Inc. C107: ©Matt Meadows/Peter Arnold, Inc. C109: ©John Keating/Photo Researchers, Inc. C110: (r) ©Randy White/USGS; (bg) ©Roger Ressmeyer/CORBIS. C111: ©Doug Wechsler/Animals Animals/Earth Scenes.

National Geographic Unit Opener D: D0 ©NOAA, colored by John Wells/Science Photo Library/Photo Researchers, Inc; D1 ©World Perspectives/Stone. **Unit D:** D2: ©Steve Terrill/The Stock Market. D4: ©G.L. Kooyman/Earth Scenes; (br) ©Price, R. -Surv. OSF/Animals Animals/Earth Scenes. D5: ©Richard Hutchings. D12: (tr) ©Runk/Schoenberger/Grant Heilman/Grant Heilman Photography, Inc.; (r) ©Yoav Levy/PhotoTake. D13: ©Ed Degginger/Color-Pic. D14: ©Wolfgang Kaehler/CORBIS. D15: ©Richard Hutchings. D16: ©Amy C. Etra/PhotoEdit. D17: ©Richard Hutchings. D18: ©Ed Degginger/Color-Pic. D22: ©Bonnie Kamin/PhotoEdit. D23: ©Richard Hutchings. D24: (tr) ©A.J. Copley/VU; (m) ©Henry W. Robison/VU; (m) ©Mark A. Schneider/VU; (br) ©Bettmann/CORBIS; (bl) ©D. Cavagnaro/VU; (br) ©Mark E. Gibson/VU; (bl) ©W. Banaszewski/VU. D27: (br) ©Jeff J. Daly/Fundamental Photographs; (m) ©Michael P. Gadomski/Dembinsky Photo Associates. D30: ©Runk/Schoenberger/Grant Heilman Photography, Inc. D33: ©Digital Stock. D34: ©Vince Streano/CORBIS. D35: ©Richard Hutchings. D38: ©Superstock. D41: ©NASA. D43: ©Richard Hutchings. D44: (tr) ©Ed Degginger/Bruce Coleman, Inc.; (tr) ©Science/VU. D45: (r) ©McGraw-Hill School Division (m) ©Paul A. Souders/CORBIS. D46: ©John H. Clark/CORBIS. D47: (br) ©DRA/Still Pictures/Peter Arnold, Inc.; (t) ©Susan Blanchet/Dembinsky Photo Associates. D50: ©Stephen Ingram/Animals Animals/Earth Scenes. D52: ©Bertram G. Murray/JR Animals Animals/Earth Scenes. D58: ©NASA/Accuweather. D61: ©Charles Palek/Animals Animals/Earth Scenes. D62: ©CORBIS-Bettmann/CORBIS. D63: (br) ©NASA/National Weather Service/AP/Wide World. D64: ©Peter Beck Pictor/Uniphoto. D68: ©Richard Hutchings. D69: ©Joyce & Frank Burek/Animals Animals/Earth Scenes. D71: ©Science/VU. D72: ©Carlos Guerrero. D73: ©Annie Griffiths Belt/CORBIS. D74: ©Joan Iaconetti/Bruce Coleman, Inc. D78: ©Richard Huthings. D80: ©Arthur Gloor/Animals Animals/Earth Scenes. D83: ©Richard Hutchings. D88: (bl) ©Science/VU (br) ©VU. D89: ©Jim Sugar Photography/CORBIS. D90: (tr) ©Don Smetzer/Stone; (br) ©Jeff Greenberg/PhotoEdit D91: ©Frost Fair on the Thames, Abraham Hondius, Museum of London, UK/The Bridgeman Art Library International Ltd. D93: ©Mark A. Schneider/Dembinsky Photo Associates. D94: (r) ©CORBIS; (tl) ©courtesy of Dr. Henry Diaz/Climate Diagnostics Ctr, NOAA. D95: ©Jim Sugar/CORBIS.

National Geographic Unit Opener E: E0, E1 ©Roger Ressmeyer/Corbis. **Unit E:** E2: ©Christine Osborne/CORBIS. E4: ©Michael T.

PERIODIC TABLE OF THE ELEMENTS

Key

6 ← Atomic number
C ← Element symbol
Carbon ← Element name

Phase at 20° C

C Solid
Br Liquid
H Gas

1	2		3	4	5	6	7	8	9
1 **H** Hydrogen									
3 **Li** Lithium	4 **Be** Beryllium								
11 **Na** Sodium	12 **Mg** Magnesium								
19 **K** Potassium	20 **Ca** Calcium		21 **Sc** Scandium	22 **Ti** Titanium	23 **V** Vanadium	24 **Cr** Chromium	25 **Mn** Manganese	26 **Fe** Iron	27 **Co** Cobalt
37 **Rb** Rubidium	38 **Sr** Strontium		39 **Y** Yttrium	40 **Zr** Zirconium	41 **Nb** Niobium	42 **Mo** Molybdenum	43 **Tc** Technetium	44 **Ru** Ruthenium	45 **Rh** Rhodium
55 **Cs** Cesium	56 **Ba** Barium		71 **Lu** Lutetium	72 **Hf** Hafnium	73 **Ta** Tantalum	74 **W** Tungsten	75 **Re** Rhenium	76 **Os** Osmium	77 **Ir** Iridium
87 **Fr** Francium	88 **Ra** Radium		103 **Lr** Lawrencium	104 **Rf** Rutherfordium	105 **Db** Dubnium	106 **Sg** Seaborgium	107 **Bh** Bohrium	108 **Hs** Hassium	109 **Mt** Meitnerium

Row labels: 1, 2, 3, 4, 5, 6, 7

Lanthanide Series

57 **La** Lanthanum	58 **Ce** Cerium	59 **Pr** Praseodymium	60 **Nd** Neodymium	61 **Pm** Promethium	62 **Sm** Samarium

Actinide Series

89 **Ac** Actinium	90 **Th** Thorium	91 **Pa** Protactinium	92 **U** Uranium	93 **Np** Neptunium	94 **Pu** Plutonium